Microsoft®

A+
Certification
Training
Kit Second Edition

PUBLISHED BY
Microsoft Press
A Division of Microsoft Corporation
One Microsoft Way
Redmond, Washington 98052-6399

Copyright © 2000 by Microsoft Corporation

Library of Congress Cataloging-in-Publication Data
A+ Certification Training Kit , Second Edition. / Microsoft Corporation.
        p. cm.
     Includes index.
     ISBN 0-7356-1109-2
     1. Electronic data processing personnel--Certification.   2. Computer
technicians--Certification--Study guides.   I. Microsoft Corporation.

     QA76.3. .A178   2000
     004.16--dc21   00-029213

Printed and bound in the United States of America.

1 2 3 4 5 6 7 8 9   WCWC   5 4 3 2 1 0

Distributed in Canada by Penguin Books Canada Limited.

A CIP catalogue record for this book is available from the British Library.

Microsoft Press books are available through booksellers and distributors worldwide. For further information about international editions, contact your local Microsoft Corporation office or contact Microsoft Press International directly at fax (425) 936-7329. Visit our Web site at mspress.microsoft.com. Send comments to *tkinput@microsoft.com*.

Macintosh is a registered trademark of Apple Computer, Inc., used under license. Intel is a registered trademark of Intel Corporation. Microsoft, Microsoft Press, MS-DOS, MSN, Windows, and Windows NT are either registered trademarks or trademarks of Microsoft Corporation in the United States and/or other countries.

Unless otherwise noted, the example companies, organizations, products, people, and events depicted herein are fictitious. No association with any real company, organization, product, person, or event is intended or should be inferred.

For Microsoft Press
Acquisitions Editor: Jeff Madden
Project Editor: Michael Bolinger

Author: James Karney

For Webfoot Productions
Project Manager: Herb Payton
Manuscript Editor: Nancy Thalia Reynolds
Technical Editor: Roger Scrafford
Typographer: Kristin Ziesemer
Proofreader: Rose Williamson
Indexer: Julie Kawabata

Contents

About This Book

Welcome to the *A+ Certification Training Kit.* This technology-based training kit is intended to provide the user with the skills necessary for A+ Certification. It is a study of the computer—its hardware and software—from its earliest beginnings, through the advent of the mainframe and personal computers, up to present-day Pentium processor-driven machines.

The computer industry has evolved and grown phenomenally since its commercial inception in the 1960s. This industry is so vast and complex that no one can claim to understand all its aspects. However, to participate in this ever-changing and growing industry, the computer technician must be able to demonstrate a level of proficiency with computers and technology. Certification is a first step in establishing your presence as a computer professional. It provides you with the opportunity to gain the skills you need, it helps you establish your knowledge base, and it gives you the confidence to get started.

Note   For more information on becoming A+ Certified, refer to the section titled "The A+ Certification Program" later in this introduction.

Each chapter in this book is divided into lessons. Each lesson ends with a brief summary, and each chapter concludes with a chapter summary and a set of review questions to test your knowledge of the chapter material.

The "Getting Started" section of this introduction provides important instructions that describe the hardware and software recommendations presented in this course. Read through the section thoroughly before you start the lessons.

Intended Audience

This book was developed for the entry-level computer technician, as well as the experienced technician who is seeking certification. For the entry-level student, it starts by explaining the basics and moves on to more complex topics. It introduces the simple concepts that underlie today's computers. Once this foundation is established, it brings you up to date with the latest technology covered by the A+ exam. For the more experienced user, it provides a fresh review and focus on what is required to meet the objectives of the A+ exam.

Prerequisites

There are no formal prerequisites such as course work or specific knowledge base. This is an entry-level course, and everything you need to know is provided in the text.

To better understand the concepts presented and to complete any exercises or practices, it would be useful to have a computer with an Intel processor and, at the very least, MS-DOS 6.2 and Windows 3.x. A Windows 95-based computer is recommended. Windows NT or other types of operating systems are not recommended because some of their features are beyond the scope of the A+ Certification Program.

About the CD-ROM

The companion compact disc contains informational aids that can be used to supplement this book. These include demonstration videos and an electronic version of the book.

The electronic version of the book requires an HTML browser. If Microsoft Internet Explorer is installed on your system (as described in the "Getting Started" section), simply double-click any of the electronic book files to view them. The demonstrations are stored as HTML files with embedded Microsoft Windows Media Player files. If your machine has standard multimedia support and an HTML browser, you can view these demonstrations by double-clicking them.

For specific information about what is included on the companion CD and how to access this information, see the README.TXT file on the CD.

Features of This Book

Each chapter opens with a "Before You Begin" section, which prepares you for completing the chapter.

The body of each chapter provides detailed coverage of the subjects you'll need to study to prepare for the test. The "Review" sections at the end of each chapter allow you to test what you have learned in the chapter lessons. They are designed to familiarize you with the types of questions you might encounter on the exam.

Chapter and Appendix Overview

This self-paced training course combines instruction, procedures, multimedia presentations, and review questions to teach you what you need to know for A+ Certification. It is designed to be completed from beginning to end, but you can choose a customized track and complete only the sections that interest you. (See the next section, "Finding the Best Starting Point for You.") If you choose the customized track option, be sure to check the "Before You Begin" section in each chapter. Any concepts or procedures that require preliminary work from preceding chapters will steer you to the appropriate chapters.

This self-paced book is divided into the following chapters:

- The "About This Book" section contains a self-paced training overview and introduces the components of this training. Read this section thoroughly to draw the greatest educational value from the self-paced training and to plan which lessons you will complete.

- Chapter 1, "Introduction to Computers," sets the background for the rest of the lessons. It provides an historic view of computers from their beginning to today's high-speed marvels. This section also explores the role of today's computer technician.

- Chapter 2, "Understanding Electronic Communication," discusses how computers communicate. It explains the differences between the language we use and the language of machines.

- Chapter 3, "An Overview of the Computer," defines the basic elements of a computer's hardware and how they interact.

- Chapter 4, "The Central Processing Unit," explains the development of the microprocessor, focusing on what differentiates each type of processor and how to identify each.

- Chapter 5, "Supplying Power to a Computer," covers power supplies, including how they work and how to troubleshoot problems.

- Chapter 6, "Primary PC Components," discusses the components that make up a motherboard, from the computer case to the BIOS (Basic Input/Output System).

- Chapter 7, "Memory," covers the various types of memory found in a computer, what memory is used for, and how to upgrade or replace it.

- Chapter 8, "Basic Disk Drives," discusses floppy disk drives and hard disk drives. It explores mass storage devices, how they work, and their limitations.

- Chapter 9, "High-Capacity Disk Drives," discusses the barriers imposed by early MS-DOS-based computers and how the new large drives have overcome these barriers. It also covers CD-ROM and SCSI drives.

- Chapter 10, "Expansion Buses," defines the computer bus, examines the major effect it has had on the development of the computer, and why that is.

- Chapter 11, "The Display System: Monitors and Adapters," covers the various monitors and displays, how they work, and how to troubleshoot them.

- Chapter 12, "Printers, Modems, and Cables," discusses all the devices that attach to a computer. It focuses on the two most common: printers and modems.

- Chapter 13, "The Basics of Electrical Energy," covers electricity and how it relates to the computer. A computer technician does not need to be an electrical engineer, but does need to be able to perform basic tests and to work safely. This chapter provides the reader with a grounding in these issues.

- Chapter 14, "Upgrading a Computer," covers the basic tools and techniques used to perform common upgrades to a computer, including computer disassembly and reassembly.

- Chapter 15, "Software: MS-DOS and Windows 3.x," is an introduction to software and operating systems. This section focuses on the early operating system MS-DOS and how Windows 3.x overcame some of its limitations.

- Chapter 16, "Windows 95 and Beyond," discusses this innovative operating system by Microsoft. It presents the differences between Windows 95 and MS-DOS-based operating systems along with an introduction to how it works.

- Chapter 17, "Managing and Troubleshooting Windows," covers the various tools provided by the Windows 95 operating system that a computer technician uses to manage and troubleshoot a computer.

- Chapter 18, "Connectivity and Portability," takes a look at how to expand the usefulness of a computer. It discusses the basics of how a computer network functions and explores the features of portable (laptop and notebook) computers.

- Chapter 19, "Maintaining Computer Hardware," covers the techniques and procedures used by a service technician to maintain a computer. It also looks at some safety and environmental issues and how to address them.

- Chapter 20, "Staying on Top of Your Profession," focuses on the computer technician and gives some tips on how to keep up with this rapidly evolving profession. It also takes a look at the customer service aspect of being a service professional.

- Appendix A, "Questions and Answers," lists all the review questions from each chapter of the book, including the page number where the question appears, and provides suggested answers.

- Appendix B, "Table of Acronyms," lists a number of acronyms relevant to the A+ Certification exams.

- The Glossary provides concise definitions of terms used throughout this book that are relevant to the A+ Certification exams.

Finding the Best Starting Point for You

Because this book is self-paced, you can skip some lessons and visit them later. But note that some sections require an understanding of the concepts presented in previous sections (prerequisites are noted at the beginning of each chapter).

If:	Follow this learning path:
You are preparing to take the A+ Certification exam and have no experience	Read the "Getting Started" section. Then work through Chapters 1 through 20 in order.
You are preparing to take the A+ Certification exam and are experienced with computer repair	Read the "Getting Started" section. Be sure to focus on the exam objectives as presented in the "The A+ Certification Program" section of this introduction, "About This Book." Then work through the remaining chapters in any order you wish. Be sure, however, to cover all the chapters.
You'd like to review information about specific topics for the exam	Use the "Where to Find Specific Skill Areas in This Book" section that immediately follows this table.

Where to Find Specific Skill Areas in This Book

The following tables provide a list of the skill areas measured on the A+ Certification exam. The tables list the skill and where in this book you will find the lessons related to that skill.

A+ Core Service Technician Examination

The objectives for the core exam focus on computer hardware. Information relevant to the core exam objectives can be found in every chapter in this training kit, except in those that cover specifically MS-DOS or Windows.

Skill Area Measured	Location in Book
Installation, Configuration, and Upgrading	Any chapter containing information specific to devices (printers, monitors, drives, and so on). Focus on Chapters 8–12 and 14.
Diagnosing and Troubleshooting	Any chapter containing information specific to devices (printers, monitors, drives, and so on). Focus on Chapters 8–13.
Safety and Preventive Maintenance	Focus on Chapters 13 and 19. Other safety and preventive maintenance tips are found in the sections that cover a specific device.
Motherboard/Processor/Memory	Chapters 4, 6, and 7.
Printers	Chapter 12.
Portable Systems	Chapter 18.
Basic Networking	Chapter 18.
Customer Satisfaction	Chapter 20.

A+ DOS/Windows Service Technician Exam

The majority of information for this exam is found in Chapters 15, 16, and 17. Specific information regarding a device will be found in the chapter that covers that device.

Skill Area Measured	Location in Book
Function, Structure, Operation and File Management	Chapters 15, 16, and 17.
Memory Management	Chapters 15, 16, and 17. Also see Chapter 7.
Installation, Configuration, and Upgrading	Chapters 15 and 16.
Troubleshooting	Chapters 15 and 17.
Networks	Chapters 15, 16, and 17. Also see Chapters 12 and 18.

Getting Started

This self-paced training course contains hands-on procedures to help you learn about computer hardware and software. Although it is not a requirement to have a computer and software to complete the course, you will need one available for practice. It is recommended that you not use a computer that contains any important data that needs to be saved. Some of the concepts in this book require complete reformatting of the operating system, during which all data will be lost.

Hardware Requirements

This course builds knowledge that begins with early technology. Therefore, almost any computer will provide some level of skill building. In fact, a new computer with a Pentium II processor and full Plug and Play capability will be something of a detriment because it is overly capable for our purposes and does not require the interaction necessary for building these basic skills. However, to get the most out of this course, your computer should have the following minimum configuration (all hardware should be on the Microsoft Windows 95 Hardware Compatibility List):

- 486 DX processor and motherboard
- 16 MB of RAM
- 500-MB hard disk drive
- 3.5-inch floppy disk drive
- CD-ROM drive (8x minimum recommended)
- A mouse or other pointing device
- A simple printer

Software Requirements

The following software is required to complete the procedures in this course:

- MS-DOS versions 5.0 or later (version 6.2 recommended)
- Windows 3.1
- Windows 95 and later

To view the electronic version of the book, you will need Microsoft Internet Explorer 4.01 or later. A version of Microsoft Internet Explorer 5 that allows you to view the electronic version of the book is supplied on the companion CD. See the README.TXT file on the companion CD for instructions on how to use this supplied version of the Internet Explorer browser to view the electronic version of the book.

About the Electronic Book

The companion CD also includes an electronic version of the book that you can use to search and view on-screen as you work through the exercises. See the README.TXT file on the companion CD for instructions on how to install and/or use the electronic version of this book.

The A+ Certification Program

A+ Certification is a testing program sponsored by the Computing Technology Industry Association (CompTIA) that certifies the competency of service technicians in the computer industry. Many computer hardware and software manufacturers, vendors, distributors, resellers, and publications back the program.

Earning A+ certification means that you possess the knowledge, skills, and customer-relations expertise that are essential for a successful computer service technician. The exams cover a broad range of hardware and software technologies, but are not related to any vendor-specific products.

Benefits of Certification

For most individuals entering the computer industry, A+ Certification is only the first step. If your goal is to enter the profession of computer service and repair, this might be all the certification you need. However, if you are interested in becoming an MCSE (Microsoft Certified Systems Engineer), this course provides just the foundation you need to get on your way with confidence.

As an A+ Certified Technician, you will receive many benefits, including:

- **Recognized proof of professional achievement.** The A+ credential asserts that the holder has reached a level of competence commonly accepted and valued by the industry.

- **Enhanced job opportunities.** Many employers give hiring preference to applicants with A+ Certification. Some employers require A+ as a condition of employment.

- **Opportunity for advancement.** The A+ credential can be a plus when an employer awards job promotions.

- **Training requirement.** A+ Certification is being adopted as a prerequisite to enrollment in certain vendors' training courses. Vendors find they can cut their training programs by as much as 50 percent when they require that all attendees are A+ Certified.

- **Customer confidence.** As the general public learns about A+ Certification, customers will request that only certified technicians be assigned to their accounts.

- **Companies benefit from improved productivity.** Certified employees perform work faster and more accurately. Statistics show that certified employees can work up to 75 percent faster than noncertified employees.

- **Customer satisfaction.** When employees have credentials that prove their competency, customer expectations are more likely to be met. More business can be generated for the employer through repeat sales to satisfied customers.

The A+ Exam Modules and Domains

To become certified, you must pass two test modules: the Core and the A+ DOS/Windows module (includes Windows 3.x and Windows 95). Individuals are permitted to take the test as often as they like, but in the case of A+ Certification, the Core and one specialty module must be passed within 90 calendar days of each other in order for the candidate to become certified.

This text prepares you to master the A+ exams. By completing all course work, you will be able to complete the A+ Certification exams with the confidence you need to ensure success. More importantly, you will be able to conduct your business with the knowledge that you are among the best and that you really "know your stuff."

Core Exam

This examination measures essential competencies for a microcomputer hardware service technician with six months of on-the-job experience. It is broken down into eight sections (called domains). The following table lists the domains and the extent to which they are represented.

Domain	Percent of Examination
1.0—Installation, Configuration, and Upgrading	30
2.0—Diagnosing and Troubleshooting	20
3.0—Safety and Preventive Maintenance	10
4.0—Motherboard/Processors/Memory	10
5.0—Printers	10
6.0—Portable Systems	5
7.0—Basic Networking	5
8.0—Customer Satisfaction*	10

*This Domain will be scored but will not impact final pass/fail score.

1.0 Installation, Configuration and Upgrading

This domain tests the knowledge and skills needed to identify, install, configure, and upgrade microcomputer modules and peripherals. Included is the ability to identify and configure IRQ, DMA, I/O addresses, and set switches and jumpers.

- Identify basic terms, concepts, and functions of system modules, including how each module should work during normal operation.
- Identify basic procedures for adding and removing field-replaceable modules.
- Identify available IRQ, DMA, and I/O addresses and procedures to configure them for device installation.
- Identify common peripheral ports, associated cabling, and their connectors.
- Identify proper procedures for installing and configuring IDE/EIDE devices.
- Identify proper procedures for installing and configuring SCSI devices.
- Identify proper procedures for installing and configuring peripheral devices.
- Recognize the functions and effective use of common hand tools.
- Identify procedures for upgrading BIOS.
- Identify hardware methods of system optimizations and when to use them.

2.0 Diagnosing and Troubleshooting

This domain tests the candidate's knowledge and skills in diagnosing and troubleshooting common problems and system malfunctions, and requires knowledge of the symptoms relating to common problems.

- Identify common symptoms and problems associated with microcomputers.
- Identify basic troubleshooting procedures and good practices.

3.0 Safety and Preventive Maintenance

This domain tests skills regarding safety and preventive maintenance. Safety includes identifying potential hazards to personnel and equipment. Preventive maintenance includes preventive maintenance products, procedures, environmental hazards, and precautions to take when working on a microcomputer system.

- Identify the purposes of various types of preventive maintenance products and procedures.
- Identify procedures and devices for protecting against environmental hazards.
- Identify the potential hazards and proper safety procedures in relation to laser and high voltage equipment.
- Identify items that require special disposal procedures in order to comply with environmental guidelines.
- Identify ESD (electrostatic discharge) precautions and procedures.

4.0 Motherboard/Processors/Memory

This domain tests skills related to specific terminology, facts, and ways and means of dealing with classifications, categories, and principles of motherboards, processors, and memory in a microcomputer system.

- Identify the differences between the popular CPU chips.
- Identify the categories of RAM and their locations and physical characteristics.
- Identify the most popular motherboard.
- Identify the purpose of CMOS.

5.0 Printers

This domain tests knowledge and skills related to printers.

- Identify the basic concepts, printer operations, printer components, and field replaceable units.
- Identify care and service techniques common to printers.
- Identify the types of printer connections and configurations.

6.0 Portable Systems

This domain tests skills related to the use of portable computers. It focuses on the unique features and problems associated with portables.

7.0 Basic Networking

This domain tests the skills and knowledge of basic network concepts and terminology.

- Identify basic networking concepts, including how a network works.
- Identify procedures for swapping and configuring network interface cards.
- Identify ramifications of repairs on the network.

8.0 Customer Satisfaction

This domain tests the skills and knowledge of customer relations and satisfaction.

- Distinguish effective from ineffective behaviors.
- Recognize communication skills.
- Recognize how to instill customer confidence.

A+ DOS/Windows Service Technician Examination

Also referred to as the Microsoft Windows/DOS Specialty Exam, this test measures essential operating-system competencies for a break/fix microcomputer hardware service technician with six months of on-the-job experience. It examines a basic knowledge of MS-DOS, Windows 3.x, and Windows 95, including how to install, configure, upgrade, troubleshoot, and repair microcomputer systems. It is broken down into five sections (domains). The following table lists the domains and the extent to which they are represented.

Domain	Percent of Examination
1.0—Function, Structure, Operation, and File Management	30
2.0—Memory Management	10
3.0—Installation, Configuration, and Upgrading	30
4.0—Diagnosing and Troubleshooting	20
5.0—Networks	10

Note   In terms of operating systems, Windows 95 is covered in about 75 percent of the operating-system exam materials, while MS-DOS & Windows 3.x are covered in about 25 percent of the materials.

1.0 Function, Structure, Operation, and File Management

This domain tests skills and knowledge of operating systems.

- Identify the operating system's functions, structure, and major system files.
- Identify ways to navigate the operating systems and how to get technical information.
- Identify basic concepts and procedures for creating and managing files and directories in MS-DOS and Windows.
- Identify the procedure for viewing files and changing file attributes, and the ramifications of these changes.
- Identify the procedures for basic disk management.
- Identify how the operating system stores information on the hard disk drive in file allocation tables.

2.0 Memory Management

This domain tests the skills and knowledge of the various types of memory and how to manage them.

- Differentiate between types of memory.
- Identify typical memory conflict problems and how to optimize memory use.

3.0 Installation, Configuration and Upgrading

This domain tests the skills and knowledge of installing, configuring, and upgrading MS-DOS, Windows 3.x, and Windows 95.

- Identify the procedures for installing MS-DOS, Windows 3.x, and Windows 95. Bring the software to a basic operational level.
- Identify steps to perform an operating system upgrade.
- Identify the boot sequences for MS-DOS, Windows 3.x, and Windows 95.
- Identify how Windows 95 uses Plug and Play and how it functions.
- Identify procedures for loading/adding device drivers and the necessary software for the devices.
- Identify the procedures for changing options, configuring, and using the Windows printing subsystem.
- Identify the procedures for installing and launching typical Windows and non-Windows applications.

4.0 Diagnosing and Troubleshooting

This domain tests the skills and knowledge of diagnosing and troubleshooting problems related to MS-DOS, Windows 3.x, and Windows 95.

- Recognize and interpret the meaning of common error codes.

- Identify the steps required to correct a startup or boot problem.

- Identify the steps required to create an emergency boot disk with utilities installed.

- Recognize Windows-specific printing problems and identify the procedures to correct them.

- Recognize and categorize common problems and identify their possible causes.

- Identify the purpose of and procedures of using various MS-DOS and Windows-based utilities and command switches to diagnose and troubleshoot problems.

- Identify the procedures to install and configure MS-DOS applications and potential problems in Windows 95.

- Identify concepts relating to viruses and virus types.

5.0 Networks

This domain tests the skills and knowledge of the network capabilities of MS-DOS and Windows.

- Identify the networking capabilities of MS-DOS and Windows, including procedures for connecting to the network.

- Identify concepts and capabilities relating to the Internet and basic procedures for setting up a system for Internet access.

Registering for the A+ Exams

The tests are administered by Sylvan Prometric. They have hundreds of authorized testing centers in any of the 50 states in the U.S. and in 150+ other countries worldwide. To register for the test call: 1-800-77-MICRO (1-800-776-4276).

When you call, please have the following information available:

- Social Security number or Sylvan Prometric ID number (provided by Sylvan Prometric)
- Mailing address and telephone number
- Employer or organization
- Date on which you wish to take the test
- Method of payment (credit card or check)

The test is available to anyone who wants to take it. Payment is made at the time of registration, either by credit card or by requesting that an invoice be sent to you or your employer. Vouchers and coupons are also redeemed at that time.

C H A P T E R   1

Introduction to Computers

About This Chapter

We begin our introduction to computers with a brief history of how they evolved. Although this course and the A+ exam focus on the modern electronic computer, many principles used in the early computational machines still apply to their modern successors. With a summary of computer development and discussion of the role of today's computer professional, this chapter lays the foundation for the chapters that follow.

Before You Begin

There are no prerequisites for this chapter.

Lesson 1: The Development of the Computer

In this lesson, we take a brief look at the development of the computer. By understanding its origins, you'll gain an appreciation for both the complexity and simplicity of today's computers.

After this lesson, you will be able to:

■ Describe the major milestones in the development of the modern computer.

Estimated lesson time: 15 minutes

Many of us think only in terms of electronic computers, powered by electricity. (If you can't plug it in, is it a computer?) But as the definition in *Funk & Wagnalls Standard College Dictionary* makes clear, to "compute" is to "ascertain (an amount or number) by calculation or reckoning." In fact, the first computers were invented by the Chinese about 2500 years ago. They are called *abacuses* and are still used throughout Asia today.

The Abacus

The abacus, shown in Figure 1.1, is a calculator; its first recorded use was circa 500 B.C. The Chinese used it to add, subtract, multiply, and divide. But the abacus was not unique to the continent of Asia; archeological excavations have revealed an Aztec abacus in use around 900 or 1000 A.D.

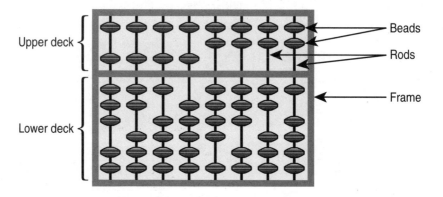

Figure 1.1   The first computer

The Analytical Engine (A Pre-Electronic Computer)

The first mechanical computer was the analytical engine, conceived and partially constructed by Charles Babbage in London, England, between 1822 and 1871. It was designed to receive instructions from punched cards, make calculations with the aid of a memory bank, and print out solutions to math problems. Although Babbage lavished the equivalent of $6,000 of his own money—and $17,000 of the British government's money—on this extraordinarily advanced machine, the precise work needed to engineer its thousands of moving parts was beyond the ability of the technology of the day to carry out. It is doubtful whether Babbage's brilliant concept could have been realized using the available resources of his own century. But if it had been, it seems likely that the analytical engine could have performed the same functions as many early electronic computers.

The First Electrically Driven Computer

The first computer designed expressly for data processing was patented on January 8, 1889, by Dr. Herman Hollerith of New York. The prototype model of this electrically operated tabulator was built for the U. S. Census Bureau and computed results in the 1890 census.

Using punched cards containing information submitted by respondents to the census questionnaire, the Hollerith machine made instant tabulations from electrical impulses actuated by each hole. It then printed out the processed data on tape. Dr. Hollerith left the Census Bureau in 1896 to establish the Tabulating Machine Company to manufacture and sell his equipment. The company eventually became IBM, and the 80-column punched card used by the company, shown in Figure 1.2, is still known as the Hollerith card.

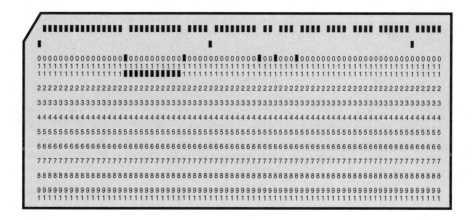

Figure 1.2   Typical 80-character punched card

The Digital Electronic Computer

The first modern digital computer, the ABC (Atanasoff–Berry Computer), was built in a basement on the Iowa State University campus in Ames, Iowa, between 1939 and 1942. The development team was led by John Atanasoff, professor of physics and mathematics, and Clifford Berry, a graduate student. This machine included many features still in use today: binary arithmetic, parallel processing, regenerative memory, separate memory, and computer functions. When completed, it weighed 750 pounds and could store 3000 bits (0.4 KB) of data.

The technology developed for the ABC machine was passed from Atanasoff to John W. Mauchly, who, together with engineer John Presper Eckert, developed the first large-scale digital computer, the Electronic Numerical Integrator and Computer (ENIAC). It was built at the University of Pennsylvania's Moore School of Electrical Engineering. Begun as a classified military project, ENIAC was destined to prepare firing and bombing tables for the U.S. Army and Navy. When finally assembled in 1945, ENIAC consisted of 30 separate units, plus power supply and forced-air cooling. It weighed 30 tons, used 19,000 vacuum tubes, 1500 relays, and hundreds of thousands of resistors, capacitors, and inductors. It required 200 kilowatts of electrical power to operate.

Although programming ENIAC was a mammoth task requiring manual switches and cable connections, it became the workhorse for the solution of scientific problems from 1949 to 1952. ENIAC is considered the prototype for most of today's computers.

Another device important to computer history is the Colossus I, an early digital computer built at a secret government research establishment at Bletchley Park, Buckinghamshire, England, under the direction of Professor Max Newman. Colossus I was designed for a single purpose: cryptanalysis—breaking codes. Using punched paper tape input, it scanned and analyzed 5000 characters per second. Colossus became operational in December 1943 and proved to be one of the most important technological aids to victory in World War II. It enabled the British to break the otherwise impenetrable German "Enigma" codes.

The 1960s and 1970s marked the era of the mainframe computer. Using the technology of ABC, ENIAC, and Colossus, large computers and emerging companies came to dominate the industry.

As these highlights show, the concept of the computer has indeed been with us for quite a while. The following table provides an overview of the evolution of modern computers—it is a timeline of important events.

Note Don't worry if you are not familiar with some terms in this timeline; they are explained in the chapters that follow, as well as in the glossary.

Year	Events
1971	The 4004—the first 4-bit microprocessor—is introduced by Intel. It boasts 2000 transistors with a clock speed of up to 1 MHz (megahertz).
1972	The first 8-bit microprocessor—the 8008—is released.
1974	The 8080 microprocessor is developed. This improved version of the 8008 becomes the standard from which future processors will be designed.
1975	Digital Research introduces CP/M—an operating system for the 8080. The combination of software and hardware becomes the basis for the standard computer.
1976	Zilog introduces the Z80—a low-cost microprocessor (equivalent to the 8080).
	The Apple I comes into existence, although it is not yet in wide use.
1977	The Apple II and the Commodore PET computers, both of which use a 6502 processor, are introduced. These two products become the basis for the home computer. Apple's popularity begins to grow.
1978	Intel introduces a 16-bit processor, the 8086, and a companion math coprocessor, the 8087.
	Intel also introduces the 8088. It is similar to the 8086, but it transmits 8 bits at a time.
1980	Motorola introduces the 68000—a 16-bit processor important to the development of Apple and Atari computers. Motorola's 68000 becomes the processor of choice for Apple.
1981	The IBM personal computer (PC) is born; it contains a 4.7-MHz 8088 processor, 64 KB (kilobytes) of RAM (random access memory) and is equipped with a version of MS-DOS 1.0 (three files and some utilities). Available mass-storage devices include a 5.25-inch floppy drive and a cassette tape drive.
1982	Intel completes development of the 80286—a 16-bit processor with 150,000 transistors.
	MS-DOS 1.1 now supports double-sided floppy disks that hold 360 KB of data.

(continued)

continued

Year	Events
1983	IBM introduces the XT computer with a 10-MB hard-disk drive.
	MS-DOS 2.0 arrives—it features a tree-like structure and native support for hard-disk drive operations.
1984	The first computer with an 80286 chip—the IBM AT—enters the market. It is a 6-MHz machine with a 20-MB hard-disk drive and a high-density, 1.2-MB 5.25-inch floppy-disk drive.
1985	MS-DOS 3.2, which supports networks, is released.
1986	The first Intel 80386-based computer is introduced by Compaq; it features a 32-bit processor with expanded multitasking capability (even though no PC operating system yet fully supports the feature).
1987	MS-DOS 3.3 arrives, allowing use of 1.44-MB 3.5-inch floppy-disk drives and hard-disk drives larger than 32 MB.
1988	IBM introduces the PS/2 computer series. A complete departure from previous machines, its proprietary design does not support the hardware and software available on IBM PCs or clones.
	Microsoft (with the help of IBM) develops OS/2 (Operating System 2), which allows 32-bit operations, genuine multitasking, and full MS-DOS compatibility.
	Microsoft releases MS-DOS 4.0.
1989	Intel introduces the 80486 processor; it contains an on-board math coprocessor and an internal cache controller (offering 2.5 times the performance of a 386 processor with a supporting coprocessor).
1991	MS-DOS 5.0 offers a significantly improved DOS shell.
1992	The Intel i586 processor, the first Pentium, is introduced, offering 2.5 times the performance of a 486.
	IBM expands OS/2, and Microsoft Windows is introduced.
1993	MS-DOS 6.0 arrives. The term "multimedia" (the inclusion of CD-ROM drives, sound cards, speakers, and so forth, as standard equipment on new personal computers) comes into use.
1994	Intel delivers the first 100-MHz processor. COMPAQ Computer Corporation becomes the largest producer of computers.
1995	Windows 95, code-named Chicago, is introduced by Microsoft. It features 32-bit architecture.
	IBM has now shipped over one million OS/2 Warp software packages.
	The Internet, having expanded far beyond its beginnings as a network serving government and university institutions, is now in everyday use by the rapidly growing population with access to a modem.
	Computer prices drop as performance increases. IBM purchases Lotus (maker of the popular Lotus 1-2-3 spreadsheet).

continued

Year	Events
1995–1996	Software manufacturers scramble to make their products compatible with Windows 95.
1997	Microprocessor speeds exceed the 200-MHz mark. Hard-disk drive and memory prices fall while basic system configuration sizes continue to increase.
	CD-ROM drives and Internet connections have become standard equipment for computers.
1998	Personal computer performance continues to soar, and PC prices continue to fall. CPU speeds exceed 450 MHz, and motherboard bus speeds reach 100 MHz.
	Multimedia and Internet connections have become the de facto standard for new PCs.
	Entry-level machines are priced near the $500 mark.
	Universal Serial Bus (USB) is introduced.
	Windows 98 becomes the standard operating system for most new personal computers.
1999	Processors exceed 600 MHz.
	Microsoft readies Windows 2000 for release in February 2000, as Internet shopping doubles over the holiday season.

Lesson Summary

The following points summarize the main elements of this lesson:

- The concepts that form the basis of computer technology have a long history that stretches back 2500 years.

- Rudimentary, electrically powered computers were first developed in the 1950s and 1960s.

- The "standard" personal computer has undergone several stages of evolution, characterized by improvements to the processor, internal architecture, and types of storage devices.

Lesson 2: The Role of a Computer Service Professional

As computers have evolved, so has the role of the computer technician. This lesson takes a look at the contemporary technician's role in maintaining and servicing computers.

After this lesson, you will be able to:

- Define your role as a modern computer technician.

Estimated lesson time: 5 minutes

Matching the rapid pace of change in the industry, the role of the computer professional is constantly changing, too. Not too many years ago, all that was needed to repair a computer was a screwdriver, needle-nose pliers, the documentation for the computer, a boot disk with a few utilities, and a good MS-DOS reference manual. Although these tools are still fundamental to the job, to be ready for all situations, a technician has to travel with an entire library of technical manuals (a laptop computer with a CD-ROM drive and modem helps, too). The screwdriver is still the standard repair tool, but the technician is confronted with a wider array of case types, motherboard designs, processor types, and operating systems—and a wider array of customer needs. Today's computer professional needs to be a technician, a scholar, and a diplomat rolled into one, as you can see by the table that follows.

Title	Skills
Technician	You are able to troubleshoot and repair hardware and software efficiently and quickly.
Scholar	You have the wisdom and perseverance to seek answers to what you don't know and build your base of knowledge. Learning never stops.
Diplomat	You are able to instill in the user (your customer) the confidence that you are in control and can fix things, even when you are encountering them for the first time. You are able to resolve the problem, even if your customer's (lack of) understanding of the computer might be part of that problem.

Lesson Summary

The following points summarize the main elements of this lesson:

- To be competent, the computer technician of today must master a variety of skills.
- Understanding how a computer functions and how the owner plans to use it are just as important to a technician as familiarity with parts and workbench tools.

Chapter Summary

The following points summarize the key concepts in this chapter:

The Development of the Computer

- The concepts that form the basis of computer technology have a long history that stretches back 2500 years.

- Modern computers have followed the growth and technology of the electronics industry.

The Role of a Computer Service Professional

- The role of the computer technician has paralleled the evolution of the computer.

- A computer technician must combine troubleshooting and repair skills with on-the-job learning and customer support.

Review

1. Give an example of an early electronic computer.

2. What are the three roles that today's computer service professional needs to assume?

CHAPTER 2

Understanding Electronic Communication

About This Chapter

Communicating is the act of giving, transmitting, or exchanging information. A key element in developing a device such as a computer is establishing a method of communication, both internally (for the transfer of information between hardware components) and externally (with the outside world). In this chapter, we discuss how a computer processes data and communicates (transmits information) with its user. Understanding this process is fundamental to understanding how computers work.

Before You Begin

There are no prerequisites for this chapter.

Lesson 1: Computer Communication

In this lesson, we examine the fundamentals of electronic communication and explore how computer communication differs from human communication.

After this lesson, you will be able to:

- Understand how a computer transmits and receives information.
- Explain the principles of computer language.

Estimated lesson time: 20 minutes

Early Forms of Communication

Humans communicate primarily through words, spoken and written. From ancient times until about 150 years ago, messages were either verbal or written in form. Getting a message to a distant recipient was often slow, and sometimes the message (or the messenger) got lost in the process.

As time and technology progressed, people developed devices to communicate faster over greater distances. Items such as lanterns, mirrors, and flags were used to send messages quickly over an extended visual range.

All "out of earshot" communications have one thing in common: they require some type of "code" to convert human language to a form of information that can be packaged and sent to the remote location. It might be a set of letters in an alphabet, a series of analog pulses over a telephone line, or a sequence of binary numbers in a computer. On the receiving end, this code needs to be converted back to language that people can understand.

Dots and Dashes, Bits and Bytes

Telegraphs and early radio communication used codes for transmissions. The most common, Morse code (named after its creator, Samuel F. B. Morse), is based on assigning a series of pulses to represent each letter of the alphabet. These pulses are sent over a wire in a series. The operator on the receiving end converts the code back into letters and words. Morse code remained in official use for messages at sea almost to the end of the twentieth century—it was officially retired in late 1999.

Morse used a code in which any single transmitted value had two possible states: either a dot or a dash. By combining the dots and dashes into groups, an operator was able to represent letters, and by stringing them together, words. That form of on-off notation can also be used to provide two numbers, 0 and 1. Zero represents no signal, or off; and one represents a signal, or on, state.

This type of number language is called *binary notation* because it uses only two digits, usually 0 and 1. It was first used by the ancient Chinese, who used the terms *yin* (empty) and *yang* (full) to build complex philosophical models of how the universe works.

Our computers are complex switch boxes that have two states and use a binary scheme as well. The value of a given switch's state—on or off—represents a value that can be used as a code. Modern computer technology uses terms other than yin and yang, but the same binary mathematics creates virtual worlds inside our modern machines.

The Binary Language of Computers

The binary math terms that follow are fundamental to understanding PC technology.

Bits

A *bit* is the smallest unit of information that is recognized by a computer: a single on/off event.

Bytes

A *byte* is a group of eight bits. A byte is required in order to represent one character of information. Pressing one key on a keyboard is equivalent to sending one byte of information to the CPU (the computer's central processing unit). A byte is the standard unit by which memory is measured in a computer—values are expressed in terms of kilobytes (KB) or megabytes (MB). The table that follows lists units of computer memory and their values.

Memory Unit	Value
Bit	Smallest unit of information, shorthand term for binary digit
Nibble	4 bits (Half of a byte)
Byte	8 bits (Equal to one character)
Word	16 bits on most personal computers (longer words possible on larger computers)
Kilobyte (KB)	1024 bytes
Megabyte (MB)	1,048,576 bytes (Approximately one million bytes or 1024 KB)
Gigabyte (GB)	1,073,741,824 bytes (Approximately one billion bytes or 1024 MB)

The Binary System

The binary system of numbers uses the base of 2 (0 and 1). As described earlier, a bit can exist in only two states, on or off. When bits are represented visually:

- 0 (zero) equals off.
- 1 (one) equals on.

The following is one *byte* of information in which all eight *bits* are set to zero. In the binary system, this sequence of eight zeros represents a single character—the number 0.

```
0     0     0     0     0     0     0     0
```

The binary system is one of several numerical systems that can be used for counting. It is similar to the decimal system, which we use to calculate everyday numbers and values. The prefix "dec" in the term "decimal system" comes from the Latin word for ten and denotes a base of ten. That is, the decimal system is based on the ten numbers zero through nine. The binary system has a base of two, the numbers zero and one.

Counting in Binary Notation

Every schoolchild learns to count using the decimal system. There, the rightmost whole number (the number to the left of the decimal point) is the "digits" column. Numbers written there have a value of zero to nine. The number to the left of the digits column (if present) is valued from ten to ninety—the "tens" column. Ten is the factor of each additional row in the decimal system of notation. To get the total value of a number, we add together all columns in both systems: 111 is the sum of 100+10+1.

Note   A *factor* is an item that is multiplied in a multiplication problem. For example, 2 and 3 are factors in the problem 2 × 3.

In our more common decimal notation, the values of numbers are founded on a base of ten, starting with the rightmost column. Any number in that position can have a value ranging from zero to nine. In the next column to the left, the values range from 10 to 99; and in the column to the left of that, values range from 100 to 999. Binary notation uses a system of right-to-left columns of ascending values, but in which each row has only two-instead of 10-possible numbers.

Under the binary system, the first row to the right can be only zero or one; the next row to the left can be two or three (if a number exists in that position). The columns that follow have values of four, then eight, then sixteen, and so on, each column doubling the possible value of the one to its right. Two is the factor used in the binary system, and—just like decimal—zero is a number counted in that tally. Examples of bytes of information (eight rows) follow.

Byte—Example A

The value of this byte is zero because all bits are off (0 = off).

```
0     0     0     0     0     0     0     0     8     bits
128   64    32    16    8     4     2     1     #     values
```

Byte—Example B

In this example, two of the bits are turned on (1 = on). The total value of this byte is determined by adding the values associated with the bit positions that are on. This byte represents the number 5 (4 + 1).

```
0     0     0     0     0     1     0     1     8     bits
128   64    32    16    8     4     2     1     #     values
```

Byte—Example C

In this example, two different bits are turned on to represent the number 9 (8 + 1).

```
0     0     0     0     1     0     0     1     8     bits
128   64    32    16    8     4     2     1     #     values
```

Those who are mathematically inclined will quickly realize that 256 is the largest number that can be represented by a single byte.

Because computers use binary numbers and humans use decimal numbers, A+ technicians must be able to perform simple conversions. The following table shows decimal numbers and their binary equivalents (0 to 9). You will need to know this information. The best way to prepare is to learn how to add in binary numbers, rather than merely memorizing the values.

Decimal Number	Binary Equivalent
0	0000
1	0001
2	0010
3	0011
4	0100
5	0101
6	0110
7	0111
8	1000
9	1001

Numbers are fine for calculating, but today's computers must handle text, sound, streaming video, images, and animation as well. To handle all of that, standard codes are needed to translate between binary machine language and the type of data being represented and presented to the human user. The first common code-based language was developed to handle text characters.

Parallel and Serial Devices

The telegraph and the individual wires in our PCs are serial devices. This means that only one element of code can be sent at a time. Like a tunnel, there is only room for one person to pass through at one time. All electronic communications are—at some level—serial, because a single wire can have only two states: on or off.

To speed things up, we can add more wires. This allows simultaneous transmission of signals. Or, to continue our analogy, it's like adding another set of tunnels next to the first one; we still have only one person per tunnel, but we can get more people through because they are traveling in parallel. That is the difference between parallel and serial data transmission. In PC technology, we often string eight wires in a parallel set, allowing eight bits to be sent at once. This means that a single "send" can represent up to 256 numbers $2^8 = 256$. That is the same number of values found in the ASCII code system (discussed in the next paragraph). Figure 2.1 illustrates serial and parallel communication.

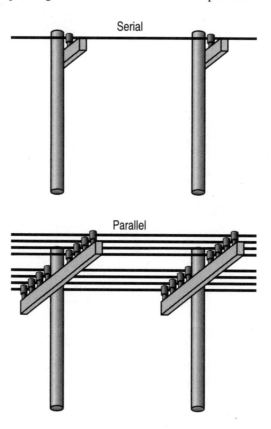

Figure 2.1   Serial and parallel communication

ASCII Code

The standard code for handling text characters on most modern computers is called *ASCII* (American Standard Code for Information Interchange). The basic ASCII standard consists of 128 codes representing the English alphabet, punctuation, and certain control characters. Most systems today recognize 256 codes: the original 128, plus an additional 128 codes called the *extended character set*.

Remember that a byte represents one character of information; four bytes are needed to represent a string of four characters. The following four bytes represent the text string 12AB (using ASCII code):

```
00110001    00110010    01000001    01000010
1           2           A           B
```

The following illustrates how the binary language spells the word "binary":

```
B           I           N           A           R           Y
01000010    01001001    01001110    01000001    01010010    01011001
```

Note It is very important to understand that in computer processing the "space" is a significant character. All items in a code must be set out for the machine to process. Like any other character, the space has a binary value that must be included in the data stream. In computing, the absence or presence of a space is critical and sometimes causes confusion or frustration among new users. Uppercase and lowercase letters also have different values. Some operating systems (for example, UNIX) distinguish between them for commands, while others (for example, MS-DOS) translate the uppercase and lowercase into the same word no matter how it is cased.

The following table is a complete representation of the ASCII character set. Even in present-day computing, laden with multimedia and sophisticated programming, ASCII retains an honored and important position.

Symbol	Binary 1 Byte	Decimal	Symbol	Binary 1 Byte	Decimal
0	00110000	48	V	01010110	86
1	00110001	49	W	01010111	87
2	00110010	50	X	01011000	88
3	00110011	51	Y	01011001	89
4	00110100	52	Z	01011010	90
5	00110101	53	A	01100001	97
6	00110110	54	B	01100010	98
7	00110111	55	C	01100011	99
8	00111000	56	D	01100100	100
9	00111001	57	E	01100101	101
A	01000001	65	F	01100110	102
B	01000010	66	G	01100111	103
C	01000011	67	H	01101000	104
D	01000010	68	I	0110100	105
E	01000101	69	J	01101010	106
F	01000110	70	K	01101011	107
G	01000111	71	L	01101100	108
H	01001000	72	M	01101101	109
I	01001001	73	N	01101110	110
J	01001010	74	O	01101111	111
K	01001011	75	P	01110000	112
L	01001100	76	Q	01110001	113
M	01001101	77	R	01110010	114
N	01001110	78	S	01110011	115
O	01001111	79	T	01110100	116
P	01010000	80	U	01110101	117
Q	01010001	81	V	01110110	118
R	01010010	82	W	01110111	119
S	01010011	83	X	01111000	120
T	01010100	84	Y	01111001	121
U	01010101	85	Z	01111010	122

Note   All letters have a separate ASCII value for uppercase and lowercase. The capital letter "A" is 65, and the lowercase "a" is 97.

Keep in mind that computers are machines, and they do not really perceive numbers as anything other than electrical charges setting a switch on or off. Like binary numbers, electrical charges can exist in only two states—positive or negative. Computers interpret the presence of a charge as one and the absence of a charge as zero. This technology allows a computer to process information.

Lesson Summary

The following points summarize the main elements of this lesson:

- Computers communicate using binary language.

- A bit is the smallest unit of information that is recognized by a computer.

- ASCII is the standard code that handles text characters for computers.

Lesson 2: The Computer Bus

This lesson discusses the set of hardware lines, or conductors, by which data is transferred internally in the components of a computer system.

After this lesson, you will be able to:

- Understand the concept of an electronic bus.

Estimated lesson time: 5 minutes

For efficient use of system resources, most communications within a computer need to occur at a much quicker rate than processing signals one at a time would allow. Therefore, the computer moves information through a *bus*. Several types of buses are used within a computer, and they are discussed more fully in later chapters. For now, let's simply look at what a bus is and how it works.

A bus is a group of electrical conductors (usually wires) running parallel to one another that can carry a charge from point a to point b. These conductors can be copper traces on a circuit board or wires in a cable. Usually, they are found in multiples of eight (8, 16, 32, 64, and so on). Early computers used eight conductors for the main system bus, thereby allowing the transmission of eight bits, or one byte, of information at a time. Figure 2.2 illustrates an 8-bit and a 16-bit bus.

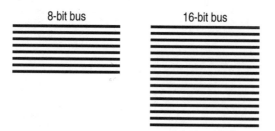

Figure 2.2   Computer bus

The physical configuration of a bus isn't as important as its function. A bus provides a common path along which to transmit information in the form of code. It allows any device to receive or send information to any other device on the same bus. This is not unlike the telegraph system in which a single wire was strung from one end of the country to the other. Any town that tapped into the wire could exchange information with any other town also connected to the wire.

Another familiar example of a bus system is the electrical wiring in a home or office. The 110-volt AC outlets are wired with three wires—hot, neutral, and ground—that run in parallel from one outlet to another. Each time a device is plugged in, it is connected to the bus (in parallel). (See Figure 2.3.)

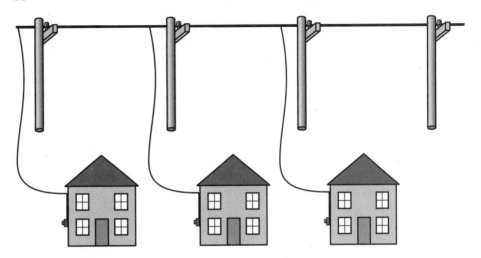

Figure 2.3   Connecting to a bus

Remember: in a computer, a bus is a set of parallel wires or lines to which the CPU, the memory, and all input/output devices are connected. Everything in a computer is connected to a bus. The actual number of wires, or lines, in a bus can vary from one computer to another or even from one part of a computer to another. The bus contains one line for each bit needed to give the address of a device or a location in memory. It also contains one line for each bit of data being transmitted from device to device.

A manufacturer might also use additional lines for power or other communication within the computer. When we speak of buses within a computer (data bus, expansion bus, or address bus), we are speaking of a specific numbers of wires, dedicated to a specific purpose—connecting parts of the computer to each other for the exchange of data between components.

Lesson Summary

The following points summarize the main elements of this lesson:

- A bus is the physical means by which data is made to move inside a computer.

- A bus can take on many different shapes (wires, flat cables, circuit traces), but it is basically a group of parallel wires.

Chapter Summary

The following points summarize the key concepts in this chapter:

Computer Communication

- Computers communicate using binary language.
- An A+ technician must be able to convert decimal numbers to binary and binary numbers to decimal.
- ASCII is the standard code that handles text characters for computers.

The Computer Bus

- A computer uses a bus to move data from one device to another.

Review

1. What is the definition of a bus in a computer?

2. What is the purpose of the computer bus?

3. Define the term "digital."

4. Describe the difference between serial and parallel communication.

5. What is binary code language?

6. How does ASCII use binary code to represent numbers or characters?

7. Define a bit.

8. Define a byte.

9. Which decimal number does the following binary number represent: 00001001?

10. What do ones and zeros represent in computer operation?

11. Computer buses are usually found in multiples of _____ wires or traces.

C H A P T E R   3

An Overview of the Computer

About This Chapter

In this chapter, we begin our study of computer hardware with a general overview of personal-computer design. We go on to define the hardware components that a computer professional can expect to encounter every day—the computer parts that you actually touch.

Before You Begin

If possible, while you work through this chapter, have a PC at hand, with its case open. Take a look at each piece of hardware and try to identify its function as you work through this lesson.

Lesson 1: The Three Stages of Computing

In this lesson, we discuss the three stages of computing and how they relate to the constituent parts that make up the modern personal computer.

After this lesson, you will be able to:

■ Describe the three stages of computing.

Estimated lesson time: 5 minutes

A modern computer looks like a complicated device. It is constructed of many hardware components connected with what seem to be miles of interwoven wires. Despite this apparent complexity, however, a computer, just like a calculator, handles information in three stages: *input*, *processing*, and *output*. (See Figure 3.1.) Each piece of hardware can be classified in one (and sometimes two) of these three stages. We can also use these three stages to classify any aspect of a computer's operation or the function of any of its components. During the troubleshooting phase of a repair job, it is often useful to categorize a problem according to which of the three stages it occurs in.

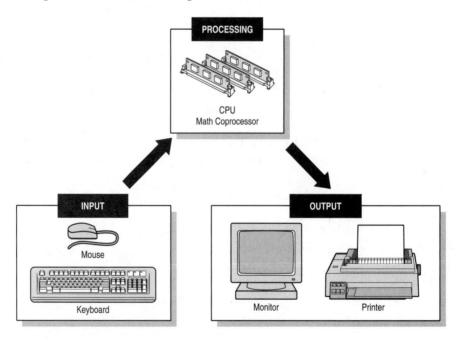

Figure 3.1   Three stages of computing

Input

Input is the first stage of computing. Input refers to any means that moves data (information) from the outside world into the processor. Today's PC can support a wide variety of input devices; keyboards, mouse devices, voice recognition devices, sound cards, modems, scanners, tape drives, CD/DVD drives, and video cameras are some of the most common.

Processing

Processing is the second stage of computing: the actual manipulation of data by the computer. Computers were designed initially as tools to carry out the tedious task of "number crunching" and then, later, to store large amounts of often redundant data. Today, computers not only fulfill ever-expanding scientific and business roles, but they also fill our lives with education, entertainment, organization, information processing, and—occasionally—frustration. As we enter this new century, computers have become a necessity of life and are often taken for granted. Even for people who do not own or use a personal computer, they are an increasing part of everyday life. And computer technology hides in many everyday appliances. Microprocessors run most of our mechanical and electronic devices, including cars, cameras, VCRs, microwave ovens, telephones, and the checkout system at the supermarket.

Output

Output is the third stage of computing. All the input and processing in the world won't do us any good unless we can get the information back from the computer in a comprehensible and usable form. Output devices today come in many forms: monitors, printers, fax machines, modems, plotters, CD-recordable discs, sound cards, and more.

Input, Processing, and Output

Whenever you sit down at a computer and run an application—whether it is a game, spreadsheet, database, or word processor—you are an active part of the input, processing, and output operation of that computer. The following table provides some examples.

Application	Function
Word processor	Input: Typing your words.
	Processing: Formatting the text (such as wordwrap and fonts).
	Output: Storing the text and allowing you to retrieve or print it.
Spreadsheet	Input: Typing or providing numbers (such as sales figures).
	Processing: Applying one or more formulas to the data.
	Output: Displaying the results of the calculation in numeric or graphical form.
Database	Input: Typing information into a data form.
	Processing: Indexing and storing the data records.
	Output: Producing reports showing selected data records.
Game	Input: Moving your chess piece.
	Processing: Computer calculating how to respond to your move.
	Output: Computer making a move.

Lesson Summary

The following points summarize the main elements of this lesson:

- All computer hardware can be classified according to its primary function: input, processing, or output.
- Any time you sit down at a computer and run an application, you are using the input, processing, and output stages of computing.

Lesson 2: Components of a Computer

In this lesson, we take a look at the different components of a computer system.

After this lesson, you will be able to:

- Define the primary components that make up a computer.

Estimated lesson time: 10 minutes

As you might expect, the components of a computer reflect the function of the machine—specifically, the three stages of computing, as outlined in Lesson 1. Let's examine the components.

Input

The following table lists the devices that are used to put information into the machine.

Device	Description
Keyboard	The primary input device for a computer.
Mouse	Used with graphical interface environments to point and select objects on the system's monitor. Can be purchased in a variety of sizes, shapes, and configurations.
Scanner	Converts printed or photographic information to digital information that can be used by the computer. Works similarly to the scanning process of a photocopy machine.
Microphone	Works like the microphone on a tape recorder. Allows input of voice or music to be converted to digital information and saved to a file.
CD-ROM	Compact disc–read only memory: stores large amounts of data on a compact disc that can be read by a computer.

Processing

The CPU (central processing unit) is the heart and brain of the computer. This one component or "chip" is responsible for all the number crunching and data management. It is truly the centerpiece of any computer. It is so important that whole generations of computer technology are based and measured on each "new and improved" version of the CPU.

When we refer to the CPU, we are usually speaking of the processor. But the CPU also encompasses several other components that support it with the management of data. These components, when working in harmony, make up the computer we know today. The following table lists these components.

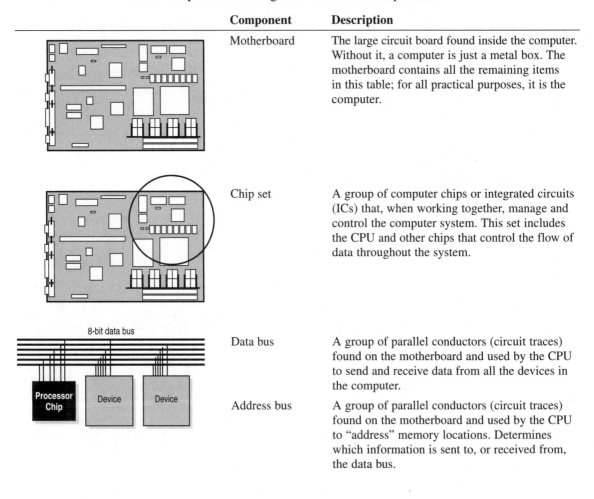

Component	Description
Motherboard	The large circuit board found inside the computer. Without it, a computer is just a metal box. The motherboard contains all the remaining items in this table; for all practical purposes, it is the computer.
Chip set	A group of computer chips or integrated circuits (ICs) that, when working together, manage and control the computer system. This set includes the CPU and other chips that control the flow of data throughout the system.
Data bus	A group of parallel conductors (circuit traces) found on the motherboard and used by the CPU to send and receive data from all the devices in the computer.
Address bus	A group of parallel conductors (circuit traces) found on the motherboard and used by the CPU to "address" memory locations. Determines which information is sent to, or received from, the data bus.

continued

	Component	Description
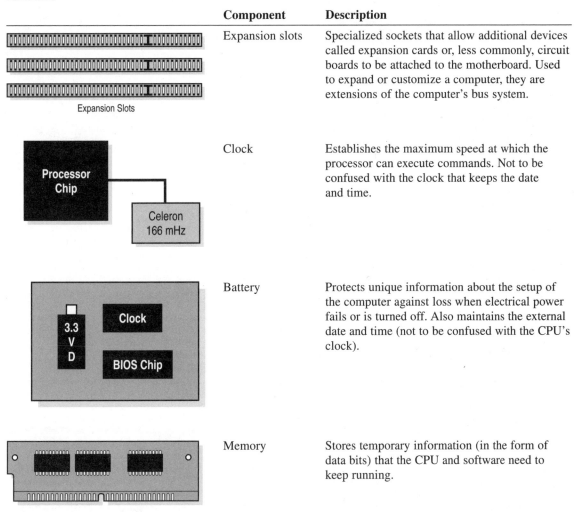	Expansion slots	Specialized sockets that allow additional devices called expansion cards or, less commonly, circuit boards to be attached to the motherboard. Used to expand or customize a computer, they are extensions of the computer's bus system.
	Clock	Establishes the maximum speed at which the processor can execute commands. Not to be confused with the clock that keeps the date and time.
	Battery	Protects unique information about the setup of the computer against loss when electrical power fails or is turned off. Also maintains the external date and time (not to be confused with the CPU's clock).
	Memory	Stores temporary information (in the form of data bits) that the CPU and software need to keep running.

Output

The following table lists some common devices, known as *peripherals*, used exclusively for output.

Device	Description
Printer	Generates a "hard copy" of information.
Monitor	The primary output device. Visually displays text and graphics.
Plotter	Similar to a printer, but uses pens to draw an image. Most often used with graphics or drawing programs.
Speakers	Reproduce sound. Optional high-quality speakers can be added to provide improved output from games and multimedia software.

Input and Output

Some devices handle both input and output functions. These devices are called *input/output (I/O)* devices, a term you will encounter quite often.

Device	Description
Floppy-disk drive	Mechanism to read and write to low-capacity, removable, magnetic disks. Used to store and easily transport information.
Hard-disk drive	High-capacity internal (and sometimes external) magnetic disks for storing data and program files. Also called fixed disks.
Modem	Converts computer data to information that can be transmitted over telephone wires and cable lines. Allows communication between computers over long and short distances.
Network card	An expansion card that allows several computers to connect to each other and share information and programs. Also called network interface card (NIC).
CD recorder	Also called CD/R. You can create a CD with this device, but you can only write to a section of the disc once. Variations on this type of device include CD-RW (CD Read/Write) drives. These products allow you to read, write, and overwrite a special CD-ROM-type disc.
Tape drive	Large-capacity, magnetic, data-storage devices. Ideal for backup and retrieval of large amounts of data. Works like a tape recorder and saves information in a linear format.

Lesson Summary

The following points summarize the main elements of this lesson:

- All computer hardware can be classified by primary function (input, processing, or output).

- Some hardware devices combine multiple functions (input and output).

- Some hardware devices, such as network and modem cards, expand the communication abilities of a computer.

- Data-storage capabilities have been increased with the use of CD-ROM and CD/R.

Lesson 3: Support Hardware

Lesson 2 covered the basic hardware that makes up a computer. There are, however, additional components needed to support safe computer operation. In this lesson, we look at several devices that protect and enhance the value of a computer.

After this lesson, you will be able to:

- Identify additional support hardware for a computer.
- Understand the functions of some of the add-on hardware.

Estimated lesson time: 5 minutes

In addition to the devices that support a computer's data-processing functions, there are others that enhance its operation and performance. The following table lists some of these devices.

Device	Description
Power supply	Converts a local power source (typically 110 volts AC in the U.S.) to 3.3, 5, or 12 volts DC.
Switch box	Allows the user to manually or automatically switch cable connections so that one computer can use several printers or devices with one parallel port.
Surge suppressor	Used to prevent large power spikes (for instance, lightning) from damaging a computer.

(continued)

continued

	Device	Description
	UPS	Uninterruptible Power Supply—Acts as both a surge suppresser (to prevent high-power spikes) and a power leveler to provide the computer with a constant source of power. Can even provide power during a power failure or interruption (although the duration depends on the UPS and the computer's power consumption) so that the user can safely save data before shutting down.
	Case	The box that houses most of the system must provide an environment that minimizes electrical interference to other electronic devices in the area. It should provide a proper heat level for safe operation and bays and connections for drives, circuit boards, and I/O devices.

Don't let the term "supporting role" lead you to underestimate the importance of these components. How important are roads to commerce, or water to a city? Without a reliable power source, modern PCs would not exist. The internal power supply keeps a clean current running to the system.

Lesson Summary

The following points summarize the main elements of this lesson:

- Support equipment protects a computer or makes it easier to operate.
- Support equipment, such as the power supply, is critical to the operation of the computer.

Chapter Summary

The following points summarize the key concepts in this chapter:

The Three Stages of Computing

- Computing occurs in three stages: input, processing, and output.
- All computer hardware can be classified in one or more of these stages.

Components of a Computer

- An input device retrieves data from an outside source and brings it into the computer for processing.
- A processing device takes information and alters it in some useful manner.
- An output device takes the altered information and stores or displays it.

Support Hardware

- Computers require additional components to protect operations and ensure optimal performance.
- Use of surge suppressors and uninterruptible power supplies can protect computers from damage caused by power spikes and surges.

Review

1. Describe the three stages of computing and the role of each.

2. What is the purpose of the central processing unit (CPU)?

3. Describe two devices that process information inside a computer.

4. What is a chip set?

5. Name and describe three input devices.

6. What type of device is a scanner?

7. Describe three output devices.

8. What is I/O?

9. Name three I/O devices.

CHAPTER 4

The Central Processing Unit

About This Chapter

This chapter presents an overview of the central processing unit (CPU), which functions as the "brain" of the personal computer. Like the brain, the CPU is a complicated, highly integrated component performing many simultaneous functions. Understanding the principles that underlie the workings of the microprocessor is critical to understanding the computer and its operation.

Before You Begin

You should be familiar with the terms and concepts introduced in Chapter 1, "Introduction to Computers," and Chapter 2, "Understanding Electronic Communication."

Lesson 1: Microprocessors

A *microprocessor* is an integrated circuit that contains a complete CPU on a single chip. In this lesson, we examine the microprocessor from its inception to the current state-of-the-art chip. It is important for a computer technician to understand the development of the processor and what makes each version different from its predecessors. This knowledge gives us an understanding of the enhancements each new design offers over earlier ones and how the system components can take advantage of the new features.

After this lesson, you will be able to

- Describe how a microprocessor works.
- Define different types of processors and describe their advantages and limitations.

Estimated lesson time: 40 minutes

Computer technicians, fortunately, aren't required to design microprocessors, only to understand how they work. Microprocessors can be viewed as little black boxes that provide answers or perform a variety of chores on command. We also need to understand the external data bus, because it is the means by which the CPU accesses system resources.

The External Data Bus

In previous lessons, you learned that information is transmitted throughout a computer by binary code traveling through a bus. The *external data bus* (also known as the external bus or simply data bus) is the primary route for data in a PC. All data-handling components or optional data devices are connected to it; therefore, any information (code) placed on that bus is available to all devices connected to the computer.

As mentioned in Chapter 1, "Introduction to Computers," early computers used eight conductors (an 8-bit data bus), which allowed for the transfer of 1 byte of information at a time. As computers evolved, the width of the external data bus increased to 16, 32, and finally to the current width of 64 conductors. The wider bus lets more data flow at the same time, just as adding more lanes to a highway allows more cars to move through a point in a given amount of time.

Figure 4.1 shows a CPU attached to its motherboard. The motherboard is the main circuit board, which contains the external data bus and connection for expansion devices that are not part of the board's basic design. The expansion slots act as "on ramps" to the external bus. Expansion cards, once commonly known as "daughter cards," are placed in slots on the motherboard. Other forms of onramp are the slots that hold memory or the sets of pins used to attach drive cables. Connectors on the motherboard grant access to the data bus for keyboards, mouse devices, and peripheral devices like modems and printers through the use of COM and LPT ports.

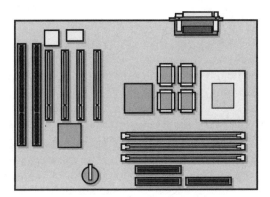

Figure 4.1   Motherboard

To understand how a computer moves data between components, visualize each device on the data bus (including the CPU) connected to the bus by means of a collection of on/off switches. By "looking at" which conductors have power and which ones do not, the device can read the data as it is sent by another device. The on-off state of a line gives the value of 0 (on) or 1 (off). The wires "spell out" a code of binary numbers that the computer interprets and then routes to another system component or to the user by means of an output device such as a monitor or printer. Communication occurs when voltage is properly applied to, or read from, any of the conductors by the system. Figure 4.2 illustrates a data bus connected to a CPU and a device.

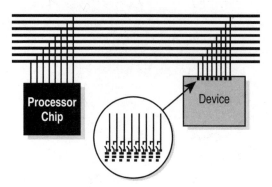

Figure 4.2   External data bus

Coded messages can be sent into or out of any device connected to the external data bus. Think of the data bus as a large highway with parallel lanes. Extending that analogy, bits are like cars traveling side by side—each carries part of a coded message. Microprocessors are used to turn the coded messages into data that performs a meaningful task for the computer's user.

Note   All hardware that uses data is connected in some way to the data bus, or to another device that is connected to the data bus.

The CPU

The CPU is the part of a computer in which arithmetic and logical operations are performed and instructions are decoded and executed. The CPU controls the operation of the computer. Early PCs used several chips to handle the task. Some functions are still handled by support chips, which are often referred to collectively as a "chip set." Figure 4.3 shows a close-up of a CPU and other chips on a motherboard.

Figure 4.3   CPU

Although it is not necessary to know exactly what goes on inside the processor, learning a few terms that you will encounter as a computer professional will be helpful to you in the discussion that follows.

Transistors

Transistors, the main components of microprocessors, are small, electronic switches. The on/off positions of the transistors form the binary codes discussed earlier in this lesson. Although transistors might seem simple, their development required many years of painstaking research. Before transistors were available, computers relied on slow, inefficient vacuum tubes and mechanical switches to process information. The first large-scale computers took up a huge amount of space, and technicians actually went inside them to "program" by turning on and off specific tubes!

Many materials, including most metals, allow electrical current to flow through them—these are known as electrical conductors. Materials that don't pass electrical current are called insulators. Pure silicon (which is used to make most transistors) is a *semiconductor*; its degree of conductivity can be adjusted, or modulated, by adding impurities during production.

Transistor switches have three terminals: the source, the gate, and the drain. When positive voltage is applied to the gate, electrons are attracted, forming an electron channel between the source and the drain. Positive voltage applied to the drain pulls electrons from the source to the drain, turning the transistor on. Removing the voltage turns it off by breaking the pathway.

In the late 1950s, a major development in transistor technology took place. A team of engineers put two transistors on a silicon wafer, creating the world's first integrated circuit and paving the way for the development of compact computers.

Integrated Circuits

An *integrated circuit (IC)* is an electronic device consisting of a number of miniature transistors and other circuit elements (resistors and capacitors, for instance). An IC functions just as a large collection of these parts would, but it is a fraction of the size and uses a fraction of the power. ICs make today's microelectronics possible. The original transistors were small plastic boxes about the size of a peanut (outside its shell), and could handle only one function. The word "integrated" denotes that IC devices combine many circuits—and some of their functions—into one package. A prime example of this technology is the microprocessor.

Microprocessors

On November 15, 1971, Intel shipped the commercial microprocessor, Model 4004. It ran a product called the Busicom calculator. The 108-KHz 4004 had 2300 transistors and a 4-bit data bus and could address 640 bytes of RAM. Computer engineers quickly took advantage of the potential this new type of chip offered, leading the way to the first personal computers.

A year later, the Intel 8008 appeared. *Radio Electronics Magazine* reported that hobbyist Don Lancaster used an 8008 to build what is considered the first personal computer. The article called it a "TV typewriter."

The Intel 8080 appeared in 1974. It sold then for $400, and now sells for about one dollar. It powered traffic lights, but of more interest to our discussion is the fact that it formed the core of the Altair computer of 1975. It was sold in kit form for $395 and was named for a world in the Star Trek TV series. Figure 4.4 shows a picture of the 8080 die. By today's standards, it was very weak: 6000 transistors, an 8-bit bus, and a 2-MHz clock speed. It could address 64 K of RAM, and users programmed the Altair by throwing manual switches located on the case.

Figure 4.4   The Intel 8080 Microprocessor

Microprocessor Design

Before going further into microprocessor-development history, it is important to discuss in general terms how they operate. Microprocessors are usually divided into three subsystems: the control unit (CU), the arithmetic logic unit (ALU), and the input/output unit. The term CPU is used to denote a combined CU and ALU, contained in a single package.

The advent of the control unit marked a radical improvement in processor design, allowing CPU operations to be based in part on code provided by an external program like a BIOS (basic input/output system). This extended the ability of a PC to use new hardware components that were not part of the original design.

The ALU is just what its name implies—the part of the IC that handles the basic, math functions of computation. The I/O unit fetches data from the outside and passes data back to the external bus.

Registers

Registers are temporary memory storage areas used during data manipulation. Physically, registers are rows of microscopic switches, which are set on or off. Each row forms a binary number: off = 0, on = 1. Hence (reading from right to left) off.off.on equals the number 1. Off.on.on equals the number three (0+2+1). The CPU uses registers like scratch pads, to hold data while it works on a task. Changes in data during an operation are also stored in a register, then sent out to other components as the job is finished. The number and width of a register varies from one type of machine to another. The wider the register, the more bits the machine can handle at one time—just as with the width of the external bus. As register width moved from 4 to 8 to 16 to 32 to 64 bits, PCs increased in performance.

Codes

Computers use various binary-based codes to represent information. In Chapter 2, "Understanding Electronic Communication," we saw how ASCII code is a binary representation of characters on a keyboard. These codes are sent on the external data bus by a system component to be read by other devices. Press a key on a PC keyboard and an ASCII code is generated and sent over the data bus. Transferring information to and from the CPU (and other hardware) is only the first step in manipulating data.

Other codes tell the PC how to display data on the monitor, talk to devices such as printers, and take in data streams from scanners. Each of those operations requires system resources and the manipulation of binary numbers.

In addition to the code that requires data, special *machine code* is required in order for the CPU to turn the string of numbers into something useful to an application. As with the data code, this machine code is sent in the form of binary numbers on the data bus. The CPUs in turn are different enough that a code system must be written specifically for each of them.

The Clock

Timing is essential in PC operations. Without some means of synchronization, chaos would ensue. Timing allows the electronic devices in the computer to coordinate and execute all internal commands in the proper order.

Timing is achieved by placing a special conductor in the CPU and pulsing it with voltage. Each pulse of voltage received by this conductor is called a "clock cycle." All the switching activity in the computer occurs while the clock is sending a pulse. This process somewhat resembles several musicians using a metronome to synchronize their playing, with all the violinists moving their bows at the same time. Thanks to this synchronization, you get musical phrasing instead of a jumble of notes.

Virtually every computer command needs at least two clock cycles. Some commands might require hundreds of clock cycles to process. Figure 4.5 shows an external data bus with a CPU and two devices. Notice that the crystal or clock is attached to the CPU to generate the timing.

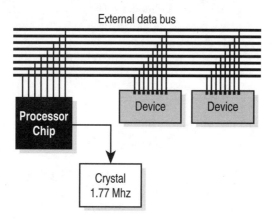

Figure 4.5   CPU with clock

Clock Speed

It is common for computers to be marketed to consumers based on features that show off their best points. One principal selling point is the system clock rate—measured in megahertz (MHz) or millions of cycles per second. The clock rate suggests how many commands can be completed in two cycles (the minimum time required to execute a command). The process of adding two numbers together would take about four commands (eight clock cycles). A computer running at 450 MHz can do about 44 million simple calculations per second.

Clock speed is determined by the CPU manufacturer and represents the fastest speed at which the CPU can be reliably operated. The Intel 8088 processor, as used in the original IBM PC, had a clock speed of 4.77 MHz. Today's processors have clock speeds that run up to and, in some, exceed 750 MHz.

Note   Remember that this speed is the CPU's *maximum* speed. If you place too many clock cycles on a CPU, it can fail or overheat and stop working.

The system crystal determines the speed at which a CPU operates. The system crystal is usually a quartz oscillator, very similar to the one in a wristwatch. You can find the system crystal soldered to the motherboard. Look for a silver part, usually with a label that indicates the crystal speed.

Important   A computer has two clocks: one to set the speed and timing and a second clock to keep time for date/time calculations. They are two entirely different devices.

Memory

The CPU's ability to hold large amounts of information at once is very limited. To compensate, additional chips are installed in the computer for the sole purpose of temporarily storing information that the CPU needs. These chips are called random access memory (RAM). The term *random access* is used because the CPU can place or retrieve bytes of information in or from any RAM *location* at any time. RAM is explored in greater detail in Chapter 7, "Memory."

Address Bus

The word "location" is italicized in the last paragraph to underscore the importance of location in PC memory operations. The content of RAM is changing all the time, as programs and the computer itself use portions of it to note, calculate, and hold results of actions. It is essential for the system to know what memory is assigned to which task and when that memory is free for a new use. To do so, the system has to have a way to address segments of memory and to quickly change the holdings in that position. The portion of the PC that does this is the *address bus*.

Think of the address bus as a large, virtual table in which the columns are individual bits (like letters) and each row contains a string of bits (making up a word). The actual lengths of these words will vary depending on the number of bits the address bus can handle in a single pass. Figure 4.6 shows a table containing 1s and 0s. Each segment is given an address, just like the one that identifies a home or post office box. The system uses this address to send data to or retrieve data from memory.

1 byte

1	0	0	0	0	0	0	1
0	0	0	0	0	0	0	0
1	1	0	0	0	0	1	1
0	0	0	0	0	0	0	0
0	0	0	0	0	0	0	0
0	0	0	1	0	1	1	1
1	1	1	1	1	1	1	1
1	0	0	0	0	0	0	1
1	1	1	1	1	1	1	1
0	0	0	0	0	1	1	1

Figure 4.6 Memory spreadsheet

Like all the other buses in a PC, this one is a collection of conductors. It links the physical memory to the system and moves signals as memory is used. The number of conductors in the address bus determines the maximum amount of memory that can be used (memory that is *addressable*) by the CPU. Remember that computers count in binary notation. Each binary digit—in this case, a conductor—that is added to the left will double the number of possible combinations.

Early data buses used eight conductors and, therefore, 256 (2^8) combinations of code where possible. The maximum number of patterns a system can generate determines how much RAM the data bus can address. The 8088 used 20 address conductors and could address up to 1,048,576 bytes of memory locations, or 2^{20}. Today's PCs can address a lot more than that, and, in many cases, the actual limiting factor is not the number of patterns, but the capacity of the motherboard to socket memory chips. In all cases, the total amount of memory is the factor of 2^X, where X = the number of connectors.

The CPU does not directly connect to the memory bus, but sends requests and obtains results using the system's memory controller. This circuitry acts as both postmaster and translator, providing the proper strings of data in the right order, at the right time, and in a form the CPU can use. As mentioned before, any write or read action will require at least two clock cycles to execute. (It can require more clock cycles on systems that do not have memory tuned to the maximum system clock speed. In that case, the PC will have to use additional clock cycles while it waits for the memory to be ready for the next part of the operation.)

Figure 4.7 shows a diagram of the process with the CPU and RAM stack on the external data bus. The address bus is connected to the memory controller. It fetches and places data in memory.

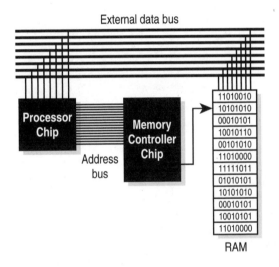

Figure 4.7 CPU and RAM

How Microprocessors Work

Current CPUs, such as the Intel Pentium III, are collections of millions of switches and bus pathways. They operate all kinds of machines, in addition to PCs, and are found in cameras, cars, microwave ovens, TVs, and all kinds of gadgets. Here, however, we are interested only in how they work inside a PC. Let's look at a simple task: adding two numbers such as 2 and 2 together and obtaining their sum (2 + 2 = 4). The CPU can do math problems very quickly, but it requires several very quick steps to do it. Knowing how a CPU performs a simple task will help you understand how developments in PC design have improved PC performance.

When the user pushes a number key (in a program like Calculator, which can add numbers), the keystroke causes the microprocessor's prefetch unit to ask for instructions on what to do with the new data. The data is sent through the address bus to the PC's RAM and is placed in the instruction cache, with a reference code (let's call it 2 = a).

The prefetch unit obtains a copy of the code and sends it to the decode unit. There it is translated into a string of binary code and routed to the control unit and the data cache to tell them what to do with the instruction. The control unit sends it to an address called "X" in the data cache to await the next part of the process.

When the plus (+) key is pressed, the prefetch unit again asks the instruction cache for instructions about what to do with the new data. The prefetch unit translates the code and passes it to the control unit and data cache, which alerts the ALU that an ADD function will be carried out. The process is repeated when the user presses the "2" key.

Next (yes, there's still more to do), the control unit takes the code and sends the actual ADD command to the ALU. The ALU sums "a" and "b" are added together after they have been sent up from the data cache. The ALU sends the code for "4" to be stored in an address register.

Pressing the equal sign (=) key is the last act the user must execute before getting the answer, but the computer still has a good bit of work ahead of it. The prefetch unit checks the instruction cache for help in dealing with the new keystroke. The resulting instruction is stored, and a copy of the code is sent to the decode unit for processing. There, the instruction is translated into binary code and routed to the control unit. Now that the sum has (finally) been computed, a print command retrieves the proper address, registers the contents, and displays them. (That involves a separate flurry of activity in the display system, which we won't worry about.)

As you can see, a microprocessor must go through many more steps than human beings are required to take, merely to arrive at the conclusion that 2 + 2 = 4. The computer must execute a complicated dance in order to manage the code, place it, and fetch it in memory; then it has to be told what to do with it. Yet the result usually appears as fast as you can type the request. You can see that clock cycles and, hence, processor speed, have a significant effect on performance. Other issues that affect performance include memory access and speed, as well as the response time of components such as the display system.

PC Microprocessor Developments and Features

PC microprocessor design grows more complex with each generation, and CPU packaging keeps changing to provide room for additional features and operating requirements. Microprocessors have evolved from the 4004 described earlier into today's high-speed Pentiums. Each new processor has brought higher performance and spawned new technology. Six basic elements are customarily used to gauge the performance and capability of a CPU design:

- Speed: The maximum number of clock cycles measured in megahertz. The higher the speed, the quicker a command will be executed.

- Number of transistors: More switches, more computing power.

- Registers: The size (in bits) of the internal registers. The larger the registers, the more complicated the commands that can be processed in one step.

- External data bus: As data bus size increases, so does the amount and complexity of code (information) that can be transferred between all devices in the computer.

- Address bus: The size of the address bus determines the maximum amount of memory that can be addressed by the CPU.

- Internal cache: The internal cache is high-speed memory built into the processor. This is a place to store frequently used data instead of sending it to slower devices (speed is relative in computers) such as RAM and hard disk drives. It is built into the processor and has a dramatic effect on speed. We cover cache in more detail later in this lesson.

Intel has held most of the PC CPU market share since the original IBM PC was introduced. Closely following each new Intel launch, rivals such as Advanced Microdevices (AMD) and Cyrix have offered alternative chips that are generally compatible with the Intel models. This development, in turn, drives prices down and spurs a new round of CPU design. Another player is Motorola, a firm that manufactures the microprocessors used in the Apple family of computers, among others.

Intel's 8086 and 8088: The Birth of the PC

We have already introduced the "pre-PC" CPUs. Now we take a look at the models that have powered one of the most dramatic developments of the modern world: the inexpensive, general-purpose computer.

On June 6, 1978, Intel introduced its first 16-bit microprocessor, known as the 8086. It had 29,000 transistors, 16-bit registers, a 16-bit external data bus, and a 20-bit address bus to allow it to access 1 MB of memory. When IBM entered the computer business, the 8086 was too powerful (and expensive) to meet its requirements.

Intel then released the 8088 processor, which was identical to the 8086 except for an 8-bit external data bus, and a slower top clock rate. This meant that 8-bit components (more common at the time) could be used for the construction of PCs, and 8-bit applications written for earlier machines could be converted for PC use. The following table compares the 8088 and 8086 chips.

Chip	Number of Transistors	CPU Speed (MHz)	Register Width	External Data Bus	Address Bus	Internal Cache
Intel 8088	29,000	4.77–8	16-bit	8-bit	20-bit	None
Intel 8086	29,000	4.77–10	16-bit	16-bit	20-Bit	None

The early 8088 processors ran at 4.77 MHz, while later versions ran at 8 MHz. The 8086 and 8088 processors came as a 40-pin DIP (dual inline package) containing approximately 29,000 transistors. The DIP is so named because of the two rows of pins on either side of the processor, as shown in Figure 4.8. These fit into a set of slots on a raised socket on the motherboard. The small u-shaped notch at one end of a DIP-style CPU denotes the end that has pin 1. During installation, you well need to be sure to line it up correctly, or you might have to repeat the process.

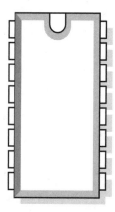

Figure 4.8 DIPP (Dual Inline Package Processor) used for 8086, 8088, and 80286 CPUs

Note The 8088 and 8086 are software-compatible—they can run exactly the same programs (assuming the PCs that use them don't have other complicating factors). The benefit of using an 8086 is its 16-bit external data bus. This allows an 8086-based computer to execute the same software faster than an 8088 computer with the same clock speed.

The early IBM personal computers based on the 8086 and 8088 chips featured:

- 16 KB of memory.
- Cassette tape recorder or floppy disk drive for program and data storage.
- Nongraphics monochrome monitor and monochrome display adapter (MDA).

Soon, a new industry was born as third-party vendors started manufacturing add-ons and improved models of the basic design. Graphics cards with color and better resolution, clocks, additional memory, and peripherals, such as printers, extended the features of the new appliance. "Clones" offered some of these extras at very competitive prices, as a way to attract buyers who wanted a lower price and did not need the comfort of purchasing from a big name like IBM.

Note   A clone is a computer that contains the same microprocessor and runs the same programs as a better-known, more prestigious, and often more expensive machine.

Most of the 8088 and 8086-based PCs used some variation of MS-DOS. The variations limited the growth of the software market because of the compatibility issues they presented between versions of MS-DOS. Buyers had to be sure that a program would run on their specific version of MS-DOS.

As users found more ways to take advantage of the PC's power, developers and owners alike soon felt the limitations of the original IBM PC design. The engineers who created it never envisioned the need for more than 16 K of RAM. "Who would ever need more than that?" one is quoted as saying. The cassette drive was never a big seller; most buyers opted for one or two 5.25-inch floppy disk drives, and many soon craved color graphics and the space of the "massive" 5- and 10-MB hard disk drives.

To meet that growing demand, IBM introduced a more robust PC, the XT (eXtended Technology), that could take advantage of a hard disk drive and came with either a monochrome or four-color display and more RAM. Clone makers soon followed suit.

The 80286 and the IBM PC AT

In February, 1982, Intel introduced the 80286 6-MHz microprocessor (later pushing the clock speeds to 10 and 12.5 MHz), commonly called the 286, with a 24-bit address path. In 1983, IBM unveiled its PC AT (Advanced Technology) computer, based on the 286. It had a larger, boxier design, came with a standard hard drive, and a new expansion slot format, rendering older add-on cards obsolete.

The AT could run the same applications as the PC XT (8088), but run them faster. The use of a 24-bit address path allowed the 286 to access up to 16 MB of memory. The clone-makers soon followed suit, taking advantage of third-party versions of the 286. Chip makers Harris and AMD produced versions of the 286 that could run at up to 20 MHz.

Computers based on the 80286 chip featured:

- Two memory modes (real and protected).
- 16 MB of addressable memory.
- Clock speeds up to 20 MHz.
- Reduced command set (fewer program commands to do more work).
- Multitasking abilities.
- Virtual memory support.

Virtual Memory

Virtual memory is the art of using hard disk space to hold data not immediately required by the processor; it is placed in and out of RAM as needed. Although using virtual memory slowed the system down (electronic RAM is much faster than a mechanical hard drive), it allowed the 286 to address up to 1 GB (gigabyte—one thousand megabytes) of memory (16 MB of actual memory and 984 MB of virtual memory). Virtual memory required the use of operating systems more advanced than MS-DOS, leading to the development of products such as Microsoft Windows, IBM OS/2, and SCO's PC version of UNIX.

Real Mode vs. Protected Mode

The 286 might have made older hardware outdated, but Intel had no desire to invoke industry ire and slow the adoption of the new chip by requiring all-new software applications. The result was a CPU with two operating modes: real and protected.

In *real mode,* sometimes called compatibility mode, a 286 emulates the 8086 processor and addresses only the first 1 MB of memory. This mode is used to run older software. *Protected mode* allows access to all memory on the system, physical and virtual. In protected mode, a program can write only to the memory allocated to it, with specific memory blocks allocated to different programs.

This mode can go well beyond the 16 MB of "true" memory, opening up the possibility of multitasking—running more than one program at a time.

This development required new, more powerful operating systems and applications, but they were slow in coming. By the time they arrived on the market, the 286 was functionally obsolete, but it paved the way for today's powerful multitasking environments such as Windows 95 and 98, Windows NT and 2000. Another major drawback to the 286's memory management scheme was its need to reboot the system when changing between real and protected modes.

The original 286 processor came packaged in DIP (already shown), PGA (pin grid array), and PLCC (plastic leadless chip carrier) designs. The PLCC can be recognized by the arrangement of thin legs around its perimeter. The PLCC's major advantage is its stronger leads (pins), which make it more difficult to damage during removal or installation. PLCCs became popular because they made it easier to upgrade a PC with a faster CPU.

Note PGA and PLCC models look very much alike, but CPUs designed for some types can't be socketed in the other type. Verify the type you need before ordering or attempting a replacement or upgrade (see Figure 4.9).

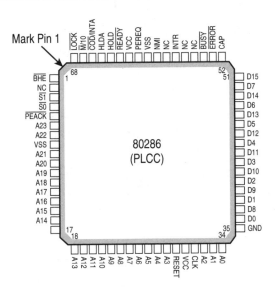

Figure 4.9 Plastic Leadless Chip Carrier (PLCC) CPU Package

The 80386 Arrives

On June 16, 1985, Intel introduced the original 80386 (commonly known as the 386). This true 32-bit processor was equipped with a 32-bit external data bus, 32-bit registers, and a 32-bit address bus. The first models shipped with a clock speed of 16 MHz, and the CPU sported 275,000 transistors. It could directly address 4 GB of RAM, and 64 TB (terabytes—a terabyte is approximately one trillion bytes) of virtual memory. According to Intel, the 386 could hold an eight-page history of every person on earth in that address space. The 386 was a true generational leap in PC computing, with true multitasking capability—it really could run more than one program at a time. That was due to a third memory mode, called *virtual real mode,* that allowed independent MS-DOS sessions (called "virtual machines") to coexist on the same system at once. It spawned a host of programs called "memory managers" designed to optimize (and trouble-shoot) the more complex world of virtual memory.

The original 80386 chips shipped with speeds of 12 or 16 MHz. Intel produced faster versions—25 and 33 MHz, while AMD manufactured a 40-MHz variant. The 386 provided both the real and protected mode available in the 286.

By April of 1989, the 386 was running at clock speeds of 33 MHz, and Intel was calling it the 80386DX to distinguish it from a lower-cost model, the 386SX.

The 386SX: A Scaled-Down Version

The 386SX came on the scene in June, 1988. Intel wanted to increase the sales of 386-based machines without dramatically dropping the price of its flagship CPU. The result was the introduction of a scaled-down model for "entry-level" computers. It had a 16-bit external data bus and a 24-bit address bus (it could address only 16 MB of memory). The 16-bit configuration allowed it to be used as an upgrade chip for existing 16-bit motherboards, thereby providing an easy transition to the next generation of computers.

The following table compares members of the 80386 chip family from Intel and rival AMD. The AMD 80386DXLV is notable as the first PC CPU with an internal cache.

Chip	Number of Transistors	CPU Speed (MHz)	Register Width	External Data Bus	Address Bus	Internal Cache
Intel 80386SX	275,000	16–25	32-bit	16-bit	24-bit	None
Intel 80386DX	275,000	16–33	32-bit	32-bit	32-bit	None
AMD 80386DX	275,000	20–40	32-bit	32-bit	32-bit	None
AMD 80386DXL	275,000	20–33	32-bit	32-bit	32-bit	None
AMD 80386DXLV	275,000	20–33	32-bit	32-bit	32-bit	8 KB

Note   The terms "SX" and "DX" are not acronyms; they do not stand for longer terms.

386 Packaging

The 386 was usually placed in either a PLCC package or a PGA package. This type of mount can be found with the 80386, 486, and some older Pentiums up to 166-MHz models. The pins are evenly distributed in concentric rows along the bottom of the chip (see Figure 4.10).

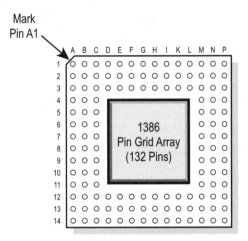

Figure 4.10   PGA (Pin Grid Array)

PGA chips go into regular PGA or the popular ZIF (zero insertion force) sockets. Care must be used when inserting or removing CPUs from a PGA mount—it is very easy to bend the pins if you do not pull perfectly straight up from the socket or have a slight uneven push downward. ZIF mounts are a bit better, but much tech time has been wasted straightening pins, and it is possible to ruin a CPU! PGA mounts are often "hidden" under a CPU fan, which presents another hurdle during repair or upgrade.

A variation of the PGA is the SPGA (staggered pin grid array). It looks almost the same, but with (surprise!) staggered rows of pins. This allows engineers to place more connectors in a smaller area. It also adds emphasis to the caution given earlier about not bending pins through careless removal or insertion.

Both the PGA and SPGA have three pointed corners and a "snipped corner" on one side. Use that corner to line the chip with the socket. If it does not go in smoothly—double check!

Laptop Designs and the Plastic Quad Flat Pack

Some forms of portable PC have existed from the days of the 8088. The early models, such as the Osborne and the original Compaq, were known as "luggables"—tipping the scales at close to 30 pounds. Their cases looked more suited for holding sewing machines than computers. Modern laptop computers started to gain popularity with the advent of the 386 chip and the use of flat screen monitors incorporated in the design, rather than conventional video tubes.

To seat 80286, 80386, and 486 CPUs (the latter are covered in the section that follows) on the more compact laptop motherboards, many vendors use plastic quad flat pack (PQFP) mounts, which are also more secure than traditional socket types designed for systems that will not be moved as much. PQFPs require a submount called a "carrier ring" (see Figure 4.11). PQFPs require a special tool for placing or removing a CPU. Be sure to get the tool before attempting repairs on PQFP-mounted CPUs.

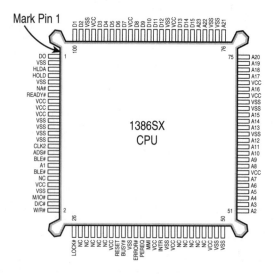

Figure 4.11   PQFP (Plastic Quad Flat Pack)

80486

April 10, 1989, brought us the 80486 line of processors. Once again, the rallying cry was "better and faster." By this time, applications like CorelDRAW, Adobe PhotoShop, and desktop-publishing tools like PageMaker and Ventura Publisher were generating more interest in faster systems. Microsoft Windows was gaining popularity and on its way to becoming the standard desktop environment.

The 486 processor started life at 25 MHz and could address 4 GB of RAM and 64 TB of virtual memory. It is the first PC CPU to break the 1-million transistor mark with 1,200,000. It provided a built-in math coprocessor (older PC CPUs offered separate math coprocessors as an option—usually with a similar number ending in a 7 rather than a 6). The combination speeded up graphics programs that used floating-point math.

The 486SX and Beyond

Once again, Intel sought a way to increase sales without weakening the price of the flagship version of its 486DX CPU, so it added an SX version in April, 1991. This time, the company achieved its goal by removing the math coprocessor, reducing the number of transistors to 1,185,000. Users could upgrade the SX to a 486DX by adding an optional OverDrive processor to restore the missing component.

The 486 label was attached to other chip designs during its active development phase, both by Intel and third-party chip makers. The 486SL, a variant with a 20- to 33-MHz clock and 1.4 million transistors, debuted in 1992. It was very popular in high-performance laptop computers, running at lower voltage (3.3 volts instead of 5 volts) than the usual 486. The small (and for that time) powerful machines also included System Management Mode (SMM), which can dim the LCD screen and power down the hard disk drive—extending the life of the battery.

System Memory Management

System Memory Management (SMM) is a hardware-based function that allows the microprocessor to selectively shut down the monitor, hard drives, and any other peripherals not in use. SMM works at the chip level; the microprocessor can be operating in real, protected, or virtual 8086 mode. SMM is transparent to all software running on the system, which decreases the likelihood of lockups.

Clock-Doubling Debuts

The need for speed spurred the introduction of new models of the 486 family through the spring of 1994, the last variations being the DX2 and DX4. These chips were models with faster clock speeds of up to 100 MHz. The processors were either 25- or 33-MHz versions that had been altered to run internally at double or triple their external speed. For example, the DX4 version of the 486 33-MHz processor ran at 33 MHz externally, but at 100 MHz internally (3 x 33.3 MHz). This meant that internal operations, such as numeric calculations or moving data from one register to another, occurred at 100 MHz, while external operations, like loading data from memory, took place at 33 MHz.

Slower external clock speeds allowed existing motherboard and memory designs to be used. Upgrades were less expensive, and new machines based on the DX technology could quote faster benchmarks at lower costs. The DX4 offered 16 KB of on-board cache, further boosting performance. The DX2 50-MHz-based machines should not be confused with machines designed around the 50-MHz 486DX processor—the latter performed much better.

Vendors such as AMD rode the wave with their own editions of the 486 for users feeling a need for greater speed. The following table lists the most popular 486 chips and third-party work-alikes.

Chip	CPU Speed (MHz)	Register Width	External Data Bus	Address Bus	Internal Cache
Intel 80486DX	25, 33, 50	32-bit	32-bit	32-bit	8 KB
Intel 80486DX/2	50, 66	32-bit	32-bit	32-bit	8 KB
Intel 80486DX/4	75, 100	32-bit	32-bit	32-bit	16 KB
Intel 80486SX	16, 20, 25	32-bit	32-bit	32-bit	8 KB
Intel 80486SL	16, 20, 25	32-bit	32-bit	32-bit	8 KB
AMD AM486DX	33, 40	32-bit	32-bit	32-bit	8 KB
AMD AM486DXLV	33	32-bit	32-bit	32-bit	8 KB
AMD AM486DX2	50, 80	32-bit	32-bit	32-bit	8 KB
AMD AM486DX4	100, 120	32-bit	32-bit	32-bit	8 KB
AMD AM486DX "Enhanced"	120, 133	32-bit	32-bit	32-bit	16 KB W/B
AMD AM486DXL2	50, 80	32-bit	32-bit	32-bit	8 KB
AMD AM486SX	33, 40	32-bit	32-bit	32-bit	8 KB
AMD AM486SXLV	33	32-bit	32-bit	32-bit	8 KB
AMD AM486SX2	33	32-bit	32-bit	32-bit	8 KB
CYRX CX486DX	33	32-bit	32-bit	32-bit	8 KB W/B
CYRX CX486DX2	50–80	32-bit	32-bit	32-bit	8 KB W/B
CYRX CX486DLC	33–40	32-bit	32-bit	32-bit	1 KB W/B
CYRX CX486SLC	20–33	32-bit	32-bit	32-bit	1 KB W/B
CYRX CX486SLC2	50	32-bit	32-bit	32-bit	1 KB W/B

Note   W/T (write-through) and W/B (write-back) cache are explained in Chapter 7, "Memory."

Heat Sinks and Fans

The 486 is notable for one other item, the addition of a standard heat sink and, usually, a fan mounted on the CPU and powered by the PC. To maintain stable operation, the PC must provide proper cooling for the 5486 and newer CPUs. Failure of the cooling apparatus can lead to erratic behavior and—uncorrected—can damage the chip. If a customer complains of strange noises inside the PC, the CPU fan is a good place to look. As their bearings age, they start to whine.

Pentium

By 1993, Windows was standard, and users expected a lot more from PCs in performance and features. Increasing software sophistication led to increasing memory usage and hard disk drive requirements. The market was ready for a major upgrade in CPUs, and Intel once again addressed that need. The new Pentium processor signaled a radical redesign of both the CPU and naming conventions.

With their CPUs identified by numbers, Intel faced a business problem: numbers cannot be trademarked. The company's strategy was to substitute a trademarkable name, "Pentium," for their upcoming chips that would otherwise have been named "586." The word is based on the Latin word for the number five, and this chip would have been the 80586. The original design has been revamped several times since 1993, and now there are Pentium IIs and IIIs. Like the older PC CPUs, the Pentium has spawned its share of clones, leading to entry-level PCs priced under $400.

The Pentium (Series I) offers the following features:

- Speeds of 60 to over 200 MHz.
- 32-bit address bus and 32-bit registers.
- 64-bit data path to improve the speed of data transfers.
- Dual pipeline, 32-bit data bus that allows the chip to process two separate lines of code simultaneously.
- At least 8-KB write-back cache for data and an 8-KB write-through cache for programs. (Types of caches are explained in more detail in Chapter 7, "Memory.")
- "Branch prediction"—in which the program cache attempts to anticipate branching within the code. The CPU stores a few lines of code from each branch so that when the program reaches the branch, the Pentium already has the code stored within the cache.

The following table lists the first generation of Pentium and Pentium-compatible chips.

Chip	Speed (MHz)	Register Width	External Data Bus	Address Bus	Internal Cache
Intel Pentium	60, 66	32-bit	64-bit	32-bit	8 KB W/B and 8 KB W/T
Intel Pentium	75	32-bit	64-bit	32-bit	8 KB W/B and 8 KB W/T
Intel Pentium	90, 100	32-bit	64-bit	32-bit	8 KB W/B and 8 KB W/T
Intel Pentium	120, 130	32-bit	64-bit	32-bit	8 KB W/B and 8 KB W/T
Intel Pentium	150, 166	32-bit	64-bit	32-bit	8 KB W/B and 8 KB W/T
Intel Pentium	180, 200	32-bit	64-bit	32-bit	8 KB W/B and 8 KB W/T
CYRIX 6x86(P-rating)	100, 120, 133, 200	32-bit	64-bit	32-bit	8 KB W/B and 8 KB W/T
AMD K5 (P-rating)	75, 90	32-bit	64-bit	32-bit	8 KB W/B and 8 KB W/T

Note   W/T (write-through) and W/B (write back) caches are explained in Chapter 7, "Memory." P-rating is a standard method of rating chips by their equivalency to a Pentium chip. It avoids direct comparison of clock speeds. Each processor is tested on an identical system and measured accordingly. If a chip performs 1.5 percent slower than a Pentium chip, it gets the same rating as the next lower chip.

Mass-producing reliable P66 Pentiums proved difficult, and many were rejected during quality control. The faulty chips were stable at clock speeds of 60 MHz, so Intel sold them as the P60. Some users change their P60 processor clock speed to 66 MHz by changing a jumper on the motherboard. This might work, but computer performance and longevity can be unpredictable.

Intel continued to use the 0.8-micron manufacturing process (the ability to draw lines as fine as 1/1000 of a millimeter on the die, about 16,000 lines per inch), begun with the 486, to fit 3.1 million transistors on the Pentium chip. The P66 used considerable power and consequently generated a large amount of heat. Operating a reliable heat sink and fan became critical with the advent of the Pentium.

The Pentium 75 was released in 1994. These chips were made using a 0.6-micron manufacturing process (approximately 21,000 lines and spaces per inch) and, as a result, they required considerably less power, despite an additional 200,000 transistors. Intel was able to change the power supply from 5 volts to 3.3 volts (the DX4 also had a reduced power supply), which reduced by nearly one half the amount of heat produced. The P90 and P100 processors were released at this time. These processors ran internally at 1.5 times the external speed (60 or 66 MHz, which was the fastest system board). A P75 processor was also released for use in lower specification machines and laptop computers.

Superscalar Technology

The main components of a processor—registers, decoders, and ALUs (arithmetic/logic units)—are collectively known as the *instruction pipeline*. To carry out a single instruction, a processor must:

- Read the instruction.
- Decode the instruction.
- Fetch operands (for math functions).
- Execute the instruction.
- Write back the results.

Early processors carried out these steps one at a time. Combining these steps into a single clock cycle, a process known as *pipelining*, thereby increases the speed of processing. *Superscalar technology* allows the Pentium to have two instruction pipelines—called U and V. The U pipeline can execute the full range of Pentium instructions, while the V pipeline can execute a limited number. When possible, the Pentium processor breaks up a program into discrete tasks that are then shared between the pipelines, thus allowing the Pentium to execute two simple instructions simultaneously. Software must be specifically written to take advantage of this innovative feature, which is known as *multithreading*.

Pentium On-Board Cache

The original Pentium series came with two 8-KB caches—one for data and one for program code, compared with the single 8-KB cache on the 486 (16 KB on the DX4). As described with the 486 chip, the cache uses a technique called "branch prediction" to improve its ability to guess what data or program code will be required next by the processor.

Intel's Competitors

Competitors have moved away from simply making clones of the Intel processors. They are currently designing their own processors with unique features:

- NextGen Nx586
- AMD AmSx86
- Cyrix 6x86
- IBM 6x86

RISC (Reduced Instruction Set Computing)

Until recently, all the Intel processors had been based on a CISC (complex instruction set computing) architecture. Processors based on RISC (reduced instruction set computing) have been used in high-powered machines since the mid-1980s. Intel has produced its own version of a RISC-based processor that uses a much smaller and simpler set of instructions, greatly enhancing the speed of the processor.

Pentium Pro

Intel made CPU selection even more complex with the introduction of the Pentium Pro, offering varied features, in different models, of the Pentium design. This processor was aimed at a 32-bit server and workstation-level applications such as computer-aided design (CAD), mechanical engineering, and advanced scientific computation. The Pentium Pro was packaged with a second speed-enhancing cache memory chip, and boasted 5.5 million transistors. First available in November, 1995, it incorporated an internal RISC architecture with a CISC-RISC translator, three-way superscalar execution, and dynamic execution. While compatible with all the previous software for the Intel line, the Pentium Pro is optimized to run 32-bit software. Its pin structure and mount differ from the basic Pentium, requiring a special ZIF socket. Some motherboards have sockets for both Pentium and Pentium Pro, but most machines use motherboards designed for one or the other. The package was a 2.46-inch by 2.66-inch 387-pin PGA configuration to house a Pentium Pro processor core and an on-board L2 cache. Although mounted on one PGA device, they are two ICs. A single, gold-plated copper/tungsten heat spreader gives them the appearance of a single chip.

The main CPU and 16-KB first-level (L1) cache consist of 5.5 million transistors; the second chip is a 256- or 512-KB second-level (L2) cache with 15 million transistors. A 133-MHz Pentium Pro processes data about twice as fast as a 100-MHz Pentium.

One reason for the better performance is a technology called *dynamic execution*. Before processing, the data flow is analyzed and sequenced for optimal execution. Then the system looks ahead in the program process and predicts where the next branch or group of instructions can be found in memory, then processes up to five instructions before they are needed. By using a technique known as *data-flow analysis*, the Pentium Pro can determine dependencies between data items so they can be processed as soon as their inputs are available, regardless of the program's order.

Pentium MMX

Soon, more choices were on the way. About the time the 166-MHz Pentiums shipped, Intel introduced MMX (multimedia extension) technology, designed to enhance performance of data-hungry applications like graphics and games. With larger data and code caches, Pentiums with MMX technology can run non-MMX-enhanced software approximately 10 to 20 percent faster than a non-MMX CPU with the same clock speed.

To reap the full benefits of the new processor, MMX-enhanced software makes use of 57 special multimedia instructions. These new MMX operators use a technology called *single instruction multiple data (SIMD)* stream processing. SIMD allows different processing elements to perform the same operations on different data—a central controller broadcasts the instruction to all processing elements in the same way that a drill sergeant would tell a whole platoon to "about face," rather than instruct each soldier individually.

The MMX chips also take advantage of dynamic branch prediction using the *branch target buffer* (BTB) to predict the most likely set of instructions to be executed.

The MMX Pentium processor is also more compatible with older 16-bit software than is the Pentium Pro; consequently, it soon doomed the Pro to the backwaters of PC computing. All later versions of the Pentium have incorporated some variation of MMX and improved on it. The original Pentium desktop line ended with the 233-MHz MMX release in June of 1997.

Pentium II

By 1997, multimedia was becoming mainstream, and high performance in a graphical user environment was critical to CPU market success. Intel upped the ante with its competitors in 1997 with a radical redesign. The first 233-MHz, 7.5 million-transistor, Pentium II processor incorporated MMX technology and was packaged with a high-speed cache memory chip. Intel released Pentium II versions operating at speeds of up to 450 MHz.

The Pentium II incorporated the features of its older designs and added a number of enhancements. Among these are:

- Multiple Branch Prediction: predicts program execution through several branches, accelerating the flow of work to the processor.
- Data-flow Analysis: Creates an optimized, reordered schedule of instructions by analyzing data dependencies between instructions.
- Speculative Execution: Carries out instructions speculatively and, based on this optimized schedule, ensures that the processor's superscalar execution units remain busy, boosting overall performance.

- Single-edge connector (SEC) cartridge packaging: Developed by Intel, this enables high-volume availability and offers improved handling protection and a common form factor for future high-performance processors. This development resolved problems caused when pins were accidentally bent during installation or removal of CPUs.

- High-performance Dual Independent Bus (DIB) architecture (system bus and cache bus).

- System bus that supports multiple outstanding transactions to increase bandwidth availability. It also provides "glueless" support for up to two processors. This enables low-cost, two-way symmetric multiprocessing, providing a significant performance boost for multitasking operating systems and multithreaded applications. Many inexpensive motherboards offer two Slot 1 sockets, making it easy to build a dual processor system for use with operating systems like Windows NT or 2000.

- 512-KB unified, nonblocking, L2 cache: Improves performance by reducing average memory access time and providing fast access to recently used instructions and data. Performance is enhanced through a dedicated 64-bit cache bus. The speed of the L2 cache scales with the processor core frequency. This processor also incorporates separate 16-KB, L1 caches: one for instructions and one for data.

- Models available in 450, 400, and 350 MHz: Support memory caches for up to 4 GB of addressable memory space.

- Error correction coding (ECC) functionality on the L2 cache bus: for applications in which data intensity and reliability are essential.

- Pipelined floating-point unit (FPU): supports the 32-bit and 64-bit formats specified in IEEE (Institute of Electrical and Electronics Engineers) standard 754, as well as an 80-bit format.

- Parity-protected address/request and response system bus signals, with a retry mechanism for high data integrity and reliability.

Variations on a Theme: The Intel Celeron CPUs

As it had in the past, Intel faced competitors who sold CPUs with similar performance at lower prices. Most high-priced desktop computers and servers were sold with a Pentium of one sort or another, but home and entry-level were another matter. Enter a variation of the SX concept—the Celeron.

Models available in 500, 466, 433, 400, 366, and 333 MHz have expanded Intel processing into the market for computers selling under $1,200.

All the Intel Celeron processors are available in PGA packages. The versions operating at 433, 400, 366, 333, and 300A MHz are also available in single-edge processor packages.

Key features include:

- MMX media enhancement technology.
- Dynamic Execution Technology.
- A 32-KB (16-KB/16-KB) nonblocking, L1 cache for fast access to heavily used data.
- Celerons operating at 500, 466, 433, 400, 366 and 333 MHz include integrated 128-KB L2 cache.
- All Celeron processors use the Intel P6 microarchitecture's multitransaction system bus at 66 MHz. Processors at 500, 466, 433, 400, 366 and 333 MHz use the Intel P6 microarchitecture's multitransaction system bus with the addition of the L2 cache interface.
- Like the Pentium family, the Celerons offer multiple branch prediction, data-flow analysis, and speculative execution.

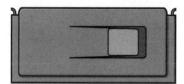

Figure 4.12   Intel Pentium II in SEC Package

Xenon, the Premium Pentium

Intel has labeled a new CPU brand to denote high-end server and high-performance desktop use. First introduced in June, 1998, the Xenon line commands a premium price and offers extra performance-enhancing technology. The Pentium II models incorporate 7.5 million transistors, clock speeds to 450 MHz, bus speeds of 100 MHz, full-speed L2 caches in varying sizes up to 2 MB, new multiprocessing capabilities, and compatibility with previous Intel microprocessor generations. All models use the SEC package.

Pentium III Processor

The Intel Pentium III processor is the newest member of the P6 family. With 28 million transistors, speeds from 500 to 733 MHz, and system bus speeds of 100 to 133 MHz, they mark a significant jump in PC CPU technology. They employ the same dynamic execution microarchitecture as the PII—a combination of multiple branch prediction, data-flow analysis, and speculative execution. This provides improved performance over older Pentium designs, while maintaining binary compatibility with all previous Intel processors. The Pentium III processor, shown in Figure 4.13, also incorporates MMX technology, plus streaming SIMD extensions for enhanced floating-point and 3-D application performance. It also utilizes multiple low-power states, such as AutoHALT, Stop-Grant, Sleep, and Deep Sleep to conserve power during idle times.

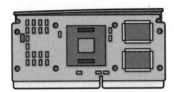

Figure 4.13   The Intel Pentium III Processor

Intel offers a Xenon version of the Pentium III processor at 550 MHz, aimed at high-performance workstations and servers.

Motorola

Motorola has been the mainstay CPU for Apple computers. The 68000 processor was introduced in 1979 as a 32-bit chip with a 16-bit data path. At that time, the 68000 outperformed the Intel 8086. In 1982, the 68010 arrived, adding virtual memory support and a cache capable of holding three instructions.

1984 saw the advent of the Macintosh II-series computer, which used the 68020 processor. It was the first full 32-bit chip, with a 32-bit data path, math coprocessor, and the ability to access up to 4 GB of RAM. Introduced in the same year as Intel's 80286 processor, the Motorola ran faster. However, it lacked the market share and third-party support to gain real marketplace momentum. PC clones offered more programs and at lower cost than the Apple offerings.

The 68030 chip, introduced in 1987, provided increased data and instruction speed. This was comparable to the 80386 chip. The 68040 processor was introduced (in the Macintosh Quadra) as a competitor to the 80486. It has internal caches for data and program code.

The Power PC processor was developed jointly by IBM, Motorola, and Apple. The name stands for performance optimization with enhanced RISC. The chips in this family of processors are suitable for machines ranging from laptop computers to high-powered network servers. It can run MS-DOS software without using emulation.

Lesson Summary

The following points summarize the main elements of this lesson:

- The microprocessor is the centerpiece of today's computers.

- Understanding the development and progression of the processor is essential in understanding how to mix older technology with new technology.

- The three key elements that go into measuring a CPU's performance are its speed, address bus, and external data bus.

- The development of the 80286 processor introduced the concepts of real and protected modes and allowed the use of up to 16 MB of memory.

- The development of the 80386 processor brought about 32-bit processing and allowed up to 4 GB of memory.

- The 80486 processor is a souped-up version of the 80386 and introduced the use of cache memory.

- The Pentium chip began a new line of processors and technology, incorporating RISC and true multithreading capabilities in an Intel microprocessor for the first time.

- Pentium MMX technology was developed to meet the needs of today's multimedia world.

- The Intel Pentium III further extended PC performance with advanced cache technology and streamlined code handling.

- Several players are currently competing with Intel for the processor market (NextGen, AMD, Cyrix, IBM), but Intel has the largest market share.

- Today's standard processor is the Pentium III, with processor speeds of 500 MHz and greater.

Lesson 2: Replacing and Upgrading Chips

A computer technician is commonly expected to upgrade computers. Because the CPU is the "brain" of a computer, replacing this single component can bring new life to an aging system. Replacing the chip is easy, but understanding the possible scenarios for a successful upgrade can be more challenging.

After this lesson, you will be able to:

- Decide whether a CPU is worth upgrading.
- Find the type of CPU required for upgrade.
- Install a new CPU.

Estimated lesson time: 15 minutes

Replacing a CPU can be very simple, but it is important to first carefully consider whether to do so. If you do decide to replace it, you will need to take care to avoid damaging the chip during installation. Before undertaking this process, always ask yourself, "What CPUs can be put on this motherboard?" The best source for an answer is the documentation packaged with the computer or motherboard. If the customer does not have the motherboard manual and you do not have a reference, the document should be available on the manufacturer's Web site.

Possible Upgrade Scenarios

There are a number of issues to think about when deciding whether to upgrade a CPU or replace a machine altogether. Perhaps the most important issue is the "value" of the upgrade. Will the suggested upgrade meet the operational requirements for that computer? There are limits to what can be upgraded and the results that can be expected from the upgrade. A poor upgrade can lead to total failure and, ultimately, require replacement of the motherboard. Again, the best source of information regarding CPU upgrades is the documentation that comes with the motherboard. The following table lists several possible scenarios for upgrading a CPU.

Existing CPU	Recommendation
8086/8088	Cannot be upgraded.
80286	Replace the motherboard with a new 486 or Pentium.
80386SX	Same as for 80286. Replace the motherboard.
80386DX	CPU has limited use—very slow. Upgrade to a Pentium motherboard.
486SX	If it has a good L2 cache (greater than 64 KB) and room to upgrade RAM, and VESA Local Bus (see Chapter 10, "Expansion Buses"), consider an AMD486DX/4 or a new Pentium motherboard.
486DX	Same as for 486SX.
486DX/2	Pentium upgrade chips will give you some improvement.
486DX/4	Same as for 486DX/2.
Pentium	Replace a Pentium 60, 66, or 75 with a faster CPU.

On average, it is more cost effective to replace an entire motherboard than it is to upgrade a CPU. However, you have to judge for yourself. Make sure that the new motherboard will fit into the computer case (check size and alignment of expansion buses) before starting the installation. Be sure that the power supply of the old case and new motherboard are of the same type with the proper connectors (such as AT, ATX). Always make sure that you can return a CPU and motherboard to the vendor if it won't fit. Be sure to determine this before you open the packaging or attempt to install. Keep in mind that many suppliers charge a restocking fee of 15 to 20 percent for returns.

Inserting a CPU

Several types of CPU sockets are sold. The three most common are:

- Low-insertion force (LIF).
- Zero-insertion force (ZIF).
- Single-edge connector (SEC).

LIF Socket

Removing an old CPU from a LIF socket is a muscular business! Luckily, there are special tools that are designed for this. However, a flat-head screwdriver, or a plate cover for an expansion card slot, will also work—just be sure to pry evenly around the CPU or you will risk damaging the CPU, the socket, or both.

Note   There is a notch in one corner of a LIF socket. The CPU will also have a notch and a dot in one corner, designed to help align the CPU correctly. The index corner of the CPU must line up with the notch on the socket. Firmly press the CPU into the PGA socket, making sure all the pins are lined up.

ZIF Socket

The ZIF socket, shown in Figure 4.14, was the most popular mount for desktop and tower PCs with 486 and early Pentium CPUs.

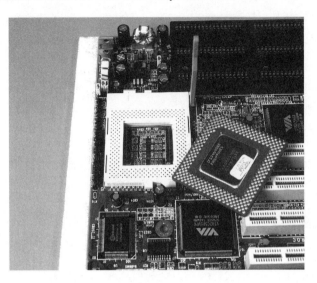

Figure 4.14   ZIF socket with CPU inverted showing matching pins

A ZIF socket has a lever arm that allows for simple removal and installation of CPUs. ZIF sockets were introduced during the early 1990s as a safe means of providing a user-friendly CPU upgrade. The first ZIF socket had 169 pins and was used on 486SX systems. These systems were sold with a 486SX chip already installed in a PGA socket and provided a ZIF socket for a 486 overdrive chip. (An *overdrive chip* is a special processor designed to increase the speed of 486 computers. It works similarly to the standard clock-doubling processors—DX2 and DX4—used on 486 motherboards.) Often, this is a good method of increasing the speed of a computer without replacing the motherboard.

The following table describes the types of ZIF sockets.

CPU Type	Number of Pins	Pin Layout	Voltage
486SX/SX2, DXUDX2, DX40DPR	169	17 x 17 PGA	5v
SX/SX2, DX/DX2, DX40DPR, Pentium OverDrive	238	19 x 19 PGA	5v
SX/SX2, DX/DX2, DX40DP, Pentium OverDrive	237	19 x 19 PGA	5v/3.3v
Pentium 60/66	273	21 x 21 PGA	5v
Pentium 75/90/100/120	320	37 x 37 SPGA	3.3v
486 DX4, Pentium OverDrive	235	19 x 19 PGA	3.3v
Pentium 75-200	321	21 x 21 SPGA	VRM

Note ODPR stands for overdrive processor replacement. PGA is a pin grid array. SPGA is a staggered pin grid array, and VRM is a voltage regulator module.

Upgrade Advice

Be very careful when handling a CPU or any exposed IC. Static discharge can damage or ruin the chip. Be sure to use a wrist-grounding strap or other approved antistatic device. Take great care to not bend any pins, and make sure the CPU is properly lined up to seat Pin 1 by using the code notch.

Caution If you encounter any resistance, stop at once and figure out what is wrong.

Check the memory and bus speed required for the new CPU before attempting to boot the PC after the procedure. It might require new RAM and will most often demand that a jumper be set on the motherboard before operating at the new speed.

SEC Package/Slot 1 Upgrades

The Pentium II and III series are most commonly packaged in a SEC. This package, shown in Figure 4.15, is very simple to work with. You will need a motherboard mount and might have to purchase a fan and heat sink before installing the CPU. Check the manual for jumper-setting adjustments, and follow the simple directions that come with the CPU.

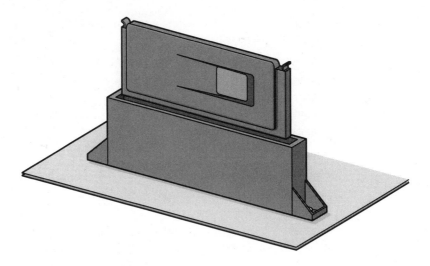

Figure 4.15   Pentium Processor in an SEC Package and Slot 1

The actual task involves seating two plastic pins, sliding two guides over the sides of the CPU, then pushing the frame and CPU into the slot on the board. With dual CPU boards, you need to know which slot to use, and you might have to place a special card (which comes with the motherboard) in the second CPU position if it is to remain empty.

Caution   Be sure to properly mount the cooling system, and make sure the fan works before running the new CPU for any amount of time or closing the case. Failure to ensure proper heat removal will destroy the CPU very quickly!

Lesson Summary

The following points summarize the main elements of this lesson:

- Replacing a CPU is usually a simple task.
- It is important to consider the limitations and potential of an upgrade before deciding to replace a CPU.

Chapter Summary

The following points summarize the key concepts in this chapter.

Microprocessors

- The CPU (central processing unit)—a microprocessor—is the centerpiece of today's computers.

- Clock speed is only one determining factor in identifying overall performance of a processor.

- Processors are generally defined by their speed, the size of the external data bus, and the size of the address bus.

- The development of the 80286 processor introduced the concepts of real and protected modes and allowed the use of up to 16 MB of memory.

- The development of the 80386 processor brought about 32-bit processing and allowed up to 4 GB of memory.

- The 80486 processor is a souped-up version of the 80386 and introduced the use of cache memory.

- The Pentium chip began a new line of processors and technology, incorporating RISC and true multithreading capabilities in an Intel microprocessor for the first time.

- The Intel Pentium III further extended PC performance with advanced cache technology and streamlined code handling.

- Today's standard processor is the Pentium III, with processor speeds of 500 MHz and greater.

Replacing and Upgrading Chips

- It is important for a computer technician to know the technological advances made by each successive generation of computers.

- Simply upgrading the CPU can often lengthen the lifespan of a computer.

Review

1. What is the language of the computer?

2. What is an external data bus?

3. Describe an integrated circuit (IC).

4. Define a clock cycle.

5. What are the advantages of a Pentium processor over a 486?

6. What is the difference between "SX" and "DX" in a 386 chip?

7. Which kind of a computer uses the Motorola 68040 chip?

8. Define "microprocessor."

9. In computer code language _____ means on and _____ means off.

10. Define clock speed.

11. What is the function of the address bus?

12. Microprocessor chips (CPUs) are manufactured in a variety of sizes and shapes. Name as many different kinds as possible.

13. Name the basic types of CPU sockets and give a brief description of each.

14. If a customer brought you an old Pentium 60 and asked you to install a new processor, what would your advice be? Why?

CHAPTER 5

Supplying Power to a Computer

About This Chapter

The power supply is an often-underrated part of a computer. Electronic components require a steady electrical current, free of surges or drops. The power supply is the part responsible for providing clean, constant current.

Before You Begin

No specialized knowledge is required; however, a fundamental understanding of terms related to power and electricity such as voltage and wattage is helpful when learning about power supplies.

Lesson 1: Power Supplies

This lesson presents basic information about power supplies for computer systems. We take a look at the different sizes of power supplies, how to connect them to a computer (motherboard and related devices), and how to deal with the safety considerations that arise. As a certified computer technician, you will often be called upon to troubleshoot, identify, and replace power supplies.

After this lesson, you will be able to:

- Define the current and voltage requirements for a computer power supply.
- Identify a replacement power supply.
- Specify the correct surge suppressors for a computer system.
- Specify a backup power supply for a computer system.

Estimated lesson time: 15 minutes

Overview of Power Supplies

A standard power supply draws power from a local, alternating current (AC) source (usually a wall outlet) and converts it to either 3.3 or 5 volts direct current (DC), for on-board electronics, and 12 volts DC for motors and hard drives. In all cases, it delivers both positive and negative DC to the computer. Power supplies must "condition" the power, smoothing out any radical changes in its quality. Many homes and offices have power that fluctuates far more than the delicate parts of a PC can tolerate and survive. Most PC power supplies also provide the system's cooling and processor fans that keep the machine from overheating.

If the computer's power supply is providing reliable, clean power and its own cooling fan works, all is well. If the power supply or its fan should fail or cause erratic behavior by the PC, the power supply must be replaced. (While it is possible to remove and replace a power-supply fan, the low cost of a power supply makes it more practical to replace the power supply itself.)

Many newer supplies have a universal input that will accept either 110 VAC (volts alternating current), 60 Hz (U.S. standard power), or 220 VAC, 50 Hz (European/Asian standard). When replacing a power supply, there are three things to consider: physical size, wattage, and connectors. This chapter covers the basics of power supplies.

Note   A hertz is a measure of unit frequency: one cycle per second equals one hertz. A kilohertz (Kz) is 1000 cycles per second; a megahertz (Mz) is a million cycles per second.

Power-Supply Sizes

Power supplies are available in a few standard sizes and shapes. However, the names for power supplies are anything but standard. They are based on the types of case they will be used in and the types of motherboard connections they will support. This is because different styles of cases place items such as plug fittings, mounting screws, and fans in different places.

A few years ago, a new type of motherboard cable power fitting began to appear on the market. The older models are known as AT-style, and the newer ones are known as ATX. We cover both in this chapter, because you will need to be able to work with either one. The ATX design simplifies the placement of connections, so there is little to worry about with case compatibility. The main issues to be aware of are how much wattage the PC needs to power its parts and how many connectors for peripherals are required. Generally speaking, older Pentium-based computers and all 486-based and earlier PCs used AT supplies; almost all Pentium II and later-based systems use ATX supplies. The ATX design is preferred for two reasons:

- The on/off power control circuit (not the button) on ATX boards is built into the motherboard. On AT PCs, it comes from the power supply.

- AT power supplies connect to the motherboard through a pair of six-wire connectors. ATX power supplies connect through a single 20-pin connector.

A few motherboards and power supplies provide both AT and ATX fittings and switch support. They are rare, but will open up more options if you have to repair such a system. Generally, you should use ATX for all replacements, if possible.

It's a good idea to compare the existing power supply to the new one. Make sure that they are physically the same size, have the same connectors, and that the new one has at least the same power rating. Some high-quality power supplies offer "silencer" fans, that are much quieter than most models.

Power-Supply Wattage

Power supplies are rated according to the maximum sustained power (given in watts) that they can produce. A *watt* is a unit of electrical power equivalent to one volt-ampere. It is important to keep in mind that the power supply must produce at least enough energy to operate all the components of the system at one time.

Don't rely on the computer's operating consumption alone, which can be obtained by adding the requirements for the devices in the PC. Remember that a much larger drain occurs as the machine powers up, when hard drives and other heavy feeders simultaneously compete for the available startup power. Most general-use computers require 130 watts while running and about 200–205 watts when booting. Sound cards, modems, and (worst of all) monitors attached with an accessory plug in the case can push a weak power supply to its limit and beyond.

Servers and high-performance workstations often have an abundance of RAM, multiple drives, SCSI (Small Computer System Interface) cards, and power-hungry video adapters, along with one or more network cards. They often demand power supplies of 35–500 watts.

Caution   The label on a power supply that says "Don't Open" means just that! Opening a power supply is dangerous. It is better to completely remove and replace a defective power supply as needed.

Power-Supply Connectors

Power supplies employ several types of connectors; all are easy to identify and use. On the outside of the computer enclosure, a standard male AC plug and three-conductor wire (two power wires and a ground) draws current from a wall outlet, with a female connection entering the receptacle in the back of the power supply. On the inside are three types of connectors: the power main to the motherboard (which differ, as mentioned, in AT and ATX models) and two types of four-pin fittings to supply 5 volts and 3.3 volts of power to peripherals such as the floppy disk and hard disk drives. Let's take a close look at each in turn.

AT-Style Connections to the Motherboard

A pair of almost identical connectors, designated P8 and P9, link the power supply to the motherboard (see Figure 5.1). These connectors are seated into a row of six pins and matching plastic guides, or "teeth," on the motherboard. The P8 and P9 connectors *must* be placed in the proper orientation. The motherboard manual will show which fitting is for P8 and P9. If the connectors are not marked, make sure that the two black wires on each plug are side by side and that the orange wire (on P8) and the two red wires (on P9) are on the outside as you push them into place.

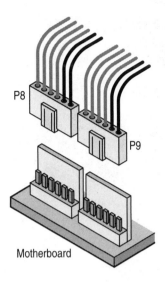

Figure 5.1   P8 and P9 connectors and motherboard fitting

The following table of power cables shows voltage values for each of the color-coded wires on P8 and P9. The ground wires are considered 0 volts; all voltage measurements (see Chapter 13, "Basic Electricity") are taken between the black wires and one of the colored wires.

Cable Color	Supply In	Tolerance
Yellow	+12	±10%
Blue	−12	±10%
Red	+5	±5%
White	−5	±5%
Black	Ground	N/A

Note   Some computer makers employ proprietary power connections that require a special power supply. To install the new part, you will need to follow the instructions that are included with the computer.

Remember to install the P8 and P9 plugs so that the black wires are side by side. Installing them on the wrong receptacle can damage both the motherboard and the power supply. Figure 5.2 shows the P8 and P9 connectors and a motherboard.

Note   Some power supplies have a third P-style connector. This is not used except on a very few motherboards and can be ignored on those where it is found . If you run into one, refer to the manual that came with the part for instructions on its requirements and installation.

Figure 5.2   Connecting P8 and P9

ATX Motherboard Connections

The newer ATX main power connection is much easier to install. A single 20-wire plug is set into a fitted receptacle and secured with a catch on the side of the plug that snaps over the fitting. Figure 5.3 shows the parts being seated. A small, flat-tip screwdriver is a handy tool for easing the pressure on the catch to remove the plug. In some cases, it can be used during installation as well.

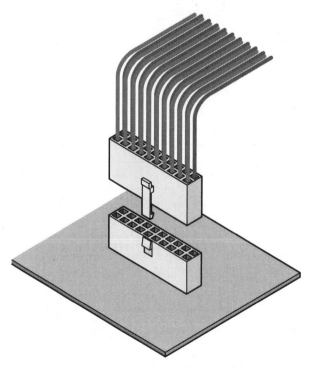

Figure 5.3   Placing an ATX plug in its motherboard receptacle

Connections to Peripheral Hardware

Two standard types of connectors can connect to peripheral hardware:

- **Molex connector:** This is the most commonly used power connector. It provides both 12-volt and 5-volt power. Hard disk drives, internal tape drives, CD-ROM drives, DVD (digital video disc) drives, and older 5.25-inch floppy disk drives all use this fitting. The Molex connector has two rounded corners and two sharp corners to ensure that it will be properly installed.

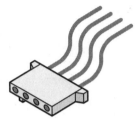

Figure 5.4   Molex connector (not to scale)

- **Mini connector:** Most power supplies provide one or more "mini" connectors (see Figure 5.5). The mini, shown in Figure 5.4, is used primarily on 3.5-inch floppy-disk drives. It has four pin-outs and, usually, four wires. Most are fitted with keys that make it difficult, but not impossible, to install upside down. Be sure to orient the connector correctly; applying power with the connector reversed can damage or destroy the drive.

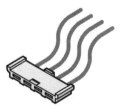

Figure 5.5   Mini connector (not to scale)

Two- and Three-Pin Mini Plugs

A less common type of power connector is used to connect the fan of a Pentium II or III processor to the motherboard for power, to connect a CD-ROM drive to a sound card, and to provide power for 3.5-inch floppy disk drives. These connectors have two or three wires which are usually red and black or red, yellow, and black.

Caution   Do not connect power-carrying mini plugs to audio or data devices such as a CD or a sound card, because you might damage or destroy those devices.

Extenders and Splitters

PCs can run out of power connections, and large cases can have drives beyond the reach of any plug on the supply. A good technician has a quick solution on hand to both of these common problems: extenders and splitters.

Extenders are wire sets that have a Molex connector on each end; they are used to extend a power connection to a device beyond the reach of the power supply's own wiring. *Splitters* are similar to extenders, with the exception that they provide two power connections from a single power supply connector.

Lesson Summary

The following points summarize the main elements of this lesson:

- Power supplies come in a variety of sizes and shapes.
- There are two types of main power connectors: AT and ATX.
- A power supply must be capable of handling the requirements of the computer and all internal devices.
- Be careful when attaching some connectors—if connected incorrectly, they can damage the computer.
- Do not open the power-supply housing!
- Keeping a few splitters and extenders in the repair kit can help the technician easily solve some common problems.

Lesson 2: Power-Supply Problems

Power-supply problems can come from both internal and external sources. Failure of a power supply can be caused by failure of components within the computer (internal), but the most common failures come from the power source itself (external). In this lesson, we look at common problems associated with power supplies and what you, as a technician, can do about them.

After this lesson, you will be able to:

- Determine the types of problems that can be caused by power supplies.
- Know when to check and when to replace a power supply.
- Plan how to protect your system from external power-supply problems.

Estimated lesson time: 10 minutes

Power Failures

Power supplies are affected by the quality of the local power source. Common power delivery problems such as spikes, surges, sags, brownouts, and blackouts affect the stability and operation of the main power supply and are passed on to the computer. While most users don't notice sudden changes in the quality of electrical power, computers and other sensitive electronics do and while we can't fully control these problems, there are a few things we can do to protect our equipment and data and ensure a reasonably clean electrical supply.

Problem	Description
Surges	These are brief (and sometimes catastrophic) increases in the voltage source (very high voltage for a very short time). They can originate with the power source (the local power company), but most often are due to lightning strikes.
Spikes	Spikes are very short overvoltage conditions. Spikes are measured in nanoseconds, while a surge is measured in milliseconds.
Sags	These are brief decreases of voltage at the power source.
Brownouts	If a sag lasts longer than one second, it is called a brownout. The overloading of a primary power source can cause brownouts. Some brownouts are "scheduled" by power companies to prevent overloading of circuits and potential catastrophic failure of the system.
Blackout	This is a complete power failure, which can be caused by equipment failure (local or regional) or accidental cutting of power cables. When the power returns after a blackout, there is a power spike and danger of a power surge.

Power-Protection Devices

Surge suppressors are devices used to filter out the effects of voltage spikes and surges that are present in commercial power sources and smooth out power variations. They are available from local computer dealers and superstores. A good surge suppressor will protect your system from most problems, but if you purchase an economy model, it might not work when you need it most. Keep in mind that almost nothing will shield your hardware from a very close lightning strike.

Note   Most power strips with surge protection have a red indicator light. If the light goes out, this means that the unit is not providing protection. Most power strip/surge protectors should be replaced every year or so. If the light starts flashing before then, the power strip is failing and should be replaced.

When evaluating the quality of surge suppressors, look for performance certification. At a minimum, it should have an Underwriters Laboratory (UL) listing and power ratings. A high-quality unit will also provide protection for phone/fax/modem and network connections. These units protect up to a point; however, for complete protection from power fluctuations and outages, the uninterruptible power supply (UPS) is recommended.

A *UPS* is an inline battery backup. When properly installed between a computer and the wall outlet, a UPS device protects the computer from surges and acts as a battery when the power dips or fails. It also provides a warning that the power is out of specification (above or below acceptable levels). Many models can also interact with the computer and initiate a safe shutdown in the event of a complete power failure. They do this by means of software that runs in the background and is set in action by a signal through one of the computer's COM ports when the power goes down.

The amount of time that a UPS device can keep a system running is determined by battery capacity and the power demands of the equipment connected to it. A more powerful UPS device will need its own line and circuit breaker. One of the principal power drains is the monitor. To keep a system online as long as possible during a power failure, turn off the monitor immediately after the failure commences.

When recommending a UPS, take into consideration how much protection is needed as well as the importance of peace of mind to the user. The VA rating (voltage x amps = watts) must be sufficient to supply the computer and all its peripherals with power for long enough to safely shut down the system. The easiest way to calculate this number is to total the power rating (watts) for *all* pieces of equipment that are to be connected to the UPS, as shown in the following table.

Device	Power Rating (Watts)	Connected to UPS	Power Required
Computer	200–350	Yes	250
Monitor	80–100	Yes	80
External modem	5.5	No	0
External backup drive	50	Yes	50
Total	330–500	—	380

Caution   Never plug a laser printer into a UPS unless the UPS is specifically rated to support that type of device. Laser printers can easily require more power than an underspecified UPS is able to provide; the printer, the UPS, and the computer could all be endangered if the printer is connected to the UPS power source.

Power-Supply Problems

The most easily recognized problem is a complete failure of the power supply. This is easy to detect because in the event of a failure, the computer will not begin to boot up (no lights, no sound). If there is apparently no power, be sure to check the power source and the plug at both ends: the outlet and the computer.

If you are experiencing intermittent failures such as memory loss, memory corruption, or unexplained system crashes, don't rule out the power supply. It is often the culprit. Fortunately, it is easy to check and replace.

Good power supplies have line-conditioning circuits, but these might not be sufficient enough in locations where the power source has substantial quality flaws. If you have problems with several systems, or if a second power supply still does not fix a related complaint, add a UPS with good line-conditioning features.

Lesson Summary

The following points summarize the main elements of this lesson:

- Power-supply problems can be caused by component failures within the power supply or from the power source.

- Two devices protect against external power problems—surge suppressors and UPSs.

Chapter Summary

The following points summarize the key concepts in this chapter:

Power Supplies

- The key to specifying the proper size of a power supply for a computer is to add together the power requirements for all the components. It is important to be sure to add extra power to allow for boot up.

- Electrical power is measured in watts.

- Proper installation of the P8 and P9 connectors is important to prevent damage to the motherboard. The black (ground) wires must be installed side by side.

- Molex and mini connectors are used to connect power to devices such as floppy disk and hard disk drives.

Power-Supply Problems

- The flow of power into a computer must be managed in order to prevent damage and/or loss of data.

- Surge suppressors will eliminate some higher-than-normal voltage problems.

- High-quality UPS devices will eliminate most power fluctuations caused by too much or too little voltage.

- Check power supplies when there are unusual problems with memory and PC operations that do not quickly point to another cause.

Review

1. Explain the difference between spikes, surges, and sags.

2. What are the two types of power-supply connectors to the motherboard?

3. What are the two types of power-supply connectors to devices such as drives?

4. Name two benefits of having a UPS on a system.

5. Describe the difference between a brownout and a blackout.

6. When you purchase a UPS, what is the most important thing to consider?

7. Will all surge suppressors provide protection against lightning strikes?

8. What is the best defense against spikes caused by lightning?

9. What is the most important thing to remember when connecting a P8 and P9 connector to a motherboard?

10. Explain the difference between the mini connector and the Molex connector.

11. Describe the best way to make sure a new power supply matches the one you are replacing.

12. What is the primary use of mini connectors?

13. A computer power supply has both 5-volt and 12-volt outputs. The 5-volt output is used to power _____, and the 12-volt output is used to power _____.

C H A P T E R   6

Primary PC Components

About This Chapter

In earlier lessons, we provided an overview of the computer. In this chapter, we focus on the computer's infrastructure. We begin with the centerpiece of the computer, the motherboard, also known as the mainboard. The motherboard is the key member of the hardware infrastructure. It is a large circuit board that serves as a home for the CPU and all its associated chips, including the chip set and RAM, and connects them to the rest of the physical elements and components of the computer.

Before You Begin

Although this chapter can be studied independently, it is suggested that you review the preceding chapters, which discuss microprocessors, basic input/output, and how power gets to the system, before reading this material.

Lesson 1: Computer Cases

The case, or chassis, which is usually made of metal, holds all the primary electronics of the personal computer (PC) and often all the drives as well.

After this lesson you will be able to:

- Identify the primary types of PC cases.
- Explain how the case helps to protect the PC and surrounding devices from electromagnetic interference.

Estimated lesson time: 5 minutes

The Computer Case

To casual users, the PC is a metal container, attached by a few cables to a keyboard, mouse, and monitor. In fact, the case is more than just a box to house a computer. It often represents the identity of a specific brand of computer, and, sometimes, it is even part of the reason we purchase a particular computer. We do, after all, want something that looks good, especially if we are spending a lot of money on it.

Early computer cases were little more than boxes that sat on the desk and served as monitor stands. Today, some manufacturers build "designer" computers that come in fancy colors and command premium prices.

The real value of a case does not lie in the label, color, or how pretty it looks. The case houses all the internal components, offers access to the outside world (ports and connectors), and protects the PC's delicate circuits from damage and electromagnetic interference. And it protects surrounding devices, such as TVs, from the PC's EMI.

Note *Electromagnetic interference (EMI)* is a newer term for *radio frequency interference (RFI)*. EMI is any radio frequency that is emitted from an electrical or electronic device that is harmful to the surrounding equipment or that interferes with the operation of another electrical or electronic device. A computer interferes with radio, telephone, or TV reception when it generates EMI. Any high-quality computer will contain special circuits and grounding to prevent emissions into the surrounding area. Running a computer without its cover is a sure way to generate EMI.

As computer technicians, we don't usually concern ourselves with the computer case; we simply deal with whatever our customer already has. However, when it comes to recommending a computer for purchase, the size and configuration of the case should be considered. Depending on the business application, the difference between a tower and a desktop design could be important.

When considering the case, there are three general rules to follow:

- The bigger the box, the more components it can hold (the greater the expansion potential) and, often, the better the airflow (essential for cooling). Large cases are easier to work with.

- The more compact the box, the less expansion potential it has; working on it is often much more difficult, and usually airflow is reduced.

- Smaller cases that come with a power supply usually have lower wattage, once again reducing the number of internal devices that can be installed.

Important   It is *not* a good idea to run a computer for extended periods of time with the case open or removed entirely. This not only produces EMI, but also results in improper airflow and reduced cooling of the system components.

Working with Cases

In any repair job that involves inspecting or replacing internal components, the technician has to open the case. That used to be very simple; the technician would remove four screws in the back of the computer with a Phillips screwdriver, then pull the case's covering shroud forward to reveal the contents. Today, however, cases come in a variety of forms, with screws in the front or back, fancy plastic bevels in front, and featuring one of several types of metal wraps—some in several parts, some in a single piece.

The majority of cases still open the old-fashioned way. But if you find yourself with one of the exceptions and can't locate screws in the back, check to see if the plastic cover in the front can be pulled off. If so, that should reveal three or four screws. Then see if the main cover can be pulled forward. If not, look for screws that secure one or more of the side panels. Some side panel designs are great for granting easy access to our next topic, motherboards. This style of case allows one to inspect or remove the motherboard without having to remove the entire outer covering.

Lesson Summary

The following points summarize the main elements of this lesson:

- The case of the PC defines the size, shape, and configuration of the motherboard, the amount of expansion possible, and the space into which hard drives and other internal accessories can be fitted.

- To prevent EMI and ensure system components are properly cooled, you should avoid running a computer without its cover.

Lesson 2: Motherboards

The motherboard is the PC's center of activity. All devices in a computer are in some way connected to the motherboard. It hosts the largest single collection of chips of any PC component and serves as the "street system" for the grid of wires that link all the components, making it possible for them to communicate.

After this lesson, you will be able to:

- Identify a motherboard and its functions.
- Locate and define the components of a motherboard.
- Safely remove and replace a motherboard.

Estimated lesson time: 15 minutes

The Motherboard

The motherboard (one is shown in Figure 6.1) defines the computer's limits of speed, memory, and expandability. A computer needs more than just a CPU and memory. To accept input from the user, it needs devices, such as a keyboard and a mouse. It also needs output devices, like monitors and sound cards, to cope with the powerful graphics and sound capabilities of the programs available today. A computer also needs "permanent" storage devices, such as floppy disk drives and hard disk drives, to store data when it is turned off. It is the function of the motherboard to provide the connectivity for all these devices, as well as for the CPU, RAM, and support ICs.

Figure 6.1   Motherboard with CPU

The motherboard is usually the largest circuit board found inside the computer case. Motherboards come in a variety of shapes. One size does not fit all, and careful attention to size and location of mounting holes is required before installing a new motherboard in an older computer. A motherboard needs to fit in the space allotted for it, be secure in its mounts, be properly grounded, receive sufficient ventilation (for cooling of the CPU and other heat-sensitive components), and must not conflict with other hardware. When considering the purchase of a new motherboard (see Lesson 2: Replacing and Upgrading Chips in Chapter 4), keep these things in mind:

- Most "generic" motherboards will fit into "generic" computers. One good reason to consider purchasing a PC clone is that it is easier to upgrade.

- There are two major categories of motherboards: AT and ATX. The main difference between them lies in the type of power supply and main power switch each requires. When you order a new motherboard, be sure to first verify that it is compatible with the case and power supply to be used.

- If you are working on a brand-name computer, you might be required to purchase a new motherboard or other custom components from the same manufacturer.

- Before buying a motherboard, check its technical references to be sure that the new board will fit and will be compatible with any of the RAM and expansion cards the owner intends to use. Often, this information can be found in the owner's manual. If not, check the manufacturer's Web site, if one is available, or check other online resources such as technical libraries. A Web search using the keyword "motherboard" will yield sites dedicated to computer hardware.

- For all practical purposes, you cannot repair motherboards. They should be replaced if physically or electrically damaged. Your customer will get new technology, usually for a price lower than the cost of the repair.

- Because it is often the most difficult part of a system to replace (you have to remove all the equipment that is connected to it), check all other internal and external components before removing or replacing the motherboard.

- When obtaining a replacement, be sure to factor in the cost of all critical options found on the existing motherboard. Some have built-in SCSI (Small Computer System Interface) or display adapters that might not be common. In that case, either make sure the new board offers the same level of support or install the appropriate add-on card(s) to bring the system up to the existing level of operation.

Chip Sets

A motherboard comes with a variety of support chips soldered in place. The primary elements constitute the *chip set* and are designed to work with the CPU. These chips are highly complex and coordinated ICs that help the CPU manage and control the computer's system. When replacing a CPU, you must make sure that it is compatible with the chip set and supported by the motherboard. If not, the computer won't work. A basic chip set (see Figure 6.2) consists of a:

- Bus controller.
- Memory controller.
- Data and address buffer.
- Peripheral controller.

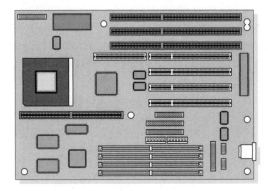

Figure 6.2   Motherboard with chip set

On a more modern motherboard, you will find chips to control things such as cache memory and high-speed buses. You will also find boards with fewer individual chips because the manufacturer has incorporated several functions into one chip.

Keep in mind that there is a wide range of features and costs to choose from when you select a motherboard. You will need to keep up to date on the types of processors, memory design, CPUs, and expansion slots available in order to recommend and obtain the right product for your customers.

Lesson Summary

The following points summarize the main elements of this lesson:

- Motherboards come in many sizes and shapes, but generic boards are available that fit most clone computers.
- The motherboard determines the limits of the computer's capabilities.
- Chip sets are unique to each motherboard design and work with the CPU to manage and control the computer's system.
- You should make sure any new motherboard is compatible with CPU, RAM, and any other critical hardware and features that are not being upgraded at the same time.

Lesson 3: ROM BIOS

In addition to the chip set, you will find other chips called *ROM BIOS*. A ROM BIOS chip contains data that specifies the characteristics of hardware devices, such as memory and hard disk and floppy disk drives, so the system can properly access them. This lesson explores ROM BIOS and what it does.

After this lesson, you will be able to:

- Identify the different types of ROM.
- Modify the CMOS settings in a computer.
- Identify POST codes and take appropriate corrective action when a problem is identified.

Estimated lesson time: 30 minutes

ROM BIOS

ROM (read-only memory) is a type of memory that stores data even when the main computer power is off. This is necessary so that the system can access the data it needs to start up. When stored in ROM, information that is required to start and run the computer cannot be lost or changed. The *BIOS*, software in the form of programs stored on ROM chips, is used during the startup routine to check out the system and prepare to run the hardware. The *system BIOS* is a ROM chip on the motherboard used by the computer during the startup routine (boot process) to check out the system and prepare to run the hardware. The BIOS is stored on a ROM chip because ROM retains information even when no power is being supplied to the computer. The downside of storing data in an older computer's ROM is that we have to change a chip to update information.

More recent systems use a technology called flash ROM or flash BIOS that allows code in the core chips to be updated by software available through the BIOS or motherboard supplier. Check the Internet site for the supplier if you suspect your ROM chip has flash ROM technology; the software and instructions are generally downloadable.

Caution   Upgrade a BIOS only when necessary! Be sure to follow all precautions included with the motherboard manual and instructions for the upgrade. Improper installation can render the motherboard useless.

BIOS (also referred to as firmware) can be subdivided into three classes, depending upon the type of hardware it controls.

- The first class, called core chips, includes support for hardware that is common to all computers, is necessary, and never changes.

- The second class, called updatable chips, encompasses hardware that is also common and necessary, but that might change from time to time.

- The third class of chips includes anything that is not included in one of the first two classes.

Core Chips

Look on any motherboard: ROM chips for the core chips are found everywhere. They are distinctive because they are in DIP (dual inline package) form and are almost always labeled. These chips are commonly used for the keyboard, parallel ports, serial ports, speaker, and other support devices. Each ROM chip contains between 16 and 64 KB of programming.

Updatable Chips

Several devices on a computer often contain their own flash BIOS or updatable ROMS. These include SCSI controllers and video cards. Because this information is subject to change (for instance, you can upgrade a hard disk drive or change a video card), it is stored on a special chip called the *CMOS* (complementary metal-oxide semiconductor). This chip gets its name from the way it is manufactured, not from the information it holds.

Unlike other ROM chips, CMOS chips do not store programs; they store data that is used by the BIOS for the programs needed to talk to changeable hardware. The CMOS chip also maintains date and time information when power to the computer is off.

The CMOS chips can store about 64 KB of data. However, to store the data needed to boot a computer requires only a very small amount of memory: about 128 bytes. If the data stored on the CMOS is different from the hardware it keeps track of, the computer, or part of it, will probably not work. For example, if the hard disk drive information is incorrect, the computer can be booted from a floppy disk, but the hard disk drive might not be accessible. The technician or owner will have to reset the CMOS values before the computer can use the device if it is not properly defined in the CMOS registry.

The information contained in a CMOS chip will depend on the manufacturer. Typically, CMOS contains at least the following information:

- Floppy disk and hard disk drive types
- CPU
- RAM size
- Date and time
- Serial and parallel port information
- Plug and Play information
- Power Saving settings

Important   It is critical that the core information on a CMOS chip be correct. If you change any of the related hardware, the CMOS must be updated to reflect those changes.

Updating CMOS

To make changes to a CMOS chip, you need to run a CMOS setup program. This application is independent of the operating system, because it must work even if an operating system is not loaded, or even if there is no form of disk drive. The way to start this program depends on the manufacturer of the BIOS, not the manufacturer of the computer. Manufacturers of motherboards purchase the BIOS from other companies, most of which specialize in making these chips. Many different computer suppliers use the same BIOS. The BIOS manufacturer and version number is the first thing you see displayed when you boot up your computer. Figure 6.3 shows examples of startup information for three different types of BIOS chips.

```
AMIBOS (C) 1996 American Megatrends Inc.,

PRESS <DEL>, IF YOU WANT TO RUN SETUP

                OR

(C) American Megatrends Inc.,
40-0100-006259-00101111-060692-SYMP-F

                OR

Phoenix BIOS TM A486 Version 1 03 (225B)
Copyright © 1985-1996 Phoenix
Technologies Ltd.
All Rights Reserved
```

Figure 6.3   BIOS information

Although several companies write BIOS code and sell it to computer makers, three companies—American Megatrends (AMI), Phoenix, and Award—dominate the BIOS market. Motherboard vendors might use one supplier for a series of products; however, it is not uncommon for a manufacturer to change sources within a series due to design or cost considerations. A good technician should be familiar with the basic CMOS setup procedures for BIOSs manufactured by all three.

Because of its flexibility, the Hi-Flex BIOS, manufactured by AMI, has taken a large share of the computer market. Motherboard manufacturers can purchase a basic BIOS from AMI and then add setup parameters to meet the needs of their products. For this reason, the number of setup parameters available on one computer can differ from those on another computer that is based on the same motherboard. Award competes directly with AMI, providing very flexible BIOS chips. Award was the first BIOS to heavily support PCI (Peripheral Component Interconnect) motherboards.

Phoenix is considered a manufacturer of high-end BIOS. Phoenix creates individual BIOS chips for specific machines. As a result, Phoenix BIOS chips have fewer setup parameters available. These chips are commonly used in machines with proprietary motherboards, such as laptops. Vendors can tune the BIOS for performance, basing new code on the Phoenix core.

There are several ways to determine who the BIOS manufacturer is:

- Watch the monitor when the computer boots. A BIOS screen will usually be displayed, indicating the manufacture and version number. (This screen might not be visible if the computer is warm-booted. In that case, power off the unit and restart.)

- Check the computer or motherboard manual. Most include a section on entering the setup program and setting options.

- Remove the cover of the computer and look at the chip. Most BIOS chips have a manufacturer's label.

- Try a good third-party utility program. These products are available at almost any software store. A Web search for a key phrase such as "BIOS diagnostic" will yield the names of a number of them.

- Reboot the computer and hold down several keys at once or unplug a drive. This will often cause an error and prompt you to get into the setup program. Unplugging the keyboard will accomplish the same goal with less work; however, you won't be able to make adjustments on most systems with the keyboard inoperative.

A Typical CMOS Setup

Every CMOS setup program looks slightly different. Do not be too concerned about the differences—all BIOS routines contain basically the same information. Take your time and be comfortable searching around the setup programs. Most of the CMOS setup programs are text-based, so you will have to use keystrokes to navigate through the information. However, some newer machines use a Windows-like CMOS setup (they have the look of a Windows environment and will let you use a mouse to select changes).

The Most Common Ways to Access BIOS Setup Programs

- For AMI, press DELETE when the machine first begins to boot.
- For Phoenix, press CTRL+ALT+ESC or F2 when requested.
- For Award, you can usually follow either of the first-mentioned procedures.

Motherboard makers can change the key combinations to access the CMOS setup. This can be especially true for brand-name computers, and manufacturers are not likely to publish the information on the start-up screen.

Note   If all else fails, try any of these key combinations: CTRL+ALT+INSERT, CTRL+A, CTRL+S, CTRL+F1, and F10.

Let's look at some typical screens from a Phoenix BIOS setup program. They are good examples of how typical CMOS settings are presented and adjusted.

Figure 6.4 shows the first screen of this CMOS setup. From this point, you can select alternate pages (Advanced, Security, Power) or adjust any of these individual items: floppy disk drive, hard disk drive, date and time, or RAM settings.

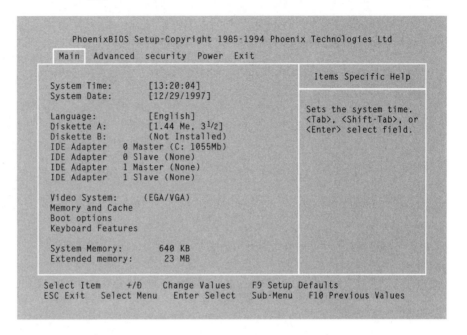

```
              PhoenixBIOS Setup-Copyright 1985-1994 Phoenix Technologies Ltd
              Main  Advanced  security  Power  Exit

                                                          Items Specific Help
         System Time:        [13:20:04]
         System Date:        [12/29/1997]
                                                      Sets the system time.
         Language:           [English]               <Tab>, <Shift-Tab>, or
         Diskette A:         [1.44 Me, 3¹/₂]          <Enter> select field.
         Diskette B:         (Not Installed)
         IDE Adapter    0 Master (C: 1055Mb)
         IDE Adapter    0 Slave (None)
         IDE Adapter    1 Master (None)
         IDE Adapter    1 Slave (None)

         Video System:       (EGA/VGA)
         Memory and Cache
         Boot options
         Keyboard Features

         System Memory:        640 KB
         Extended memory:       23 MB

         Select Item    +/Ð    Change Values     F9 Setup Defaults
         ESC Exit    Select Menu   Enter Select   Sub-Menu   F10 Previous Values
```

Figure 6.4   Main screen

The hard disk drive setup screen (Figure 6.5) is where individual hard drive parameters are set. Today, most hard drives based on IDE (Integrated Device Electronics) can be automatically detected by the BIOS. The CMOS settings are then made by the BIOS automatically. However, you should still know how to do this manually, to be able to work with an older machine and in case the setup program fails in its recognition.

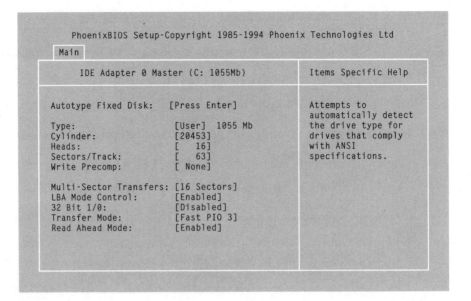

Figure 6.5   Hard disk drive setup screen

The Advanced screen (Figure 6.6) leads to more advanced setup parameters. A lot of customization can be achieved using these settings. Pay careful attention to any warnings that come up before you make any changes to device settings. If you don't understand a setting, it is best to leave it on the default option.

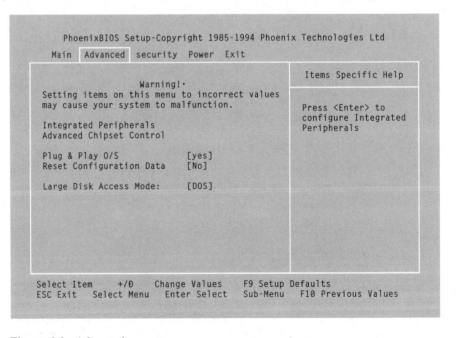

Figure 6.6   Advanced screen

The Security screen allows you to set security parameters. Be careful: once you set a password, you have to remember that password to change the security parameters. If you encounter a situation in which an owner has set and forgotten a password, you will have to flush and reset the CMOS to the factory default settings. Check the motherboard manual for information on how to do this. It usually involves changing jumper settings twice.

Notice in Figure 6.7 that the virus check reminder option is disabled. If you find a CMOS virus checker enabled, turn it off. This is especially important during operating system and program installation. If you are certain that no virus software is on the computer, yet you continue to get error messages warning you to turn off all antivirus software, the CMOS virus checker is the source of these erroneous messages. If you find this happening, disable the CMOS virus checker. Of course, if you still get the message you should check for a real virus. Figure 6.7 shows a Security screen.

Tip These built-in CMOS virus checkers actually do very little to protect your system. For the best possible protection against viruses, be sure to install a good Windows 95 or 98 antivirus program and update it regularly.

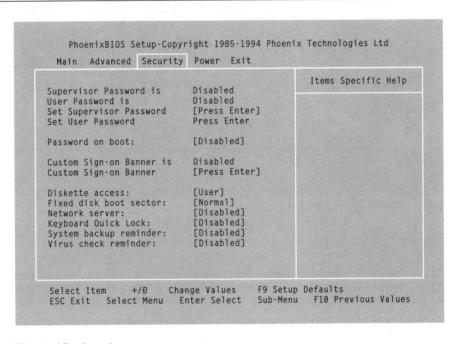

Figure 6.7 Security screen

The Power screen, shown in Figure 6.8, allows the user to set up any power conservation options provided by the manufacturer. These features typically include setting a time limit for reducing power to the monitor and hard disk drive.

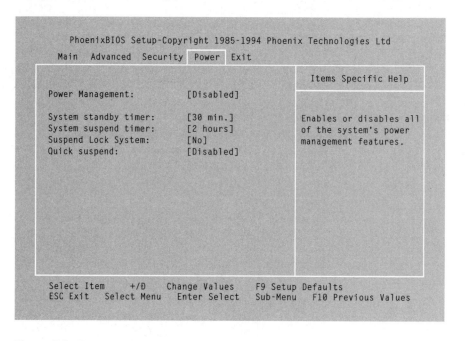

Figure 6.8   Power screen

Maintaining CMOS

Losing CMOS information is, unfortunately, a common problem. If the information on the CMOS chips is erased or corrupted, the computer will not be able to boot and/or you'll get nasty-looking errors. Some of the more common reasons that CMOS data is lost include the following:

- The on-board battery has run out.
- Cards have been removed or inserted without regard to preventing ESD.
- Improper handling of the motherboard has caused electrical short circuits or failure due to ESD.
- Something has been dropped on the motherboard.
- There is dirt on the motherboard.
- The power supply is faulty.
- There have been electrical surges.

The following types of errors indicate lost or corrupt CMOS data:

- CMOS configuration mismatch
- CMOS date/time not set
- No boot device available
- CMOS battery state low
- Cannot locate hard disk drive or floppy disk drive

It is wise to back up the CMOS setup just as you back up important data. One way to do this is to write down the information (especially before making hardware changes). There are many third-party CMOS save-and-restore utility programs available.

Note Many newer machines that run Windows 95 and 98 and offer Plug and Play place less emphasis on the CMOS. The BIOS information is stored with the device and is automatically detected at boot.

The CMOS Battery

The CMOS chip requires a small trickle voltage from a battery to keep its memory alive. When the battery gets low or runs out of current, the computer will experience a sudden memory loss and thus lose settings. It might not be able to find the floppy disk or first hard disk drive and therefore signify an error indicating that it cannot find the system or non-system disk.

The voltage of CMOS batteries ranges from 3 to 6 volts. Check the motherboard or the motherboard documentation to determine the actual battery requirements. Batteries come as either on-board (NiCad batteries, soldered in place or in a fixture, that last from five to seven years) or external (nonrechargeable AA alkaline batteries that last from two to four years). The 3-volt lithium watch battery is becoming very popular with motherboard suppliers. Many of these are mounted in a special holder so that the battery can be easily changed; however, some manufacturers solder them in place.

The first clue that the battery is weakening is that the CMOS clock begins to slow down. Go to a C prompt and type **time.** If you notice the clock is slow, it's time to change the battery.

Note   Remember that an MS-DOS machine (this includes one running
Windows 95 or 98) uses the CMOS clock only to get the date upon startup.
After the computer is running, MS-DOS uses the memory refresh timer on the
memory controller to keep time. This works well, but because the refresh timer
is not very accurate about seconds, you will lose one or two seconds per day.
If you never turn off a computer, it could lose time. Do not confuse this with a
bad battery. When you reboot, the computer will update itself to the correct time
from the CMOS. If the CMOS battery is low, it will still show the incorrect time.

When the CMOS battery dies completely, you will get lost CMOS errors, as
previously described. If you reload the CMOS data and the errors return, you must
change the battery. Although the computer will hold CMOS information during
the week, sometimes, over the weekend—when the computer is turned off for
two days—the CMOS data will be lost. Do not let these seemingly "intermittent"
problems fool you. And sometimes, before a battery dies, but after it has started
to fail, it will still be able to hold CMOS settings for a short time after the computer is off. Any time a computer loses the CMOS information more than once in
a week, replace the battery immediately—if only to eliminate the battery as the
source of the problem. After replacing the battery, you must run the setup utility
and restore any CMOS settings.

Note   The CMOS chip contains a capacitor that allows replacement of the battery
without losing data. For motherboards with soldered on-board batteries, there
is usually a connection that allows you to add an external battery to replace a
worn-out internal one. Be sure that the external battery has the same voltage as
the on-board battery you are replacing. Some of the older PCs use a battery pack
with four AA cells or a single nine-volt battery. These should be replaced with
a special PC battery pack to ensure longer life.

The best source of information about replacing a CMOS battery is the documentation that comes with the motherboard.

Today's computers are becoming less reliant on battery backup for CMOS. With
Windows 95 and 98 and Plug and Play technology, devices come with their own
BIOS, which the system reads each time the computer is booted. This does not
eliminate the need for CMOS or batteries, but it minimizes the impact of a battery
failure. At the very least, you will still need to retain the date-and-time information.

All Other Chips

It would be impossible to put all the necessary BIOS information for every
conceivable piece of hardware on one chip. It would also be impractical, as
new devices are released almost monthly. Upgrading a machine would require
a new BIOS chip (or a new version of the flash BIOS) every time. Fortunately,
there are other ways to handle this challenge.

ROM Chips with BIOS

BIOS can be put on the hardware device itself. Many new add-on boards such as display adapters, network interfaces, and sound cards have their own on-board ROM chip. Since the system BIOS doesn't have a clue about how to talk to the device, this card brings its own BIOS.

Loading Device Drivers

Did you ever wonder why (almost) every newly purchased device comes with an installation disk? Did you ever notice the line(s) DEVICE= in the CONFIG.SYS file (a text file found in the root directory of the hard disk drive) or how often a program writes information to Windows 98 or 2000 Registry?

Using device drivers is the most popular way to provide BIOS support for hardware. A device driver is a program that acts as an interface between the operating system and the control circuits that operate the device. For example, Windows has "generic" code that opens a file, but the driver for the disk drive takes care of low-level tasks like positioning the read head, reading or writing blocks of data, and so on. Thus, applications programmers don't usually have to worry about these details and can assume that any hardware supported by a device driver will work. Every time the computer is booted up, the CONFIG.SYS file is read and the device drivers are loaded from the hard disk drive into RAM.

Some examples of device drivers in CONFIG.SYS are:

```
DEVICE=C:\DOS\HIMEM.SYS
DEVICE=C:\DOS\EMM386.EXE NOEMS
DEVICEHIGH =C:\SCSI\ASPIPP3.SYS /D /Z
DEVICEHIGH =C:\DOS\DRVSPACE.SYS
DEVICEHIGH =C:\CDROM\MTMCDAI.SYS /L=001
```

Loading device drivers in CONFIG.SYS is a requirement for machines running MS-DOS. The Windows 95, 98, and 2000 operating systems have their own drivers that are loaded as part of startup. (Drivers are covered in more detail in Chapter 15, "Software: MS-DOS and Windows 3.x" and Chapter 16, "Windows 95 and Beyond.") Occasionally, drivers become outdated or have problems. You can obtain new drivers directly from the device manufacturer (frequently from their Web sites).

Note Even hardware that installs without a setup disk can be changing the registry if it is a Plug and Play device that is recognized by the operating system. Erratic problems can occur if a device is improperly identified. Under Windows 95, 98, or 2000, check under the System section of Control Panel to identify possible conflicts.

POST—Power-On Self Test

Every time a PC is turned on or reset using the Reset button or Windows Restart command, the computer is rebooted and reset to its basic operating condition. The system BIOS program starts by invoking a special program (stored on a ROM chip) called the *POST (power-on self test)*. The POST sends out standardized commands that check every primary device (in more technical terms, it runs an internal self-diagnostic routine).

The POST has two stages:

- Test 1 occurs before and during the test of the video.
- Test 2 occurs after the video has been tested.

This division determines whether the computer will display errors by beeping or showing them on the screen. The POST does not assume the video works until it has been tested. The POST does assume that the speaker always works, but in order to let you know that the speaker is working, all computers beep on startup. Depending on the BIOS type, the POST might also sound a single beep when it's done, to let you know the boot process was successful. If something goes wrong, the POST sends a series of beep codes to let you know what the problem is or where to start looking for it.

Beep Codes Before and During the Video Test

The purpose of the first POST test is to check the most basic components. The exact order, number of tests, and error states will vary from product to product. In a healthy system, the POST reports by using a series of beep codes and screen messages to convey that all components are working. Then it transfers control to the boot drive, and the operating system is loaded. The POST is a good indication that the hardware is in working order.

If a problem occurs, the POST routine attempts to report the problem. This is also done by beep codes and (if possible) screen prompts. Some error codes are specific to chip sets or custom products, and the exact message and its meaning can vary from system to system. (See the POST code references in the system manual that shipped with the PC or the motherboard to obtain references for detailed error messages and beeps.) The following table lists the basic beep codes for AMI and Phoenix BIOSs.

Number of Beeps	Possible Problem
1	DRAM refresh failure
2	Parity circuit failure
3	Base 64 KB or CMOS RAM failure
4	System timer
5	Processor failure
6	Keyboard controller or Gate A20 error
7	Virtual mode exception error
8	Display monitor write/read test failure
9	ROM BIOS checksum error
10	CMOS RAM shutdown register failure
1 long, 3 short	Conventional/extended memory test failure
1 long, 8 short	Display test and display vertical and horizontal retrace test failure

Troubleshooting After a Beep

After a beep code has been recognized, there are a few things you can do to troubleshoot the error. The following table suggests some solutions. Keep in mind that in many cases it can be less expensive to replace the motherboard than to replace a chip.

Problem	Solution
RAM refresh failure Parity error RAM bit error Base 64-KB error	Reseat and clean the RAM chips. Replace individual memory chips until the problem is corrected.
8042 error (keyboard chip) Gate A20 error	Reseat and clean keyboard chip. Check operating system. Replace keyboard. Replace motherboard.
BIOS checksum error	Reseat ROM chip. Replace BIOS chip.
Video errors	Reseat video card. Replace video card.
Cache memory error	Reseat and clean cache chips. Verify cache jumper settings are correct. Replace cache chips.
Any other problems	Reseat expansion cards. Clean motherboard. Replace motherboard.

Note   Many computers will generate beep codes when the only problem is a bad power supply! Turn the computer off and on three or four times to see if the same beep code is generated every time. If so, it's probably a legitimate beep code that concerns the hardware and not the power supply.

Since early 1996, some BIOS programs have eliminated many beep codes. However, beep codes can still be found as part of the A+ Certification exam.

Error Messages—After the Video Test

After successfully testing the video, the POST will display any error messages on the screen. These errors are displayed in one of two ways: numeric error codes or text error messages.

Numeric Error Codes

When a computer generates a numeric error code, the machine locks up and the error code appears in the upper-left corner of the screen. The following table lists some common numeric error codes, but it is a good idea to check the manual before beginning repairs based on a beep code or error message.

Error Code	Problem
301	The keyboard is broken or not plugged in.
1701	The hard disk drive controller is bad.
7301	The floppy disk drive controller is bad.
161	The battery is dead.
1101	The serial card is bad.

Text Error Codes

BIOS manufacturers have stopped using numeric error codes and have replaced them with about 30 text messages. Instead of numbers, you get text that is usually, but not always, self-explanatory.

How Bad Is It?

There are two levels of error codes during POST: fatal and nonfatal. As the name implies, fatal errors will halt the system without attempting to load the operating system. Memory problems or a faulty disk or display adapter are examples of fatal errors. Nonfatal errors like a "missing" floppy disk drive will still result in the system attempting (and often succeeding) to load the operating system.

In most cases, the POST procedure does a good job of testing components. If it gives a clean bill of health to the hardware, its failure to boot will often lie in the operating system. You can use a bootable floppy disk in most cases to access the hard disk drive, or boot Windows using the Safe Start approach (press the F8 key just after the POST completes) and check for conflicting settings.

POST Cards

More difficult to resolve is a hardware problem that keeps the POST from issuing any report at all. When you face one of these, you will find that this is where a POST card earns its keep. These special diagnostic expansion cards monitor the POST process and display all codes (usually in two-digit hexadecimal format) as the system runs the POST. The technician can then decode this information using the manufacturer's manual. More advanced models can also be used to run advanced series of tests to isolate erratic problems.

When choosing a POST card, be sure that it will work with the types of machines you plan to test. Most are based on the ISA slot and work with most Intel CPUs. That means they should help with AT and later-based PCs that use the x86 processors. Basic models give only POST codes. More advanced models also can check DMA (direct memory access), IRQ (interrupt request), and port functions. Some come with fancy diagnostic software. The more features, the higher the price tag. But a POST card will save a lot of time and frustration, making it a worthwhile addition to any PC toolkit.

Lesson Summary

The following points summarize the main elements of this lesson:

- Understanding ROM BIOS is key to keeping a computer up and running.
- CMOS setup defines the data a computer needs to communicate with its hardware (such as its drives).
- The CMOS battery maintains BIOS data when computer power is turned off.
- POST cards can quickly repay their expense by helping to isolate problems when the POST routine fails to provide a report.

Chapter Summary

The following points summarize the key concepts in this chapter:

Computer Cases

- The function of the case is to house the computer's internal components, connect the computer to the outside world with ports and connectors, and to protect the computer from damage.

- To prevent electromagnetic interference, avoid running a computer without the cover on.

Motherboards

- The motherboard defines the capabilities of a computer.

- Not all motherboards are the same. Some manufacturers have proprietary motherboards that can be used only in their own computers. They will also require proprietary parts for expansion. Generally, these motherboards are of higher quality (and price).

ROM BIOS

- BIOS chips are used to provide data to the CPU; this data tells the CPU how to operate specific devices.

- CMOS is a BIOS chip that can have its data updated. The CMOS setup program is used to make these changes.

- CMOS chips require a battery to save the data when power to the computer is off.

- Some of the newer BIOS chips are updatable. These are called flash BIOS.

- A device driver is a program that acts as an interface between the operating system and the control circuits that operate the device.

- On machines running MS-DOS, device drivers are loaded by the CONFIG.SYS file.

- Computers running Windows 95, 98, or 2000 load their own device drivers and do not require a CONFIG.SYS file.

- POST is used to check a computer before it boots.

- POST errors are indicated by beeps before the video is checked and by text after the video check.

Review

1. What is the main function of the motherboard?

2. Name the typical chips found in a chip set.

3. What is EMI?

4. What are ROM chips used for?

5. Name the three types of ROM chip.

6. Describe what makes the CMOS special.

7. How can a technician use the POST beep codes?

8. What is a device driver?

9. What information is contained in the CMOS?

10. Define the POST and describe its function.

C H A P T E R   7

Memory

About This Chapter

In earlier chapters, we learned that the CPU and motherboard (bus and controllers) are critical components that help determine the overall speed with which a computer can process data. This chapter looks at another important system component and performance factor: memory.

Technicians are often asked to upgrade PCs by adding more memory, and memory conflicts or errors commonly prompt calls for assistance by users. Understanding how memory works, how to choose the right memory for a given system, and how to troubleshoot memory problems is critical to success as a computer technician.

Before You Begin

A clear understanding of microprocessors, motherboards, and computer buses, covered in earlier chapters, is required before beginning this chapter.

Lesson 1: ROM and RAM

As a computer technician, you will encounter various types of memory. This lesson defines the different types of memory, shows you how to locate memory in a computer, and discusses how to expand or add new memory.

After this lesson, you will be able to:

- Identify the various types of memory.
- Define the types of memory and describe their advantages and disadvantages.
- Specify the correct memory upgrades for a given computer.

Estimated lesson time: 40 minutes

Defining Memory

A host of terms and acronyms relate to the memory technology used in personal computers. A technician must understand the key concepts involved and be able to identify the distinctions between the major memory components, and to distinguish between memory and storage.

All computer memory is used to hold binary strings of data destined to be manipulated by the CPU. Think of memory as a vast bank of switches with two positions: on or off. Off is given the value of "0"; on is given the value of "1." This allows the switches to hold binary data based on whether they are open or closed. By stringing a series of switches together, larger numbers and code values can be represented.

Nonvolatile and Volatile Memory

There are two major classes of computer memory: nonvolatile and volatile. *Nonvolatile memory* is retained even if the power is shut off. The setup data held in CMOS, discussed in the preceding lessons, is a good example of nonvolatile memory. If the data is lost when the computer loses power, the memory is said to be *volatile*.

Active memory is a state in which a block of code or data is directly accessible to the CPU for reference or manipulation. When data is located outside the system's active memory, it is said to be "in storage." Storage devices include floppy disk and hard disk drives, optical media, and tape units.

Active memory is faster than storage because the information is already on the system, there are fewer physical (and no mechanical) operations involved in obtaining the data, and the CPU has direct control over the memory.

ROM: Read-Only Memory

ROM (read-only memory) is nonvolatile memory, generally installed by the vendor of the computer during the process of manufacturing the motherboard or secondary components that need to retain code when the machine is turned off. With the use of ROM, information that is required to start and run the computer cannot be lost or changed.

ROM is used extensively to program operation of computers, as well as in devices like cameras, and controls for the fuel injectors in modern cars. However, ROM plays a limited role in the PC. Here, it holds the instructions for performing the POST routine and the BIOS information used to describe the system configuration. For more detailed information, refer to Chapter 6, "Primary PC Components."

In most cases, a technician will need to be concerned with ROM only if it has failed and requires replacement, needs to be upgraded, or if it conflicts with other memory installed in the system. The actual code in ROM is not usually in the direct control of a repair person or technician.

RAM: Random Access Memory

RAM (random access memory) is what is most often referred to when PC memory is discussed. RAM is the form of volatile memory used to hold temporary instructions and data for manipulation while the system is running. The term "random" is applied because the CPU can access or place data to and from any addressable RAM on the system. If power to the system is lost, all RAM is lost as well.

Usually, when referring to RAM, we are speaking of some variation of DRAM (dynamic random access memory) or the newer SDRAM (synchronous DRAM). These are the most common forms of RAM used in the modern PC.

DRAM works by using a microscopic capacitor and a microscopic transistor to store each data bit. A charged capacitor represents a value of "1," and a discharged capacitor represents a value of "0." A capacitor works like a battery—it holds a charge and then releases it. Unlike a battery, which holds a charge for months, the tiny capacitors in DRAM hold their charges for only fractions of a second. Therefore, DRAM needs an entire set of circuitry just to keep the capacitors charged. The process of recharging these capacitors is called "refreshing." Without refreshing, the data would be lost. This is another reason why DRAM is called volatile memory.

All PC CPUs handle data in 8-bit blocks. Each block, known as a byte, denotes how many bits the CPU can move in and out of memory at one time. The number is an indication of how rapidly data can be manipulated and arranged in system memory. But don't confuse this byte with the amount of system memory, which is usually expressed in megabytes (MB). System memory is the total amount of active memory that is available to the CPU as a temporary work area.

Each transaction between the CPU and memory is called a *bus cycle*. The amount of memory that a CPU can address in a single bus cycle has a major effect on overall system performance and determines the design of memory that the system can use. The width of the system's memory bus must match the number of data bits per cycle of the CPU.

All computers have some form of memory controller, which handles the movement of data to and from the CPU and the system memory banks. The memory controller is also responsible for the integrity of the data as it is swapped in and out. There are two primary methods of ensuring that the data received is the same as the data sent: parity and error-correction coding (ECC).

Parity

Parity is a method of ensuring data integrity that adds an extra bit (the parity bit) along with each 8-bit bus cycle. There are two kinds of parity: even and odd. Both use a three-step process to validate a bus transaction; however, they do it in opposite ways.

- In step one, both methods set the value of the parity bit based on the even or odd number that represents the sum of the data bits as the first step.

- In step two, the string goes into DRAM.

- And in step three, the parity circuit checks the math. If the parity bit matches the parity bit of the number that represents the sum of the binary string sent, the data is passed on. If it fails the test, an error is reported.

ECC

A more robust technology, *ECC* can detect errors beyond the limits of the simpler parity method. It adds extra information about the bits, which is then evaluated to determine if there are problems with individual bits in the data string.

Access Speed

Access speed, denoted in nanoseconds (ns), is the amount of time it takes for the RAM to provide requested data to the memory controller. Here, smaller is better. Be sure to buy RAM that is at least as fast as that listed as standard for the computer in question.

A typical total response time for a 70-ns DRAM chip is between 90 and 120 ns. This includes the time required to access the address bus and data bus. Most 486- and Pentium-based machines use either 70-ns or 60-ns DRAM chips, although 50-ns chips are now available. The access speed of a chip is usually printed on the chip (often as part of the identification number).

Here are a few important things to remember about access speed when adding memory:

- Any add-on memory should be the same speed or faster (lower number) as any existing memory.
- You cannot mix memory modules with different speeds in the same bank.
- You should check the motherboard specifications for the recommended memory chip speed.

RAM Packaging

Over the years, the way memory has been packaged and placed on the motherboard has changed several times. Early versions of RAM were installed as single chips, usually 1-bit wide dual inline package (DIP), as shown in Figure 7.1. In some cases, this was soldered right onto the motherboard, but most often it was seated in a socket, offering a simpler method of removal and replacement. Some older machines have special memory expansion cards that contain several rows of sockets. These cards are placed in a slot on the motherboard.

To upgrade or add memory, new chips had to be individually installed on the motherboard (eight or nine chips per row—nine chips if using parity). This could be challenging, because each chip has 16 wires that need to be perfectly aligned before insertion into the base. The notch in one end denotes the side that has pin 1.

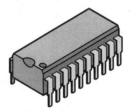

Figure 7.1   A DIP DRAM Chip

As the amount of memory and the need for speed increased, manufacturers started to market modules containing several chips that allowed for easier installation and larger capacity. These modules come in a variety of physical configurations. Technicians must be able to identify both the type and amount of memory a computer requires for optimum performance.

Tip   The latter is very easy if the PC is operational: simply boot the system and note the memory values given during the POST. In some cases, this is also a useful way to determine if a memory block is improperly installed. If that is the case, the computer might fail to boot or the POST might report a lower figure than the actual amount of RAM present.

SIPPs

One of the first module forms of DRAM, the *SIPP (single inline pin package)* is a printed circuit board with individual DRAM chips mounted on it, shown in Figure 7.2. Physically, a SIPP module looks like a rectangular card with a single row of pins along one edge. The SIPP had a very short time in the sun, due to the fragile nature of these pins.

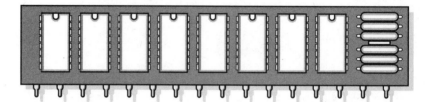

Figure 7.2   SIPP

Caution   SIPPs have a row of pins along one side. These pins are easily broken, and care should be taken to avoid damaging them during installation.

SIMMs (30-pin)

SIMMs (single inline memory modules) quickly replaced SIPPs, because they are easier to install. They are similar to SIPPs with one exception—they require no pins; 30-pin SIMMs have 30 contacts in a single row along the lower edge (see Figure 7.3). A 30-pin SIMM can have as few as two, or as many as nine, individual DRAM chips. While SIMM modules can have pin counts as high as 200, in PCs, 30- and 72-pin versions are the most common.

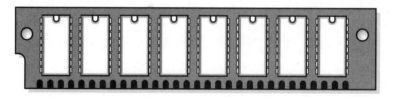

Figure 7.3   30-pin SIMM

Caution   Avoid touching the contacts on SIMMs, and use proper handling to reduce the risk of damage from electrostatic discharge (ESD).

Memory Configuration

The capability of the computer's CPU, its memory chip configuration, and its operating system all play roles in how the computer's memory is allocated. Technicians should understand the terms and processes involved, both for their own benefit and in order to explain the details to a customer if the question arises.

As mentioned earlier, the CPU processes data in byte-wide (8-bit) pieces. The power of a processor is often expressed by how many such pieces it can handle at a time. For example, the Intel Pentium is a 64-bit CPU, meaning that it can handle 64 bits at once. That amounts to 8 bytes (8 x 8). These terms always refer to byte-wide memory (8 bits).

It's important to remember that each 30-pin SIMM always supplies 8 data bits (one byte) per CPU clock cycle, no matter how many megabytes it holds. When the bus cycle demand is greater than the number of bits a module provides, a bank of modules equal to the bit width must be used to feed the data demands of the CPU and fill the entire data bus. An 8-bit data bus (8086 or 8088) needs 8-bit-wide memory to fill one bank. A 16-bit data bus requires 16-bit-wide memory to fill one bank, and so on. If you are installing 30-pin SIMMs (each is 8 bits wide) on a 16-bit machine, you would need two rows of chips to completely fill the data bus.

Note A 286 processor needs two rows of chips to make one bank. A 386DX and a 486 have 32-bit external data buses—four rows to make a bank. The Pentium and Pentium Pro each have 64-bit external data buses—eight rows of 8-bit-wide memory to make one bank. Each of the rows that make a bank must be filled with identical chips (size and speed). See Figure 7.4.

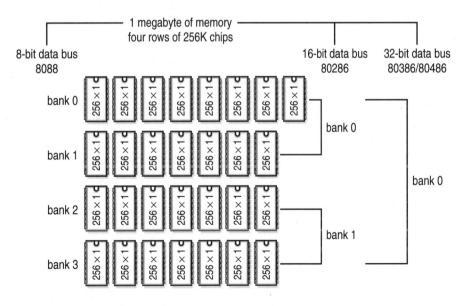

Figure 7.4 Banking

Most motherboards provide several rows of slots for adding memory, often referred to as banks. Be careful with the word "bank." It is used to describe the necessary rows of chips, as well as the slots into which they are inserted.

SIMMs usually require matched pairs to form a bank of memory, whereas DIMMS require only one card. To calculate the number of SIMMs needed to make one bank, use the following formula: Divide the number of data bits per CPU cycle by the bit width of the module. (For 30-pin SIMMs, that is always 8 bits.) A 32-bit external data bus with 30-pin SIMMs requires 32 (the width of the data bus) divided by 8 (the number of bits per SIMM module) or 4 (30-pin SIMMs per bank).

There are some rules to follow when banking:

- All rows in a bank must be either completely filled or completely empty.
- Each bank is numbered, starting with bank 0.
- In most systems, DRAM should be installed in bank 0 before any other bank is used.
- Refer to the motherboard documentation for bank numbering and installation directions.

Specifying SIPPs and SIMMs

When speaking of DRAM SIPPs and SIMMs, we use two values to determine how much memory a unit can hold:

- **Width:** 1 bit, 4 bits (a nibble), 8 bits (a byte), or 16 bits (a word), and so on.
- **Depth:** How *deep* the chip is: 256 KB, 1 MB, 4 MB, 8 MB, 16 MB, 32 MB, and so on.

By combining the depth and width, the "size" of the DRAM chip can be determined.

Here are a few points to remember when specifying DRAM:

- When upgrading memory, you add megabytes.
- When purchasing DRAM, you buy bits.
- Calculate chip size by multiplying depth by width; the result is measured in bits.
- One KB of memory is equal to 8192 bits (1024 x 8).
- One MB is equal to 8,388,608 bits (1024 x 1024 x 8).

The following table lists common DRAM module sizes.

Chip (depth x width)	Number of Chips/Module	Memory per Module
256 KB x 1	8	256 KB
256 KB x 4	2	256 KB
256 KB x 16	1	512 KB
512 KB x 8	1	512 KB
1 MB x 1	8	1 MB
1 MB x 4	2	1 MB
1 MB x 16	1	2 MB
2 MB x 8	1	2 MB
4 MB x 1	8	4 MB
4 MB x 4	2	4 MB

The 72-Pin SIMM

With the advent of 32- and 64-bit CPUs, the bank began to take up too much space on the motherboard and added to the cost of memory. (The board that houses the chips often costs more than the DRAM chips.) Enter the 72-pin SIMMs, with 72 pins on each card. One of these is four times wider than a 30-pin SIMM, which is 8-bits wide (see Figures 7.5 and 7.6). Therefore, a motherboard requiring four rows of 30-pin SIMMs to fill one bank needs only one 72-pin SIMM. Virtually all Pentium and Pentium Pro systems use 72-pin SIMMs.

Because 72-pin SIMMs are 32 bits wide, the term "x 32" is used to describe them. A 1 MB x 32 SIMM contains 4 MB of RAM because it is 4 bytes wide. (One MB of RAM is 1,048,576 x 32, which equals 4 MB.) Remember, memory is measured in bytes, and chips are measured in bits.

Figure 7.5 A 72-pin SIMM

There are many varieties of SIMMs on the market. The following table lists some common 72-pin SIMMs.

Configuration	Memory
256 KB x 32	1 MB, no parity
256 KB x 36	1 MB, parity
1 MB x 32	4 MB, no parity
1 MB x 36	4 MB, parity
2 MB x 32	8 MB, no parity
2 MB x 36	8 MB, parity
4 MB x 32	16 MB, no parity
4 MB x 36	16 MB, parity
8 MB x 32	32 MB, no parity
8 MB x 36	32 MB, parity
16 MB x 32	64 MB, no parity
16 MB x 36	64 MB, parity

Voltage

All early PCs used 5-volt circuits to power components, including memory. Today, the trend is to use 3.3-volt power unless 5 volts are required for a specific part of the system (such as a hard disk drive). Be sure to check the voltage of the memory before installing a module.

Installing SIMMs

When installing SIMMs:

- Always use precautions to avoid ESD. Refer to Chapter 13, "The Basics of Electrical Energy," for details.

- Always handle SIMMs carefully—keep your fingers on the plastic edges. There is nothing worse than destroying a 16-MB SIMM because of static discharge.

- All SIMMs have a notch on one side that prevents them from being installed improperly. If you cannot insert the SIMM easily, it's probably backwards.

- SIMMs are inserted into the slot at a 45-degree angle along the wide side (see Figure 7.12).

- After the SIMM is securely seated in the slot, push it upright until the holding clamps on either side are secured.

Important   SIMMs are extremely sensitive to static. Be sure to handle them carefully.

Figure 7.6   Installing SIMMs

After the chip is physically installed:

- Turn on the computer. If the DRAM is installed correctly, the RAM count on the computer will reflect the new value.

- If the RAM value has not changed, probably either a bank is disabled or the SIMMs aren't installed correctly. Check the motherboard documentation to determine if a jumper needs to be changed in order to turn on the SIMM.

- If the computer does not boot and the screen is blank, the RAM was not installed correctly.

Note   When a computer is booting, the RAM count is based on units of 1024 bytes. One MB of RAM should show as 1024, 2 MB as 2048, 4 MB as 4096, and so on. Most RAM counts will stop before they get to the value expected (less than 1 MB). This is acceptable—some memory is "skipped" during the count, but it's all there.

- After the RAM is installed, and the RAM count correctly reflects the new value, the CMOS needs to be updated. On most machines, this is done automatically and no intervention is required.

If you get an error similar to "CMOS Memory Mismatch Press Fl to continue," access the CMOS with the CMOS setup program, then save and exit (changes will be automatically recorded). The CMOS will be reset.

If the system fails to boot, or reports less than the amount of memory actually installed, recheck the modules to make sure they are seated properly according to the motherboard manual and that the right type and amount are present.

Dual Inline Memory Modules

These newer modules look much like SIMMs, but come in a package with 168 pins and have a different wiring structure, so that one card can form a complete bank. These are the memory packages used on virtually all new motherboards.

Cache Memory

To *cache* is to set something aside, or to store for anticipated use. Mass storage is much slower than RAM, and RAM is much slower than the CPU. Caching, in PC terms, is the holding of a recently used or frequently used code or data in a special memory location for rapid retrieval. Speed is everything when it comes to computers. The high-speed memory chip generally used for caching is called *SRAM*.

SRAM

SRAM (static RAM) does not use capacitors to store ones and zeroes. Instead, SRAM uses a special circuit called a *flip-flop*.

The advantages of SRAM are that it is fast and it does not have to be refreshed, because it uses the flip-flop circuit to store each bit. A flip-flop circuit will toggle on or off and retain its position, whereas a standard memory circuit requires constant refreshing to maintain an on state.

The main disadvantage of SRAM is that it is more expensive than DRAM.

Internal Cache (L1)

Starting with the 486 chips, a cache has been included on every CPU. This original on-board cache is known as *Level 1 (L1)* or *internal cache*. All commands for the processor go through the cache. The cache stores a backlog of commands so that, if a wait state is encountered, the CPU can continue to process using commands from the cache. Caching will store any code that has been read and keep it available for the CPU to use. This eliminates the need to wait for fetching of the data from DRAM.

External Cache (L2)

Additional cache can be added to most computers, depending on the motherboard. This cache is mounted directly on the motherboard, outside the CPU. The external cache is also called *Level 2 (L2)* and is the same as L1, but larger. L2 can also (on some motherboards) be added or expanded. When installing any L2 cache, be sure to check the CMOS setup and enable the cache.

Write-Back vs. Write-Through

As mentioned, the primary use of a cache is to increase the speed of data from RAM to the CPU. Some caches immediately send all data directly to RAM, even if it means hitting a wait state. This is called *write-through* cache, shown in Figure 7.7.

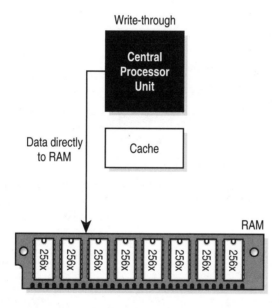

Figure 7.7   Write-through cache

Some caches store the data for a time and send it to RAM later. This is called *write-back* cache, shown in Figure 7.8.

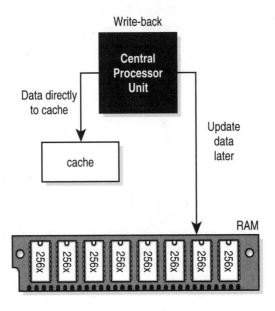

Figure 7.8   Write-back cache

Write-back caches are harder to implement but are much more powerful than write-through caches, because the CPU does not have to stop for the wait state of the RAM. However, write-through caches are less expensive.

Lesson Summary

The following points summarize the main elements of this lesson:

- There are two basic kinds of memory in a computer: ROM and RAM.
- Memory chips come in many sizes and shapes: DIPPs, SIPPs, DRAM, SRAM.
- Installing memory (RAM) is easy; however, you must be able to match the size and configuration of the memory chips to the motherboard.
- The number of memory modules needed to fill one memory bank equals the width of the external data bus (in bits) divided by the width of the SIMM (in bits).
- Cache memory is used to increase the performance of a computer.
- Cache memory (SRAM) is faster, but more expensive, than the standard DRAM; therefore, it is used in small quantities and for special purposes.
- There are two types of cache memory: L1 and L2.

Lesson 2: Memory Mapping

Computer memory has many functions. Some memory is reserved for particular uses by the processor and, if improperly allocated, will cause problems. Understanding how to identify and manage memory is key to optimizing a computer. In this lesson, you learn how memory is allocated. Later, you will learn how to apply this information and optimize computer memory (in Chapter 15, "Software: MS-DOS and Windows 3.x.")

After this lesson, you will be able to:

- Know how to use hexadecimal numbers.
- Define the different types of memory access.
- Optimize memory allocation.

Estimated lesson time: 20 minutes

The Workings of Hexadecimal Code

Chapter 2, "Understanding Electronic Communication," introduced the concept of binary notation. This is how computers count—by setting the value of a two-position switch to either 0 (off) or 1 (on). Ones and zeroes work well when machines are conversing, but that language can be somewhat confusing for computer designers and programmers. To simplify the representation of numbers and notations, designers and programmers use a numbering system called *hexadecimal notation* (also known simply as *hex*). This is a numbering system based on 16 instead of 10. Fortunately, computer technicians do not have to be experts in hexadecimal notation. You do, however, need to know how to use the numbering system as it relates to computer memory.

Hexadecimal is used to simplify notation of binary code in much the same way that we sometimes count in 5s or 10s when it is more convenient than working our way through a problem by 1s. You might ask how anyone would find it simpler to count in hex. Well, in dealing with a system that uses 8 bits, addressing counting locations in hex (a system based on eight positions) makes perfect sense.

All address buses and wires within a computer come in some multiple of 4 (8, 16, 20, 24, 32). Because there are 16 different combinations, the 16 unique characters of the base-16 numbering system are a natural choice for computer shorthand when referring to memory locations or a bus address. The following table contrasts binary notation with hex shorthand.

Binary Number	Hex Shorthand	Binary Number	Hex Shorthand
0000	0	1010	A
0001	1	1011	B
0010	2	1100	C
0011	3	1101	D
0100	4	1110	E
0101	5	1111	F
0110	6		
0111	7		
1000	8		
1001	9		

Hexadecimal Shorthand

There is no need to say:

10110110011000101101

To use hex shorthand:

- Break the 20 digits into 5 sets:

  1011   0110   0110   0010   1101

- Give each 4-character set its hex shorthand:

  1011   0110   0110   0010   1101
  B   6   6   2   D

  Hex shorthand = B662D

To represent all the possible addresses for the 20-bit address bus, we use 5 hex values (0 to F) that map to their binary equivalents, from all 0s:

0000   0000   0000   0000   0000
0   0   0   0   0

to all 1s.

1111   1111   1111   1111   1111
F   F   F   F   F

Each of the possible memory locations for the Intel 8088 can be represented by 5-digit hexadecimal values, starting at 00000 and ending at FFFFF.

Memory Allocation

Previously in this chapter, we discussed memory in terms of the chips themselves. In this section, we look at how that memory is allocated for use by the CPU. This is called *memory mapping* and uses hexadecimal addresses to define ranges of memory.

 Run the **memory** video located in the **demos** folder on the CD accompanying this book to view a presentation of memory allocation.

The original processors developed by Intel were unable to use more than 1 MB of RAM, and the original IBM PC allowed only the first 640 KB of memory for direct use. MS-DOS applications were written to conform to this limitation. As application requirements grew, programmers needed to optimize the use of memory to make the most of the available space. This 1 MB of memory was divided into two sections. The first 640 KB was reserved for the operating system and applications (designated as conventional memory). The remaining 384 KB of RAM (designated as upper memory) was earmarked for running the computer's own housekeeping needs (BIOS, video RAM, ROM, and so on). Although some early PC clones had firmware that could make direct use of the upper memory block available to programmers, actually doing so would result in hardware and software incompatibility issues (see Figure 7.9)

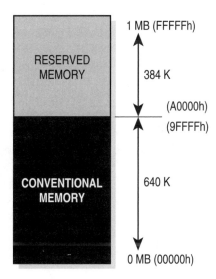

Figure 7.9   IBM PC/MS-DOS Memory map

Under MS-DOS and Windows 3.*x*, the 640-KB area must be kept as free as possible for program use. MS-DOS memory optimization ensures that MS-DOS applications have as much of this memory as possible. The MS-DOS limitations no longer apply to Windows 95 in 32-bit mode and newer operating systems. However, they are still an important part of running MS-DOS, Windows 3.*x*-based programs on older machines or in MS-DOS compatibility mode with the more advanced operating systems.

Types of Memory Access

When we speak of memory in a computer, we are generally speaking of its RAM, because ROM cannot be written to by either the system or applications. Although we have only one source of RAM, under MS-DOS-based operating systems, it is divided into smaller groups depending on how it is used.

Extended Memory Specification (XMS)

RAM above the 1-MB address is called *extended memory*. With the introduction of the 80286 processor, memory was addressable up to 16 MB. Starting with the 80386DX processor, memory was addressable up to 4 GB. Extended memory is accessed through an extended memory manager (HIMEM.SYS for MS-DOS or a third-party utility such as 386MAX).

Conventional Memory

Conventional memory is the amount of RAM, typically 640 KB, that is addressable by an IBM PC or compatible machine operating in real mode. (Real mode is the only operating mode supported by MS-DOS.) Conventional memory is located in the area between 0 and 640 KB. Without the use of special techniques, conventional memory is the only kind of RAM accessible to MS-DOS programs.

MS-DOS Protected Mode Interface (DPMI)

MS-DOS Protected Mode Interface (DPMI) is a specification that allows multiple applications to access extended memory at the same time and has been endorsed by most memory-manager producers and applications developers. Windows uses the DPMI specification.

Expanded Memory Specification (EMS)

This technique, developed by Lotus/Intel/Microsoft (LIM), uses a 64-KB section of memory (usually in upper memory) to provide a "window" in which data can be written. Once in this area, the data can be transferred to the expanded memory. The memory chips are located on an expansion card installed inside the computer. The data is paged or swapped to and from the CPU through this window (see Figure 7.10).

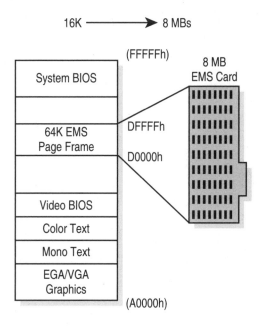

Figure 7.10   Expanded memory

Expanded memory can provide up to 32 MB of additional memory, and because it is loaded from a 64-KB section, it is below the 1-MB limit and therefore MS-DOS can recognize it.

MS-DOS applications must be specifically written to take advantage of expanded memory. Windows applications do not use expanded memory; 80386 and newer processors can emulate expanded memory by using memory managers such as EMM386.EXE and HIMEM.SYS.

High Memory Area (HMA)

An irregularity was found in the Intel chip architecture that allowed MS-DOS to address the first 64 KB of extended memory on machines with 80286 or higher processors. This special area is called the *high memory area*. A software driver called an "A20 handler" must be run to allow the processor to access the HMA. MS-DOS uses HIMEM.SYS for this purpose. The only limitation is that HIMEM.SYS can load only a single program into this area. Typically, MS-DOS is loaded into HMA to free conventional memory (see Figure 7.11).

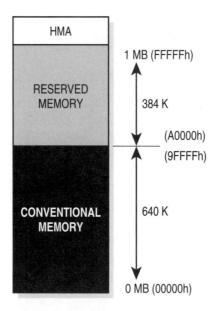

Figure 7.11   High memory area

Protected Mode

Beginning with 80286 processors using an operating system such as OS/2 or Windows, a computer can create "virtual machines," providing all the functionality of a standard computer in real mode but allowing multiple tasks to take place at the same time. This is called *protected mode* because the processor, memory, and other hardware are "protected" from the software application taking direct control of the system by the operating system, which allocates memory and processor time.

Real Mode

In *real mode* (MS-DOS), a computer can perform only one operation at a time and an application expects full control of the system. Real mode operates within the MS-DOS 1-MB limitation.

Shadow RAM

Many high-speed expansion boards use shadow RAM to improve the performance of a computer. *Shadow RAM* rewrites (or shadows) the contents of the ROM BIOS and/or video BIOS into extended RAM (between the 640-KB boundary and 1 MB). This allows systems to operate faster when application software calls any BIOS routines. In some cases, system speed can be increased up to 400 percent (see Figure 7.12).

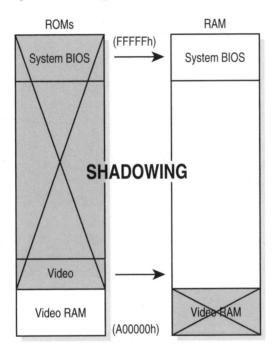

Figure 7.12   Shadow RAM

Upper Memory Area (UMA)

The *upper memory area* (UMA), the memory block from 640 KB to 1024 KB, is designated for hardware use, like video RAM, BIOS, and memory-mapped hardware drivers that are loaded into high memory. Refer to Chapter 15, "Software: MS-DOS and Windows 3.x," for details.

Upper Memory Blocks (UMB)

The unused addresses in upper memory, known as *upper memory blocks (UMB)*, can be divided into blocks. These empty blocks have no RAM associated with them and are simply reserved space. This unused space is valuable because, unlike expanded and extended memory, MS-DOS can run programs in UMB.

Virtual Control Program Interface (VCPI)

The memory-management specification, known *as Virtual Control Program Interface (VCPI)*, accesses extended memory for MS-DOS-based applications. It allows only one application to control extended memory and does not support multitasking. Windows is not compatible with the VCPI specification.

Determining Usable Memory

The MS-DOS command MEM (MEM.COM) provides information about the amount and type of memory available (see Figure 7.13). It provides a quick way to determine how all of the different areas in physical memory are being used and the total amount of RAM actually active on the system.

```
Memory Type                          Total    =    Used    +    Free
Conventional                         640 KB        122K          518K
Upper                                155K           41K          144K
Reserved                             128K          128K            0K
Extended (XMS)                     7,269K        2,486K        4,783K
Total Memory                      81,259K       21,777K        5,415K
Total under 1 MB                     795K          163K          632K
Largest executable program size              518K (530,096 bytes)
Largest free upper memory block              114K (116,352 bytes)
```

Figure 7.13   MEM.COM

Most MS-DOS and many early Windows systems load numerous device drivers and TSR (terminate-and-stay resident) programs using the CONFIG.SYS and AUTOEXEC.BAT routines during the boot cycle. These programs are, by default, loaded into conventional memory, taking up valuable space. Memory management techniques are used to load these device drivers and TSRs into the upper memory, allowing more lower memory to be made available to applications.

To determine which device drivers and TSRs are loaded, use the command:

```
MEM/C
```

The "/c" is a classify switch. This determines how much conventional memory a certain real-mode program is using (see Figure 7.14).

```
Name               Total   =   Conventional  +  Upper Memory

MSDOS      21,581 (21K)     21,581  (21K)          0   (0K)
HIMEM       1,168  (1K)      1,168   (1K)          0   (0K)
EMM386      3,120  (3K)      3,120   (3K)          0   (0K)
IFSHLP      3,872  (4K)      3,872   (4K)          0   (0K)
NECIDE     20,544 (20K)     20,544  (20K)          0   (0K)
ANSI        4,208  (4K)      4,208   (4K)          0   (0K)
COMMAND     2,928  (3K)      2,928   (3K)          0   (0K)
GUARD       9,360  (9K)      9,360   (9K)          0   (0K)
MSCDEX     36,244 (36K)     36,244  (35K)          0   (0K)
SHARE      17,904 (17K)     17,904  (17K)          0   (0K)
DOSKEY      4,144  (4K)      4,144   (4K)              0(0K)
SETSERV       512  (1K)          0   (0K)        512   (1K)
VSDINIT     4,192  (4K)          0   (0K)      4,192   (4K)
SMARTDRV   30,368 (30K)          0   (0K)     30,368  (30K)
KEYB        6,944  (7K)          0   (0K)      6,944   (7K)
Free      646,768(632K)    530,208(518K)    116,560(114K)
```

Figure 7.14   MEM/C

You can also use the Memory button provided with MSD.EXE (Microsoft Diagnostics) to determine the amount and allocation of memory (see Figure 7.15).

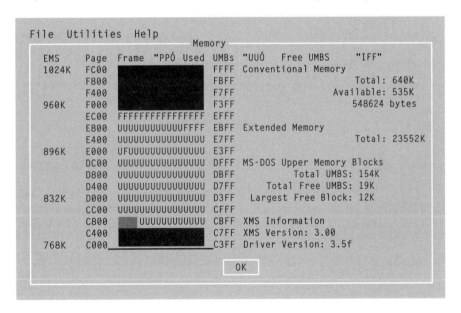

Figure 7.15   Microsoft Diagnostics

Note Hexadecimal notation is used by Microsoft Diagnostics. *U* represents areas of the UMA which are used by TSRs and device drivers.

Lesson Summary

The following points summarize the main elements of this lesson:

- Hexadecimal notation is used as shorthand for writing binary numbers.

- Memory is defined in terms of the physical characteristics of the chips and how the memory is allocated for use.

- The MS-DOS operating system can address only the first 1 MB of memory.

- Expanded memory was an early method of adding memory to an MS-DOS-based system. It paged, or swapped, 64-KB chunks of data through a window (a 64-KB block of memory in the upper memory area) to an expansion card.

- Extended memory, used by Windows 3.*x* and newer systems, allows the addressing of memory above the MS-DOS limit and has virtually replaced expanded memory.

- Understanding memory allocation and the different memory locations is key to optimizing a computer's memory.

- The MS-DOS command MEM.COM is a utility that provides information about memory allocation.

Chapter Summary

The following points summarize the key concepts in this chapter:

ROM and RAM

- ROM is a form of nonvolatile memory that is used in PCs to hold POST commands.

- RAM is the memory that is used by the CPU to temporarily hold data that is currently used by the system. It is cleared any time the system is powered down or rebooted.

- RAM chips come in many sizes and shapes. It is important for the computer technician to be able to identify the different types and calculate how many chips, banks, or rows of memory modules are needed to upgrade a computer.

- The number of SIMMs required is based on the width of the data bus.

Mapping Memory

- Memory (RAM) is allocated to different parts of the CPU. A computer technician uses a memory map to describe how memory is allocated.

- Hexadecimal numbers are used to identify the location of memory on a memory map.

- MS-DOS can access only the first 1 MB of memory.

- Several commands, such as MEM.COM, are used to identify memory allocation in a computer.

- A computer technician must know the difference between conventional and high memory.

Review

1. What is hexadecimal shorthand used for?

2. Define the following terms: conventional memory, expanded memory, extended memory, HMA, shadow RAM.

3. Describe the difference between ROM and RAM.

4. How many 30-pin SIMM boards are required for one bank of memory on a computer with a 486 processor?

5. What is the difference between "write-through" and "write-back" cache?

6. What is DRAM?

7. Define access speed.

8. Describe the major difference between SIPPs and SIMMs.

9. Define cache memory.

10. One of the differences between DRAM and SRAM is that SRAM does not have to be refreshed. What does this mean, and how does it affect the cost of each type of chip?

C H A P T E R   8

Basic Disk Drives

About This Chapter

This chapter is all about drives—disk drives—which come in assorted sizes and shapes. The first disk drives were physically large, small in capacity (limited in the amount of data they could store), and very expensive. Today, disks drives are physically small, large in capacity, and very inexpensive.

The history of disk drives is long and complex. In this chapter, we begin our exploration by first looking briefly at the history and development of disk drives. We start with the most basic of drives (the floppy disk drive), and continue through the early hard disk drives, examining their complexities and limitations along the way.

Before You Begin

Before starting this chapter, you should review the discussions of memory, hexadecimal notation, and BIOS operations in Chapters 6 and 7.

Lesson 1: Floppy Disk Drives

The most basic input device is the floppy disk drive. It is perhaps the only computer component that has retained its original technology. Other than increased storage capacity and the adoption of a hard plastic shell, the floppy disk drive still works essentially the same way (in terms of cabling and BIOS configuration) it did 10 years ago. In this lesson, we explore this venerable standard.

After this lesson, you will be able to:

- Describe floppy disk drive technology.
- Troubleshoot a floppy disk drive problem.

Estimated lesson time: 20 minutes

The Basics of Floppy Disk Drives

IBM developed the first floppy disk drives for its System 370 machines, which came out around 1972. These drives used 8-inch floppy disks. The same basic design was adapted by companies such as Wang for the dedicated word-processing machines used in the 1970s and early 1980s. The 5.25-inch floppy disks that accompanied the early personal computers came shortly thereafter. Floppy disks were included in personal computers before hard disk drives, mostly out of economic considerations. The cost of an early PC hard disk drive was more than the total cost of a system today and took a half day to prepare and install.

Today's floppy disks (see Figure 8.1) are made of flexible plastic and coated with a magnetic material. To protect the disk from dust and physical damage, it is packaged in a plastic or coated paper case. The main reason for the popularity of floppy disk drives and disks is that they provide inexpensive read/write (R/W) removable media. The data stored on a floppy disk can be moved from one computer to another, provided both have the same type of drive. In general, it is a good idea to protect your data by always keeping two copies of any data file that you create (the original and a backup), and the floppy disk is an excellent medium for backing up, storing, or distributing copies of relatively small files, such as word-processing documents.

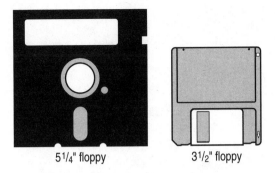

5¼" floppy   3½" floppy

Figure 8.1   Floppy disks

The following table describes various floppy disks and their capacities.

Disk Size	Capacity	Description
5.25-inch	160 KB	Single-sided single-density—the first model.
5.25-inch	360 KB	Double-sided single-density.
5.25-inch	720 KB	Double-sided double-density.
5.25-inch	1.2 MB	Double-sided high-density.
3.5-inch	720 KB	Double-sided double-density.
3.5-inch	1.44 MB	Double-sided high-density—today's standard.
3.5-inch	2.88 MB	Double-sided quad-density. This format has never really gained in market share and is not common on today's PCs.

The only major differences between the 5.25-inch and the 3.5-inch disk drives (other than physical size) are that the 5.25-inch drive has a slot connector and the 3.5-inch drive has a pin connector for engaging and spinning the disk, and they use different power plugs and voltages.

All floppy disk drives are connected to the motherboard's external data bus by a 34-conductor ribbon cable, shown in Figure 8.2. This cable has a seven-wire twist in lines 10 through 16. This ensures that when two floppy disk drives are attached, the drive-select and motor-enable signals on those wires can be inverted to "select" which drive becomes the active target. The other wires carry data and ground signals. The connector end of the cable with the twist *always* goes toward the drives.

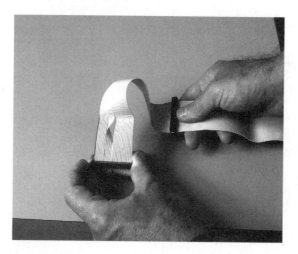

Figure 8.2   Floppy disk drive cable with a twist

Early BIOS was developed to recognize one or two floppy disk drives. No more than one 34-pin cable for floppy disk drives can be installed in a single system without resorting to special hardware. When a floppy disk drive is installed on the end connector (near the twist), the drive is logically designated as the *A drive* by BIOS. The drive attached in the middle of the cable is always the *B drive*. The BIOS will not recognize a B drive unless an A drive is physically installed.

The number 1 red wire must be connected to the number 1 pin on the drive. If this is not correctly installed, the drive will not work (although no damage can be done by installing the connector backward).

Note   If you install a new drive and notice that the indicator light comes on and stays on, the cable is most likely backward.

The power connection for a floppy disk drive, shown in Figure 8.3, is either the large Molex type connector on the 5.25-inch drive (see Chapter 5, Lesson 1: Power Supplies for details) or the smaller mini connector, on the 3.5-inch drive. A large number of power supplies, designed primarily for tower systems, provide a special connector exclusively for 3.5-inch floppy disk drives. This connector is a two-strand connection that provides a 5-volt power connection to the 3.5-inch drive.

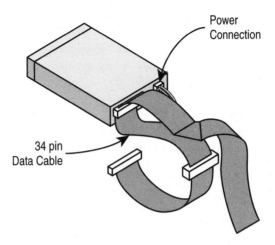

Power
Connection

34 pin
Data Cable

Figure 8.3 Floppy disk drive cable connections

After you physically install a floppy disk drive, you need only set the proper CMOS settings for the type and position (first or second) and the installation will be complete. In CMOS setup, select the drive (A or B) and enter the correct capacity. (CMOS stands for complementary metal-oxide semiconductor.)

Note   Many older CMOS chips won't have settings for 1.44 MB or 2.88 MB 3.5-inch floppy disk drives because they were developed before these drives were introduced. Also, the 5.25-inch drives are virtually obsolete, and the CMOS of the future might not have settings for them. Several third-party utilities will allow the CMOS to accept the necessary values to support these drives.

Keeping a Floppy Disk Drive Running

Although floppy disk drives are usually rugged and dependable, they do take a lot of abuse and sometimes they fail. Some failures are simply caused by improper use, some by overuse combined with a lack of cleaning, and sometimes the mechanism just stops working.

Floppy disk drives fail more than any other part of a computer system. They are highly susceptible to failure because their internal components are directly exposed to the outside world. Often, there is only a small door or slot that separates the R/W heads from dust, grime, and cigarette smoke. Floppy disk drives are often the victims of inverted disks, paper clips, and other foreign objects that can cause mechanical damage.

Floppy disk drives are inexpensive and easy to replace. The only preventive maintenance required is to keep the floppy disk drive *clean*! Excellent cleaning kits are available in most computer and discount stores. To achieve the best performance from a floppy disk drive in a high-use or industrial environment, schedule monthly cleaning.

Always an Exception

One unusual floppy disk drive solution that appeared as the 3.5-inch models gained dominance was the hybrid 3.5/5.25 drive. This married the slots for both formats in a single housing. They install just like a single drive.

Errors Caused by the Floppy Disk

If a floppy disk drive doesn't work, the first thing you suspect should be the floppy disk.

To check a floppy disk, follow this procedure:

1. First, make sure the disk is not write protected. The hole on the right top corner of a 3.5-inch disk (viewed from the front) should be closed. On a 5.25-inch disk, the notch on one side should be visible (not covered).

2. Try another disk.

3. Try a new (formatted) disk.

4. Try someone else's disk—one that is known to work on another computer (first make sure there is no critical data on the disk).

5. If two or more disks are unreadable, the drive is suspect; try going to MS-DOS and reading a directory using the DIR command.

Caution   Never test a drive by using a disk that contains important data! If the drive is bad, it may destroy any disks placed into it.

Detecting Data Errors on a Disk

If you can read data from one disk, but not another, the problem is the floppy disk. *Throw it away*. Data errors on floppy disks generally result in an error message that ends with the words "Abort, Retry, Fail." The process for repairing floppy disks is identical to the process for repairing hard disk drives drives, should there be data on the disk that must be recovered (see "ScanDisk" in Lesson 2, later in this chapter).

Check the CMOS Setting

Occasionally, the CMOS settings for floppy disks cause problems with drive operations. Any of the following errors indicates a possible CMOS setup problem:

- General failure reading drive A: (or B:)
- Not ready error reading drive A: (or B:)
- Insert disk for drive A: (or B:) and press any key when ready

BIOS makers often use the 3.5-inch high-density disk drive as the default CMOS setting for the A drive. With this BIOS, failure of the CMOS battery, or even accidental erasure of the CMOS, will still allow most floppy disks to work. Always double-check the CMOS if you are experiencing a recurrent floppy disk drive failure. It is quick, easy, and might save you time.

Tip It is possible for the CMOS to be corrupted by a software or hardware conflict and yet appear to be fine. If all else fails, reset the CMOS and reinstall the CMOS setup (check the motherboard manual for the jumper or disconnect the battery).

Check/Change the Floppy Disk Drive Cable

Cables wear out, work themselves loose, and are sometimes improperly installed. Check out both the data cable and the power jack as causes of the errant floppy disk drive before moving on to the controller.

Change the Floppy Disk Drive Controller

Floppy disk drive controllers are durable and highly resistant to failure and therefore should be the *last* components to blame. Left alone, they generally cause no problems. However, if they have recently been handled, such as during a move or repairs to the computer, they can be suspect. They are extremely sensitive to shock and static discharge.

In the event of a loose data cable or power plug, the POST (power-on self test) will return "FDD Controller Failure" or "Drive Not Ready" errors. (For more information about POST, refer to Chapter 6, "Primary PC Components.") Verify all the connections and try again. If the connections are good, try removing and reseating the controller (beware of electrostatic discharge). If the same errors continue, replace the controller. Floppy disk drives and controllers are inexpensive.

When replacing a floppy disk drive controller (see Figure 8.4), keep in mind that most of these controllers on pre-Pentium machines are bundled as part of a combination I/O card. These cards include some (often all) of the following: hard disk drive controllers, serial ports, parallel ports, and joystick ports. If the new card contains any duplicate ports (they already exist elsewhere on the computer), a potential for conflict will exist.

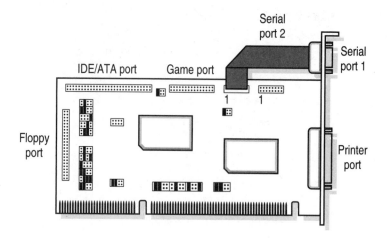

Figure 8.4   I/O card with floppy disk controller

Tip   Be sure to disable all other devices on the card that are already installed on the computer when installing I/O cards. If not disabled, the I/O card can cause conflicts. If you have a new card with improved devices, disable or remove the older item.

Replace the Floppy Disk Drive

When replacing floppy disk drives, be sure to throw away the old drive. Floppy disk drives are inexpensive compared to other components in the computer. Consider purchasing them in quantity and saving money. It is not a bad idea to have a spare floppy disk drive and I/O card available for testing purposes.

Note   As a rule, floppy disk drives fail more than any other part of a computer system except the floppy disk itself.

Lesson Summary

The following points summarize the main elements of this lesson:

- The 3.5-inch floppy disk drive has become an industry standard.

- Floppy disk drive technology has not changed much over the years.

- Floppy disk drives fail more than any other part of a computer system. Floppy drive parameters must be properly set in the system CMOS.

- When a drive fails to read or write, first check each individual medium, then the CMOS settings, and cable; as a last option, replace the drive itself.

Lesson 2: Hard Disk Drives

Hard disk drives are mass storage devices. Virtually all of today's computers have at least one hard disk drive. The first hard disk drives were small in capacity, physically large, and expensive, by today's standards; they were about 4 inches tall, 5.25 inches wide, 8 inches long, and weighed almost 10 pounds. In 1981, IBM introduced the XT computer with a 10-MB hard drive, and new owners wondered what they would do with all that space. Today, a new hard disk drive can fit in your pocket and hold over 17 GB of data. In this lesson, we examine hard disk drives, from the early versions to today's mini-monsters.

After this lesson, you will be able to:

- Explain the operation of a hard disk drive.
- Define the different types of hard disk drives, including their advantages and disadvantages.
- Partition a hard disk drive.
- Troubleshoot hard disk drives.

Estimated lesson time: 45 minutes

Physical Characteristics

Run the **hdrive** video located in the **demos** folder on the CD accompanying this book to view a presentation of the inner workings of a hard disk drive.

The first form of PC mass storage was the magnetic tape drive. Although tape proved a good medium for storing large amounts of data, it had some significant limitations. The typical cassette drive cartridge was easily damaged. Further, gaining access to the data was slow due to the way data is organized on tape, as a long stream of ones and zeroes, an arrangement known as "sequential." Because tapes were hundreds of feet long, users often had to run the entire length of the tape to find the data they were seeking. Although by providing random access (the ability to go directly to any point on the data surface), floppy disks are a major improvement, they are too slow and too limited in capacity for modern applications.

The original concept behind the hard disk drive was to provide a storage medium that held large amounts of data and allowed fast (random) access to that data. Data on a hard drive can be accessed directly, without requiring the user to start at the beginning and read everything until finding the data sought.

The first IBM hard disk drives came out in the late 1970s and early 1980s and were code-named "Winchester." The original design concept included two 30-MB units in one enclosure: 30-30 (hence "Winchester"). The PC-XT was the first personal computer to include a hard disk. They were called "fixed disks" because they were not removable. (Old mainframe computers had hard platters that *were* removable.) The Winchester technology is the ancestor of all PC fixed disks.

Hard disk drives are composed of several platters, matched to a collection of R/W heads and an actuator. Unlike floppy disk drives, a hard disk drive assembly is housed in a sealed case, which prevents contamination from the surrounding environment. Each case has a tiny aperture with an air filter. This allows the air pressure to be equalized between the interior and the exterior of the drive.

The platters are usually made of an aluminum alloy and have a thin magnetic-media coating on both sides. After coating, the platters are polished and given another thin coating of graphite for protection against mechanical damage caused by physical contact between the data heads and the platter surface.

The R/W heads "float on a cushion of air" above the platters, which spin at 3500 to 12,000 rpm. The distance (flying height) between the heads and the disk surface is less than the thickness of a fingerprint.

Storing Data

As noted in previous chapters, data is stored using binary code. Within the computer's memory, ones and zeroes are stored as electrical impulses. On magnetic media, the ones and zeroes can be stored as either magnetic or nonmagnetic areas on the drive surface. Although there are magnetized and nonmagnetized positions on the hard disk drive, the ones and zeroes of the binary code are stored in terms of *flux reversals*. These flux reversals are actually the transitions between magnetized and nonmagnetized positions on the hard drive surface.

Early hard disk drives used a method of encoding called FM (frequency modulation). FM technology is based on timing. To differentiate a 1 from a 0, it measures the time the drive head spends in a magnetized state. For FM to work, it requires every 1 or 0 to be preceded by a *timing bit*. The early FM drives worked well, but all the extra bits added to the work and slowed the process of data transfer. In order to improve efficiency and speed of the data transfer, the FM was replaced by an improved version that reduced the number of timing bits required. This new technology was called MFM (modified frequency modulation). MFM uses the preceding data bit to indicate whether the current bit is a 1 or a 0, thus reducing the number of timing bits by more than 50 percent.

Another method used to place data on hard disk drives is run-length limited (RLL) encoding. RLL replaces the timing bits with patterns of 1s and 0s that represent longer patterns of 1s and 0s. Although this looks inefficient, the elimination of the timing bits speeds overall performance.

Tip Unless you're working with hard disk drives manufactured before 1989, it is not necessary to know which type of data encoding is used.

Actuator Arms

The goal of a hard disk drive is to quickly and directly access data stored on a flat surface. To do this, two different motions are required. As the disk spins, the R/W heads move across the platter perpendicularly to the motion of the disk. The R/W heads are mounted on the ends of the actuator arms (much like the arm of an old record player). A critical element in hard disk drive design is the speed and accuracy of these actuator arms.

Early hard disk drives used a *stepper motor* to move the actuator arms in fixed increments or steps. This early technology had several limitations:

- The interface between the stepper motor and actuator arm required that slippage be kept to a minimum. The greater the slippage, the greater the error.

- Time and physical deterioration of the components caused the positioning of the arms to become less precise. This deterioration eventually caused data transfer errors.

- Heat affected the operation of the stepper motor negatively. The contraction and expansion of the components caused positioning accuracy errors. (Components expand as they get warmer and contract as they cool. Even though these changes are very small, they make it difficult to access data, written while the hard drive is cold, after the disk has warmed up.)

- The R/W heads need to be "parked" when not in use. Parking moves the heads to an area of the disk that does not contain data. Leaving the heads on an area with data can cause that data to be corrupted. Old hard disk drives had to be parked with a command. Most drives today automatically park the heads during spin-down.

Note   Older hard disk drives require that the heads be parked before moving the computer. It is recommended that you use the appropriate command to park the heads. The actual command can vary depending on the drive manufacturer, but you can try typing PARK at an MS-DOS prompt.

Hard disk drives with stepping motor actuator arms have been replaced by drives that employ a linear motor to move the actuator arms. These linear *voice coil motors* use the same type of voice coil found in an audio loudspeaker, hence the name. This principle uses a permanent magnet and a coil on the actuator arm. By passing electrical current through the coil, it generates a magnetic field that moves the actuator arm into the proper position.

Voice coil hard disk drives offer several advantages:

- The lack of mechanical interface between the motor and the actuator arm provides consistent positioning accuracy.
- When the drive is shut down (the power is removed from the coil), the actuator arm, which is spring-loaded, moves back to its initial position, thus eliminating the need to park the head. In a sense, these drives are self-parking.

There is a drawback: because a voice coil motor can't accurately predict the movement of the heads across the disk, one side of one platter is used for navigational purposes and so is unavailable for data storage. The voice coil moves the R/W head into an approximate position. Then the R/W heads on the reserved platter use the "map" to determine the head's true position and make any necessary adjustments. This is why hard drive specifications list an odd number of heads.

Head to Disk Interference

Head to Disk Interference (HDI) is a fancy term for *head crash*. These terms describe the contact that sometimes occurs between the fragile surface of the disk and the R/W head. This contact can cause considerable damage to both the R/W head and the disk. Never move a hard disk drive until it is completely stopped; the momentum of the drive can cause a crash if it is moved or dropped during operation.

Picking up a disconnected hard disk drive that is still spinning is not a good idea either. The rotation force of the platters can wrench it out of your hands, and the drive is not likely to survive the trip to the floor.

Geometry

Hard disk drives are composed of one or more disks or platters on which data is stored. The *geometry* of a hard drive is the organization of data on these platters. Geometry determines how and where data is stored on the surface of each platter, and thus the maximum storage capacity of the drive. There are five numerical values that describe geometry:

- Heads
- Cylinders
- Sectors per track
- Write precompensation
- Landing zone

Write precompensation and landing zone are obsolete, but often seen on older drives. Let's take a look at each of these components.

Tip   All hard disk drives have geometry. Knowledge of the geometry is required to install or reinstall a hard drive.

Heads

The number of heads is relative to the total number of *sides* of all the platters used to store data (see Figure 8.5). If a hard disk drive has four platters, it can have up to eight heads. The maximum number of heads is limited by BIOS to 16.

4 Platters
8 Heads

Figure 8.5   Drive heads

Hard disk drives that control the actuator arms using voice coil motors reserve a head or two for accuracy of the arm position. Therefore, it is not uncommon for a hard disk drive to have an odd number of heads.

Some hard disk drive manufacturers use a technology called *sector translation*. This allows some hard drives to have more than two heads per platter. It is possible for a drive to have up to 12 heads but only one platter. Regardless of the methods used to manufacture a hard drive, the maximum number of heads a hard drive can contain is 16.

Cylinders

Data is stored in circular paths on the surface of each head. Each path is called a *track*. There are hundreds of tracks on the surface of each head. A set of tracks (all of the same diameter) through each head is called a *cylinder* (see Figure 8.6). The number of cylinders is a measurement of drive geometry; the number of tracks is not a measurement of drive geometry. BIOS limitations set the maximum number of cylinders at 1024.

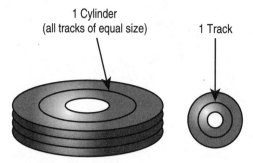

Figure 8.6   Cylinders

Sectors per Track

A hard disk drive is cut (figuratively) into tens of thousands of small arcs, like a pie. Each arc is called a sector and holds 512 bytes of data. A sector is shown in Figure 8.7. The number of sectors is not important and is not part of the geometry; the important value is the number of sectors per track. BIOS limitations set the number of sectors per track at 63.

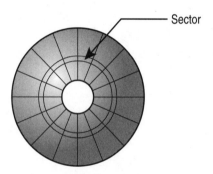

Figure 8.7   Sector

Write Precompensation

All sectors store the same number of bytes: 512; however, the sectors toward the outside of the platter are physically longer than those closer to the center. Early drives experienced difficulty with the varying physical sizes of the sectors. Therefore, a method of compensation was needed—the *write precompensation value* defines the cylinder where write precompensation begins.

Note   The write precompensation value is now obsolete, but is often seen on older drives.

Landing Zone

A landing zone defines an unused cylinder as a "parking place" for the R/W heads. This is found in older hard disk drives that use stepper motors. It is important to park the heads on these drives to avoid accidental damage when moving hard disk drives.

CHS Values

Cylinders, heads, and sectors per track (see Figure 8.8) are known collectively as the CHS values. The capacity of any hard disk drive can be determined from these three values.

Figure 8.8   Cylinders, heads, sectors per track

The maximum CHS values are:

- 1024 cylinders.
- 16 heads.
- 63 sectors per track.
- 512 bytes per sector.

Therefore, the largest hard disk drive size recognized directly by the BIOS is 504 MB. Larger drive sizes can be attained by using either hardware or software translation that manages access to the expanded capacity without direct control by the system BIOS.

1024 x 16 x 63 x 512 bytes/sector = 528,482,304 bytes (528 million bytes or 504 MB)

There are many hard disk drives that are larger than 504 MB. These drives manage to exceed this limitation in one of two ways: either they bypass the system BIOS (by using one of their own) or they change the way the system BIOS routines are read. (For a fuller discussion of this, refer to Chapter 9, "High-Capacity Disk Drives.")

Hard Disk Drive Types

The original personal computer design did not include hard disk drives. Hard disk drives were reserved for large mainframe computers and remained highly proprietary in design. Today, there are four types of hard drives, each with its own method of installation.

ST506

The very first hard disk drives for personal computers used the ST-506/412 interface. It was developed by Seagate Technologies in 1980 and originally appeared with the 5-MB ST-506 drive. The ST-506 was priced at $3,000 and had a capacity of 5 MB. The ST-506/412 was the only hard drive available for the IBM computer and was the first to be supported by the ROM BIOS chip on the motherboard.

ESDI

The ESDI (Enhanced Small Device Interface) was introduced in 1983 by the Maxtor Corporation. This technology moved many of the controller functions directly onto the hard disk drive itself. This greatly improved data transfer speeds. Some ESDI controllers even offered enhanced command sets, which supported autosensing of the drive's geometry by the motherboard's ROM BIOS. The installation of ESDI drives was almost identical to the installation of ST-506 drives. The high cost of ESDI drives and advances in other drive technologies spelled their doom. Today they are obsolete.

IDE/EIDE

The IDE (Integrated Drive Electronics) drive arrived on the scene in the early 1990s and incorporated the benefits of both its predecessors. IDE quickly became the standard for computers. It supports the ST-506 standard command set, and its limited controller functions build directly on the drive's logic board. This results in a much less expensive design. Most new motherboards have the IDE connections built in; thus, the chips are part of the board design.

Western Digital and Compaq developed the 40-pin IDE ISA pinout specification. ANSI (the American National Standards Institute) standards committees accepted the standard as the Common Access Method (CAM) AT. The official name for these drives is now ATA/CAM (AT Attachment/Common Access Method). The terms IDE and ATA/CAM are interchangeable.

Enhanced IDE (EIDE) adds a number of improvements to the standard IDE drives, including:

- Increased data throughput.
- Support of storage devices other than hard disk drives.
- Up to four IDE devices instead of just two. This actually allows the BIOS to support two controllers (each with two drives).
- Support for hard disk drives larger than 528 MB.

Note   EIDE is the standard for most hard disks in today's personal computers. A new type of EIDE, U-DMA 66, doubles the base speed of existing EIDE drives on motherboards that have a 66-MHz bus (hence the name).

SCSI

The Small Computer System Interface or SCSI (pronounced *scuzzy*) has been around since the mid-1970s in one or more forms. It is the most robust of the hard disk drive interfaces, and is popular on network servers and high-performance workstations. Apple adopted SCSI as its expansion bus standard. The original SCSI standard allowed up to seven peripheral devices to be daisy-chained (connected in a series) to one common bus through a single host adapter connected to the computer bus. SCSI-2 upped that to 15, and some adapters allow multiple chains for even more devices.

The SCSI bus functions as a communications pathway between the computer system bus and the SCSI device controller. That improves performance, because the card takes over the low-level commands and frees the system bus during operations that do not involve RAM. A SCSI adapter uses its own BIOS and firmware to talk to its devices, then uses a software interface layer and drivers to communicate with the operating system. There are two software interface layers: ASPI (Advanced SCSI Programming Interface) and CAM (Common Access Method). CAM is now obsolete, and ASPI comes with Windows and other operating systems. In most cases, you won't have to worry about loading the drivers unless you are updating them or installing a new card that does not have native drivers available to the operating system.

Note   Most SCSI cards can be configured to mimic the ST-506 hard disk drive and talk directly to the PC BIOS. This lets you install a SCSI hard drive without additional drivers. You will need the ASPI or CAM software to get full use of advanced SCSI performance features or to attach non-hard disk drive SCSI peripherals to the system.

SCSI usually costs more than other hard disk drive interfaces, but is the only one that allows both internal and external connections on the same adapter. It also allows you to attach more types of devices than any other interface. A single chain can include hard drives, CD-ROM and other optical drives, scanners, and tape drives.

Installation and Setup

All boot devices must be configured outside the operating system (Windows 95 and 98, Windows NT, or MS-DOS) regardless of the level of Plug and Play compatibility. (Devices such as disk drives and CD-ROMs that are used to boot must be configured at the BIOS and hardware level because they typically contain the operating system and must run properly before the operating system can be started.)

Installation of a hard disk drive consists of five simple steps:

1. Physical installation and cabling
2. CMOS setup
3. Low-level formatting (if required)
4. Partitioning
5. Formatting

Cabling

Just as there are different types of drives, there are different cabling requirements for each. Let's look at the three most common types.

ST-506

The ST-506 uses a 34-connector control cable (daisy-chained for dual drives) and a 20-connector data cable for each drive. The 34-wire control cable has a twist in it for line 25 through 29 configuration (similar to the floppy disk drive cable); this twist determines which hard disk drive is hard drive 0 and which is hard drive 1. The drive at the end is drive 0.

IDE/EIDE

The IDE uses a simple 40-pin cable that plugs into the controller and into the drive (see Figure 8.9). There are *no* twists. IDE controllers identify the two drives as either master or slave. Drive makers use different methods to set up their drives. The most common system uses jumpers. Setting these jumpers serves the same function as the twist used with other drive cables: it identifies whether the drive is master or slave. Other drives use switches, and some new drives use software to determine which is the dominant drive. Be sure to check the manufacturers' specifications to properly set up the drive.

U-DMA 66

A special version of the 40-pin IDE cables is used for U-DMA 66. Be sure to obtain and install it if you are working with one of these newer drives. It is also 40-pin, but has a blue connector on one end and a black one on the other. All the other installation and cabling procedures are the same as for traditional IDE devices.

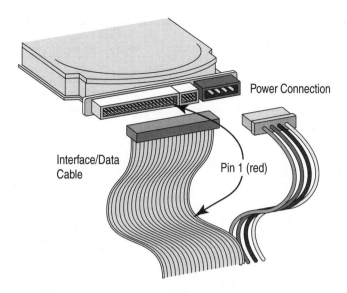

Figure 8.9 IDE connections

Tip When installing a new secondary hard disk drive in a system, be sure to set the new drive as slave and verify that the first drive is set to master. The documentation supplied with the drive should provide the necessary information. Often, this information is printed on the label of the drive. Both drives must be properly configured before the system is started. If the drives are not properly jumpered, they won't work.

If you don't know how to set the jumpers (see Figure 8.10), try calling the hard disk drive manufacturer (or look for its Web site on the Internet).

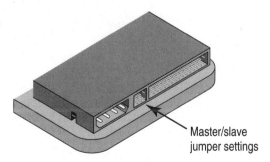

Figure 8.10 Master/slave jumper settings

Setting the System CMOS for the Hard Drive

After a hard disk drive has been installed physically, the geometry of the drive must be entered into the CMOS through the CMOS setup program before the PC will recognize the new device. This information must be entered exactly as specified by the manufacturer. Figure 8.11 shows hard disk drive configuration information in a typical CMOS. Figure 8.12 shows a subscreen of the main hard drive setup screen.

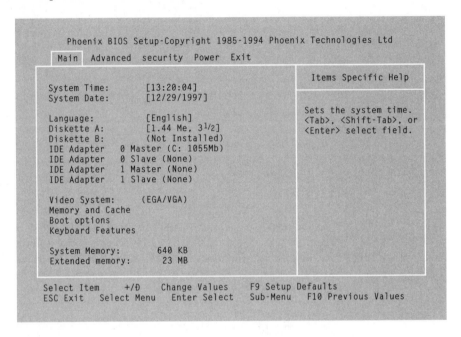

Figure 8.11   CMOS main screen

Originally, CMOS would allow for only two drives. Later versions allow up to four drives, because most new PCs have two IDE channels.

The CHS (cylinders, heads, sectors per track), along with write precompensation and landing zone, determine how the hard disk drive controller accesses the physical hard drive. The creators of the first CMOS routines for the 286 AT believed that the five different geometry numbers would be too complicated for the average user to configure, so they established 15 preset combinations of hard drive geometries. These preset combinations are called *types*. With types, the user simply enters a hard drive type number into the CMOS.

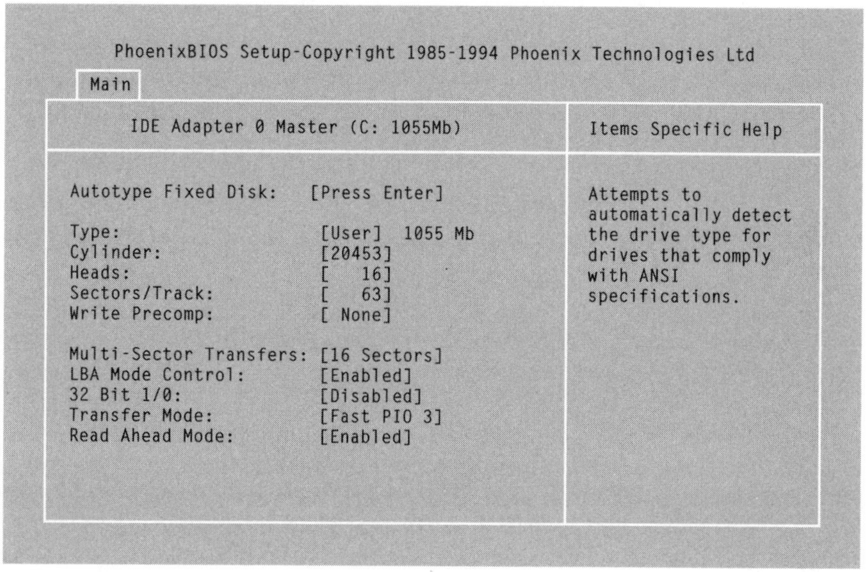

```
PhoenixBIOS Setup-Copyright 1985-1994 Phoenix Technologies Ltd
 Main

     IDE Adapter 0 Master (C: 1055Mb)          Items Specific Help

  Autotype Fixed Disk:   [Press Enter]         Attempts to
                                               automatically detect
  Type:                  [User]  1055 Mb       the drive type for
  Cylinder:              [20453]               drives that comply
  Heads:                 [  16]                with ANSI
  Sectors/Track:         [  63]                specifications.
  Write Precomp:         [ None]

  Multi-Sector Transfers: [16 Sectors]
  LBA Mode Control:      [Enabled]
  32 Bit 1/0:            [Disabled]
  Transfer Mode:         [Fast PIO 3]
  Read Ahead Mode:       [Enabled]
```

Figure 8.12 Hard disk drive setup screen

This system worked well for a period of time, but with each new hard disk drive that manufacturers designed, a new type also had to be created and added to the list. BIOS makers continued to add new types until there were more than 45 variations. To deal with this issue, Setup routines now include a *user* type. This allows manual entry of the geometry values, increasing both the flexibility and complexity of hard drive installation.

CMOS setup is easy with IDE drives. Most CMOS chips today have a setting known as IDE *autodetection,* which runs the `identify drive` command, gathering and setting the proper geometry values. To use it, simply connect the drive to the computer, turn it on, and run the CMOS. The `identify drive` command instructs the drive to transmit a 512-byte block of data containing the following information:

- Manufacturer
- Model and serial numbers
- Firmware revision number
- Buffer type indicating sector buffering or caching capabilities
- Number of cylinders in the default translation mode
- Number of heads in the default translation mode
- Number of sectors per track in the default translation mode
- Number of cylinders in the current translation mode
- Number of heads in the current translation mode
- Number of sectors per track in the current translation mode

Important   Be sure to save your settings before you exit the setup program.

What happens if wrong data is entered into the CMOS? For example, what if a 1.2-GB hard disk drive is installed and the CMOS is set up to make it a 504-MB hard drive? When you boot the computer, you will see a perfect 504-MB hard drive. You will need to correct the entry to obtain proper use of the drive. It should not be left improperly entered, and it might not be accessible by the system.

If the computer you are working on does not support autodetection, you must be able to determine the geometry of a drive in order for it to be installed.

There are many ways to determine the geometry of a hard disk drive:

- Check the label. The geometry or type of many hard drives will be labeled directly on the hard drive itself.
- Check the documentation that came with the hard drive. All drives have a model number that can be used to obtain the geometry parameters either from the manufacturer or a third party. The hard drive manufacturers usually reserve a section of their Web site for providing configuration data and the setup utilities available for download.
- Contact the manufacturer. Many manufacturers have toll-free phone numbers.

After a drive is installed, it must be assigned a drive name or letter that is unique. There are several drive-naming conventions that help identify this unique name. If only one hard disk drive is installed, it must be configured as drive 0, or master. If a second drive is installed, it is recognized as hard drive 1, or slave. Many CMOS configurations use the terms C: and D:. Under all versions of MS-DOS and Windows, hard drive 0 is recognized as C; hard drive 1 is recognized as D.

As more drives are added to a system, (including tape, CD-ROM, and network drives), the names of existing drives might change. For example, installing a portable drive such as an Iomega Zip drive can change a CD-ROM from the D drive to the E drive. When the portable drive is removed, the CD-ROM will once again be the D drive. Keep in mind the difference between *logical* and *physical* drives. A physical drive is the hardware—it can be divided into two or more logical drives. (See the "Partitioning" section later in this lesson.) Drives on a network server are also logical drives. Write down the configuration and keep track as changes in the system are made. The only drive letters that are fixed are the A and B drives, which are always the floppy disk drives, and the C drive, the boot drive where the MS-DOS operating system resides.

Note This confusion in drive letters can also confuse the operating system, making it hard or impossible for it to locate drivers. In such cases, you might need to reinstall the drivers before the system can make use of the affected hardware, and a Windows 95, 98, or 2000 machine might automatically start in Safe Mode. Check the System/Device manager option in the Control Panel after the PC is operational and look for duplicate hardware items or items with flags noting missing or inoperable conditions.

Low-Level Formatting

Low-level formatting means to create all the sectors, tracks, cylinders, and head information on the drive and is the third step in installing hard disk drives; generally it applies only to older drives. Low-level formatting by the end user has virtually been eliminated with today's drives (it's done at the factory).

A low-level format performs three simultaneous functions:

- It creates and organizes the sectors, making them ready to accept data.
- It sets the proper interleave (records the sector header, trailer information, and intersector and intertrack gaps).
- It establishes the boot sector.

Every hard disk drive arrives from the factory with bad spots on the platters. Data cannot be written to these areas. As the sectors are being created, the low-level format attempts to skip over these bad spots. Sometimes, it is impossible to skip over a spot so the sector is marked as "bad" in the ID field.

Caution   Low-level formatting is not required on IDE and U-DMA drives. Performing a low-level format on these devices might render the drive unusable. SCSI drives are low-level formatted using a utility that is built into the SCSI adapter card's firmware. Format a low-level drive only if it is absolutely necessary (for example, if a virus has contaminated the boot sector and that is the only remedy) and if you are sure you know and can follow the proper procedure! Remember, as soon as you issue the format command, all data on the drive will be lost.

IDE drives use a special type of low-level formatting called *embedded servo*. This type of low-level formatting can be done by the manufacturer only, or with a special utility provided by the manufacturer. When installing an IDE drive, go straight to the partitioning step after the CMOS is set up.

To continue with hard disk drive installation for MS-DOS and Windows 3.x and 95 and 98 versions, you will need a bootable floppy disk containing several programs that are required to prepare the new drive. (For Windows NT and 2000, alternate methods that are not part of the current A+ test are available. You can also use the procedure listed below to prepare a drive for use with those operating environments.)

To create a bootable floppy disk, a computer is required that has an installed working hard disk drive, or floppy disk drive, and a compatible operating system. Be sure to use the same operating system on the floppy disk as the one you'll use for the new drive.

Insert a floppy disk into the A drive and type:

```
format a: /s
```

This will copy system files to the disk, making it a bootable disk.

The next step is to copy the necessary files from the MS-DOS directory to the floppy disk. The default location for these files is the C:\DOS directory for MS-DOS and the C:\Windows\Command directory for Windows 95 and 98. Copy these files:

```
format.com (or format.exe)
fdisk.com
```

This bootable disk can be used for partitioning and high-level formatting as discussed in the following sections.

Partitioning

Partitions are *logical* divisions of a hard drive. A computer might have only one physical hard drive (called hard drive 0), but it can have anywhere from one to 24 logical drives, identified as C to Z.

Partitions exist for two reasons:

- To divide the disk into several drive letters to make it easier to organize data files. Some users separate data, programs, and operating-system files onto different drives.

- To accommodate more than one operating system.

When MS-DOS was first designed to use hard disk drives, the largest hard drive that could be used was 32 MB (because of the way MS-DOS stored files on the hard drive). Partitioning was included in MS-DOS 3.3. This allowed for the development of larger physical hard drives by creating multiple logical drives of up to 32 MB each. Starting with MS-DOS 4.0, the partition size was increased to 512 MB. Beginning with MS-DOS 5.0, the partitions can be as large as 2 GB. Windows 98 and 2000 support much larger drive sizes, and many new disks exceed 20 GB.

Note Some hard disk drives that exceed 4 GB might not work with an older computer, BIOS, or operating system. They will physically function, but the whole drive cannot be accessed—disk access will be limited to the largest size that can be recognized by that system.

Primary and Extended Partitions

There are two types of partitions: primary and extended. The *primary* partition is the location where the boot information for the operating system is stored. To boot from a hard disk drive, it must have a primary partition. Primary partitions are for storage of the *boot sector,* which tells the computer where to find the operating system. The name of the primary partition is C.

The *extended* partition is for a hard disk drive, or part of a hard disk drive, that does not have an operating system. The extended partition is not associated with a "physical" drive letter. Instead, the extended partition is further divided into logical drives starting with D and progressing until drive letter Z is created. (Remember: A and B are reserved for floppy disk drives.)

Newer operating systems can use all of the drive as a single primary partition. The logical drive concept was invented to allow older versions of MS-DOS and Windows to make use of drives that exceeded their maximum drive size.

The following table provides examples of partitions:

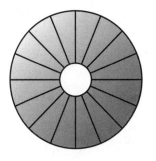

One 500-MB physical drive with one partition:

C (primary drive)

One physical drive and one logical drive

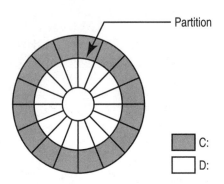

Partition

C:

D:

One 1-GB physical drive with two partitions:

C (400-MB primary drive)

D (600-MB extended drive)

One physical drive and two logical drives

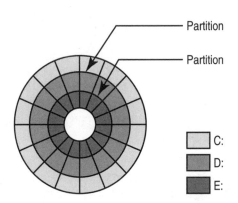

Partition

Partition

C:

D:

E:

One 4.3-GB physical drive with three partitions:

C (1-GB primary drive)

D (1.65-GB extended drive)

E (1.65-GB extended drive)

One physical drive and three logical drives

How to Partition

The FDISK utility is used to partition a drive. After the drive is installed and the CMOS is updated, run FDISK to partition the drive(s).

Figure 8.13 shows the FDISK startup screen.

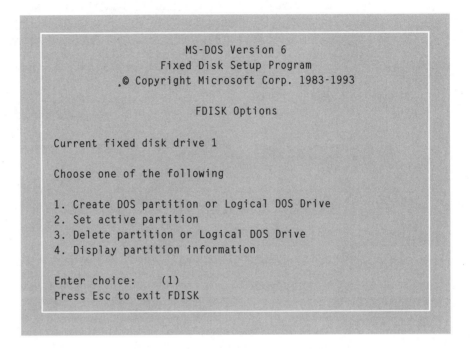

```
                     MS-DOS Version 6
                   Fixed Disk Setup Program
               .© Copyright Microsoft Corp. 1983-1993


                        FDISK Options


    Current fixed disk drive 1


    Choose one of the following


    1. Create DOS partition or Logical DOS Drive
    2. Set active partition
    3. Delete partition or Logical DOS Drive
    4. Display partition information


    Enter choice:    (1)
    Press Esc to exit FDISK
```

Figure 8.13   The FDISK startup screen.

The function of lines 1, 3, and 4 is clear. Line 2 sets the active partition. The active partition is the partition where the BIOS will look for an operating system when the computer is booted.

Don't confuse the primary partition with the active partition. On a computer with a single operating system, the primary and active partitions are usually the same. A computer with dual-boot capability might have separate partitions for each operating system. In that case, the active and primary partitions might not be the same.

The primary partition is where MS-DOS (or the Windows boot information) is stored on the hard disk drive, and the active partition is where the operating system is stored on the hard drive. (If MS-DOS is the only operating system, the primary partition and active partition are the same.) Other operating systems—Windows NT, Windows 2000, and OS/2, for instance—can exist on an extended partition.

Advanced operating systems can create a special partition called a *boot partition*. When the computer boots, a menu prompts the user to pick which operating system to use. The boot manager then sets the chosen partition as *active*, which starts the operating system located in that partition.

Note　MS-DOS has a limitation not shared by any other operating system: it must be placed on the primary partition, and that partition must always be named C. OS/2, UNIX, and Windows NT/2000 can boot from another drive letter, as well as from the C drive.

High-Level Formatting

The high-level format is simply called "format" (the program used to perform a high-level format is called FORMAT.COM). This is the same format command used to prepare floppy disk drives. The high-level format performs two major functions:

- It creates and configures the file allocation tables (FATs).
- It creates the root directory, which is the foundation upon which files and subdirectories are built.

File Allocation Tables (FATs)

The base storage unit for drives is a sector. Each sector can store between one byte and 512 bytes of data. Any file less than 512 bytes is stored in a single sector, and only one file can be assigned a sector. Therefore, any part of a sector left unfilled is wasted. When files are stored in more than one sector (if they are greater than 512 bytes), MS-DOS needs a way to keep track of each location and the order in which data is stored. MS-DOS also needs to know which sectors are full and which sectors are available for data, so it uses the file allocation table (FAT) to keep track of this information.

The FAT is simply an index that keeps track of which part of the file is stored in which sector. Each partition (or floppy disk) has two FATs stored near the beginning of the partition. These FATs are called FAT #1 and FAT #2. They are identical. Each FAT can be looked at as a two-column spreadsheet.

Left Column	Right Column
Gives each sector a number (in hex) from 0000 to FFFF (65,536 sectors). The left side contains 16 bits (4 hex characters = 16 bits). This FAT is called a 16-bit FAT. Floppy disk drives use 12-bit FATs because they store substantially less data.	Contains information on the status of the sector. During formatting, any bad sectors are marked with a status code of FFF7 and good sectors are marked 0000.

Sectors and Clusters

As mentioned, the CHS values limit the maximum size of a hard disk drive to 504 MB under the older PC operating systems. The 16-bit FAT can address 64,000 (2^{16}) locations. Therefore, the size of a hard drive partition should be limited to 64,000 x 512 bytes per sector or 32 MB. With this limitation, you might ask, how are larger hard drives possible?

There are two solutions to this problem. The first method, used with earlier drives (under 100 MB), was to use FDISK to break the drive up into multiple partitions, each less than 32 MB.

The second method is called *clustering*. Clustering means to combine a set of contiguous sectors and treat them as a single unit in the FAT. The number of sectors in each cluster is determined by the size of the partition. There can never be more than 64,000 clusters. To determine the number of sectors in a partition, divide the number of bytes in the partition by 512 (bytes per sector). Then divide the number of sectors by 64,000 (maximum allowable clusters). The following table provides an estimate of sectors per cluster.

Partition (in MB)	Total Bytes	Total Sectors	Sectors per Cluster	Bytes per Cluster
32	33,554,432	65,536	1	524
64	67,108,864	131,072	2	1049
128	134,217,728	262,144	4	2097
256	268,435,456	524,288	8	4194
512	536,870,912	1,048,576	16	8389
1000	1,048,576,000	2,048,000	32	16,384
2000	2,097,152,000	4,096,000	64	32,768
4000	4,194,304,000	8,192,000	128	65,536

Note   Remember: for this table, a sector is not the basic unit of storage—it is now the cluster.

How the File Allocation Table Works

When a file is saved:

1. MS-DOS starts at the beginning of the FAT and looks for the first space marked "open for use" (0000). It begins to write to that cluster.

2. If the entire file can be saved within that one cluster, the code FFFF (last cluster) is placed in the cluster's status field and the file name is added to the directory.

3. The cluster number is placed with the file name.

4. If the file takes more than one cluster, MS-DOS searches for the next open cluster and places the number of the next cluster in the status field. MS-DOS continues filling and adding clusters until the entire file is saved.

5. The last cluster then receives the end of file code (FFFF).

FAT32

Windows 98 and Windows 95 (OSR2—the final version of Windows 95, available only on new machines, also called version C) support the new FAT32 file system. FAT32 can create partitions up to 2 terabytes (two trillion bytes) in size (much larger than the 2-GB limit of FAT16) and uses smaller clusters than FAT16. This results in a more efficient use of space on a large hard disk.

When deciding whether to use FAT32, take the following into consideration:

- Don't use FAT32 on any partition that other operating systems—except for Windows 95 OSR2—will use.

- MS-DOS, Windows 3.x, the original release of Windows 95, and Windows NT clients can read FAT32 partitions shared across a network.

- If you dual boot between Windows 98 and another operating system (such as Windows NT 4.x), the drive C partition cannot be FAT32.

- You cannot compress FAT32 partitions.

- Windows 98 MS-DOS mode fully supports FAT32, so you can run most MS-DOS-mode games and applications from FAT32 partitions.

- Some older applications written to FAT16 specification might not display disk space larger than 2 GB.

- Do not use any utilities that do not support FAT32. This could result in data loss and might corrupt the file system on the hard drive.

Fragmentation

Fragmentation is the scattering of parts of the same disk file over different areas of the disk.

During PC use, files are opened and then saved back to disk. As mention earlier, the file is often stored in several small sections. Fragmentation is caused by the following:

1. As a file is written to sectors (clusters), it is placed in the first available location.
2. The continual addition and deletion of files begins to leave open clusters.
3. These open clusters are filled by the first part of the next file to be saved.
4. Soon, files become fragmented, or scattered, all over the drive.

This is an acceptable way to operate and causes no problems for the computer itself. However, excessive fragmentation slows down the hard disk drive because it has to access two or more areas to retrieve a file. It is possible for a single file to be fragmented into hundreds of pieces, forcing the R/W heads to travel all over the hard disk drive.

Most operating systems have either native or third-party applications that will *defragment* a drive. These should be used on a regular basis to improve performance and save wear and tear on the drive.

Disk Compression   Disk compression is offered as part of the Microsoft Plus add-on product for Windows 95, but is included in Windows 98 as the DriveSpace 3 program. It works by creating a single big file (called a compressed volume file or CVF) that acts like a virtual disk drive (with its own drive letter). Files you write to the CVF will become records within the one big file. This process is normally transparent to the user.

Note   Keep in mind that you cannot use DriveSpace 3 with partitions that use the FAT32 file system. If you wish to compress a drive under Windows 98, use the FAT16 file system when installing the drive.

Compression saves space in two ways. It:

- Eliminates the wasted cluster space used by separate disk files.
- Replaces sequences of identical values or characters in the file data with a special reference that represents the actual data, but occupies less disk space than the data itself would.

  When the data is retrieved from the file, the real values are extracted from the special references. The result can be a dramatic reduction in the disk space occupied by files, especially with uncompressed graphics files and word-processing documents.

Using compression introduces some risk because an error in the compressed volume file can make data inaccessible. It is safest not to use a compressed file for critical data, and some older programs (particularly games) might not work with compression. With DriveSpace 3 you can use the Troubleshooter to identify and fix problems.

Compression is less necessary today, because of the advent of large hard disk drives and the availability of the FAT32 file system with its smaller cluster sizes.

The elimination of fragmentation improves the speed of the hard disk drive dramatically. Running a program to eliminate fragmentation is called defragmenting a drive. The slang term "defrag" is often used. MS-DOS installations include a defragmentation program called DEFRAG. Windows 95 and 98 include a defragmentation program that can be accessed from the Start menu—select Programs, then select Accessories, and finally select System Tools.

Note   DEFRAG cannot rewrite or move systems and hidden files. These files might be program files that are copy protected and must not be moved after the program is installed. System files such as the MS-DOS core program must occupy a particular position on the disk.

Caution   Never run a defragmentation program designed for MS-DOS or Windows 3.x on a Windows 95 or 98 system. The program might not understand the Windows 95 and 98 long file names, and data might be lost.

Maintaining a Disk Drive

Being prepared for a potential failure *before* a hard disk drive fails to work properly can save lost data and time. How fully you should prepare depends on the answers to two questions:

- Can you afford to lose the data in question?
- How much time do you have to start over?

With this in mind, to minimize the impact of a hard disk drive failure:

- Perform comprehensive, frequent backups.
- Save a copy of the boot-sector and partition-table information.

You should have the following tools at hand to perform hard disk repairs:

- A list of the hard disk drive's parameters and the correct CMOS settings required.
- A bootable floppy disk with the FDISK, FORMAT, CHKDSK, and MSCDEX (if using a CD-ROM) command files. Adding EDIT or another text editor is handy for tweaking the CONFIG.SYS and AUTOEXEC.BAT files.
- Drivers needed to get the operating system running with any primary expansion cards (drive controllers, SCSI card, display adapter, and so on.)
- Good cables for the kinds of drives you might have to repair.
- CHKDSK or other hard disk inspection programs that are part of the operating system on the drive in question. Be sure to use the right version!

A number of third-party programs are also available for use with older hardware and operating systems. These programs are available at most computer software stores.

Caution   When using any third-party programs to troubleshoot/repair a drive, be sure they are certified for the hard disk drive and operating system in question. Use uncertified third-party programs only when such a step is the last resort before discarding the drive. Even then, be aware that the program may cause problems of its own. Keep the software up to date; changes in the operating system or bugs found in the utility can render the product more of a problem than a cure. If possible, back up any critical data before using the software.

Abort, Retry, Fail or Abort, Retry, Fail, Ignore Errors

The most common drive errors begin with "Abort, Retry, Fail," or "Abort, Retry, Fail, Ignore."

When you see any of the following errors, you have a drive problem:

```
Sector not found reading drive C:
Abort, Retry, Fail?

Data error reading drive C:
Abort, Retry, Fail, Ignore?

Read fault reading drive C:
Abort, Retry, Fail, Ignore?

Invalid media type reading drive C:
Abort, Retry, Fail?
```

These errors are the easiest to fix and can usually be attributed to a bad sector on the drive. When this happens, try the following.

ScanDisk

MS-DOS, Windows 3.x, and Windows 95 and 98 contain versions of the ScanDisk program. ScanDisk performs a battery of tests on a hard disk, including looking for invalid file names, invalid file dates and times, bad sectors, and invalid compression structures. In the file system, ScanDisk looks for lost clusters, invalid clusters, and cross-linked clusters. Regular use of ScanDisk can help prevent problems as well as resolve them. Windows 95- and 98-based computers will automatically run ScanDisk any time the operating system is improperly shut down—that is, when the power is turned off before the system is allowed to complete its shutdown procedures.

Verify the Media

Most SCSI drives have a program built into the controller that will verify the hard disk drive and make repairs if a sector has become unusable or unstable. Boot the PC and watch for a prompt to enter the SCSI BIOS setup (usually CTRL+A). Then choose Disk Utilities and the option to verify or inspect the drive. Do not select the low-level format option. After the program is finished, reboot the computer and see if the problem is resolved. If the disk fails verification, it might need to undergo low-level formatting or be replaced.

CMOS Errors

At times, the system CMOS becomes unstable. This can result in the following error messages:

```
CMOS configuration mismatch
```
```
No boot device available
```
```
Drive not found
```
```
Missing operating system
```

Checking the CMOS is quick and easy. It is a good idea to always have a backup of the CMOS data on paper.

Note   After boot up, if you receive the message "Strike F1 key to continue," this indicates that your system configuration is invalid and you will need to check the CMOS settings.

Connectivity Errors

Connectivity problems (when something is not connected or plugged in) usually appear when you boot up a computer. Look for the following messages:

```
HDD Controller failure
```
```
No boot device available
```
```
Drive not found
```

Connectivity errors are overcome by inspecting the entire connection system (including power). You might want to try removing and reseating the controller if you get an HDD controller failure.

Tip   As a computer technician, you should keep an extra controller and cables around. Often, substituting a good cable or controller is the quickest way to solve a hard disk drive problem.

Lost Boot and Partition Information

It is possible for a drive to lose partition information. Look for these errors:

```
Invalid partition table
```

```
Corrupt boot sector
```

```
Non-system disk or disk error
```

Boot and partition information is stored on sectors and can fail. If the partition table or boot sector is corrupted, the best solution is to restore the data on the drive from a backup copy after repartitioning the drive and reloading the operating system.

Lesson Summary

The following points summarize the main elements of this lesson:

- The maximum storage capacity of a hard disk drive is determined by its geometry.
- CHS values define the geometry of a hard disk drive.
- The largest hard disk drive recognized by the BIOS will vary with the age of the system.
- Proper CMOS settings are required for hard disk drives.
- There are two types of partitions—primary and extended.
- A cluster is the basic unit of storage.
- The FDISK program is used to partition drives.
- Microsoft ScanDisk is a useful tool for diagnosing and repairing many disk problems.
- The proper drive information must be held in CMOS for proper drive operation.

Chapter Summary

The following points summarize the key concepts in this chapter:

Floppy Disk Drives

- The first disk drives were floppy disk drives. The technology of floppy disks has changed little in the past decade.

- Floppy disk drives are designated as A or B. The drive letter designation is determined by the location of the drive on the cable.

- Floppy disk drives fail more than any other part of a computer system.

Hard Disk Drives

- The three major steps in installing a hard disk drive are to partition the drive, set the CMOS settings, and format the drive.

- FDISK is used to partition hard disk drives. A computer technician should be familiar with the use of FDISK and partitioning.

- The geometry of a hard disk drive (CHS values) determines its storage capacity.

- There are two type of partitions (primary and extended). MS-DOS must be on the primary partition.

- The active partition is where the operating system is stored. The active partition is usually (but not always) the primary partition.

Review

1. What is the purpose of an IDE drive?

2. How many drives can be connected to a single IDE connector?

3. What is the best method of determining the number of drives available on a computer?

4. What three things should be checked when a floppy disk drive fails?

5. What is the best way to ensure long life from a floppy disk drive?

6. When you purchase a new floppy disk drive controller, what can you expect to receive with it?

7. Other than physical size, what are the only differences between a 5.25-inch floppy disk drive and a 3.5-inch floppy disk?

8. What type of cable is used to connect a floppy disk drive to the external data bus?

9. What is the proper way to install a floppy disk drive cable?

10. To which pin must the Number 1 wire of the floppy disk drive cable be connected?

11. You've received the following error message: "General failure reading Drive A:". What is the most likely problem?

12. Are floppy disk controllers sensitive to ESD?

13. You receive an error message that ends with "Abort, Retry, Fail?" What is the most likely cause of the error?

14. Why is a voice coil actuator arm better than a stepper motor actuator arm?

15. Define hard disk drive geometry.

16. What is the best way to determine the geometry of an unknown drive?

17. Describe HDI.

18. BIOS limits the number of heads to _____.

19. BIOS limits the number of cylinders to _____.

20. How many bytes of data does a sector hold?

21. What is the maximum number of sectors per track?

22. What does CHS stand for?

23. What type of drive is standard on today's personal computer?

24. Name the characteristics of the different hard disk drive types.

25. What is a partition? What are the two types of partition?

26. Define a cluster.

27. What is the FAT and how does it work?

28. What is fragmentation?

29. How can you minimize the impact of a hard disk drive failure?

30. What is the function of ScanDisk?

C H A P T E R   9

High-Capacity Disk Drives

About This Chapter

This chapter picks up where the previous chapter left off; we continue our look at disk drives, moving on to more advanced technologies. The lessons in this chapter cover CD-ROM drives, newer and larger hard disk drives, and Small Computer System Interface (SCSI) drives.

Before You Begin

Before starting this chapter, you should review Chapter 8, "Basic Disk Drives."

Lesson 1: CD-ROM Drives

The CD-ROM (compact disc read-only memory) is a technology taken directly from the audio world that has become standard equipment for computers. This lesson covers the basics of installing and using CD-ROM drives.

After this lesson, you will be able to:

- Define the advantages of using CD-ROMs.
- Install and operate a CD-ROM drive.

Estimated lesson time: 30 minutes

Advantages of CD-ROM Drives

If a hard disk drive holds more information than a floppy disk drive, accesses the information faster, and reads and writes information, then why do we need CD-ROM drives? The answer is simple: a compact disc can hold large amounts (650 MB) of removable data and can be mass-produced at a very low cost.

The CD has become the medium of choice for software distribution by manufacturers. DVD (digital video disc) technology is beginning to replace traditional CD-ROM technology on many new PCs, but DVD drives can read CD-ROM. It is expected that CD-ROM will be a standard distribution method for the foreseeable future.

An entire software package can be stored on one CD. For example, the early versions of the Microsoft Office Suite were supplied on 32 floppy disks. Today, the entire program suite and its manuals are stored on a single CD. It is also much faster to install a CD. The user simply starts it up, enters any required information, and comes back later; it's no longer necessary to feed disk after disk into the computer. When they were introduced, CDs held large databases such as encyclopedias. Today, they are used for every possible type of data, from national phone directories and software libraries to collections of clip art, music, and games. The following table lists the advantages of storing data on a CD.

Advantage	Description
Large storage capacity	Up to 650 MB of data fit on a single 5-inch disc. (Smaller than the original 5.25-inch floppy disk, a CD holds almost 2000 times as much information.)
Portability	The CD is a portable medium.
Data cannot be changed	A CD is read-only, which prevents accidental erasure of programs or files.
Sturdiness	More durable than the standard 5.25-inch or 3.5-inch disks, CDs are not magnetic media and thus are not subject to the same dangers posed by proximity to electrical sources or magnets.
Special capabilities	CD-ROMs are audio-capable, allowing special compression of audio, image, and video data. They can be used to play standard audio CDs and have the capacity to store and record video data.

Development of the CD

The development of the computer CD roughly paralleled the audio (music) CD:

- In 1979, the CD, as a storage medium, was introduced in the audio industry.

- In 1985, the CD came to the computer industry. Development was slow because the hardware was too expensive for most manufacturers and users.

- In 1991, the CD-ROM/XA standard was enhanced, and multimedia requirements for hardware were specified.

- In 1993, high-quality video playback came to the computer.

- Today, the price of CD-ROM drives continues to drop, while their speed climbs. Approximately 85 percent of all computers include an internal CD-ROM drive as standard equipment. Most software packages are shipped in CD-ROM versions (3.5-inch disk versions are available but usually only by special order, and often they do not contain all the extras of the CD version).

About CD-ROM Standards

The CD-ROM world makes use of several standards. These are usually referred to by the color of the cover of the volume issued by the ISO (International Organization for Standardization) committee—for example, the White Book, Yellow Book, and so on. ISO formats are discussed in more detail later in this lesson.

CD-ROM Technology

CD-ROMs store data as a series of 1s and 0s, just like a floppy disk or a hard disk drive. However, instead of using magnetic energy to read and write data, CD readers and writers use laser energy. There are two major advantages to using lasers:

- There is no physical contact between the surface of the CD and the reading device.
- The diameter of the laser beam is so small that storage tracks can be written very close together, allowing more data to be stored in a smaller space.

Hard Disk Drives vs. CD-ROMs

With the cost of hard disk drives falling and the amount of available data storage rising, the hard drive is still king of the storage media. Optical data-storage devices hold their place as removable media and as the media of choice for archival data storage.

A CD platter is composed of a reflective layer of aluminum applied to a synthetic base that is composed of polymers. A layer of transparent polycarbonate covers the aluminum. A protective coating of lacquer is applied to the surface to protect it from dust, dirt, and scratches.

Note   CD-recordable (CD-R) discs use materials other than aluminum. They often have a yellow or green cast on the data side. Not all CD-ROM readers are able to read these discs—some older readers based on IDE (Integrated Drive Electronics) are incompatible with CD-R technology.

Data is written by creating pits and lands on the CD's surface. A *pit* is a depression on the surface, and a *land* is the height of the original surface. The transition from a land to a pit, or a pit to a land, represents a binary character of 1. Lands and pits represent binary 0. The reading of data is based on timing—the speed at which the CD is rotating—and the reflection of light. If no data is on the disk, the reflectivity will not change and the CD will read a series of binary 0s. There are approximately 4 to 5 million pits per CD. They are arranged in a single outward-running spiral (track) approximately 3.75 miles (6 kilometers) long. The distance between each element is 1.6 thousandths of a millimeter.

Connecting a CD-ROM Drive

A CD-ROM drive is a peripheral device and must be connected to the bus of the computer through a controller. There are several ways to install a CD-ROM drive.

Adapter Boards

Some CD-ROM manufacturers provide a proprietary adapter board made specifically for their product. These boards are supplied with the drive and are not usually interchangeable. The early CD-ROM drives used either SCSI or a special version of a parallel port. Most modern CD-ROM devices are either IDE or SCSI.

Sound Cards with CD-ROM Interface

Many add-on sound cards have built-in CD-ROM controllers. Most sound cards come with a 15-pin female connector known as the MIDI (Musical Instrument Digital Interface) connector. Some of the newer cards come with a SCSI interface. Sound cards with the built-in controller interface were very useful for earlier computers that did not have a controller available on the motherboard. Because today's motherboards have the ability to connect four IDE devices, a sound card with a controller is generally not required.

Tip If you purchase a sound card with a controller and you already have a CD-ROM drive installed, be sure to disable the controller on the sound card. This will prevent IRQ (interrupt request) and other potential conflicts.

SCSI Host Adapter

The SCSI interface is the most advanced CD-ROM interface and often operates at higher data transfer rates than other interfaces. A single card can handle both internal and external drives, including CD-ROM and other optical devices. A detailed discussion of SCSI drives is found later in Lesson 3: SCSI Drives. A SCSI CD-ROM drive can be installed in any SCSI chain. You can purchase SCSI adapters that connect directly to a parallel port on the computer.

IDE

New computers have primary and secondary IDE connectors as part of the motherboard and BIOS setup. It is becoming commonplace to install CD-ROM drives on the secondary controller.

Audio Capability

Any CD-ROM drive that meets the Yellow Book standards (created by the audio industry for sound and adopted by the computer industry) has the ability to play back audio. Most CD-ROM drives contain the circuitry and chips to convert digital audio data into sound data. Most drives and sound cards also have a headphone jack, as well as audio jacks to connect to a stereo system. The only requirement is that the drive support the ISO 9660 standard for the file system. ISO 9660 is also known as the High Sierra Format. The ISO 9660 format is a standard for writing data to a CD-ROM for use in a cross-platform environment. This standard is compatible with MS-DOS, Windows, UNIX, Macintosh, and other operating systems.

Access Time

When purchasing or recommending a CD-ROM drive, you need to consider two values. The first is data transfer rate. The long-time standard for transfer rate has been 150 KB per second, and this is the basis for measuring CD-ROM drives today. A 2X CD-ROM drive operates at 300 KB per second, a 4X at 600 KB per second, and so on. A typical CD-ROM drive today will operate at 24X or 32X (4.8 MB per second) or faster. A hard disk drive typically operates between 800 KB and 1.8 MB per second.

The second value to look at is the drive's mean access time. This is the time it takes the head to move over half the tracks. Typical access time is 200 to 400 milliseconds (ms). Today's CD-ROM drives can have faster data transfer speeds than many hard drives, but their mean access time is 20 or so times slower. This means that while a CD-ROM drive will outperform the hard disk drive for copying or loading a large chunk of contiguous data, it will be beaten by the hard drive on random access tasks.

Although the transfer rate increases in multiples, the mean access time does not. The following table lists transfer rates and access speeds for some common CD-ROM drives.

CD-ROM Speed	Transfer Rate	Access Speed
4X	600 KB per second	220 ms
6X	900 KB per second	145 ms
8X	1200 KB per second	100 ms
12X	1800 KB per second	125 ms
16X	2.4 MB per second	100 ms
24X	3.6 MB per second	95 ms

Installing a CD-ROM Drive

Installing a CD-ROM drive is a four-step process.

1. Install the drive controller card, if needed. Follow the instructions with the card.
2. Install the CD-ROM drive in the computer case.
3. Attach the data and power cables.
4. Install the necessary drivers and set up the CD-ROM drive.

Controller Cards

The most difficult part of installing a CD-ROM drive is determining which controller card is best for the system. The controller card should be selected before buying the CD-ROM drive because it must be compatible with both the CD-ROM drive and the motherboard's expansion slot. There are several ways to ensure this:

- Use the secondary IDE controller on the motherboard.
- Install a new controller card (this might be supplied with the CD-ROM drive).
- Install the CD-ROM drive in an existing SCSI chain.
- Install a new SCSI host adapter and create a new SCSI chain.
- Use an existing sound card with a CD-ROM connection.

A quick review of how the computer is currently equipped will guide you in the selection of the proper card. In most cases, there will be a SCSI or IDE interface available. Whatever card arrangement you choose, be sure to disable any other possibly conflicting cards. Confirming the extent of the computer's resources before purchasing a new CD-ROM drive could save you the time and frustration of having to return or exchange it.

Installing the Drive Internally

A CD-ROM drive can be mounted easily in any computer that has an open bay for a 5.25-inch disk drive. Physical installation is as simple as installing a floppy disk drive. Most new CD-ROM drives come with a hardware kit, which includes a combination of screws and brackets.

Make sure you have all the tools and parts before beginning. These include:

- The CD-ROM drive.
- The correct cables.
- The appropriate hardware (including special mounting rails for the PC's case).
- A flat-head screwdriver.
- A Phillips screwdriver.
- Needle-nose pliers or tweezers (for jumper settings).

Connecting the cables for a CD-ROM drive is as simple as installing a floppy disk drive. There are two cables—a flat ribbon cable (for data) and a power cable. Be sure to connect the flat ribbon cable to the correct location on both the controller and the CD-ROM drive (the red wire going to pin 1). If there are no available power cables, use a Y power splitter cable (this will split a single Molex connector into two connectors; these are discussed earlier in Chapter 5, Lesson 1: Power Supplies). There might also be an audio out cable (two to four wires) that connects to a sound card (see Figure 9.1). This connection will allow you to take full advantage of the audio capabilities of the CD-ROM drive.

If you are adding an IDE-style CD-ROM drive, be sure to set the master/slave jumper as required (see Chapter 8, Lesson 2: Hard Disk Drives). For SCSI drives, you must set the proper SCSI ID using either a jumper or switch and make sure the chain is properly terminated.

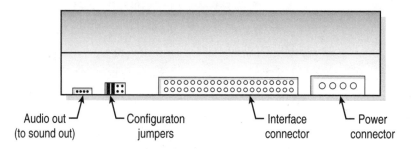

Audio out   Configuraton   Interface   Power
(to sound out)   jumpers   connector   connector

Figure 9.1   Cable connections to a typical CD-ROM drive

Software Setup

The file structure for a CD-ROM drive is different from the directory used by the MS-DOS FAT (file allocation table). Therefore, a special driver is necessary for MS-DOS to be able to recognize this device as a drive. A standard device driver supplied by the manufacturer (for BIOS) might also be required.

Windows 3.x

Microsoft's MSCDEX.EXE, an MS-DOS resident application, provides the required translation and also specifies the device driver required by the device. The following changes in CONFIG.SYS and AUTOEXEC.BAT will do the job.

- Changes to CONFIG.SYS

  To load the device driver, type the following line and include the directory and driver for the CD to be installed. (The exact name and location of the your driver file might be different from what is shown in this example.)

  ```
  device=C:\CDROM\MTMCDAI.SYS /D:MSCD001
  ```

  To ensure drive number assignment space, type the following line. (Note that the last drive letter assignment and, therefore, the number of drives, can be limited by assigning a lower value letter).

  ```
  lastdrive=z
  ```

- Add the following line to AUTOEXEC.BAT:

  ```
  c:\dos\mscdex.exe /d:mscd001 /1:e /m:10
  ```

This instruction provides the location of the driver and any switches required to set up the driver. You might have to consult the documentation for the CD-ROM drive to determine which, if any, switches are required.

Many CD-ROM drive installation disks will make these changes automatically. (Additional information for configuring CONFIG.SYS and AUTOEXEC.BAT is found in Chapter 15, "Software: MS-DOS and Windows 3.x.")

Windows 95 and 98

Windows 95 and 98 use a 32-bit protected-mode driver called VCDFSD.VXD. This driver replaced MSCDEX.EXE, the MS-DOS real-mode driver. When adding a new CD-ROM drive after Windows 95 has been installed, be sure to use the Add New Hardware wizard. This wizard will properly identify and set up the CD-ROM drive. With the Windows 95 and 98 Plug and Play feature, installing a new CD-ROM drive is simple—the operating system will recognize the drive and run the install wizard automatically.

Note If you intend to use a CD-ROM drive in the MS-DOS mode (from a bootable disk), the real-mode drivers will have to be installed and added to the CONFIG.SYS and AUTOEXEC.BAT files of the boot disk.

Tip You can use a Windows 98 startup disk to obtain the files required to recognize a CD-ROM drive. Be sure that the PC has the proper software licenses to use those files.

Multimedia

The term *multimedia* embraces a number of computer technologies, but refers primarily to video, sound, and the storage required by these large files. Basically, multimedia is a combination of graphics, data, and sound on a computer. In all practicality, the concept of adding multimedia simply means adding and configuring a sound card, a video card, and a CD-ROM drive to a system.

Microsoft formed an organization called the Multimedia PC Marketing Council in 1991 to generate standards for multimedia computers. The council created several multimedia PC (MPC) standards, and it licenses its logo and trademark to manufacturers whose hardware and software conform to these guidelines.

The Multimedia PC Marketing Council formally transferred responsibility for its standards to the Multimedia PC Working Group of the Software Publishers Association (SPA). This group includes many of the same members as the original MPC Marketing Council. The group's first creation was a new MPC standard.

The MPC Marketing Council originally developed two primary standards for multimedia: MPC Level 1 and MPC Level 2. Under the direction of the SPA, the first two standards have been replaced by a third, called MPC Level 3 (MPC 3), which SPA introduced in June 1995. (There are currently no plans for the publication of any additional MPC standards.) These standards define the minimum capabilities for a multimedia computer. The following table presents these standards.

	MPC Level 1	MPC Level 2	MPC Level 3
Processor	16 MHz 386SX	25 MHz 486SX	75+ MHz
RAM	2 MB	4 MB	8 MB
Hard disk	30 MB	160 MB	540 MB
Floppy disk	1.44 MB 3.5-inch	1.44 MB 3.5-inch	1.44 MB 3.5-inch
CD-ROM	Single-speed	Double-speed	Quad-speed
Audio	8-bit	16-bit	16-bit
VGA video resolution	640 x 480; 16 colors	640 x 480; 64,000 colors	640 x 480; 64,000 colors
Other I/O	Serial; parallel; MIDI; game	Serial; parallel; MIDI; game	Serial; parallel; MIDI; game
Software	Microsoft Windows 3.1	Microsoft Windows 3.1	Microsoft Windows 3.1
Date introduced	May 1993	1994	June 1995

You should consider the MPC 3 specification as the bare minimum for any multimedia system today. Specifically, a recommended system exceeds the Level 3 standards in several areas such as RAM, hard disk size, and video capability. Note that although speakers are not technically part of the MPC specification, sound reproduction does require external speakers! The built-in speaker used for POST beep codes is not sufficient for this quality of sound.

Video-Capture Software

With the advent of multimedia computers and software, manipulating full-motion video was the next logical step. A modern high-speed multimedia computer has become standard equipment in the moviemaking industry. Today, even amateur filmmakers can use their computers to give home movies a touch of professionalism.

Video-capture software provides an interface that allows users to import and export video formats in order to edit them with their computers. This software allows a user to view audio waveforms and video images, create files, capture single frame or full-motion video, and edit video clips and still frames for content and effects.

File-editing functions such as zoom, undo, cut, paste, crop, and clear can be used to edit audio and visual files. Users can also set the compression controls to the type of format desired and determine the capture rates. The capture rate for full-motion video (equivalent to what you would find in TV or on the big screen) is 30 frames per second (fps), but some systems might not be able to reach this potential. Professional systems include very large, very fast hard disk drives for data buffering. A typical user of video-capture software might realize a frame-capture rate of only up to 15 fps without adding an arsenal of hardware to enhance the system.

Note   Most new PCs will far exceed the basic multimedia requirements listed above. The A+ test current at the time of writing should not, however, go beyond these features. For now, you should still be able to describe the MPC features for the exam.

Lesson Summary

The following points summarize the main elements of this lesson:

- A CD-ROM drive is now a standard component of a computer system.
- CD-ROM data transfer rates are based on a factor of 150 KB per second.
- Installing a CD-ROM drive is as easy as installing a floppy disk drive.
- The proper drivers must be loaded before a CD-ROM drive can be accessed by the processor.
- To run a CD-ROM drive from MS-DOS, the real-mode drivers must be loaded.
- A CD-ROM drive is an essential part of the multimedia standard.

Lesson 2: Advanced Hard Disk Drives

Chapter 8, "Basic Disk Drives," covered the basics of hard disk drives. In this lesson, we broaden our discussion of hard disk drives to include the newer large-capacity drives and cover several of the newest methods.

After this lesson, you will be able to:

- Configure the newer large-capacity hard disk drives.
- Define the limitations of hard disk drives.
- Identify the advantages and disadvantages of SCSI connections.

Estimated lesson time: 30 minutes

Limitations of Early Hard Disk Drives

The original basic hard disk drives—specifically the ST-506—were relatively simple to install because the primary input/output commands were handled by the PC AT system BIOS. They used the routines built into the original IBM AT and the same interface command set as the original ST-506 hard drive. As drive capacities grew, they required many changes in setup to get around the limitations imposed by earlier models. Often, these changes added to the workload of the processor, which had a net effect of slowing down the processing of data. The result was a search for new methods to overcome those bottlenecks, which in turn led to other design considerations that had to be addressed. Storage technology is still evolving. Drives increase in capacity and speed, causing changes in PC design and operating-system support to take advantage of the larger-capacity, faster drives.

IDE and EIDE Drives

IDE (Integrated Drive Electronics) drives have been in use since the late 1980s. The purpose of the IDE was to integrate the drive controller with the drive itself rather than use a separate controller card. The ATA (Advanced Technology Attachment—the official name for IDE drives) standard is based on the original IBM AT standard for hard disk drives. ATA drives use the same interface command set as the original ST-506 drives and are handled by the system BIOS built in to the original IBM AT. ATA was, and is, a good command set, but its limitations led to its decline as a viable hard drive interface. These limitations set the stage for the development of the Enhanced Integrated Drive Electronics (EIDE). The EIDE drive system was developed with two essential objectives: increasing the size of available disk drives and increasing the speed of data transfer between the host and the disk drive.

The EIDE specification:

- Increased the numbers of drives available to the average computer.
- Increased the data transfer rate.
- Allowed for non-hard disk drives such as CD-ROM, ZIP, and tape drives to be configured to EIDE standards and used from an EIDE controller.
- Broke the 528-MB storage capacity limit of the ATA standard.

Note The above remarks apply only to IDE-style drives. SCSI drives and how they deal with the size and number of drive issues are covered later in this chapter.

Let's examine these improvements in detail.

Number of Drives

The ATA standard allows two hard disk drives to connect to one common controller. IBM set aside (reserved) I/O address 1FOh and IRQ 14 for the use of hard disk drive controllers. IBM also reserved I/O address 170h and IRQ 15 for a second controller (two more hard drives). Early computers had no BIOS support for this second controller. The BIOS installed on newer computers takes full advantage of both controllers, allowing up to four EIDE devices. (You'll find a fuller discussion of addresses and IRQs in Chapter 10, "Expansion Buses.")

Most SCSI controllers offer the ability to use IRQ 13 for hard disk drive support without the use of special drivers. To do so, the SCSI card must be set with boot BIOS enabled, and the hard disk drive must be properly formatted for the operating system in question.

Data Transfer Rate

ATA drives transfer data to and from the hard disk drive and memory using standardized protocols called *PIO (Programmed Input/Output)* modes. With PIO, data is exchanged between the main memory and a peripheral device, not by means of DMA (direct memory access), but with in-and-out instructions through the CPU. The Small Forms Factor (SFF) standards committee defined these data transfer rates as PIO mode 0, PIO mode 1, and PIO mode 2. ATA drives can use PIO mode 0, 1, or 2. With each improved PIO standard, the efficiency and speed of data transfer increased. The original ATA drives could transfer data from the hard disk drive to RAM at a maximum rate of roughly 3.3 MB per second. Speed increases to 5.2 MB per second, and then 8.3 MB per second and beyond, followed shortly thereafter.

Non-Hard Disk Drives

The original controllers allowed only for hard disk drives—and just two of them. The ATAPI (AT Attachment Packet Interface) was developed by an independent industry group to allow non-hard disk drives (CD-ROM drives and high-speed streaming tape units) access to the ATA interface.

The 528-MB Limit

Early BIOSs had a limitation on the maximum CHS (cylinder, head, and sector) values allowed, and the ATA standard added to that. As a result, for several years the maximum hard disk drive size was restricted to 528 MB. The following table shows how CHS limits are determined.

	BIOS Limit	IDE (ATA) Limit	Maximum Usable Limit
Cylinders	1024	65,536	1024
Heads	255	16	16
Sector/track	63	255	63
Maximum capacity	8.4 billion bytes	136.9 billion bytes	528 million bytes

Important   There are two ways to look at 528,000,000 bytes—the marketers' way (528 MB means 528 million bytes) or the literal way, which takes into account that there are 1,048,576 bytes per megabyte (1024 bytes x 1024 bytes). The second way, which is more accurate, yields a value of 528,000,000 divided by 1,048,576—a total of 504MB. Also be aware that an operating system will have to use part of the space for its housekeeping functions, as well as command and system files. The actual usable space for application and data files might be considerably smaller.

EIDE

As mentioned, EIDE stands for Enhanced Integrated Drive Electronics. This term specifies the incorporation of four major upgrades to the ATA/IDE specification:

- LBA (Logical Block Addressing) translation standards for BIOSs to support IDE drives larger than the old limit of 528 MB.

- Industry standards for improved data throughput to and from IDE drives— PIO modes 3 and 4.

- Industry standard instruction sets that allow CD-ROM drives and tape back-ups to connect to the same controller using the ATAPI standards.

- Use of the old, mostly unused IBM standard for a secondary controller calling IRQ 15 and I/O address 170h.

Overcoming the 528-MB Barrier

There are several methods used to overcome the 528-MB barrier that affects hard disks. When developing these methods, the difficult task was to create novel ways to access more data and maintain backward compatibility. In most cases, the designers found ways to address larger drives while "fooling" the operating system into functioning as if the drive were still within the proper limits.

When working with high-capacity drives, the computer professional must understand these different methods and apply the best method for the situation at hand. This is especially true if you encounter a situation in which different oversized drives are installed in an older system; these older systems often require special drivers or partitioning software. Using multiple hard disk drive drivers can confuse older operating systems due to incompatibilities. Never use drive data compression software in such cases without being sure that all the code involved is compatible.

Important   The new super-large hard disk drives might not work with some older machines. They will run, but will not take advantage of the extra-high capacity.

Logical Block Addressing (LBA)

Logical Block Addressing (LBA) is a means of addressing the physical sectors on a hard disk drive in a linear fashion. A translating BIOS detects the capacity of the drive and manipulates the CHS values so that the cylinder value is always less than 1024. Here's how it works:

- Before LBA (limit 528):

    capacity = cylinders x heads x sectors per track

    528,482,304 = 1024 x 16 x 63 x 512

- With LBA:

    cylinders = capacity divided by (heads x sectors per track)

When the computer boots up, an enhanced drive parameter table is loaded into memory. When data is transferred, this table intercepts the request and converts the system's CHS values to LBA values that the computer's BIOS can handle.

Enhanced CHS Translation

Enhanced CHS is a standard that competes with LBA. This standard allows drives to be manufactured a little faster and more easily than LBA. The standard is supported by IBM and other manufacturers.

Fast ATA

Fast ATA means using PIO mode 3, and Fast ATA-2 means using PIO mode 4. It is a technique used by Seagate Technologies (and others) to compete with EIDE. Fast ATA drives will support either LBA or CHS drive translation to break the 528-MB barrier.

Logical CHS and Physical CHS

Logical Cylinders, Heads, and Sectors (LCHS) is a value used by the operating system (MS-DOS, Windows 95 and 98, OS/2, and so forth) to determine the size of the hard disk drive. Physical Cylinders, Heads, and Sectors (PCHS) is a value used within the device to determine its size. A translating BIOS and/or the operating system use different algorithms to determine the address of the data.

DMA Transfer

Direct memory access (DMA) is a transfer method that, although not a PIO mode, also works to overcome the size limitations of hard disks. DMA bypasses the CPU to transfer data directly into memory. This is the preferred way to move large chunks of data in a multitasking environment. UNIX and Windows NT take advantage of DMA transfers. These transfers can function by using either the DMA controller on the ISA (Industry Standard Architecture) bus or a bus mastering controller that takes over the expansion bus and bypasses the built-in DMA controller.

DMA data transfers can be either 16 bits (single word) or 32 bits (double word) wide. The transfer width depends upon the data bus used—ISA, EISA, or VLB (see Chapter 10, "Expansion Buses," for details). DMA data transfer for ATA hard disk drives is extremely rare.

Using DMA data transfer can lead to data loss. However, data loss should be a concern only when transferring partitioned and formatted hard disk drives between computers that use different BIOSs to make the translation. The following table shows the various DMA modes.

DMA Modes	Physical CHS	Logical CHS
Cylinders	2304	576
Heads	8	32
Sectors/track	63	63
Capacity	594.5 million bytes	594.5 million bytes

Breaking the 8.4-GB barrier

Hard disk drives larger than 8.4 GB require a BIOS that supports enhanced interrupt 13h extensions for very large drives. Which method is used will depend on the system's age, operating system, and the drive in question. Newer machines come with built-in support in the system BIOS. There are three methods you can use to enable this function on older PCs that do not come with native support:

- Upgrade the system BIOS.
- Install a hard disk drive adapter with Int 13h support.
- Use a software program from the drive maker to allow the system to access the drive.

Depending on the system BIOS, you might not be able to display the entire size of the drive while in BIOS/CMOS Setup. Check the manual for the BIOS and operating environment for more details.

While the procedures just described will let the system recognize the drive, the maximum partition size will still be determined by the operating system in question. Be sure to check the procedures for the version you will be using with any third-party software. Newer versions of Windows (98, NT, and 2000) allow very large partitions.

If you use an older FDISK to prepare the drive, you will not be able to use the entire contents as a single volume. If you use Microsoft's FAT12- or FAT16-based FDISK, the largest single partition will still be 2.1 GB unless a third-party partitioning program is used. New versions of Windows can access partitions greater than 2.1GB, but if you plan to use a dual-boot configuration, be sure that any partition is compatible with the operating system you want to use to view the files it contains. NTFS and FAT32 partitions are not visible to older versions of Windows, MS-DOS, or UNIX.

Ultra DMA

While questions about the latest incarnation of ATA/DMA drives are not likely to appear on the current A+ Exam, a good computer technician should be conversant with them and expect to see them as part of the certification renewal process. Ultra DMA/33 is a faster drive technology that can be used on virtually any Pentium motherboard. Ultra DMA/66 offers raw data transfers at twice the speed of its DMA/33 older sibling. It requires a compatible system bus on the motherboard (or a special controller card), BIOS, and special IDE cable certified for that speed. They are easy to identify. One 40-pin connector is blue, the other black. Most are also labeled for Ultra DMA/66.

Installing EIDE Drives

Installing an EIDE drive is similar to installing an ATA drive; however, your pre-setup examination should consider secondary controllers, proper translations, and verifying PIO modes on older systems. Before undertaking an installation, it is a good idea to collect all the information from the new drive as well as from the existing drive. Consider all the options on paper before removing any screws. If you don't have enough information on hand, consult the drive manufacturer or the Internet. If you are installing a very new EIDE or UDMA drive on an old system, make sure the motherboard, PCI (Peripheral Component Interconnect) bus, cables, and IDE interface are compatible with the drive specification.

Secondary Controllers

Many EIDE I/O cards support secondary controllers, allowing for up to four ATA devices, as mentioned earlier. Before installing a card, be sure that jumper settings are set properly (see Figure 9.2). Secondary controllers are always set at I/O address 170h and IRQ 15.

Many cards come preset with the secondary controller disabled. Also check the advanced CMOS settings to make sure that any secondary controller enable/disable options are set to enabled.

Note   Some EIDE controller cards require that the CMOS options for secondary port hard disk drives be left as "Not Installed." Be sure to read all documentation that comes with these cards.

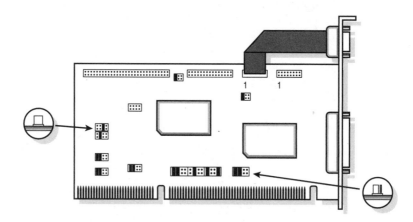

Figure 9.2   Controller card with jumpers

Secondary IDE interface and on-board channels are best suited for use with CD-ROM, DVD, or tape drives. Many secondary controllers on older machines run at a lower PIO mode (0 or 1) than the primary controller (3 or 4). It is always best to check the documentation first.

LBA or CHS?

Most BIOSs can support both LBA and CHS. Enhanced BIOS allows the system to get around the MS-DOS limitation of 528 MB per hard disk and is the easiest way to install an EIDE drive. An enhanced BIOS will support either the Western Digital LBA mode or the Seagate Extended CHS mode.

Note The two translation options are not interchangeable. It is not possible to partition a drive in one computer using one option and move it to a system that uses the other option. Also, see the earlier information about drives of over 8.4-GB capacity. CHS settings are not "real" for drives larger than that size, and they must use some form of controller, system, or third-party software translation to work.

What if a computer does not support either CHS or LBA? Most newer large-capacity drives will provide a disk manager disk, or the ability to make one from the drive itself. (If the information is on the disk, you will be able to access a small MS-DOS partition with the data. The instructions for accessing this data are very specific and must be followed according to the manufacturer's requirements.) This software, when installed properly, performs the same task as CHS or LBA. When using this method, you need to first answer this question: Is the drive in the master or slave position?

- If it is in the slave drive, install the appropriate driver in the CONFIG.SYS file.

- If it is in the master drive, the driver must be loaded *before* anything else, including the CONFIG.SYS file. This is done by changing the Dynamic Drive Overlay (DDO) in the master boot record. The software provided by the drive manufacturer should make these changes for you.

There are some drawbacks to using this method rather than LBA or CHS:

- Microsoft no longer supports the use of DDO software.

- When booting up from a floppy disk, for the hard disk drive to be accessible, the device must be loaded from the floppy disk's CONFIG.SYS file.

- A virus might attack the master boot record, where this file resides. This can cause some serious problems and at the very least will require reinstallation of the DDO file. Always keep a bootable, virus-free floppy disk on hand.

- The driver that allows use of a large, hard disk drive might also use a large chunk of conventional memory. The tradeoff might not be worth it.

- Many hard disk drive repair programs cannot be used with DDO.

- The software might cause conflicts with the operating system or other drivers.

Setting PIO Mode

There are five PIO modes. A drive must be set properly to achieve the best performance. The following table shows the parameters of PIO modes.

PIO Mode	Cycle Time in Nanoseconds (ns)	Transfer Rate (MB per second)
0	600	3.3
1	383	5.2
2	240	8.3
3	180	11.1
4	120	16.6

Answer the following questions before setting the mode:

- What is the fastest mode supported by the hard disk drive?
- What is the fastest mode supported by the controller?
- What is the fastest mode supported by the BIOS or device driver?

Caution   The maximum achievable PIO will be limited by the slowest component. Setting a mode that is too fast will not damage the driver, but it might damage your data.

To set up the PIO mode:

- Determine the PIO of the drive. This is preset by the manufacturer and cannot be changed.
- Determine the fastest speed your controller can handle. Most hard disk drives can support PIO mode 2. If you're using an ISA card, PIO mode 2 is the highest PIO available. The two fastest PIO modes, 3 and 4, must be run from either a VL bus (VESA local bus) or a PCI controller. Be careful with on-board controllers! On PCI systems, almost all on-board controllers are PCI; on VESA machines, they are VL bus.
- Set up the BIOS on the CMOS. If auto setup is available, use it.

  PIO modes 3 and 4 use a hardware flow control called IORDY (I/O ReaDY), also known as IOCHRDY. This setting allows the drive to slow down the data transfer as the head moves across the disk.

Other Settings

There are several other drive settings that are not necessarily limited to EIDE, but are generally associated with these larger hard disk drives.

Multiple Block Reads

The ATA standard requires each drive to activate its IRQ (see Chapter 10, "Expansion Buses," for details of IRQ) every time it sends one sector of data. This process helps to verify good data transmission, but it slows down the computer. Multiple block reads speed up the process by reading several sectors of data at a time.

Many BIOS chips have multiple block read as an advanced feature. Enabling multiple block read can be done with third-party utilities as well. Multiple block read can also be installed using a device driver that comes with a hard disk drive controller. Always use multiple block read, if possible.

32-Bit Access

Providing 32-bit disk access is a major speed improvement over MS-DOS for the Windows 3.x and Windows for Workgroups 3.11 environments. Every time an operation is performed under Windows, Windows must use the BIOS routines to access the hard disk drive. To do this, it creates a virtual MS-DOS world, a "bubble" of conventional memory that looks and runs just as if the machine were running MS-DOS.

Enabling 32-bit file access allows Windows 3.x to talk directly to the ROM BIOS, using a protected-mode driver called VFAT.386 (found in the Windows\System directory). VFAT.386 is loaded using the [386Enh] section of the SYSTEM.INI file. With the 32-bit file loaded, Windows does not have to create an MS-DOS "bubble" to talk to the hard disk drive.

For 32-bit file access to work in older versions of Windows:

1. Enter the line

   ```
   device=c:\windows\ifshlp.sys
   ```

   into your CONFIG.SYS file. This loads the 32-bit file access driver.

2. In the SYSTEM.INI file, add two lines to the [386enh] section:

   ```
   device=vfat.386
   device=vcache.386
   ```

(These protected-mode drivers replace MS-DOS FAT functions and SMARTDRV.EXE functions.)

Note   Windows 95 and later versions of that operating system automatically install a 32-bit file access driver. 32-bit file access is transparent to EIDE and requires no special settings.

There are some other potential problems with Windows 3.x and large drives. Windows 3.x uses a file called *WDCTRL for 32-bit disk access. This file is enabled from the SYSTEM.INI [386enh] section. This driver predates LBA and will generate the error: "32 file access validation failed." If this happens, *WDCTRL needs to be updated. Most EIDE controllers and all drives now come from the factory with a disk of software. If not, look up the Web site of the hard disk drive manufacturer and download the driver.

Whenever possible, check the CMOS, look for a 32-bit disk access option, and enable it.

Lesson Summary

The following points summarize the main elements of this lesson:

- Originally, hard disk drives were limited to storage capacity that did not exceed 528 MB.
- Using new technology, the old hard disk drive limit has been exceeded.
- Modern computers allow up to four IDE drives to be installed on built-in controllers.
- Properly setting PIO will enhance the performance of a drive.
- 32-bit disk access provides a major speed improvement for disk drives.

Lesson 3: SCSI Drives

The Small Computer System Interface (SCSI) has become the mass-storage device of choice for large network installations. SCSI was first introduced in Chapter 8, Lesson 2: Hard Disk Drives, and has many advantages over standard IDE and EIDE drives. SCSI is the favored drive for high-end workstations, network and Internet servers, and the Macintosh line of personal computers. In many installations, the advantages far outweigh the slight extra effort in configuration. In this lesson, we explore the advantages and uses of a SCSI system.

After this lesson, you will be able to:

- Define the advantages and disadvantages of a SCSI system.
- Determine whether a SCSI system is best for your client.
- Set up a SCSI system.

Estimated lesson time: 30 minutes

SCSI was introduced in 1979 as a high-performance interface, allowing connection of both internal and external devices. Because it runs on virtually any operating system, it was adopted by the ANSI Standards Committee and is now an open standard in its third generation.

At its core, SCSI is a simple design. A single card, the host adapter, (or a chip set on the motherboard) connects up to 15 devices. These devices can be attached inside or outside the PC using standard cables and connectors. SCSI is the only interface that can connect such a wide variety of devices. Communication between the devices and the host adapter is done without involving the CPU or the system bus until data must be passed to one or the other.

This design frees expansion slots and reduces the number of interrupts and memory addresses needed, while cutting down the number of drivers required. Less-robust solutions, such as IDE and EIDE, are little more than switching stations, relying on the PC's CPU to manage the data bus. SCSI host adapters are true subsystems with advanced commands that can order and route data to improve performance.

SCSI-1

In the late 1970s, Shugart Associates developed an interface to handle data transfers between devices, regardless of the type of device. The interface operated at the logical—or operating system—level instead of at the device level. This new interface was called the Shugart Associates System Interface, or SASI—the precursor to SCSI.

In June 1986, the ANSI X3.131-1986 standard known as SCSI-1 was formally published. This was a very loose definition, with few mandates. As a result, manufacturers of SCSI products developed a variety of competing designs.

SCSI-1 supported up to seven devices on a chain (plus the host adapter). Each device transferred data through an 8-bit parallel path. Compatibility of SCSI drives was nearly impossible because many SCSI devices had their own custom commands on top of the limited SCSI standard.

You might encounter older SCSI adapters, drives, and peripherals that are based on the original SCSI-1 standard. In reality, this standard amounts to little more than a few agreed-upon commands. The wide range of proprietary drivers, operating system interfaces, setup options, and custom commands made true compatibility a real problem and gained SCSI a bad reputation on the PC platform. It was, however, popular with Apple and UNIX developers, who could work with a limited range of devices.

In most cases it is best to upgrade any SCSI-1 devices to SCSI-2. If circumstances require you to work on an early SCSI product, you will have to contend with both hardware and driver issues. Check the Web site of your SCSI device's manufacturer for possible new drivers.

SCSI-2

The limited acceptance, but great potential, of SCSI-1 led to a more robust standard with a range of commands and a layered set of drivers. The result was a high-performance interface that began to take over the high-end market. It was the interface of choice for fast hard disk drives, optical drives, scanners, and fast tape technology.

One of the most important parts of the SCSI-2 specification is a larger (and mandatory) standard command set. Recognition of this command set (18 commands) is required for a device to be SCSI-2 compliant. The Common Command Set (CCS) made compatibility of multivendor devices possible. The CCS also introduced additional commands to more easily address devices such as optical drives, tape drives, and scanners.

SCSI-2 also supports:

- Wide (16-bit) SCSI.
- Fast SCSI.
- Fast/Wide (combines fast and wide features).
- Ultra (32-bit) SCSI SI-2.
- Backward compatibility with SCSI-1.

Fast SCSI-2

This standard uses a fast synchronous mode to transfer data, doubling the data transfer speed from 5 MB/s to 10 MB/s. Wide SCSI doubles that again.

Plug and Play SCSI adapters first arrived with the advent of the SCSI-2 standard. Today, all new SCSI host adapters are Plug and Play. The SCSI-2 standard took a long time to gain final approval, requiring agreement by many vendors. As a result, you might run into products labeled "Draft SCSI-2." In almost all cases, you can get these products running on any SCSI-2 or later system if you get the appropriate drivers from the vendor or the maker of the host adapter or operating system.

SCSI-3

To speed up the pace of development, the SCSI Committee approved a "fast track" system for the SCSI-3 standard. It let a subcommittee handle most of the work, and new subsections were adopted without waiting for the publication of the entire SCSI definition.

That bright idea, plus the advent of the PCI bus and mature Plug and Play operating systems, has made it easy to install components and given users excellent control and flexibility. All SCSI-3 cards have ways to support existing SCSI-2 devices. Some of the highlights of current state-of-the-art SCSI technology on the desktop include the following seven features:

High-Performance Products

The success and stability of the SCSI standard makes it an ideal platform for developing high-performance products. SCSI's robust, reliable interface and advanced commands allow manufactures to build "best-of-breed" products to take advantage of its power. The fastest hard disk drives and CD-ROM devices traditionally show up first, sporting a SCSI interface. The most advanced scanners are SCSI-based, and many optical products come only in SCSI versions. Even when non-SCSI versions reach the market, they generally under-perform their SCSI siblings.

Plug and Play Installation

Well-designed SCSI cards are recognized and drivers are installed automatically with Plug and Play operating systems such as Windows 98, Windows NT, 2000, and the Macintosh OS. Most SCSI-based peripherals provide Plug and Play setup. The first time the system is booted up after they are added to a SCSI chain, the system notices the new device and asks for the product's setup disk.

Simple Expansion

Adding external devices is as simple as connecting an industry standard cable and power cord. If users decide to add additional host adapters, they can share the same drivers, reducing system overhead.

Advanced Management

SCSI products generally offer a range of tools to tune the bus and devices attached to it. For example, many host adapters have firmware that provides the ability to format and inspect hard disk drive reliability and define custom settings for each device on the chain. Operating-system utilities are provided to check the status of a device and enable advanced features.

SCAM Support

This SCSI acronym stands for "SCSI configured auto-magically." Most new SCSI products are SCAM enabled, meaning that the user does not have to worry about setting the ID numbers for them, because they will configure themselves, using an open ID position on the SCSI chain.

Note   Even if a hard disk drive is SCAM enabled, you might have to set an ID on multidrive PCs, because the host adapter will need it to determine which drive is the normal boot device.

Connect/Disconnect

This command allows a SCSI device handling a large amount of data or performing complex operations to disengage from the host adapter's bus while performing the task, allowing other devices free access until it is finished.

Tag Command Queuing

SCSI devices with this feature can reorder how blocks of data are moved on the bus to speed transfer. The way it functions can be compared to letting a shopper with only a few items move to the head of the checkout line, to reduce the average wait time per shopper.

SCSI and IDE Compared

Feature	SCSI	UDMA/IDE
Devices per channel	7/15 per chain	2 per chain
Maximum potential throughput for major classes of SCSI and IDE	160 MB per second (Ultra 160) 80 MB per second (Ultra2) 40 MB per second (Wide SCSI)	66 MB per second (UDMA) 33 MB per second (UDMA) 16.7 MB per second(Fast ATA)
Connection types	Internal and external	Internal only
True bus mastering	Yes	No
Operate more than one I/O device at a time?	Yes	No
Advanced commands (such as tag command queuing, connect/disconnect)	Yes	No

Noise and SCSI

Any electrical signal other than data is called *noise*. Due to the many signals and electrical devices present, the interior of a computer is a noisy place. Computer manufacturers do many things to contain the noise inside the case, including adding shielding and grounding. Anything inside, or directly connected to, a computer is either a contributor to or a victim of the noise.

Because of the high data transfer speed, products using the SCSI-2 and later standards can be very sensitive to noise. Cables tend to act as antennae for noise. For this reason, proper cabling and minimizing of cable length are needed to maintain low noise in a SCSI system. Any noise spread through either the electrical power cables or the data cable is called "common-mode" noise.

A single-ended device communicates through only one wire per bit of information. This one wire is measured, or referenced, against the common ground provided by the metal chassis. Single-ended devices are vulnerable to common-mode noise (they have no way of telling the difference between valid data and noise). SCSI-1 devices are all single-ended.

Some SCSI-2 and SCSI-3 devices are differential-ended. These products employ two wires per bit of data—one wire for the data and one for the inverse of the data. The inverse signal takes the place of the ground wire in the single-ended cable. By taking the difference of the two signals, the device is able to reject common-mode noise in the data stream.

Caution   Under no circumstances should you try to connect single-ended and differential-ended devices on the same SCSI chain. You might fry the single-ended device and, if the differential-ended device lacks a security circuit to detect your mistake, you will probably smoke it as well.

Troubleshooting a Device Conflict

Determine which is the offending device by taking the following measures:

- Load only the device drivers for the SCSI devices.
- If the problem still occurs, use the F8 key to determine which driver conflicts. (Press F8 when starting MS-DOS or Windows 95 or 98—this will allow step-by-step confirmation of the startup process.)
- If the device driver is an executable file, try running it with the "/?" option. This will usually show a variety of command-line switches for the device driver (for instance, MOUSE.EXE /?). For more details on MS-DOS commands programs and switches, see Chapter 15, "Software: MS-DOS and Windows 3.x."

Here are some ways to correct the problem after you've found it:

- Look in the manuals or "readme" files of both devices. The problem might be a common one with a known solution.
- Try a variety of switches to see if any of them solves the problem.
- Attempt to find an updated driver for one or both of the devices (the Internet is a good place to look).
- If none of those solutions fixes the problem, you might be forced to choose between the devices or go to a multiple boot configuration.

Memory Management

SCSI host adapters typically have their own ROM chips. For MS-DOS systems, put the appropriate "X=" statements in the EMM386.EXE line of the CONFIG.SYS and the appropriate EMMEXCLUDE= statement in the SYSTEM.INI file. (For more details about configuring these files, see Chapter 15, "Software: MS-DOS and Windows 3.x.") A missing or erroneous "exclude" statement can cause intermittent lock-up problems.

Costs and Benefits of SCSI

Initially, the cost of a SCSI system and SCSI devices is greater than IDE. However, there are several environments in which a SCSI system might justify the increased cost. Some ideal uses for SCSI include:

- File servers.
- Workstations (both graphical and audio).
- Multitasking systems.
- Systems moving large amounts of data between peripheral devices.
- Systems with a large number of peripheral devices.
- Systems requiring fault tolerance (mostly file servers).

The Future of SCSI

SCSI continues as the device of choice for systems in which speed and compatibility are important. The ability of the SCSI format to provide fast and efficient fault tolerance for network systems through the use of RAID (redundant array of independent disks) will keep it as the drive of choice for networks. Although it is not required, the SCSI drive is generally preferred over IDE by Windows NT system designers for its performance and flexibility. SCSI continues to be more expensive than IDE, but SCSI's ability for RAID, hot plugging (changing drives without shutting down a system), and machine independence will keep it popular for workstations and servers.

Setting Up a SCSI Subsystem

There are several steps in setting up a SCSI-based system or adding a new SCSI peripheral to an existing system. Performing these steps in the proper order, without shortcuts, is the key to a fast, easy installation.

Start with the Host Adapter

SCSI cards come in a wide variety of sizes, shapes, and configurations. Some offer one connection, others have four. Options include secondary or even tertiary channels—RAID, cache RAM, and so forth. Be sure that the card will be able to service the devices planned for it. Set any jumpers first, then install the SCSI adapter card in the appropriate expansion slot.

Set the SCSI IDs, Termination, and Peripheral Cabling

Write down the ID for each device—including the host adapter—as it is assigned. After the IDs are set, verify termination for each end of the chain. Finally, attach the cables—first to the host adapter, then to the closest internal device—and move outward on the chain. Repeat the process for the external devices.

External devices usually use some form of switch to set the ID. Most allow setting IDs from 0 through 7 only. You might need to adjust that with internal devices that often allow a wider range of ID numbers. Cable types include: 50-pin Centronics type, SCSI-2 D-Shell 50, and 68-p type connectors. Make sure the last device in the chain is properly terminated.

Internal SCSI devices are installed inside the computer and are connected to the host adapter through an interior connector on the host adapter. Check the connection diagram to be sure the fitting is the right one for that type of device. The options are a 50-pin ribbon cable (similar to a 40-pin IDE cable) and two similar 68-pin cables. Be sure to use the right type of 68-pin cable: one is for ultra-low voltage differential (LVD), and the other is for single-ended (SE) drives. They are NOT interchangeable.

Important   SCSI devices connected incorrectly (for instance, with the cable plugged backwards) can be damaged! Be sure the red or blue strip on the cable is facing toward pin 1. Some SCSI devices allow only a proper connection.

Power Up One Device at a Time

A good practice is to connect the power to one device, power up, and check for problems. Then power additional devices one at a time and make sure everything is working and without conflict.

Load Operating System Drivers and SCSI Software

Finally, load any software required to allow the operating system to recognize the new hardware and take full advantage of its features.

Using a cable with enough connectors enables you to easily link multiple internal devices. You can have up to eight (numbered 0 through 7) devices, or 16 (numbered 0 through 15, depending on the host adapter and the devices) on a single SCSI chain. Don't forget that one position in each SCSI chain is taken up by the host adapter. Figure 9.3 shows a SCSI chain.

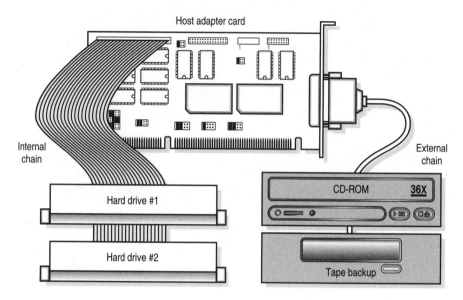

Figure 9.3   SCSI Chain

The exact number of devices will vary depending on a number of conditions. The host adapter must support the number selected, the installer must be able to set proper IDs, and the cables and connectors must be compatible. Older adapters allow only seven total IDs, and the card will use one, leaving you with six devices. Some SCSI devices have limited ID options. Many older products have only seven possible settings; some scanners or optical products are factory-set to an ID. Given the range of cable options and performance considerations, you might have to limit the number of devices on a single chain to get maximum performance.

Setting SCSI IDs

A simple SCSI chain works like a network, and—like a network—each device requires its own unique address. But unlike a network, setting an address on a SCSI chain is simple. A SCSI device can have any ID number in a range recognized by the host adapter, as long as no other device on the same chain has been set to the same number.

In SCSI numbering conventions:

- The host adapter is typically set to SCSI ID 7. (This is a de facto standard, not a requirement.)

- There is no mandated order for the use of SCSI IDs, but the SCAM feature will use a preestablished pattern of IDs if one is available.

- The ID of a bootable hard disk drive may be preset by the host adapter manufacturer. Most manufacturers use SCSI ID 0, although a few are configured to SCSI ID 6.

Setting a SCSI ID for a device is accomplished using jumpers or switches located on, or inside, the SCSI device. Typically, all internal SCSI hard disk drives use jumpers to set their IDs. External devices usually (but not always) have switches. Some SCSI devices have automatic ID and termination, using SCAM.

Caution Some external devices will offer a limited number of choices. This lack of choices could cause some problems when the chain is full. You might then have to adjust other drive IDs in order to find a unique ID for the new drive.

If you plan to utilize a SCSI drive as your C drive (this is required if you want to boot into MS-DOS from this drive), it must be configured as a bootable drive. This is done by either specifying the host adapter as the "bootable" SCSI ID or setting the host adapter to emulate a standard AT-style controller.

Logical Unit Numbers (LUN)

It is possible to have a single SCSI ID support more than one device. *Logical unit numbers* (LUNs) can be used to provide a unique identifier for up to seven subunits per ID number. These are used primarily in hard disk drive arrays to create one large logical drive out of several smaller physical drives. LUNs require highly specialized software and are most often found in network servers running NetWare, Windows NT, or UNIX.

Termination

Whenever you send a signal through a wire, some of that signal will reflect back up the wire, creating an echo. To *terminate* a device simply means to put a terminating resistor on the ends of the wire. The purpose of this terminator is to prevent the occurrence of this echo. Two kinds of termination are used in SCSI technology: active and passive. Most older (and all SCSI-1) devices use passive termination. Proper termination of a SCSI device requires special consideration. Older hardware can be damaged by improper termination but, more often, lack of proper termination will result in a boot failure or the failure of the system to recognize a device that has been connected to the SCSI chain.

On most devices within a computer, the appropriate termination is built into that device. On other devices, including SCSI chains and some network cables, termination must be set during installation. The only absolute termination rule is that both ends of the chain must be terminated and that devices that are not on either end must not be terminated. Most SCSI devices come equipped with some form of termination. For most internal products, jumpers can be set to enable termination and connectors can be attached to cables that lead to one of the two SCSI connectors on an external device. Internal Ultra-SCSI 80 and Ultra-SCSI 160 drives do not have termination options on the actual devices. Their termination is handled by a termination block on the end of the cable.

Most new SCSI host adapters are equipped with autotermination circuitry, which polls the chain and sets the proper termination at their ends (or middles). On older cards, you might have to set jumpers. Check the manual for any SCSI device you are installing for instructions on how to set termination and ID before powering it up.

Lesson Summary

The following points summarize the main elements of this lesson:

- SCSI was introduced in 1979 as a system-independent means of mass storage.
- A SCSI chain is a series of devices that work through a host adapter.
- SCSI chains can have up to 8 devices, including the host adapter (or 16, depending on the configuration) connected together.
- SCSI chains must be terminated on both ends.
- SCSI is used with many different types of peripherals, including printers, scanners, hard disk drives, and tape units.
- Bus mastering is a method used by SCSI to transfer data independently of the CPU.
- RAID uses several SCSI hard disk drives to provide improved performance and fault tolerance for data storage.

Chapter Summary

The following points summarize the key concepts in this chapter:

CD-ROM Drives

- CD-ROM data transfer rates are based on a factor of 150 KB per second.

- Before a CD-ROM drive can be accessed by the processor, the proper drivers must be loaded.

- To run a CD-ROM drive from MS-DOS, the real-mode drivers must be loaded.

Advanced Hard Disk Drives

- For many years, hard disk drives were limited to 528 MB.

- There are four ways to overcome the 528-MB Barrier: LBA, Enhanced CHS translation, Fast ATA, and DMA transfer.

- EIDE controllers and I/O cards support up to four EIDE drives including hard disk drives, tape drives, CD-ROM drives, and removable disk drives.

SCSI Drives

- SCSI chains can have up to eight devices, including the host adapter (or 16, depending on the configuration) connected together.

- SCSI chains must be terminated at both ends.

- Each device in a SCSI chain must have a unique ID.

- RAID uses SCSI drives to provide improved data storage and fault tolerance.

Review

1. Name four methods of overcoming the 528-MB hard disk limitation.

2. How do multiple block reads speed up a computer?

3. How many devices can be installed on a SCSI chain?

4. What is the effect of improper termination on a SCSI chain or device?

5. What is the BIOS protocol for SCSI devices?

6. Sometimes the SCSI device driver conflicts with other drivers. What steps need to be taken to resolve the problem?

7. Describe three advantages of using a CD-ROM drive.

8. What are the four steps required to install a CD-ROM drive?

9. Is a 16X CD-ROM drive 16 times faster than a 1X? Why?

10. How would you determine which type of CD-ROM to install in a computer?

11. Why would you use the MSCDEX.EXE real-mode driver with Windows 95?

12. Instead of using magnetic energy for storing data, a CD-ROM uses
    _____ technology.

13. Name some possible controller card combinations.

14. What software is required for a CD-ROM drive installation?

C H A P T E R   1 0

Expansion Buses

About This Chapter

The success of the personal computer is due largely to its ability to expand to meet the changing needs and economic requirements of the user. In this chapter, we describe the array of expansion buses that help to expand the system and that work with an ever-growing number of enhancements, including modems, video cards, and portable drives. We also discuss conflicts within the computer—how they are created and reconciled.

Before You Begin

This chapter requires knowledge of processors, motherboards, and the binary/ hexadecimal number systems. If you are not familiar with these concepts, take some time to review earlier chapters.

Lesson 1: Understanding Expansion Buses

Expansion buses are used to connect devices to the motherboard using the motherboard's data bus. They allow the flow of data between that device and other devices in and connected to the computer. Early computers moved data between devices and the processor at about the same rate as the processor. As processor speeds increased, the movement of data through the bus became a bottleneck. Therefore, the design capability of the buses needed to evolve, too. This lesson discusses that evolution.

After this lesson, you will be able to:

- Identify the different types of expansion buses in a computer.
- Identify the difference between the system bus and the expansion bus.

Estimated lesson time: 30 minutes

Development of the Expansion Bus

As discussed earlier in Chapter 4, "The Central Processing Unit," every device in the computer—RAM, the keyboard, network card (NIC), sound card, and so forth—is connected to the external data bus. Expansion slots on the motherboard are standardized connections that allow the installation of devices not soldered to the motherboard. The function of an expansion slot is to provide configuration flexibility when devices are added to a computer.

Whether a device is soldered to the motherboard or connected through an expansion slot, all integrated circuits are regulated by a quartz crystal. The crystal sets the timing for the system, giving all parts access to a common reference point for performing actions. Most CPUs divide the crystal speed by two. (If the CPU has a 33-MHz speed, a 66-MHz crystal is required.) Every device soldered to the motherboard—keyboard chip, memory controller chip, and so on—is designed to run at the speed (or at half the speed) of the system crystal.

CPU speeds increased as technology improved, while the speeds of expansion cards remained relatively constant. It was not practical to redesign and replace every expansion card each time a new processor was released—this would have been complicated and expensive for manufacturers. (And, of course, the additional expense would have been passed along to the consumer.) The commitment of the industry to maintain backward compatibility further complicated design tasks, because any new technology would have to run the older, slower devices.

To resolve this dilemma, designers have divided the external data bus into two parts:

- **System bus**: This supports the CPU, RAM, and other motherboard components. The system bus runs at speeds that support the CPU.

- **Expansion bus**: This supports any add-on devices by means of the expansion slots and runs at a steady rate, based on the specific bus design.

Dividing the bus enhances overall system efficiency. Because the CPU runs off the system clock, upgrading a CPU requires changing only the timing of the system bus, while the existing expansion cards continue to run as before. There is usually a jumper setting that changes the system clock speed to match the CPU. The ability of the motherboard to make this change sets the limit for the processor speed. Next, we take a look at the evolving types of expansion buses.

Industry Standard Architecture (ISA)

The first-generation IBM XT (with the 8088 processor) had an 8-bit external data bus and ran at a speed of 4.77 MHz. These machines were sold with an 8-bit expansion bus (PC bus) that ran at 8.33 MHz (see Figure 10.1).

Figure 10.1   8-bit PC bus slot

IBM took steps that fueled the rapid development of the personal-computer market. Their engineers framed the PC's design as an open system, using standard, off-the-shelf components. That allowed third-party developers to manufacture cards that could snap into the PC bus. IBM also allowed its competitors to copy the PC bus.

With this move, IBM established the *Industry Standard Architecture (ISA)* interface, thus generating the market for clones. A host of third-party developers worked to create products that enhanced the basic machine's features and to keep prices much lower for add-ons than competing proprietary systems such as those from Apple. Without this push, the PC market would have grown more slowly and probably would have been limited to businesses with the money to pay for the more expensive products.

IBM wanted to include a new expansion bus—one that would be compatible with previously released devices—with the release of its AT (Advanced Technology) PC, featuring Intel's 80286 16-bit processor. To accomplish this, the designers added a bus that allowed insertion of either an 8-bit card or a 16-bit card. This change resulted in the standard 16-bit ISA slot. This new 16-bit bus officially ran at a top speed of 8.33 MHz, but on some Peripheral Component Interconnect (PCI)-based systems the actual rate for ISA slots proved to be as high as about 10 MHz. (PCI is discussed later in this lesson.)

Note   The term "ISA" did not become official until 1990. Therefore, the 8-bit slot is called the XT, and the 16-bit slot is called the AT. When we refer to an ISA slot or an ISA card, we generally mean the 16-bit AT-style interface. The speed of the slots remained at about 7 MHz.

Problems with the ISA Design

The ISA design is one of the most enduring elements of the PC. It can be found on virtually all systems, from the second-generation IBM PC to machines built today. But it suffers from two major shortcomings: lack of speed and compatibility problems stemming from card design.

As CPU performance increased and applications became more powerful, card designers sought an interface that would allow add-on cards to keep up with the need for improved hard drives, display adapters, and similar products.

Expansion cards must make use of system resources in an orderly way, so that they do not conflict with other devices. When demands for these system resources are not coordinated, the system might behave erratically or even fail to boot up. Formerly, ISA cards often used a bewildering array of jumpers and switches to set addresses for memory use or the IRQ locations they would use.

The need to overcome the expansion card's slowness and compatibility problems led to a search for a new, standard expansion card interface—one that everyone could agree on and that would gain user acceptance.

Micro Channel Architecture (MCA)

In 1986, the market came to be dominated by the new 386 machines with their 32-bit architecture. Most PC manufacturers stuck to the same basic ISA design and MS-DOS. Expansion devices based on ISA technology for the 286 AT class machines could be placed in a new 386 clone without problems.

IBM, however, was feeling the pinch of competition from cheaper clones, and sought to retain its dominance in the PC market. IBM designers produced a new version of the PC, the PS/2 (Personal System/2) and created a proprietary expansion bus called *Micro Channel Architecture (MCA)* as part of the design. Running at 10 MHz, it offered more performance and provided a 32-bit data path. It was also totally incompatible with older ISA cards.

A feature of MCA is its ability to "self-configure" devices. Unlike devices that use technology in which the PC configures itself automatically to work with peripherals such as monitors, modems, and printers, an MCA device always comes with a configuration disk. When installing a new device in an MCA computer, insert the configuration disk (when prompted), and the IRQs, I/O addresses, and DMA channels will be configured automatically. (IRQs, I/O addresses, and DMA channels are discussed in detail in the next lesson.) An MCA bus is shown in Figure 10.2.

The PS/2 never gained enough market share to compete with the 386. MCA cards were few and far between, and more expensive than competing interface designs.

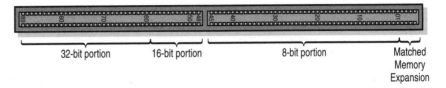

| 32-bit portion | 16-bit portion | 8-bit portion | Matched Memory Expansion |

Figure 10.2 MCA bus

MCA is now a lost technology. As a computer technician, you will not encounter MCA on new computers. However, it is still found in some older machines, and you will need to know how to identify it. If a customer brings in a PS/2 machine for service, be sure to obtain the configuration disks for the computer as well as any MCA cards that go with it.

Enhanced ISA (EISA)

In 1988, an industry group answered the challenge of MCA and released a new open standard called *Enhanced ISA* (EISA—pronounced "ee-suh"). It's a 32-bit, 8-MHz standard.

Unlike MCA, EISA uses a variation of the ISA slot that accepts older ISA cards, with a two-step design that uses a shallow set of pins to attach to ISA cards and a deeper connection for attaching to EISA cards. In other words, ISA cards slip part-way down into the socket; EISA cards seat farther down.

Caution Be very careful to line up cards being placed in an EISA slot precisely and push straight down! If you try to angle the card in, it can be very difficult to seat and you might damage either the connector or the slot.

Although EISA is faster and cheaper than MCA, it never gained much more acceptance than MCA.

Confusion between MCA and EISA technology—along with a limited need for cards that ran at the faster rate and the fact that only a few display, drive controller, and network cards were made available—led to the early demise of both bus technologies. Figures 10.3 and 10.4 show how the slot design of the two technologies differs.

Figure 10.3 Top view of ISA and EISA bus

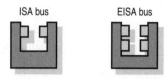

Figure 10.4   Cross section of ISA and EISA bus

VESA Local Bus (VLB)

The problems posed by MCA and EISA designs meant that developers needed an improved bus architecture to speed up graphics adapter performance and keep up with the evolving technologies as new 32-bit operating systems such as Microsoft Windows 3.1 gained popularity. The latter's graphical user interface (GUI) required a much faster display adapter, because every pixel (not just lines of character data) had to be represented and refreshed. About the same time, laser printers and graphics programs like PageMaker and CorelDRAW fostered the "desktop publishing revolution." The hardware industry developed the *VESA local bus (VLB)* to meet the need for a faster expansion interface. (VESA, the Video Electronics Standards Association, was the driving force behind the new bus technology.) Found only in 386 and 486 machines, the VLB had a short lifespan. The cards based on this design are connected directly to the system-bus side of the PC's external data bus (see Figure 10.5).

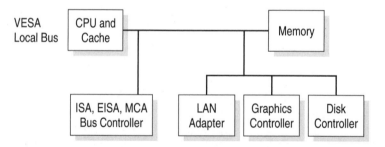

Figure 10.5   VESA local bus design

The speed of the system data bus is based on the clock rate of the motherboard's crystal. During the heyday of the VLB, this was usually 33 MHz, and VLB cards usually ran at half that rate, far outpacing the ISA bus. Some cards ran as fast as 50 MHz, using the full speed of the souped-up system bus. That often caused system crashes, because 50 MHz was outside the VLB specification.

The chip design for the VLB controller was relativity simple, because many of the core instructions were hosted by the ISA circuits already on the motherboard, but the actual data passes were on the same local bus as the one used by the CPU.

The design specification provides two other performance-boosting features: *burst mode* and *bus mastering.* In burst mode, VLB devices gain complete control of the external data bus for up to four bus cycles, passing up to 16 bytes (128 bits) of data in a single burst. Bus mastering allows the VLB controller to arbitrate data transfers between the external data bus and up to three VLB devices without assistance from the CPU. This limit of three devices also limited the maximum number of VLB slots to three and called for the use of a coprocessor. Display-system design is covered in more detail in Chapter 11, "The Display System: Monitors and Adapters."

The actual connectors on the motherboard resemble an ISA slot with an additional short slot aligned with it. On systems that support this interface, one to three slots are located on the side of the motherboard closest to the keyboard connection.

Peripheral Component Interconnect (PCI)

Peripheral Component Interconnect (PCI) allows developers to design cards that will work in any PCI-compatible machine. It overcomes the limitations of ISA, EISA, MCA, and VLB, and it offers the performance needed for today's fast systems.

At first glance, there are many similarities between PCI and the older VLB specifications. Both are local bus systems with 32-bit data paths and burst modes. Also, the original PCI design operates at 33 MHz—roughly the same speed as the VLB. But the important differences between them gained PCI its dominant role in expansion-bus technology. These differences stem from the following features:

- The PCI design's special bus and chip set are designed for advanced bus mastering techniques and full arbitration of the PCI local bus. This allows support of more than three slots.

- The PCI bus has its own set of four interrupts, which are mapped to regular IRQs on the system. If a PC has more than four PCI slots, some will be sharing interrupts and IRQs.

Note   In Windows 95 or with poorly designed PCI cards (both are becoming rarities), the shared addresses can lead to system conflicts and resource problems. Install PCI cards one at a time to minimize problems. Also, be aware that on many systems not all PCI slots offer full bus mastering. Check the owner's manual for details, especially on machines with more than four slots. In general, the PCI slots closest to the keyboard connector are the best choices for full bus mastering.

- The PCI bus allows multiple bus-mastering devices. Advanced controllers such as SCSI (Small Computer System Interface) cards can incorporate their own internal bus mastering and directly control attached devices, then arbitrate with the PCI bus for data transfers across the system bus.

- Autoconfiguration lets the PC's BIOS assign the IRQ linking the card to the system bus. Most PCI cards have no switches or jumpers to set, speeding installation and preventing many hardware conflicts.

Most PCs on the market today have one or more ISA slot for backward compatibility; however, most expansion cards are now built using the PCI interface. Although Intel was the original driving force behind PCI development, a PCI standards committee maintains the specification, and it is an open design—anyone can design hardware using PCI without being required to pay royalties.

Variations on a Theme: Differences in PCI Versions

The earlier discussion makes PCI sound like a technician's dream interface: fast, reliable, and doing most of the work itself. In most cases, that's true; still, there is always a "but." PCI has gone through many changes, and there are some features to be aware of when you work with one:

- The early PCI motherboards often have jumpers and BIOS settings that must be set to enable proper PCI operation. These are most often found on Pentium 60-MHz and 66-MHz machines.

- The PCI bus speed is not fixed. Newer chip sets can drive it—and the cards on it—at 66 MHz. At full performance, the PCI bus can deliver data transfers at up to 132 MB per second.

- PCI is not used only by PCs. Macintosh and some other non-PC-style computers incorporate PCI. Manufacturers appreciate this feature because it allows them to design core technology and port it to different models, with little effort and using the same production line. Although that's good, you need to be sure that a card is actually designed for the machine you are working on, even if it fits.

Keep in mind that PCI is evolving. That fact will help to keep it a viable interface for the foreseeable future, but it might also lead to incompatibilities between new cards and older machines.

Accelerated Graphics Port (AGP)

In the early days of PCI, the major market for that technology was the high-performance display adapter. The popularity of PCI led to its dominance of the expansion-bus market for card manufacturers. Today, the PCI market includes network cards, sound cards, SCSI adapters, UDMA controllers, and DVD interfaces. That posed a problem for display-card designers: having more cards on a single bus slowed down the performance, just when the increasing popularity of 24-bit graphics and 3D rendering called for greater demands on the display system. The search was on for yet another interface; this time, the solution was a single slot—tuned for the display adapter. Once again, Intel led the way and developed the *Accelerated Graphics Port (AGP)*.

The AGP removes all the display data traffic from the PCI bus and gives that traffic its own 525-MB per second pipe into the system's chip set and, from there, straight to the CPU. It also provides a direct path to the system memory for handling graphics. This procedure is referred to as Direct Memory Execute (DIME). The AGP data path is shown in Figure 10.6.

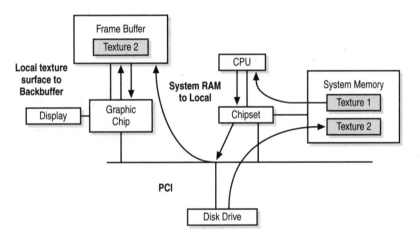

Figure 10.6 AGP Direct Memory Execute offers priority access to display data

The AGP slot, if present, is the only one of its kind on the motherboard and is usually the slot closest to the keyboard connector (see Figure 10.7). It is set forward of the back PC's case than the PCI slots. APG connectors are found only on Pentium II-based and later computers or on similar CPUs from non-Intel vendors.

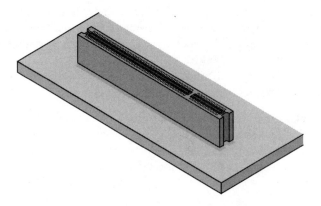

Figure 10.7   An AGP slot on the motherboard

Universal Serial Bus (USB)

The newest addition to the PC bus collection, the *universal serial bus (USB)* connects external peripherals such as mouse devices, keyboards, joysticks, scanners, and digital cameras to the computer. The USB port is a thin slot; most new motherboards offer two, located near the keyboard. They can also be provided through an expansion card.

USB supports *isochronous* (time-dependent) and *asynchronous* (intermittent) data transfers. Isochronous connections transfer data at a guaranteed fixed rate of delivery. This is required for more demanding multimedia applications and devices. Asynchronous data can be transferred whenever there is no isochronous traffic on the bus. USB supports the following data transfer rates, depending on the amount of bus bandwidth a peripheral device requires:

- 1.5 megabits per second (Mbps) for devices, such as a mouse or keyboard, that do not require a large amount of bandwidth.

- 12 Mbps isochronous transfer rate for high-bandwidth devices such as modems, speakers, scanners, and monitors. The guaranteed data-delivery rate provided by isochronous data transfer is required to support the demand of multimedia applications and devices.

USB devices can be attached with the computer running. A new device will usually be recognized by the operating system, and the user will be prompted for drivers, if drivers are required. Bear in mind that USB is a new standard, and some early USB ports and chip sets do not properly support some newer devices. Problems with embedded USB ports are not generally worth repairing. It is usually better to install a new USB interface card.

Lesson Summary

The following points summarize the main elements of this lesson:

- Expansion buses provide a way of connecting devices to the motherboard.
- ISA architecture could accommodate both 8-bit and 16-bit expansion cards.
- MCA was a proprietary architecture for IBM's PS/2 computers.
- EISA 32-bit architecture could accommodate older ISA expansion cards.
- VLB employed burst mode and bus mastering to boost performance.
- PCI architecture makes use of autoconfiguration to let the PC's BIOS assign the IRQ linking the card to the system bus.
- AGP architecture removes display data traffic from the PCI bus.
- USB architecture supports both isochronous (time-dependent) and asynchronous (intermittent) data transfers.
- Expansion buses have changed to keep up with increases in processor speed.
- A computer technician must know how to identify the various expansion buses (ISA, MCA, EISA, PCI, AGP, and USB) to ensure compatibility and know how to maximize performance when upgrading a computer.

Lesson 2: Configuring Expansion Cards

In the previous lesson, we discussed the different kinds of expansion buses. The purpose of these buses is to accept expansion cards. Internal and external computer hardware, such as disk drives and monitors, can be connected to the computer's motherboard by means of these expansion cards. As we learned in earlier lessons, the expansion buses connect to an external data bus. All devices are connected to the same communication bus. In this lesson, we look at how the computer keeps track of each device and controls the flow of data.

After this lesson, you will be able to:

- Define addresses.
- Describe the attributes and limitations of an IRQ.
- Identify the causes of conflicts within a computer.
- Locate and resolve hardware conflicts.

Estimated lesson time: 30 minutes

I/O Addresses

The bus system establishes a connection between the CPU and expansion devices and provides a path for the flow of data. The computer needs a way to track and control which device is sending data and which device is receiving; without such a means—the bus system—there would be complete chaos. The first step to establishing orderly communication is to assign a unique I/O address to each device.

Note Everything in a computer, whether hardware or software, requires a unique name and address for the CPU to be able to identify what is going on. Bus-mastering devices might seem to get around this requirement, but they have their own controllers that track local traffic and "talk" to the CPU as needed.

I/O addresses are patterns of 1s and 0s transmitted across the address bus by the CPU. The CPU must identify the device before any data is placed on the bus. The CPU uses two bus wires—the IOR (Input/Output Read) wire and the IOW (Input/Output Write) wire—to notify the devices that the address bus is not being used to specify an address in memory, but rather to read to or write from a particular device. The address bus has at least 20 wires. However, when the IOW or IOR wire has voltage, only the first 16 wires are monitored.

To allow communication directly between the CPU and a device, each device responds to unique patterns or code built into it. If the CPU needs to check the error status of a hard disk drive controller, for instance, it activates the IOW wire and puts the correct pattern of 1s and 0s onto the address bus. The controller then sends back a message describing its error status.

All I/O addresses define the range of patterns assigned to each device's command set. The device ignores all commands outside its range. All devices must have an I/O address, and no two devices can have overlapping ranges. Basic devices on the address list have preset I/O addresses that cannot be changed. Other devices must be assigned to the open addresses, and they must be configured at installation. The following table lists standard PC I/O port address assignments.

PC/XT Port	Used By	PC/XT Port	Used By
000h–00Fh	DMA chip 8237A	2F0h–2F7h	Reserved
020h–021h	PIC 8259A	2F8h–2FFh	COM2
040h–043h	PIT 8253	300h–31Fh	Prototype adapter
060h–063h	PPI 8255	320h–32Fh	Hard disk controller
080h–083h	DMA page register	378h–37Fh	Parallel interface
0A0h–0AFh	NMI mask register	380h–38Fh	SDLC adapter
0C0h–0CFh	Reserved	3A0h–3AFh	Reserved
0E0h–0EFh	Reserved	3B0h–3BFh	Monochrome adapter/ parallel interface
100h–1FFh	Unused	3C0h–3CFh	EGA
200h–20Fh	Game adapter	3D0h–3DFh	CGA
210h–217h	Extension unit	3E0h–3E7h	Reserved
220h–24Fh	Reserved	3F0h–3F7h	Floppy disk controller
278h–27Fh	Parallel printer	3F8h–3FFh	COM1

AT Port	Used By	AT Port	Used By
000h–00Fh	First DMA chip 8237A	278h–27Fh	Second Parallel interface
020h–021h	First PIC 8259A	2B0h–2DFh	EGA
040h–043h	PIT 8253	2F8h–2FFh	COM2
060h–063h	Keyboard controller 8042	300h–31Fh	Prototype adapter
070h–071h	Real-time clock	320h–32Fh	Available
080h–083h	DMA page register	378h–37Fh	First parallel interface
0A0h–0AFh	Second PIC 8259A	380h–38Fh	SDLC adapter
0C0h–0CFh	Second DMA chip 8237A	3A0h–3AFh	Reserved
0E0h–0EFh	Reserved	3B0h–3BFh	Monochrome adapter/ parallel interface
0F0h–0FFh	Reserved for coprocessor 80287	3c0h–3CFh	EGA
100h–1FFh	Available	3D0h–3DFh	CGA
200h–20Fh	Game adapter	3E0h–3E7h	Reserved
210h–217h	Reserved	3F0h–3F7h	Floppy disk controller
220h–26Fh	Available	3F8h–3FFh	COM1

I/O addresses have several important characteristics to remember:

- I/O addresses have 16 bits; they are displayed with a hexadecimal number.
- By convention, the lead 0 is dropped (because all I/O addresses have it).
- Hexadecimal I/O addresses must use capital letters; they are case sensitive.

Setting I/O Addresses

Run the **jumpers** video located in the **demos** folder on the CD accompanying this book to view a presentation of how jumpers are used to configure expansion cards.

As mentioned, each device in a computer must have an I/O address. If a device qualifies as a basic device, it will have a standard, preset I/O address. The default setting for the I/O address will work and no changes are required.

If a device is *not* a basic device, and does not conform to the PCI Plug and Play specification on a Plug and Play–compatible system, read the manual that came with it. The manual will explain how to set the I/O address and define the limits for that device. I/O addresses are set by changing jumpers, switches, or through use of software.

On Plug and Play systems, PCI cards are self-configuring, and usually no intervention is needed to set I/O addresses for those cards. It is possible for Plug and Play cards to conflict with older ISA cards, which don't recognize the Plug and Play devices. If you are confronted with this problem, refer to the cards and the motherboard manual for possible resolution.

Managing I/O Addresses

Devices assigned overlapping I/O addresses usually do not respond to commands and stop functioning. In such a scenario, a modem will dial but not connect; a sound card will start to play but will stop; a mouse pointer will appear but the mouse will not move. I/O overlaps can sometimes cause the machine to lock up intermittently.

I/O overlaps never happen independently. They usually appear immediately after a new device is installed. The best way to prevent I/O address overlaps is to document all I/O addresses. There are many commercially available programs that will check the I/O addresses for every device on your computer. You can also use Microsoft Diagnostics (MSD), a program provided with MS-DOS.

Note   If you are running Windows 95 or Windows 98 or the Windows NT operating system, you can use the Device Manager or System Information to locate and resolve IRQ and address conflicts. (See Chapter 16, "Windows 95 and Beyond," for more information on the Device Manager.)

Interrupt Request

The I/O address and the address bus establish a method of communication. The next step is to prevent multiple devices from "talking" at the same time. If the CPU needs to communicate with a device, BIOS routines or device drivers can use I/O addresses to initiate conversations over the external data bus.

Controlling the flow of communication is called *interruption*. Every CPU has a wire called the INT wire. If voltage is applied to the wire, the CPU interrupts what it is doing and attends to the device. For example, when a mouse button is pressed, the CPU attends to the interrupt request, invoking the necessary BIOS routine to query the mouse.

Because the CPU has only one interrupt wire and must handle many peripheral devices, a specific type of chip, called the 8259 chip, is present on the system to help the CPU detect which device is asking for attention. Every device that needs to interrupt the CPU is provided with a wire called an *IRQ* (*interrupt request*). If a device needs to interrupt the CPU, it goes through the following steps:

1. The device applies voltage to the 8259 chip through its IRQ wire.
2. The 8259 chip informs the CPU, by means of the INT wire, that an interrupt is pending.
3. The CPU uses a wire called an INTA (interrupt acknowledge) to signal the 8259 chip to send a pattern of 1s and 0s on the external data bus. This information conveys to the CPU which device is interrupting.
4. The CPU knows which BIOS to run.

The 8088 computers used only one 8259 chip (see Figure 10.8), which limited these computers to using only eight available IRQs. Because a keyboard and system timer were fixtures on all computers, these IRQs were permanently wired into the motherboard. The remaining six wires were then made part of the expansion bus and were available for use by other devices.

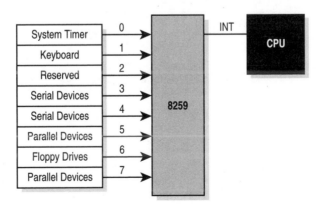

Figure 10.8 8259 chip with IRQ assignments

Starting with the generation of computers based on the 286 chip, two 8259 chips were used to add eight more available IRQs (see Figure 10.9). These new wires were run to the extension on the 16-bit ISA expansion slot (the 8-bit XT slot was extended to a 16-bit XT slot). Because the CPU has only one IRQ wire, one of the IRQs is used to cascade the two 8259 chips together. This gives a total of 15 available IRQs.

Note   When a device is *cascaded*, this means that data is passed through a common path between two devices, usually on to another destination. The term denotes a situation much like water cascading over a waterfall on its journey to the sea.

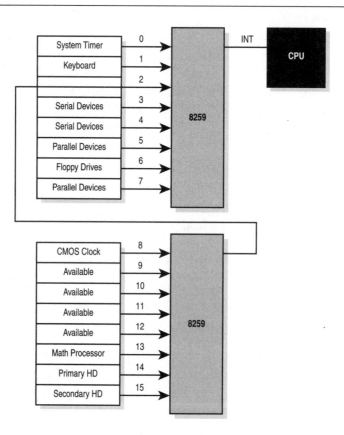

Figure 10.9   Cascading 8259 chips

Notice that the cascade removes IRQ 2. IRQ 9 is directed to the old IRQ 2 wire. Any older device designed to run on IRQ 2 will now run on IRQ 9. Some important facts to remember about IRQs include the following:

- IRQ 2 and IRQ 9 are the same IRQ.
- Three IRQs are hardwired (0—system timer, 1—keyboard controller, and 8—real-time clock).
- Four IRQ assignments are so common that no computer or device manufacturer dares to change them for fear their devices will cause conflicts (6—floppy disk controller, 13—math coprocessor, 14—primary IDE controller, and 15—secondary IDE controller).
- Four IRQs default to specific types of devices but can be changed: IRQ 3—COM2 and COM4, 4—COM1 and COM3, 5—LPT2, and 7—LPT1. (See table that follows.)
- The rest (IRQs 2/9, 10, 11, and 12) are not specific and are available for use.

Note The 8259 chips no longer exist on a motherboard. Their functions have become part of the multifunction chips called chip sets that perform all the functions of the 8259 chips and more. However, the information provided in the preceding section is still useful for understanding how this portion of the chip set operates. Also, the IRQ assignments generally are the same.

The following table provides typical IRQ assignments.

IRQ	Function	Available for Change
IRQ 0	System timer	No
IRQ 1	Keyboard controller	No
IRQ 2/9	Available	Yes
IRQ 3	COM2, COM4	Usually
IRQ 4	COM1, COM3	Usually
IRQ 5	LPT2	Usually
IRQ 6	Floppy disk controller	No
IRQ 7	LPT1	Usually
IRQ 8	Real-time clock	No
IRQ 10	Available	Yes
IRQ 11	SCSI/available	Yes
IRQ 12	Available	Yes
IRQ 13	Math coprocessor	If there is no math coprocessor
IRQ 14	Primary IDE controller	No
IRQ 15	Secondary IDE controller	Usually

Setting IRQs

Devices lacking a fixed or standard IRQ (except for newer PCI cards in compatible PCs) must have their IRQs set during installation. Read the accompanying manuals to learn about these. Setting IRQs is one of the first topics discussed in any device's installation instructions. The manual will tell you not only how to set the IRQ, but also the limits, if any, of the device.

Just like I/O addresses, IRQs can be set using hardware, software, or a combination of both. The best way to ensure that no two devices share the same IRQ is to document the IRQs for each device you install in a computer and file that documentation in a location in which you can find it easily if it is needed. As an example, suppose one of your customers has recently installed a sound card that now locks up when a parallel-port tape backup unit is used on the system. This strongly indicates an IRQ conflict. You need merely to check the sound card and the tape backup IRQ settings you have on file and change one if necessary.

Important   Some devices have a limited number of IRQ settings; you might need to change the IRQs of other devices in order to free one of these IRQs.

Direct Memory Access (DMA)

The CPU runs the BIOS, operating system, and applications, as well as handling interrupts and accessing I/O addresses. This requires the CPU to move a lot of data. This data movement is necessary, requiring considerable CPU power and time, but it is also very simple. Moving data is a waste of the CPU's resources.

To reduce this waste, another chip is installed to work with the system CPU. It is called a *direct memory access (DMA)* chip. The only function of the DMA chip (the 8237 chip) is to move data. It handles all the data passing from peripherals to RAM and vice versa.

DMA transfers are not automatic. Hardware and device drivers must be designed to take advantage of this chip. Originally, DMA was used only to transfer data between floppy disk drives and RAM; early computers had only four wires and one DMA chip. Any device requiring DMA had to send a request, just like an IRQ.

DMA channels use the same rules as IRQs. Just as with the 8259 chip, DMA availability soon became a problem because an insufficient number of channels was available. A second DMA chip was added for 286-based computers. Just like the second IRQ chip, these two are cascaded, allowing a total of eight DMA channel assignments (usually referred to simply as DMA channels). The floppy disk drives on all computers use DMA channel 2.

Setting DMA Channels

Fortunately, not many devices use DMA. Sound cards, a few SCSI controllers, and some CD-ROM drives and network cards do require DMA. Just as with IRQs and I/O addresses, DMA can be set by means of either hardware or software. However, manufacturers started using DMA for devices other than the floppy disk drive only recently. As a result, almost all devices set DMA through software (although some still use jumpers). If two devices share the same DMA channel and "talk" at the same time, the computer will lock up. The following table provides DMA channel assignments.

DMA Channel	Function
0	Available
1	Available
2	Floppy disk controller
3	ECP parallel/available
4	First DMA controller
5	Second sound card
6	SCSI/available
7	Available

Managing DMA

DMA and IRQ work in the same way; therefore, DMA conflicts look and act exactly like IRQ conflicts. Always check for IRQ conflicts first. (It is possible for a computer professional to spend hours trying to solve IRQ problems when the source of the problem is actually the DMA.) If you are sure all IRQs are correct, yet the computer continues to experience a problem, check the DMA. There is very little diagnostic software for resolving DMA problems, so it is important to maintain careful documentation.

COM and Ports

IBM created preset combinations of IRQs and I/O addresses for serial and parallel devices. These preset combinations are called *ports*. The word "port" simply means a portal or two-way access. The preset combinations are called COM ports for serial devices and LPT ports for parallel devices.

The purpose of a port is to make installation easier. Modems and printers, therefore, do not require IRQ or I/O settings. When assigned to an active port (as long as no other device is using that port), they will work. The following table lists standard ports.

Port	I/O Address	IRQ
COM1	3F8	4
COM2	2F8	3
COM3	3E8	4
COM4	2E8	3
LPT1	378	7
LPT2	278	5

Most computers are manufactured to offer built-in physical ports with cable connections available either directly to the motherboard or in an expansion slot. In this case, the standard port addresses and IRQs are assigned to them. This makes it possible to install an external device simply by plugging in the port and assigning addresses to the device. If necessary, these ports can be disabled (by using CMOS setup), freeing their I/O addresses and IRQs for another device.

For example, suppose you want to install a new internal modem on a machine that has two external serial ports on the motherboard. By disabling one of these ports, you have made its address and IRQ available for use by the internal device. Simply assign the device to the now-free port.

Installation Problems with COM Ports

Assume you have a modem set to COM1. You buy a network card that comes out of the box with a default setting of IRQ 4. You realize the network card and the modem will conflict, and the computer will lock up. What do you do?

You will have to change the IRQ on one of the devices. The network card is probably the best choice, because the modem is installed and already working.

COM Ports

The original 8088-based IBM PCs were equipped with two serial ports: COM1, set to IRQ4, and COM2, set to IRQ3. While those two IRQs are still the standard for COM ports 1 and 2, many BIOS routines will allow different IRQ assignments or even allow an unused port to be disabled. Because of the limited number of IRQ addresses available, any additional COM ports would have to share IRQs with existing ports. COM3 shared the interrupt of COM1 (IRQ4), and COM4 shared the interrupt of COM2 (IRQ3). To enable use of these additional ports, COM3 was assigned I/O address 3E8-3EF, and COM4 was assigned I/O address 2E8-2EF. This sharing was possible because the IRQ-sharing devices would be unlikely to use them at the same time.

Today we have many other ways of adding printers and other peripherals to PCs, but such conflicts can still be a problem with modems and UPS (uninterruptible power supply) devices that might need simultaneous access.

Note   The first rule for setting IRQs is to ensure that two devices never share the same IRQ. The only exception is that two (or more) devices can share an IRQ if they never "talk" at the same time! Common IRQ conflicts occur between a serial mouse, sound card, modem, and/or serial printer. (Remember that PCI devices can share an IRQ if it is managed by the same PCI controller.)

LPT Ports

LPT ports are for parallel data connections. The name is derived from their original use with printers (LPT—line printer). The original IBM standard LPT port did not provide bidirectional communications (talkback) and was designed solely for one-way data streams to a printer. The standard addresses are IRQ 7 for LPT1 and IRQ 5 assigned to LPT2, if it is present. IRQ 5 quickly became the favorite for devices like sound cards and other add-ons. Today, many devices are made that can use the parallel plug in the back of a computer, thus reducing costs. These devices (tape backups, SCSI drives, or modems) use bidirectional communication and, therefore, need an interrupt. This situation is easing as USB connections replace many of the parallel designs.

Installing Expansion Cards

The rules for installing expansion cards are simple:

- First read the manual.
- Document addresses and DMA and IRQ settings for any non-Plug and Play device.
- Keep the IRQs, DMAs, and I/O addresses unique.

Windows 95, Windows 98, and Windows 2000 support Plug and Play. In most cases, you can insert a Plug and Play card into the proper type of expansion slot and turn on the computer. Windows will find the card and guide you through the setup. The savvy computer professional documents and keeps track of the IRQ, DMA, and I/O addresses, in case a conflict arises with a Plug and Play device on the system.

Windows 95 and Windows 98 use Hardware Properties, under the System Information/Device Manager option in the Control Panel, which does a good job of identifying (and allowing) changes to these settings.

Tip   A good way to document a computer is to print a complete list of the computer's hardware settings from this Hardware Properties dialog box.

Note   For Plug and Play to work, the computer must have a Plug and Play BIOS, and the operating system and the device card must be Plug and Play–compliant.

Lesson Summary

The following points summarize the main elements of this lesson:

- Every device in a computer needs a unique name and address.
- In order for the CPU to identify which devices need to use the data bus, it monitors the IRQs.
- Generally, no two devices can use the same IRQ or DMA channel.
- Most conflicts during an installation of a new device are caused by IRQ conflicts.
- BIOS routines or device drivers can use I/O addresses to initiate "conversations" over the external data bus by means of an interrupt request (IRQ).
- DMA handles all the data passing from peripherals to RAM and vice versa.
- COM ports are for serial devices; LPT ports are for parallel devices.
- The computer technician should document addresses and DMA and IRQ settings for any non-Plug and Play device installed in a computer.

Chapter Summary

The following points summarize the key concepts in this chapter:

Connecting Devices to the Motherboard

- Expansion slots are standardized connections that provide a common access point for installing devices.

- The different types of expansion bus architecture are the ISA, MCA, EISA, VESA VLB, and PCI.

- USB architecture supports both isochronous (time-dependent) and asynchronous (intermittent) data transfers.

- PCI architecture makes use of autoconfiguration to let the PC's BIOS assign the IRQ linking the card to the system bus.

- AGP architecture removes display data traffic from the PCI bus.

Configuring Expansion Cards

- In order for a CPU to keep track of its devices and communicate with them, a unique I/O address must be assigned to each device.

- In order to prevent devices from "talking" to the CPU at the same time, an IRQ number is assigned to the devices that informs the CPU which device is requesting its attention. It is recommended that you memorize as many of the typical IRQ assignments as possible.

- The DMA chip moves data, handling all the data passing from peripherals to RAM and vice versa.

- To avoid problems similar to IRQ conflicts, no two devices should have the same DMA channel assignment.

- COM ports are used for serial devices (such as modems) and LPT ports are used for parallel devices (such as printers). COM ports put these devices in direct communication with the CPU and make installation easier.

Review

1. Why does a computer need an expansion bus?

2. Name the available expansion buses.

3. What happens if two non-PCI devices use the same I/O address?

4. How many IRQs are available on most PCs?

5. Under what conditions would a second modem—installed and assigned to COM3—not work?

6. Identify the two divisions of the external data bus and describe the purpose of each.

7. What is the standard that governs computer buses?

8. What is the difference between ISA and EISA cards?

9. Why was VESA created?

10. What is bus mastering?

11. Describe ways in which the PCI bus is better than previous technologies.

12. How does the CPU use I/O addresses?

13. What is the I/O port address of COM2?

14. What are the functions of IRQs?

15. List as many of the standard IRQ assignments as you can.

16. What is the function of the DMA chip?

17. Why is it important not to assign an IRQ to more than one device?

18. What is the difference between COM ports and LPT ports?

19. Why is it important to document IRQs, DMAs, and I/O addresses?

C H A P T E R   1 1

The Display System: Monitors and Adapters

About This Chapter

Early personal computers employed text-based displays, offering green, white, or amber characters against a black background. Today the average PC monitor can provide life-like colors and reproduce images of near-photographic quality. This dramatic change is the result of radical improvements in monitors and the display-adapter technology that drives them. This chapter discusses how these devices work in unison to provide an acceptable display.

Before You Begin

An understanding of the principles of memory and expansion cards is essential. If you need a refresher course on these subjects, review Chapters 7 and 10.

Lesson 1: Monitors

This lesson discusses the computer's most obvious and necessary output device: the monitor. It is important for the computer technician to understand the basics of how monitors work and are adjusted. In many cases, a simple modification can correct a problem; in others, the intervention of a specially trained technician is required.

After this lesson, you will be able to:

- Identify the various types of monitors.
- Recognize the components of monitor resolution.
- Determine the amount of video memory your system requires.
- Troubleshoot common monitor problems.

Estimated lesson time: 20 minutes

Basic Monitor Operation

A monitor operates fundamentally like a TV set, except that it is designed to receive signals from a card in the PC, rather than a broadcast signal. The quality of a monitor's display is influenced by a variety of design factors and the features of its companion adapter card.

Caution   Repairing the inside of monitors is a job more in the realm of a TV repairman than a computer technician. Monitors generally carry warnings that they contain no user-serviceable parts for good reason. Although we discuss the inner workings of monitors in this chapter, that should not be taken as an invitation to probe inside them, where the risk of serious electrical shock is high.

The Cathode-Ray Tube

The cathode-ray tube (CRT) is the main component of a traditional monitor. The rear of the CRT holds a cylinder that contains one or more *electron guns*. Most color monitors have three guns in back—one for each of the colors red, green, and blue. This combination (usually referred to as RGB) allows the visual production of all colors.

The wide end of the CRT is the display screen, which has a *phosphor coating* (a substance that can emit light when hit with radiation). When active, the guns beam a stream of charged electrons onto the phosphorus coating. When the coating is hit with the right amount of energy, light is produced in a pattern of very small dots. This same technology is used in X-ray imaging, oscilloscopes, and other CRT devices. Similarly, monitors emit X-radiation. There is one dot for each primary color (RGB), and the dots are grouped in patterns close together. The name for a collection of all dots in a specific location is a *pixel* (which stands for picture element).

Image Formation and Refresh Rates

The human eye perceives the collection of pixels painted at the front of a CRT as a compound image, in much the same way as it interprets the pattern of ink dots in a newspaper halftone as a photograph. The term *persistence* is used to define how long the phosphors on the screen remain excited and emit light.

The image on the screen is not painted all at once. The stream is directed in rows, usually starting in an upper left corner. A series of *rasters* (a rectangular pattern of lines) are drawn down the face of the screen until the beam reaches the lower right, whereupon the process starts over. The persistence rate must hold for long enough to allow formation of a complete image, but not so long that it blurs the dots painted in the next pass.

These raster passes take place very quickly. The time required to complete a vertical pass is called the *vertical refresh rate (VRR)*; the time required to pass once from left to right is known as the *horizontal refresh rate (HRR)*. Generally speaking, faster is better. Too slow a vertical rate can cause flicker, which is not only annoying, but can lead to eye strain. The larger the CRT, the faster the refresh rate must be to cover the entire area within the amount of time needed to avoid flicker. At 640 x 480 resolution, the minimum refresh rate is 60 Hz; at 1600 x 1200, the minimum is 85 Hz. The refresh rate, shown in Figure 11.1, is produced by both the monitor and display adapter.

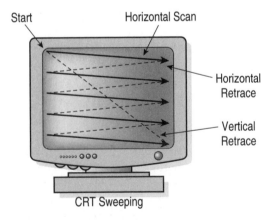

Figure 11.1 Horizontal and Vertical Refresh Rates

Early monitors had fixed refresh rates. In 1986, NEC introduced the first *multifrequency* monitor that could automatically adjust the refresh rate to take advantage of the highest rate supported by the display adapter of that time. NEC used the term "multiSync" to describe its line of multiple frequency monitors. Today, this feature is standard on most monitors.

Caution   Do not exceed the approved refresh rate for a monitor, even if the adapter can produce a higher scan of the screen. The result will be an unstable or unreadable image, which can damage a monitor very quickly.

The direction and point of contact of the electron stream on the phosphor display are determined by deflection coils coupled with a series of magnetic fields generated by a ring of electromagnets placed around the narrow end of the tube. This collection is called the *yoke,* because it forms a yoke around the tube.

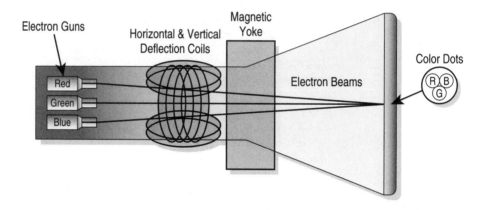

Figure 11.2   Cathode-ray tube (CRT)

Note   The CRT-based monitor has been around for a long time; recently, its successor, the liquid crystal display (LCD) monitor, has started to show up on desktops.

Screen Resolution and Pitch

The term *resolution* refers to the degree of detail offered in the presentation of an image. The method of measurement varies, based on the medium—photographic lenses, films, and paper are measured using lines per inch, while computer-monitor manufacturers express resolution in pixels per inch. The greater the number of pixels per inch, the smaller the detail that can be imaged, and, consequently, the sharper the picture.

Monitor resolution is usually expressed as "a" x "b" where "a" is the number of horizontal pixels, and "b" is the number of vertical pixels. For example, 640 x 480 means that the monitor resolution is 640 pixels horizontally by 480 pixels vertically. Modern monitors usually offer a variety of resolutions, with different refresh rates. Price and quality should be compared at the maximum for both, along with two other factors, dot pitch and color depth (the latter is covered in the next lesson).

Dot pitch is a term used to define the diagonal distance between the two closest dots of the same color, usually expressed in millimeters. The smaller the pitch, the greater the number of dots, and the more well-defined the image that results. The values for dot pitch are generally reflected in the monitor's price, and are getting smaller as manufacturing technology improves. You should match the monitor's dot pitch and maximum resolution numbers to the needs of the customer, and install a graphics display card that will meet or exceed them.

Note   Do not confuse pixels with dots. A pixel is the smallest image unit the computer is capable of printing or displaying. It is usually the first number given in screen resolution: horizontal pixels x vertical raster lines. For example: 640 x 480 is the standard VGA resolution of 640 pixels per line, 480 lines deep.

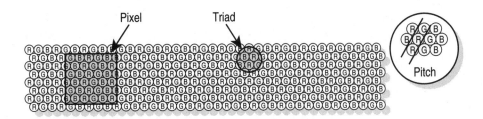

Figure 11.3   Color dots on a monitor

Other Considerations in Choosing Monitors

Cost and Picture Area

There is a direct link between the size of the picture tube and the cost of the monitor. The CRT is the most expensive part of the monitor. GUI operating systems have increased the demand for big screens, to allow for more working area so that the user can have more applications open at once, or more working room for graphics.

Bandwidth

When referring to computer monitors, the term *bandwidth* is used to denote the greatest number of times an electron gun can be turned on and off in one second. Bandwidth is a key design factor, because it determines the maximum vertical refresh rate of a monitor. It is measured in MHz. Higher numbers are better. The lower the resolution, the faster the bandwidth. When comparing products, remember to measure bandwidth at the same resolution for each product.

Interlacing

Interlacing refreshes the monitor by painting alternate rows on the screen and then coming back and sweeping the sets of rows that were skipped the first time around. This increases the effective refresh rate, but can lead to eyestrain. Interlacing is found on less expensive monitors, and should be avoided unless achieving the very lowest initial cost is the client's key concern.

Power-Saving Features

Because they are the highest consumers of electrical current in the average PC, most new monitors provide some level of power-saving technology. Consequently, VESA has established a standard set of power economy controls to reduce power use when the monitor is idle. These are collectively referred to as *Display Power-Management Signaling (DPMS) modes*.

DPMS technology uses monitors to gauge activity levels of the display. If there is no change in the data stream from the adapter, as set in either the BIOS or operating system controls, the monitor is switched to inactive status. The goal is to reduce power consumption, while minimizing the amount of time required to restore the display to full intensity when needed. The following table lists DPMS stages, arranged in the order ranging from most to least power used.

Monitor Status	Video Signal Sent	Monitor Activity Level	Amount of Power Saved	Recovery Time to Normal Display
On	Yes	Active	None	N/A
Standby	No	Inactive	Fair	Minimal
Suspend	Yes	Inactive	Good	Long
Off	No	Inactive	Excellent	Longest (Virtually the same as full power)

Frequently turning a monitor on and off places stress on the components. DPMS reduces the need to use the mechanical switch to turn the device on or off. Clients without power-saving systems in place should be advised to turn on the display only when it is first needed, and to turn it off at the end of each workday.

DPMS can be configured in one of three ways: using hardware, software, or a combination of both. When configuring a system for a new monitor, check the manufacturers' manuals for recommendations on appropriate settings and setup instructions.

Tuning the Monitor's Display

In most cases, the monitor must be adjusted for a proper picture when the screen resolution or refresh rate is changed or a new display card is added to the system. The following table lists typical monitor adjustments.

	Vertical height	Allows adjustment of the top and bottom of the image. Image height changes.
	Vertical center	Allows adjustment of the location of the image between the top and bottom of the active viewing area.
	Pincushion	Adjusts the center of the image (vertically) to eliminate or reduce bowing in or out of the display image.
	Horizontal width	Allows adjustment of the size of the image on the horizontal axis.
	Horizontal center	Allows the image to be horizontally centered.
	Keystone	Allows adjustment of the top and bottom edge widths so that the image is square.
	Degaussing	Available on newer, larger monitors. Demagnetizes the CRT to prevent an electron beam from bleeding over to an adjacent dot, causing shadowing and/or loss of color control.

Important   When using the degaussing button, hold it down for only one or two seconds: longer use could harm the monitor.

Some monitors offer advanced adjustment screws that allow the user, without opening the monitor shell, to tune the settings that are usually available only with interior controls. Adjust these tools only if you understand the process and after you have reviewed the instructions in the product's manual. Any internal repairs or adjustments to the monitor that require opening the shell should be left to properly trained technicians with the appropriate tools and training.

Caution   Working inside a monitor is dangerous. The high voltages inside a monitor can cause *sudden death or serious injury*. It's important to realize that monitors contain their high-voltage charge even when they're not operating or even plugged in. A monitor can hold its charge for days. Before you can work safely inside the monitor, such energy must be discharged. Remember that this is often best left to someone who specializes in repairing monitors.

Monitor Maintenance

Monitor care and troubleshooting are usually simple tasks. Here are some general guidelines to follow:

- Make sure the enclosure is properly ventilated. Covering the opening on the case can lead to overheating. Dust the unit at regular intervals.

- Clean the face of the CRT gently: Follow the instructions in the product manual. In most cases, this means dusting the glass with a clean soft cloth. Do not use window cleaners that contain solvents on the unit.

- Make sure that all driver settings are kept within the operating guidelines of the product. Never operate at higher resolutions or refresh rates than those specified by the vendor, and stay within the limits of the display adapter.

- Use any automatic energy-conservation features supported by the hardware and operating system. Employ a screen saver on older models that lack energy-saving features. If possible, do not turn the monitor on and off more than twice a day.

- When a monitor fails to operate or produces an improper image, check the following:

  1. Check all cables, including power and display.

  2. Check the front panel controls. Make any appropriate minor adjustments that are needed.

  3. Check and, if needed, reinstall the display drivers. Make sure all settings are within the required limits. Reinstall by returning to a plain 16-color, VGA display mode and adding resolution; then increase the refresh rate.

  4. Try another display adapter; then, if the problem is still unresolved, try another computer.

  5. If the monitor still shows problems, refer to a specialist for further tests.

Lesson Summary

The following points summarize the main elements of this lesson:

- The CRT is the main component of a monitor.

- Price, screen size, resolution, and refresh rate are primary considerations when purchasing a monitor.

- Resolution is a combination of horizontal pixels, vertical lines, and the refresh rate.

- Color depth indicates the maximum number of colors that can be shown.

- The higher the refresh rate, the more subtle the display will appear to the viewer, and the less flicker will be present.

- A CRT has very high voltage and should be serviced only by trained personnel.

Lesson 2: Display Adapters

The monitor is only half of a computer's display system; it must be matched to a display adapter (also commonly referred to as a graphics adapter, video card, or video controller). This lesson discusses the different types of display adapters and design issues that affect quality and performance.

After this lesson, you will be able to:

- Identify the different types of display adapters.
- Understand display memory and how it affects quality and performance.
- Select the right card for a monitor.

Estimated lesson time: 25 minutes

Evolution of the Display Adapter

The display adapter has gone through several major evolutions as the nature of PC computing has changed from simple word processing and number crunching, to the graphics-intensive world of Windows and multimedia.

The First PC Display Cards

The two "official" video cards for the early 8088-based IBM personal computers (the PC and XT) were matched to the limited capabilities of the early monitors. The *Monochrome Display Adapter (MDA)* offered a simple text-based monochrome display. This adapter produced an 80-character-wide row of text at a resolution of 720 x 350 pixels. Shortly after that, the *Color/Graphics Adapter (CGA)* card appeared. It provided up to four "colors" (actually, just different intensities of the monitor's active color: amber, green, or white). In four-color mode, CGA provided a resolution of 320 x 200 pixels. Using just two colors allowed a resolution of 640 x 200 pixels.

With the release of the *Enhanced Graphics Adapter (EGA)* card, the IMB PC AT became the first PC really able to use color. This adapter was an improved version of CGA, offering a top resolution of 640 x 350 with 16 colors in text-only mode, and 640 x 200 with two colors in graphics mode. The EGA also ushered in the era of video conflicts. It was not fully backward-compatible with CGA and MDA, and some programs would display improperly or even lock up the system. The MDA, CGA, and EGA cards all shared the same connection, a 9-pin d-shell male fitting.

The human eye can distinguish 256 shades of gray and about 17 million variations in color in a scene, the minimum required to produce true photographic realism on a screen. EGA did not even come close. It's aim was to offer the ability to incorporate color in pie charts and other forms of business graphics. Although the first graphics programs did arrive to make use of the EGA's graphics capability, serious computer graphics had to wait for better hardware.

Memory and the Arrival of the Display Coprocessor

A brief digression to explain pixel depth and video memory demands will help you understand what follows. Both the MDA and CGA adapters were equipped with 256 KB of *DRAM (dynamic random access memory)*. The amount of memory on a display card determines the amount of color and resolution that it can image and send to the monitor. As the desire for better graphics and color displays increased, so did the complexity of graphics cards and with them, memory requirements and cost.

Remember that the image on the monitor is a collection of dots called pixels. Each image placed on the screen requires that code be placed in the adapter's memory to describe how to draw it using those dots and their position in the grid. The MDA cards featured a *lookup table (LUT)* for each character. For MDA adapters, a code number for that symbol and each position on the grid was stored in memory, and the card had a chip set that told it how to construct each of those items in pixels. The MDA and CGA cards each had 265 KB of memory, just enough to map the screen at their maximum resolution. That's why the CGA card had two different modes: the more colors used, the more memory was required. When it displayed four colors instead of two, the resolution had to drop.

The MDA card was a 1-bit device. In other words, each pixel used 1 bit, valued either 0 or 1 to represent whether a given position on the screen (a pixel) was on or off. To represent colors or shades of gray, a card must use memory to describe color and intensity. This attribute of the display, measured in bits, is known as *color depth*. Color depth multiplied by resolution (the number of horizontal pixels multiplied by the number of vertical rows on the screen) determines the amount of memory needed on a given display adapter.

The adapters that followed the EGA cards to market all offered more colors and, very quickly thereafter, higher resolution. That, in turn, required more processing. The MDA, CGA, and EGA cards all relied on the host computer's CPU. Although that was sufficient in the days before widespread use of graphical interfaces and lots of color, with the advent of the graphical user interface (GUI), all that changed.

The new generation of display cards started the practice of including their own display coprocessors on-board. Coprocessors, which have their own memory, are tuned to handle tasks that would usually slow down the PC, and many display cards use bus mastering to reduce the amount of traffic on the system bus and to speed display performance. Video coprocessing is also called "hardware acceleration." This uses one or more techniques to speed up the drawing of the monitor image. For example, one or more screen elements can be described without using calculations that have to determine the placement of every pixel on the screen.

These new graphics chips were designed to do one thing: push pixels to the screen as efficiently as possible. At first, the cards that used them were expensive and often prone to memory conflicts with the host CPU. Their growing popularity led to rapid advances in design. In the mid-1990s, a new graphics card was introduced on the market almost every day, and a new processor almost every ten days.

Today, high-performance graphics adapters are the norm. While there is no longer a mad rush to market, the graphics coprocessor is a key element of fast Windows performance. Next, we return to our review of standards and see how the industry progressed to today's world of high-speed, full-color computing.

The Advent of Advanced Display Systems

Graphics artists, engineering designers, and users who work with photorealistic images need more than a coarse, 16-color display. To tap into this market, which was using $40,000 workstations, PC vendors needed more powerful display systems. IBM offered a short-lived and very complicated engineering display adapter, the *Professional Graphics Adapter (PGA)*. It required three ISA (Industry Standard Architecture) slots, and provided limited three-dimensional manipulation and 60 frames-per-second animation of a series of images. It was also very expensive and a dismal failure in the marketplace.

The reason was the advent of the *Video Graphics Array (VGA)* standard. All the preceding cards were digital devices; the VGA produced an analog signal. That required new cards, new monitors, and a 15-pin female connector. It allowed developers to produce cards that provided the user with up to 262,144 colors and resolutions up to 640 x 480.

The VGA card quickly became commonplace for a PC display system, and the race was on to produce cards with more colors, more resolution, and additional features. VESA (Video Electronics Standards Association) agreed on a standard list of display modes that extended VGA into the high-resolution world of color and high photographic quality we know today. The standard is known as SVGA (Super VGA). The SVGA sets specifications for resolution, refresh rates, and color depth for compatible adapters. On Pentium and later PCs, an SVGA adapter is the standard for display adapters. The minimum resolution needed for SVGA compatibility is 640 x 480 with 256 colors, and most modern adapters usually go far beyond that.

High-Color, True-Color, Photorealism, and Multimedia Displays

The SVGA specification for 256 shades of gray is in the basic SVGA specifications for true photographic reproduction of monochrome images; it's the number of shades that the human eye expects in a grayscale photo. Color requires the same number of shades for each color in the image to achieve the same level of visual realism. To get 256 shades requires an 8-bit memory address system inside the card, $2^8 = 256$. In the early days of SVGA, vendors worked to increase color quality without significantly increasing cost.

In color mode, an 8-bit card can't display all the colors in a full-color picture, so a LUT is used to figure the closest match to a hue that can't be represented directly. Although this method isn't ideal, it was for several years the state of the art on desktop PCs. Then, early in the age of the 486 processor, came the 16-bit SVGA card, which allowed approximately 64,000 colors. More bits require more memory, more processing requirements, a bigger LUT, and more money. These cards were tuned to be used with bigger monitors, 15 to 17 inches at 800 x 600 or 1024 x 768 resolution. The new systems were too expensive for average users, but graphics professionals and power users generated a large enough market to fuel development.

Short-Lived Standards

During the early days of VGA and SVGA, three other graphics-card standards were introduced by IBM for the PS/2. Although they never gained significant market share or full support among adapter developers, they did increase the demand for higher resolution and faster performance. The following list presents the highlights of the evolution of PC graphics standards:

- 8514/A, a 256 color competitor to VGA, with some hardware acceleration capability, offered 640 x 480 resolution in noninterlaced mode, and 1024 x 768 resolution at 43.3 Hz in interlaced mode.

- XGA, the eXtended Graphics Array, offered a resolution of 1024 x 768 in 8-bit (256-color) mode, and 640 x 480 in 16-bit mode (high-color). It came with 1 MB of memory and limited bus mastering.

- XGA/2 boosted the high-color mode to 1024.768 mode and increased the available refresh rates.

True Color Arrives

The SVGA adapters were a stepping stone; the growing popularity of Microsoft Windows and scanners pushed the demand for cards that could deliver color of photographic quality. In the early 1990s, several manufacturers introduced add-on cards that could be attached to SVGA cards to deliver 16.7 million colors. Soon after, stand-alone products that offered both SVGA resolution and true-color operation arrived. These adapters, known as true-color or 24-bit displays, come with coprocessors, lots of memory, and in true color mode have 256 shades (8-bits) available for each of three colors: red, green, and blue. By mixing them, the system can display 2^{24} colors. Eight bits are used in each of the three color channels. Some monitors use traditional 15-pin cables, and some use BNC bayonet cables, with a separate cable for each RGB color, and one each for vertical and horizontal synchronization. The latter are found on many high-performance systems.

True-color cards originally sold for $3,000 or so, but within two years were under $800; now they are available for $150 or less. To add value, the better cards now have TV output ports that send a National Television Standards Committee (NTSC) signal that can be used to record images from the monitor onto a VCR or TV set. Multimedia cards are equipped with a TV tuner, letting the owner view TV programs on the monitor, or watch DVD (digital video disc) movies on a PC. One reason for the dramatic lowering of prices and added features stems from the mass production of the coprocessors, which reduced their cost to the manufacturer; another factor is the decreasing cost of video memory.

Video Memory

As mentioned earlier, the amount of memory on a display adapter is a major factor in determining the screen resolution and color depth that the card can manage. Just as with system RAM, the video memory must be able to operate at a speed that can keep up with the processor, and the demands of the system clock. If the display adapter is too slow at updating the image on the monitor, the user is left waiting or is presented with jerky mouse movements and keystrokes that appear in delayed bursts rather than as typed.

Fast Page DRAM

Early video cards used *fast page-mode (FPM) DRAM*, a series of chips that were basically the same as the RAM used on the early PC's motherboard. This memory form was fine for MDA and CGA cards, and even the 8514/A, but with the higher resolution, increasing pixel depth, and faster refresh rates of VGA displays and beyond, vendors sought improved memory models to get the most performance out of their video coprocessors.

VRAM

Enter dual-ported memory in the form of *VRAM (Video RAM)*. It can read and write to both of its I/O ports at the same time. It allows the processor to talk to the system bus and the monitor simultaneously: fast, but very expensive. VRAM showed up in the best cards, but vendors wanted a low-cost option as well. Some vendors just used FPM (fast page-mode) DRAM, leaving the user to discover that, at high resolution, the display was too slow for efficient operation. These cards did sell well in the low-end market, as they allowed the budget-minded user to operate in low-color modes for most tasks, switching only to higher color depth for projects that required high-color or true-color mode. Users who regularly worked in high-color or true-color mode often would quickly consider an upgrade.

EDO DRAM

An alternate is *EDO (Extended Data Out) DRAM*, which can begin reading a new set of instructions before the preceding set of instructions has been completed. This is a common form of system DRAM that boosts performance to about 15 percent above conventional DRAM.

WRAM

WRAM (Window Random Access Memory, unrelated to the Microsoft operating system) is a high-speed variant of VRAM that costs less to produce and boosts performance by about 20 percent beyond regular VRAM. VRAM and WRAM have become the standard memory types for high-end display adapters.

SGRAM

The mid-range display market makes use of *SGRAM (Synchronous Graphics RAM)*. As the name implies, it is tuned to the graphics-card market, offering faster transfers than DRAM, but not as fast as VRAM and WRAM.

MDRAM

Multibank DRAM (MDRAM) is the final stop on our tour of memory acronyms. It uses interleaving (the dividing of video memory into 32KB parts that can be accessed concurrently) to allow faster memory input/output to the system without expensive dual-porting. It is also a more efficient type of chip that is practical to produce in sizes smaller than a full megabyte. A vendor can save money by just buying the amount needed to actually draw the screen. This saves about 1.75 MB per card for a resolution of 1024 x 768.

The table below lists the standard memory requirements for the most common resolutions and pixel depths used today. As pointed out in the previous paragraphs, keep in mind that the minimum amount of memory for MDRAM is usually less than for other types of RAM. Some graphics cards offer additional memory, and even incorporate different types of RAM on the same card. In such cases, some of the memory might be used for features other than merely imaging the picture to be sent to the CRT in pixels.

Display Drivers

Minimum Memory Requirements for Common Display Resolutions

Screen Resolution	8-Bit (256 color)	16-Bit (65-KB color)	24-Bit (16.7 Million Color)
640 x 480	512 KB	1 MB	1 MB
800 x 600	512 KB	1 MB	2 MB
1024 x 768	1 MB	2 MB	4 MB
1280 x 1024	2 MB	4 MB	4 MB
1600 x 1200	2 MB	4 MB	6 MB

Text-based adapters under MS-DOS don't need software drivers to interface between the operating system and the image on the screen. Windows, OS/2, and other graphics-rich environments do need drivers. In addition, controls are needed to adjust the refresh rate, resolution, and any special features the card offers. These needs are handled by the use of display drivers, a software layer that marries the card and monitor to the operating environment.

When installing a new card or operating system for a client, be sure to check the manufacturer's Web site for the latest display drivers. Not only will you reduce the likelihood of problems in using the new addition, but you will find that most new cards incorporate setup routines that can make quick work of getting a new display running.

Lesson Summary

The following points summarize the main elements of this lesson:

- Display adapters have gone through significant changes since the first PCs entered the marketplace.
- SVGA is considered the standard for applications today. The increasing use of graphical operating systems fueled the need for bigger monitors, higher resolution, and more colors.
- The coprocessor is a key factor in graphics-adapter performance.
- 24-bit cards are required to offer photorealistic color displays.
- Memory is a limiting factor in resolution and color depth.
- Drivers are the link between the display hardware and the operating system.
- The type and amount of memory have direct impact on video performance. Less memory means fewer colors, and slower memory types mean poorer performance.

Lesson 3: Choosing and Troubleshooting Display Systems

Matching the components of the display system to the needs of the computer owner is critical to user satisfaction when upgrading or purchasing a system. Knowing the basic steps to troubleshooting a display is key to effecting a quick repair when a component fails to operate properly. This lesson sets out the basic steps to follow in selecting the right class of display hardware for a client, proper care, and troubleshooting common problems.

After this lesson, you will be able to:

- Understand the basic criteria used to advise a customer about display-system options.
- Troubleshoot common display problems.

Estimated lesson time: 10 minutes

Helping a user pick the right display is relatively simple, despite the variety of monitors and adapters on the market.

The display is the part of the system the user interacts with and "sees" the most, and is a major factor in overall performance. Within limits, the buyer needs to get the best display possible.

The CRT size determines the maximum viewable area. For users who will work in only one program at a time, or who don't need high-resolution, a basic monitor should suffice. Graphics intensive applications and multitasking call for larger monitors with faster refresh rates, and display cards to match.

Users who will be using graphics-intensive applications designed for drawing and painting or for CAD and games, will prefer a fast graphics adapter, usually with VRAM or WRAM and high resolution and refresh rates.

Multimedia systems can benefit from cards that offer TV out (usually in the form of an RCA jack that lets the signal be displayed on a regular TV set using the NSTC format), TV tuner, and hardware DVD acceleration.

The usual trade-offs between cost and performance apply, but less than in the days of $3,000 high-end cards. Today, a user can purchase a fast, high-quality adapter for $250 to $300, and can purchase acceptable speed with true-color display for $150 without the extras and expensive memory types.

In recommending a display system, start with your customers' needs, followed by their preferences, and match the two as closely as possible to the available budget. Keep in mind that the display adapter is only part of the equation. Cost can be contained by using a smaller monitor or by accepting slower refresh rates. Cutting the cost excessively can leave clients with a display that does not support the tasks they perform, or that might lead to user eyestrain from the flicker that occurs at slower-than-acceptable refresh rates for the selected resolution.

Troubleshooting Display Systems

When MDA cards were standard, display systems gave technicians few problems. If the cable was properly attached and the monitor was working, the user got a picture. Today, the wide range of card options and the mix of resolutions, refresh rates, and operating systems lead the user to require help with displays more often.

In spite of the increasing complexity of display systems, most problems can be traced to a few common sources: cables improperly connected or damaged; lack of power; improper monitor adjustment; corrupt or incorrect drivers; and memory conflicts with other components. The following checklist can help you troubleshoot the common display problems you are likely to encounter:

- Cables: Verify that both the power and monitor-display adapter cables are properly attached. Failure to attach them properly can lead to having no picture at all or to an erratic image with incorrect colors. If the monitor cable has been removed and reseated, bent pins could be the problem. Make sure power is reaching both the PC and the monitor, and that they are turned on.

- Make sure that the adapter is properly seated in the expansion slot.

- Boot the system. If you get an image during the POST (power-on self test), but the computer does not load the operating system, suspect memory or driver problems. The same is true if the system repeatedly hangs during Windows operation. Try working in Safe mode. If that succeeds, reinstall the drivers and use Device Manager in the Control Panel System applet to resolve any hardware or memory conflicts.

- Reset the card to the 640 x 480 in 16-color VGA mode at the 60-Hz refresh rate. If the card works in Normal Mode, in Windows, at these settings, yet fails at higher resolution, color depth, or refresh rates—check the drivers and the capabilities of the display components.

Caution   Do not exceed the approved refresh rate for a monitor, even if the adapter can produce a higher scan of the screen. The result will be an unstable or unreadable image, which can damage a monitor very quickly.

If all these enumerated attempts fail, try a different display adapter and/or monitor, or test the hardware set on a different PC to see if one of the components has failed and must be repaired or replaced. In most cases, an out-of-warranty card is not worth repairing; a monitor that has failed should be examined by a specialist.

Lesson Summary

The following points summarize the main elements of this lesson:

- Choosing a new display system or upgrading components is a matter of matching the user's needs to the available hardware within the budget allowed.

- Price is not the sole issue when buying a display system. The quality of a display is a major factor in the performance and usability of the computer.

- PC display problems can cause a variety of symptoms on a system, from screen distortion to failure of the machine to boot.

- Using a step-by-step approach and walking through possible problem/solution combinations offers a quick way to resolve many display-related difficulties.

Chapter Summary

The following points summarize the key concepts in this chapter:

Displays

- The CRT (cathode-ray tube) is the main component of a monitor. The slender end of the cylinder contains an electron gun, and the larger end is the display screen.

- Resolution is a measurement of the detail of images produced by the monitor. It is measured in dots per inch.

- The monitor is the primary consumer of power in a computer system.

- A monitor can be dangerous and should never be worked on without being discharged first.

Video Cards

- The video card is the interface between the expansion bus and the monitor.

- The PGA, VGA, and SVGA monitors each use a 15-pin, three-row, female DB connector.

- Coprocessors are used to speed up graphics-intensive displays.

Video Memory

- The amount of video memory on a display card determines the maximum resolution/color depth that the video card can provide.

- Several types of DRAM are used for video memory; VRAM and WRAM are used for high-performance displays.

Review

1. Describe the three elements that make up one dot of color.

2. What is the advantage of interlacing? Is it worth doing?

3. Should a monitor be turned on and off, or left on all day?

4. What is the "standard" type of video card used with today's computers?

5. What is the formula for calculating the required memory for a monitor/video card combination?

6. What does CRT stand for?

7. What are HRR and VRR?

8. Define resolution.

9. What is bandwidth?

10. Why is it dangerous to open the monitor's cover?

11. Name four common sources of video problems.

12. Explain one similarity and one difference between VRAM and WRAM.

13. What is a raster?

14. What type of connector is used for an SVGA monitor?

C H A P T E R   1 2

Printers, Modems, and Cables

About This Chapter

This chapter expands on the discussion in Chapter 10, "Expansion Buses," by defining and exploring some of the PC's most popular add-ons. Printers are the second most common output devices (after monitors), and modems have moved from the exotic to the essential with the rise of the Internet. These two peripheral devices are connected to the computer through cabling and connectors, which are also covered in this chapter.

Before You Begin

Because the devices discussed in this chapter are connected to the computer by means of expansion buses, it is suggested that you review Chapter 10. Specifically, you should be familiar with the different types of expansion buses and how to configure IRQs and addresses.

Lesson 1: Printers

Printers are considered standard PC components; they are often bundled with computers and sold to consumers as part of a complete package. The most common add-ons, printers are manufactured in several popular forms. Like other devices, each type has unique advantages and disadvantages. This lesson covers all types and aspects of printers.

After this lesson, you will be able to:

- List the various types of printers and their advantages and disadvantages.
- Possess a working knowledge of laser printers.
- Troubleshoot printer problems.
- Identify the differences between parallel and serial printers.
- Understand expansion cards and how to use them.

Estimated lesson time: 45 minutes

Printer Basics

Printers have virtually replaced the typewriter in the contemporary office. The simplest printers are designed for the bargain-seeking home user, while the most complex are designed for production use, producing over 60 pages per minute and offering features like collating, stapling, and internal two-sided printing.

When evaluating printers, you should keep the following issues in mind:

- **Printer resolution:** Resolution is usually measured in dots per inch (dpi). This indicates the number of vertical and horizontal dots that can be printed; the higher the resolution, the better the print quality.
- **Speed:** This is usually given in pages printed per minute, where the page consists of plain text with five percent of the printable page covered in ink or toner.
- **Graphics and printer-language support:** If the device is used to print graphics, it should support one or more of the popular printer languages, such as Adobe PostScript and Hewlett Packard's LaserJet PCL (Printer Control Language).
- **Paper capacity:** The number and types of paper trays available, the number of pages that can be placed in them, and the sizes of pages that can be printed all vary widely among printers. Some smaller units hold as few as 10 sheets, while high-volume network printers hold several reams in different sizes. Some printers can also be set to automatically choose which tray to use based on the type of paper best suited for a job.

- **Duty Cycle:** This is the number of sheets of paper the printer is rated to print per month. It is based on a plain-text page with five percent coverage and does not include graphics.

- **Printer memory:** Laser printers that will be used to print complex graphics and full-color images require larger amounts of memory than those which print simple text only. In many cases, this memory can be added as an option.

- **Cost of paper:** Will a printer require special paper? Some printers must use special paper to produce high-quality (photo-quality) images or even good text. Some paper stocks are too porous for ink-jet printers and will cause the ink to smear or distort, causing a blurred image.

- **Cost of consumables:** When comparing the cost of various printers, be sure to calculate and compare the total cost per page for printing, rather than just the cost of a replacement ink or toner cartridge.

Common Printer Terms

You should familiarize yourself with these basic terms used with printer communication:

- **ASCII (American Standard Code for Information Interchange):** A standard code representing characters as numbers, used by most computers and printers.

- **Font:** A collection of characters and numbers in a given size, usually expressed in style name and size, and expressed in points (pts.)—for example, Times Roman 10 pt. bold (One point equals 1/72 inch.) Although many people think that bold and italic are variations of the same font, technically they are different fonts. Some printers are sold with limited fonts, such as bold only or no-bold varieties of the typefaces.

- **LPT (Line Printer Terminal) Port:** Term that describes parallel printer ports on a computer.

- **PCL:** Hewlett-Packard's printer-control language for printers.

- **PostScript:** The most common page-description language (PDL). A method of describing the contents of a page as scalable elements, rather than bitmapped pixels on the page. The printer is sent a plain ASCII file containing the PostScript program; the PostScript interpreter in the printer makes the conversion from scale to bitmap at print time.

- **Resolution Enhancement:** Technology that improves the appearance of images and other forms of graphics by using such techniques as modifying tonal ranges, improving halftone placement, and smoothing the jagged edges of curves.

- **Portrait:** The vertical orientation of printing on a piece of paper so that the text or image is printed across the 8.5-inch width of the paper.

- **Landscape:** The horizontal orientation of printing on a piece of paper so that the text or image is printed across the 11-inch width of the paper.

- **Duplexing:** The ability to print on both sides of a page. This cuts operating costs and allows users to create two-sided documents quickly.

Printer Ports

Although some printers make use of serial, SCSI (Small Computer System Interface), and other interfaces to communicate with a PC, most today use the standard parallel printer port, or one of its bidirectional variations. Two other common communication methods are the USB (universal serial bus), covered in Chapter 10, "Expansion Buses," and a network interface.

The standard parallel port uses cable with a 25-pin female connector on one end and a Centronics-compatible D-Shell fitting on the other. You simply connect the Centronics-compatible end of the printer cable to the printer and attach the 25-pin plug to an LPT port on the computer. (Cables and connectors are discussed in detail later in Lesson 3.) Although parallel ports are relatively trouble-free, they have some disadvantages:

- The data transfer rate is 150 KB. This is slow compared to network cards and other high-speed interfaces.

- Parallel communication consumes system resources because it relies on the PC's system bus and CPU for transport and management.

- There are no standards for parallel cables or ports. Although parallel port configurations follow a few common practices, this form of communication remains the source of compatibility problems.

- Parallel cables usually have a maximum effective length of 10 feet. This can be extended by using a booster device, but at added cost.

Impact Printers

In the early days of PC printing, the most commons forms of printers were dot-matrix and daisy-wheel designs. Both these designs create an impression by striking an inked ribbon with enough force to place ink on the page. In this, they function very much like typewriters. Except for a few special cases, impact printers (one is shown in Figure 12.1) have been replaced by ink and laser technology.

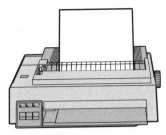

Figure 12.1   Impact printer

Dot-Matrix Printers

The most popular impact printer is the dot-matrix variety. Dot-matrix printers form characters as raster images on paper by pressing pins onto an inked ribbon, which then is pressed onto paper. Dot-matrix printers use an array of pins (commonly 9 or 24 pins) which are made of stiff wire. The higher the number of pins, the more dots per square inch and the higher the print quality. The pins are held in a print head that travels on a rail in front of a roller that transports the paper. The pins are controlled by electromagnets; dots are created when power is applied to selected electromagnets in the print head, forcing the desired pin away from a magnet in the print head. The pins strike an inked ribbon, which then strikes the paper. As the individual dots are struck, a character is formed. Each character produced by the print head is made up of several rows and columns of dots. (See Figure 12.2.) High-resolution dot-matrix printers use more dots to form one character.

The dot-matrix printer is still used in some commercial environments where its ability to inexpensively create multipage forms is appreciated. The pins have enough impact to be used with carbon paper, making it easy to obtain two or more copies so that one can be given to a customer or kept for accounting, filing, or other purposes.

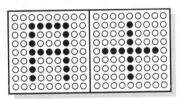

Figure 12.2   Dot-matrix letters formed from dots.

Maintaining a dot-matrix printer is very simple:

- Change the ribbon.
- Keep the printer clean.
- Keep the print head clean.
- Replace the print head if it fails.

Troubleshooting a dot-matrix printer usually requires a reference manual. There are so many printers on the market that no single guide will suffice to help a computer technician troubleshoot all printer problems. If a manual for a particular printer is unavailable, check the printer itself for instructions (sometimes there are diagrams inside the printer). Usually, a thorough inspection of the mechanical parts will uncover the problem. The following table lists common problems encountered with dot-matrix printers, and possible causes.

Symptom	Possible Cause
Printer does not function at all.	No AC power is getting to printer. Fuse is blown.
Device does not print although power is on.	Printer is not online. Printer is out of paper. Printer cable is disconnected.
Printer won't go online.	Printer is out of paper. (Check connections.)
Paper slips around platen.	Paper is not being gripped properly. (Adjust paper-feed selector for size and type of paper.)
Head moves, but does not print.	Ribbon is not installed properly or is out of ink.
Head tears paper as it moves.	Pins are not operating properly. (Check pins; if any are frozen, the head needs to be replaced.)
Paper bunches up around platen.	There is no reverse tension on paper.
Paper has "dimples."	Paper is misaligned, or the tractor feed wheels are not locked in place.
"Paper/Error" indicator flashes continuously.	There is an overload condition.
Printout is double-spaced or there is no spacing between lines.	Printer configuration switch is improperly set. (Make sure it isn't set to output a carriage return or linefeed after each line.)
Printer cannot print ASCII characters above code 127.	Printer configuration switch is improperly set.
Print mode cannot be changed.	Printer configuration switch is improperly set.

Daisy-Wheel Printers

Once popular, the daisy-wheel printer is now a rare form of impact printer. A daisy-wheel device prints characters one at a time using a circular printer element that produces letter-quality output. Each printer element contains characters of only one font, which means that every time you want to change fonts (for example, from Courier to Times Roman), you must manually change the element. In this respect, these printers are similar to some electric typewriters; these devices produced clean type, along with lots of noise and often a great deal of vibration. If a client has a daisy-wheel printer that needs repair or replacement, consider recommending a laser printer instead.

Thermal Printers

A thermal printer heats spots on paper with an array of tiny, fast-acting heating elements. At one time, these printers were an inexpensive alternative to dot-matrix printers for the low-end, low-volume market, even though their paper costs were much higher. Early fax machines, today's non-plain-paper fax machines, and some label makers are examples of thermal printers. For uses other than faxing, this type of printer is rare, too. You might find it used to print simple sales receipts.

Thermal Wax-Transfer Printers

A thermal wax-transfer printer uses heat to bond a wax-based pigment to paper. These printers usually have resolutions of 150 or 300 dpi. At one time, these devices were used for color graphics and photo-reproduction; more recently, they have been replaced by ink-jet and color laser printers, which are less expensive to own and operate.

The bewildering assortment of transport rollers, heating arrays, and electronics make field repair of these printers impractical, except by a specially trained technician equipped with special tools.

Ink-Jet Printers

 Run the **inkjet** video located in the **demos** folder on the CD accompanying this book to view a presentation of ink-jet printers.

Ink-jet printers have replaced dot-matrix printers, in the low-end market, and thermal wax printers for the low-end color market. Many computer manufacturers and large computer stores offer an ink-jet printer as part of a computer-system package deal.

Ink-jet printers spray ink onto paper in order to form images. They produce good-quality printing and—compared to dot-matrix and wax printers—they are relatively fast. They also require little maintenance beyond cleaning and ink-cartridge replacement. What makes them so attractive is their ability to easily produce color as well as standard black-and-white images.

Important   When installing a new ink-jet cartridge or replacing the cartridge on an existing ink-jet printer, follow the instructions carefully! The cartridge is not just a simple ink container. It must be properly pressurized, and there are sensors on the unit (small metal plates) that must line up with contacts on the cartridge transport. Read the product manual for details.

When recommending an ink-jet printer, the cost of printing as well as the cost of the printer itself should be considered. The cartridges are usually more expensive per page than those for a laser printer.

You might find it cost-effective to equip an office with more than one kind of printer. Many offices have a heavy-duty, high-speed, black-and-white laser printer for text printing, an aging dot-matrix printer for forms and labels, and a color ink-jet printer for graphics. It is also common to find several printers available on the local office network.

If a printer fails to operate, the first step in determining the source of the problem is to decide if the problem lies with the printer or with the computer. The best place to start is at the printer, with a visual inspection. Look for simple issues, like a tray out of paper or a paper jam. Most printers have either an LED (light-emitting diode) panel or lights that warn of common problems.

If visual inspection of the printer does not turn up an obvious fault, proceed to the printer's self-test program. In most cases, you can initiate this routine by holding down a specified combination of control keys on the printer (check the owner's manual for diagnostic procedures) while you turn it on. If a test page prints successfully, the problem is most likely associated with the computer, the cabling, or the network. The following table lists some typical problems encountered with ink-jet printers and their possible causes.

Symptom	Possible Cause
Power is on but device does not print.	Printer is not online. Printer is out of paper.
Printer won't go online after user has replaced ink cartridge.	Cartridge is installed incorrectly. Printer cable is disconnected.
Printer is plugged in, but all indicator lights are off and the printer appears to be dead.	Check the drive mechanisms and motors for signs of binding. They might need to be replaced. Fuse is blown. (Check the power supply's fuse and replace with on of the same type and rating, if necessary.)
Print head does not print.	Ink reservoirs are empty. (Check the ink supply and replace the ink cartridge as necessary.)
Paper does not advance.	Paper-handling hardware is jammed. (Check the control panel to confirm that the printer is online. If so, you will need to inspect the paper-handling motor and gear train. You can do this by setting the printer offline and pressing down the form-feed button.)

Laser Printers

Run the **laser** video located in the **demos** folder on the CD accompanying this book to view a presentation of laser printers.

The laser printer has become the dominant form of computer output device, with models ranging from personal, low-volume desktop printers to behemoths that fill half a room and serve hundreds of users, churning out reams of pages every day.

All laser printers follow one basic engine design, similar to the ones used in most office copiers. They are non-impact devices that precisely place a fine plastic powder (the toner) on paper. Although they cost more to purchase than most ink-jet printers, they are much cheaper to operate per page, and the "ink" is permanent. (Most ink-jet images are, at best, water-resistant.)

Primary Components of a Laser Printer

A laser printer is a combination of mechanical and electronic components. Although the internal workings of the printer generally are not a concern of the average PC technician, you should be familiar with the parts and processes involved in their operation.

Paper Transport

The paper path for laser printers ranges from a simple, straight path to the complicated turns of devices with options such as duplexers, mailboxes, and finishing tools like collators and staplers. The goal is the same for all these devices—to move the paper from a supply bin to the engine where the image is laid on the paper and fixed to it, and then to a hopper for delivery to the user. Most printers handle a set range of paper stocks and sizes in the normal paper path, and a more extensive range (usually heavier paper or labels) that can be sent though a second manual feed, one sheet at a time. When users fail to follow the guidelines for the allowed stocks, paper jams often result.

Logic Circuits

Laser printers usually have a motherboard much like that of a PC, complete with CPU, memory, BIOS, and ROM modules containing printer languages and fonts. Advanced models often employ a hard disk drive and its controller, a network adapter, a SCSI host adapter, and secondary cards for finishing options. When upgrading a printer, check for any updates to the BIOS, additional memory requirements for new options, and firmware revisions.

User Interface

The basic laser printer often offers little more than a "power on" LED and a second light to indicate an error condition. Advanced models have LED panels with menus, control buttons, and an array of status LEDs.

Toner and Toner Cartridges

To reduce maintenance costs, laser printers use disposable cartridges and other parts that need periodic replacement. The primary consumable is toner, a very fine plastic powder bonded to iron particles. The printer cartridge also holds the toner cylinder, and often the photosensitive drum. The cartridge requires replacement when the level of toner is too low to produce a uniform, dark print. Some "starter" cartridges shipped with a new printer print only 750 sheets or so, while high-capacity units can generate 12,000 or more pages. Keep in mind that what constitutes a "page" is based on a five-percent coverage area, less than a standard letter and far below that of a page of graphics or images.

Photosensitive Drum

The photosensitive drum is a key component and usually is a part of the toner cartridge. The drum is an aluminum cylinder that is coated with a photosensitive compound and electrically charged. It captures the image to be printed on the page and also attracts the toner which is to be placed on the page.

Important   The drum should not be exposed to any more light than is absolutely necessary. Such exposure will shorten its useful life. The surface must also be kept free of fingerprints, dust, and scratches. If these are present, they will cause imperfections on any prints made with the drum. The best way to ensure a clean drum is to install it quickly and carefully and leave it in place until it must be replaced.

The Laser

The laser beam paints the image of the printed page on the drum. Before the laser is fired, the entire surface of the photosensitive drum, as well as the paper, are given an electrical charge carried by a pair of fine wires.

Primary Corona

The primary corona charges the photosensitive particles on the surface of the drum.

Transfer Corona

The transfer corona charges the surface of the paper just before it reaches the toner area.

Fuser Rollers

The toner must now be permanently attached to the paper to make the image permanent. The fuser rollers—a heated roller and an opposing pressure roller—fuse toner onto the page. The heated roller employs a nonstick coating to keep the toner from sticking to it. The occasional cycling heard in many laser printers is generated when the fuser rollers are advanced a quarter turn or so to avoid becoming overheated.

Erase Lamp

This bathes the drum in light to neutralize the electrical charge on the drum, allowing any remaining particles to be removed before the next print is made.

Power Supply

Laser printers use a lot of power and so should not be connected to a UPS (uninterruptible power supply) device. The high voltage requirements of the imaging engine and heater will often trip a UPS. In addition to the motors and laser print heads, the printer also has a low DC voltage converter as part of the power package for powering its motherboard, display panel, and other more traditional electronic components.

Drivers and Software

Most laser printers ship with a variety of software that includes the basic drivers that communicate with the operating system, diagnostic programs, and advanced programs that allow full control of all options as well as real-time status reporting. A recent trend in network laser printing is allowing print-management tools and printing to work over the Internet. A user can send a print job to an Internet site or manage a remote print job using a Web browser.

The Mechanics of Laser Printing

Now that you know the major parts of the printer, here's a quick survey of how the laser printer works and the components needed to handle each task. (Some of these tasks occur simultaneously in actual printing.)

Communicating

The following sequence occurs as computer-to-printer communication is established:

1. The operating system sends a request to the printer and is informed that the printer is online and ready to accept data.

2. The PC starts sending data.

3. During the printing process, the printer—if it is able to handle bidirectional communications—informs the computer of any problems encountered while handling the print job so the user can address the complaint. These messages might include an out-of-paper condition, paper jam, or low toner.

4. After the entire job has been sent, the printer acknowledges the receipt of all data and waits for the next request.

Many printers can store more than one job, and network printers often have hard disk drives that can hold common jobs to allow the printer to print without being connected to a PC.

Warming Up

The printer might delay accepting the job or printing the first page while it warms up its rollers and the imaging drum.

Raster-Image Processing

The image (text and graphics) to be made is converted into a series of raster lines that can be drawn much the same way as the image is formed on the PC's monitor. The data is stored in memory, waiting for the send command.

Paper Feeding

The printer moves a sheet of paper from the proper tray onto a series of rollers, through the imaging and fixing areas, and to the output hopper.

Drum Cleaning and Charging

Any residual toner from past jobs is scraped from the printer's photosensitive drum. A fine wire (the primary corona) produces a negative electrical charge across the entire face of the drum. The image is set in raster lines as a series of fine dots on the drum.

Imaging the Drum

The information from the raster-image processor is read from memory and sent to the print engine, one line at a time. The laser sets a positive charge in the areas of the image to be filled with toner.

Transferring Toner to the Drum

A film of fine plastic power is placed on the toner transfer roller, which is turning close to the photosensitive drum. This toner is then attracted to the positively charged areas of the drum.

Transferring Toner to the Paper

The corona wire places a positive electrical charge on the paper as it moves close to the drum. The toner is attracted to the page, forming an image.

Fusing the Toner

The page passes through a pair of rollers. The roller on the side toward the toner that has been placed on the page is heated just enough to melt the plastic toner particles onto the page without smearing. The roller on the other side supplies the needed pressure.

Finishing and Output

After the toner has been fused to the paper, the next step is usually to transport the page to the output tray. However, if other options—such as a duplexer or collator—are available, the page might be routed through a separate path, based on the options for the current print job, and then sent out to the tray. Figure 12.3 shows the process of laser printing.

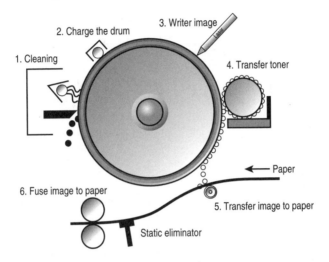

Figure 12.3   The laser printing process

Laser Printer Resolution

The quality of a laser printer is directly related to its resolution, given in dpi. Horizontal resolution is determined by how fine a line can be focused on the drum by the laser (the number of dpi across the page); vertical resolution is based on the increment by which the photosensitive drum is turned for each pass of the raster line.

In most cases, resolution is given as a single number, indicating that both the horizontal and vertical increments are the same. The first laser printers offered 300 dpi resolution; printers today commonly offer 600 and 1200 dpi. The higher the number, the sharper the detail and the more memory required to image the page. In general, the human eye cannot distinguish between 600 dpi and 1200 dpi text on bond paper, but the higher resolution does benefit images and drawings by providing a smoother transition between tones and curved lines.

Tip   Many laser printers offer a "toner saver" that uses a lower-resolution draft mode, thereby extending the life of a toner cartridge by placing less toner on each page.

Troubleshooting Laser Printer Problems

Properly installed laser printers are quite reliable when operated and maintained within the guidelines set by the manufacturer. Still, given the combination of mechanical parts, the variety of steps in printing, and the innovative ways some users use the printer, problems do occur. The following table lists a few problems that can be encountered with laser printing and their possible causes.

Symptom	Possible Cause
Ghost images appear at regular intervals on the printed page.	Photosensitive drum is not fully discharged. Previous images used too much toner, and the supply of charged toner is either insufficient or not adequately charged to transfer to the drum.
Light ghosting appears on pages.	Previous page(s) used too much toner; therefore, the drum could not be properly charged for the image (called developer starvation).
Dark ghosting appears on pages.	Drum is damaged.
Page is completely black.	Primary corona, laser scanning module, or main central board has failed.
Random black spots or streaks appear on page.	Drum was improperly cleaned; residual particles remain on drum.
Marks appear on every page.	Drum is damaged and must be replaced.
Printing is too light (appears in a column-like streak).	Toner is low.
Memory overflow error.	Not enough RAM—printing resolution too high.
Characters are incomplete.	Print density is incorrect. (Adjust the darkness setting on the toner cartridge.)
Mass of melted plastic is spit out.	Wrong transparency material is used (see section on transparency, later in this lesson).
Pages are creased.	Paper type is incorrect.
Characters are warped, overprinted, or poorly formed.	There is a problem with the paper or other media or with the hardware. (For media: avoid paper that is too rough or too smooth. Paper that is too rough interferes with fusing of characters and their definition. If the paper is too smooth, it can feed improperly, causing distorted or overwritten characters. For hardware: run the self-test to check for connectivity and configuration problems.)
After clearing a paper jam from the tray, printer still indicates a paper jam.	Printer has not reset. (Open and close the cover.)
Paper continues to jam.	Problem with the pickup area, turning area, and registration (alignment) area. (Look for worn parts or debris.)

Ghosting

The term ghosting is used to describe unwanted images that are produced on the printed page at regular intervals. This usually occurs when the drum is not fully discharging or is being saturated with excess toner. One remedy is to print one or two totally black pages; this will pull the toner off on the drum and onto the paper. If the problem persists, try using a new toner cartridge (if the toner is part of the cartridge assembly). If those steps fail, the printer will require servicing by a trained technician, who is able to adjust the internal settings that regulate toner levels during printing.

Printing on Transparencies

When printing on transparencies, use only materials approved for laser printers. Laser printers generate far more heat than other types of printers—using the wrong material can cause serious damage.

Caution   Printing on transparencies can be hazardous to the printer. Improper material might melt and damage the internal components of a laser printer.

Hardware Problems

Most laser printers offer the ability to print a page or more of diagnostic and configuration information. If you suspect a hardware problem, print these sheets. Check for status lights, menu warnings, or error messages. The manual should list steps to be taken in troubleshooting the common problems that are indicated by the printer's display. The variety of error codes that exist, the result of different options on printers, even from the same vendor, makes a detailed listing beyond the scope of this volume and beyond the skills required for the exam. Refer to the printer's manual for details concerning codes for a given printer.

Lesson Summary

The following points summarize the main elements of this lesson:

- Dot-matrix, ink-jet, and laser printers are the most widely used printers today.

- As a computer technician, you can expect to encounter printing problems.

- The key components of a laser printer are the power supply, photosensitive drum, eraser lamp, primary corona, laser, transfer corona, logic circuits, paper transport, and fuser.

- Laser printing involves several steps: preparing the drum, imaging the page in memory, placing toner, and heating that toner to fix it on the page.

Lesson 2: Modems

Once an expensive and complicated option, the modem is now an integral part of the modern PC, thanks to the popularity of the Internet, faxes, and e-mail.

After this lesson, you will be able to:

- Define how modems transmit data.
- Define the difference between serial and parallel data transfer.
- Install a modem.
- Troubleshoot basic modem and communication problems.
- Set up and test a modem.

Estimated lesson time: 45 minutes

Modem Basics

A modem is a peripheral device that enables computers to communicate with each other over conventional telephone lines, ISDN cable lines, or even without wires. The word *modem* comes from combining the words MOdulator and DEModulator. In radio parlance, to *modulate* a signal is to change the frequency (FM) or amplitude (AM) of a carrier (fixed signal) by superimposing a code (voice or other information) on top of the signal. The reverse is to *demodulate*, to remove the fixed signal and have the superimposed code remain. For many years, this has been an effective way to communicate over long distances, using both wires and radio waves.

The following table defines some basic terms used with modem communication.

Term	Definition
Baud rate	The number of events, or signal changes, that occur in one second. It was used as an early measurement of how fast a modem can send data, because at that time, modems transmitted data at a speed equal to the baud rate (one bit per cycle). Today's high-speed modems use complex signals to send more data; therefore, data transfer can exceed baud rate. The baud rate is limited by the capability of copper wires to transmit signals.
bps	Stands for bits per second—the speed at which a modem transmits data. Typical rates are 14,400; 28,800; 33,600; and 56,600 bps. These numbers represent the actual number of data bits that can be transmitted per second.
Browser	Software used to explore sites on the World Wide Web using the HyperText Transfer Protocol (HTTP).

continued

Term	Definition
Bulletin board service (BBS)	Interactive software that offers the ability log directly onto a remote computer to post and retrieve messages, and to upload and download files. Some BBSs offer the opportunity to chat live with other members who are online at the same time. The Internet has diminished the importance of BBS software.
Download	The act of transferring a file from a remote computer (host) to a local computer (client). When downloading, you are receiving a file.
DTMF	Stands for dual-tone multifrequency, the technology behind the tones of a touchtone phone.
Internet	A worldwide, online network that links computers by means of the TCP/IP protocol. (See entry for TCP/IP later in this table.)
Internet server	A computer/software combination that provides a gateway and supporting services for linking other computers to the Internet.
IP	Stands for Internet Protocol—the network protocols used to define how data is transmitted on the Internet.
IP address	Stands for Internet Protocol address—a unique, 32-bit address that identifies every network and host on the Internet. (A host is the TCP/IP network interface within the computer, not the computer itself; a computer with more than one network interface card—NIC—can have more than one IP address, one for each card.)
ISDN	Stands for Integrated Services Digital Network, a digital telephone connection like a modem that uses digital links and offers speeds about five times that of an analog modem. The ISDN system is a packet system that can also handle voice communication.
ISP	Stands for Internet service provider—a host computer that you can dial into over a modem to connect to the Internet.
Logging on	The process of sending the appropriate signals and gaining access to a remote computer over a modem or other remote connection.
Modem	A device for converting a computer's digital data stream to and from an analog form so that it can be sent over a telephone line.
Offline	Status of a computer that is not connected to another device over a modem or other telecommunications device.
Offline reader	A program designed to display e-mail messages or other information that has been downloaded to one computer from another.

(continued)

continued

Term	Definition
Online	An active connection between two computers, making possible the exchange of data.
POTS	Stands for Plain Old Telephone Service, a common term that denotes the basic analog phone network as compared to newer digital networks used for packet transfer of data.
Protocol	A set of rules that govern the transfer and verification of data between two or more systems.
Proxy server	A computer/modem/software combination that manages Internet traffic to and from a local area network (LAN) and can provide other features, such as document caching and access control.
Settings (modem)	Configuration required by the telecommunications software in order for data to be transmitted. Usually 8 bits, no parity, 1 stop bit (8N1) will work. Some BBSs require special terminal emulation, a software configuration that mimics the operation of proprietary mainframe terminals like the VT100.
Sysop	The system operator of a BBS (pronounced SIS-op).
TCP/IP	Stands for Transmission Control Protocol/Internet Protocol—the name given to a collection of protocols that were designed in the 1970s for use on the large-scale, mixed-platform environment that became the Internet.
Telecommunications	The ability to transmit data over telephone lines to a remote computer. Often abbreviated as "telecom."
Telecommunications software	An application that allows two computers to communicate with each other. Both computers must use compatible software for communication to take place.
Upload	The ability to transfer a file from a local computer to a remote computer. When uploading, you are sending a file to another computer.
Webmaster	A person who manages a Web site on the Internet's World Wide Web. The Webmaster's duties are analogous to those of a BBS.

Communication

Two basic problems arise from using modems to transmit data. The first problem is that, as we saw in Chapter 4, computers transfer data using 8, 16, or 32 parallel wires or buses, while telephone systems use only two wires. (See Figure 12.4)

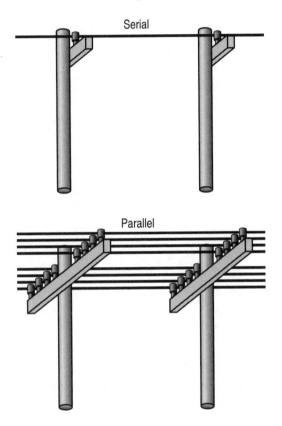

Figure 12.4   Serial and parallel communication

The second problem is that telephone and radio systems use analog signals (based on waveforms), and computers use digital signals, either on or off, as shown in Figure 12.5.

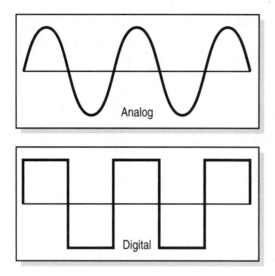

Figure 12.5   Analog and digital signals

A modem resolves both of these problems by acting as an analog-to-digital (A/D) converter as well as a modulator/demodulator.

Serial/Parallel Conversion

Virtually all personal computers use a family of chips produced by National Semiconductor to run serial ports. Known as UARTs (universal asynchronous receiver-transmitters), these chips convert an 8-bit wide parallel data path to a 1-bit wide serial path.

The UART has gone through several major changes during the PC era, and there are many different types of UARTs with different functions. The following table lists several of the more common ones.

Chip	Description
INS8250	The original chip used in the IBM PC, the INS8250 operated at speeds up to 56 kilobits per second (Kbps). The 8250A and 8250B incorporated fixes for minor bugs in the original design, but the 8250 series was unreliable at speeds over 9600 bps.
16450	Designed for 286-based PCs, the 16450 is the first UART that reliably operated at 9600 bps and above.
16550	The 16550 allowed use of more than one DMA channel to achieve improved throughput over the 16450.
16550A	An improved version of the 16550, the 16550A is the only UART installed on today's computers. It adds support for First in-First Out (FIFO) communication. This is the only UART that should be installed in current PCs or add-on cards that are used to provide expansion card-based COM ports.

Determining which UART chip is installed in a computer can be easily accomplished by using the MSD (Microsoft Diagnostics) utility that comes with MS-DOS, Windows 3.x, and Windows 95 and Windows 98 (Windows Device Manager). Select COM Ports from the MSD main menu. (See Figure 12.6.)

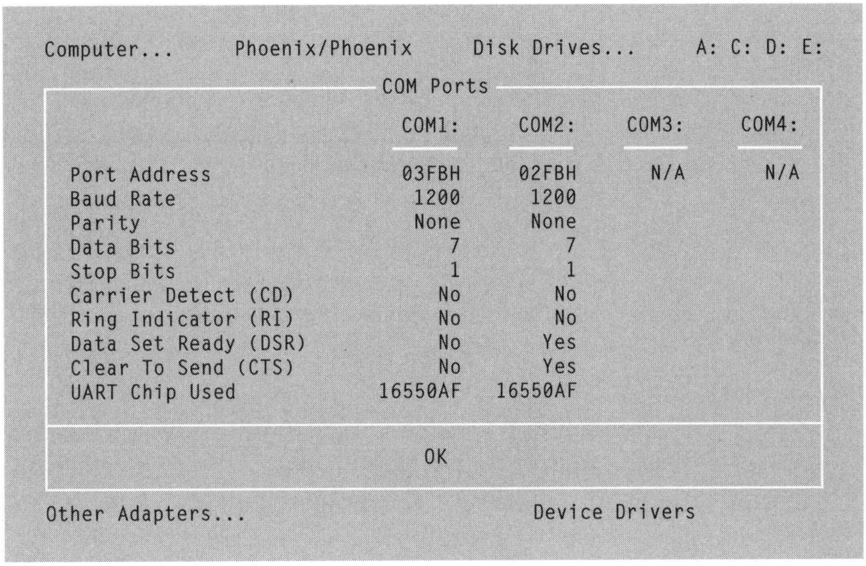

```
Computer...      Phoenix/Phoenix      Disk Drives...      A: C: D: E:
                          COM Ports
                         COM1:     COM2:     COM3:     COM4:

    Port Address         03FBH     02FBH      N/A       N/A
    Baud Rate            1200      1200
    Parity               None      None
    Data Bits            7         7
    Stop Bits            1         1
    Carrier Detect (CD)  No        No
    Ring Indicator (RI)  No        No
    Data Set Ready (DSR) No        Yes
    Clear To Send (CTS)  No        Yes
    UART Chip Used       16550AF   16550AF

                           OK

Other Adapters...                    Device Drivers
```

Figure 12.6 MSD utility—COM ports

Digital Communication

The movement of data from one computer to another over telephone lines is a multistep process. The first step is to convert the data from parallel to serial form. Then the digital information must be broken into uniquely marked packets (this allows the receiving computer to distinguish one byte from another).

Asynchronous Communication

Asynchronous communication is any data transmission that does not link the two devices with a common data clock. This is useful because the length of time between sending a packet and its receipt on the other end can vary between the communicating devices. A signal called a *start bit* is sent at the beginning of each segment, and a signal called a *stop bit* is sent at the end. These let the receiving device note the boundaries (beginning and end) of a transmission packet. Early PC modems were almost always asynchronous devices operating at speeds of no more than 18,000 bits per second.

Synchronous Communication

Synchronous communication sends data blocks at strictly timed intervals that are monitored at both ends. Modems operating at speeds up to 56 Kbps over standard telephone audio lines are usually synchronous devices.

Many protocols are used for PC-to-PC modem communication. Kermit, Xmodem, Ymodem, and Zmodem are four common ones. The following is a summary of how these protocols work:

1. Before a modem sends any data, a communication link must be established. To do this, the modem sends a series of standardized bytes—called sync bytes—to the device it is to communicate with.

2. The modem on the other end receives the sync bytes.

3. The receiving modem perceives that it is receiving sync-byte data and synchronizes with the incoming data.

4. After sending the sync bytes, the sending modem adds a start-of-text (STX) character.

5. The data bytes are sent. The data in synchronous transmission is processed in packets or in blocks of fixed length, depending on the protocol used.

6. Each packet ends with an end-of-text (ETX) character and two error-checking characters called CRC (cyclical redundancy check) characters or BCCs (block check characters).

7. The receiver then responds with an ACK—acknowledgment character—if the data is good, or a NAK—negative acknowledgment—if transmission errors have occurred.

Note   In asynchronous communication, the receiving modem does not respond—it just reads the data and acts on it—unless a timing error is reported. In synchronous modes the receiving modem *must* respond.

Parity

Asynchronous communication packets have an optional *parity* bit that is used for error detection. The parity bit is used by the receiving port to verify whether the data is intact or has been corrupted. There are two types of parity:

- **Even parity**: The sending computer counts the 1s in the data part of the packet; if the number of 1s is even, the parity bit is 0—this makes the total number of bits even. If the number of 1s in the data part of the packet is odd, the parity bit is set to 1—again making the total number of bits even. The receiving port counts the data bits and compares its answer to the parity bit. If the two fail to match, an error is reported, and a request to retransmit the packet is passed to the sending computer.

- **Odd parity**: This works in exactly the same way as even parity, except that the total number of bits must be odd.

The use of parity bits is optional. The quality of data transmission and telephone lines has improved to the extent that parity bits are no longer required. However, if data accuracy is critical and/or telephone-line quality is questionable, use parity.

Hardware

Now that we've seen how modems send and receive data, we examine the hardware involved.

Internal Modems

The entire modem and even its serial port can be accommodated on a single expansion card. This configuration offers lower cost than that of an external modem, but is more prone to compatibility problems with either the on-board UART or the COM port IRQs.

USB Modems

Most new PCs offer two universal serial bus (USB) ports, either of which can be used to attach a modem. USB is a hot swap (the device can be added or removed without powering down the PC), Plug and Play interface (See Chapter 10, "Expansion Buses,") well suited to this task. To install a modem this way, usually all that is required is to attach a USB cable between the modem and PC, connect the phone-line cable between the modem and a wall jack, and load the modem-driver software from the manufacturer's configuration disk when prompted.

External Analog Modems

The original modems used a pair of cups to cradle a telephone handset over a built-in speaker and microphone; in this way, the modem would send and receive tones acoustically, and the telephone handset would relay the tones. Today, the external modem is usually a rectangular box with a row of status lights on the front, a speaker to give audible feedback, and a number of ports on the back. Two of those ports are telephone jacks—one to connect to the wall line and the other to pass the telephone signal to a phone for regular voice conversations when the modem is not in data mode. A third port on the back of the modem is a serial port using a standard 25-pin RS-232 connector that passes data to and from a serial port on the PC.

ISDN Terminal Adapters

Until about 30 years ago, the North American telephone network was an analog system connecting phones by means of a grid of copper wires. Today, the long line sections (intercity telecom lines) are part of a packet-based, digital switching system, but the final run from the local switch to most homes is the aged copper-wire POTS line.

ISDN is an all-digital phone connection that uses special high-quality phone lines to ensure clean, high-speed, data transfers—directly to the user's home or business. Both voice and data are carried by bearer channels (B channels) with a maximum speed per channel of 64 Kbps. A companion data channel (D channel) handles signaling at 16 Kbps (or 64 Kbps, depending on service provided by the carrier).

Note   In the context of ISDN communications, "K" means 1000; in other computing contexts, "K" means 1024.

ISDN connections do not make use of a modem. Instead, a device called a terminal adapter (TA) serves as the interface for both computers and analog phones served in a location. Most small-business and residential customers make use of a TA that has a 25-pin serial connection to attach to a computer serial port and that also provides analog telephone connections for two lines.

ISDN is complicated to install and should be set up using the help of a vendor or the local telephone company. After installation, ISDN functions like a high-speed modem, offering not only faster data transfers, but faster connections to remote ISDN providers such as ISPs. Because each TA unit is completely digital, there is no testing of the nature of the remote source by the hardware to establish the maximum connection rate (as with a modem), and links are typically established in under three seconds.

The RS-232 port

External modems and TAs communicate with their host computers by means of an RS-232 communications port. The RS-232 standard was developed by the Electronics Industry Association (EIA) for low-speed data communication; the standard defines a series of signals that are sent between two telecommunications devices to indicate line and transmission status. The following table shows the most common signals.

Signal	Definition
CTS	Clear to Send
DCD	Data Carrier Detected
DSR	Data Set Ready
DTR	Data Terminal Ready
RI	Ring Indicator
RTS	Request to Send
RTSRD	Request to Send/Receive Data

RS-232 Cables

RS-232 connections can make use of either 25-pin or 9-pin connectors. On many PCs, the end attaching to a modem or TA has a 25-pin connector, while the PC has a 9-pin connector. The following table presents the layout and signals for both.

Description	Pin Outs on 9-Pin Cable	Pin Outs on 25-Pin Cable	Signal	Direction
Protective Ground	—	1	—	—
Transmitted Data	3	2	TD	DTE→DCE
Received Data	2	3	RD	DCE→DTE
Request to Send	7	4	RTS	DTE→DCE
Clear to Send	8	5	CTS	DCE→DTE
Data Set Ready	6	6	DSR	DCE→DTE
Signal Ground (Common)	5	7	—	—
Data Carrier Detected	1	8	DCD	DCE→DTE
Data Terminal Ready	4	20	DTR	DTE→DCE
Ring Indicator	9	22	RI	DCE→DTE
Data Signal Rate Detector	—	23	DSRD	DCE↔DTE

Telephone-Line Basics For Modems

Modem connections to the telephone service are made using two wires (*ring* and *tip*) that are used in a standard telephone jack. The wires are named for the plug wires used in the original telephone lines by which telephone operators would manually connect two telephones at the phone company switchboard. There are two versions of the telephone jack:

- **Half-duplex:** The RJ-11 has only two wires, which make up one line. Therefore, only one signal can be sent or received at a time.

- **Full-duplex:** The RJ-12 uses four wires to make up two lines; it can be used to simultaneously send and receive.

Multifunction Modems

Most modems offer some form of fax capability, along with software that adds functions beyond the average, small, stand-alone fax machine. Such a modem is usually labeled a fax/modem. They can store faxes, both incoming and outgoing, for reference or online reading. Most allow direct faxing of a document from a word processor, generally by using the print command to send the pages to the modem, where they are converted on the fly to the bitmap form used to send and receive fax transmissions. Many programs let you to automatically attach a predesigned cover sheet with each fax.

Another addition to the basic data out/data in modem is voice mail. Here, the PC and telephone work just like an answering machine. If the phone rings and the modem does not detect either a data or fax tone, it switches modes and streams a recorded message (the outgoing message). The caller can be prompted to record a message for the owner, and in some cases the modem will even forward a pager call or fax with the message contents.

Modem Installation

With the advent of Plug and Play technology, Windows 98 and Windows 2000, and the USB port, installing a modem has become a simple process. Summaries of the general installation process for both internal and external modems follow.

Note   A good technician always reviews the product documentation before setting up a modem to ensure proper operation and the inclusion of all desired features.

Internal-Modem Expansion Card

As with installing any card or internal board, remember to take the proper precautions against electrostatic discharge (ESD), and, of course, back up your data before you open the computer case. Follow these steps:

1. Document: Check the current IRQ settings and I/O addresses in the computer. Make a note of available IRQs and addresses.

2. Configure IRQ and I/O settings for non–Plug and Play compliant systems: Set the modem to an unused COM port and IRQ.

3. Install the board: Physically install the board in an available expansion-bus slot.

4. Install any software: Follow the software setup routine and, if needed, fill in the modem settings and any dial-up connections the user requests for Internet access or for logging on to a remote system. To avoid generating any security concerns, do not ask for or accept account passwords. Show the user how to set that part of the connection personally.

   For older Windows 3.x or MS-DOS machines and non-Internet connections under Windows 95 and later versions, additional work might be required. Here is a sample of how this part of a typical Windows 3.x SYSTEM.INI file might look:

```
[386enh]
COM3Irq=5
COM3Base=03E8
```

5. Set up the command set: Any software that will access the modem must know the correct command set to use for that modem. This means identifying the type of modem so the software will use the correct AT commands. When all else fails, try using a Hayes-compatible modem.

6. Document your work: Write down *all* the new settings and changes.

External Modem

External modems are easier to install than internal modems because they do not run the risk of conflicting COM ports.

1. Connect to a COM port: Choose either COM1 or COM2. Be sure to confirm that the COM port you are using is assigned to the connector on the computer. If the computer is using a serial mouse, that will be using one of the COM ports, too, and this sets up a potential conflict. You can also use COM3 or COM4 if they are properly installed and configured.

2. Plug in the cabling: Connect the modem to its power source and to the computer. You will also have to connect a telephone line (RJ-11) from the wall jack to the modem.

3. Configure software: Configure the software to select the required COM port and the type of modem (command set) used by the specific modem installed.

Modem Speeds

When installing and using a modem, the primary factor to consider is speed. The multimedia World Wide Web requires far more speed than the simple data transfers of just a few years ago. Modem speed is measured in baud and bps.

Baud Rate

As mentioned earlier, baud rate refers to how fast a modem can transmit data. Technically, the baud is the number of voltage or frequency changes that can be made in one second. When a modem is working at 300 baud, this means that the basic carrier frequency has 300 cycles per second. Due to restrictions imposed by the physics of the wiring, a dial-up phone line can go up to 2400 cycles, a baud rate of 2400.

If each cycle is one bit, the fastest rate at which data can be transmitted is2400 bps. However, by using different types of modulation, more than one bit can be transmitted per cycle. Earlier modems used the baud rate to measure their speed. (See Figure 12.7.)

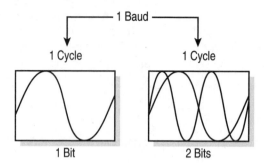

Figure 12.7   Baud

Bits per Second

The actual modem speed, or rate, that data is transmitted, is measured in bits per second. If a modem modulates one bit for each baud cycle, then the modem speed is 2400 bps. If a 2400-baud modem modulates two bits for one cycle of time, the modem is said to have a speed of 4800 bps (not a baud rate of 4800). If four bits are modulated with one cycle of time, then a modem speed of 9600 bps is achieved.

Note   Do not confuse baud with bps.

Modem speed standards are designated by the Comité Consultatif Télégraphique et Téléphonique (CCITT), an international body that develops fax and modem standards. The CCITT is now a branch of the International Telecommunications Union—Telecommunication Standardization Sector (abbreviated as ITU-T). The following table lists the standard rates designated by the CCITT.

CCIT Term	bps
V.21	300
V.22	1200
V.22bis	2400
V.23	1200 bps in one direction and 75 bps in the other
V.29	9600
V.32	4800 and 9600
V.32bis	14,400
V.32fast	28,800
V.34	28,800
V.42bis	38,400

Note   The term "bis" refers to the second revision of the standard.

Fax Speeds

Faxes are transmitted using one of several variations of an international standard. These standards are divided into four groups.

Groups 1 and 2

Groups 1 and 2 are based on 300-baud communication rates. They pertain to analog devices and do not include a modem. Group 1 transmits one page in six minutes. Group 2 transmits one page in three minutes.

Group 3

Group 3 is for digital equipment and can use the same modem for data and fax. Not all modems in this group are compatible. Group 3 is comprised of several subclasses as shown in the following table.

CCIT Term	bps
V.21 Channel 2	300
V.27 Turbo	4800
V.29	9600
V.17	14,400

Group 4

Group 4 allows the highest resolution to date (400 by 400, up to 1200 dpi). These speeds are for use with digital telephone circuits, ISDN, or leased lines.

Information Transfer Protocols

Communication relies on protocols. In order to ensure clear and clean communication without any errors, the device on each end must follow a very strict set of rules. If either device violates any of the rules, the communication will fail. These rules are called *File Transfer Protocols (FTPs)*.

All the necessary protocols should be included with the software that came with the modem. After communication is established with the host (usually the computer that receives the call), it can be asked what type of protocol to use. The call initiator can then select the matching protocol before starting a file transfer. *Both computers must use the same protocol.* There are five basic protocols used by modems.

ASCII

This protocol uses the standard ASCII character set, just like typing directly from a keyboard. ASCII protocol has no error-checking or compression features. It is simple, uncomplicated, and is used just to get simple character-based data. It is not a good protocol for transferring program files.

Xmodem

Xmodem is the next level of protocol. The advantage of Xmodem is that it includes error detection, which makes it more suitable for transferring program files. It transfers 128-byte blocks of data and one checksum (error-checking) character. The receiving computer calculates a new checksum and compares it to the one transmitted. If they are the same, the receiving computer transmits an ACK. If they are different, it sends back a NAK, and the transmitting computer then retransmits the data block. The protocol uses parity error checking, which is not perfect. If two errors were to occur—that is, if the first error were to change the parity bit, and the second error were to change it back to its original state—the second would cancel the first, and no error would be reported. The result can be a corrupted file or random characters on the display.

Ymodem

Ymodem is faster than Xmodem. Ymodem transfers data in 1024-byte blocks; therefore, less time is required to verify data with ACKs and NAKs.

Zmodem

Zmodem shares all the features found in Xmodem and Ymodem protocols. It also adds a few new features, including crash recovery, automatic downloading, and a *streaming* file transfer method. This is the protocol of choice for most situations.

Kermit

This protocol is rarely used today. It was the first of the synchronous protocols for uploading and downloading data to and from a mainframe computer.

Handshaking

Did you ever wonder what all that noise means that occurs when analog modems or fax machines begin to communicate? They are handshaking—or negotiating the rules (protocols) of communication. Because not every modem and computer is exactly the same, there must be some way for the two machines to determine how to communicate. That is what happens in that short burst of information between the two modems: decisions are made about what transmission speed to use (the fastest speed of the slowest device), how the data will be packaged, and who will control the transfer. If any of the parameters cannot be satisfied by both machines, the negotiations will fail and both parties will disconnect.

Tip   If you experience communication difficulty between two modems, be sure that you have not limited one of them to parameters that the other is unable to meet. For example, if one modem has a minimum speed restriction imposed by the software, it might need to be changed before it can communicate with other modems.

Connections between a sending device (sometimes referred to as Data Communications equipment or DCE) and a receiving device (Data Terminal Equipment or DTE) are called *handshaking signals*. They ensure that each sending and receiving device is in sync with the other. The flow control of data between modems is handled by the modems themselves. However, the local flow control between modem and COM port can be set by the user. There are two types of flow control:

- **Hardware flow control:** This takes advantage of some of the extra wires in the serial connection between the modem and COM port. These wires are used to let the other device know that the DCE is ready to send or receive data. The wires are named RTS (Request to Send) and CTS (Clear to Send). Hardware handshaking is sometimes referred to as RTS/CTS.

- **Software flow control:** This uses special characters known as XON and XOFF to let the other device know that the DCE is starting to send data or that the data transmission is finished. Software handshaking is slower and not as dependable as hardware handshaking. Only some very old modems use software handshaking. If given a choice, always use hardware flow control.

Modem Standards

As with every other communication device, standards are needed to ensure that both sides "speak the same language." Modems have their own set of standardized communication conventions.

Error Detection

Some modems offer various forms of hardware error detection and correction. Such features usually require matching firmware in the modems at both ends.

Data Compression

Data compression is a means of shrinking files into smaller packets, which results in faster connections and requires less space on the host and client machine for storage. Some modems can perform "on-the-fly" data compression; both modems must be able to understand the compression for it to work. On-the-fly compression will significantly enhance the amount of data sent between modems during a given time period. There are now a variety of industry standards for data compression, based in part on the work done by various Internet-related committees.

Communication Standards

There were no standards during the early days of modem communication. The only way to ensure data transmission was to place identical modems at the sending and receiving ends of the transmission. Compatibility was a great concern, and proprietary modems were the norm.

Today, modems comply with several standards. There are two sources for these standards:

- Manufacturers have placed specifications of their modem functions in the public domain. These specifications can now be copied and used by any manufacturer. If enough manufacturers use a specification, it becomes a standard on its own merits.

- Standards committees are formed when there is enough interest expressed by users, vendors, or regulatory committees to develop a set of rules for a class of data or modems.

Early Bell Standards

Bell Telephone produced the first generally accepted modem standards (103 and 212A); they developed out of the market-dominant position of the telephone company in telecommunications. To compete, other vendors offered products that would recognize the Bell command set. This scenario occurred more than once.

CCITT Standards

The CCITT modem standards are commonly known as Vdot standards (because each is named using the letter "V" followed by a decimal point and a number). The Vdot standards set out detailed requirements for the use of various modem speeds, incorporation of data-compression schemes, and error correction.

MNP Standards

The MNP standards (Micron Network Protocols—named for Micron, the company that developed them) set forth a series of error-correction methods.

Modem-Speed Standards

The following table compares the standards set by the aforementioned organizations.

Standard	Baud	bps	Comment
Bell 103	300	300	U.S. and Canadian standard, now largely obsolete.
Bell 212A	600	1200	U.S. and Canadian standard.
V.21	300	300	Similar to B 103. However, B 103 modems are not compatible with V.21.
V.22	600	1200	Incompatible with 212A. This standard is primarily used outside the U.S.
V.22bis	600	2400	Offers world-wide compatibility.
V.23		1200/75	Provides split data transmission.
V.29		9600	Used for Class 3 fax machines.
V.32	2400	4800/9600	Provides error correction. Full-duplex.
V.32bis	2400	14,400	An improved version of V.32.
V.32fast	2400	28,800	An extension of V.32 and V.32 bis.
V.34 or V.fast	2400	28,800	Allows optional higher speeds of 31.2 Kbps and 33.6 Kbps.

Error-Detection and Data-Compression Protocols

In addition to speed standards, some CCITT standards include error-detection and data-compression protocols. The following table shows the standards that include error detection.

Standard	Baud	bps	Type	Comments
V.42	2400	2400 and up	Error correction	
MNP 1–4	2400	2400 and up	Error correction	
V.42 bis	2400	9600/38.4K	Data compression	V.42 must be present.
MNP 5	N/A	N/A	Both	

56-K Modems

Telephone lines are capable of carrying 56 Kbps of data; however, conversion from analog to digital signals and back comes with a price. That price is a speed limit of 33.6 Kbps. Because many telephone systems are now digital, it is possible to transmit, in some instances, at a full 56 Kbps in one direction. The return data, however, is still limited to 33.6 Kbps. For these reasons, it is unlikely that you can achieve a full data transfer rate with a 56-K modem (56-K refers to a modem that transmits at 56 Kbps). In order to achieve the best performance, the following conditions must be met:

- Digital to analog conversion should be limited so that it takes place only once within the network. Each conversion slows the communication process.
- The host must be connected digitally.
- Both modems must support the 56-K technology.

There are currently three 56-K modem standards: K56flex, x2, and V.90. Unfortunately, these standards are not compatible at 56 K, so in order to achieve the highest possible speed, both modems must use the same standard. Several companies developed the K56flex standard, and U.S. Robotics developed the x2 standard. Currently, the V.90 standard is replacing both the K56flex and the x2, and most 56-K modems can be upgraded to this standard. If you have a 56-K modem and want to upgrade to V.90, check the manufacturer's Web site for instructions and download the appropriate software.

Modem Commands

Just like the early computers that needed MS-DOS commands to tell them what to do, modems also need commands; also, programmers needed a standard command set to incorporate the use of modems into their software. Unfortunately, there are no true standard command sets for modems because manufacturers are free to create their own. There is, however, one set of commands that has been accepted as a de facto standard. Most modems today are Hayes-compatible. In the early 1980s, Hayes developed the AT command set.

These commands are very useful as diagnostic tools for today's computer professional. To use these commands, make sure the communication software is loaded and the computer is in terminal mode. Unless the modem is set up to autoconnect (online mode), it will be in command mode and ready to accept AT commands. The following table lists some of the more useful AT commands used by computer professionals.

Command	Function
AT	Lets you know that your modem is plugged in and turned on. The modem should respond with OK.
ATE1	Echoes the command on the screen.
ATE0	Turns off the echo to the screen. Some modems will not run correctly when the echo is on.
ATH	Takes the telephone off the hook. Should elicit a reply of OK or 0 from the modem, or a dial tone and an OH indicator if it's an external modem.
ATM1	Turns the speaker on for the dial tone. ATL0 is the lowest volume. ATL2 is medium volume.
ATM0	Turns the speaker off.
ATD	Takes the phone off the hook and dials a number if one is included with command (for example, ATDT555-2222). The second "T" is for tone; substitute "P" for a pulse phone. Include a "W" (ATDTW) to instruct it to wait for a dial tone before dialing. Include a comma anywhere after the command to instruct it to pause before continuing to dial.
ATQ0	Enables result codes. A troubleshooting aid. Type "ATV1" prior to this command and you will get back verbose result codes (OK-BUSY-CONNECT 2400,9600-COMPRESSION:V.42bis).

continued

Command	Function
ATQ1	Disables result codes.
ATH, ATH0	Hangs up the modem.
ATX	This resets your modem to a predefined state. You can configure your own reset state. If it wasn't set previously, it can be reset to the factory's default setting.

Troubleshooting

It can be very frustrating when a modem does not function as expected. However, follow these simple guidelines to determine whether the modem is really broken or something else is the culprit.

Possible Cause	Possible Solution
New hardware was added to the computer and now the modem doesn't work.	Check for IRQ and/or I/O conflicts.
New software was added to the computer and now the modem doesn't work.	Check for IRQ and/or I/O conflicts. Cards that were configured for software can be inadvertently changed by corrupted software or by the installation of new software.
The software says there is no modem.	Make sure the software is looking at the correct port. Reconfigure or reinstall the software (there might be a corrupt driver).
Modem works sporadically.	Try another modem type. Check the phone lines.
Modem does not hang up the phone line.	A power surge (lightning) can cause this problem. If manual disconnect and reconnect allows the modem to work, replace or repair the modem.

Lesson Summary

The following points summarize the main elements of this lesson:

- Modems convert parallel digital data to and from serial analog data.

- Modem speeds are based on bps (bits per second).

- CCITT (now ITU-T) establishes standards for modem communication.

- AT commands are used to manually communicate with and test a modem.

- Modems can be installed internally or externally.

- The primary modem problem is IRQ conflicts.

Lesson 3: Cables and Connectors

Cables and connectors are critical to the operation of any computer peripherals. A computer professional must be able to identify and understand the various types of cables and connectors. This lesson discusses common connectors and their functions.

After this lesson, you will be able to:

- Identify cables and connectors by their names and functions.

Estimated lesson time: 20 minutes

Parallel Printer Cables

Parallel printer ports and cables are used to connect printers and other add-on items such as CD-ROMs, tape drives, and scanners. Centronics Corporation invented the most common type. It is an 8-bit parallel connection with handshaking signals between the printer and the computer—these tell the computer when to start or stop sending data. A standard printer cable is configured with a 36-pin Centronics connector on the printer end and a standard 25-pin "D" (male) on the computer end. A standard 25-pin "D" (female) connector found on the back of the computer designates it as a parallel port. (See Figure 12.8.)

Figure 12.8   Standard 25-pin D connector

The original parallel port was designed only to send information to printers and was unidirectional. However, some bidirectional communication was possible by manipulating the handshaking lines. Today, computer manufacturers have developed updated versions that allow better bidirectional communication while maintaining the original Centronics specification. The Institute of Electrical and Electronic Engineers (IEEE, pronounced "I triple E") developed a standard—IEEE 1284—to oversee the standardization of these ports.

There are three bidirectional standards used today:

- **Bi-Tronics:** This modified Centronics connection was created by Hewlett-Packard. It utilizes bidirectional communication, allowing the printer to send messages to the computer (out of paper, paper jam, and so forth).

- **EPP (enhanced parallel port):** This features 2 MB per second data transfer rates, bidirectional 8-bit operation, and addressing to support multiple (daisy-chained) peripherals on a single computer.

- **ECP (extended capabilities port):** This was developed by Hewlett-Packard and Microsoft. It features 2 MB per second data transfer and bidirectional 8-bit operation. ECP will specify whether transmitted information consists of data or commands for the peripheral. ECP supports CD-ROM and scanner connections, RLE (Run Length Encoded) data compression, and DMA support to increase transfer speed and reduce processor overhead.

Note   The EPP and ECP standards often have to be enabled in the CMOS setup before the specified port can use them.

IEEE 1284 Printer Modes

A vast array of printers is available, and in order to ensure that you are obtaining optimum performance, the printer, the printer driver, and the software using the printer must be configured for the same mode. The following table describes various printing modes and their capabilities.

Mode	Capabilities	Speed	Notes
Compatibility	8-bit output. Hardware handshaking. No DMA.	100–200-KB per second out	Original parallel port
4-bit	4-bit input using some of the printer's hand-shaking lines.	100–200 KB per second out; 40–60 KB per second in	HP Bi-Tronics mode
8-bit	8-bit I/O bidirectional.	80–300 KB per second	Original bidirectional port
ECP	8-bit I/O. Can use DMA.	>2 MB per second	Scanners and high-speed printers
EPP	8-bit I/O.	Up to 2 MB per second	Very flexible modes of operation

Parallel Pin Assignments

Just like modem cables, it is important for printer cables to have the correct pin connections. The following table describes the standard parallel pin assignments for the computer-end (25-pin) and the printer-end (Centronics) connectors.

Computer	Direction of Data Flow	Printer	Name	ID	Function
1	→	1	Strobe	STROBE	Sends data to printer.
2	→	2	Data bit 0	DBO	
3	→	3	Data bit 1	DB1	
4	→	4	Data bit 2	DB2	
5	→	5	Data bit 3	DB3	
6	→	6	Data bit 4	DB4	
7	→	7	Data bit 5	DB5	
8	→	8	Data bit 6	DB6	
9	→	9	Data bit 7	DB7	
10	←	10	Acknowledge	ACK	Printer acknowledges receipt of data.
11	←	11	Printer busy	BUSY	
12	←	12	Paper error	PE	
13	←	13	Select	SLCT	Indicates printer is online.
14	←	14	Auto feed	AUTOFD	
15	←	32	error	ERROR	
16	→	31	Reset Printer	INIT	
17	←	36	Select input	SLECT IN	
—	←	18	5v		5 volts available from some printers.
18–25	←	16, 19–30, 33	Ground		Sometimes to pin 17.

Serial Port Cables

A serial port allows a computer to send data over long distances by converting parallel data to serial data. Typical computers will have one or two serial ports, usually designated as COM1 and COM2. The "standard" port is a 9-pin male connector on the computer, shown in Figure 12.9. (There are also 25-pin cables available.)

Figure 12.9   Standard 9-pin D connector

The following table describes the pin connection for the 9-pin and 25-pin serial cable connectors.

9-pin	25-pin	Name	ID	Function
	1	Shield		
3	2	Transmitted Data	TX	Data sent from computer.
2	3	Receive Data	RX	Data sent to computer.
7	4	Request to Send	RTS	Computer is ready to send.
8	5	Clear to Send	CTS	"Other end" is ready to receive
6	6	Data Set Ready	DSR	"Other end" is ready to receive.
5	7	Signal Ground	SG	GND.
1	8	Data Carrier Detected	DCD	The modem has detected a signal from another modem.
4	20	Data Terminal Ready	DTR	Computer is ready to send.
9	22	Ring Indicator	RI	Modem detects line ringing.

Null-Modem Cables

Null-modem cables are used to directly connect two computers together without the need for a modem. The transmit and receive wires in the cable (wires 2 and 3) are switched to make the computers "think" they are using modems.

SCSI Cables

SCSI cables come in a variety of sizes depending on the type of SCSI used and the manufacturer of the device. Typically, internal cables are flat ribbon types and external cables are shielded bundles.

Keyboard Cables

Another peripheral device with a cable that we encounter and yet never think about is the keyboard. Because there are different types of keyboard cables (and connectors) and because, on occasion, the technician might encounter a problem with a keyboard connector, they are worthy of mention.

Keyboards are manufactured in two different styles with different cables and connectors. Earlier versions used a 5-pin DIN connector (DIN stands for Deutsche Industrie Norm, the German national standards organization), and most new keyboards use a 6-pin DIN connector, the same as is used on a PS/2 mouse. Connectors are available to convert the 5-pin DIN to a 6-pin mini-DIN. Although they have a different number of pins, they use the same wires and pin outs. Data is sent serially to the keyboard using the keyboard interface. Data is written to the controller's input buffer to accomplish this. Keyboard data passes through pin 2 of the connector, while clocking signals move through pin 1. A keyboard reset, which can be connected to the system's reset line, is included at pin 3. Ground and +5-volt DC connections are applied to the keyboard through pins 4 and 5.

Identifying Cables and Connectors

Because printers and modems can both use 9-pin and 25-pin connectors and cables, a computer technician must be able to identify the function of the cables by their connectors. Other devices, such as monitors and game ports, use 15-pin connectors. Cable identification can be confusing, but it is important. The following table summarizes how to identify common cables and connectors.

Function	Computer Connector	Cable Connector
Communication (serial)	9-pin or 25-pin male	9-pin or 25-pin female
Printer (parallel)	25-pin female	25-pin male
Monitor (VGA and SVGA)	15-pin female (three rows of pins)	15-pin male (three rows of pins)
Monitor (MGA and CGA)	9-pin female	9-pin male
Game port (joystick)	15-pin female (two rows of pins)	15-pin male (two rows of pins)
Keyboard	5-pin DIN female or 6-pin DIN female (PS/2)	5-pin DIN male or 6-pin DIN male (PS/2)

Troubleshooting Cables

Cables and connectors are a very common source of problems. Here are a few suggestions for troubleshooting:

- If a peripheral device doesn't work, always check the cables, especially if the device has been working recently.
- Always check for loose connections.
- Check for bent or broken pins on the connector. Bent pins can sometimes be repaired; however, they will always be susceptible to damage later, because the pin has been weakened. It is a good idea to mark these connectors and use them with care. A better idea is to replace them.
- If a connector or cable doesn't fit or if you have to push hard to make the connection, something is wrong. Either a connector has been damaged or it is not the right match.
- Check for worn or frayed cables. Replace if necessary.
- Make sure you have the right cable. Some, such as null-modem cables, look just like standard communication cables, but will not work with a modem.
- Always be wary of "homemade" cables.

Summary of Connectors

Computers use a large variety of connectors for various peripherals. The following table offers a summary of the most common connectors and their uses.

Name	Uses
DB-9	Serial ports—external modem, mouse, printer.
DB-25	Parallel port—printer, scanner, removable drive.
RJ-11	Standard telephone connector—2 wires.
RJ-12	Standard telephone connector—4 wires—used with dual phone connections.
RJ-45	Network connector.
PS/2 (mini-DIN)	Mouse, scanners.
Centronics	Printers.
USB	Universal serial bus—Technology that allows multiple peripherals to be attached to one cable. Popular devices are keyboards, mouse devices, modems, video cameras, and Zip drives.

Lesson Summary

The following points summarize the main elements of this lesson:

- There are many different types of computer cables and connectors. It is important for the computer technician to be able to identify each of them.

- The evolution of a technology often brings modification to cables, the way they are wired, and their length.

- Distinguishing between a male or a female connector is often the key to identifying the connector's function.

- Loose or poorly connected cables are often the cause of computer problems.

Chapter Summary

The following points summarize the key concepts in this chapter:

Printers

- The three most commonly encountered types of printers are dot-matrix, ink-jet, and laser printers.

- As a computer technician, you can expect to encounter printing problems on a regular basis.

- Most printer problems can be resolved quickly by checking for paper jams, expended consumables, or improper use.

- The key components of a laser printer are its power supply, photosensitive drum, eraser lamp, primary corona, laser, transfer corona, and fuser.

Modems

- Modems convert parallel digital data to and from serial analog data.

- Modem speeds are based on bps (bits per second).

- CCITT (now ITU-T) establishes standards for modem communication.

- AT commands are used to manually communicate with and test a modem.

- Modems can be installed internally or externally.

- The primary modem problem is IRQ conflicts.

Cables and Connectors

- There are many different types of computer cables and connectors. It is important for the computer technician to be able to identify each of them.

- Distinguishing between a male or a female connector is often the key to identifying the connector's function.

- Loose or poorly connected cables are often the cause of computer problems.

Review

1. Name three types of printers and describe their advantages and disadvantages.

2. The dot-matrix printer is an _____ printer. Name at least one advantage of this type of printer. Name at least one disadvantage.

3. What are the six steps of laser printing?

4. Which components are usually included in a laser printer's replaceable toner cartridge? Why?

5. What causes black spots to appear on a document that has been printed on a laser printer? How can this problem be resolved?

6. What is the IEEE 1284 standard?

7. What kinds of signals do telephones use? What kinds of signals do computers use?

8. What is the purpose of a modem?

9. Which AT command is used to take the phone off the hook?

10. What is the difference between baud and bps?

11. What is the name of the chip that converts data from parallel to serial?

12. Name three transfer protocols.

13. What is Zmodem? What are its advantages over other protocols?

14. Define handshaking.

15. What are AT commands and how can a computer technician use them?

16. Explain the difference between half-duplex and full-duplex. What makes them different? Where or when is each used?

17. What is the difference between synchronous and asynchronous communication?

18. Why are fax standards different from modem standards?

19. Describe a null-modem cable.

20. In addition to the cost of the printer, what other costs should be considered when purchasing a printer?

21. What does bps stand for?

22. Identify as many cables and connectors as you can.

23. What type of connector is used for a parallel port on the computer?

24. What type of connector is used for a parallel port on the printer?

CHAPTER 13

The Basics of Electrical Energy

About This Chapter

Computers run on electrical energy. Without it, a computer might as well be a paperweight. Because every component of a computer needs power to run (whether plugged into a wall outlet or a battery), a computer professional must understand the basic principles that govern electricity and electrical energy. This chapter introduces you to these principles.

Before You Begin

There are no prerequisites for this chapter.

Lesson 1: Power

The energy or power to drive a computer is derived from electricity. Whether it uses 110 volts alternating current (AC), the U.S. standard, 220 volts AC, the European standard, or direct current (DC) from a battery, a computer is useless without a steady, reliable source of power. When we encounter problems with a computer, it is crucial for us to be able to test the entire power system. This lesson covers the basics of power and electricity.

After this lesson, you will be able to:
- Explain the difference between electricity and electrical energy.
- Define the terms used to measure electrical energy.
- Identify basic electric and electronic components.
- Perform basic and advanced electrical energy tests.

Estimated lesson time: 45 minutes

Understanding Electricity and Electrical Energy

What is electricity? The meaning of the word varies with the user. Electricity to physicists is the primal property of nature, and they call the power delivered at the wall socket and stored in batteries electrical energy. Most people, including computer technicians, are less fussy, often using the term electricity to refer to both:

- the form of energy associated with moving electrons and protons.
- the energy made available by the flow of electric charge through a conductor.

For our discussion, we mostly talk about the flow of energy used to run computers—electrical energy—and not worry about the fine points of scientific philosophy.

Some Definitions

For our discussion we employ the following definitions:

- Electricity: The form of energy associated with charged particles, usually electrons.
- Electric Charge: When charged particles move in tandem, fields are generated, producing energy.
- Electrical Circuit: The path taken by an electrical charge.
- Electric Current: When an electric charge is carried, or flows through a conductor (like wires), it is known as a current. A current-carrying wire is a form of electromagnet. Electric current is also known as electron flow.

- Power: The rate at which an amount of energy is used to accomplish work. Electrical power is measured in watts, which is determined by multiplying voltage by current.

- Conductors: Materials that can carry an electrical current. Most conductors are metals.

- Resistance: A quality of some materials that allows them to slow the speed of an electrical current, producing heat, and sometimes light, in the process.

- Insulators: Materials that prevent or retard the electrical current of electrons.

- Ampere: A measurement of current strength, equal to 1 Coulomb per second. Coulomb's Law: two charges will exert equal and opposite forces on each other. Opposite charges attract and like charges repel.

- Ohm: A unit of electrical resistance. Ohm's Law states that voltage is equal to the product of the current times the resistance, or Voltage = Current x Resistance.

- Volt: The unit of electromotive force, or potential energy, that when steadily applied against a resistance of 1 ohm, produces a current of 1 ampere.

- Voltage: The potential energy of a circuit.

Ohm's LAW

In addition to defining terms, we need to understand some basic principles that are applied in testing electrical devices. One formula that all computer professionals should know is *Ohm's Law*. From this formula, or a derivation of this formula, all basic power calculations can be performed.

Ohm's Law states that the current (electrons) flowing through a conductor, or resistance, is linearly proportional to the applied potential difference (volts). A conductor is any medium, usually metal, that allows the flow of electrical current. Resistance is any device or media that resists the flow of electrons. In mathematical terms, this means:

Resistance: $R = V/I$

Current: $I = V/R$

Volts: $V = IR$

In these formulas, R = Resistance in Ohms (Ω), V = Voltage, and I = Current in Amperes.

Note   In some cases you may find E used instead of V in formulas expressing Ohm's Law. The E stands for "electromotive force," and is often used by engineers as a more precise technical term for their measurements.

By memorizing any one of these formulas, the other two can be easily derived using simple algebra. For example, the voltage (potential energy of the circuit) is equal to the amperage (the current or flow of electricity) multiplied by any resistance to that flow of electricity. The more resistance there is in a circuit, the lower the current flow for a given voltage.

PCs and Electrical Power

That PCs use electrical power to operate is no surprise, even to the casual user. The technician must understand the different types of electrical energy and how they work inside the PC. A PC's electrical power can come from a wall outlet, in the form of alternating current, or from a battery in the form of direct current.

AC Power (Alternating Current)

AC power is what most people think of as electricity. It comes from the wall, and powers most of our lights and household appliances.

AC power is man-made, using generators. As the wire coil inside the generator rotates, it passes by each pole of unit magnet(s) producing an electric current. When it passes the opposite pole, the current reverses, or *alternates*, the direction of flow (see Figure 13.1). The number of revolutions made by the generator per minute is called its frequency. In the United States, power companies run their systems at 60 turns per second to produce a high-voltage, 60Hz (cycles per second) alternating current as they rotate. The power system drops the voltage in stages before it is connected to the consumer's home or business.

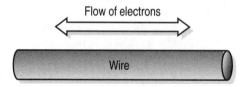

Figure 13.1   Flow of electrons

The power company delivers AC power to our homes or businesses with three wires. Two of the wires are *hot*, meaning that they carry a charge. One, the bare wire that runs from the breaker box to the power pole, is *neutral*. The measured voltage between the two hot wires is between 220 and 240 volts AC (VAC), while the measured voltage between either of the hot wires and the neutral wire is between 110 and 120 VAC. These voltages, which are called *nominal* voltages, can vary by plus or minus (±) 10 percent (see Figure 13.2).

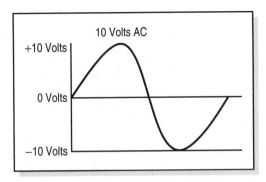

Figure 13.2   AC volts

Typical electrical outlets are connected between one of the hot wires and the neutral wire. These outlets are usually three-prong connections. The smaller rectangular hole is the hot, the larger rectangular hole is the neutral, and the small round hole is called the *ground*. The ground wire is used as a safety wire. In the event of a short circuit, a large flow of current (amps) is discharged all at one time. This short, high flow of current will burn out circuits unless it can be safely sent somewhere else. Electricity will always seek the path of least resistance to ground. By providing this wire, a short circuit will cause less damage by providing a path for safe dissipation of the current. To provide a safe working environment for the computer and yourself, make sure that this wire is properly installed.

Older structures might have two-wire electrical outlets without the ground wire. An electrical outlet without grounded plugs and the third ground wire is unacceptable for use with a computer (see Figure 13.3). An extension cord without a ground wire is also unacceptable.

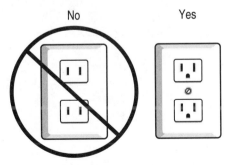

Figure 13.3   The proper type of outlet includes a ground

Caution   A short circuit can cause physical damage to equipment and personnel. It can cause a fire, component damage, permanent disability, or even death. The ground plug provides a direct connection to ground, giving the electricity an alternate path away from equipment and people.

DC Power (Direct Current)

Alternating current is used for transporting low-cost power to end users. But a computer's electronic components won't run on AC power—they need a steady stream of direct current. The PC's power supply performs several tasks, but the main function is to convert AC into DC. A computer's power supply combines two components to handle this job: a *step-down transformer* and an *AC/DC converter*. The AC adapters used for laptop computers, many low-cost ink-jet printers, and many other consumer electronics do the same thing—turn alternating current into lower-voltage direct current.

As we have seen, DC is electrical energy that travels in a single direction within a circuit. (The electrical energy in a thunderstorm is another example, but not very practical in electronic applications.) DC current flows from one pole to another, hence it is said to have *polarity* (see Figure 13.4). The polarity indicates the direction of the flow of the current and is signified by the "+" and "–" signs (see Figure 13.5).

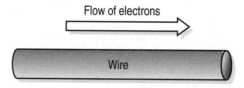

Figure 13.4   DC power

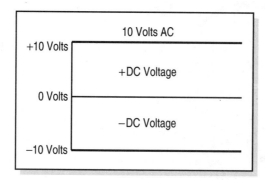

Figure 13.5   DC voltage

Measuring Electricity

A computer professional should know how to use a multimeter—sometimes called a VOM (Volt-Ohm Meter) or a DVOM (Digital Volt-Ohm Meter). An electrical test meter is probably the best (and most practical) tool for troubleshooting electrical problems. It is not necessary to be an "electronic technician" to use this tool effectively.

The Multimeter

A multimeter is an instrument that is used to measure several aspects of electricity. All multimeters are designed to provide at least four major measurements:

- AC voltage
- DC voltage
- Continuity
- Resistance

A multimeter consists of two probes, an analog or digital meter, and a multi-position switch to select the type of test you wish to perform.

Testing AC Power

On any new building installation, failure to properly test AC outlets can result in damaged or destroyed equipment, as well as possible injury and electrocution. In the event a wiring error was made that causes the voltage to be outside of the specifications (either two high or too low), problems are sure to arise. Don't take for granted that the building power supply provides the correct voltage, or that all of the other inputs are wired correctly.

When testing an AC power source, check these three things:

- Is the *hot* wire sending the correct voltage, and is it wired to the correct pin?
- Is the *neutral* wire connected to ground and to the correct pin?
- Is the *ground* wire connected to ground and to the correct pin?

Testing AC Outlets with a Multimeter

The first step when testing an AC outlet is to set up the multimeter. Then you need to know how to read the meter. You can also use special equipment if the multimeter does not provide enough information.

Setting Up the Meter

Basic multimeter usage with AC circuits is quite straightforward:

1. Attach the black test lead to the negative (–) marked hole. In some low-cost meters, leads are permanently attached to the meter.

2. Attach the red test lead to the volts (+) hole. Be careful—if this lead is placed in the wrong hole (ohm or amp) it can cause permanent damage to the meter.

3. Set the selector switch to AC volts (this choice is often denoted by red lettering). If there are multiple selections, use the highest setting possible (if voltage is unknown), or select one level higher than the estimated voltage. For standard household outlets, 200 VAC is a good selection. Some digital meters use "Auto-range" and don't need any selection except AC volts.

Reading the Meter

After the meter is set up, you are ready to test a wall outlet. There are three tests to perform. With AC voltage, it does not matter which lead is placed in which connector:

- **Hot to Neutral:** Place one lead in hot (smaller of the two vertical slots) and the other in neutral (larger of the vertical slots). The reading should be between 110 and 120 volts AC.

- **Hot to Ground:** Place one lead in hot (smaller of the two vertical slots) and the other in ground. The reading should be between 110 and 120 volts AC.

- **Neutral to Ground:** Place one lead in neutral (larger of the two vertical slots) and the other in ground. The reading should be 0 volts.

Using AC Testers

An alternate method for testing electrical outlets is to purchase an AC tester. These small devices are made especially for testing outlets and can be purchased at any home improvement or electronics outlet store. By simply inserting the tester into an outlet, all voltages for all combinations can be tested at the same time. Many testers provide several LEDs that tell whether or not each function passes the test. This device is not as accurate as a multimeter but it is more convenient. It will provide a pass/fail indication rather than an accurate voltage reading.

Testing AC Ripple

The function of the power supply is to convert AC to DC voltage. When working properly, a pure DC signal will be produced. However, sometimes, as the power supply ages, its ability to produce pure DC falters. A power supply uses electrolytic capacitors (discussed later in this lesson) to filter or smooth the voltage after it has been converted from AC to DC. These capacitors are second only to fuses as the part of a power supply most likely to fail. When an electrolytic capacitor begins to fail, it allows more and more AC voltage to pass through. This small amount of AC voltage is superimposed on top of the DC voltage and called *noise* or *ripple*. To test for ripple, set a meter to read AC. Then connect a .1μfd (microfarad) capacitor to the red lead. With the power turned on, measure the DC voltage. Any ripple present will be displayed as AC voltage.

Testing Resistance

Resistance is an opposition to the flow of current through a conductor. Resistance is measured in *ohms*. The symbol for an ohm is Ω. Resistance is measured by placing one lead of the meter on each side of the circuit or component to be measured. Taking resistance measurements for a component while it is still soldered in its circuit can lead to inaccurate readings because any other component connected to the circuit can affect the total resistance measured. Unlike voltage checks, you should test resistance with the power off. If a meter is set up to read resistance, you will damage it if you connect it to an electrical outlet.

Note Be careful when measuring resistance. If the meter is set too high or the resistance is too high for the meter, you will get an inaccurate reading. Also, before taking a measurement, be sure that any charge stored in a capacitor is properly discharged. Refer to the applicable product manual for details.

Testing Continuity

Continuity is a term used to indicate whether or not a connection exists between one point in a circuit and another. It is used to determine the presence of breaks in wires and electrical circuits.

If no continuity setting is available, use the resistance setting (see the next section). If the multimeter measures infinite resistance, there is no continuity. This indicates a break in the line. If the multimeter shows little or no resistance, there is continuity and the circuit is complete.

Testing DC Voltage

Testing for DC voltage is the same as testing for AC voltage, but with one important difference: DC voltage is sensitive to polarity. As mentioned earlier, DC voltage has a positive pole (+) and a negative pole (–). When measuring DC voltage, it is important to place the positive (red) lead on the positive side and the negative (black) lead on the negative side of the circuit. If the leads are positioned backwards, the polarity of the reading will be the opposite of what it should be.

Caution   When using an analog meter (one with a dial and needle), connecting the leads backward will cause the needle to move in the opposite direction, possibly damaging the meter.

Testing a Power Supply

Many computer problems blamed on the operating system or hardware component are really power problems (see Chapter 5). In some cases, it is the power produced and transmitted by the electric utility that will require line conditioning. The quickest way to resolve this is by adding a quality UPS (discussed in Chapter 5, Lesson 2: Power-Supply Problems) with line-conditioning circuits. Before adding one, test the power supply to make sure it is functioning properly.

Note   Find out if the client is having any problems with flickering lights, intermittent problems with other appliances, or is using a power strip with too many connections for the rated use; improper loading of the circuit, not the PC itself, can be the problem.

A bad power supply can cause intermittent lockups and unexpected computer reboots. Erratic problems encountered during booting and changed or erased CMOS information can also be traced to a failing power supply. Bad power supplies have been known to destroy data on mass-storage devices. There are two types of tests for power supplies: a basic test used to verify voltages and an advanced test for checking its internal components.

Basic Voltage Test

The only purpose of this test is to verify the existence and value of voltages. With time, most power supplies show their age by a reduction in voltage. This voltage drop will show itself in both the 5-volt and the 12-volt outputs, but is more pronounced on the 12-volt side.

Prepare the Meter for the Test

Again, meter preparation is quite simple:

1. Connect the black lead to the common (–) connector and the red lead to the voltage (+) connector.

2. Turn the test selector to DC volts. If the meter has an AC/DC switch, be sure it is set to DC. If the meter does "auto range," set the range to 15-to-20 volts.

Testing the Voltages

The best place to check voltage is at the power supply's P8/P9 or ATX power connectors (see Chapter 5, "Supplying Power to a Computer"). For P8/P9 systems use the instructions below:

1. Place the meter's black (ground) lead on the black wire connection and its red (positive) lead on the yellow (+12 volt) connection.

2. Record the voltages. A good power supply will provide a voltage between 11 and 13 volts DC.

3. Replace the power supply if the voltage reading is less than 10.

Note   Be sure to reverse the leads when using an analog meter to check negative voltages. This is not necessary with a digital meter because it will simply show a negative sign with the reading.

When No Voltage Is Present

If you have completed the basic voltage test and no voltage is present, the problem may not be the power supply. It might, instead, be caused by an excessive load on the system due to another piece of hardware. To determine if that is the case, try the following procedure.

Isolating the Problem

First you should test the hardware:

1. Disconnect the Molex leads from the power supply.

2. Connect the meter leads as described in the previous sections.

3. Turn off the AC power.

4. Disconnect all the Molex plugs from the devices.

5. Turn the power back on. If power is present at the motherboard, one of the devices is bad and is causing a drain on the power supply.

6. Reconnect each Molex plug, one at a time, and test the power. When the power drops out, you have located the offending device.

Advanced Testing

The basic test is designed to quickly isolate the power supply as a problem. In most cases, if the test proves the power supply to be defective, it may be more cost-effective to replace the power supply than to try to repair it. Advanced testing requires a working knowledge of power supplies and removal of the power supply and its cover.

There are three sections to a power supply: the *switching network*, the *transformer,* and the *voltage regulator* (see Figure 13.6).

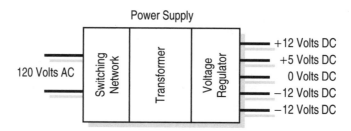

Figure 13.6   Power supply

The Switching Network

AC power coming from the power company is imperfect. It is not uncommon to have sudden increases in voltage called *spikes* or decreases in voltage called *sags* (see Chapter 5, "Supplying Power to a Computer").

To smooth out the power sent to the electronic components, a PC has basic line conditioning capability—a switching network. The better the power supply, the more sophisticated the network. The main components found in a switching network are a fuse, capacitors, rectifiers, and switching transistors (see Figure 13.7).

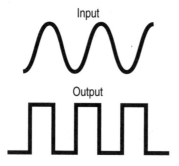

Figure 13.7   Switching network

The switching network performs the following three tasks:

- Filters electrical noise (spikes, sags).
- Eliminates frequency changes (ensuring that current stays at a constant 60 cycles).
- Converts AC *sine wave* signals to AC *square wave* signals.

The Transformer

The transformer reduces the voltage of the *square wave* DC into separate 12-volt and 5-volt square wave AC circuits (see Figure 13.8).

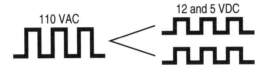

Figure 13.8   Transformer voltage

The Voltage Regulator

The voltage regulator receives the low-voltage AC outputs of the transformer and converts them to clean DC power. The main components in this section are rectifiers, capacitors, and coils.

The voltage regulator section performs three functions:

- It uses rectifiers (diodes) to convert the square wave AC output of the transformer into DC output (see Figure 13.9).
- It regulates the voltage to a constant output level and uses capacitors to remove any ripples that are present.
- It monitors the amount of current used by the computer circuits and adjusts the switching network using a special circuit called the feedback circuit. This compensates for variations in load on the power supply.

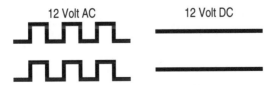

Figure 13.9   Regulator section voltage

> **Caution** Do not open the power supply while it is plugged in, and do not open the power supply until it has been discharged. The power supply can carry dangerous levels of power even when disconnected. Only a properly trained technician should ever open a PC power supply. Given the cost of a power supply, there is no good reason to disassemble one; defective units should be replaced.

Electronic Components

As a computer professional, you should be familiar with the more common types of electronic components within a power supply. Here is a description of the basic components found on circuit boards inside a computer.

Fuse

Before the advent of the circuit breaker, fuses were common in the home and office. A fuse serves one purpose—to fail—and thus cut the flow of power in the event of a current load that has exceeded the safe capacity of the system components to absorb. While fuses come in many shapes and sizes, a PC fuse is almost always a small, clear glass tube with metal caps on each end and a wire inside the tube to electrically connect the two caps (see Figure 13.10). In general, the thicker the wire, the more current it can conduct before failing. When a fuse fails, the wire will melt or be broken. You can check for a "blown" fuse by seeing if the wire is intact or broken. The amperage (A) rating (stamped on the metal cap) indicates the maximum current the wire is rated to conduct. Be sure not to exceed to the rated limits of the PC design for a fuse, because an excess power load can damage or destroy the system.

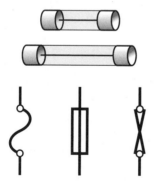

Figure 13.10   Fuses

If a fuse in a specific location fails more than once or repeatedly, the system is being overloaded, and you need to isolate the problem causing the failure. Fuses are often found on power supplies and many external components. If a fuse fails, try first replacing it with another of the same rating. If the replacement also fails, the fault probably lies with the motherboard or another internal part.

Capacitors

A capacitor is an electrical component used to hold an electrical charge. In photography, electronic flashes use capacitors to build up power before a picture is taken and to vary the amount of power used in a flash to control the exposure. In PCs, they are often used to regulate the flow of current to areas of the system circuits for a short period of time. Some are fixed-capacity models, whereas others can absorb or hold variable amounts of power. The amount of electrical current a capacitor can control is called capacitance, measured in microfarads (see Figure 13.11).

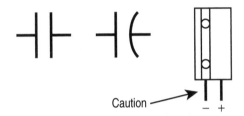

Figure 13.11   Capacitors

Most PC power supplies employ an *electrolytic* capacitor. These devices are able to retain a significant charge for long periods. You should work with such components only if you are properly trained to know how to release any residual charge before disconnecting, testing, removing, or replacing one. Failure to follow safe procedures can result in injury or death to you, and damage to the system. These capacitors have a distinct polarity (negative and positive) to their two leads.

Caution   Before you test a capacitor you must discharge the power supply. Failure to discharge can create a serious hazard to you and your equipment.

Rectifiers and Diodes

Rectifiers are devices that convert AC power into a DC form (rectification). A diode is a device that lets current flow in only one direction (see Figure 13.12). Two or more diodes connected to an AC supply will convert the AC voltage to DC voltage.

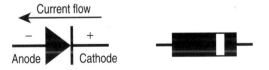

Figure 13.12   Diodes

Single diodes are generally used to convert AC current to pulsating DC current (see Figure 13.13). Two diodes working in parallel produce half-wave rectification, resulting in a pulsating direct current. Four diodes produce full-wave rectification, with a continuous stream of pulses.

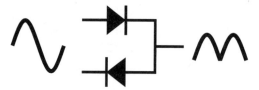

Figure 13.13   Half-wave rectifier

Normally, a computer technician does not test at this level; however, diodes can be tested with a multimeter. With the power turned off, test for resistance across both leads of the diode. Then reverse the leads of the multimeter and test again. A good diode will exhibit low resistance in one direction and high resistance in the other.

Transistors

The invention of the compact, power-efficient, and reliable transistor created the modern electronics industry; replacing bulky, power-hungry, and temperamental vacuum tubes. Transistors are basically a pair of diodes connected in series with an "on-off" switch (see Figure 13.14). Varying the voltage sent to a transistor turns the switch on or off. Early computers used vacuum tubes as switches and were so large that technicians could actually step inside the larger ones to plug in or remove the tubes in order to program them.

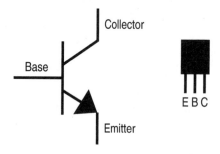

Figure 13.14   Transistors

Transistors can be tested; however, this often requires special equipment. Due to the reliability of transistors, a computer technician normally does not need to do this level of testing.

Transformers

The most common forms of electrical transformers are step-down or step-up devices. A step-down transformer decreases the transformer's voltage on the output side; a step-up model increases it. Both have a primary wire coil connected to other coils—secondary coils—joining two or more AC circuits.

Electronic transformers generally contain stacks of thin metal-alloy sheets, known as laminations, with coils of copper wire wound around them. They are commonly employed in a circuit along with a rectifier which, as we have seen, supplies DC power to the equipment. In the PC power supply, the transformer's secondary coils are used to provide 12-volt, 5-volt, and 3.3-volt outputs used by various components (see Figure 13.15).

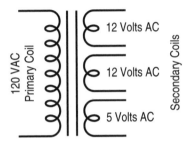

Figure 13.15   Transformer

Testing a Transformer

As noted, a transformer is made up of several coils of wire. Because each coil in the transformer is continuous, each can also be tested for continuity. Follow these steps:

1. Disconnect the power.

2. Discharge all capacitors.

3. Check the bottom of the circuit board of the power supply to be sure all leads have been disconnected. The primary connections, as well as the secondary connections, can be located below the transformer.

4. Configure the multimeter to measure continuity (or resistance).

5. Simultaneously touch each lead of a multimeter to one of the pairs of contacts.

A good transformer will show a reading of low resistance. A very high reading could indicate that one of the coils is broken.

Inductors (Coils)

Inductors, commonly called coils because of their shape, are loops of conductive wire (see Figure 13.16). Current passing through the inductor sets up a magnetic field. This field reduces any rapid change in current intensity. Inductors can also be used to distinguish between rapidly and slowly changing signals in a circuit.

Figure 13.16 Coil

Testing a Coil

Since an inductor is simply a wire coil, it can be tested for continuity in much the same way as a transformer is tested.

Visually inspect the wire for deterioration. If it shows signs of breakage or burned areas, it should be replaced. If the wire looks good, follow up with a conductivity test. Turn the system power off. Disconnect one lead to the coil (this might require a soldering iron) and connect one meter lead to each end of the coil. A null or low reading indicates continuity. A reading of high or infinite resistance indicates a lack of continuity. Replace the coil.

Lesson Summary

The following points summarize the main elements of this lesson:

- Ohm's Law is the basic formula for power calculations.

- There are two types of power: alternating current (AC) and direct current (DC).

- A multimeter is used to measure volts, amps, continuity, and resistance.

- A computer technician should be familiar with the various electronic components found on a power-supply circuit board.

- In a new installation, a computer technician should never assume that the power supplied in the wall outlets is correct. Always test and be sure.

- Be careful with large electrolytic capacitors. They can store electrical charges and must be discharged before it is safe to work with them.

Lesson 2: Electrostatic Discharge (ESD)

This lesson discusses a phenomenon that can damage or ruin sensitive electronic equipment—electrostatic discharge (ESD), sometimes referred to as static electricity. Fortunately, it is one of the easiest things to protect against.

After this lesson, you will be able to:

- Define ESD (electrostatic discharge).
- Avoid ESD.

Estimated lesson time: 15 minutes

Causes of Electrostatic Discharge

The human body has an electric field and under the right (and very easy to obtain) conditions can generate a tremendous amount of voltage, often referred to as static electricity.

ESD occurs when an imbalance in the amounts of positive and negative electrical charges on the surface of an object is released. The most dramatic example of ESD is lightning, which splits trees as easily as it lights up the sky. The amount of energy released when you touch a metal object can be quite large. The buildup of energy with nylon clothes can easily reach 21,000 volts. About 750 volts are required to produce a visible spark with ESD, while a mere 10 volts or so can ruin a computer chip.

The actual amount of energy in a given ESD event depends on the types of materials involved (wool fabrics generate less than nylon), the humidity (low humidity offers less resistant to the discharge), the amount of physical energy (friction) involved, and how quickly the energy is released.

Note   ESD does not have to be seen (a spark) to do damage to electronic components. Voltages lower than 10 volts can damage some parts.

ESD Damage

Over the years, engineers have produced smaller and smaller components, which operate at lower and lower voltages. Their goal is to reduce size, cost, and operational heat production. Those are worthy goals, but because of reduced component size, they present a smaller target with less resistance to power surges. This makes the parts more susceptible to damage from ESD.

The amount of damage and resulting problems caused by ESD can be divided into three categories:

- **Catastrophic Failure:** This is sometimes referred to as "frying" or "smoking" a part because of the heat (and sometimes the noise and smoke) generated during the failure. Mishandling and misapplication of a power source, cable, or test instrument are the most likely causes. Care in opening, installing, cabling, and testing are the best ways to prevent this type of ESD damage.

- **Upset Failure:** An ESD can produce an erratic fault in a component. This kind of problem is very difficult to detect and repair, because the failure is intermittent. It is easy to blame the operating system or a program operation for the data loss or system crash. The best way to diagnose and correct this type of problem is to remove and replace suspected parts until the failure stops appearing.

- **Latent Failure:** This type of failure weakens the actual transistor. The part will seem normal in most operations and will frequently pass quality control and conformance tests. Like upset failures, these can be very difficult to isolate.

Preventing ESD

Prevention is the best defense against ESD, and the first step of prevention is to understand the source. The number one cause of ESD damage is improper handling of electronic devices. A semiconductor device can be damaged by ESD during handling before it is installed.

The key to ESD prevention is to keep all electronic components—and yourself—at a common electrical potential. This usually means ground potential, or zero volts. Maintain a habit of "grounding" yourself to the computer chassis whenever you attempt a repair. There are times when it is not practical, or convenient, to wear a ground strap. At such times, touching a part of the metal chassis before removing devices will bring you and the computer chassis to a common voltage. Don't move around while installing or handling a part; doing so can generate additional voltages, negating any effort you have made to eliminate ESD.

All repair shops and workbenches should have proper ESD-suppression devices, and technicians should use them whenever working with exposed parts. These devices include:

- **Antistatic mats:** Nonconducting pads placed on the work surface and on the floor in front of the work area.

- **Antistatic wristband:** A wristband with a grounding strap connected to the chassis of the PC.

- **Antistatic pouches:** A sealed, antistatic pouch used to store any sensitive electronic device, including hard disk drives, when they are not installed in a computer.

- **Antistatic pad:** An insulating foam pad in which individual chips with exposed pins should be embedded when they are not installed in a computer.

Caution   AC voltage can kill. Although the power used by the computer components is no more than 12 volts DC, many computers have 110 volts AC wired from the power supply to the on/off switch at the front of the computer case. This wiring can present a hazard. Never disconnect or remove boards from a computer with the power applied. This can damage the components.

Caution   Safety precautions are different for computer monitors. Never work on a monitor with the cabinet removed, power applied, and a wrist strap on; a wrist strap coming in contact with the high voltage wire (30,000 volts) can cause electrocution.

Lesson Summary

The following points summarize the main elements of this lesson:

- ESD damages computer components.

- ESD can occur without detection.

- ESD can be prevented.

Lesson 3: Safety and Electrical Power

Computers are electronic equipment and therefore consume electricity. Although most components in a computer operate on low voltages—in the safe range between 3.3 and 12 volts DC—the main power source and the monitor use high voltages. This lesson sets out some basic high-voltage electrical safety guidelines.

After this lesson, you will be able to:

- Identify high-voltage hazards.
- Define some common guidelines for electrical safety.

Estimated lesson time: 5 minutes

Electrical Safety Is Your Responsibility

Standard wall outlets in the U.S. provide a nominal 120 volts AC and are rated to deliver currents between 15 and 20 amps. Under certain conditions, it is possible to receive a lethal shock from much lower voltages than these. Inside a computer, and especially the monitor, voltages as high as 30,000 volts can exist—even *after* the power is turned off.

It is vital to follow basic electrical-safety guidelines when servicing a computer. There is no substitute for good old common sense. However, here are a few tips:

- When in doubt about the correct way to safely service a part of a computer, don't do it. Have an experienced professional do the necessary work.
- Always use grounded outlets and power cords.
- Switch the power off and disconnect all equipment from its power source before removing any covers.
- Always replace blown fuses with fuses of the correct rating and type.
- Do not work alone—you might need help in an emergency.
- Remove all jewelry and any wristwatch. These are conductors and can cause short circuits.
- Have trained personnel service computer power supplies and monitors; these devices use and store potentially lethal voltages (often for days or longer).
- Work with one hand. Using two hands can cause a direct circuit, via your heart, from one object to another.

In the U.S., common AC wiring uses the following color coding:

Connection	Color
Live or hot	Black
Neutral	White
Ground	Green or bare copper

Caution   Color codes for AC wires and DC wires can be different. For example, the *ground* wires on the P8 and P9 connector for an AT-style motherboard are black.

Lesson Summary

The following point summarizes the main elements of this lesson:

- Electrical safety is your responsibility. Be sure to follow all safety guidelines listed for the devices you work with, and do not work inside of products such as monitors or power supplies without special training.

Chapter Summary

The following points summarize the key concepts in this chapter:

Power

- Ohm's Law states that the current flowing through a conductor, or resistance, is linearly proportional to the applied potential difference (volts).

- Electricity is delivered to our homes and businesses as AC (alternating current). Computers use DC (direct current).

- Electricity always seeks the path of least resistance to ground. An electrical outlet or an extension cord without a ground wire is unacceptable for use with a computer.

- A multimeter is an instrument used to measure electrical voltage, current, resistance, and continuity.

Electrostatic Discharge (ESD)

- Electrostatic discharge (ESD) depends on the types of materials and the amount of friction involved, the humidity, and how quickly the energy is released. ESD can cause damage to computer parts. Always take preventive measures when working around a computer.

Safety and Electrical Power

- It is vital to follow basic electrical-safety guidelines when working around electrical and electronic devices. Remember—electrical safety is your responsibility.

Review

1. What is Ohm's Law?

2. What is the formula for Ohm's Law?

3. What is the difference between AC and DC?

4. What instrument is used to measure the various components of electricity?

5. How do you test for continuity?

6. What is "AC Ripple?" How do you test for it?

7. Describe ESD and how to prevent it.

8. What is a latent failure? What makes it especially troublesome?

9. What is a catastrophic failure?

10. When working with a computer, when is it acceptable to use an AC power supply that is not grounded?

C H A P T E R   1 4

Upgrading a Computer

About This Chapter

Computer upgrades are among the most common tasks performed by a computer technician. With new technology coming out every day, it is a constant struggle to stay up to date. Before you can upgrade or repair a computer, you must know how to take it apart. A thorough understanding of how to disassemble a computer and put it back together is required by any computer professional. This chapter provides guidelines for successfully disassembling, upgrading, and reassembling a computer.

Before You Begin

Before starting this chapter, you should review the previous chapters, which cover the physical components of a computer. Also review Chapter 13, "The Basics of Electrical Energy," especially Lesson 2: Electrostatic Discharge (ESD).

Lesson 1: Computer Disassembly and Reassembly

In this lesson, we look at the tools and practices required by a computer technician to physically take apart a computer and successfully put it back together. Although this lesson mentions software that you should have and know how to use, software is covered more deeply in Chapters 15, "Software: MS-DOS and Windows 3.x," and 16, "Windows 95 and Beyond."

After this lesson, you will be able to:

- Develop a systematic and logical approach to repairing a computer.
- Identify and describe the basic tools and procedures for working on a computer.
- Identify basic procedures for adding and removing computer components.

Estimated lesson time: 20 minutes

Preparation

Knowledge and preparation are the primary ingredients for a successful, efficient, and profitable upgrade or repair. Before attempting any work on a computer, it is wise to know what you are working with and to have a good understanding of the problem, or task, at hand. Ten minutes to an hour of preparation can save hours of endless guessing and frustration.

Documentation is the key to preparation. If adequate documentation is not readily available, your first step is to collect or create it. When you finish a job, don't forget to save the documentation, including an account of what you did and any problems you encountered.

Documentation to Collect Before Starting the Job

The following list provides examples of the types of documentation you should assemble before you begin a repair.

- A computer configuration sheet. A sample computer configuration sheet is shown in Figure 14.1 in Lesson 2 of this chapter.
- Copies of the computer and/or motherboard documentation.
- A list of all installed expansion cards. If possible, include the date on which they were originally installed.
- Copies of the operating-system documentation (especially if you are not familiar with the system).
- A plan of action. Writing down a checklist of tasks and related tools and parts *before* starting a project can help you keep focused and stay on target. Remember, plans can always be changed; but without a plan, you could find yourself wandering aimlessly through the project and perhaps getting side-tracked or lost.

Questions to Ask Yourself Before Starting the Job

Carefully consider the following questions before you open the case of any computer:

- Is this the right computer?

- Why am I taking it apart?

- Do I have everything necessary to do the job?

- Do I need more information before starting this job?

- Might any components of this machine be proprietary hardware? If so, do I have the right tools and parts to do the job?

- Do any of these tasks require the assistance of a third party—for example, monitor adjustment?

Recommended Hardware

A computer professional does not need a large toolbox; only a few basic hand tools, a handful of floppy disks are required to solve most computer problems. Most PCs can be opened and most parts removed and replaced with a pair of screwdrivers. Be careful when working on a proprietary machine, however—special tools are often required. A small canvas bag or a briefcase will generally be sufficient to carry everything you need.

The following table lists and describes the hand tools that will meet most needs.

Tool	Description
Screwdrivers	Two of each (one large and one small) flathead (regular) and Phillips (sometimes called a cross) screwdrivers are usually sufficient. *Avoid magnetic screwdrivers:* although they are convenient for picking up lost screws, their magnetism can cause problems.
Torx driver	Used to remove the odd star-shaped screws found on some proprietary computers. Sizes T-10 and T-15 should meet the needs of most computers.
Tweezers	Very convenient for picking up small parts (for instance, screws). You might consider the long plastic variety; these don't conduct electricity and hence won't create any short circuits.
Needlenose pliers	Can be used to pick up dropped items and to hold or loosen screws, nuts, and bolts.
Chip removers	Although optional, these are very useful when changing video RAM or other (older) RAM chips that are pushed into a socket.
Tube for small parts	A short plastic tube (with caps on both ends) will keep loose screws and small parts from wandering.
Compressed air	A can of compressed air is helpful to remove dust.

(continued)

continued

Tool	Description
ESD tools	An antistatic wristband is a must. Antistatic mats and antistatic bags are also helpful.
Multimeter	A small, digital meter that is capable of measuring volts (AC and DC) and ohms (resistance or continuity) is all that is needed.
Flashlight	A small (bright) light for illuminating those hard-to-get-at places.
Nut driver set	Sizes 3/16-inch, 7/32-inch, and 1/4-inch.
Hemostats	Good for picking up and holding small parts. Straight hemostats will work most of the time. However, curved ones will get into those small places that the straight ones can't reach.
POST Card	A POST card can be used to see what the error messages during system start are being sent when no data is being sent to the display.

Recommended Software

Don't feel compelled to carry an entire arsenal of arcane software. A small number of commonly used programs can serve most of your needs.

Bootable Floppy Disk

You'll want to compile and carry bootable floppy disks for each operating system that you encounter. These should contain the following files:

- ATTRIB.EXE
- **COMMAND.COM**
- DEFRAG.EXE
- EDIT.COM
- EMM386.EXE
- EXPAND.COM
- **FDISK.EXE (.COM)**

- **FORMAT.EXE (.COM)**
- HIMEM.SYS
- LABEL.COM
- MEM.EXE
- MEMMAKER.EXE
- **MSCDEX.EXE**
- **MSD.EXE (.COM)**

- QBASIC.EXE
- SCANDISK.EXE
- SHARE.EXE
- SIZER.EXE
- SMARTDRV.EXE
- **SYS.COM**

Note   These files will just barely fit on one 3.5-inch high-density floppy disk. Files listed in **bold** are essential.

A Windows 98 startup disk is also a good item to carry. This is a bootable disk that will also load all drivers needed to run a CD-ROM on most PCs.

Tip   The utility MSD.EXE is a good diagnostic tool that can determine which hardware options are installed on a computer system without the need for you to remove the case. MSD.EXE is also a great tool for diagnosing software conflicts.

Operating-System Disk

Make sure copies of the original operating-system disk (or CD) are available. If it becomes necessary to install one or more components that were left out during the original installation, the computer might require verification of serial numbers (the original disk #1) before any additional files can be installed. Windows 95 and 98 and Windows NT strongly recommend that you create a rescue disk in case there are any problems with corrupt files in the operating system. It is a good practice to ensure that you have this disk available.

Note   A rescue disk is unique to the computer for which it was created. Therefore, a new one must be made for each computer in service.

Software Utilities

There are many good-quality utility programs available today. These programs allow the experienced user to find and correct a multitude of problems. However, caution should be used when "correcting" a problem that has been identified by the software. The software might consider something a problem simply because it does not recognize it. ("If I don't know what it is, it must be bad.") In some cases, the cure is worse than the disease. Also, keep in mind that one utility will not solve every problem. As a computer professional, you will do far better to master one good software system than to have a box full of utilities that you don't know how to run effectively. Don't forget good old MS-DOS; it is full of commands that are usually forgotten or never used.

Caution   Older versions of utility programs are designed to work with MS-DOS and Windows 3.x. They can wreak havoc on a Windows 95 or Windows 98 system. You must also be especially careful if you're running later versions of Windows 95 or Windows 98 that use the FAT32 file system, because most utilities are designed to handle the traditional FAT16.

You should never run any application to "tune" a system that is not specifically designed for that version of the operating system. That applies triple to advanced 32-bit operating systems such as Windows 98 and Windows 2000.

Among the handiest utilities have around are virus-checking programs that are compatible with each operating system you work with, such as disk and video display diagnostic programs.

Disassembly

Disassembling a computer is a straightforward task. In most cases, you will need to remove little more than the outer cover or shroud of the case to gain access to the memory, expansions slots/cards, and the CPU. Because there are many manufacturers, each seeking to establish its own unique marketing identity, each brand has some custom components or layout. The best strategy for efficient disassembly is to locate and use the manual that came with the computer.

Often, manuals don't provide a lot of technical information, but they usually tell you how to remove the cover. The extent to which you will have to disassemble a computer depends on the specific problem or repair. Following the following procedure will help you establish a routine for completely and efficiently disassembling most computers:

1. Make a complete backup of necessary operating-system and working files.
2. Document the system (hardware and software).
3. Create a clean work area with plenty of room and light.
4. Gather all the necessary tools for the job.
5. Implement safety procedures. (See Chapter 13, "The Basics of Electrical Energy," and Chapter 19, "Maintaining Computer Hardware," for details.)
6. Turn off the computer.
7. Disconnect the power cables.
8. Wear an antistatic wrist strap.
9. Locate the screws for the cover—check the manual to discover the location of the screws (sides or back).
10. Remove the screws. It's a good idea to store them in a box or plastic tube to keep them from getting lost.
11. Remove the cover from the computer.
12. Document the location of expansion cards and drives.
13. Remove all the cards and place them in antistatic bags.
14. Document the location and connections for each drive (pay special attention to the red wire on the data cables—this identifies the location of pin 1 on the device and driver).
15. Remove the data and power supply cables.
16. Remove the drives from their appropriate bays—look on their sides for the screws (check the manuals).
17. Remove the motherboard.

Reassembly

Run the **preassem** video located in the **demos** folder on the CD accompanying this book to view a presentation of all the hardware components that go into a personal computer.

To reassemble a computer, you simply follow the same procedures as for disassembly, but in the reverse order. When installing components, remember the following:

- Do not force connectors into place—if they don't fit easily, they are probably in the wrong place.
- Expansion cards often require some force or side-to-side movement to fit into place, but do not force them.
- When removing cables, remember the pin 1 locations. Check notations on the circuit boards, and look for the red wire on the ribbon cables.
- Connect the cables to the drives *before* installing them in the bays.
- Test the system before replacing the cover.

Lesson Summary

The following points summarize the main elements of this lesson:

- By following a systematic plan, you can simplify the process of disassembling and reassembling a computer.
- Establishing and maintaining good documentation and having the right hardware and software tools are the keys to a successful upgrade.
- Following safety procedures will ensure that no damage is done to you or the computer.

Lesson 2: Upgrading a Computer

In today's world of constant change, the most frequently performed task by a computer professional is to upgrade old systems to the latest technologies. This ability to expand and upgrade a computer can prolong the life and utility of a system. However, sometimes even the simple addition of a new piece of software can lead to hardware conflicts and the subsequent need for an upgrade, as a computer owner tries to squeeze one more year out of "old faithful." This lesson discusses many aspects of computer hardware upgrades.

After this lesson, you will be able to:
- Describe the principles behind upgrading a computer.
- Define the limits of and expectations for upgrading a system.

Estimated lesson time: 30 minutes

Run the **mboard** video located in the **demos** folder on the CD accompanying this book to view a presentation of a personal computer's motherboard subsystem.

Run the **assembly** video located in the **demos** folder on the CD accompanying this book to view a presentation of components being assembled into a personal computer.

As discussed in Lesson 1, before you begin to upgrade any computer, you need to document the system. You should create and maintain files that document all computers for which you are responsible. Figure 14.1 provides a sample configuration sheet. Use it as a model to create your own.

Sample Computer Configuration Sheet

Computer Name	
BIOS	

Primary User(s)	

Processor	

RAM		Cache	
Monitor		Video Card	
Sound Card		Modem	

Device	IRQ	I/O Base Address	DMA Channel	Device Drivers
	2/9			
	3			
	4			
	5			
	7			
	10			
	11			
	12			
	13			
	15			

Drive	Cylinders	Heads	Sector/Track	Capacity	Partitions

Software Operating System: DOS _ Windows 3.x _ Windows 3.11 _ Windows 95 _ Windows 98 _

Attach copies of: CONFIG.SYS _   AUTOEXEC.BAT

Figure 14.1 Sample configuration sheet

Memory, Memory, Memory

Does this computer have enough memory? This is the question that most frequently causes users to seek a computer upgrade. As programs and hardware get faster and are required to process more graphics and animation, the need for memory is as important as the need for speed.

Memory upgrades are perhaps the simplest to perform, but they can be very confusing without advance planning. Purchasing the right memory for the job is more than half the process of the upgrade. Before installing memory, there are five things to consider:

- Memory chip format
- Memory speed
- EDO RAM
- Parity
- Cache memory

The best source of information—which should be checked *before* obtaining memory—is the documentation that comes with the computer's motherboard. This source will generally list the type of memory required, how many SIMMs are required, and their location on the motherboard. If this information is not available, open the case and look. Some documentation provides a chart that includes exactly what memory has been installed and what is needed to upgrade to a given level. The following table gives you an idea of the kind of chart you might come across.

On-board	Bank 0	Bank 1	Total
8 MB			8 MB
8 MB	4 MB	4 MB	16 MB
8 MB	8 MB	8 MB	24 MB
8 MB	16 MB	16 MB	40 MB
8 MB	32 MB	32 MB	72 MB
Disabled	64 MB	64 MB	128 MB

Note   You can add memory with SIMMs (single inline memory modules) or DIMMs (dual inline memory modules).

SIMM Formats

SIMMs are provided in two basic, physical formats: a 30-pin and a 72-pin chip. Format is the first consideration, because the chips must fit into the motherboard. This configuration, along with the size of the processor, determines how many SIMMs are required to fill one bank.

The 30-pin formats contain memory in 8-bit chunks. This means that a 32-bit processor requires four SIMMs to fill one bank. Typical 32-bit processors consist of two banks of SIMMs and therefore eight slots. (See Figure 14.2.)

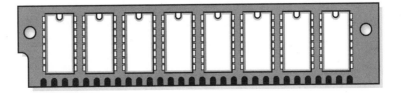

Figure 14.2   30-pin SIMM

A 72-pin format is larger and supplies memory in 32-bit chunks. Only one SIMM is required for a 32-bit machine. A Pentium processor has a 64-bit data path and requires a 72-pin SIMM. (See Figure 14.3.)

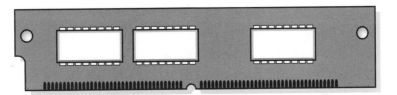

Figure 14.3   72-pin SIMM

Memory is normally sold in multiples of 8 MB. However, some machines will have 8 MB of "on-board" memory (usually soldered in place on the motherboard). When memory is soldered in place, it cannot be changed but this should not be considered a problem; it can be disabled. A computer equipped with this on-board memory can provide 8 MB of memory to the system without having any SIMMs installed in the slots. For such computers, installing 16 MB of RAM too would yield a total of 24 MB of RAM; if 64 MB were to be added, the total RAM would be 72 MB, and so on. In general, the idea of hardwiring memory on a system has died out on desktop PCs.

DIMM Formats

DIMMs are much easier than SIMMS to install or remove, because they require only one card, which is simply pushed into a module slot. The "key" cut into the edge that goes into the slot prevents the card from being inserted the wrong way. The one problem you face is choosing from the wide variety of memory types available. When ordering a new DIMM, you must know exactly the memory type supported by the system. DIMMs are found in larger memory sizes than SIMMs, ranging to 256MB and beyond for single cards.

Memory Speed

Memory speed is the amount of time required to access data and is measured in nanoseconds (ns); each nanosecond equals one billionth of a second. Two important considerations arise when addressing memory speed:

- The lower the number, the faster the chip speed.
- All chips in the same computer should run at the same speed.

Typical chip speeds are 50, 60, 70, and 80 nanoseconds. Be sure to check the motherboard documentation or the existing chips to determine the correct speed to use.

EDO RAM

The EDO RAM (extended data out read only memory) chip is used extensively with Pentium processors. This chip can improve read times and overall performance by up to 30 percent. This performance gain is possible because the chip continues to output data from one address while setting up a new address.

Parity

Parity is used to check the reliability of data. It requires one additional bit (chip). Memory can be purchased with or without parity. With parity, it will cost about 10 percent more. Be sure to check the machine specifications or the existing chips to determine if parity is required. Parity and nonparity chips cannot be mixed; however, some computers allow parity to be turned on or off (BIOS setup).

Cache

Cache memory can be found as either L1 or L2. The L1 cache is built into the processor and cannot be changed. The L2 cache, on the other hand, can be either built into the processor, or built onto the motherboard, sometimes both. In most cases, cache memory is fixed, but some machines allow L2 cache to be upgraded or expanded. Cache memory is sometimes found on older motherboard (as DIPPs—dual in-line packages). Check the motherboard documentation to determine what, if any, upgrades can be made to the cache.

Important   You need to take special care when installing DIPP chips. They are sensitive to ESD, can easily be installed backwards (look for pin 1 alignment), and the pins can be broken or bent during insertion.

Installing RAM

Installing RAM is a simple process. The only problem is that the slots are not always easily accessible. Sometimes you will need to relocate wires temporarily or even remove expansion cards. This simple procedure usually works:

1. Turn off the computer.
2. Disconnect all external devices (AC power and monitor power).
3. Follow the appropriate ESD safety procedures.
4. Remove the cover of the computer.
5. Locate the SIMM banks and determine that you have the correct size, speed, and quantity of SIMMs.
6. Insert the SIMMs in the slot at a 45 degree angle (backwards) and then snap it into the upright position, as shown in Figure 14.4. Be sure that the "notch" in the SIMM matches the slot. If it doesn't fit easily, it is probably installed incorrectly!

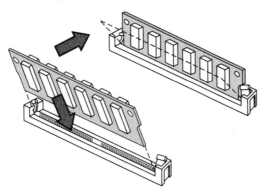

Figure 14.4   Installing a SIMM

7. When the SIMM is in an upright position, be sure that the metal retaining clip snaps into position. This clip holds the SIMM in place and must be opened before any SIMM can be removed.
8. Replace any temporarily removed or relocated wires or expansion cards. Check others to make sure they have not been loosened or disconnected.
9. Replace the cover of the computer.
10. Reconnect the power, monitor, and any other needed external devices, and start the computer.

The computer should recognize the new memory and either make the correction or automatically go to the setup program. In many cases, you need only exit setup to save the changes.

CPU Upgrades

Installing a new CPU is becoming less common as the prices of new motherboard/CPU combinations (and even new machines) continue to drop. In many cases, installing additional memory is a more effective upgrade than installing a new CPU. Still, as a technician, you need to know how to update the CPU in an existing machine.

In many cases, upgrading a CPU is as simple as removing the old one and inserting the new one. First, you need to determine whether the CPU can be upgraded and, if so, to what? The answer to this question lies in the motherboard. The motherboard must have the appropriate socket, data bus, address bus, and crystal to support the new CPU. Consult the documentation that comes with the motherboard—this documentation usually contains a table that defines which CPUs can be installed. If you are unable to find the documentation, or the processor that you want to install is not listed (because it's of newer vintage than the documentation), you will need to consult the motherboard manufacturer either through the company's Web site or with a phone call to the company's tech support department. Be sure to check on any required jumper settings and BIOS upgrades at the same time.

A small upgrade, going from one level of the same CPU family to another, is usually no problem. But if you want to upgrade a 386 to a Pentium, or a Pentium to a Pentium III, a new motherboard is the only answer. The same is true if the CPUs are coming from different chip makers. Refer to Chapter 4, Lesson 2: Replacing and Upgrading Chips, for possible scenarios.

General Procedure for Installing a CPU

Perhaps the most difficult part of upgrading a CPU is determining the limits imposed by the motherboard. But after the decision is made and you have the new processor in hand, the actual installation is quite easy. Follow this general procedure to install a CPU:

1. Turn off the computer and unplug the power cord.
2. Disconnect external devices (AC power and monitor power).
3. Follow the appropriate ESD safety procedures.
4. Remove the cover of the computer.
5. Locate the socket for the CPU. It might be on the motherboard or on a removable processor card.

6. Remove the old processor. This may require special tools for older processors. Pentium II and III packages are Slot 1 designs, which slide into a slot much like those used for an expansion card. The original Pentiums (60-166 MHz) and Pentium Pro models usually have a ZIF (zero-insertion-force) socket. The ZIF socket is opened by moving the handle to the upright position. (This should not require force.) The CPU can then be easily removed.

7. Install the new processor. Be certain to align the chip properly (this is critical!). Pin 1 on the CPU must fit pin 1 in the socket. There are several ways to identify this pin. Various chip manufacturers, and different versions of a manufacturer's chips, use different methods to mark installation orientation. Slot 1 CPU packages, for example, have a key in the slot, and it fits only one way. Other CPUs have similar schemes appropriate to their socket design. Look for a key pinhole in one corner, a blunt edge on one corner of the socket, a dot, a corner with a pin arrangement that differs from the others, or some other identifying mark. Align this mark with the corner of the socket that contains a blunt edge. If you encounter any resistance or you have to apply any pressure when inserting the CPU, recheck the chip's orientation and alignment, and reinsert the chip. After the chip is in place, secure the ZIF handle. You might need to check the documentation to make sure the chip is installed correctly.

8. Set any jumpers or switches on the motherboard. Check the documentation.

9. Replace the cover and power up the computer.

10. Reconnect any peripherals (keyboard, mouse, monitor).

11. Make changes to the CMOS setup, if required.

Some CPU upgrades also require the installation of a new voltage regulator and/or cooling fan. Be sure to check the motherboard and CPU documentation for this possibility. Failure to install these parts with the new CPU might destroy the CPU.

Note If you are working with a motherboard that has the ability to hold more than one CPU, both CPUs must be of the same type and from the same manufacturer if more than one is actually installed. In addition, on Pentium II and later systems, most such motherboards have a special card that must be inserted in any empty CPU slot, and the appropriate slot must be used for a single CPU configuration.

Expansion Cards

Installing an expansion card is one of the most common system upgrades. Adding faster video cards, more ports, or improving sound quality are common reasons for plugging in a new card. (See Figure 14.5.) Before installing (or purchasing) an expansion card, it is a good idea to make sure it will work in the system to be upgraded, and that appropriate drivers are available for the operating system to be used.

Figure 14.5   Motherboard and expansion card

Ask these questions first:

- Is adding a new card the most cost-effective way to make this upgrade, given the type of device and performance/capacity desired? In some cases a USB (universal serial bus) peripheral can offer the same features without requiring the case to be opened.

- Are there any expansion slots available? If no slots of the type required are available, you will have to make some room. To do that, you will need to do one of three things: replace separate, single-port cards with one multifunction card that provides all port connections; use a SCSI card and a chain of SCSI devices, if available; or use USB. if available.

- Will the card fit in the type of slot available? Does it match the bus type of the motherboard?

- Are there any available I/Os and IRQs in the system? If so, write them down.

- Is there enough memory (RAM and hard-disk) available to run the device and its software?

- Does the card require a DMA (direct memory access) channel? If so, is one available?

- What are the potential conflicts with other cards and devices?

- Will the software operating system support this card? If so, are all the necessary drivers provided with the operating system or will they have to be provided with the card?

After you have determined that the expansion card will work, the installation is a simple three-step process:

1. Set any jumpers or switches for IRQ and I/O addresses.
2. Install the card and cables.
3. Install any software for the card.

Step 1 (IRQ and I/O setup) is perhaps the most confusing and frustrating part. This is especially true if the computer has not been properly documented.

Important Be sure to cover all slots. A missing expansion-slot cover can cause a computer to overheat. Be sure that no screws or other items are left loose inside the case that could possibly short out a component after the case is closed.

General Procedure for Installing an Expansion Card (Non–Plug and Play Capable)

A card that is not Plug and Play capable is a bit more complicated than one that is.

1. Read the documentation that comes with the card and note any special requirements or limitations *before* you start the installation.
2. Check the computer documentation (run MSD or other diagnostic program) and determine which IRQs and I/O addresses are available. Check the computer documentation (run MSD or other diagnostic program) and determine which IRQs and I/O addresses are available.
3. Configure any jumpers or switches on the card. (See Figures 14.6 and 14.7.) Note that some cards might require changes in order to prevent conflicts and allow all devices to work.

Figure 14.6 Switches

Figure 14.7 Jumpers

4. Turn off the computer and unplug the power cord.

5. Follow the appropriate ESD safety procedures.

6. Remove the cover of the computer.

7. Install the card in a free slot. (See Figure 14.8.) Power up the computer, note any conflicts, and make adjustments as necessary. Remember to remove power and use ESD precautions when making changes.

Figure 14.8 Installing an expansion card

8. Replace the cover.

9. Install any software drivers or applications.

General Procedure For Installing An Expansion Card (Plug And Play)

The latest technology available for installing expansion cards is called Plug and Play. This is an independent set of specifications developed by a group of hardware and software companies that allow the user to make configuration changes with minimal adjustment. Simply install the card, turn on the computer, and use the device.

In order for Plug and Play to work, the device must be able to identify itself and its system requirements to the system. The operating system will then set the device and make any other adjustments, such as reconfiguring other devices, as required. In order for a Plug and Play device to work immediately, you must be sure that the computer hardware—motherboard, BIOS, and other components—the operating system, and the device are Plug and Play–compliant.

Tip   If a device is Windows 95–compliant, it is Plug and Play–compliant, too, and can take full advantage of operating in a Windows 95 environment.

Note   In many systems you must enable Plug and Plug features in the system CMOS. (Failure to have the right settings will make installing a Plug and Plug card a difficult task.)

Drives

Installing a new drive is not difficult. However, you must answer a few questions before purchasing a new drive:

- Will the drive physically fit inside the computer? Some desktop cases have only enough space for one hard disk drive, or the available space might be occupied by another device (a CD-ROM drive or floppy disk drive). If there is not enough space, you will have to consider alternatives such as external SCSI (Small Computer System Interface) drives, USB drives, and parallel port interface drives.

- Will the computer's BIOS and operating system support the size (storage capacity) of the drive?

- Will the drive controller support the new drive? A second or updated controller might be required.

- Are there sufficient cables (data and power) to install the drive?

Procedure for Installing an IDE Drive

Installing an IDE (Integrated Drive Electronics) drive will require some hardware and software preparation to get it running properly. Hardware preparation includes ensuring that you have the correct drive, a place to physically install it, and the proper cables to connect it. Software preparation includes at least a bootable MS-DOS disk containing a minimum of FORMAT and FDISK. A Windows 95 or 98 startup disk will do the job. If you don't already have such a disk, be sure to create one before removing the old drive. Follow these steps to install the drive:

1. Collect all the necessary documentation for the drive and the computer.
2. Turn off the computer and unplug the power cord.
3. Follow the appropriate ESD safety procedures.
4. Open the case of the computer.
5. Set the jumper for the drive. Consult the documentation that came with the drive. It must be set to single use or master or slave. If this is a second drive, both drives might require jumper settings.
6. Connect the cable to the drives. The end connector should be plugged into the master drive. Be sure the cable orientation is correct (pin 1 goes to the red wire).
7. Connect the power cable. (See Figure 14.9.)

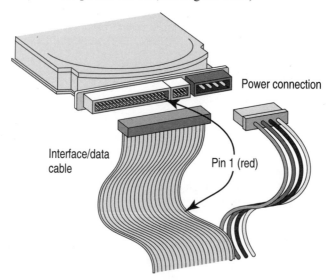

Figure 14.9   Cable Connections

8. Install the drive in its bay.

9. Reconnect the power, boot up the computer, and run the CMOS setup utility. The CMOS must be set to recognize the new drive. See the manufacturer's documentation for proper configuration. Don't forget that drives larger than 528 MB (approximately) will require logical block addressing (LBA).

Note It might be advisable to set up and test a drive before final installation in the bay. Be careful to avoid ESD or placing the drive in a position that will cause excessive heat build-up. Large capacity drives, especially SCSI and older ESDI (Enhanced Small Device Interface) drives, can generate a lot of heat. It might be necessary to position a small fan to send a current of air over the drive's logic board when running a hard disk drive out of a computer or drive case.

Some larger drives installed in older machines might require the use of disk-management software. This software is usually provided with the drive (in some cases, it's already loaded in the drive). Follow the instructions provided by the manufacturer to extract and use this software. It's especially important to document the use of such software, and to make sure it is included on any boot/rescue floppy you prepare for such a system.

To complete the installation:

1. Boot the computer from the bootable floppy disk and run FDISK to set the partition (or partitions).

2. Format the drive. If it is the only drive or the bootable drive, it must be formatted with the system files.

3. Replace the cover of the computer.

The drive is now ready for software to be installed.

Motherboards

Installing a new motherboard is one way to completely overhaul a computer. (See Figure 14.10.) In many cases, it is the most inexpensive way to get a new computer. This type of upgrade usually works best with IBM clones. Many of the larger manufacturers use proprietary motherboards that can only be replaced with one made by the same manufacturer to ensure compatibility with other components.

Figure 14.10   Motherboard

Before deciding to undertake this major overhaul, there are several questions to answer:

- Will the motherboard fit into the existing case? Check the size and alignment of mounting holes (plastic standoffs that keep the circuitry from contacting the case).

- Does the motherboard have the same built-in COM and LPT ports?

- Does the motherboard have a built-in video card?

- Will the existing expansion cards fit the motherboard's expansion bus slots? Are there enough slots available to accommodate the existing cards? The expansion slots should go toward the back of the computer, where the openings are located.

- Is the power connector located on the same side as the power supply? It should be as near to the power supply as possible.

- Will the existing drives (CD-ROM, IDE, or SCSI) work with the controllers on the motherboard?

- Will the SIMMs on the old motherboard work with the new motherboard?

- Will the upgrade meet your current and future requirements?

Installing a new motherboard is a major task and requires complete disassembly, reassembly, and setup of the computer and all its devices. You will put everything covered so far in this lesson into practice when you replace a motherboard. The best advice is to prepare everything ahead of time and to take good notes while disassembling the old motherboard.

Replacing a Motherboard

Replacing a motherboard is probably the most difficult task (from the perspective of physically replacing parts) that a computer technician will take on. It amounts to no less than building a computer, because it will, in many cases, require complete disassembly first. Although complex, if you carry out the following procedure one step at a time, you should not face any problems.

1. Complete an installation checklist and make sure all the necessary parts are available and will fit into the computer.

2. Follow the "disassemble a computer" steps set out in Lesson 1; these include removing all the screws and standoffs (taking care to keep them in a safe place) and the old motherboard.

3. Check all the settings on the new motherboard.

4. Install the new motherboard. Position the standoffs and make sure they align with the case and the motherboard. Verify that the motherboard is positioned correctly (expansion slots facing the back of the computer). Carefully tighten the screws. Visually check to be sure that the motherboard does not touch the case. (See Figure 14.11.)

Figure 14.11   Motherboard in case

5. Reconnect the case switches. Use the notes taken during disassembly to verify they are in the right place.

6. Follow the steps for computer reassembly set out in Lesson 1.

7. Test to be sure that the computer boots up.

8. Complete the final testing and close the case.

Lesson Summary

The following points summarize the main elements of this lesson:

- Performing upgrades is one of the computer technician's most commonly performed tasks.

- Good documentation (before and after) is an essential requirement for upgrading.

- A computer technician should be familiar with the steps required to upgrade memory, CPUs, expansion cards, hard drives, and motherboards.

Chapter Summary

The following points summarize the key concepts in this chapter:

Computer Disassembly and Reassembly

- Preparation is the key to a successful upgrade or repair. Document the system setup, including hardware and software, using a computer configuration sheet before you begin the project.

- Prepare a plan of action before beginning a project and stick to it.

- Make sure you have an adequate toolkit, including a bootable floppy disk and any utilities you may need.

- Always create a complete backup of the system you are going to be working on *before* you begin.

- Implement safety precautions, including ESD prevention.

- Follow the steps for disassembly and reassembly.

Upgrading a Computer

- Memory upgrades are probably the simplest and most common upgrades performed by a computer technician.

- Installing a new CPU is a common way to upgrade older computers. Installing a new expansion card is another common upgrade.

- Before installing (or purchasing) new parts, make sure the parts will work with the system you intend to upgrade.

- Installing a new hard drive is not difficult. However, certain procedures need to be followed.

- Installing a new motherboard is one way to completely overhaul a computer.

Review

1. Describe a basic sample toolkit for the computer professional.

2. What is a Torx driver used for?

3. How many bootable floppy disks are needed for a computer professional's tool kit?

4. You are only going to check the memory chips. Do you need to follow ESD (electrostatic discharge) safety practices?

5. SIMMs are available in two physical configurations. What are they?

6. You have an extra 16 MB of RAM on a single 30-pin SIMM, and a friend has a computer and needs more memory. What do you need to check in order to determine if this memory module can be used on your friend's computer?

7. What is parity? Can parity chips be mixed with nonparity chips?

8. Can L1 cache memory be upgraded?

9. Your client wants to install an internal modem. How would you determine whether this internal modem could be installed on your client's machine?

10. A friend just got a bargain on a new Plug and Play sound card and wants to install it on her 486SX computer. Will it work?

11. How do you determine whether to upgrade the CPU or install another motherboard?

12. What is the advantage of Plug and Play?

13. What are the four requirements that must be addressed before installing a new drive in a computer?

C H A P T E R   1 5

Software: MS-DOS and Windows 3.x

About This Chapter

The term *software* refers to any program (set of instructions) that directs a computer to carry out a task or function. Software can be divided into two categories: operating systems and applications. Operating-system software is used to manage hardware, data, and application software. No computer can run without an operating system. MS-DOS, Windows 3.x, Windows 95, Windows 98, Windows NT, Windows 2000, OS/2, and UNIX are examples of operating systems.

Applications are the tools employed by users. Application software programs (such as Microsoft Word, Access, Excel, and so forth) use the operating-system software enabling users to create, manipulate, and present data. This chapter focuses on the earlier operating-system software—MS-DOS and Windows 3.x. Although MS-DOS and Windows 3.x are somewhat outdated, they remain the foundation from which the newer 32-bit operating systems like Windows 95, Windows 98, and Windows 2000 evolved. Many fundamental concepts and conventions used with today's operating systems stem from these beginnings. As an A+ technician aspirant, you will find some questions regarding MS-DOS and Windows 3.x on the exam.

Before You Begin

Some experience using MS-DOS and Windows is recommended before studying this chapter; intermediate or expert level experience is *not* required. However, you should be able to perform the basic tasks of operating a computer, using a mouse, and navigating through screens.

Lesson 1: Operating System Basics

After this lesson, you will be able to:

- Define an operating system.
- Describe the difference between MS-DOS, Windows, and Windows NT.

Estimated lesson time: 20 minutes

An operating system is a special software program that is loaded into a computer at startup and is responsible for running the computer. It manages all the hardware, and provides an interface between the computer's hardware and the user.

MS-DOS

DOS stands for disk operating system. The full proper name is preceded by the name of the manufacturer—for example, MS-DOS (for Microsoft and also used by "clone" makers) or PC-DOS (for versions specific to the IBM Personal Computer). This version was also sometimes referred to as IBM-DOS. All versions of DOS are actually the product of Microsoft development. The modern computer professional must be familiar with MS-DOS because MS-DOS remains at the heart of Windows. Although increasingly more configuration can be done through the Windows interface, there comes a time when every computer professional is faced with a screen of MS-DOS commands. Windows 98—the most current operating system—is more independent of MS-DOS than prior versions of Windows. However, every PC still requires AUTOEXEC.BAT, CONFIG.SYS, and various initialization files. So there remains a need for the computer professional to be familiar with MS-DOS.

DOS has been produced by three suppliers, and the versions are so similar that they are considered as one operating system. The three brands of DOS are:

- **MS-DOS**, produced by Microsoft—the most popular
- **PC-DOS**, produced by IBM
- **DR-DOS**, produced by Novell

Proprietary DOS

Many computer manufacturers, especially in the early days of the 8088 and 80286 processors, produced their own versions of DOS. These were actually tweaked versions that contained additional commands or utilities specific to their hardware. Such versions might be required to run these machines and will require software that is compatible as well.

DOS was originally designed to load an operating system from a floppy disk to a computer with no hard drive (before hard drives were common). Today, any reference to DOS is synonymous with MS-DOS.

The following table provides a version history of MS-DOS.

Version	Introduced	Features
1.0	August 1981	Distributed on one floppy disk (required 8 KB of RAM).
1.1	May 1982	Added supported for 320-KB double-sided disks.
2.0	March 1983	Introduced support for hard disks, directories, background printing, and the ability to add device drivers.
3.0	August 1984	Increased support for hard disks larger than 10 MB and 1.2-MB floppy disks.
3.1	March 1985	Added networks and file sharing.
3.2	January 1986	Included support for 3.5-inch floppy disks.
3.3	April 1987	Added new commands and international support.
4.0	February 1988	Added support for hard disks greater than 32 MB, the MEM command, and MS-DOS Shell.
5.0	May 1991	Added memory management tools, help, undelete, unformat, task swapping. This was the last version to come with a printed manual.
6.0	March 1993	Included new features such as MEMMAKER, multiple boot configurations, Windows UNFORMAT and UNDELETE, virus protection, and backup. MEMMAKER is a utility that is used to modify the system's CONFIG.SYS and AUTOEXEC.BAT files, so that device drivers and memory-resident programs take up less conventional memory space.
6.2	October 1993	Included ScanDisk, MSD utilities, enhanced diagnostics.
7.0	December 1995	Not really a stand-alone product; provided the command-level environment included with Windows 95.

Some computer manufacturers have produced OEM (original equipment manufacturer) versions of MS-DOS. For the most part, these versions have been cosmetically modified for specific use with their computers (such as a "splash screen" that shows the company logo during boot up). Care should be taken when using any computer with one of these operating systems—some incompatibilities with software written for MS-DOS might exist. You should be careful when substituting a generic DOS for MS-DOS if you are reformatting a hard disk drive or reinstalling the operating system. Make such a substitution only after you have verified that the generic version is compatible with all of the computer's hardware and software; the generic version might not provide the necessary support.

MS-DOS includes three programs that are required to make a drive or floppy disk bootable:

- **IO.SYS:** The interface between the hardware and the operating-system code
- **MSDOS.SYS:** The main operating-system code
- **COMMAND.COM:** The interface between the user and the operating-system code

---

Note   IO.SYS and MSDOS.SYS are hidden files that are not usually visible when you examine a disk directory.

In addition to the three core files, MS-DOS uses two other startup files. These files are not required to start the machine, but they add any additional startup configuration required by the user or applications. These files are:

- **CONFIG.SYS:** Loads extra hardware and device drivers not built into the IO.SYS.
- **AUTOEXEC.BAT:** Loads terminate-and-stay-resident (TSR) programs selected by the user and sets up the environment variables such as TEMP and PATH.

Note   If a user complains that a machine is not loading MS-DOS, especially after installing new hardware or software, disable these two files as a first diagnostic step. In many cases, drivers or procedure calls are conflicting or corrupting system memory.

Microsoft Windows

Microsoft Windows 3.1 is not, in itself, an operating system. Windows 3.1 is an operating environment that uses MS-DOS as its foundation. Unlike Windows 3.1, Windows 95 is an operating system that incorporates MS-DOS. The purpose of Windows 3.1 was to make the computer more user-friendly by providing a GUI (graphical user interface). The GUI uses icons or pictures to display command information, rather than requiring the user to type a command. Windows is designed to be used extensively with a mouse or other pointing device (it can be used entirely with a keyboard—but that's not recommended).

Windows did not get off to a fast start. In fact, it was not generally accepted until the release of version 3.0. The first version, 1.0, was released in 1985, followed by version 2.0 in 1987. Version 1.0 provided a graphical interface and little else. Version 2.0 was used predominantly by the engineering, design, and graphics/ desktop publishing communities. It wasn't until the release of version 3.0 in the early 1990s that this operating environment became popular. This jump in popularity can be attributed to an increasing software base with applications that overwhelmed the features in the MS-DOS environment—faster graphics cards, and improved memory management. The best-known and most-used 16-bit version of Windows is 3.11, released in the spring of 1992.

All applications written to Windows standards provide a common user interface:

- The menu system offers the same basic commands.
- Selecting text or objects is done in a similar manner.
- Clicking and dragging mouse functions are the same.

This commonality shortens the user's learning curve for unfamiliar applications. On a programming level, application developers have access to a toolbox of Windows routines, so they do not have to reinvent the wheel every time they want to invoke a menu or dialog box.

Windows uses a sophisticated memory-management system that makes better use of memory and allows the user to run multiple applications concurrently. This form of multitasking allows the user to have more than one application open and switch between them, even cutting and pasting data from one open window to another. One of the restrictions of DOS is that it was designed to run on an 8086 machine, with a conventional memory limit of 640 KB of RAM. Windows overcomes this restriction by implementing new modes of memory utilization.

Operating Modes

With the release of the 80286 processors, the CPU was able to address more than 1 MB of RAM, thus breaking the DOS barrier. This was good, but the market was still dominated by MS-DOS-based programs that worked within this limit. The release of Windows solved this problem by allowing it to operate in several modes—thus accommodating both the old and new worlds—and fostering a whole new market for memory managers to help overcome the hurdles in configuring them.

Real Mode

The original intention of Microsoft Windows was to provide an MS-DOS-based GUI. The first versions did not include memory-management functions and did not multitask. They were designed only for starting programs and managing files while operating within the MS-DOS limit of 1 MB of RAM. Later versions, however, moved outside the 1-MB limit but continued to support this MS-DOS mode until version 3.1 appeared. This MS-DOS mode is called *real mode* and is now virtually obsolete. However, some older MS-DOS applications and hardware still require the use of real mode. Support of real-mode applications and hardware is part of downward compatibility. Even in the Windows 95 environment, you will encounter terms such as "real-mode driver," which refers to operating at this level.

Note   If any real-mode drivers are loaded in Windows 95, the system will be forced into the same mode: compatibility mode. This will slow down the machine and limit memory utilization. In general, you should stay in 32-bit mode.

Standard Mode

Windows 2.0 broke out of the MS-DOS 1-MB barrier by making use of 286-level *protected mode* of operation. Protected-mode Windows could address up to 16 MB of RAM. Although MS-DOS programs could run only in the first megabyte of memory, specialized programs were written that would run in (and only in) the extended memory controlled by Windows. The term "protected mode" refers to using *protected memory*. (Standard mode is run with the processor in protected mode.) Along with Windows protected mode came the now-famous "GPF" (General Protection Fault). Encountering this error generally means that some portion of the Windows protected mode has been violated (for example, the program is trying to write data outside the portion of memory allocated to it).

Microsoft expanded the concept behind Windows by adding support for standardized graphics, fonts, I/O devices, and memory mapping; together these are known as resources. Windows is a resource manager. In the MS-DOS environment, applications developers handled these tasks themselves. Because Windows has these resources built in, it is an easy environment for writing programs. By breaking the MS-DOS barrier (engaging 286 protected mode), Windows running in standard mode takes control of many the hardware functions. This means that programs do not have to write the code directly to control devices, only to ask Windows to use them.

MS-DOS programs can run only in real mode. Running 286 protected mode worked well for the special programs, but once in protected mode, it was not possible to return to real mode without resetting the CPU (only the CPU—not the computer). The MS-DOS program would unload when you switched back to Windows. These versions (1.0 and 2.0) of Windows could run only one MS-DOS program at a time.

Windows Runtime Version

Certain applications (like Aldus PageMaker) could be purchased with a "runtime" version of Windows. This allowed a program that required a Windows environment to run on computers that did not have the full version of Windows installed.

386 Enhanced Mode

The 386 protected mode can address up to 4 GB of memory, supports virtual memory, and allows multiple MS-DOS programs to run simultaneously. Beginning with Windows for Workgroups 3.11, only 386 enhanced mode is allowed in Windows for full operation. Real mode is still used in a limited way for advanced diagnostics and development.

As mentioned, Windows is a resource manager. It treats everything in the computer as a resource. Resources include memory, video, serial ports, and sound. All resources are presented to Windows through *device drivers*. Device drivers are simply files that know how to talk to Windows. When loaded, they allow Windows and a device to communicate. Almost all device drivers are stored in the \Windows\System directory. These drivers can be easily identified by their file extensions, which are .DRV or .386. Drivers with the extension .DRV are designed to work in standard and enhanced mode. Drivers with the extension .386 work only in enhanced mode.

Just like MS-DOS, Windows consists of three core files: KRNL386.EXE, USER.EXE, and GDI.EXE. These programs allocate and keep track of all system resources requested by the applications. They use a number of 64-KB storage areas of extended memory (called *heaps*) to keep track of which application is using which resource. They also have some ability to take away or reallocate resources (mainly RAM) from one application to another.

Applications are resource consumers. They must request access to any resource using very standardized subroutines called the *application programming interface (API)*. Another file called a dynamic-link library (DLL) can speak to the Windows core directly. These small files store subroutines that either come with the compiler that created the application, or are made by the programmer. DLL files always end with the extension .DLL. Loss or corruption of DLL files will cause an application to lock up or prevent it from loading.

Note   Some programs come with custom versions of DLLs that overwrite the standard DLL of the same name. If a problem occurs after loading a new application, installing a repair update of Windows might correct the problem, but can also render the new program useless. In such cases, you will need to consult with the program vendor or check the Microsoft Knowledge Base for more information on a fix.

When a program starts, it loads a small piece called a "stub" in conventional memory. This stub asks for RAM from KRNL386.EXE, which then allocates the amount of RAM as long as it is available. This area of RAM is known as a *segment* and its location is stored in a heap. Once loaded, a program can ask for resources as required. As long as there are resources to give, Windows will give them.

RAM is the most important resource that Windows must manage. As most users know, there never seems to be enough memory. Windows provides a way to gain memory when there is none. It uses *virtual memory*. Virtual memory means the ability to make something other than RAM chips hold data. Windows can create a special file (called a *swap file*) on the hard disk drive to act as a RAM chip. While running, Windows prioritizes programs and caches the lesser-used ones to the hard drive, thus allowing the most active program to use actual RAM.

To get around the problem of resetting the CPU in order to run an MS-DOS program, these later versions of Windows have the ability to run what is known as virtual 8086 mode. Virtual 8086 mode is an extension of 386 protected mode that allows for the creation of virtual 8086 machines. A virtual 8086 machine is a segment of RAM that operates as if it's an 8086 computer. Windows will run itself in one virtual machine (VM) and allocate another virtual machine to an MS-DOS program. Using several virtual machines, Windows can overcome the limitations of running only one MS-DOS program at a time.

Windows for Workgroups 3.11

Windows for Workgroups is an upgrade to Windows 3.1. It works and runs just like Windows 3.1 but has a few enhancements such as better networking capabilities for sharing files and printers. It also includes two utility programs: Schedule+ and Mail Service.

Windows 95 and Windows 98

Unlike earlier versions of Windows, Windows 95 and Windows 98 are true operating systems. The details of configuring and using both are included in Chapters 16 and 17.

Windows NT

In the summer of 1993, Microsoft released another operating system primarily for the professional market. When it was first introduced, it was used in relatively simple network installations. Over several revisions, it has been enhanced to support the needs of corporations ranging in size from small to large and, now, the needs of the Internet and intranets. As an operating system, Windows NT provides a high degree of networkability as well as high security levels not available in other operating systems. Windows NT uses the same GUI as Windows 3.x; therefore, making it an easy upgrade for anyone proficient in using the Windows operating system.

There are several versions of Windows NT, ranging from 3.0 through 4. In addition, there are Service Packs; inline fixes that do not change the version number. Windows NT provides three levels of operating system in each of the later versions:

- **Workstation:** A powerful, robust operating system with limited networking to allow sharing of printers and files for the professional user.

- **Server:** A complete LAN host with a variety of sophisticated features for managing users and access to printers, files, RAID installations, and other shared resources.

- **Advanced Server:** The enterprise edition that adds tools for complex network environments.

Windows 2000

The most recent addition to the Windows family, Windows 2000, is the replacement for Windows NT, adding Plug and Play support, better multimedia tools, and advanced Internet support. Like Windows NT, it comes in three versions: Workstation, Server, and Advanced Server.

Note   Be careful when upgrading to Windows NT or Windows 2000. They are not merely more powerful versions of Windows 98, but more robust, completely new environments. Not all applications and hardware are compatible with them. Be sure to consider all the advantages and disadvantages before making the decision to upgrade. Then check the Microsoft Web site for the latest version of the compatibility list.

Lesson Summary

The following points summarize the main elements of this lesson:

- An operating system provides the interface between hardware and user.
- MS-DOS is one of the first operating systems and was, for a long time, widely accepted as the standard.
- MS-DOS has limitations, notably, the 1-MB barrier.
- Early versions of Windows were operating environments that ran on top of MS-DOS.
- There are three files that make up the core operating system of MS-DOS: IO.SYS, MSDOS.SYS, and COMMAND.COM.
- Windows has three modes: real mode, standard mode, and 386 enhanced mode.

Lesson 2: MS-DOS

Lesson 1 presented the basics of operating systems—what they are and what they do. It also provided a summary of two important operating systems: MS-DOS and Windows 3.1. This lesson takes us one step further. By knowing how to configure an operating system, a computer technician can gain optimal performance from a machine. This lesson covers configuration of the MS-DOS operating system. It is not intended to be a complete course in MS-DOS; however, some important techniques useful to the computer professional are pointed out. Gaining an understanding of MS-DOS and being able to use an MS-DOS manual as a reference are requirements for the computer professional. Learning MS-DOS requires perseverance and hands-on experience.

Note   Many book and computer/software stores offer books that describe the various software operating systems. A reference book for each operating system is a necessary component of the computer professional's technical library.

After this lesson, you will be able to:

- Use basic MS-DOS commands to increase the performance of a computer.
- Optimize the MS-DOS CONFIG.SYS and AUTOEXEC.BAT files.
- Optimize conventional memory in a MS-DOS machine.

Estimated lesson time: 45 minutes

The Boot Process

In computer terms, *boot up* means to start or get going. In Chapter 6, we discussed POST (power-on self test). Once POST is complete (the basic hardware is determined to be OK), the computer loads software that tells it how to run. This software is the operating system (OS). The boot sequence for operating systems will vary. Several steps are involved in the MS-DOS system startup process:

1. The ROM BIOS looks for an operating system. It checks for the presence of IO.SYS and MSDOS.SYS, first searching the A (floppy disk) drive and then the C drive.

2. The operating system processes the CONFIG.SYS file (if present). The CONFIG.SYS contains information to configure the system environment including special memory management overlays and hardware drivers.

3. COMMAND.COM is loaded.

4. The operating system processes the AUTOEXEC.BAT file (if present). The AUTOEXEC.BAT loads programs and user-defined settings.

5. If no programs (such as Windows) have been invoked, COMMAND.COM presents the active-drive prompt and waits for a command.

The process of starting from a no-power condition is called a *cold boot*. Occasionally, a system might require a reset—for instance, when the computer locks up or runs out of memory. Resetting can be accomplished without turning off the computer by holding down the CTRL, ALT, and DEL keys at the same time. This is called a *warm boot*.

MS-DOS Terms and Commands

MS-DOS, like UNIX, uses a command-line or text-based user interface. This means that the user must memorize and type commands in order to interface with the operating system. Not exactly a user-friendly operating system, which is why Windows has come to dominate the market. Even today, the computer professional should know how to use and navigate in the MS-DOS environment. When Windows fails, using MS-DOS is often the best way to access any recoverable data and begin the repair process.

Key MS-DOS Terms

As with any operating system, it is important to understand the language or terms used. As mentioned, this is not a complete course in MS-DOS and there is no substitute for an MS-DOS manual. The following table presents some of the important terms and concepts you might encounter when working with MS-DOS.

Term	Description
.bat	An extension that indicates a batch file.
.com	An extension used to identify a file as an executable program file.
.exe	An extension used to identify a file as an executable program file.
Backslash (\)	A symbol used to separate each directory level, for instance C:\Windows\Utilities. For this reason, it is a reserved character and cannot be used as part of a file name.
Case sensitivity	The ability of the operating system to distinguish between uppercase and lowercase letters. MS-DOS commands are not case-sensitive. Traditionally, MS-DOS commands have been represented in documentation as uppercase. While you can type MS-DOS commands in either upper- or lowercase, we are representing them in this book as uppercase.
Cursor	Anytime you are entering data, whether in an application or in an MS-DOS command, the cursor (usually a small flashing line) indicates the place where the next character will be inserted. It is a good idea to always know where your cursor is.
Default drive	Each drive in a computer has its own letter designation. The default drive is the active drive. Unless otherwise specified, any commands act upon the default drive. The current default drive is indicated by the MS-DOS prompt. For example, if you want to see a directory (the command is DIR) of files on the A drive and the default drive is C, you need to type DIR A: otherwise you will see a directory of the C drive.

continued

Term	Description
Directory	Directories—known as folders in the Windows and Macintosh environments—are locations for storing files. Every disk contains a main directory known as the *root directory*. Below the root directory is a hierarchical structure of other (sub)directories.
MS-DOS prompt	The MS-DOS prompt usually displays the active drive letter (for instance, C:) and directory. This indicates that the operating system is ready to accept the next command. (The prompt is user-changeable.)
Drive pointers	MS-DOS assigns letters to each drive during the boot process.
Entering Commands	You can type a command and press ENTER to execute it. If you make a mistake, correct it by using the BACKSPACE or DEL keys. Use ESC to start a command again. Use the F3 key to repeat a command.
Error messages	Brief technical messages that are displayed when an error occurs.
Filenames (also filespecs)	A filename is made up of three parts—a name of up to eight characters, a period, and an extension of up to three characters. The name can include any number, character, or the following symbols: _()~'!%$&#. Spaces cannot be used in MS-DOS filenames. Example: MYFILE.DOC
Greater than (>)	This symbol is used to indicate that a command can be redirected to an output device. For example, to redirect the directory command to a printer, type: DIR > LPT1.
Path	The address to a file. The path consists of the drive name, the location of the file in the directory structure, and the filename. Example: C:\Mystuff\Myfile.doc.
Prompt	The command prompt—user interface provided by COMMAND.COM to signal to the user that the computer is ready to receive input (for example: C:\> or A:\>).
Switches	Many MS-DOS commands can be used with a switch ("/" followed by a letter) to invoke special functions. Because no comprehensive manuals are available after MS-DOS 5, when you follow a command with a space and "/?", a list of parameters and switches available for that command is displayed.
Syntax	Syntax is the arrangement and interrelationship of words in phrases and sentences. In computer jargon, it is the correct format in which to type a command. In MS-DOS, every letter, number, and space has a value. The most common problem when typing MS-DOS commands is adding or leaving out a letter or character. Simple typing mistakes are the most common cause for "Bad command or filename" errors.
Wildcards	The question mark (?) matches any character in a specified position, and the asterisk (*) matches any number of characters up to the end of the filename or extension. For example, to search for files beginning with the letter "A," the command would be DIR A*.* or A?????.* (the second command would find a file that starts with the letter A and any other five characters).

MS-DOS Commands

MS-DOS commands are found in two varieties and locations. The *internal MS-DOS commands* are stored within the COMMAND.COM file and are always available. These provide key commands needed to access files and manage the operating system. The *external MS-DOS commands* are larger utilities stored as .COM or .EXE files in the MS-DOS directory. External MS-DOS commands must be on the current drive, some other drive whose location is stored in the PATH variable (that is, they can be in any directory as long the directory name and location is included in the path statement in the AUTOEXEC.BAT file), or be named with the complete path to the executable file to be run. The following table lists examples of commonly used internal MS-DOS commands.

Command	Function
CHDIR or CD	Changes the directory. (For example, cd\word would take you to the "word" subdirectory.)
CHKDSK	Examines the FAT (file allocation table) and directory structure on a drive, checking for errors and inconsistencies that can keep you from accessing a file. It also locates lost clusters and can convert them into files for later deletion. It can also reclaim wasted space.
CLS	Clears the screen.
COPY	Copies files or disks. To copy all files from the "myfiles" subdirectory to the A (floppy) drive, the command would be: copy c:\myfiles*.* a:
DATE	Changes the system date.
DEL	Deletes files. (Example: c:\del myfile.txt).
DIR	Lists a directory of files.
DIR /P	Views directories, one page at a time. (Directories can be quite long.)
DIR /W	Displays wide format in columns—only the filename is listed; not size, date, or time.
DIR /W /P	Displays large directories in columns, one page at a time.
DISKCOMP	Compares two disks. The syntax is: a:\ diskcomp a: b: or diskcomp a: a: (the computer will prompt you to insert the second disk to be compared).
MKDIR or MD	Makes a directory.
PROMPT	Changes the appearance of the cursor.
REN	Renames a file.
RMDIR or RD	Deletes a directory. This works only if the directory is empty of all files including hidden ones.
TIME	Changes the system time.
TYPE	Displays (types) a text file.
VER	Displays the version of MS-DOS in use.

The following table lists examples of commonly used external MS-DOS commands.

Command	Function
DISKCOPY	Makes a copy of a complete disk. Requires that both the source and the destination disk have the same format.
EDIT	This command invokes the text editor program. This program is useful for making changes to text files such as editing CONFIG.SYS and AUTOEXEC.BAT.
FORMAT	Prepares a disk for receiving files. Places a root directory on the disk.
FORMAT /S	Formats a disk as a system disk.
UNDELETE	Will (sometimes) recover a deleted file. Works only if the disk has not been modified since the file was deleted.
XCOPY	Copies the contents of one disk to another disk. Does not require both disks to have the same format. (Note that it will not copy hidden files unless you use the /h switch.)

Getting Help in MS-DOS

The later versions of MS-DOS (4.0 and newer) provide some online help. There are two ways to access this information. You can type the word "help" followed by a space and the command, or type the command with the /? switch. In either case, you will get information regarding the proper syntax and available options for the command.

Optimizing MS-DOS

Understanding how to configure and optimize an MS-DOS computer might seem like a waste of time in view of the newer operating systems available like Windows 95, Windows 98, Windows NT, and Windows 2000; however, one must remember that MS-DOS is the basic building block of the operating environment for the vast majority of IBM-compatible computers. All IBM-compatible computers today have evolved from this standard. The limitations imposed by MS-DOS and the need to provide backward compatibility have a lot to do with how today's computers operate.

Configuring MS-DOS

As mentioned in Lesson 1, the job of configuring how MS-DOS runs on a specific computer is done by modifying the CONFIG.SYS and AUTOEXEC.BAT files. During the boot process, MS-DOS looks for these files and executes any commands or loads any drivers properly called for within them. The CONFIG.SYS file is run first and sets up and configures the computer's hardware components. The AUTOEXEC.BAT file executes commands and loads TSR programs.

Note   TSRs are used for a wide variety of tasks in MS-DOS and almost always realign the memory stack. This can quickly lead to problems with the operating environment if they do not behave well, escalating exponentially with each additional TSR. If you run into strange problems, the first place to look is in the TSR used on the system.

If problems are encountered during startup, the CONFIG.SYS and AUTOEXEC.BAT files can be bypassed by pressing F5 as soon as the message "Starting MS-DOS" appears on the screen. Alternatively, pressing F8 will allow processing the files one command at a time (with the option to bypass specific commands), making troubleshooting possible. If you bypass a command and the computer boots, you have isolated the problem.

CONFIG.SYS Commands

The following table lists several CONFIG.SYS settings and their functions.

Setting	Function
BUFFERS	Allocates reserved memory for transferring information to and from the hard disk.
COUNTRY	Enables MS-DOS to use country conventions for times, dates, and currency. Example: COUNTRY=044,437,C:\DOS\COUNTRY.SYS
	(You do not need to use this in the United States unless you wish to use an alternate convention.)
DEVICE	Loads a device driver into memory. DEVICE=C:\DOS\EMM386.EXE
DEVICEHIGH	Loads a device driver into upper memory.
MS-DOS	Loads part of MS-DOS into upper memory area. DOS=HIGH, UMB
FCBS	Specifies the number of file control blocks (FCBS) that MS-DOS can have open at the same time.
FILES	Specifies the number of files that MS-DOS can hold open concurrently. FILES=60
INSTALL	Loads a memory-resident program. INSTALL=C:\DOS\SHARE.EXE/F:500 /L:500
LASTDRIVE	Specifies the maximum number of drives the computer can access. LASTDRIVE=Z
MOUSE.SYS	Loads a mouse driver.
NUMLOCK	Specifies whether the NUM LOCK key is on or off when MS-DOS starts.
SHELL	Specifies the name and location of the command interpreter. The interpreter converts the typed command to an action. The default for MS-DOS is COMMAND.COM.
SWITCHES	Specifies special options in MS-DOS. The /N switch will disable the use of the F5 and F8 keys to bypass startup commands (used for security).

Here is a sample CONFIG.SYS listing:

```
DEVICE=C:\WINDOWS\HIMEM.SYS
DEVICE=C:\DOS\EMM386.EXE NOEMS
DOS=HIGH, UMB
BUFFERS=20
FILES=80
FCBS=4,0
LASTDRIVE=Z
DEVICE=C:\CDROM\NEC2.SYS /D:MSCD001 /V
```

AUTOEXEC.BAT Commands

The following table lists several commands that you'll find in the
AUTOEXEC.BAT file.

ECHO	Displays commands as they are executed. @ECHO OFF: Suppresses the display of commands as they are executed.
PAUSE	Stops the execution of AUTOEXEC.BAT and displays the message "Strike any key to continue."
PATH	Defines the search path for program commands.
SET	Displays, sets, or removes MS-DOS environment variables.
SMARTDRV	Provides disk caching.
KEYB	Configures a keyboard for a specific language.
SHARE	Starts the Share program, which will install the file sharing and locking capabilities.
DOSKEY	Loads the DOSKEY program. You can use the DOSKEY program to view, edit, and carry out MS-DOS commands that you have used previously.
MOUSE.EXE	Loads a mouse driver.
PROMPT	Sets the display of the command prompt.

Here is a sample AUTOEXEC.BAT listing:

```
@ECHO OFF
PATH C:\DOS;C:\WINDOWS;C:\
DOSKEY
SMARTDRV
UNDELETE /LOAD
VSAFE
MSAV
```

Tip   Here are a couple of useful tricks to try when working with CONFIG.SYS and AUTOEXEC.BAT. If you want the computer to ignore a command line, enter REM before that statement. For example: `rem mouse.exe` would tell the computer to ignore that line and the MOUSE.EXE file would not be loaded. Before editing existing CONFIG.SYS or AUTOEXEC.BAT files, copy them to a different directory or make a copy of each, but with a .OLD extension to the filename (AUTOEXEC.OLD and CONFIG.OLD). This way, you will have the current configuration data at hand if something goes amiss.

Optimizing Memory

As discussed in Chapter 7, the original processors developed by Intel were unable to use more than 1 MB of RAM. Therefore, MS-DOS applications were written to conform to this limitation. As application requirements grew, a means of optimizing the use of memory was required in order to get the most out of the space available. This 1 MB of memory was divided into two sections; 384 KB of RAM (designated upper memory) was designated for running the computer (BIOS and video RAM and ROM), and 640 KB was reserved for applications, designated conventional memory. (See Figure 15.1.)

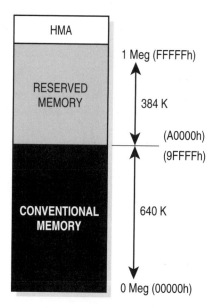

Figure 15.1   Memory map

The MS-DOS limitation means it is essential that the 640 KB area be kept as free as possible. MS-DOS memory optimization ensures that MS-DOS applications have as much of this memory as possible. Lesson 2 of Chapter 7 provides a detailed look at the types of memory used by MS-DOS and Windows. Please refer to that section for a fuller discussion.

The MS-DOS command MEM (MEM.EXE) provides information about the amount and type of memory available. (See Figure 15.2.)

```
Memory Type                      Total  =   Used  +   Free
Conventional                    640 KB      122K      518K
Upper                            155K        41K      144K
Reserved                         128K       128K        0K
Extended (XMS)                 7,269K     2,486K    4,783K
Total Memory                  81,259K    21,777K    5,415K
Total under 1 MB                 795K       163K      632K
Largest executable program size          518K (530,096 bytes)
Largest free upper memory block          114K (116,352 bytes)
```

Figure 15.2   MEM Command

The bottom line in optimization of memory for MS-DOS programs is that they require conventional memory in order to run, and conventional memory is in short supply. You can make more conventional memory available to your programs by minimizing how much memory MS-DOS, installable device drivers, and other memory-resident programs use. There are several ways to free conventional memory for use by programs:

- Run MS-DOS in extended memory instead of conventional memory.
- Streamline the CONFIG.SYS and AUTOEXEC.BAT files so they don't start unnecessary memory-resident programs.
- Run device drivers and other memory-resident programs in the upper memory area instead of in conventional memory.

Lesson Summary

The following points summarize the main elements of this lesson:

- Two files (CONFIG.SYS and AUTOEXEC.BAT) are used to custom-configure an MS-DOS operating system.
- MS-DOS programs operate only in conventional memory.
- Good memory management is the key to successfully operating an MS-DOS system.

Lesson 3: Windows 3.x

As mentioned at the beginning of this chapter, Windows is an operating environment that resides on top of MS-DOS. It brings with it two distinct advances. First, it is a graphical interface that frees us from remembering all those commands (we use icons or pictures instead) and second, it gives us the ability to get around some of the limitations of MS-DOS. Although more user friendly, it brings with it additional requirements for configuration.

Note   Calling Windows 3.x an operating system is a common, but incorrect, practice. It is really an extension of MS-DOS, and needs MS-DOS to run. This is not true with Windows 98, Windows NT, or Windows 2000. They are full-fledged operating systems, not just an interface and memory management overlay. (The .x notation indicates that the remark applies to all versions of an operating system. For example Windows 9.x would apply to both Windows 95 and 98.)

As with the lesson on MS-DOS, this lesson is not intended to offer a complete course in Windows 3.x. However, some important techniques useful to the computer professional are pointed out. Gaining an understanding of Windows 3.x, and being able to use a Windows manual as a reference, is a requirement for the computer professional.

After this lesson, you will be able to:

- Configure Windows 3.1.
- Edit Windows initialization files.
- Configure virtual memory.

Estimated lesson time: 40 minutes

Windows Features

Along with Windows came many new features. As a resource manager, it handles all the common or shared functions (like printing), making application programming, hardware manufacture, and computer operation easier. As long as a device or application meets the Windows standard, it is available to share its operation or data with other compliant applications or hardware.

The following table lists some of the primary features of Windows 3.1 and 3.11.

Feature	Function
Customizable user environment	Such features as colors, background pictures, screen savers, mouse settings, startup programs, and the Program Manager can be changed to appear and run according to the user's preferences.
Data sharing	Using Dynamic Data Exchange (DDE), information can be shared from one application to another. Object linking and embedding (OLE) allows embedding of information from one application in another application's file.
Icons	Windows uses small pictures called icons to represent programs or objects.
Multitasking	By allocating processor time to each application, Windows allows multiple applications to run at the same time. Each application is assigned a priority with the one currently in use receiving the most processor time.
Network awareness	Windows can recognize disk and print resources provided by network systems. It is compatible with Novell, NetWare, Banyan Vines, DEC Pathworks, and Unix/Linux.
Virtual memory	In an MS-DOS environment, programs are limited to the amount of physical memory (RAM) available in the computer. With Windows, part of the hard drive can be used as a swap file, in place of RAM. Using a swap file is slower than RAM; however, it does expand the capability of the computer.

Minimum Requirements for Running Windows

Windows was designed to take advantage of improvements in hardware and to overcome limitations imposed by MS-DOS. Therefore, before Windows is installed on a computer, it must meet several *minimum* hardware requirements. Minimum means just that—Windows will run with these parameters, but performance might not be optimal. The following table lists the minimum requirements of Windows 3.1.

Feature	Minimum Requirement	Comment
Processor	80386	Must have enhanced mode—the faster the better!
Memory	2 MB	Windows runs, but is severely curtailed with only 2 MB; 4MB makes it usable; 8 MB or more is desirable.
MS-DOS version	3.10	The higher the MS-DOS version, the more tools that are available.
Free disk space	8 MB minimum install; 10.5 MB full install	Needs 20 MB or more for the swap file—the less RAM the computer has, the more free disk space is needed.

(continued)

continued

Feature	Minimum Requirement	Comment
Floppy disk		Not required to run Windows, but necessary for installing programs and saving data. One 3.5-inch drive.
Display adapter	VGA	Any VGA or better.
Printer		Optional—might have to install the driver software.
Mouse	Optional	Difficult to use without a mouse, but it can be done. Any compatible mouse will work; however, the appropriate driver software might be needed.

Installing and Configuring Windows 3.x

There might be occasions when, as an A+ technician, you are required to install or make configuration changes to a Windows 3.1 system. This section points out some of the key issues that you could encounter when working with Windows 3.x operating systems.

Windows Setup

A standard Windows 3.1 setup or installation is done by placing the Windows Disk #1 in floppy drive A and typing:

```
a:\setup
```

Several switches can be used with the setup command that allow special options to be chosen:

- **SETUP /A:** Places Windows on a network server for installation across the network or for file sharing. Files are designated as read-only.
- **SETUP /B:** Set up for a monochrome display—useful with older laptops.
- **SETUP /I:** Windows will start without performing any automatic hardware detection.
- **SETUP /N:** Sets up a shared copy of Windows on a workstation.
- **SETUP /P:** This can be run from within Windows (winsetup /P for 3.11 version) and will rebuild the default Program Manager groups (Main, Accessories, Games).

Express setup installs the program to C:\Windows directory, selects hardware automatically, chooses U.S. English as the default language, allows selection of printer(s), and configures existing applications.

Custom setup installs the program, but allows the user to choose many options such as drive and directory, hardware, country, optional components, and to confirm changes to startup files. Windows automatically sets up icons and program groups for any application it finds.

Note Applications that are made specifically for Windows (such as Microsoft Office and Lotus SmartSuite) should be installed after Windows has been installed.

After Windows is installed, type **Win** from any directory and Windows will load. To configure Windows to automatically start when the computer boots, add WIN as the last statement in the AUTOEXEC.BAT file.

Windows Operating System Files

When loading, Windows uses the following files:

- **WIN386.EXE:** Handles virtual memory and MS-DOS applications; converts extended to expanded memory if required.

- **KRNL386.EXE:** Controls and allocates system resources, I/O and memory management, multitasking, and application launching.

- **USER.EXE:** Controls input and output, including mouse, keyboard, sound, timer, and COM ports. Also provides the Windows user interface.

- **GDI.EXE:** Manages display graphics and printing.

- **Core files:** Windows loads dynamic-link libraries (DLLs) that provide the core Windows functionality. (As mentioned in Lesson 1, a DLL is a shareable library of executable code modules.)

- **System resources:** Each DLL has a storage area in a 64-KB heap. If these heaps are full, you will receive "out of memory" error messages. Closing applications should relieve the problem.

- **Windows Device Drivers:** As briefly mentioned, drivers are small programs that connect Windows to the hardware. This allows applications to be independent of devices. When a new piece of hardware is added to a system, this driver needs to be installed (it's usually provided on a floppy disk with the device). Information on device drivers is recorded in the SYSTEM.INI file.

- **Font Files:** Windows provides three types of font files. Each font contains a complete character set for a particular typeface. Vector fonts are designed as a set of lines drawn between two points. Each character represents a mathematical model that can be scaled to virtually any size. Raster fonts are bitmap fonts made up of a set of dots. Each character or set of dots is "painted" on the screen or printer. Because each character requires separate data for each size, only limited scaling is possible. TrueType fonts are made from an "outline" of each character. When printing (on the screen or on a printer), these outlines are filled in. TrueType fonts are supported by all printers and provide WYSIWYG (What You See Is What You Get).

Windows Configuration

Proper configuration of Windows is critical for optimal performance. There are three methods for managing or changing Windows configuration: Control Panel, Windows Setup, and .INI files.

Control Panel

The primary method for changing the Windows configuration (and the one familiar to most users) is to use the Control Panel. This is a Windows application (found in the Main Program Group) that provides a visual way to make changes.

By selecting icons and using the associated dialog boxes, a user can customize the working environment. The following items can be changed from the Control Panel:

- Screen colors
- Other desktop options (such as screen savers and wallpaper)
- Fonts
- Printer
- Keyboard
- Mouse
- International settings
- COM port settings
- Network settings
- Date and time
- Sounds (used by system)
- Drivers for hardware
- Multitasking and virtual memory settings

Windows Setup

Windows setup will operate from within Windows if it is already loaded—click the Setup icon in the Main Group. Or it will start from MS-DOS—type **SETUP** when in the Windows directory. Using setup should be done only by experienced computer users. The results of improper setup can be disastrous—Windows won't run. If this happens, you can use the MS-DOS version of setup. From an MS-DOS prompt, change to the Windows directory and type the command **SETUP**.

Windows Initialization Files

The third method for modifying Windows configuration is to edit the Windows .INI files. As with the setup method, this should be used only by experienced operators. The Windows .INI files, which are found in the Windows directory of the bootable drive, initialize (configure) everything from device drivers to applications. Windows itself creates at least three .INI files, and any application can create initialization files of its own. Knowing how and what to edit in these files is critical to repairing and optimizing the performance of a computer.

You can use any text editor to edit .INI files. (MS-DOS provides a program for editing text files called EDIT. This program can be run from the MS-DOS prompt.) All .INI files are broken up into logical areas called groups. Each group starts with a line of text, in square brackets, called a group header. Underneath each group are its settings. They are organized as item=settings.

For example, see the following PROGMAN.INI file:

```
[Settings]
Order= 4 21 13 25 3 8 17 29 27 7 15 6 14 16 10 18 32 23 22 20 11 12 9
19 24 26 28 5 2 30 1
SaveSettings=1
AutoArrange=0
Window=28 22 628 433 1

[Groups]
Group1=C:\WINDOWS\MAIN.GRP
Group2=C:\WINDOWS\ACCESSOR.GRP
Group5=C:\WINDOWS\STARTUP.GRP
Group8=C:\WINDOWS\PROSHARE.GRP
Group13=C:\WINDOWS\LOTUSAPP.GRP
Group14=C:\WINDOWS\DIGITAL.GRP
Group15=C:\WINDOWS\MODERNAG.GRP
Group7=C:\WINDOWS\SOUNDIMP.GRP
Group10=C:\WINDOWS\PHONEBOO.GRP
Group18=C:\WINDOWS\DESIGNCA.GRP
Group20=C:\WINDOWS\ALDUS.GRP
Group12=C:\WINDOWS\APPLICAT.GRP
Group17=C:\WINDOWS\UTILITIE.GRP
Group4=C:\WINDOWS\MICROSOF.GRP
Group6=C:\WINDOWS\LOGITECH.GRP
Group21=C:\WINDOWS\IOMEGA.GRP
Group22=C:\WINDOWS\PARSONST.GRP
Group23=C:\WINDOWS\PHOTOENH.GRP
Group25=C:\WINDOWS\WINZIP.GRP
Group27=C:\WINDOWS\QUICKBOO.GRP
Group29=C:\WINDOWS\ADOBEACR.GRP
Group16=C:\WINDOWS\FAXWORKS.GRP
Group32=C:\WINDOWS\IMS2.GRP
Group3=C:\WINDOWS\NETSCAP0.GRP
Group11=C:\WINDOWS\FIRSTCLA.GRP
```

```
Group9=C:\WINDOWS\FAX.GRP
Group19=C:\WINDOWS\PROGRAMS.GRP
Group24=C:\WINDOWS\DESKTOP.GRP
Group26=C:\WINDOWS\SYSTEMTO.GRP
Group28=C:\WINDOWS\DOCUMENT.GRP
Group30=C:\WINDOWS\MULTIMED.GRP
```

Windows uses two .INI files for configuration: SYSTEM.INI and WIN.INI. The SYSTEM.INI is the Windows version of the MS-DOS CONFIG.SYS file. It initializes all the resources. The WIN.INI file is like the AUTOEXEC.BAT used by MS-DOS. It defines the "personalization" of Windows such as screen savers, colors, fonts, associations, and how resources will interact with applications. The WIN.INI file is also the dumping ground for settings that do not seem to have a home anywhere else. The information stored in these two files holds the secret to operating, optimizing, and troubleshooting Windows. Even though Windows has SYSTEM.INI and WIN.INI, it still uses the CONFIG.SYS and AUTOEXEC.BAT files of MS-DOS for the basic setup of devices and the computer. Windows also needs to use the MS-DOS files to configure the machine so that it (Windows) can run.

Windows 3.x and Windows 95 offer a utility called SYSEDIT.EXE in the Windows\System directory that lets you edit the context on the WIN.INI, SYSTEM.INI, CONFIG.SYS, and AUTOEXEC.BAT files quickly within Windows, using a notepad-like editor.

Note   Starting with Windows 95, most of the tasks performed by SYSTEM.INI and WIN.INI are now performed by the Registry.

Configuring the SYSTEM.INI File

To know SYSTEM.INI is to understand Windows. This file is the primary hardware configuration file for Windows. During installation, Windows creates all the sections in SYSTEM.INI, which, for the most part, should never be changed. However, one section—[386Enh]—is *very* important. Most of the problems associated with Windows (as opposed to Windows applications) that users encounter can be directly attributed to problems within this section.

The [386Enh] section stores all the values for 386 Enhanced Mode. Some of the more important items are:

- `32BitDiskAccess=On/Off`: 32-bit disk access can be turned off here if Windows won't start. If Windows won't start and you suspect this is the problem, use the win /d command. By starting Windows with this switch, you bypass 32-bit access. If Windows is OK, then turn this option off through the Virtual Memory/Change Menu in the Control Panel 386 Enhanced Menu, or just change *on* to *off*.

- `ComXIRq=Number`: This is where a COM port number and the port's IRQ are defined. Useful with devices that require nonstandard COM ports.

- `EMMExclude=XXXX-XXXX`: This command tunes the operation of the EMM range by excluding memory ranges that are required for specific drivers, thereby avoiding possible conflicts. Before Plug and Play, this command was often the only way to get some device drivers to load. Note that whenever an `item=XXXX-XXXX` statement is used in an EMM386 line or in the CONFIG.SYS file, an equivalent EMMExclude statement is required in this section of the SYSTEM.INI file.

- `EmmInclude=XXXX-XXXX`: This command is the reverse of the preceding EMM command, allowing one to force inclusion of memory areas that might otherwise be left unused.

- `Max:Bps=768`: Intermittent General Protection Faults (GPFs) can be caused by too few breakpoints. If this line is not in [386Enh] add it.

The following is an example of the [386Enh] section of a SYSTEM.INI file:

```
[386Enh]
device=vhhscand.386
device=C:\Netscape\system\vntstimd.exe
device=C:\Netscape\system\vtcprac.386
device=C:\Netscape\system\pdwcomm.386
device=C:\Netscape\system\dial.386
device=SYMEVNT.386
32BITDISKACCESS=on
device=*vpowerd
ebios=*ebios
device=vsndsys.386
mouse=*vmouse, msmouse.vxd
device=*vpd
woafont=dosapp.fon
netheapsize=60
device=cs$cbuf.386
device=vpmtd.386
device=*vshare
COMIrqSharing=on
COM3Base=03E8
COM4Base=02E8
COM2FIFO=1
COM1Irq=4
COM1Base=03F8
COM2Irq=3
COM2Base=02F8
COM4Irq=2
MinTimeslice=20
WinTimeslice=100,50
WinExclusive=0
Com1AutoAssign=2
Com2AutoAssign=2
LPT1AutoAssign=60
keyboard=*vkd
device=*enable
```

The [Boot] section lists the drivers that must be loaded when Windows starts. Windows might not work if you incorrectly modify or delete one of these settings.

Configuring the WIN.INI File

The WIN.INI file is not required, and Windows will run without it. However, it can be helpful. Two important commands used in WIN.INI are:

- `Load=`
- `Run=`

These lines autoload programs when Windows starts. They act like a hidden Startup Group. (Any program icon placed in the Startup Group of the Program Manager will automatically start when Windows is started.) If a program continues to automatically load and run, and it has no icon in the Startup Group, it's being loaded in WIN.INI. The difference between Load and Run is that programs invoked by Run will start minimized.

Note   Systems that have been upgraded to Windows 95 and 98 from Windows 3.1 might still have this file. Although it is not required—nor will Windows 95 or 98 create this file—Windows will use the file if it already exists. In that case, any Run and Load statements in this file will be activated as it was previously by Windows 3.1.

The WIN.INI file contains settings that affect the appearance of the Windows desktop, printer selections, and network connections. To edit this file, use the Control Panel or open it in any text editor (the Windows application Notepad will do the job). Close and save the file after you're done editing it.

Note   Windows needs to be rebooted before any changes to WIN.INI take effect. Be very careful when editing—a single typo will cause an error or unexpected results.

The WIN.INI file contains several sections of related settings. Each section is defined by its header, which is displayed in square brackets [Windows]. Within each section are entries in the format `keyname=value`:

- Keyname is the name of the setting.
- Keynames are made up of digits and letters with no spaces.
- Keynames must be immediately followed by an equal sign (=).
- Value can be an integer, a string, or a quoted string.
- Comments are preceded by a semicolon (;) and they work like the REM statements in CONFIG.SYS or AUTOEXEC.BAT files.
- Always backup the WIN.INI file before editing.

The [Windows] section of the WIN.INI file makes changes to the Windows environment—for example which applications run when Windows is started, and how information appears on the screen. Some of its parameters are:

- `DoubleClickHeight=<pixels>`: Specifies the height (in pixels) that the mouse can move between clicks when it is double-clicked. Default is 4. If movement exceeds this value, the double-click will be interpreted as two single clicks.

- `DoubleClickWidth=<pixels>`: Specifies the width (in pixels) that the mouse can move between clicks when it is double-clicked. Default is 4. If movement exceeds this value, the double-click will be interpreted as two single clicks.

- `Load=<filename(s)>`: Specifies applications to run (minimized) when Windows is started. Can include one or more filenames or applications—each must be separated by a space.

- `MenuDropAlignment=<0-or-1>`: Specifies whether menus open right-aligned or left-aligned with the menu title. 0 means left-aligned and 1 means right-aligned.

- `Programs=<extensions>`: Defines which files Windows considers to be applications. Defaults are .COM, .EXE, .BAT, and .PIF files.

- `Run=<filename(s)>`: When started, Windows will run any application listed.

The [Desktop] section contains optional settings that control the appearance of the screen background and the positioning of windows and icons on the screen. Most of these setting can be changed using the Control Panel.

The [Fonts] Section of WIN.INI describes the fonts to be loaded when Windows starts.

Configuring the CONTROL.INI File

All sections in the CONTROL.INI file can be changed from the Control Panel. This is the recommended method. The following are the sections in the CONTROL.INI file:

- **[Current]:** The current color scheme.

- **[Color schemes]:** Descriptions of color schemes.

- **[Patterns]:** Descriptions of the desktop patterns.

- **[Installed]:** Installed device drivers.

- **[Screen Saver]:** The current password used by the active screen saver (encrypted).

- **[Screen Saver.xxxxx]:** Individual screen saver settings.

- **[Don't load]:** This setting can be used to exclude items that are displayed in the Control Panel. List the name of the section to be excluded followed by "=1".

For example, you might want to edit the CONTROL.INI file directly if the screen-saver password has been forgotten. The screen-saver password can be removed by changing the following:

```
[Screen Saver.Screen Save Name]
PWProtected=1          (change to =0 to remove password protection)
[ScreenSaver]
Password=139xhfn9      (encrypted password - delete to remove password)
```

Configuring the PROGMAN.INI File

This file controls the settings for the Program Manager Group files. Adding a section to PROGMAN.INI called [Restrictions] will add some protection for the group files. If these statement are not present, the value is assumed to be the default of 0, which means that the opposite of the statement will happen. The commands and syntax are:

- NoRun=1: Disables the File Run command.
- NoClose=1: Prevents the user from exiting Windows.
- NoSaveSetting=1: Prevents the Program Manager layout from being saved on exit.
- NoFileMenu=1: Removes the File menu from the Program Manager.
- EditLevel=x: From 0, the default, to 4, establishes higher levels of restrictions.

Note   Setting attributes as "read-only" can protect individual groups. To do this, locate the .GRP file in the File Manager, select File, next select Properties, and then check the Read Only check box.

Using Sysedit

Windows provides a program for editing the system files (AUTOEXEC.BAT, CONFIG.SYS, WIN.INI, SYSTEM.INI). This program resides in the Windows directory and is called Sysedit. Windows does not provide an icon for this program in the standard setup. However, if no icon exists, Sysedit can be run by selecting File and then Run from the Program Manager, and then typing **Sysedit** and pressing ENTER. If an icon does not exist, it can be created by selecting New from the File menu in the Program Manager.

Configuring Virtual Memory

As mentioned earlier in this chapter, virtual memory allows the processor to use the hard drive to simulate RAM. Applications can access this simulated memory through virtual addresses mapped onto physical addresses, which can be either in RAM or on the hard disk.

Virtual Memory Manager

All virtual memory is controlled by the Virtual Memory Manager (VMM). The VMM divides memory into 4-KB pages and then maintains a page table to keep track of where everything goes (in RAM or on the hard drive). When the amount of free RAM reaches a critical level, a portion of RAM is set aside for page swapping. Windows uses a temporary or permanent swap file on the disk for writing the least recently used page frames of physical RAM.

Temporary Swap File

A temporary swap file is recommended when a computer is low on disk space because the file can increase or decrease in size as necessary. The temporary file is called \Windows\Win386.swp, and it's deleted when you exit Windows.

Permanent Swap File

When disk space is not a problem, a permanent swap file is recommended. Permanent swap files are faster to access than temporary swap files because they use contiguous blocks (clusters) of the hard disk drive to store data.

Sizing Virtual Memory

The required size of virtual memory varies with every machine and depends upon the memory requirements of the applications that will be run at the same time. When setting up virtual memory, consider the following:

- Total memory requirements of the computer should equal RAM plus the size of the swap file.

- The maximum swap file should not be larger than three times the size of RAM memory.

- Maximum total virtual memory should not be larger than four times the size of RAM.

To determine the actual memory requirements for a machine, add together all the memory requirements for each application to be run concurrently and add an extra 1 MB each for MS-DOS and Windows.

Swap File Settings

Swap files are modified using the Control Panel's 386 Enhanced icon. Select the Virtual Memory button on the right side of the dialog box. The following settings are recommended:

- **Drive:** Use the disk drive with the most available space. Do not select any removable drives such as floppy disk drives or Zip drives (they are too slow).

- **Type:** For best performance, use a permanent swap file (be sure to defragment the drive first—this will provide a space for a contiguous file).

- **Space Available:** Calculate the recommended size. Consult your application manuals to determine the amount of memory required to run each of them. Use a value large enough to support the workload on the computer, but do not exceed the recommended maximum size as suggested by Windows in the Virtual Memory dialog box.

- **32-bit access:** Use 32-bit access if available. It requires a Western Digital WD1003, or compatible, drive. Using 32-bit disk access allows Windows to talk directly to the hard drive, (thereby skipping the requirement to open an MS-DOS session), which then talks to the BIOS and then to the drive. 32-bit file access can be used with Windows 3.11 or Windows for Workgroups. It works the same as 32-bit disk access and can often speed up drive access. 32-bit file access is not hardware-sensitive and can often work when 32-bit disk access won't.

Note   If the drive controller is not compatible, this option will not be available.

Out of Memory

"Out of memory" messages from Windows usually means "out of conventional memory." However, it can also mean there is a shortage of virtual memory. Try closing files or increasing virtual memory as a temporary fix. If the message continues to appear, even after a reboot, the memory usage of the system should be evaluated and modified if needed.

Improving Hard Disk Drive Speed

In addition to improving memory, the operation of Windows can be enhanced by speeding up the hard disk drive speed by using disk cache and RAMDrive.

RAMDrive is an MS-DOS utility that lets you use memory (RAM) to create a virtual disk. This was a good method for improving performance when applications were run from a floppy disk. You could create a virtual drive and copy the application to this drive. Then, by running from the virtual drive, you would experience a dramatic increase in performance. The problem with this system is that each time you turn the computer off and then back on, you have to re-create the drive and copy the files. A RAMDrive is the opposite of a swap file. It is RAM that thinks it is a drive. As with any drive, RAMDrive has a drive letter, and the user can read, write, copy, and delete to and from it.

Installing a disk cache is one of the best methods for improving the performance of Windows. A disk cache is similar to a memory cache, except that it works between the mass-storage devices (hard disk drives, CD-ROM drives, and floppy disk drives) and RAM. Most applications use the same files over and over again. By creating a disk cache, the computer takes a piece of extended memory and uses it to hold the repetitive files. Because access to RAM is faster than disk access, the overall performance of the system improves. The most popular disk cache is SMARTDRV.EXE which comes with MS-DOS.

Tip   Using disk caching can be problematic: it is the exact opposite of virtual memory. Disk caching uses memory to improve performance, and virtual memory uses disks to improve performance. As a computer technician, you will have to strive to achieve the best compromise between the two, based on the situation.

Tweaking SMARTDRV.EXE

SMARTDRV.EXE can be run by simply adding it to the AUTOEXEC.BAT file, but it can be made to perform even better by adding a few switches. The performance of the disk cache is measured by its *hit rate,* the percentage of time that data requested by the operating system is already in the cache; therefore, it doesn't have to be read from the hard disk drive. A good hit rate will be between 75 and 90 percent. A good SMARTDRIVE configuration (in the AUTOEXEC.BAT file) looks something like this:

```
SMARTDRVE a- b- 1024 256 /B:32
```

"a- b-" means not to cache the floppy drives (floppy disks usually don't contain files that are repeated often).

"1024 256" sets the size for the cache. The rule for cache size is to make it equal to one-quarter the size of the total RAM (up to 2 MB), as shown in the following table. Performance gained by using SMARTDrive tends to drop off after 2 MB.

RAM (MB)	Cache
<1	None
1	256 KB
2	512 KB
4	1 MB
8	2 MB
16	2 MB
>16	2 MB

"/B:32" increases the look-ahead buffer if the hard drive is maintained in a defragmented state. The default value is 16 without the /B option.

Other SMARTDrive options are shown in the following table.

Switch	Description
/E	Changes the number of bytes processed by SMARTDrive.
/L	Loads low—by default, SMARTDrive loads in high memory. This switch forces it to load into low memory.
/N	Doesn't wait for the C prompt upon lazy write. This is very risky because the system can return to the C prompt without flushing the cache. If the computer is turned off, data can be lost.
/Q	Quiet mode—does not show anything on the screen when loading SMARTDrive.
/U	Does not load the CD-ROM cache.
/V	Verbose mode—shows everything on the screen when loading SMARTDrive.
/X	Turns off lazy writing. A lazy-writing disk cache stores saved data in the cache and waits until the system has slowed down before writing to the disk. The file is not really saved, and if the computer is turned off for any reason before the data is actually saved, data will be lost.

A few switches also enable SMARTDrive tools. When SMARTDrive is running, enter the following at the MS-DOS prompt for the listed result:

Command	Result
SMARTDRV /S	Returns the current hit rate.
SMARTDRV /R	Forces immediate flush of all lazy-write data in cache.
SMARTDRV /R	Flushes and restarts the cache.

Vcache

Windows 3.11 and Windows for Workgroups include a replacement for SMARTDrive. This replacement is a protected-mode disk cache called "Vcache." Vcache is set by making changes in the Virtual Memory (Change button) window, found in the Virtual Memory Setup dialog box (the 386 Enhanced icon in the Control Panel). Vcache runs up to eight times faster than SMARTDrive. The only disadvantage is that it does not cache the CD-ROM. However, it does run with SMARTDrive (simply configure SMARTDrive to cache only the CD).

Temp Files

Many applications need to store data on a temporary basis. To do this, temporary files are created and stored in the same directory. All temp files have the extension .TMP and are usually found in the Windows/Temp directory. This directory can be changed at any time by adding the statement SET TEMP=<PATH> to the AUTOEXEC.BAT file.

It is a good idea to periodically clean out the temp files by deleting them. Be careful when doing this, because one or more of them might be in use. In general, as long as you delete any temporary files created before the current computer session, they will not be in use. There are two ways to automatically remove temporary files. One is to create a batch file to delete the contents of the temporary directory and run it from the AUTOEXEC.BAT file. The other is to create a RAMDrive and store the temporary folder in that drive.

To make a RAMDrive, and command Windows to save all temp files to the RAMDrive, add the following to the AUTOEXEC.BAT file:

```
Device=c:\dos\ramdrive 1024
md d:\temp
SET TEMP=d:\temp
```

Note Which drive letter you use depends on the system and which drive letter is the next available.

Memory Configuration

Most intermittent lockups and General Protection Faults can be blamed on poor MS-DOS memory management. To minimize the possibility of lockups and GPFs, Windows provides a few solutions that you should be familiar with.

EMMExclude and EMMInclude

If you have exclude or include statements (such as to accommodate memory reserved for video cards) in your CONFIG.SYS file, they need corresponding EMMExclude and EMMInclude lines in your SYSTEM.INI file under the [386Enh] section.

Translation Buffers

Windows needs UMB (upper memory block) space for what are known as its *translation buffers*. Translation buffers are small storage areas of RAM that are used to support MS-DOS applications and networks. If you are loading a lot of devices into UMBs, you should add WIN= statements to the EMM386.EXE line of the CONFIG.SYS (to identify memory location). For example:

```
DEVICE=C:\DOS\EMM386.EXE  WIN=C800=C900FF
```

Running MS-DOS Applications from Windows

By running MS-DOS in a virtual 8086 machine, Windows remains in memory and active. Therefore Windows functions like Cut, Copy, and Paste can be used between MS-DOS applications and the Windows application. Switching between the MS-DOS application and the Windows application is carried out in the same way as between any two Windows applications, by pressing the ALT and TAB keys at the same time. MS-DOS applications can be run either using the full screen or inside a window. To make an MS-DOS application operate properly, Windows uses a .PIF (Program Information File) to hold the necessary data to set up the virtual machine.

Most MS-DOS applications are provided with their own .PIFs that include the optimum settings. When these are provided, they should be used. Usually, .PIFs are located in the same directory as the program executable file. If no .PIF is provided, Windows will use its default .PIF. If there are problems running the program, or no .PIFs exist, the current .PIF can be modified or a new one created. To create or modify this file, use the .PIF editor utility provided by Windows.

Settings for .PIFs

The following table sets out settings available for MS-DOS .PIFs.

Setting	Description
Advanced options	Additional options made available by clicking the Advanced button. Options include setting the multitasking priority, adding more memory options, and allowing Windows to quit with the application open.
Close window on exit	If box is unchecked, the window will stay open when the application terminates.
Display usage	Determines whether the application is to be run in a window or full screen.
Execution	Selects whether the program is to be run in the background (with other Windows applications running) or exclusively (suspends all other applications).
Memory	Sets the minimum amount of conventional memory required for the application to start. Use 0 for "not needed" and −1 for "no limit."
Optional parameters	Includes switches or other command settings.
Program file name	Includes the drive, path, and filename of the MS-DOS program.
Startup directory	Specifies the working directory for the application.
Video memory	Selects text, low graphics, or high graphics. This ensures that Windows sets aside enough memory for the video mode used by the application.
Window title	This title will be displayed on the Window title bar.

Troubleshooting Windows 3.x

Windows 3.x problems can be divided into three distinct groups: lockups (the computer locks up without any errors—in other words, the machine simply refuses to operate); GPFs; and erratics (strange behavior by programs or devices apart from locking up or generating errors).

Lockups

Lockups are simple: the machine no longer responds to input and doesn't display any errors. Lockups tend to indicate fairly serious hardware problems and need to be dealt with aggressively, because there is a risk of data corruption and loss.

Note   Unlike Windows 3.x, if a single applications locks up in Windows 95 or 98, it does not lock up the whole computer. You can press CTRL+ALT+DEL to get to the Task dialog box and close the offending application.

Symptoms of a lockup are:

- The mouse pointer doesn't move. (Hint: if the mouse doesn't work, try the keyboard; this will confirm whether the problem is caused by the mouse or a lockup.)
- Keyboard controls don't work.
- The machine seems to be frozen.

There are a few common causes of lockups.

Incorrect Drivers

Using incorrect drivers are among the most common causes of lockups and inter-mittent program crashes. Make sure that video cards, hard disk drives, sound cards, and so forth are using the proper drivers. Always back up old drivers when you are updating, just in case you have problems. That way at least you can go back to a working machine if the new driver locks up your machine.

Power Supply

Lockups created by power supplies tend to be intermittent. The system locks up for no apparent reason—no particular application or function seems to cause the problem. If the power supply is the problem, the errors will show up in MS-DOS, Windows, or any other operating systems that you use.

If a power supply is the suspect, turn off the machine, turn it back on, and walk away for ten minutes. If, after you come back, the machine is still locked up, the power supply is the problem.

Corrupted Files

Corrupted files are files that have been damaged by bad hard disk drives, floppy disks, CD-ROMs, or corrupted software.

The major symptom of a corrupted file is that the lockup takes place at the exact same time, every time, in the execution of a particular file. For example, suppose that every time you start an application, it locks up when it reaches a certain point. Run ScanDisk to determine whether the problem is with the hard disk. If running ScanDisk doesn't correct the problem, try reinstalling the application in another directory so that it does not write over the same area of the hard disk.

Note   Corrupted files can be created by improperly shutting down Windows. You should never simply shut off a computer; close all applications and properly stop the operating system first.

If you click an icon and receive an "application not found" error, this typically indicates that the software needs to be reinstalled, or that the application has been moved and the icon can no longer find it.

Corrupted Swap Files

Lockups caused by corrupted swap files tend to show themselves when Windows is first starting or when it is shutting down. Turn off the swap files and try restarting Windows. If you can get into Windows, find the 386SPART.PAR file and erase it. Windows will give an error on startup, but it will start up. Defragment the drive, and re-create the swap file.

Bad RAM

Bad RAM lockups are easily detected—if a RAM chip is so bad that it can cause a lockup in Windows, the HIMEM.SYS file will detect it. Reboot the computer and watch HIMEM.SYS while it's loading—use the F8 key if necessary. If the RAM is bad, you will see an error message like: "HIMEM has detected unreliable XMS memory at XXXX:XXXXXXXX."

Note   Lockups due to bad RAM chips look a lot like power-supply lockups. Most RAM problems show up as errors or GPFs.

IRQ and DMA Conflicts

Lockups generated by IRQ and DMA conflicts are created when the two hardware devices begin to speak at the same time. Not all IRQ and DMA conflicts manifest themselves as lockups. Remember that IRQ/DMA conflicts don't happen on machines that were "working fine before." Invariably, these lockups take place on computers on which a device has recently been added or changed.

General Protection Faults

General Protection Faults (GPFs—also known to old-time Windows users as "The Blue Screen of Death") fall into four categories.

Memory-Management Problems

Memory-management problems show up as GPFs in KRNL386.EXE. Typically, these are found in machines that are running MS-DOS applications and have been incorrectly configured. Pay particular attention to the proper use of exclude statements on the EMM386.EXE line.

GDI Errors

GDI (Graphical Device Interface) errors indicate a resource-heap overflow. A GPF caused by a GDI heap overflow can be visually exciting. Typically, these occur on machines with animated screen savers that run along with some mini-mized high-powered applications such as PowerPoint or Excel. Usually, the animated part of the screen saver will disappear. Deactivating the screen saver will often cause all the icons to turn into white squares, or parts of the desktop to disappear. This is caused by the GDI heap losing all data about the attributes of each icon. With resource-heap overflows, the only surefire cure is to quit trying to do so many things at once, or to upgrade to Windows 9x, Windows NT, or Windows 2000 which do not have resource heaps limited to 64 KB each. In this case, the addition of RAM (the usual cure for not being able to run all the programs you want at the same time) will not help. Remember, RAM is only one of the computer's resources.

Application-Specific Errors

Application-specific errors are frustrating because there is nothing you can do to make them go away. In order to fix these errors, the application software must be repaired at the source. When these errors occur, contact the company that makes that software—often there is a "patch" (which can usually be downloaded from the company's Web site) available to repair the problem.

If a GPF is created by bad RAM, it will occur over and over again at a specific memory address. You will be able to detect this by writing down the exact message on the GPF screen. If the address noted in the message is the same, time after time, you can suspect bad RAM.

Erratic Behavior

When the computer begins to act strangely, this is known as "erratic behavior." Video cards are notorious for erratic behavior that can be as innocuous as colored dots on the screen (wherever the mouse has been moved) to the occasional glitch after installing the latest video driver.

Printer drivers can create problems by causing the printer to spew forth nonsense characters that bear no resemblance to the original text or graphic image.

To resolve these problems, you must first identify the problem driver. For video drivers, go into the Control Panel and select the Microsoft VGA driver. It is very slow but will cause no problems. After the driver has been identified, go online (either through the Internet or directly with the company) and verify that you are using the latest version for your particular device. Also check for an odd setting in the .INI file that goes with the driver. The .INI file will share the same name as the driver, but not all drivers have .INI files.

Lesson Summary

The following points summarize the main elements of this lesson:

- Windows 3.x is an operating environment that runs on top of MS-DOS.
- Windows uses a GUI (graphical user interface) instead of the command line interface of MS-DOS.
- In addition to the MS-DOS configuration files, Windows uses .INI files.
- WIN.INI, SYSTEM.INI, and CONTROL.INI are the primary configuration files for Windows.
- Sysedit is used to modify system files.
- Windows also uses DLL (dynamic-link library) files to configure and run applications.
- MS-DOS applications will run in Windows, but might require special settings to run properly. A .PIF file is used to create these settings.
- Windows uses protected mode to allow the multitasking of applications.
- General Protection Faults (GPFs) occur when an application tries to use resources allocated to other applications.

Chapter Summary

The following points summarize the key concepts in this chapter:

Operating System Basics

- MS-DOS is considered synonymous with the term DOS, even though there were other disk operating systems produced.

- The three programs that constitute the core operating system of MS-DOS are IO.SYS, MSDOS.SYS, and COMMAND.COM.

MS-DOS

- CONFIG.SYS loads extra hardware and device drivers that are not built into the IO.SYS file.

- It is important that you are familiar with the steps involved with the boot process.

Windows 3.x

- Windows 3.x is not an operating system, but provides a common user interface for applications written to its standards.

- It is important that you are familiar with the different modes of Windows and how (and where) they function.

- Windows runs on top of MS-DOS. It is an MS-DOS-based program that provides a graphical user interface (GUI).

- It is important that you know the different areas of memory.

- Windows provides three types of fonts: vector fonts, raster fonts, and TrueType fonts.

- There are three methods for managing or configuring Windows: the Control Panel, Windows Setup, and Windows .INI files.

- Sysedit is a program for editing the system files (AUTOEXEC.BAT, CONFIG.SYS, WIN.INI, and SYSTEM.INI).

- PROGRAM.INI controls the settings for the Program Manager Group files.

- Virtual memory allows the processor to use the hard drive to simulate RAM.

- A popular disk cache is SMARTDRV.EXE. It is provided as part of MS-DOS and is activated by entering it into the CONFIG.SYS file.

- Windows uses a .PIF (Program Information File) to hold the necessary data to set up the virtual machine.

- Windows 3.x problems can be divided into three distinct groups: lockups, GPFs, and erratic behavior.

Review

1. What does DOS stand for?

2. What was DOS created to do?

3. Which version of MS-DOS is bundled with Windows 95?

4. Describe the core operating systems within MS-DOS.

5. What are the two MS-DOS startup files?

6. Which MS-DOS command is used to determine the amount of free space left on a disk?

7. Describe the difference between real mode and protected mode.

8. Windows provides a GUI for the user. What does "GUI" stand for? What is its advantage over the older MS-DOS system?

9. Describe the three kinds of fonts used in a Windows environment.

10. Name five settings that can be changed from the Windows Control Panel.

11. Which wildcard character can be used to replace a single character in a search string?

CHAPTER 16

Windows 95 and Beyond

About This Chapter

Just as the microprocessor has evolved over time, so have software and operating systems. As covered in the previous chapter, MS-DOS, as an operating system, and Microsoft Windows, as an operating environment, have become cornerstones of the computer market. Although MS-DOS was limited by restrictions affecting memory and ease of configuration, Windows—residing on top of MS-DOS— was able to overcome many problems. However, it still retained some restrictions.

To solve this problem, Microsoft developed Windows 95, creating a new operating system from the ground up. Then, to keep abreast of the ever-changing needs of technology and the phenomenal growth of the Internet, Microsoft responded with an upgrade: Windows 98. This chapter provides the basics of managing the Windows 95 environment. To gain the high level of proficiency required of today's computer professional, it is recommended that you go on to obtain advanced training and build a library of references after completing this chapter.

Note   While this chapter focuses on the Windows 95 operating system, enhancements brought about by Windows 98 are also mentioned. Windows 98 shares many features with Windows 95; however, because Windows 98 is not a subject on the A+ Certification test, we do not examine it deeply. The same is true for Windows NT and 2000. Because they are not part of the current exam, we do not cover them in detail.

Before You Begin

This chapter assumes you are familiar with the operation and configuration of MS-DOS and Windows 3.x. At the very least, you should read and master Chapter 15, "Software: MS-DOS and Windows 3.x."

Lesson 1: A New Operating System

In this lesson, we take a look at the Windows 95 operating system and examine what makes it so different from the Windows 3.x operating system.

After this lesson, you will be able to:

■ Identify the basic differences between Windows 95 and 98 and earlier versions of the Windows operating system.

Estimated lesson time: 15 minutes

As covered in Chapter 15, "Software: MS-DOS and Windows 3.x," Windows 3.x is an operating *environment* created on top of MS-DOS to provide a graphical user interface (GUI) and other features that make it easier to run programs and manage files. Windows 95 is a complete operating *system* that includes an improved GUI as well as other useful features. It has a unique desktop appearance and features multimedia and Internet access.

Windows 95 is dramatically different from Windows 3.x. Installing devices, managing memory, optimizing the system, and troubleshooting are handled in a completely different way than in Windows 3.x.

Although Windows 95 will run most MS-DOS and Windows 3.x software, and even bears some superficial resemblance to those operating systems, it is constructed very differently. Windows 95 is comprised of two products: a DPMI (DOS Protected Mode Interface—an improved MS-DOS) and the protected mode GUI. The MS-DOS part of Windows 95 looks and acts pretty much like the old MS-DOS; however, because it is DPMI-compliant, it can support use of extended memory even though it does not support multitasking.

When you first boot up Windows 95, you see the message "Starting Windows 95." At this point, Windows is starting the DPMI. After the DPMI is loaded, Windows 95 loads the GUI. Notice that it is not necessary to use the GUI to boot up to Windows 95; this is important because many computer repair functions, particularly for the hard disk drive, are handled at a MS-DOS prompt.

DOS 7

MS-DOS is available in Windows 95, although it resides in the background, and many novice users will never use it directly in command mode. MS-DOS external commands can be found in the Windows\Command directory of the bootable drive. Its unofficial name is MS-DOS 7. The IO.SYS and MSDOS.SYS from older versions of MS-DOS are still there, but their functions are completely different. All the functions of MSDOS.SYS and IO.SYS have been combined together into IO.SYS, and MSDOS.SYS has been turned into a hidden, read-only text file in the root directory of the boot drive. MSDOS.SYS is used as a startup option. Configuring and using MSDOS.SYS is covered in detail in Lesson 3 of this chapter.

COMMAND.COM remains and still performs basically the same functions as the old COMMAND.COM: to provide the command prompt. When the computer boots up and says "Starting Windows 95," press the F8 key and select "Command Prompt Only" to get to an MS-DOS 7 prompt. Type **VER** and you will see "Windows 95."

The Windows 95 GUI

The Windows 95 GUI is a protected-mode overlay of the MS-DOS 7 shell. It loads its *own* device drivers. It does not need to load device drivers from CONFIG.SYS unless Windows 95 does not have a built-in protected-mode driver for a particular device. Windows 95 also has support for FILES, BUFFERS, DOS=UMB, and just about every other setting found in CONFIG.SYS. Assuming that there are Windows 95 drivers available, there is no need for a CONFIG.SYS file. The GUI loads a protected-mode driver for most CD-ROMs, has VCACHE for disk caching, and protected-mode mouse support for Windows 95, Win 3.x, and MS-DOS applications. As with CONFIG.SYS, there is no requirement for AUTOEXEC.BAT.

The Virtual Memory Manager (VMM) supports memory usage both at the MS-DOS 7 level and the GUI. At the MS-DOS 7 level, VMM does little more than load a simple MS-DOS. When the GUI is loaded, VMM takes advantage of the power of 386 (and better) protected mode to create virtual machines (VMs)—one for Windows 95 and one for any MS-DOS program running in Windows 95. Along with the VMM is the Installable File System (IFS), which provides support for hard drives, CD-ROMs, and network drives. The IFS also provides the support for long filenames. The IFS runs both for MS-DOS 7 and the GUI.

While the GUI is running, the main functions of Windows 95 are handled by three core operating components:

- **The kernel:** loads applications, handles all aspects of I/O, and allocates virtual memory.
- **The user component:** handles all input from the user—mouse, keyboard and so forth.
- **The graphical device interface (GDI) modules:** provide routines that draw the images on the display.

Windows 95 applications use the operating system as a pool of resources (memory, modem, video, and printer). Programs or dynamic-link libraries (DLLs) make "calls" to these three modules whenever they need to place something on the screen, check the status of the mouse, use memory, or gain access to anything else they might need. This operates similarly to Windows 3.x. However, there are also major improvements:

- Most functions run in full 32-bit protected mode. Win 3.x functions run in 16-bit real mode.
- Windows 95 runs as a preemptive multitasker, allocating time to each program. Win 3.x offered a cooperative multitasking feature that made it possible for programs to take turns using processor time.
- In Windows 95, GDI and the user component use fixed memory areas called heaps to keep track of all resources. Heaps for Windows 3.x are 64 KB in size. Improvements with hardware and applications have proven that 64 KB is often too little and frequently causes problems. Windows 95 heaps are variable in size and no longer subject to this restriction.
- The user interface is at the top of the Windows 95 architecture. Windows 95 can use either its default interface, the Windows 3.x interface, or another interface. Old Windows and MS-DOS applications run within the GUI.

The Windows 95 File Structure

Disk structures have not changed in Windows 95. Partitions are still exactly the same, so the MS-DOS 7 bootable files of Windows 95 must still be installed to the C drive. Windows 95 still uses 16-bit FAT (FAT16) formats for hard disk drives and floppy disk. The FDISK and FORMAT commands are still used to set up hard drives. A hard drive that was partitioned with FDISK and formatted with an older version of MS-DOS is exactly like a Windows 95 drive. Windows 95 OSR2 and Windows 98 support 32-bit FAT (FAT32). This file system improves storage efficiency by reducing cluster sizes on large partitions. The following table shows the Windows 95 versions and their appropriate file system.

Version	Description
Version A	The original Windows 95 release—intended for upgrading from Windows 3.1. Uses FAT16 file system.
Version B	The OEM (original equipment manufacturer) version—intended for installation on new computers only. Uses FAT16.
OSR2	The final version of Windows 95 (sometimes referred to as Version C)—intended for installation on new computers only. Uses FAT32 file system. End users cannot buy this version as a retail product.

32-Bit VFAT

Disk access is provided through the 32-bit VFAT (virtual file allocation table). Unlike the 16-bit FAT used in previous versions, VFAT is a virtual device driver that operates in protected mode. This provides more reliability and works with a greater variety of hardware. Don't confuse 32-bit VFAT with 32-bit FAT, which has to do with how data is stored on a hard disk partition (the cluster size) while VFAT has to do with how files are accessed.

Note   VFAT was formerly known as 32-bit file access in Windows 3.1.

Long Filenames

In MS-DOS and Windows 3.x, filenames were in what is called an 8.3 ("eight dot three") format. That is, the filename itself was restricted to a maximum of eight characters in length, and the extension to a maximum of three characters in length. Filename and extension are connected by a period, or "dot." Windows 95 supports long filenames (LFNs). The LFN removes the 8.3 filename limitation of older MS-DOS and Windows operation systems. In a regular MS-DOS 8.3 file specification directory, all file records are stored in 32-byte records. Ten of these 32 bytes are "reserved." The other 22 bytes are used to store information on starting clusters, creation date, and creation time, and 11 bytes are for the filename itself. LFNs exist on FAT partitions by chopping the filename into 12-byte chunks (stealing one of the "reserved" bytes) and allowing up to 13 chunks, creating a filename of up to 255 characters.

When an LFN is saved, the system creates a short name that conforms to the 8.3 standard. Then, each 12 characters is cut off and stored in its own directory section. The directory entries that make up the long filename are called LFN entries. These must be backwardly compatible with MS-DOS programs and with MS-DOS itself.

Note   Windows takes the first six characters (no spaces) of the filename, adds a tilde (~), a number, and then the extension. If two or more files have the same first six characters, the number is incremented by one for each. For example, two files named "long file name one.txt" and "long file name two.txt" would become "longfi~1.txt" and "longfi~2.txt."

To make LFNs compatible with MS-DOS means to make sure that MS-DOS ignores the LFN entries in the directory structure. This is achieved by giving LFN entries the bizarre attribute-combination of hidden, read-only, system, and volume label. There is nothing in the MS-DOS code that tells it what to do if it runs into a file with this combination of attributes, so MS-DOS will not interfere with them.

Caution   Older disk utilities are incompatible with long filenames and will try to erase the LFN entries. It is critical that any disk utility that tries to diagnose the directory structure, including the SCANDISK that is included with MS-DOS 6 and earlier, should never be run on a computer with LFNs. The SCANDISK that comes with Win 95 is compatible with LFNs.

The Registry

The main difference between Windows 95 and Windows 3.x is the Registry. The Registry consists of two binary files called SYSTEM.DAT and USER.DAT that are located in the Windows directory. Because they are hidden read-only files, they are prevented from being accidentally removed or changed. The Registry holds information on all the hardware in the computer, network information, user preferences, and file types, as well as anything else that pertains to Windows 95. The idea of the Registry is to have one common database for everything that comprises the computer. The Registry is designed to replace CONFIG.SYS and AUTOEXEC.BAT, as well as every .INI file (especially WINDOWS.INI and SYSTEM.INI). Windows 95 still reads these files at boot up to provide backward compatibility with Win 3.x programs that use them.

Windows 95 Enhancements

Windows 95 is dramatically different from any of the Windows 3.x series—not only in its look, but because it provides many enhancements that make it even more versatile and user-friendly. For an A+ technician, proficiency in using the Windows 95 environment requires a great deal of study and hands-on experience.

Windows 95 represents an evolutionary step in operating the system. The following table compares the features of Windows 3.x, Windows 95, and Windows 98. (The A+ Certification does not include Windows 98 at this time; it is included for reference only.)

Windows 3.x	Windows 95	Windows 98
A 16-bit program.	A 32-bit program.	A 32-bit program.
An MS-DOS-based application that supplements an operating system.	An operating system.	An operating system.
All hardware upgrades require a software driver to be installed in order for the new hardware to work with Windows.	Supports Plug and Play hardware installation. Allows user to simply plug in new hardware and let Windows 95 configure it.	Supports Plug and Play hardware installation. Allows user to simply plug in new hardware and let Windows 98 configure it. Expanded hardware support for USB (universal serial bus), IEEE1394 serial bus, ACPI (Advanced Configuration and Power Interface) and DVD (digital video disc), Windows Driver Model (WDM), Multiple Display Support, and more.
Supports filenames up to only 8.3 format, such as filename.doc or spreadsh.xls.	Supports filenames up to 250 characters.	Supports filenames up to 250 characters.
Supports only multitasking.	Supports both multitasking and multithreading (running several processes in rapid sequence within a single program).	Supports both multitasking and multithreading.
Cannot run the new 32-bit applications.	Can run older Windows and MS-DOS applications, plus the new 32-bit applications written specifically for Windows 95 and Windows NT.	Can run older Windows and MS-DOS applications, plus the new 32-bit applications written specifically for Windows 95 and Windows NT.
Program Manager and program group-centered interface.	Document and work-centered interface.	Document and work-centered interface. Optional Web-like interface.
Designed to be a stand-alone, single-user computer interface.	Designed to be an interactive terminal on a local area network (LAN), wide area network (WAN), or remote or dial-up connection.	Designed to be an interactive terminal on a local area network (LAN), wide area network (WAN), or remote or dial-up connection.
Uses Program Manager as the starting point.	Designed around a Start button used to launch a program or open a document.	Designed around a Start button used to launch a program or open a document.
Windows for Workgroups provided limited support for communication and networking.	Integrated support for communication and networking. Provides TCP/IP (Transmission Control Protocol/Internet Protocol) and PPP (Point-to-Point Protocol) support.	Improved support for communication and networking. Network-card friendly (supports Network Driver Interface Specification—NDIS). Supports PPTP (Point to Point Tunneling) and VPN (Virtual Private Network). Supports Windows Sockets 2.0, Web-based Enterprise management (WBEM), and much more.

Advantages of Windows 95

There are several changes, not readily visible to the user, that make Windows 95 superior to the older versions of Windows.

Windows 95 has a better system of managing computer resources: memory (RAM), video RAM, hard disk drives, and network communications.

Programs designed to run on Windows 95 carry out tasks effortlessly. They tend to be faster, more efficient, and less likely to crash than with earlier Windows programs.

Microsoft's goal was to build a backward-compatible 32-bit operating system that allowed people to continue using their favorite MS-DOS programs and existing hardware. Some additional advantages of Windows 95 are:

- **User-definable interface:** The desktop is completely and easily customized by the user.
- **New accessories:** The standard Windows accessory package has been improved and expanded.
- **Interconnectivity:** It is designed to run as part of any network system.
- **Direct cabling:** Any two computers with Windows 95 and a free COM or parallel port can be connected for data sharing. One computer acts as a host and shares its files with the other.

Lesson Summary

The following points summarize the main elements of this lesson:

- Windows 95 is an operating system.
- The new GUI is more user-friendly than the Windows 3.1 interface.
- Early versions of Windows 95 are 16-bit operating systems and utilize 32-bit VFAT.
- The final version of Windows 95 (OSR2) and Windows 98 can run either 16-bit or 32-bit FAT systems (32-bit is the default).
- Windows 95 fully supports Plug and Play.
- Windows 95 supports multitasking and multithreading.
- One of the advantages of Windows 95 is its improved communication and networking capabilities.

Lesson 2: Installing and Configuring Windows 95

In this lesson, we take a look at how to set up Windows 95.

After this lesson you will be able to:
- Upgrade and install Windows 95.
- Describe the Windows 95 boot-up process.

Estimated lesson time: 45 minutes

Installing Windows 95

Windows 95 can be installed as an upgrade to Windows 3.x; from MS-DOS; on a new machine; or as a dual-boot system with either Windows 3.x, Windows NT, or other operating systems. Each method has unique requirements and limitations. The basic process is the same for all installations, but you must be sure that you understand the differences that do exist so that the final result is the solution you or your client needs. In many cases, you might have to compromise to achieve the best results.

Hardware Requirements

The minimum recommended requirements (and you should be familiar with these for the Certification test) differ from the practical requirements to run Windows 95. Let's look at both.

Minimum Requirements

The minimum requirements recommended by Microsoft and covered by the test are:

- A 386DX personal computer or better.
- At least 4 MB of random access memory (RAM).
- At least 40 MB of hard disk space reserved for the operating system.

By selecting the typical Windows setup, Windows 95 uses 30 MB of hard disk space and reserves at least 8 to 10 MB for swap space on the hard disk. Windows 95 still needs to create a VM environment and the more hard disk space available, the better Windows 95 operates.

If your computer suddenly gives you a number of different read/write error messages or its performance declines dramatically, it is possible that you don't have enough hard disk space to handle the swapping requirements of Windows 95. The first step in troubleshooting such conditions is to free up hard disk space and defragment the hard disk drives.

What You Really Need

In order to run Windows 95 with the applications commonly found on a desktop such as word processors, spreadsheets, and databases, you should not use anything less than:

- A 486DX 66-Mhz machine.
- 8 MB of RAM or more.
- A 520-MB hard disk drive.

Tip   Windows 95 will start outperforming Windows For Workgroups on a 486 computer after you increase RAM from 8 MB to 16 MB.

Additional Hardware

It is recommended that the following additional hardware be included on a Windows 95 installation:

- Modem and/or network interface card (NIC).
- Microsoft Mouse or compatible pointing device.
- Sound card and speakers.

How Much RAM Is Enough?

The amount of RAM really needed depends on the user and which applications are to be run. Typical Microsoft Office users can usually work quite well with 8 MB of RAM. Moderate users of the Copy and Paste commands will need to increase RAM to at least 16 MB. If users require their applications to be a click away (all running at the same time), they will need 32 MB of RAM. In the 32-bit Windows world, additional RAM will always boost performance. Remember:

- You can never have too much RAM.
- RAM is the key to optimization of Windows.
- The simplest and least expensive way to improve the speed and performance of any computer is to add RAM.
- Moore's Law: Processing power doubles every 18 months (from Gordon Moore, cofounder of Intel).
- Parkinson's Law of Data: Data expands to fill the storage space available (from the original Parkinson's Law: Work expands to fill the time available).

Upgrading from Windows 3.x (Windows 95 Version A)

Windows 95 installation is a relatively painless affair (in most cases) and requires minimal intervention. Before starting an installation, consider the following:

- The more complicated the system, the more complicated the installation.
- Incompatible hardware is probably the number one cause of installation problems.
- Conflicting software is probably the number two cause of installation problems.
- Patience and persistence are two requirements for a Windows 95 upgrade.

Before you start the installation, consider the following:

- Back up, back up, back up! Make copies of all the current system files—.INI, .GRP, AUTOEXEC.BAT, CONFIG.SYS, .DLL, and all critical data files. You can use the MS-DOS version of MSD (Microsoft Diagnostics) to record (and print) a complete configuration of the system.
- The best tool for an installation is a pad of paper and a pencil. Write everything down. Document, document, document!
- It is probably better to remove any questionable hardware and software before starting the installation. Be sure to back up any data files and check the integrity of the installation disks. Reinstall after Windows 95 is up and running.
- Check the Microsoft Internet Web site for its incompatible hardware list. Search: www.microsoft.com.
- Be sure to turn off all TSRs (terminate-and-stay-resident programs) and active programs before starting the installation.
- Check the CMOS (complementary metal-oxide semiconductor) setup for any antivirus programs and deactivate. Windows 95 installation does not like virus protection. You will need to open the BIOS setup and disable virus checking before proceeding. While you are there, document your CMOS.

Windows 95 Installation Process

The Windows 95 installation process can be divided into five distinct steps:

Step 1—Startup and System Check

Run the SETUP.EXE from either the CD (best choice) or Disk 1. Windows 95 is shipped on CD; if your computer does not have a CD-ROM drive, you can request the floppy disk version from Microsoft. The setup process goes like this:

1. SETUP looks through the system for a previous version of Windows. If you are installing the upgrade version, it must find the previous version of Windows or it will not install.

2. SETUP runs SCANDISK. You must correct any disk problems before continuing the install. If problems are encountered, run SCANDISK again after they are repaired.

3. SETUP confirms that the system is ready to accept a new operating system (OS).

4. SETUP checks for the presence of an extended memory manager (HIMEM.SYS) and a disk cache (SMARTDrive). If they are not present, it loads XMSMMGR.EXE and SMARTDrive.

5. SETUP checks for any TSR programs and device drivers.

6. If SETUP was started from MS-DOS and this is an upgrade, it copies the basic Windows 3.1 files to a temporary directory (WININSTO.400). It uses the old GUI to get started.

7. SETUP looks for a directory named Old_dos.x and asks if you want to remove it.

8. SETUP adds the following to the AUTOEXEC.BAT file:

```
@if exist c:\wininst0.400\suwarn.bat call c:\wininst0.400\suwarn.bat
@if exist c:\wininst0.400\suwarn.bat del c:\wininst0.400\suwarn.bat
```

If for any reason the installation process aborts, this will display a warning that Windows 95 was not installed completely and that you need to rerun SETUP and choose the Safe Recover option.

Step 2—Information Collection

This step runs the Installation wizard, which presents a step-by-step series of dialog boxes. The purpose of this process is to collect any custom information required, including:

- The directory in which to install Windows 95.
- Which components to install.
- Your name and company name.
- Any network configurations.

SETUP creates a text file named SETUPLOG.TXT in the root directory. This file stores the requested information.

Step 3—Hardware Detection

SETUP attempts to automatically determine all hardware—IRQs, addresses, DMA (direct memory access), and so forth. If the hardware is Plug and Play–compatible, the detection manager simply queries the BIOS for the information. With legacy (the older non–Plug and Play) devices, it is more complicated (and dangerous). This low-level detection can cause device drivers to go haywire and cause delays to the system. Therefore, Windows looks for "hints" of these devices. This is called safe detection.

Hardware devices are divided into four classes: sound cards, SCSI (Small Computer System Interface) controllers, network adapters, and proprietary CD-ROM drives. Windows SETUP will look in the following places for information about these devices:

- The DEVICE= lines in CONFIG.SYS
- Device drivers residing in memory
- The hard drive, for files that might be associated with a driver (*.drv, for instance)
- Read-only memory strings
- Warnings in MSDET.INF that spell out prescribed actions

Remember, SETUP is looking for "hints." If it makes an incorrect assumption, problems can occur when Windows 95 tries to run for the first time. (Consider uninstalling any questionable legacy devices before starting the Windows 95 installation.) The data found during the search is stored in a file called DETLOG.TXT in the root directory of the C drive. It is not deleted at the end of setup, and can be examined if you like.

After finding all the devices, SETUP creates the Registry (the database for this information). During this process, go get a cup of coffee and a doughnut. This might take awhile, and you will need a break, anyway.

Step 4—Startup Disk Creation and File Installation

SETUP next asks if you want a startup disk created. (It is highly recommended that you select "yes.") This will create a bootable floppy disk with several useful files. This is also called an emergency startup disk, and you can create one at any time, on any Windows 95 computer, by selecting the Startup Disk tab of the Add/Remove icon found in the Control Panel.

The following files are put on the emergency startup disk:

- ATTRIB.EXE
- CHKDSK.EXE
- COMMAND.COM
- DEBUG.EXE
- DRVSPACE.BIN
- EBD.SYS
- EDIT.COM
- FDISK.EXE
- FORMAT.COM
- IO.SYS

- MSDOS.SYS
- REGEDIT.EXE
- SCANDISK.EXE
- SCANDISK.INI
- SYS.COM
- UNINSTALL.EXE

After creating the startup disk, SETUP checks the SETUPLOG.TXT file and begins copying all the necessary files from the CD (or floppy disks) to the hard disk.

Note If you are installing Windows 95 or 98 on a laptop that can support only a CD-ROM or a floppy disk drive in a single bay, you can defer creating the emergency startup disk by choosing cancel when the dialog box that prompts you to insert a floppy disk appears.

Step 5—Windows Configuration

Now that everything has been copied to the hard disk drive, Windows 95 needs to set itself up to take over the operating system duties. Configuration is a multistep process as Windows:

- Replaces the Master Boot record with the Windows 95 version.
- Renames several system files: IO.SYS to IO.DOS; MSDOS.SYS to MSDOS.DOS; COMMAND.COM to COMMAND.DOS.
- Copies the Windows 95 operating system files: replaces IO.SYS and MSDOS.SYS with IO.SYS.

Now, the computer reboots, invoking a special routine used only when Windows 95 is run for the first time. This process:

- Combines all virtual device drivers into one file called VMM32.VXD.
- Loads the Run-Once module, which configures the hardware.
- Installs any network information (if required).
- Converts any Program Group files from Windows 3.x into Windows 95 shortcuts for the Start menu.
- Runs wizards for configuration of printers and other peripherals.
- Initializes the Windows 95 Help system.
- Enables MS-DOS program settings.
- Sets the date and time properties.
- Reboots to set final hardware configuration.

Performing a Clean Installation

A clean installation is perhaps the best way to install Window 95. Before undertaking a clean installation, make sure you have:

- A bootable floppy disk with all the necessary files (FORMAT.COM, FDISK.EXE, and so forth).

- A disk with all the files necessary to run any hardware such as the CD-ROM drive or SCSI controller.

- A startup disk. This disk should include an AUTOEXEC.BAT file with a MSCDEX.EXE line that points to the location of the MSCDEX.EXE file, and a CONFIG.SYS file that loads the CD driver. See the example at the end of this section.

- Disk #1 from your Windows 3.x disk set, if you are upgrading from Windows 3.x. SETUP will ask to see this disk to verify that this is an upgrade. When asked, insert the disk in the floppy drive and tell Windows 95 where to look for the information.

- Back up copies of all your programs and data because this type of installation requires that you wipe everything off the hard disk drive.

If you are going to complete a clean installation on an existing drive, you will need to remove all the files. You can simply erase (delete) them, or reformat the drive (the best choice because all hidden files will also be removed).

Whether you erase the drive or install a new drive, you need to follow the instructions for installation on a new computer or hard drive.

The following is an example of an AUTOEXEC.BAT file on a boot disk:

```
MSCDEX /D:MSCD001 /V
```

The following is an example of a CONFIG.SYS file on a boot disk:

```
DEVICE=A:\CDPRO\VIDE-CDD.SYS /D:MSCD001
```

Note   This example disk also contains a folder (CDPRO) with the driver for the CD-ROM drive (VIDE-CDD.SYS).

Installing Windows 95 on a New Computer or Hard Drive

Windows 95 version B is an OEM product designed specifically for installation on new machines or new hard drives. It does not require an existing version of Windows 3.x to be present in order to install. It was replaced with the OSR2 (OEM Service Release 2) version. The primary difference between version B and OSR2 is that the latter uses a 32-bit FAT (versions A & B use 16 bit-FAT). Because this installation takes place on a new drive with no other installed software, potential software conflicts are avoided.

Windows 98

Today, new OEM computers come with Windows 98 preloaded. It is highly unlikely that you will be able to locate a copy of Windows 95 in any local computer store. Windows 98 can be installed on a new computer or as an upgrade to MS-DOS, Windows 3.1, or Windows 95. If you wish to retain your Windows 95 settings when upgrading, be sure to start the installation from Windows 95.

For your convenience, here is the complete process of installing a new hard disk drive and the Windows 95 operating system from scratch. You will need the following for the installation:

- A hard disk drive (preferably new) with the manufacturer's specifications (CHS values and jumper settings)
- Bootable floppy disk—aWin95 startup disk (can be made from any Windows 95 computer)
- Device drivers for the CD-ROM drive: MSCDEX.EXE and the driver that came with the CD-ROM drive
- Windows 95 OEM CD-ROM

Follow these steps to install the hard disk drive and put Windows 95 on it:

1. Set up all the jumpers according to the manufacturer's specifications. Identify the drive as master or slave.
2. Physically install the drive. (See Chapters 8 and 9 to refresh your memory on hard disk drives.)
3. Connect the cables (power and data).
4. Start the computer and open the CMOS setup.
5. Set the CMOS either using the CHS values established by the manufacturer or using Auto-detect (the preferred method).
6. Reboot the computer using the Win95 startup disk.
7. Run FDISK from the floppy disk and partition the drive.
8. Format the C partition by typing:

```
Format C: /S
```

9. Format any other partitions.
10. Remove the floppy disk and reboot the computer.
11. Install the CD-ROM drivers on the new C drive.
12. Confirm operation of the CD-ROM.
13. Install Windows 95 from the CD. Follow instructions with the documentation.

Optional Install

This optional install method will speed up the installation process and allow for easy addition of drives and Windows 95 programs not installed during the initial installation. However, it requires an additional 40 MB of hard disk drive space. The process is as follows:

1. After installing the CD-ROM driver, make a directory (name it "Win95") on the C drive, and copy all the files in the Win95 directory on the CD into this folder.

2. Install Windows 95 from the new folder on the C drive by typing the following command:

```
C:\win95\setup
```

Installing a Dual-Boot System

You can install Windows 95 on a disk that already has Windows 3.1 or Windows NT. Let's look at both options.

Windows 3.1 and Windows 95

Windows 95 can be installed without removing the Windows 3.x system. The main advantages of this approach are that Windows 95 installs cleanly and the Windows 3.x files are left intact. You will still be able to run old programs that Windows 95 doesn't like.

There are two considerations to keep in mind when creating a dual-boot computer:

- Windows 3.x and Windows 95 must be installed in different directories (for instance, install Windows 95 in a Win95 directory).

- It requires lots of hard disk space. Not only must both operating systems be on the hard disk drive, many programs will have to be installed twice— once for Windows 3.x and once for Windows 95. This is because not all program configurations will migrate across two operating systems.

To run the old system, press F8 when you see the "Starting Windows 95" message during boot up. The menu you will see is shown in Figure 16.1.

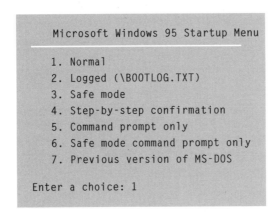

```
         Microsoft Windows 95 Startup Menu

      1. Normal
      2. Logged (\BOOTLOG.TXT)
      3. Safe mode
      4. Step-by-step confirmation
      5. Command prompt only
      6. Safe mode command prompt only
      7. Previous version of MS-DOS

  Enter a choice: 1
```

Figure 16.1   Windows 95 Startup menu

Select number 7 (8 if running a network), and the old version of MS-DOS will boot. You can then change to the Windows 3.x directory and start the earlier operating system.

Note   Another method for setting up a dual-boot computer is to create two partitions on the hard disk drive (or have two hard drives) and install one operating system in each. On startup, you can then select which partition to boot up. Using this method, you will keep both operating systems completely separate and reduce the chances of contamination.

Dual-Booting with Windows NT

Windows 95 and Windows NT share the same machine quite well and dual-booting is no problem. However, you must consider the following:

- The hard disk drive must have a Windows 95 FAT16 partition. NT will run in Windows FAT16, but Windows 95 will not run on NTFS (NT file system).
- Drive compression for Windows 95 and Windows NT differs and is incompatible. Therefore, you cannot install Windows NT on a Windows partition that uses drive compression.

To avoid reinstalling all the Windows 95 applications in Windows NT, do the following:

- In the Windows NT Control Panel, open the system icons.
- In the System dialog box, highlight the Path line in the System Environment Variables section. Move down to the Value text box and add the following string to the end of the existing value:

```
c:\windows;c:\windows\system
```

The Boot Process from Power Up to Startup

There are twelve steps to a successful startup of Windows 95.

1. **Powering on:** The system microprocessor executes the ROM BIOS code and initiates the POST (power on self-test). A single beep means success.

2. **Finding a boot sector:** The BIOS checks the A drive for a boot sector; if there is no disk in the floppy disk drive, it checks the C drive.

3. **Running the boot program:** BIOS runs IO.SYS (or IO.SYS and MSDOS.SYS), initializes some device drivers, and performs a few real-mode chores.

4. **Reading MSDOS.SYS:** Remember, this is not the same as with MS-DOS (it is a text file with setup information). After collecting the information from MSDOS.SYS, you will see the "Starting Windows 95" message.

5. **Reading CONFIG.SYS:** Commands are processed in CONFIG.SYS file and load real-mode devices.

6. **Reading AUTOEXEC.BAT:** Commands are processed in AUTOEXEC.BAT.

7. **Reading the Registry:** The Registry data is read and drivers and settings are loaded. The following table describes some of the drivers that can be specified by the Registry along with their functions. They could also be loaded using the CONFIG.SYS file.

Setting	Function
BUFFERS=30	Determines the number of file buffers to create—for backward compatibility.
DOS=HIGH	Loads MS-DOS into high memory.
DRVSPACE.BIN or DBLSPACE.BIN	Disk compression.
FCBS=4	Determines the number of file control blocks that can be open at one time—for backward compatibility.
FILES=30	Determines the number of file handles to create—for backward compatibility.
HIMEM.SYS	Loads real-mode extended memory manager.
IFSHLP.SYS	Installable file system helper—helps load VFAT and other Windows 95 installable file systems.
LASTDRIVE=Z	Determines the last drive letter that can be assigned to a disk drive—for backward compatibility.
SETVER.EXE	The operating system version. If an MS-DOS program needs a special version of MS-DOS, this setting can "lie" to MS-DOS so the program will run.
SHELL=COMMAND.COM /P	Determines the name of the command-line interpreter.
STACKS=9,256	Determines the number of stack frames and the size of each frame—for backward compatibility.

Caution Don't use values less than these defaults.

8. **Switching to Protected Mode:** The processor switches to protected mode and loads protected-mode drivers (VMM32.VXD).

9. **Configuring Plug and Play:** Windows now loads new device drivers detected during the initial boot phase, resolves hardware conflicts, and performs other tasks.

10. **Loading Windows 95 GUI:** The interface is loaded.

11. **Configuring Network:** Prompts for network password if applicable (or user password if user profiles are enabled).

12. **Processing Startup Folder:** Checks the startup folder and loads any programs found.

The Startup Menu—Modes of Starting

With early versions of Windows, startup problems could be resolved by booting up from a floppy disk and editing the appropriate file. With Windows 95, it's not as simple. Therefore, Windows 95 comes with a Startup menu, shown in Figure 16.2. Pressing the F8 key when the "Starting Windows 95" message appears on the screen evokes this menu.

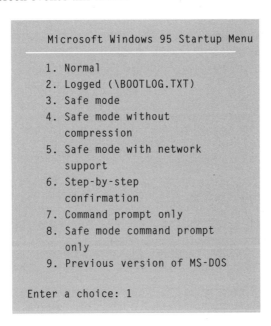

```
    Microsoft Windows 95 Startup Menu

    1. Normal
    2. Logged (\BOOTLOG.TXT)
    3. Safe mode
    4. Safe mode without
       compression
    5. Safe mode with network
       support
    6. Step-by-step
       confirmation
    7. Command prompt only
    8. Safe mode command prompt
       only
    9. Previous version of MS-DOS

Enter a choice: 1
```

Figure 16.2   Startup menu (dual boot)

Let's look at the options presented by the Startup menu.

Normal
This option loads Windows 95 in the usual fashion.

Logged (BOOTLOG.TXT)
This choice loads Windows 95 in the same way as the normal option, but it creates a boot log file (BOOTLOG.TXT) and places it in the root directory of the boot drive. It can be read with any text editor and shows all steps of the boot process, noting whether or not they were successful.

Safe Mode
If it encounters difficulty starting up, Windows 95 can (and will) load in the safe mode. Most of the time, startup problems are caused by driver conflicts or problems. Safe mode starts Windows 95 with a minimum of drivers. This mode is considered the Windows 95 troubleshooting mode. When safe mode is enabled:

- CONFIG.SYS, AUTOEXEC.BAT, and the Registry are bypassed.
- HIMEM.SYS and IFSHLP.SYS are loaded.
- MSDOS.SYS is checked for the location of the Windows 95 files.
- The command `win /d:m` (enables a safe-mode boot) is executed and COMMAND.COM is bypassed.
- Windows loads only the virtual device drivers for the keyboard, mouse, and a standard VGA display.
- The SYSTEM.INI and WIN.INI files are partially loaded (reading the shell and drivers lines in the [Boot] sections of SYSTEM.INI).
- The desktop is resized for 640 x 480 resolution.
- A dialog box appears to notify the user that safe mode is in effect.

Safe Mode Without Compression
With this option selected, safe mode is loaded but Windows doesn't load any drivers to access a compressed drive.

Safe Mode with Network Support
With this option, safe mode is loaded along with any real-mode drivers for network support.

Step-by-Step Confirmation

Step-by-step confirmation allows Windows 95 to load normally, but each command in the IO.SYS, CONFIG.SYS, and AUTOEXEC.BAT is addressed one step at a time and the operator has the option to bypass or use each item.

The following table presents a four-combination matrix that can be used to troubleshoot startup problems using the step-by-step method. Each of the columns represents combinations you should try.

Step-by-Step Prompt	A	B	C	D
Load DoubleSpace driver?	Yes	Yes	Yes	Yes
Process the system registry?	Yes	Yes	Yes	No
Create a startup log file (BOOTLOG.TXT)?	Yes	Yes	Yes	Yes
Process your startup device drivers (CONFIG.SYS)?	No	No	Yes	Yes
DEVICE=C:\WINDOWS\HIMEM.SYS?	Yes	Yes	Yes	Yes
DEVICE=C:\WINDOWS\IFSHLP.SYS?	Yes	Yes	Yes	Yes
DEVICE=C:\WINDOWS\SETVER.EXE?	Yes	Yes	Yes	Yes
Process your startup command file (AUTOEXEC.BAT)?	No	No	Yes	Yes
Load the Windows graphical user interface?	Yes	Yes	Yes	Yes
Load all Windows drivers?	No	Yes	No	Yes

If Windows starts properly when using response A, you know you have a problem with a device driver or TSR. Successful startup with option B indicates a problem with a real-mode device driver or TSR in CONFIG.SYS or AUTOEXEC.BAT. Successful boot with option C means you have a problem with a protected-mode device. And if option D is successful, you have a problem with the Registry.

Command Prompt Only

This choice boots to MS-DOS without loading the Windows 95 GUI and protected-mode drivers. It will, however, load CONFIG.SYS and AUTOEXEC.BAT.

Note   The CD-ROM drive might not work in this mode.

Safe Mode Command Prompt Only

This operates in the same way as command prompt only, but does not process the CONFIG.SYS and AUTOEXEC.BAT.

Previous Version of MS-DOS
This option is used for dual-boot systems.

To save time, you can use shortcut keys to access Startup menu options.

BootKey	Startup Menu Equivalent
F4	Previous version of MS-DOS
F5	Safe mode
SHIFT+F5	Safe mode—command prompt only
CTRL+F5	Safe mode without compression
F6	Safe mode with network support
SHIFT+F8	Step-by-step confirmation

A New Desktop Environment

With Windows 95, Microsoft has replaced the Windows 3.x Program Manager with a new format. Program groups have been replaced with a Start menu, and program icons have been replaced by shortcuts and desktop items. A shortcut is a pointer (an icon) to an object such as an executable file or a document. The desktop now truly represents a virtual desktop.

Note A common problem with a shortcut occurs when the object it is pointing to gets moved, is missing, or has become corrupted. In such cases, when a user double-clicks the shortcut, an error message pops up saying "The item (item named here) that this shortcut refers to has been changed or moved. The nearest match, based on size, date, and type is c:\pathname goes here. Do you want this shortcut to point to this item?"

Some of the features introduced in Windows 95 include:

Feature	Description
Folders	Folders have replaced MS-DOS directories and subdirectories. A folder is used to hold data and system objects and can reside within another folder, on a disk, or on the desktop.
Plug and Play	Windows 95 supports Plug and Play hardware. In some cases, additional driver software (provided by the manufacturer) is required. Look for the Windows 95 symbol on the device to determine if it is Plug and Play–compliant.
Printers folder	The Printers folder has replaced the Print Manager. This folder allows access to all aspects of printing (from setup of printers to monitoring printing activity).
Properties	All items in the Windows 95 environment are treated as objects, and they have properties. All properties can be configured. An object's settings and properties are located on the Properties sheet. The long ignored, little used, right mouse button now has a major function in the Windows 95 environment (and on the Internet.) The secondary mouse button now accesses shortcut menus and the Properties dialog boxes.
Windows Explorer	The Windows 3.x File Manager has been replaced by Windows Explorer. Explorer provides a visual representation of the computer and its components, as well as providing enhanced file-management tools.

Lesson Summary

The following points summarize the main elements of this lesson:

- Windows 95 comes in two versions: an upgrade 16-bit FAT version and an OEM 32-bit version for installation on new machines.

- Windows 95 can be dual-booted with Windows 3.x (DOS) or Windows NT. Special considerations must be taken to ensure compatibility when setting up a dual-boot system.

- Installing Windows 95 is a five-step process.

- Windows 95 has a startup menu that can be used for troubleshooting or starting with another operating system.

- Shortcut keys are provided to allow quick access to the various startup options.

- Windows 95 uses a new desktop environment for a more user-friendly operator interface.

Lesson 3: How Windows 95 Works

The first two lessons in this chapter gave you an overview of Windows 95. We looked at what makes it different from its precursors and described its distinguishing features. This lesson lets you see take a look "under the hood" and presents the basics of how the Windows 95 operating system works. It is not a complete course, but it is intended to give you a firm background in the operation of Windows 95.

After this lesson, you will be able to:

- Identify the various parts of Windows 95.
- Define the principles of the Windows 95 Registry.
- Back up the Registry.
- Identify the basics of Plug and Play technology.

Estimated lesson time: 40 minutes

The Windows 95 File Structure

As mentioned earlier in this chapter, Windows 95 disk structures are nothing new. Partitions still work in exactly the same way as they did in Windows 3.x systems, so the MS-DOS 7 bootable files of Windows 95 must still be installed to the C drive. Windows 95 still uses 16-bit FAT formats for hard disk drives and floppy disks. Hard disks formatted with Windows 95 are identical to disks formatted with MS-DOS.

Note   Using 32-bit FAT provided with Windows 95 OSR2 or Windows 98 reduces the necessity for multiple partitions because cluster size is set at a default of 4 KB.

Windows 95 has also added some new bits of file information. The best one is a "last accessed" date value that tells when a particular file was last used (includes executable files, DLLs, and other nonuser data files such as font files).

Important System Files

Windows 95 starts up differently from earlier versions of Windows. The startup relies on several files that both complement and work independently of each other. We introduced most of these files in earlier sections of this chapter. Now let's take a look at what makes them tick.

IO.SYS

This is the real-mode operating system for Windows 95. Most of the "old" CONFIG.SYS commands have been incorporated into the IO.SYS. If you recall, the IO.SYS does most of the work that was done by the CONFIG.SYS file in MS-DOS. For that reason, Windows 95 no longer requires a CONFIG.SYS.

IO.SYS includes the files:

- COMMAND.COM.
- HIMEM.SYS.
- IFSHLP.SYS.
- SETVER.EXE.

IO.SYS also includes the following commands:

- dos=high
- files=
- lastdrive=
- buffers=
- stacks=
- shell=
- fcbs=

Note   The IO.SYS file cannot be changed or overwritten. The only way to override these commands is to create a CONFIG.SYS or edit an existing CONFIG.SYS. Remember that a CONFIG.SYS file is not required with Windows 95; however, if one exists, it will take precedence over any commands or files in IO.SYS.

EMM386.EXE is a memory manager left over from Windows 3.1, and it is not loaded by IO.SYS. EMM386.EXE is an MS-DOS driver that uses extended memory to simulate expanded memory. Some older MS-DOS-based programs take advantage of this memory in order to run. If you have an application that needs EMM386.EXE in memory, you must add it to your CONFIG.SYS file.

MSDOS.SYS

As mentioned earlier in the chapter, in the days before Windows 95, MS-DOS used two system files to boot up: IO.SYS and MSDOS.SYS. The IO.SYS file provided the system initialization code, and the MSDOS.SYS file loaded basic system drivers. In Windows 95, MSDOS.SYS functions have been incorporated into the IO.SYS file. MSDOS.SYS is now a special information file. It contains two components: paths used to locate other Windows files and options to add information that helps run older MS-DOS programs. MSDOS.SYS is a text file that can be edited with any file editor. It is hidden and read-only, therefore the attributes must be changed to make the file read/write, nonhidden (the MS-DOS command `attrib -r -h filename` makes the file accessible).

To open MSDOS.SYS:

1. In Windows Explorer, select Options from the View menu to display the Options dialog box.

2. Activate the Show All Files option and click OK (this makes all hidden files visible).

3. In the Folders window, highlight the root folder (C:\).

4. Select MSDOS.SYS and right-click it.

5. Select Properties. (See Figure 16.3.)

6. Deactivate the Read-only check box and click OK.

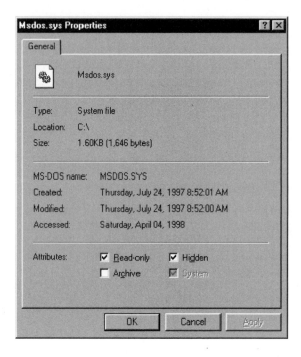

Figure 16.3   MSDOS.SYS properties sheet

The following table lists what you'll find in the [PATH] Group of MSDOS.SYS.

Setting	Function
HostWinBootDrv=C	The drive letter of the system boot drive. Always the C drive.
UninstallDir=C:\	The location of the Windows 95 uninstall file.
WinBootDir=C:\WINDOWS	The location of the Windows files needed to boot.
WinDir=C:\WINDOWS	The location of the GUI files.

The following table lists what you'll find in the MSDOS.SYS [OPTION] Group. Unless otherwise specified, the values are either 0 or 1.

Setting	Function
BootConfig=	If you have multiple hardware configurations, this allows boot up of a particular hardware configuration. For example, BootConfig=2 would start configuration 2.
BootDelay=X	Determines the number of seconds that the "Starting Windows 95" message appears during startup. Default is 2 seconds.
BootGUI=1	Sets whether to boot the Windows 95 GUI or not. 0 boots to the MS-DOS prompt.
Bootkeys=1	Sets whether to allow use of function keys at boot. 0 disables the keys.
BootMenu=0	Sets whether to load the boot menu. 1 shows the menu.
BootMenuDefault=1	Determines which of the startup menu options is highlighted automatically when you invoke the menu: 1 = Normal 2 = Logged to BOOTLOG.TXT 3 = Safe mode 4 = Safe mode with network support (if network installed). If a network is not installed, this line item will not be available and the following steps will be numbered accordingly. 4 or 5 = Step-by-step 5 or 6 = Command prompt 6 or 7 = Safe mode command prompt 7 or 8 = Previous version of MS-DOS (if BootMulti=1).
BootMulti=0	Determines whether to prompt for previous version of MS-DOS in boot menu—requires BootMenu=1.
Bootsafe=0	Forces the machine to boot in safe mode. 1 invokes safe mode.
Bootwarn=1	Sets whether to show the "You are in Safe Mode" warning message. 0 does not show the message.
BootWin=1	Determines whether to boot from your previous version of MS-DOS or Windows 95. 0 selects MS-DOS.
DisableLog=1	Enables or disables the BOOTLOG.TXT file. 0 disables the log.
DoubleBuffer=1	Sets whether to load VFAT's double buffer or not. 0 doesn't load the buffer.
Drvspace=1 or Dblspace=1	Loads DOUBLESPACE or DRIVESPACE drivers. 0 stops the drivers from loading.

(continued)

continued

Setting	Function
LoadTop=1	Loads COMMAND.COM at the top of 640 KB. 0 loads it normally.
Logo=1	Sets whether to show the animated Windows logo. 0 doesn't show the logo.
Network=1	Sets whether to add the Boot In Safe Mode With Networking menu to the startup menu. 0 doesn't show it.
SystemReg=1	Determines whether to load the system Registry. 0 prevents the Registry from loading.

Important   Older programs, especially antivirus programs, expect the MSDOS.SYS file to be larger than 1024 bytes. To make MSDOS.SYS large enough to prevent these problems, 19 lines of x's are included to keep the file size large enough for compatibility. (See Figure 16.4.)

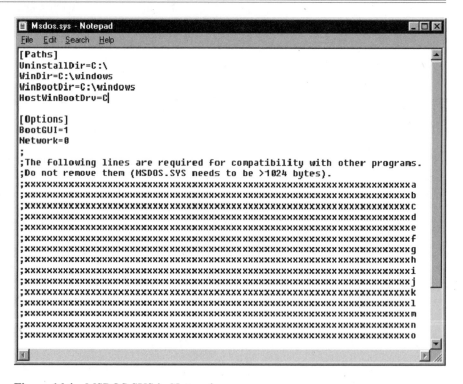

Figure 16.4   MSDOS.SYS in Notepad

CONFIG.SYS and AUTOEXEC.BAT

These two familiar files play roles very similar to those in the old MS-DOS world, with one important exception: Windows 95 automatically loads drivers and sets defaults by using the IO.SYS file and the Registry. If you have a software or hardware device that needs a driver not contained in the IO.SYS file or Registry, Windows 95 will use the commands contained within CONFIG.SYS and AUTOEXEC.BAT files.

If you edit AUTOEXEC.BAT and CONFIG.SYS to override some of the information contained in the Registry and IO.SYS file, remember to avoid the following items.

In AUTOEXEC.BAT:

- Don't include other versions of Windows in the path statements.
- Don't add SMARTDRV.SYS or other device caches. Windows 95 has built-in disk-caching.
- Don't add any statements for loading mouse drivers. Windows 95 includes mouse support.
- Don't make your network connections by using commands in the AUTOEXEC.BAT file; do it from inside Windows 95.

In CONFIG.SYS:

- Remove any `device=mouse.sys` command. Windows 95 includes mouse support.

COMMAND.COM

Windows 95 comes with a few "MS-DOS-like" real-mode components. These are necessary to get it going and get into protected mode. It provides the MS-DOS prompt (C:\) and a few internal MS-DOS commands. The following table lists COMMAND.COM's internal MS-DOS commands:

Command	Function
BREAK	Sets or clears extended CTRL+C checking.
CD and CHDIR	Changes to a different directory or displays the current directory.
CHCP	Displays the number of the active character sets.
CLS	Clears the screen.
COPY	Copies one or more files to the specified location.
CTTY	Changes the terminal device used to control the computer.
DATE	Displays or sets the current date.
DEL	Deletes the specified files.

(continued)

continued

Command	Function
DIR	Displays a list of the files and subfolders that exist in the current folder.
ERASE	Deletes the specified files.
EXIT	Quits the COMMAND.COM and returns to the previous program.
LH and LOADHIGH	Loads a program into upper memory.
LOCK	Enables direct disk access (allows storage and retrieval from disk without involving the CPU).
MD	Creates a folder or subfolder.
MKDIR	Same as MD.
PATH	Specifies which folders Windows 95 should search for executable files.
PROMPT	Changes the appearance of the command prompt.
RD and RMDIR	Deletes a folder.
REN and RENAME	Changes the name of a file or files.
SET	Displays, sets, or removes environment variables.
TIME	Displays or sets the current time.
TYPE	Displays the contents of a text file.
UNLOCK	Disables direct disk access.
VER	Displays the operating system version number.
VERIFY	Directs the operating system to verify that files are written correctly to a disk, and displays the status of verifications.
VOL	Displays the volume label and serial number for a disk.

System Commands

Many of the familiar MS-DOS prompt commands, system files, and drivers are included in Windows 95. They are found in the Windows\Command directory. The following is a list of commands and related files *not* included in the basic Windows 95 command set. Some of these commands can be loaded from the Windows 95 CD and are found in the directory Other\Olddos:

- ASSIGN
- BACKUP
- CHKSTATE.SYS
- COMP
- DOSSHELL
- EDLIN
- EGA.SYS
- EXPAND
- FASTHELP
- FASTOPEN
- GRAFTABL
- GRAPHICS
- HELP
- INSTUPP.BAT

- INTERLNK
- INTERSVR
- JOIN
- LOADFIX
- MEMCARD
- MEMMAKER
- MIRROR
- MONOUMB.386
- MSAV
- MSBACKUP
- POWER
- PRINT
- PRINTER.SYS
- QBASIC
- RAMDRIVE.SYS
- RECOVER
- REPLACE
- RESTORE
- ROMDRIVE.SYS
- SHARE
- SIZER
- SMARTMON
- TREE
- UNDELETE
- UNFORMAT
- VSAFE

BOOTLOG.TXT

As mentioned earlier, this log contains information about the Windows 95 startup process. It is a good troubleshooting tool. The BOOTLOG.TXT file contains the following sections:

- Loading real-mode drivers
- Loading VxDs system—critical initialization of VxDs
- Device initialization of VxDs
- Successful VxD initialization

Note   VxD is a Windows virtual device driver—it replaces the real-mode drivers from MS-DOS. The *x* is a variable and stands for the type of device—for example, P for printer or D for display.

The following is an example of the first 10 lines of a BOOTLOG.TXT file:

```
[000B346F] Loading Device = ATAPICD.SYS
[000B3482] LoadSuccess = ATAPICD.SYS
[000B3482] Loading Device = C:\WINDOWS\HIMEM.SYS
[000B3484] LoadSuccess = C:\WINDOWS\HIMEM.SYS
[000B3484] Loading Device = C:\WINDOWS\IFSHLP.SYS
[000B3485] LoadSuccess = C:\WINDOWS\IFSHLP.SYS
[000B3485] Loading Device = C:\WINDOWS\SETVER.EXE
[000B3486] LoadSuccess = C:\WINDOWS\SETVER.EXE
[000B348D] C:\PROGRA~1\MCAFEE\VIRUSS~1\SCANPM.EXE[000B348D] starting
[000B34D2] Loading VXD = VMM
```

Initialization Files

As explained in Chapter 15, "Software: MS-DOS and Windows 3.x," .INI files were some of the most important files in earlier versions of Windows. In Windows 95, .INI files are not nearly as important as the Registry.

The Windows 3.1 .INI system included WIN.INI, which contained information about the appearance of the Windows environment including keyboard, mouse, and display options. The SYSTEM.INI file contained information related to hardware and device options including memory options, device drivers, and networking and resource-sharing parameters.

WIN.INI and SYSTEM.INI are still used by Windows 95 to run older Windows 3.x programs that are not supported by .VXD files. With time, the use of these files will diminish. They are not required by Windows 95; they simply provide backward compatibility.

Tip   If Windows 95 is installed in its own directory and not in the root directory of the hard disk, older versions of MS-DOS can still be run by setting the `BootMulti=` statement in the [Options] section of the Windows 95 version of MSDOS.SYS. Load the earlier version of MS-DOS by pressing F4 at the "Starting Windows" screen during system startup.

The Registry

As explained in Lesson 1, the Registry is a common database composed of two binary files: SYSTEM.DAT and USER.DAT, which are located in the Windows directory. Inside the Registry is information on all the hardware in the computer, network information, user preferences, and file types, as well as virtually anything else you might run into within Windows 95.

Note   The Registry is intended to replace CONFIG.SYS, AUTOEXEC.BAT, and every .INI file. However, Windows 95 still reads all .INI files at boot up for backward compatibility with Win 3.x programs that need them.

Why the Change in Windows 95?

Windows 3.1x supported two kinds of .INI files: system initialization files and private initialization files. System initialization files controlled the Windows environment and included SYSTEM.INI and WIN.INI. Private initialization files included CONTROL.INI, PROGMAN.INI, WINFILE.INI, and PROTOCOL.INI, as well as any application .INI files. Initialization files created a bridge between the application and the Windows operating environment.

In addition to .INI files, Windows 3.1 used a host of other text files to manage operations. The files included AUTOEXEC.BAT and CONFIG.SYS. It was conceivable for a user to have more than 150 files responsible for the operation of the computer and the Windows environment.

During the development of Windows 3.11, it became apparent that a move away from the .INI files was needed. A new file type was introduced into the programming environment. The file was called REG.DAT and was the precursor to the Windows 95 Registry. REG.DAT included information used for drag-and-drop operations, object linking and embedding (OLE), and establishing associations between data files and their programs.

The binary file REG.DAT was bundled with its editor, REGEDIT.EXE. While this began the process of centralizing computer operations, REG.DAT came with some serious size limitations. It could not exceed 64 KB, which is the same limit established for the .INI files in Windows 3.11.

Accessing the Registry

The recommended way to access the Registry is through the Control Panel. It lets a user modify settings with an easy to use interface that never even mentioned the word Registry. In Windows 3.x, most such changes required modifying the SYSTEM.INI file.

Tip Everything necessary to configure the system so that it will work can be handled from the Windows 95 Control Panel. The three areas where Windows 95 preferences/settings can be viewed and configured are the Control Panel, the System Monitor, and the Registry.

Directly changing an entry (to be done only by a knowledgeable user) is accomplished with the Registry Editor, REGEDIT.EXE. To open it, type REGEDIT at a command prompt. This can be obtained by typing the command in the dialog box that appears when you choose Run from the Start menu. The Registry itself is stored in binary format, so you can't open, view, or edit the contents directly.

Microsoft tried to make the Registry as inaccessible as possible. The fact that the Registry is the central repository creates its principal weakness—once it has been corrupted, it's hard to recover settings if they haven't been backed up.

The Registry is stored in three locations:

- **SYSTEM.DAT:** Stores most of the data, including the majority of hardware and software configurations.
- **USER.DAT:** Stores data about a particular user.
- **The Virtual Registry:** Consists of a host of files that are created by Windows 95 when the system is started up. They are stored in RAM. These settings relate to many of the performance-monitoring tools such as PVIEW.EXE.

Components of the Registry

The Windows 95 Registry consists of six root keys, each of which reflects a different aspect of the configuration. Each key or branch of the Registry groups information that logically belongs together. All top-level keys are called root keys and defined and named by Windows 95. These cannot be changed. Root keys are named HKEY_XXX and can be followed by several subkeys. All other keys in the Registry are subkeys of these six primary keys. Subkeys can be added, deleted, or renamed. The six root keys are shown in Figure 16.5 and are explored in the following sections.

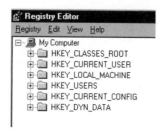

Figure 16.5 Registry root keys

HKEY_CLASSES_ROOT

This section of the Registry defines the standard-class objects used by Windows 95. Do not make any changes to this section. This is a link to the HKEY_LOCAL_MACHINE\SOFTWARE\Classes, which simply provides compatibility with the Windows 3.1 registration database. This compatibility is important if you want to run Windows 3.1 16-bit applications in Windows 95.

HKEY_CURRENT_USER

This section defines the current user settings—it's not important for repairing computers. Personalized information like fonts, some icons, and colors can be changed here. This is a link to the HKEY_USERS key. This key provides Windows 95 compatibility to applications using the Windows NT Registry structure.

HKEY_LOCAL_MACHINE

This portion of the Registry contains all the data for the system's non-user-specific configurations (including every device in the computer). This is the largest key in the Registry and the place you will perform the bulk of your system edits to optimize Windows 95 performance. Information stored here includes hardware configuration, peripheral devices, installed software, OLE compatibility, software configuration, and Windows 95 configuration. The data stored in HKEY_LOCAL_MACHINE is stored in the SYSTEM.DAT file.

HKEY_USERS

This section of the Registry is where Windows 95 keeps track of the different user settings. If your computer is not configured for multiple users, you will have a single subkey named DEFAULT. If your computer has been configured for multiple users, two profiles are created when you log on: HKEY_USERS\.DEFAULT and HKEY_USERS*user name*\user.dat. If it's a two-user system, the other user's settings are held in memory. This makes it impossible to alter user settings without logging on under their name and password.

HKEY_CURRENT_CONFIG

This key handles Plug and Play and contains information about the current configuration of a multiple-hardware-configured computer. This key works in conjunction with HKEY_LOCAL_MACHINE\Config*xxxx*, where *xxxx* is the subkey that represents the numeric value of the current hardware configuration.

HKEY_DYN_DATA

This is Registry data that is stored in RAM to speed up system configuration. A snapshot of all hardware in use is stored here. It is updated on boot up and when any changes are made in the system configuration file. This portion of the Registry is dynamic. It's where virtual device drivers are installed, where Plug and Play hardware information is maintained, and where performance statistics are calculated. Because this information is accessed and changed constantly, this portion of the Registry is never written to the hard disk. It resides in the computer's RAM.

Editing the Registry

Caution Editing the Registry directly can cause serious problems if it is not done correctly. Windows 95 provides the Control Panel and Properties sheets for editing the Registry. Microsoft recommends these methods. Microsoft does not support direct editing of the Registry.

If you feel you must edit the Registry, then back up first (see the end of this section for details on backing up the Registry). The tool used to edit the Registry is REGEDIT.EXE. (See Figure 16.6.) This program is not included in any of the menus and will not be found on the desktop. You must either activate REGEDIT.EXE through Windows Explorer or start the program from the command line.

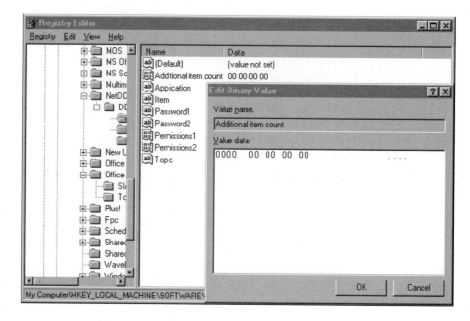

Figure 16.6 REGEDIT

The following table provides an overview of the commands in the REGEDIT.

Menu	Commands
Registry	**Import Registry File:** Allows you to take a Registry file that you've created or modified and import it into the current Registry. Importing a Registry file is often the best way to rescue a corrupted Registry or to replace the current damaged Registry with a known good backup.
	Export Registry File: Allows you to export the Registry file to a floppy disk or network location. Exporting a Registry is one of the best ways to back up your Windows 95 system.
	Connect Network Registry: Allows you to connect to a user on your network and, if you have the proper authority, modify that user's Registry. This is a very powerful feature, not necessarily one that a majority of users should have access to.
	Disconnect Network Registry: Releases the connection to a network user's Registry.
	Print: Allows you to print either the entire Registry, or just one of the keys or branches in the Registry.

continued

Menu	Commands
Edit	**New:** Allows you to create keys and assign values.
	Delete: This command allows you to delete a key, key value, or value name.
	Rename: This command lets you rename either a key or value name.
	Find: Allows you to find a particular string or key value name.
	Find Next: Finds the next value that was defined in the Find command.
View	**Status Bar:** Either hides or shows the status bar at the bottom of the screen.
	Split: This command lets you move the split bar (vertical separation) between the Key window (on the left) and the Value window (on the right).
	Refresh: This command refreshes the REGEDIT screen.

Note   The Edit command doesn't include the typical Copy, Cut, and Paste options. If you need to copy and paste in REGEDIT, you will need to use the Windows keyboard commands. Press CTRL+C for Copy, and CTRL+V for Paste. These two commands are a necessity if you do a lot of searching and replacing in the Registry.

REGEDIT's Dual Purpose

REGEDIT is more than a Windows utility program. It can be used from inside real-mode MS-DOS. This is particularly important if you have a seriously corrupted Registry file and Windows won't start. During installation, Windows 95 puts a copy of REGEDIT.EXE on the startup disk. When running REGEDIT in real mode, it doesn't have an interface—it uses a command-line format to carry out instructions. The following table lists the most common REGEDIT switches.

Switch	Function
/?	Displays the REGEDIT command-line syntax.
/L:system	Provides the location and filename of SYSTEM.DAT.
/R:user	Provides the location and filename of USER.DAT.
/E *filename* <regpath>	Creates a Registry (.REG) file.
/C *filename*	Replaces the entire Registry with the contents of your .REG.

To use REGEDIT in real mode, you'll need to tell it where your SYSTEM.DAT and USER.DAT files are located, if they are in a directory other than Windows.

Here is the syntax needed to replace an existing, corrupt Registry with the contents of the .REG file you created. Remember, this command is typed in full at the MS-DOS prompt:

```
REGEDIT [/L:system] [/R:user] /C filename
```

Using REGEDIT to Modify the Registry

Before modifying the Registry, make sure it is backed up sufficiently. When you edit the Registry, consider using the Control Panel and the applications contained inside of it to make Registry edits. The Control Panel is the wizard for updating specific parts of the Registry. A corrupted Registry is not something you can easily recover from.

Edits to the Registry can be made using either the menu or the right mouse button. Adding keys can be accomplished by simply right-clicking the key you want to add to and entering your information. Windows 95 has two restrictions you need to be aware of when adding keys:

- You cannot add a top-level key. Windows 95 creates those.
- Within a parent key, each subkey name must be unique. You can use the same subkey name in different parent keys.

Modifying the value section of the Value entry can be accomplished with a double-click on the value in the Value window. After you double-click the value, you will see one of three different dialog boxes.

Windows 95 uses multiple registers for multiuser operations, and it can be difficult to know exactly where pieces of information are stored. The System Policy Editor allows administrators to locate where information is stored.

Backing Up the Registry

Backing up the Windows 95 Registry is one of the most important parts of maintaining a personal computer. Because the Registry is so undocumented, the only way to recover from Registry errors is by restoring the Registry data. A corrupt Registry can disable a few components of a particular piece of software, or it can prevent Windows from booting. Microsoft has provided a number of different tools to back up the Registry. No single tool offers the total solution, but if used in combination they can provide a very effective backup strategy.

Every time you add a piece of software, adjust a system component, or make a new connection, the Registry is changed. The Registry is extremely dynamic and needs to be backed up any time it is changed.

There are three primary Registry backup tools available in Windows 95:

- Microsoft Configuration Backup (CFGBACK.EXE)
- Emergency Recovery Utility (ERU.EXE)
- .REG files

Microsoft Configuration Backup (CFGBACK.EXE)

CFGBACK.EXE (Microsoft Configuration Backup) is a proprietary program that creates backups that can be restored only from inside this program. CFGBACK allows you to create up to nine iterations, or different backup files, of a Registry. Once the program is installed, start it and choose the option you want to execute: Backup or Restore. One nice feature of CFGBACK is that it allows you to write a description of why the backup was run (for instance: "Before MSOffice installation" or "After MSOffice installation"). See Figure 16.7.

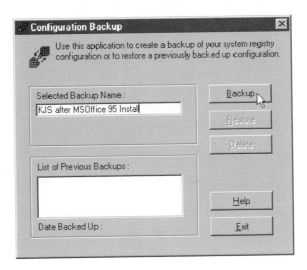

Figure 16.7   CFGBACK.EXE

Configuration Backup is available in two places: on the Windows 95 CD in the folder \Other\Misc\CFGBACK, or on the CD included with the Windows 95 Resource Kit. Either way, you need to load the file from the CD to your Windows 95 system before you can use it.

The limitations of CFGBACK.EXE include the following:

- If a Windows 95 system has multiuser settings, CFGBACK.EXE will not back up the separate user settings.
- CFGBACK.EXE will not help if Windows 95 itself cannot start. CFGBACK.EXE runs inside Windows 95, not in MS-DOS real mode. One of the best ways to bring your system back from a Windows boot-up failure is to use the .REG files created using REGEDIT.

Emergency Recovery Utility

The Emergency Recovery Utility (ERU.EXE) is available on the Windows 95 CD in the folder \Other\Misc\Eru. The ERU.EXE program backs up all critical system files, including AUTOEXEC.BAT, COMMAND.COM, CONFIG.SYS, IO.SYS, MSDOS.SYS, PROTOCOL.INI, SYSTEM.DAT, SYSTEM.INI, USER.DAT, and WIN.INI.

ERU.EXE also creates an MS-DOS real-mode file, called ERD.EXE, that you can use to restore from MS-DOS if the Windows system fails to start up.

The limitations of ERU.EXE include the following:

- When backing up to a floppy disk, ERU.EXE determines the amount of space available to perform the backup. If the disk doesn't contain enough space, it will simply not back up one of the components. Unlike the old MS-DOS BACKUP command, which could back up over multiple diskettes, ERU.EXE can back up only to a single floppy disk.

- On a multiuser system, ERU.EXE fails to create a backup of Registry settings related to the current user.

- If ERU.EXE can't find a file it is trying to back up, it will hang without giving you an error message. You are left on your own to try to figure out the problem. If it hangs, however, you can usually assume that you're missing one of the files that it's trying to back up.

Using .REG Files

One of the features of REGEDIT is its ability to export Registry information. By creating a .REG file that backs up your entire system, you can easily restore a Registry. To rescue a Registry, you use either REGEDIT in Windows or the real-mode REGEDIT found on your Rescue disk.

Tip   If you don't know where your Windows 95 Rescue disk is, you can re-create it by doing the following: Go to the Control Panel and click the Add/Remove programs applet. Inside the applet, click the Startup Disk tab and follow the instructions.

Additional Restore Techniques

Windows 95 comes with at least two other techniques you can use to restore your system. Often, these techniques are the quickest ones available to you, and offer the easiest solution.

The first technique is to let Windows try to restore your Registry. Give that a try if, during boot, you see the message shown in Figure 16.8.

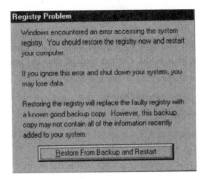

Figure 16.8   Registry problem

Note   Remember what the message says: "Restoring the Registry will replace the faulty Registry with a known good backup copy. However, this backup copy may not contain all of the information recently added to your system."

The second technique is to restore the Registry in MS-DOS mode by replacing the SYSTEM.DAT and USER.DAT files. Follow these steps:

1. Click the Start Button and select Shut Down.
2. In the Shut Down dialog box, select Restart The Computer In MS-DOS Mode.
3. After you're in MS-DOS mode, make sure you're in the Windows directory. You can change directories (folders) by typing:

```
cd \windows
```

4. Next type each of these commands as they appear in this order:

```
attrib -h -r -s system.dat
attrib -h -r -s system.da0
copy system.da0 system.dat
attrib -h -r -s user.dat
attrib -h -r -s user.da0
copy user.da0 user.dat
```

Note   These commands will change the Registry files from hidden read-only to non-hidden read/write files and then replace the original Registry files with the backup files.

5. Restart your computer.

Registry Restored But Windows Problems Remain

Not all Windows problems are attributable to a corrupt or bad Registry. Some problems relate to erroneous entries in either the SYSTEM.INI or WIN.INI files. Not everything critical to your system is stored in the Registry.

When backing up a Registry, you should also back up SYSTEM.INI and WIN.INI. If you get one of the following two error messages, it is possible that the problem lies elsewhere besides the Registry or the .INI files:

```
Registry File Was Not Found
Invalid Vxd dynamic link call from IFSMGR (03)
```

It could be that you have a missing or bad MSDOS.SYS file. If you receive one of those error messages, find your Startup disk and copy the MSDOS.SYS file from the disk to your Windows directory.

Last Resort Before Reloading Windows 95

When it was originally set up on your computer, Windows created another SYSTEM.DAT file during installation called SYSTEM.1ST. If you want, you can reload SYSTEM.1ST using the following real-mode commands:

```
attrib -r -h -s system.dat
attrib -r -h -s system.1st
copy system.1st system.dat
```

If none of these solutions work, you'll need to reload Windows.

Windows Registry

The Windows Registry is very complex, and we have touched only on some of its more important aspects. To learn more about the Registry and how to edit it, we suggest you add the following text to your technical library: *Inside the Registry for Microsoft Windows 95*, Gunter Born, Microsoft Press, 1997.

Device Drivers in Windows 95

From a developers standpoint, the ideal way to run drivers is in protected mode in Windows 95. These virtual device drivers, which have the extension .VXD, will work for most every device driver commonly found in the MS-DOS CONFIG.SYS and AUTOEXEC.BAT files.

Double-buffering and the HIMEM.SYS, SMARTDRV.EXE, SETVER.EXE, and IFSHLP.SYS programs and files are all loaded from within IO.SYS. Microsoft also provides protected-mode drivers for a broad cross section of peripheral devices.

When Windows 95 installs, it looks for real-mode drivers in CONFIG.SYS and AUTOEXEC.BAT that it can replace. The list of device drivers that can be safely replaced is stored in the text file IOS.INI (located in the Windows directory).

Important   There are roughly 300 device drivers that Windows 95 can replace, and about 300,000 device drivers that Windows 95 has never heard of. These real-mode device drivers must run, or the device they support will not operate. That is why CONFIG.SYS, SYSTEM.INI, and AUTOEXEC.BAT files still exist.

Virtual Device Drivers vs. Real-Mode Drivers

There are several reasons for eliminating real-mode drivers from the Windows memory stack:

- Real-mode drivers are 16-bit drivers. For the most part, they are slower than 32-bit drivers (although a well-written 16-bit driver can out-perform a poorly-written 32-bit driver).

- Windows 95 runs in protected mode. To use a real-mode driver, Windows must switch between real mode and protected mode (this is time consuming).

- Real-mode drivers must reside in conventional or upper memory, thus utilizing valuable resources (virtual drivers don't).

- The processor has no built-in protection for real-mode drivers.

Windows 95 includes VxDs (virtual device drivers) to replace the following Windows 3.x real-mode components:

- FAT file system (VFAT.VXD)
- CD-ROM file system (CDFS.VSD)
- SMARTDrive disk cache (VCACHE.VXD)
- Mouse driver (VMOUSE.VXD)
- Network protocols
- SHARE.EXE MS-DOS file sharing and locking support (VSHARE.VXD)
- Disk device drivers including SCSI devices

Plug and Play

The ultimate goal of any computer user is to be able to simply plug any device into a computer, turn it on, and have it work. This is the concept upon which Plug and Play is founded. A well-designed Plug and Play system would eliminate the need for jumpers, switches, and installation software. Does Plug and Play work? The answer is a resounding yes and no. In order for Plug and Play to work, the system must have three things:

- A Plug and Play BIOS
- A Plug and Play device
- A Plug and Play operating system (such as Windows 95)

Windows 95 uses the Configuration Manager (CONFIGMG.VXD) to collect BIOS information and manage the assignment of IRQ, DMA, and other settings. During each startup, the Configuration Manager searches the system for all information, checks for conflicts, and reconfigures as necessary to resolve conflicts. Any time a new device (without a driver) is detected, the Configuration Manager launches the necessary wizard to configure the device. When all is well, it simply asks for confirmation of the device and how it is to be configured. When Plug and Play doesn't work or there is a problem, the solution is usually in the Device Manager.

Device Manager

As mentioned, all Windows 95 information is stored in the Registry. The Device Manager provides a graphical view of all the devices on a computer. This is the place to find and resolve hardware problems. The Device Manager allows you to make many changes to the hardware configuration of a computer, including:

- Add or remove a device.
- View devices by IRQ, I/O port, and DMA channel.
- Print system reports.
- View individual device properties.
- Adjust a device's resources.
- Change drivers.
- Adjust settings.

To display the Device Manager, select Start, select Settings, then select Control Panel, and open the System icon. You can also right-click My Computer and select Properties from the context menu. (See Figure 16.9 for the Device Manager.)

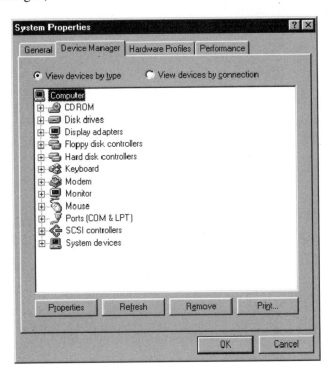

Figure 16.9   Device Manager

To see a specific device, click on the plus sign (+) to the left of the device class. (See Figure 16.10.) Any time Windows 95 sees a conflict, it denotes the device with a red X or a yellow exclamation point.

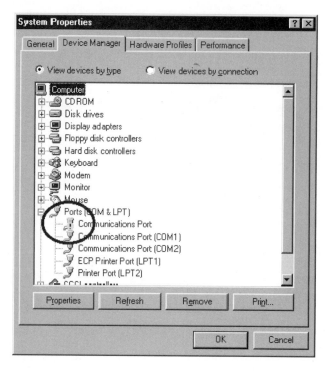

Figure 16.10   Device Manager expanded

To see a list of all IRQ and DMA channels, right-click My Computer to get Properties, click on the panel marked System Manager, and then click on the Properties dialog box below that to get the IRQ, as shown in Figure 16.11.

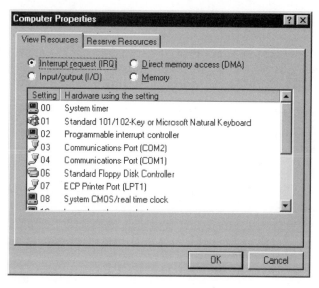

Figure 16.11   Computer properties

To document a system, select the Print command button from the Device Manager window, then select the type of printout you want (system summary, selected class or device, all devices and system summary), shown in Figure 16.12.

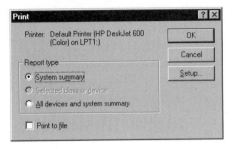

Figure 16.12   Print system summary

To view the details of an individual device, select the device and select the Properties button at the bottom of the window. Many setup options can be changed from this screen.

Note   If the device is not Plug and Play-compliant, the changes will also need to be made on the device itself.

To remove a device, simply select it from the Device Manager and click the Remove button at the bottom of the Device Manager screen. Don't forget to turn off your computer and physically remove the device from the system.

Adding New Hardware

Adding new hardware is simple—it will follow one of two processes, depending on whether or not the device is Plug and Play. Both processes use the Hardware wizard. With Plug and Play, this wizard is launched automatically when Windows detects the new device during startup. With a non-Plug and Play device, you have to start the wizard manually by using the Add New Hardware icon in the Control Panel. When installing manually, Windows asks if you want to specify the device or let Windows find it. In most cases, Windows does a good job of finding it; however, if you know the device and have the manufacturer's software for installation, it is often better to tell Windows what to do.

Installing Printers

Installing printers is similar to installing any other device. However, since several printer drivers can be installed and chosen at will from inside an application, Windows 95 uses a special wizard for printers. Printers also use standard ports (LPT1 or LPT2); therefore, setting the IRQs and I/O addresses is not an issue. A new Plug and Play printer is perhaps as close to true Plug and Play as possible. Simply plug the printer into a parallel port, turn on the printer, and boot up the computer. Windows 95 will recognize the printer (by polling the ports during startup) and launch the Install wizard. In many cases, you merely confirm that Windows has recognized the correct printer and it will do the rest.

For a non-Plug and Play printer, simply select the Add Printer icon from the Printers folder in the Control Panel. You will be asked to select the printer from a list. If the printer is not on the list, you will need to use the Have Disk option and supply the software. Options can vary depending on whether you are connecting to a network or a local printer.

Configuration Tips for Windows 95

Windows 95 is less difficult to configure than Window 3.x. The Windows 95 operating system automatically handles disk caching as well as many other configuration settings. Here are a few things to watch for when configuring Windows 95.

Make a Bootable Disk

A bootable floppy disk is just as important in Windows 95 as it is for MS-DOS. Use the Add/Remove Programs window in the Control Panel to create a startup disk. Bootable disks can also be made from the MS-DOS prompt (format a: /s) or by formatting from Windows Explorer (the Windows 95 equivalent to File Manager), just as in MS-DOS and Windows 3.x. Making a startup disk is a good idea, because the process will also copy many of the utility files used by a computer professional.

Memory Management—Support of MS-DOS Applications

DOS 7 provides built-in, protected-mode support for the main conventional device drivers such as Smartdrv, Mscdex, and the mouse. Even with this, there are still plenty of systems that need more memory to support MS-DOS applications as well as Windows 3.x programs. For example, you might encounter an office or small business that is still using an MS-DOS-based accounting system. To run this program on their new Windows 95 computers will require you to put extra effort into memory management to ensure that sufficient RAM is configured and available for this software.

PIF Files

Windows 95 no longer creates .PIF files by using the PIF editor. PIF settings are created by accessing the Properties value when a MS-DOS application is right-clicked. The major areas of concern for MS-DOS applications are the memory functions. Unlike the old PIF editor, Windows 95 now uses an Auto function. In theory, this means that Windows 95 automatically detects the amount of memory needed and allocates it. What usually happens is that *all* memory is reported to the program as available, whether the program needs it or not. Just as in the old Windows 3.x days, a lot of memory can be saved by giving the MS-DOS application only what it needs.

If the system says there is no expanded memory, it is because the NOEMS option in the CONFIG.SYS file has been added. If expanded memory support is needed in Windows 95, use EMM386 and be sure to use the RAM option. For example, use a statement like the following in CONFIG.SYS:

```
DEVICEHIGH=C:\WINDOWS\EMM386.EXE NOEMS
```

MS-DOS Mode

Windows 95 has the new MS-DOS mode that allows creation of custom CONFIG.SYS and AUTOEXEC.BAT files for tough MS-DOS applications. You can create a custom CONFIG.SYS and AUTOEXEC.BAT for any MS-DOS application but there is one problem. To run a program in MS-DOS mode, Windows 95 reboots the computer. It is better to create a good CONFIG.SYS that allows running the MS-DOS program without rebooting. Use the same memory management for Windows 95 that is used for MS-DOS and Windows 3.x. Running in MS-DOS mode is different from running in an MS-DOS session. In the MS-DOS mode, you will have to configure real-mode drivers for your mouse, CD, sound card, etc., just as you had to do with MS-DOS and Windows 3.1.

New Options in CONFIG.SYS

Although CONFIG.SYS is, in theory, no longer needed, Microsoft has added new options that give CONFIG.SYS some power in memory management.

Remember Windows (DOS 7) automatically loads the following commands and files:

- HIMEM.SYS
- IFSHLP.SYS
- SETVER
- DOUBLESPACE and/or DRVSPACE (if needed)
- DBLBUFFER for disk cache (if needed)

You can save approximately 10 KB by loading only the options needed. Only HIMEM.SYS and SETVER are needed, so create a CONFIG.SYS file and add the following:

```
DEVICE=C:\WINDOWS\HIMEM.SYS
DEVICE=C:\WINDOWS\IFSHLP.SYS
DOS=NOAUTO
```

Important   NOAUTO means "Do not autoload the drivers." If you use NOAUTO, be sure to add HIMEM.SYS and IFSHLP.SYS to the CONFIG.SYS file or it will lock up the computer.

Caching and Swap Files

Windows 95 has excellent built-in caching support for both the hard drives and CD-ROMs. It also has better support for virtual memory. Neither the cache nor the swap file are locked in size as they were in Windows 3.x. Their only drawback is that they use up a lot of hard disk space.

When configuring Windows 95, two areas need to be checked to improve the use of hard disk drive space when caching and using virtual memory. They are the File System and Virtual Memory options found in the System icon in the Control Panel. The two options are at the bottom of the System Performance window.

Setting Up Proper Caching and Performance Enhancement

Using a cache is a typical method of increasing performance. We saw in Chapter 7, "Memory," how a cache improves the performance of memory and CPU processing. There are two ways in which you can increase the performance of your drives through caching. The first is to properly set up your VCACHE, and the second is to tune your drives' cache. You can also increase performance by properly setting your swap file size.

VCACHE

The VCACHE that comes with Windows 95 is quite different from that which comes with Windows 3.x. The big difference is that the cache is "sized dynamically." As Windows needs more RAM, it takes away from the cache and vice-versa. Unfortunately, the cache-sizing algorithms are very slow, especially when used with the swap file. Therefore, the swap file needs to be limited in size. Windows does not allow any direct control over the VCACHE settings for the hard disk drive. The SYSTEM.INI commands can be changed to limit this. To set the best VCACHE size, type the following in the [386Enh] section:

```
MaxCacheSize=(X)
```

where X is one-fourth the size of your RAM, expressed in kilobytes.

Tuning the Hard Disk Drive Cache

Tuning the hard disk drive cache is a simple process. Access the System properties (the same way as for the Device Manager) and select the Performance tab. From this window, select the File Systems button at the bottom.

There are now three tabs to choose from for File System Performance: Hard Disk, CD-ROM, and Troubleshooting.

The Hard Disk Tab

This tab selects the role of the machine. (See Figure 16.13.) Choose the most common role for the computer and select OK.

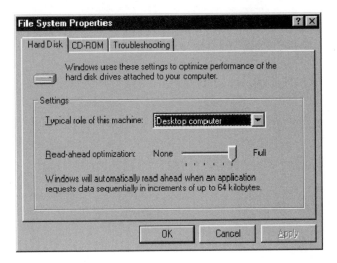

Figure 16.13   Hard Disk tab

The following choices are available on the Hard Disk tab:

- **Desktop Computer:** Typical for a desktop computer; assumes there is more than the minimum required RAM. Don't select this if you want improved system performance.

- **Mobile or Docking System:** This configuration assumes a minimum amount of RAM and that the computer is running on batteries.

- **Network Server:** This configuration assumes there is more than 16 MB of RAM and frequent hard disk access. This system is optimized for increased hard disk activities. Select this to improve system performance.

The CD-ROM Tab

The Windows settings for CD-ROMs are fine as long as you are willing to give up a lot of hard disk drive space to the CD cache. Try setting the CD-ROM to a lower setting by trying the Double-Speed Drives setting for all drives. (See Figure 16.14.) Unless you run a lot of video from your CD-ROM drive, you will not notice any difference in CD performance and will get back a megabyte of hard drive space.

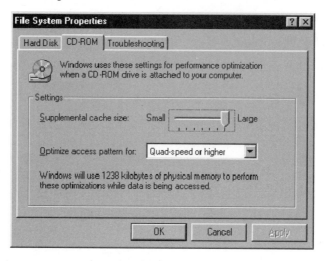

Figure 16.14   CD-ROM tab

The Troubleshooting Tab

This tab is for advanced users only. (See Figure 16.15.) It allows the user to disable several functions, therefore helping the troubleshooter isolate problems.

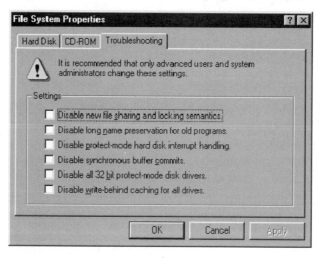

Figure 16.15   Troubleshooting tab

Setting Up the Swap File

Access the Virtual Memory option on the System Properties window. This option sets the optimal swap-file size, shrinks the information file that tells MS-DOS 7 how to boot up, and tells the computer which drive and directory to use for the swap file. Learning these options will help you time and time again.

The "Let Windows manage my virtual file settings (recommended)" option is fine, provided you have the hard disk drive space to spare. Windows 95 will shrink the swap file if you need to save data to the drive, but *very slowly*. Also, Windows 95 seems to occasionally save data to the swap file even when there is plenty of room to load it in physical memory. Windows 95 does not even use all of the allocated swap file.

Set the swap file manually to get better performance. Use the following table as a guideline:

Available RAM	Swap File Size
4 MB	30 MB
8 MB	25 MB
16 MB	15 MB
24 MB	10 MB
32 MB	8 MB
32 MB	None unless required by an application

Lesson Summary

The following points summarize the main elements of this lesson:

- MS-DOS 7, which comes with Windows 95, still uses the same three system files—IO.SYS, MSDOS.SYS, and COMMAND.COM—however, their functions are somewhat different.
- The principal visible difference between Windows 95 and Windows 3.x is the new GUI.
- The Registry is the principal operational difference between Windows 95 and earlier versions of Windows.
- The Registry is stored in three file locations: SYSTEM.DAT, USER.DAT, and the virtual registry.
- The Registry can be directly edited using REGEDIT.EXE, however, doing this is not recommended.
- Microsoft provides three ways to back up the Registry—Microsoft Configuration Backup (CFGBACK.EXE), the Emergency Recovery Utility (ERU.EXE), and REGEDIT.EXE. Each has its own advantages and limitations.
- The Device Manager is the key to managing the hardware on a Windows 95 system.

Chapter Summary

The following points summarize the key concepts in this chapter:

A New Operating System

- Windows 95 and 98 represent the new generation of operating system technology for personal computers.

- It replaces the older MS-DOS and Windows 3.x systems with a new 32-bit operating environment offering better memory management, and simplified hardware installation.

- The new desktop operating environment offers an improved user interface and easier networking tools.

- Unlike Windows 3.x (which is an operating environment), Windows is a full operating system and does not rely on MS-DOS. MS-DOS (often called MS-DOS 7.0) is available for the purpose of maintaining backward compatibility.

- Windows 95 supports long filenames, but retains a 8.3 filespec directory for backward compatibility.

- Windows 95 supports multithreading and multitasking.

Installing and Configuring Windows 95

- Installing Windows 95 is a simple process. It can be installed as an upgrade to a MS-DOS/Windows 3.x system or as a stand-alone operating system. It can also be installed in a dual-boot system with either Windows 3.x or Windows NT.

- Hardware installation is simple with support for Plug and Play. Hardware management is made simple by using the Device Manager.

How Windows 95 Works

- The Registry is the biggest difference between Windows 95 and Widows 3.x. The registry replaces the .INI configuration files used by Windows 3.x, although they can still be used to provide backward compatibility.

Review

1. Name three ways that Windows 95 differs from Windows 3.x.

2. What is Plug and Play? What is required for a component to be Plug and Play–compliant?

3. Does Windows 95 still require MS-DOS?

4. Which version of MS-DOS comes with Windows 95?

5. Is CONFIG.SYS required to install GUI drivers?

6. Why would you want to set the swap-file size in Windows 95?

7. What is the main difference between Windows 3.x and Windows 95?

8. Why can't older versions of disk utilities be used with Windows 95?

9. After turning on the power to the computer, what is the first step in the boot-up process?

10. In which directory do you find the external MS-DOS commands?

11. What is FDISK used for?

12. Define virtual memory.

13. The Registry is composed of two binary files. Name them.

14. What is the difference between an MS-DOS session and MS-DOS mode?

15. If you are running in MS-DOS mode and the CD-ROM does not run, what must you do to get it running?

16. Do you need a .PIF file to run an MS-DOS program in Windows 95?

17. What are the five steps of a Windows 95 installation?

18. Which version of Windows 95 uses FAT32?

19. What is safe mode and what is it used for?

20. What are the three Registry backup tools provided with Windows 95?

C H A P T E R   1 7

Managing and Troubleshooting Windows

About This Chapter

In Chapter 16, we began our study of the Microsoft Windows 95 operating system. We studied what makes it different from MS-DOS and previous versions of Windows, how it works, and how to install it, both as an upgrade and on a new system. One of the most powerful aspects of this operating system is its ability to manage files.

Another powerful improvement, especially useful to computer technicians, is its ability to troubleshoot hardware and software problems. Although the new Plug and Play hardware takes a lot of the work out of installing and troubleshooting, there are still times when hardware and software doesn't work correctly and we must apply our skills. Windows 95 and Windows 98 make this much easier with their many tools. In this chapter, we focus on using Windows 95 to manage files and troubleshoot problems.

Before You Begin

It is highly recommended that you review the previous Chapter 16 "Windows 95 and Beyond," before tackling this one. You should also be familiar with the operation and configuration of the MS-DOS and Windows 3.x environments covered in Chapter 15, "Software: MS-DOS and Windows 3.x." A working knowledge of the Windows 95 graphical user interface (GUI) is also helpful.

Lesson 1: Managing the Windows 95 File System

Managing files and data is a critical function of any operating system. Compared with previous operating systems, Windows 95 has a much-improved file management system. It provides two useful tools for file management: My Computer and Windows Explorer. This lesson explores these components.

After this lesson, you will be able to:

- Find and manage files.
- Manage the Recycle Bin.
- Perform basic disk and file maintenance.
- Identify and implement various troubleshooting techniques.

Estimated lesson time: 30 minutes

File Management Improvements

The Microsoft Windows 95 file system is better and faster than the Windows 3.x file system. The following table summarizes the significant improvements.

Feature	Improvement
32-bit VFAT	Disk access is provided by the 32-bit VFAT (virtual file allocation table). This virtual device works in protected mode, requiring no time-consuming mode changes every time the system needs to write to the disk.
Long filenames	Filenames can now be as long as 255 characters (including the path). Long filenames in Windows 95 are implemented without creating incompatibilities with 16-bit applications.
Demand paging	This is an advanced algorithm for paging memory to the swap file. It is faster than a permanent swap file in Windows 3.x and dynamic (adjusts according to the load on the system).
VCACHE	This 32-bit cache driver replaces SMARTDrive (a 16-bit real mode driver).
CD-ROM support	Windows 95 uses a protected mode 32-bit file system to speed up CD performance, CDFS (CD-ROM File System).
IDE and SCSI support	Windows 95 has its own EIDE and SCSI drivers so it no longer relies on third-party drivers.
Port drivers	These 32-bit drivers communicate directly with specific disk devices, thus allowing a floppy disk to be formatted in the background.

Managing Files with Explorer

Windows 95 offers two methods of locating and organizing files: My Computer and Windows Explorer. The latter is an advanced version of the Windows 3.x File Manager; Explorer is the better choice for computer professionals. There are three simple ways to open Windows Explorer:

- From the Start menu, select Programs and then select Windows Explorer.
- Right-click the Start button and select Explore.
- Right-click My Computer and select Explorer.

For the most part, Explorer works just like File Manager. Explorer looks similar to File Manager, although it lacks the drive icons (disk drives and networks in the Folder window). Unlike File Manager, which featured multiple windows for different folders, Explorer is not a Multiple Document Interface.

Windows 98 Explorer

The Windows 98 and Windows 95 OSR2 operating systems feature improved versions of Explorer. When using these systems, you will find somewhat different menus and dialog boxes than those presented in this course; however, they contain all the information covered here and more.

By default, Windows 95 hides the Explorer toolbar. To open it, select Toolbar from the View menu. This will display several tool icons. (See Figure 17.1.) These tools provide several ways of viewing information.

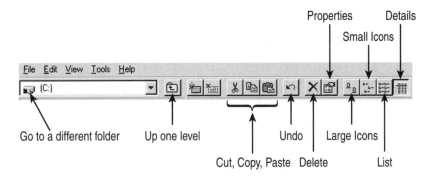

Figure 17.1   Windows Explorer toolbar

Displaying File Extensions

By default, Windows 95 does not display registered file extensions. A registered file extension is one that Explorer can "understand"—in other words, an extension that Explorer can associate with an executable program (the source of the file). So, for instance, you will not see extensions such as .EXE, .DOC, .JPG, and so forth. Any file extension that Explorer does not recognize is considered text and is displayed. With this system, Windows 95 allows users to open any file (with a registered file extension) by simply double-clicking its icon in Explorer. (See Figure 17.2.) If you try to rename a file and forget to add an extension, or if you delete the existing extension, Windows will warn you of a potential problem.

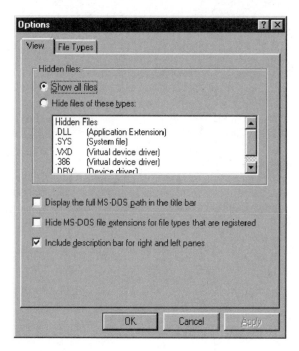

Figure 17.2   Displaying file extensions

To display all registered file extensions in the Contents window of Explorer, select Options from the View menu and remove the check from the Hide MS-DOS File Extensions box. Check Show All Files.

From this dialog box, you can also:

- Show all files, including hidden files.
- Select which files to hide.
- Display the full MS-DOS path.
- Enable or disable the description bar (displays the full path and filename of the selected file or folder).

The File Types tab of this dialog box allows you to review and edit the registered file types.

Sorting Files and Folders

The objects in the Contents window can be viewed in one of several formats. You can use the View menu on the menu bar or the View icon on the toolbar to change the view (Large Icon, Small Icon, List, or Details). When you use the List or either of the icon views, all files are displayed alphabetically by folders, then by files. However, when using the Details view, you have several options for sorting the information. By selecting Arrange Icons from the View menu, you can arrange the information in the Contents window in useful order, as shown in the following table:

By Name	Alphabetically. The default setting.
By Type	In ascending alphabetical order by file type with folders first.
By Size	In ascending numerical order by file size with folders first.
By Date	In ascending order by the last modified date with folders first.
Auto Arrange	When activated, this command sorts the objects automatically if moved or if a new one is added. This works only in icon views.

Note Clicking the Column heading of the Contents window also arranges the contents according to that column.

Moving Objects Within Explorer

One of Explorer's most useful functions is the ability to move and copy files from one location to another. Explorer uses two methods to accomplish these tasks.

Drag-and-Drop

Drag-and-drop simply means visually moving an object from one location to another. Most users know how to do this instinctively: select an object by left-clicking and holding the mouse button, move the object to a new location (the destination folder must be highlighted), and release the mouse. If you hold down the CTRL key while dragging, the object will be copied instead of moved (you'll see a small plus sign attached to the mouse pointer icon during copy operations).

Here are a few rules for drag-and-drop:

- When the source and destination folder are on the same disk, drag-and-drop moves an object. To copy the object instead, hold down the CTRL key.

- When the source and destination folders are on different disks, the object is copied. To move the object, hold down the SHIFT key.

- When the object is an executable file (.EXE), a shortcut will be created in the destination folder.

Cut, Copy, and Paste

Any file or folder (including its contents) can be cut, copied, or pasted from any folder or drive to another.

Note   To cut, copy, or paste an object, you must first select it.

There are four methods to accomplish this:

- Use the icons on the toolbar.

- Select the object to be cut or copied, and right-click it. Choose Cut from the pop-up menu, then choose the destination location, right-click, and select Paste from the menu.

- Use the key commands: CTRL+X (Cut); CTRL+C (Copy); or CTRL+V (Paste).

- Use Cut, Copy, and Paste from the Edit menu.

Note   In addition to using Explorer, you can also manipulate files using My Computer. The methods for moving, copying, and pasting are very similar.

Properties

The Properties command is probably the most important command of all. It is found throughout the Windows 95 environment and especially in Explorer. Any time you need to know more about an object, right-click the icon and choose Properties. It is usually found at the bottom of the shortcut menu. It can also be found as a command button at the bottom of a dialog box or at the bottom of the File menu in Windows. By selecting this option, you will be directed to dialog box(es) that provide the details of the object and often allow you to make changes.

Note You should always look for "Properties" when you are working with applications or objects. Often this is the key to configuring that object to work for you.

Searching

In today's multigigabyte world, finding a file is like looking for that proverbial needle in a haystack. To overcome this problem, Windows 95 has a new and intuitive Find feature. (See Figure 17.3.) Finding a file has never been easier:

- To search a particular folder, highlight the folder and, from the Tools menu, select Find, and then select Files or Folders.

- To search the entire desktop (all drives in the computer), click on any part of the Explorer window and press F3. The default selection searches the C drive, however, you can select any drive or My Computer to search the entire computer.

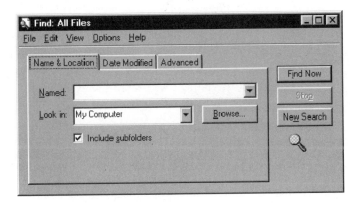

Figure 17.3 Find dialog box options

There are three methods of searching. You can search by Name and Location, Date Modified, or Advanced.

Search by Name and Location

This tab will let you search for files or folders by name. It will also let you specify the drive or folder in which to search.

Here are a few helpful hints to limit your search:

- If the filename contains a space (more than one word), enclose the name in quotation marks.
- When searching for multiple files, separate each name with a space, comma, or semicolon.
- Remember that file searches are not case-sensitive.
- Remember that all MS-DOS wildcards work with Find. (See Chapter 15, "Software: MS-DOS and Windows 3.x," for more about MS-DOS wildcards.)

Search by Date

If you don't know the name of the file, but know approximately when it was created or last modified, use this tab. There are three methods for searching with this tab. You can search:

- Between any two dates.
- During the previous x months.
- During the previous x days.

Using Advanced Search

The advanced search tab provides some additional search techniques. You can search:

- By type of file (requires a registered file extension).
- By size of file.
- For any file containing a specific word or phrase.

The Windows Taskbar

The Windows 95 taskbar provides a single location in the interface for important information. By default, it sits at the bottom of the screen, but it can be moved by the user. By clicking and dragging any portion of the taskbar that is not a button, you can move it to the top, bottom, left, or right of the screen. It is comprised of three sections.

- The notification area (also called the system tray) contains the clock (if you point your mouse at the time, the date will pop up) and any icons representing applications that are running in the background (printer, scanner, antivirus program).
- The Start Button opens programs.
- Each Open program is displayed on the taskbar as a button (between the notification area and the Start Button) that contains the program name and icon.

Note   The more open programs there are, the smaller each button appears.

The Recycle Bin

In the early days of the computer, accidental deletion of files was a common occurrence. When a file was deleted, MS-DOS did not delete the contents—it changed the first letter of the filename to a lowercase Greek letter, sigma, and changed all the file's FAT entries to 0 (the clusters could now be used by another file). Later versions of MS-DOS included an UNDELETE command, which could restore a file (provided no other file had used the clusters). However, unless the file was recovered immediately after being deleted, the chances of recovery were slim.

Windows 95 has overcome this problem by creating the Recycle Bin, which is a hidden folder that holds deleted files. The files stay safe and out of sight in this folder until they are removed from the Recycle Bin. You can restore any file by opening the Recycle Bin, selecting the file, and selecting Restore from the File menu. The Recycle Bin is a great tool, but it is not perfect. Here are some things to be aware of:

- Emptying the Recycle Bin permanently deletes the files.
- Floppy disk and network drive deletions are permanent.
- The Recycle Bin can be bypassed by holding down the SHIFT key while deleting. This permanently deletes a file.
- The Properties dialog box (right-click on the Recycle Bin icon) allows you to customize Recycle Bin activities. You can configure a Recycle Bin independently for each drive, select to remove files immediately when deleted, or set the maximum size of the Recycle Bin.

Managing Disks

In addition to managing files, a computer technician must be proficient in managing disks. Windows 95 provides several tools to make this job easier.

Disk Maintenance

Windows Explorer is as helpful in managing disks as it is in managing files. By right-clicking a disk's icon (see Figure 17.4), you can access a full menu of disk-management options.

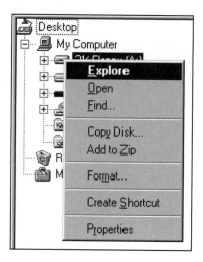

Figure 17.4   Disk management options

The two most common disk-management tools are Format and Copy.

Formatting a Floppy Disk

Follow these steps to format a floppy disk:

1. Insert a disk into the floppy disk drive.
2. From Explorer, right-click the drive containing the disk and select Format. Do not highlight the drive first—Windows 95 will not let you format if the drive is highlighted first.
3. Use the Capacity drop-down list to select the correct drive size.
4. In the Format group, choose from Quick (removes files but does not check for bad sectors), Full (removes files and checks for bad sectors), or Copy System Files Only (makes a bootable disk but does not delete any data).
5. Select any other options: Label (to add a label of less than 11 characters), No Label (to delete an existing label), Display Summary When Finished (to display a summary of the results of the formatting process), or Copy System Files (to add system files after formatting is complete).
6. Select Start and the formatting process will begin.

Copying a Floppy Disk

Follow these steps to copy a floppy disk:

1. Insert the disk to be copied in the floppy disk drive (this is the source disk).

2. From the Disk Management menu, select Copy Disk.

3. From the Copy menu, highlight the disk to be copied (source).

4. From the Copy menu, highlight the disk to be copied to (destination).

5. Click Start to begin the process.

6. When all the data is copied from the source disk into memory, you will be prompted to insert the destination disk.

7. If the destination disk is unformatted, Windows 95 will format it first.

8. When the copy process is finished, select Close.

Viewing Disk Properties

By selecting Properties from the Disk Management menu, you will be able to see statistics about the drive. Figure 17.5 shows the Disk Properties dialog box.

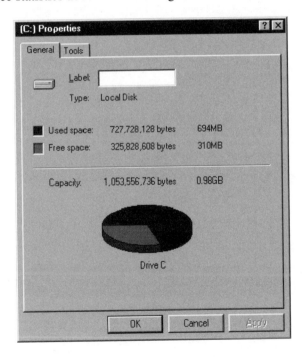

Figure 17.5 Disk Properties dialog box

By selecting the Tools tab, you can perform basic maintenance on the selected drive. You can check the:

- **Error-checking status:** This tells you when ScanDisk was last run and allows you to run ScanDisk.
- **Backup status:** This tells you when the disk was last backed up and allows you to backup.

Note   Backup hardware (tape or disk drive) must be installed before a ScanDisk backup can be performed.

- **Defragmentation status:** This group tells you when the drive was last "defragged" and allows you to defragment the disk (rearrange disk sectors so that files are stored on consecutive sectors in adjacent tracks).

Partitioning a Disk in Windows 95

Partitioning a disk increases its storage efficiency by reducing waste or cluster overhang. Basically, the smaller the drive, the more efficient it is. As discussed in Chapter 8, Lesson 2: Hard Disk Drives, the basic unit of a hard drive is a cluster, and its size depends on the size of the partition. Also, a cluster can contain data from only one file.

If you have a file that is 4000 bytes and a cluster size of 8389 bytes, you will have 4389 bytes of wasted space. By creating several smaller partitions, you will have smaller clusters and, therefore, less waste. Creating a partition in the Windows 95 environment follows the same process as with MS-DOS and is explained in detail in Chapter 8, "Basic Disk Drives." Here are a few things to keep in mind when partitioning in Windows 95:

- Use FDISK to partition a drive.
- FDISK destroys all data on the drive.
- FDISK must be run from MS-DOS. The computer must be booted from the startup disk.

FAT32

One of the advantages of using FAT32 with Windows 95 OSR2 or Windows 98 is that you can create partitions up to 8 GB and limit the cluster size to 4 KB.

Lesson Summary

The following points summarize the main elements of this lesson:

- Windows 95 provides two tools for managing files: My Computer, which is designed for the novice user, and Windows Explorer, which is intended for the more advanced user.
- Objects in Explorer can be displayed in several formats, and copied or moved as necessary.
- The Recycle Bin is a key tool for preventing accidental loss of data.
- The process for partitioning disks in Windows 95 is the same as for MS-DOS.

Lesson 2: Troubleshooting Windows 95

No application or program is perfect. The evolution from MS-DOS to Windows 3.x to Windows 95 was neither short nor simple. Windows 95 is a major improvement in the way computers operate and the way we interface with them. But to expect this operating system to solve all problems and achieve full compatibility with all hardware is not realistic—there are simply too many different hardware and software manufacturers, each with its unique approach, for one operating system to manage. As computer technicians, we must understand both the strengths and weaknesses of computer systems (hardware and software) in order to achieve the best possible performance for our clients. Fortunately, Microsoft has incorporated many tools to help us fine-tune our systems and achieve the best performance. This lesson focuses on some of the methods and tools we can use to identify problems and manage our systems.

After this lesson, you will be able to:

- Identify some of the common problems encountered while using Windows 95.
- Use System Monitor and the Resource Meter to optimize performance.
- Troubleshoot problems with MS-DOS applications.
- Troubleshoot common printer problems.

Estimated lesson time: 30 minutes

Limitations of Windows 95

You must understand how efficiently a system is operating before you can troubleshoot and tune that system. Windows 95 provides two tools for that purpose: System Monitor and Resource Meter. If they are not installed, use the Control Panel Add/Remove Programs (Windows tab) to add them to your system. After they have been installed, you can find both by selecting Programs from the Start menu, then selecting Accessories, and, finally, selecting System Tools.

The System Monitor

The System Monitor provides real-time reports about how various system processes are performing. It displays various functions in either a line graph, a bar graph, or a numeric graph. To run System Monitor, go to the Start menu, select Programs, Accessories, System Tools, and System Monitor. By default, the System Monitor shows only the Kernel Process Usage setting (the percentage of time the processor is busy).

Items can be added to or removed from the System Monitor by selecting Add Item from the System Monitor Edit menu, or using the Add button in the toolbar. Figure 17.6. shows the Add Item dialog box.

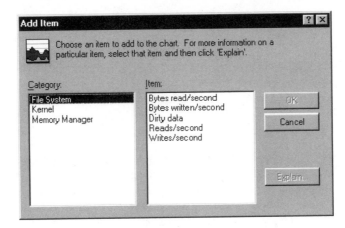

Figure 17.6   System Monitor—Add Item dialog box

Two useful items are the Kernel (which tracks CPU usage) and the Memory Manager (which tracks allocated memory, cache size, and swap file size), shown in Figure 17.7.

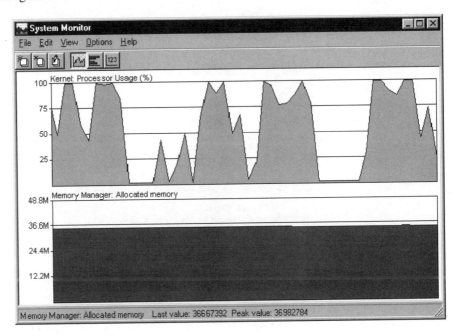

Figure 17.7   System Monitor

Both tools can help you determine whether it's time to upgrade a computer. For example, start the computer and open all the files and applications that are normally used at the same time. Turn on the System Monitor and run the system for a while. If the processor is constantly running at more than 75 percent, it might be time to upgrade. Also, if the total allocated memory (RAM, swap file, and cache) exceeds the amount of RAM in the system, it might be time to get more RAM.

Resource Meter

The Resource Meter is used to monitor (in real time) the use of system resources. When activated, it adds a small bar graph to the taskbar in the notification area indicating the percentage of free resources, based on the computer's total resources. As the bar gets smaller (fewer resources available), it will change color indicating a potential problem. If the color changes to yellow, this means that resources have dropped to 30 percent. If the color changes to red, the resources have dropped to 15 percent. If the resources drop to 10 percent, Windows warns you that the computer is in imminent danger of hanging (unable to respond to user input), so you must start closing applications to avoid losing data. Figure 17.8 shows the Resource Meter in the notification box of the taskbar.

Figure 17.8   Resource Meter

For more details, hold the mouse over the Resource Meter icon for a second or two. This will cause a banner to display that shows the individual resource percentages. You can also double-click the icon to display the Resource Meter dialog box. (See Figure 17.9.)

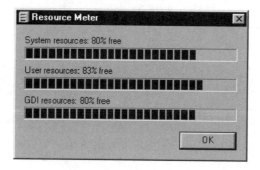

Figure 17.9   Resource Meter dialog box

You might use these tools if a customer complains of getting out-of-memory errors, or that the computer's disk drives seems to run all the time. By monitoring memory use, you can determine how much memory is required to run all the applications, and which applications are consuming the most memory. From that information, you should be able to determine the best course of action. If a client is trying to decide whether or not to upgrade a processor, you can also monitor the CPU kernel to determine just how busy it is. If it is working more than 80 percent of the time, a new processor might be warranted.

MS-DOS-Application Incompatibilities

In spite of attempts to make Windows 95 backwardly compatible, it can still experience problems running MS-DOS applications. Most MS-DOS applications run better in Windows 95 than in Windows 3.11, but very few users pushed the envelope by running MS-DOS applications with earlier versions of Windows. (Most users simply updated them and learned to use the new software.) Often, MS-DOS applications refuse to run under Windows 95 (and Windows 98) because they cannot find a version of MS-DOS they recognize.

"Wrong MS-DOS Version"

One of the most common causes for MS-DOS- and Windows-application crashes in Windows 95 is that many applications check the version number of MS-DOS before running. If the software reads the wrong version number or a version number that's in the wrong range, an error occurs and the program crashes. To get around this, Windows 95 "lies" to applications and passes the right version number.

To achieve this, Windows needs a bit of help tricking MS-DOS programs. Include the following line in the CONFIG.SYS file. Remember, lines in the CONFIG.SYS overwrite IO.SYS and SYSTEM.DAT commands:

```
device=c:\windows\setver.exe
```

With SETVER.EXE loaded, Windows 95 will report an appropriate version number to your MS-DOS application.

Tricking an old Windows 3.x application is a two-step process.

First, find the module name for the application that is crashing. To find an application's module name, start Windows Explorer and then right-click the application's executable (.EXE) file. Using Quick View, find the module name. For example, the module name for Word 6.0 is winword.

Note   QuickView is not included in a typical Windows 95 installation. To load QuickView, go to the Control Panel and select the Add/Remove Programs applet. In the Add/Remove Programs dialog box, select the Windows Setup tab, then select Accessories. Click the Details button, check QuickView on the Components list, and click the OK button.

Next, add a section to your Windows 95 WIN.INI file. Open WIN.INI using a text editor and add the following lines:

```
[Compatibility]
compiled_module_name = 0x00200000
```

For example, you would add:

```
winword = 0x00200000
```

Other MS-DOS Workarounds

Often, MS-DOS applications fail to execute because of missing drivers or the presence of Windows itself. By using the Properties tab of a program's .EXE file, you can modify many of the settings that cause your program to fail. To do this:

1. Open Windows Explorer and find the troublesome MS-DOS .EXE file.

2. Right-click with your mouse and select Properties.

3. Click the Program tab.

4. Click the Advanced button.

The Advanced dialog box will present the following options:

- **Prevent MS-DOS-based Programs From Detecting Windows:** This hides Windows in memory so MS-DOS programs can't detect it.

- **Suggest MS-DOS Mode As Necessary:** This is an on-the-fly MS-DOS-mode diagnostic. If Windows detects an application that's likely to run better in MS-DOS, it starts a wizard so that you can customize the application to run in MS-DOS.

- **MS-DOS Mode:** If this option is selected, the application will run in MS-DOS mode. Within this setting are three additional options:

  - **Warn Before Entering MS-DOS:** When entering MS-DOS mode, you should close any open Windows applications and files. This warns you to save files and close any applications that are running.

  - **Use Current MS-DOS configuration:** This uses all the current system settings that have been passed along, including settings in CONFIG.SYS, AUTOEXEC.BAT, IO.SYS, and the Registry.

  - **Specify A New MS-DOS Configuration:** This allows you to modify CONFIG.SYS and AUTOEXEC.BAT for MS-DOS mode.

This Properties tab is the Windows 95 replacement for the .PIF files used in Windows 3.x. You will find five other tabs for configuring the properties of this MS-DOS application. These tabs are:

- **General:** Provides the statistics of the file.
- **Font:** Specifies the type of font you want to use.
- **Memory:** Configures expanded and extended memory requirements.
- **Screen:** Offers options for running inside a window or full screen.
- **Misc:** Provides miscellaneous settings.

Printing Problems

It's frustrating when a printer prints random characters or only part of the data or—worst—won't print at all. To help resolve such problems, Windows 95 offers the Print Troubleshooter. This tool can be found by selecting Help from the Start menu and then choosing the Contents tab. Select Troubleshoot and display the topic: If You Have Trouble Printing. The troubleshooter will ask a series of questions that lead you through the problem and—hopefully—provide a solution.

If the Print troubleshooter doesn't solve the problem, you can try the Enhanced Print Troubleshooter (EPTS). This program is found on the Windows 95 CD. To use this program, copy the EPTS folder (and files) from the CD to the hard disk drive. Then start the program EPTS.EXE. This program operates in the same way as the standard version, but is much more detailed.

Here are some other troubleshooting tips. If the printer won't print:

- Make sure the power is turned on and the printer is online.
- Check the cable connections.
- Verify that the printer has paper.
- Clear any paper jams.
- Clear the print buffer by turning the printer off and restarting it.
- Make sure the driver and the printer are in the same mode.
- Send a print job directly to the printer (not from an application). Go to an MS-DOS prompt and send a text file directly to the printer, thus bypassing any application.
- Try printing from another application (a simple one, such as Notepad).
- Delete, then reinstall the printer.
- Try printing to a file and then copy the file to the printer port.

If the printer takes a long time to print:

- Make sure spooling is enabled and that Windows 95 is spooling to EMF files (Enhanced Metafile Spooling).
- Make sure the drive on which Windows is installed has enough disk space.
- Defragment the hard disk.
- Check the system resources—are they low?
- Upgrade the printer driver if a newer one is available (check the Web site of the printer's manufacturer).
- Make sure Windows 95 is sending TrueType fonts as outlines and not bitmaps. (Check the Fonts tab of the printer's properties sheet.)

If the printouts contain random characters:

- Be sure the printer language and type is correctly identified for the job.
- Verify that there is enough printer memory to carry out the job. It's not always easy to tell how much printer memory you need—the printer may just give you an out-of-memory error. It may be useful to either eliminate graphics from the document or select a lower print resolution (you can configure the printer from the application's Printer dialog box). This can both speed up printing and possibly eliminate errors due to limited printer memory.
- Print directly to the printer. Go to an MS-DOS prompt and send a text file directly to the printer, thus bypassing any application.
- Use raw spooling instead of EMF.
- Print one job only at a time.
- Make sure the printable region isn't larger than what is supported by the printer.

If the Print command on the File menu is dimmed:

- Verify that a printer driver is installed.

If you cannot print from a MS-DOS program:

- From the printer's Properties sheet, deactivate Spool MS-DOS Print Jobs.

Viruses

Viruses are nasty little programs that can wreak havoc on a computer and its data. The sole purpose of a virus is to replicate itself and make life miserable for computer users. Many viruses are simple annoyances, but some of them can cause irreparable harm to files.

Viruses can be caught from various sources including shareware, files downloaded from the Internet, software from unknown origins, and bulletin boards.

There are four basic types of viruses:

- **File Infectors:** These attach themselves to executable files and spread to other files when the program is run.

- **Boot Sector:** These replace the master boot record (or boot sector on a floppy disk). They write themselves into memory any time the computer is booted.

- **Trojan Horses:** These are disguised as legitimate programs, but when loaded, they begin to harm the system.

- **Macro Viruses:** These common nuisances attach themselves as executable code to documents (such as Microsoft Word documents) and run when the document is opened. (They can also attach themselves to certain kinds of e-mail.) It used to be true that you couldn't get a virus from opening a document; running a program was required. Unfortunately, this has changed thanks to the widespread use of macros by computer users. While macros are very valuable, they mean that when you open a document you *are* running a program.

Viruses have become a way of life in the computer world. With this in mind, there are several measures you can take to prevent, or at least minimize, the damage:

- Purchase a good antivirus program—there are several available. Make sure your choice is compatible with Windows 95. Old MS-DOS antivirus programs do not work well with Windows 95 and might do more damage than good.

- If the computer has a BIOS setting that allows you to disable boot-sector writes (prevent applications from writing to the boot section of the hard disk), enable it! This setting must be disabled before installing Windows 95.

- Viruses are often transmitted by floppy disks. Be careful when reading a floppy disk of unknown origin or using your disk on an unfamiliar machine.

- Currently, many viruses and macroviruses are transmitted over the Internet. Use *extreme* caution when you download files, especially if they come from sources other than a manufacturer's Web site. The most secure protection against Internet-distributed viruses is to make sure you have an antivirus program running at all times (or at least when you're downloading and first running new files).

- Trust no one when it comes to loading programs on your machine. Be aware that any program you load on your computer could contain a virus.

- Keep your antivirus program updated. Hundreds of new viruses are written and transmitted each month.

Lesson Summary

The following points summarize the main elements of this lesson:

- Windows 95 is not perfect. However, if you know its limits and use the tools provided by Microsoft, you can configure any system for optimum performance.

- System Monitor and Resource Meter are two tools that help identify performance problems.

- Not all MS-DOS applications will run with Windows 95; however, with proper configuration, most of them will.

- Windows 95 has built-in troubleshooting guides for such difficulties as printer problems.

- Be aware of viruses and take precautions.

Chapter Summary

The following points summarize the key concepts in this chapter:

Managing the Windows 95 File System

- Windows 95 introduced many improvements for simplifying file management. These include 32-bit VFAT, long filenames, VCACHE, built-in CD-ROM support, built-in EIDE and SCSI drivers, and an expanded list of 32-bit drivers.

- Windows 95 provides two programs for managing files. My Computer, with its simple Windows format, is a user-friendly utility designed for beginners. Windows Explorer is an enhanced version of the Windows 3.x File Manager. For the computer professional, mastering Explorer is the key to troubleshooting hardware and software problems.

- Windows allows extensive use of the drag-and-drop, and Cut, Copy, and Paste functions for managing files. The right mouse button provides easy access to shortcut menus.

- The Recycle Bin is an excellent tool to help prevent accidental file deletion.

Troubleshooting Windows 95

- Disk management is made simple with the new GUI.

- Windows 95 provides a number of useful tools for maintaining disks. Backup, defragmentation, and ScanDisk utilities are built into the operating system.

- Two tools—Resource Monitor and Resource Meter—are provided for monitoring and identifying resource problems.

Review

1. In Windows 95, which Windows 3.x program was replaced by Windows Explorer?

2. What utilities are provided for managing files in Windows 95?

3. How do you partition a drive in Windows 95?

4. What is the function of the Recycle Bin?

5. What is the System Monitor used for?

6. What is the Resource Meter used for?

7. Loading which file will cause Windows 95 to report an appropriate version of MS-DOS to older MS-DOS applications?

8. Identify the four basic kinds of viruses and describe how they are transmitted.

CHAPTER 18

Connectivity and Portability

About This Chapter

The ability to expand beyond the limit of a single computer in a single office has expanded the reach of the PC to global proportions. Two technologies have driven this expansion: computer networking and the portable computer. In this chapter, we first take a look at how the networks that link up computers on a global scale are put together. Then we examine the portable computer, whose introduction has allowed users instantaneous access to the computing and networking power of all the latest computer technology anywhere they go.

Before You Begin

Although there are no prerequisites for this chapter, it is highly recommended that you be familiar with all aspects of the hardware presented in earlier chapters.

Lesson 1: Networks

A *network* is defined as two or more computers linked together for the purpose of communicating and sharing information and other resources. Most networks are constructed around a cable connection that links the computers. This connection permits the computers to talk (and listen) through a wire.

After this lesson, you will be able to:

- Define basic networking concepts and describe how a network functions.
- Configure and change network interface cards.
- Define Internet terms and functions.

Estimated lesson time: 40 minutes

Basic Requirements of a Network

In order for a network to function, three basic requirements must be met: it must provide connections, communications, and services.

Connections

Connections include the hardware (physical components) required to hook up a computer to the network. Two terms are important to network connections:

- **The network medium:** The network hardware that physically connects one computer to another. This is the cable between the computers.
- **The network interface:** The hardware that attaches a computer to the network medium and acts as an interpreter between the computer and the network. Attaching a computer to a network requires an add-in board known as a network interface card (NIC).

Communications

Communications establish the rules concerning how computers talk and understand each other. Because computers often run different software, in order to communicate with each other they must speak a "shared language." Without shared communications, computers cannot exchange information, and remain isolated.

Services

A service defines those things a computer shares with the rest of the network. For example, a computer can share a printer or specific directories or files. Unless computers on the network are capable of sharing resources, they remain isolated, even though physically connected.

Networking

Next we look at how the basic elements of connections, communications, and services work together to make networks function properly:

- The connections must operate so that any computer can send or receive electrical signals (data) across the physical media that link them.

- Communications must function so that when one computer sends a message, the receiving computer can listen and understand the message.

- Computers on a network must either provide a service to other computers or make use of a service provided by other computers.

Local Area Networks

A *LAN (local area network)* is a network that covers a limited distance (usually a single site or facility) and allows sharing of information and resources. A LAN can be as simple as two connected computers, or as complicated as a large site. This type of network is very popular because it allows individual computers to provide processing power and utilize their own memory, while programs and data can be stored on any computer in the network. Some of the older LANs also include configurations that rely totally on the power of a mini or mainframe computer (a server) to do all the work. In this case, the workstations are no more than "dumb" terminals (a keyboard and a monitor). With the increased power of today's personal computer, these types of networks are rare.

The primary benefit of a LAN is its ability to share. The following table lists some of the benefits of sharing the most common resources on a LAN.

Resource	Benefit
Data	The sharing of data files that reside in a common location makes multiple-user access easier. Also, it's much easier to maintain data integrity when there is a single, central database. Large customer databases and accounting data are ideal for a LAN system.
Peripherals	Sharing printers, for example, allows more than one user to send jobs to a single printer. This is useful when there is only one high-quality printer in an office and the entire office needs to use it. It also allows one user to access multiple printers, providing cost savings in hardware and redundant resources in case one device fails. Other low usage peripherals, such as scanners and plotters, will be better utilized.
Software	Sharing a single copy of an application can be cost-effective (many software manufacturers provide site licenses—licenses for multiple users on a server). It also allows easier maintenance and upgrading.
Storage	Larger, faster disk systems can be used cost-effectively for easy backups.

In addition to the ability to share resources, LANs offer many other benefits that include:

- **Resilience:** Regular backups of the entire system greatly reduce the risk of data loss. Copying data to backup servers allows network operations to continue in the event of primary server failure.
- **Communication gateways:** Low-cost access to fax and Internet connections.
- **Electronic mail:** Cost-effective and convenient communication throughout the network.

Wide Area Networks

A *wide area network (WAN)* spans relatively large geographical areas. Connections for these sites require the use of ordinary telephone lines, T1 lines, ISDN (Integrated Services Digital Network) lines, radio waves, or satellite links. WANs can be accessed through dial-up connections, using a modem, or leased line direct connection. The leased-line method is more expensive but can be cost-effective for transmission of large volumes of data.

Types of Networks

There are essentially two types of networks. They differ in how information is stored, how security is handled, and how the computers on the network interact.

In a *peer-to-peer network*, each computer acts as either a server (sharing its data or services with other computers), or a client (using data or services on another computer) depending on the user's needs. Each user, or workstation, establishes its own security and determines which resources are available to other users. Typically these networks are limited in size (15 to 20 workstations). Microsoft Windows for Workgroups, Windows 95 and Windows 98, Windows NT Work station, Windows 2000, Novell's NetWare, UNIX, and Linux are some software packages available for peer-to-peer networking.

A *server network* requires a central server (dedicated computer) to manage access to all shared files and peripherals. This is a secure environment suitable for most organizations. In this case, the *server* is a computer that runs the network operating system, manages security, and administers access to resources. The *client* is a computer that connects to the network and uses the available resources. The two most common server operating systems are Microsoft's NT4 Server and Novell's IntranetWare. Prior to the release of Windows NT, most dedicated servers worked only as hosts. Windows NT allows the server to also operate as an individual workstation. More than one server can provide services on the network, but only one can be responsible for the security and overall operation of the network.

Network Topology

LAN design is called topology. *Topology* describes the appearance or layout of a network and how data flows through the network. There are three basic types of topologies: star, bus, and ring. In the real world, you are likely to encounter some hybrid combinations of these topologies, but for the A+ exam, we focus only on these three.

Note The illustrations that follow should not be used as exact wiring diagrams, rather as sample network designs.

Star Topology

In a *star* network (see Figure 18.1), all devices are connected to a central point called a *hub*. These hubs collect and distribute the flow of data within the network. Signals from the sending computer go to the hub and are then transmitted to all computers on the network. Large networks can feature several hubs. A star network is easy to troubleshoot because all information goes through the hub, making it easier to isolate problems.

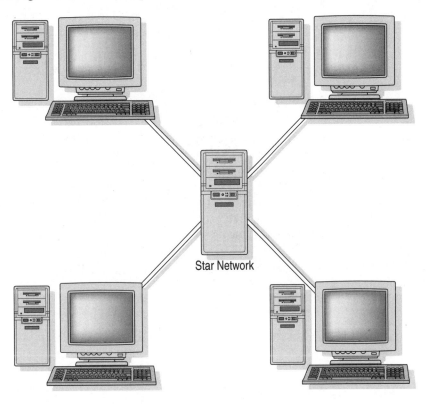

Star Network

Figure 18.1 Star topology

Bus Topology

In a *bus* network (see Figure 18.2), all devices are connected to a single linear cable called a trunk (also known as a backbone or segment). Both ends of the cable must be terminated (like a SCSI bus) to stop the signal from bouncing. Because a bus network does not have a central point, it is more difficult to troubleshoot than a star network. A break or problem at any point along the bus can cause the entire network to go down.

Note   A bus network is often referred to as an Ethernet network.

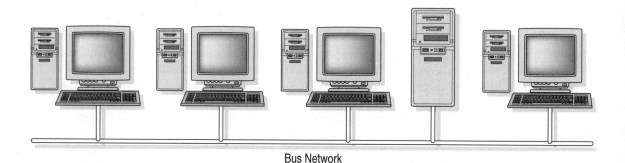

Bus Network

Figure 18.2   Bus topology

Ring Topology

In a *ring* network (see Figure 18.3), all workstations and servers are connected in a closed loop. There are no terminating ends; therefore, if one computer fails, the entire network will go down. Each computer in the network acts like a repeater and boosts the signal before sending it to the next station. This type of network transmits data by passing a "token" around the network. If the token is free of data, a computer waiting to send data grabs it, attaches the data and the electronic address to the token, and sends it on its way. When the token reaches its destination computer, the data is removed and the token sent on.

Note   This type of network is commonly called a token ring network.

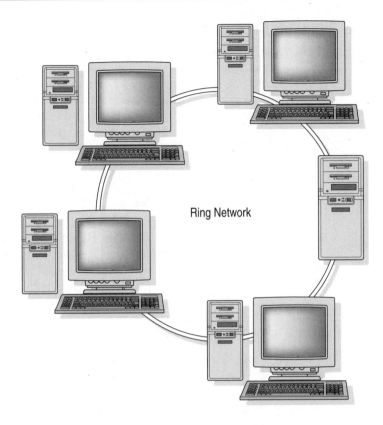

Figure 18.3   Ring topology

Network Operating System (NOS)

The network operating system (NOS) consists of a family of programs that run in networked computers. Some programs provide the ability to share files, printers, and other devices across the network. As previously mentioned, computers that share their resources are called servers; computers that use the resources on other computers are called clients. It is common to run client and server software on the same computer. This enables one user to access the resources on another computer while coworkers make use of resources on your computer.

Networking software can be a special program added on to the computer, such as Artisoft's LANtastic or Novell's NetWare, or it can be an integral part of an operating system such as Microsoft's Windows 95 or Windows 98, Windows NT, or Windows 2000.

Network Interface Cards

Network interface cards (NICs) link a computer to the network cable system. They provide the physical connection between the computer's expansion bus and the network cabling. The low-powered digital signals that transmit data inside a computer are not powerful enough to travel long distances. A network interface card boosts these signals so they can cross a network cable. The interface card also must change the form of data from a wide parallel stream—coming in 8, 16, or 32 bits at a time—to a narrow stream, moving 1 bit at a time in and out of the network port (parallel to serial conversion—see Chapter 2, Lesson 1: The Computer Bus).

The network interface card takes data from the computer, packages the data for transmission, and acts as a gatekeeper to control access to the shared network cable. Because the NIC functions as an interface between the computer and the network cabling, it must serve two masters. Inside the computer, it moves data to and from RAM. Outside the computer, it controls the flow of data in and out of the network cable system. Because the computer is typically much faster than the network, the interface card must buffer the data between the computer and cable. This means it must temporarily store the data coming from the computer until it can place it on the network.

Installation of the network interface card (see Figure 18.4) is the same as for any other expansion card. It requires setup of the system resources: IRQ, address, and software. Most cards today allow connection for either thin Ethernet or UTP (unshielded twisted-pair) cabling. Thin Ethernet uses a round BNC connector, and UTP uses a RJ-45 connector (similar to a telephone jack).

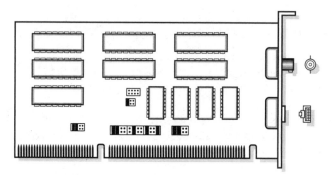

Figure 18.4   Network interface card

Installing a NIC is just like installing any other expansion card. If you are installing a Windows 95–compliant Plug and Play card in a Windows 95 or Windows 98 machine, you'll simply need to physically install the card and boot up the computer. The card will be detected and, more than likely, install itself. You might only need to answer a few questions along the way. It requires a little more work to install a NIC in an operating system that is not Plug and Play–compliant. Installing network cards includes the following steps:

1. Be sure to document any changes that you make to the existing computer. This will eliminate any confusion in the installation process and provide future reference in case of problems.

2. Determine whether the card needs IRQ, DMA (direct memory access), or address settings. Remember that you might have to configure these manually, so be sure to check the card's documentation for default settings and instructions for how to make any needed changes.

3. Determine whether the necessary settings are available on the machine on which they will be installed. If proper documentation is not available, use diagnostic software such as Microsoft Diagnostics (MSD) to determine settings. Also check your AUTOEXEC.BAT, CONFIG.SYS, and SYSTEM.INI files; they might give clues as to which settings are already in use.

4. Turn off the machine and remove the cover. Be sure to take all appropriate measures for protection against electrostatic discharge (ESD).

5. Set the NICs jumpers or DIPP (dual inline package) switches as necessary and insert the card.

6. Turn on the machine and run the setup utility provided by the manufacturer. If you are using Windows 95, Windows 98, or Windows 2000, and the NIC is not Plug and Play, you can use the Add New Hardware wizard in the Control Panel to install the drivers and set up the card. (Remember to document all settings.)

If you are replacing (upgrading) an existing NIC, follow the same steps as just described, with one addition. Before removing the card, document all its settings. Figure 18.5 shows an example of a NIC information card. You can use these cards to create a file documenting the specifics of the cards in your network.

```
Network Adapter Manufacturer: _____

Type of Adapter: (Ethernet, token ring or other) _____

    Model Number: _____

    IRQ setting: _____

    DMA setting: _____

    Speed setting (if token ring) _____

    Base memory address: _____
```

Figure 18.5   Information card

Important   An improperly configured network interface card could prohibit
network access. Check your settings carefully.

Network Cabling

All networks need cables. The three main types are twisted-pair cable (TP),
coaxial cable, and fiber-optic cable (FDDI—Fiber Distributed Data Interface).

Twisted-Pair Cable

Twisted-pair cable, shown in Figure 18.6, consists of two insulated strands of
copper wire twisted around each other to form a pair. One or more twisted pairs
are used in a twisted-pair cable. The purpose of twisting the wires is to eliminate
electrical interference from other wires and outside sources such as motors. By
twisting the wires, any electrical noise from the adjacent pair will be canceled.
The more twists per linear foot, the greater the effect.

Twisted-pair wiring comes in two types: shielded (STP) and unshielded (UTP).
STP has a foil or wire braid wrapped around the individual wires of the pairs;
UTP does not. The STP cable uses a woven-copper braided jacket, which is a
higher-quality, more protective jacket than UTP.

Figure 18.6   Twisted-pair cable

Of the two types, UTP is the most common. UTP cables can be further divided into five categories:

- **Category 1:** Traditional telephone cable. Carries voice but not data.
- **Category 2:** Certified UTP for data transmission of up to 4 Mbps (megabits per second). It has four twisted pairs.
- **Category 3:** Certified UTP for data transmission of up to 10 Mbps. It has four twisted pairs.
- **Category 4:** Certified UTP for data transmissions up to 16 Mbps. It has four twisted pairs.
- **Category 5:** Certified for data transmissions up to 100 Mbps. It has four twisted pairs of copper wire.

Twisted-pair cable has several advantages over other types of cable (coaxial and fiber-optic)—it is readily available, easy to install, and inexpensive. Among its disadvantages are its sensitivity to EMI (electromagnetic interference) and susceptibility to eavesdropping; it does not support communication at distances of greater than 100 feet; and it requires the addition of a hub (a multiple network connection point) if it is to be used with more than two computers.

Coaxial Cable

Coaxial cable (see Figure 18.7) is made of two conductors that share the same axis; the center is a copper wire that is insulated by a plastic coating and then wrapped with an outer conductor (usually a wire braid). This outer conductor around the insulation serves as electrical shielding for the signal being carried by the inner conductor. Outside the outer conductor is a tough insulating plastic tube that provides physical and electrical protection. At one time, coaxial cable was the most widely used network cabling. However, with improvements and the lower cost of twisted-pair cables, it has lost its popularity.

Figure 18.7 Coaxial cable

Coaxial cable is found in two types: thin (*ThinNet*) and thick (*ThickNet*). Of the two, ThinNet is the easiest to use. It is about one-quarter of an inch in diameter, making it flexible and easy to work with (it is similar to the material commonly used for cable TV). ThinNet can carry a signal about 605 feet (185 meters) before the signal strength begins to suffer. ThickNet, on the other hand, is about three-eighths of an inch in diameter. This makes it a better conductor—it can carry a signal about 1,640 feet (500 meters) before signal strength begins to suffer. The disadvantage of ThickNet over ThinNet is that it is more difficult to work with. The ThickNet version is also known as standard Ethernet cable.

When compared to twisted-pair, coaxial cable is the better choice even though it costs more. It is a standard technology that resists rough treatment and EMI. Although more resistant, it is still susceptible to EMI and eavesdropping.

Use coaxial cable if you need:

- A medium that can transmit voice, video, and data.
- To transmit data longer distances than less-expensive cabling.
- A familiar technology that offers reasonable data security.

A Mixed-Cable System

Many networks use both twisted-pair and coaxial cable. Twisted-pair cable is used on a per-floor basis to run wires to individual workstations. Coaxial cable is used to wire multiple floors together. Coaxial cable should also be considered for a small network because you can purchase prefabricated cables (with end connectors installed) in various lengths.

Fiber-Optic Cable

Fiber-optic cable (see Figure 18.8) is made of light-conducting glass or plastic fibers. It can carry data signals in the form of modulated pulses of light. The plastic-core cables are easier to install, but do not carry signals as far as glass-core cables. Multiple fiber cores can be bundled in the center of the protective tubing.

Figure 18.8   Fiber-optic cable

When both material and installation costs are taken into account, fiber-optic cable can prove to be no more expensive than twisted-pair or coaxial cable. Fiber has some advantages over copper wire; it is immune to EMI and detection outside the cable and provides a reliable and secure transmission media. It also supports very high bandwidths (the amount of information the cable can carry), so it can handle thousands of times more data than twisted-pair or coaxial cable.

Cable lengths can run from .25 to 2.0 kilometers depending on the fiber-optic cable and network. If you need to network multiple buildings, this should be the cable of choice. Fiber-optic cable systems require the use of fiber-compatible NICs.

Specifying the Right Cable

In order to ensure trouble-free operation, network cabling must match the system requirements. Cable specifications are based on three factors: speed, bandwidth, and length. Cables are designated with names like 10Base5. Speed is the first number in the identification—representing the maximum transmission speed (bandwidth) in Mbps. This will be 1, 5, 10, or 100. Band is the second part of the identification. It is either base or broad depending upon whether the cable is baseband or broadband. The last part of the identification refers to the cable length or cable type. If the unit is a number, it is the maximum length of the cable segments in hundreds of meters (1 meter is approximately 3.3 feet). In some cases, it can refer to 50-meter increments (1Base5 is five 50-meter increments—250 meters). In other cases, it represents cable type: T (twisted-pair) or F (fiber-optic). The following table shows the common types of cables and their specifications.

Name	Description	Type	Segment	Speed
10BaseT	Common	UTP twisted-pair	.5 to 100 meters	10 Mbps
10Base2	Ethernet ThinNet	Coaxial	185 meters	10 Mbps
10Base5	Thick Ethernet	Coaxial	500 meters	10 Mbps
100BaseT	Becoming common	Twisted-pair	.5 to 100 meters	100 Mbps

The preceding table covers the basic cable requirements for the A+ networking objective; however, there are many other forms of network connections. For example, you'll find microwave links; forms of radio; and, for small offices and homes, power-line networks (whose NICs have connectors that plug into wall sockets, allowing regular wiring to carry the signal), and telephone-line networks that use standard phone jacks to plug into existing lines. These have relatively short ranges (generally limited to one office or one floor of a building).

LAN Communication

A LAN is similar to a telephone system with one party line—not everyone can talk at the same time. The difference is that, with a LAN, the speed is so fast that it fosters the perception that many transactions are taking place at the same time. But just like a one-lane road, the heavier the traffic, the slower it moves.

Ethernet

Ethernet uses a system known as carrier sense multiple access with collision detection (CSMA/CD). It also uses the bus topology discussed earlier in this lesson. The term "carrier sense" means that the network card listens to the cable for a quiet period during which it can send messages. "Multiple access" refers to the fact that more than one computer can be connected to the same cable. And "collision detection" is the ability to detect whether messages have collided in transit (in which case neither message will arrive at its destination and both will be retransmitted).

Fast Ethernet was developed to meet the increasing demands on networks. Fast Ethernet works on the same principals as the original Ethernet, but operates at 10 times the speed. Ethernet transmits at 10 Mbps, and Fast Ethernet transmits at 100 Mbps.

Token Ring

As described earlier, a token ring network uses a "token" as the basis for deciding who can communicate on the network. Token rings transmit at 4 or 16 Mbps.

Network Protocols

A network protocol is a set of rules that govern the way computers communicate over a network. In order for computers using different software to communicate, they must follow the same set of networking rules and agreements, called *protocols*. A protocol is like a language; unless both computers are speaking and listening in the same language, no communication will take place.

Networking protocols are grouped according to their functions, such as sending and receiving messages from the NIC, or talking to the computer hardware and making it possible for applications to function in a network. Early computer networks had manufacturer-unique inflexible hardware and strict protocols. Today's protocols are designed to be open, which means they are not vendor-, hardware-, or software-specific. Protocols are generically referred to as protocol families or protocol suites because they tend to come in groups (usually originating from specific vendors).

The following is a list of standard network protocols:

- IPX/SPX (Internetwork Packet Exchange/Sequenced Packet Exchange): The NetWare core protocol developed by Novell in the early 1980s.

- NetBIOS/NetBEUI (Networked Basic Input/Output System/NetBIOS Enhanced User Interface): A local area protocol developed by IBM and refined by Microsoft; originally, the native protocol for LAN Manager and Windows NT. IBM developed NetBIOS as a way to permit small groups of computers to share files and printers efficiently. NetBIOS is the original edition; NetBEUI is an enhanced version for more powerful networks based on 32-bit operating systems.

- TCP/IP (Transmission Control Protocol/Internet Protocol): A set of standard protocols and services. It was developed by the Department of Defense beginning in the early 1970s as part of an effort to link government computers. This project led to the development of the Internet. Because TCP/IP is the foundation of the Internet, as well as the most widely used networking protocol, it is a good choice for networks.

- AppleTalk: A networking protocol utilized by Macintosh computers.

- DLC (Data Link Control) protocol: The oldest protocol of this group. IBM developed DLC to connect token-ring-based workstations to IBM mainframe computers. Printer manufacturers have adopted the protocol to connect remote printers to network print servers.

Depending on the operating systems and the function of the network you work on, you will probably use more than one network protocol. It's important to get and install LAN drivers that can switch between one protocol and another as needed. The aforementioned protocol information provides you with a rudimentary understanding of basic network techniques and terminology. However, networks are a very complicated subject, and additional training resources should be obtained before installing a network on your own.

Extending a LAN

The previous section on network cables mentioned some limits to the length of cables. The requirements of today's LANs will often exceed the capability of these cables. The following table lists several devices that can be used to extend a LAN network beyond its normal limits.

Devices	Description
Repeaters	The main purpose of a repeater is to extend the length of a network beyond its normal cable lengths. A repeater works like an amplifier to increase or boost the signal to allow transmissions over longer distances. Repeaters are used to connect network segments (groups of computers on the same network). They can also be used to connect segments composed of different media (for instance, a ThinNet segment to a fiber-optic segment).
Bridges	Bridges work like repeaters, but offer additional advantages. They can isolate network traffic or problems. Should any problems occur within one segment, the bridge will isolate that segment and not affect other segments on the network, thereby reducing the load on the network as a whole. Bridges can also link segments that are unalike (such as Ethernet and token ring).
Routers	Routers provide interconnectivity between like and unlike devices on the LAN and WAN. Routers work like bridges, but can connect networks using different protocols. They are able to select the best route from one network to another network based on traffic load. Routers determine the flow of data based on such factors as least-cost, minimum delay, minimum distance, and least congestion. Routers are generally used to create a WAN and connect dissimilar networks.
Gateways	Gateways provide all the connectivity of, and even greater functionality than, routers and bridges. A gateway usually resides on a dedicated computer that acts as a translator between two completely dissimilar systems or applications. Because gateways are both translators and routers, they tend to be slower than bridges or routers. Gateways also provide access to special services such as e-mail or fax functions.

Maintaining and Troubleshooting Networks

Maintaining and troubleshooting networks differ according to the operating system. Therefore, you will need to refer to the operating systems' manuals for detailed troubleshooting procedures. A thorough understanding of network troubleshooting is not a requirement of the A+ Certification program. (The section that follows describes some advanced certification programs that focus on networks.) As an A+ technician, you should be familiar with some generic troubleshooting concepts as presented in the following table.

Situation	Probable Cause
Reduced bandwidth	Called a bottleneck, this occurs when the network doesn't handle as much data as usual. A bottleneck is some constraint that limits the rate at which a task can be completed. If a task uses the processor, network, and disk resources, and spends more of its time transferring data to and from the disk, you could have a memory bottleneck. A memory bottleneck might require additional RAM.
Loss of data	If data transfers are incomplete or inaccurate, check to ensure that all network cabling and connectors are intact.
Slow loading of programs and files	Fragmentation (see Chapter 8, Lesson 2: Hard Disk Drives) occurs when the operating system saves, deletes, and moves information. You must defragment the drive. If slow loading persists even after defragmenting, check for memory bottlenecks.
Unauthorized software	You must manage software distribution to ensure that users are not loading unlicensed software and computer viruses on the network. One way is to load only software from a centralized location or server and then remotely copy it to local hard disk drives.
Traffic overloads	A hardware or software failure can bring a LAN to a halt, or the failure can result in more data traffic than the network is designed to handle. You might receive an error message or you might not see any signs other than poor network performance. You must have a system in place that can monitor and manage network traffic. To resolve this problem, you will need to reduce the traffic on the LAN or expand its capabilities.
Common mode failures	Some LAN-component failures affect other components. This is known as a common mode failure. For example, the on-board logic of a NIC might jumble the data format. The NIC will hand the result to the network operating system, which might not detect the error. If the network operating system puts that data into a file, the file will become corrupt.
Network-security violations	Entire books address the subject of network security alone. Every operating system is different, and every customer requires a different level of security. First determine the customer's needs, and then find and read the appropriate documentation.

Network Certification

This chapter is designed to give you a foundation in networks and a general understanding of network design and applications. Technician certification is a growing trend in the computer industry. The A+ examination touches on network terminology and design; however, some of the most popular networking certification programs are available through Microsoft and other NOS manufacturers. These companies offer many levels of certification; you should consult check manufacturer Web sites and community colleges for detailed course contents. Let's take a look at some of the available programs.

Microsoft Certified Product Specialist (MCPS)

Microsoft Certified Product Specialist (MCPS) certification is designed for advanced end users, computer service technicians, and network administrators who seek the fastest-growing certification in the computer industry. The MCPS certification is useful for those who want to demonstrate expertise with a particular Microsoft product, such as Windows NT Server or Windows NT Workstation. This is also the first step toward becoming an MCSE.

Microsoft Certified Systems Engineer (MCSE)

The Microsoft Certified Systems Engineer (MCSE) certification is the most sought-after certification in the computer industry. Qualified MCSEs plan, implement, maintain, and support information systems in a wide range of computing environments using the Microsoft Windows NT Server and the Microsoft BackOffice integrated family of server products. To become an MCSE, you must pass four core modules and two elective exams. For a detailed outline of the MCSE certification track, please visit www.microsoft.com.

Certified Novell Administrator (CNA)

The Certified Novell Administrator (CNA) certification is frequently the first credential earned by NetWare career professionals. CNA training provides you with the critical day-to-day maintenance and management skills you need to survive in the world of Novell NetWare and IntranetWare. The CNA certification is the first step to becoming a Certified Novel Engineer (CNE).

Certified Novell Engineer (CNE)

The Certified Novell Engineer (CNE) certification is currently one of the most popular credentials in the field of networking. It can give a tremendous boost to the career of any serious networking professional. Novell's certification curriculum is 50 percent industry-generic—as a Certified Novell Professional, you are qualified to support Novell-specific products as well as non-Novell products. Novell certifications are recognized worldwide as the standard of excellence for supporting Novell's Internet, Network, and GroupWare products. One of the leading vendor-certification programs in the IT industry, CNE training gives you the skills to provide high-end, solutions-based technical support.

The Internet

The *Internet*, also known as "the Net," is the most WAN in the world—a network of networks working together. This relatively new communication technology has begun to affect our lives as significantly as television and the telephone. When most people talk about using the Internet, they talk about which Web sites they have visited or who they've met online.

Most LANs make use of passwords and other forms of security, but the Internet is one of the most open networks in the world. Some common Internet uses include communication; locating lost friends and family; researching information for school or work; and locating businesses, products, or services (such as travel). The Internet can be your most valuable resource for virtually anything and everything.

A thorough knowledge of the Internet and how it works is not a requirement of A+ Certification. However, as an A+ technician, you might find that it becomes the single most valuable information tool at your disposal.

Internet Basics

The Internet is really a collection of services. Let's take a look at the most important services and the major concepts behind them.

The World Wide Web (WWW)

When people say they were "surfing" the net, they were probably visiting the collection of hyperlinked Web sites known as the *World Wide Web*. These Web sites are located around the world, and their numbers continue to grow by the thousands every day. Each Web site within the World Wide Web has a unique address called a Universal Resource Locator (URL).

Note   The World Wide Web (usually abbreviated as "the Web") is not the Internet—it is only part of the Internet. Although it is currently the largest, most popular, and fastest growing part of the Internet, it represents only a fraction of Internet services available that include FTP, Gopher, and Telnet.

Electronic Mail (E-mail)

Electronic mail, usually known as e-mail (sometimes spelled E-mail or email), is the most commonly used function of the Internet, allowing users to send and receive messages (and files) electronically to and from millions of people all over the world. Electronic mailing lists allow users to join group discussions with people who share their interests. Like regular mail (also called snail mail), e-mail is also sent to an address (a virtual one).

File Transfer Protocol (FTP)

The *File Transfer Protocol (FTP)* is a special application used for uploading and downloading files to and from the Internet.

Transmission Control Protocol/Internet Protocol (TCP/IP)

The *Transmission Control Protocol/Internet Protocol (TCP/IP)* is the language (network protocol) used by computers to talk to each other over the Net. TCP/IP has also become a common protocol for LANs. Regardless of which operating system or software is being used, your commands travel through the Internet in TCP/IP format. The services of the Internet and the World Wide Web could not be provided without TCP/IP.

Internet Protocol (IP) Address

Each machine on a network is given a unique 32-bit address. These addresses are normally expressed in decimal values of 4 bytes, separated with periods; for example, 127.0.0.1. Without a unique address, there would be conflicts and chaos. This is the same concept as the hardware addresses discussed in Chapter 10, Lesson 2: Configuring Expansion Cards, except that it is a software address. It designates the location of its assigned device (usually a NIC) on the network.

Internet Service Providers (ISPs)

Internet service providers furnish the connection between dial-up (modem) users and the Internet. While some are big names with millions of users, there are many more that serve local areas with both dial-up and hosting plans.

Uniform Resource Locators (URLs)

As mentioned, the *Uniform Resource Locator* is the Web's address system. To access a Web site, the user must enter the designated URL on the network. Each URL begins with the character sequence "http://". The letters "HTTP" are an acronym for the Hypertext Transfer Protocol, which identifies the Web site as an address. The rest of the URL is the name of the site. For example Microsoft's URL is http://www.microsoft.com. (Because it is universal, it is seldom necessary to first type the characters "http://" when typing a URL in a search engine; most engines take it for granted.)

Domain

An Internet *domain* is a site with a common general interest or purpose, often run by a single firm or institution. The domain suffix gives a general idea of the site's purpose: .com, for businesses, or .edu, for educational institutions. The following table lists common Internet domains.

Domain	Description
.com	Commercial organizations
.net	Networks (the backbone of the Internet)
.edu	Educational institutions
.org	Nonprofit organizations
.gov	US Government nonmilitary institutions
.mil	US Government armed services
.xx	Two-letter country code.

Domain-Name Server

A *domain-name server* is a computer that matches IP addresses with domain names. The domain name makes it possible for you to use the easy-to-remember domain name BigCompany.com without having to memorize the string of numbers in the IP address.

Getting Connected

These days, many computer professionals spend a lot of their time getting clients online.

The first thing you need to do to get a client connected is to make sure they have a service provider (we're assuming your client has a computer and a modem). Most people connect to the Internet using independent ISPs that provide local community-based service to Internet users, but popular national ISPs such as The Microsoft Network (MSN) are useful if you travel because many of them have 800 numbers for dial-up access, or many local numbers throughout the country. Local ISPs are great for customers who are looking for a cost-effective company that offers local (including technical) support.

You also need to consider which browser(s) to use. Most ISPs (especially the local ones) provide only the connection or gateway to the Internet. Others provide their own browser software package. Most ISPs allow you to use your choice of browsers. Some local and national ISPs provide a startup CD that includes their recommended browser, as well as FTP tools and other Internet utilities. From time to time, Web surfers will encounter pages that work only with a specific browser. In this case it might be necessary to install both browsers.

Lesson Summary

The following points summarize the main elements of this lesson:

- The three benefits provided by a network are connections, communications, and services.
- The three primary network topologies are bus, ring, and star.
- Network interface cards (NICs) provide the connection between the computer and the network cabling.
- The three network cabling types are twisted-pair, coaxial, and fiber-optic.
- Network cabling is designated by transmission speed, length, or type.
- Network protocols provide the rules for network communications.
- Networks can be extended with repeaters, bridges, routers, and gateways.
- The Internet is a valuable informational tool for an A+ Technician.

Lesson 2: Portable Computers

Portable computers, once a novelty, are now a part of everyday business life. Portable computers work and act just like the big ones except they are very compact. In this lesson, we look at those elements that make a portable computer unique.

After this lesson, you will be able to:

- Distinguish between the different categories of portable computers.
- Identify the unique components of portable systems.
- Define the unique problems of portable systems.
- Distinguish between the different types of computer cards designed for portable computers.

Estimated lesson time: 20 minutes

The category of portable computers includes laptop, notebook, and subnotebook (palmtop) computers, as well as the newest categories: PDA (personal digital assistant) and handheld computers.

Types of Portables

Portable computers are classified according to size and function. Today there are three basic types of portable computers: laptops, notebooks, and subnotebooks.

The first "portable" computers were often called "luggables." The size of a portable sewing machine, they tipped the scales at 30 pounds. Equipped with a small CRT display, they were actually a traditional PC in a slightly smaller case. The real change in portable computers came with the advent of the flat-panel display, allowing the portable to take on the now-familiar slim design. "Laptop" is the term used for the heavier version, usually offering most of the features of a full-fledged PC, but with a folding flat-panel display and integrated keyboard. Notebooks are slender devices that often lack the full range of storage as part of the normal configuration. PDAs, a special group of products offering a subset of features including e-mail, schedule-tracking, contact records, and allowing limited note-taking and Web-browsing, are beyond the scope of this chapter.

Laptop Computers

With advancements in battery technology and the advent of functional large-screen LCDs (liquid crystal displays), the first truly portable computers, referred to as *laptops*, were produced in the late 1980s. These units featured integrated AT-compatible computer boards, including I/O and video controller functions. Laptops, as mentioned, usually feature a folding LCD display and a built-in keyboard and pointing device. They also use an external power supply and a removable, rechargeable battery. Today's laptops have fairly large (2 GB or more) hard drives, a CD-ROM drive, and floppy disk drive (often the latter two are interchangeable plug-ins).

When laptops originally appeared on the market, they were the smallest portable computers made. Today, they are high-end machines that offer features and performance comparable to a desktop system.

Notebook Computers

Advancements in integrated circuit (IC) technology allowed the size of computer components to be reduced even further, and in the early- to mid- 1980s the *notebook computer* was born. Notebooks are roughly 8.75 inches deep, by 11 inches wide, by 2.25 inches thick, and designers are working to decrease the size and power consumption of these units even further. The reduction in size comes at a cost, however, and notebooks typically have smaller and less-capable displays and keyboards than laptops. A wide variety of specialty items have appeared on the market intending to overcome some of the notebook's shortcomings. Docking ports are one such item.

Docking Ports

Docking ports (also known as docking stations) are specialized cases into which an entire notebook can be inserted. This allows the notebook to be connected to desktop I/O devices such as full-sized keyboards, CRT monitors, and network connections. At the very minimum, a docking station provides an AC power source for the notebook. Docking stations are highly proprietary items that are designed for use with specific computer models. They are handy for the user who wants to maintain only one computer system and avoid the necessity of transferring information between two systems. With a docking port and a well-equipped notebook computer, it is possible to have the best of both worlds.

It is not necessary to have a docking port to use a portable computer with a full-sized keyboard, pointing device, and monitor. Most portables have standard connectors for these peripherals. Be aware that you might have to connect the devices before booting up the computer, though.

Subnotebook (Palmtop) Computers

Even smaller than the notebook computers are subnotebook computers, also known as palmtops. These tiny systems are 7 inches wide, by 4 inches deep, by 1 inch high. Due to their size, they are rather limited in function. Keyboards, for example, are too small to permit touch typing. With notebooks decreasing in cost and weight, palmtops have been losing market share and popularity.

Computer Cards (PCMCIA)

To provide laptop and notebook computers with the same expandability associated with desktop computers, the Personal Computer Memory Card International Association (PCMCIA) established several standards for credit-card-sized expansion boards that fit into small slots on these smaller machines. PCMCIA is also referred to as the PC Card bus. The PCMCIA standards have revolutionized mobile personal computers, providing them with the ability to add memory expansion cards, SCSI devices, communication hardware (for instance, modems and faxes) and many other devices that were previously unavailable to laptop and notebook computer users.

Compatibility problems surfaced along with the development of the PCMCIA card for portable computers. To overcome these incompatibilities, PCMCIA standards were created. The following table outlines the four PCMCIA types and their guidelines.

TYPE	Standard Description
Type I	This original computer-card standard is now referred to as the Type I standard. These slots work only with memory expansion cards. Type I cards are 3.3 mm thick.
Type II	Type II cards support most types of expansion devices (like communication hardware) or network adapters. Type II can accommodate cards that are 5 mm thick.
Type III	Type III slots are primarily for computers with removable hard disk drives. This standard was introduced in 1992. They are 10.5 mm thick; however, they are compatible with Type I and Type II cards.
Type IV	Type IV slots are intended to be used with hard disk drives that are thicker than the 10.5 mm Type III slot.

The PC Card itself is usually sealed in a thin metal case. One end contains the interface to the PCMCIA adapter (68 tiny pinholes); the other end might contain a connector for a telephone line, a network, or another external device.

PCMCIA (PC Card) is part of the Plug and Play standard—which means it allows you to add components without first shutting off or rebooting the computer. In short, PCMCIA buses are not configured with jumper settings (because they don't have any) but with software.

Portable Computer Hardware

Although many components in a portable computer are similar to those of a desktop system, some components are very different. The major difference between a portable system and desktop system is the display screen.

Displays

Portable computers have a flat, LCD screen that is about .5 inch thick. The display is typically the most expensive component in a portable system. Often it is more economical to replace the entire computer than to replace the screen. An LCD display is designed to operate at a specific resolution because the size of the pixels on an LCD panel cannot be changed. On a desktop system, by contrast, the signal output from the video adapter can change the resolution on the monitor, thereby changing the number of pixels on the screen. An LCD panel should be thought of as a grid ruled to a specific resolution. Transistors control the color that is displayed by each pixel. The two major types of LCD displays used in portable systems today (dual-scan and active-matrix) are defined by their arrangement of transistors.

Dual-Scan Displays

The dual-scan display (also known as a passive matrix display) consists of transistors running down the x and y axis of the screen. The number of transistors determines the screen's resolution. Each pixel on the screen is controlled by the two transistors that intersect on the x and y axis.

If a transistor fails, the entire line of pixels is disabled, leaving a black line across the screen. There is no way to repair this problem except to replace the display. The term "dual-scan" is derived from the fact that the processor redraws half of the screen at a time, which speeds up the refresh rate a little.

Dual-scan displays are considered inferior to active-matrix screens because they tend to be dimmer. They work by modifying the properties of reflected light rather than generating their own light. They are also more prone to ghost images, and make it difficult for two people to see the screen at the same time, because these displays can't be viewed well from an angle. The standard size for this type of screen is 10.5 inches (measured diagonally) with a resolution of 640 by 480. New systems are available with 12.1 inch displays that have a resolution of 800 by 600.

Active-Matrix Displays

Active-matrix displays are also known as thin film transistors (TFTs). They differ from dual-scan screens because they have a transistor for every pixel on the screen rather than just at the edges. Voltages are applied by electrodes at the perimeter of the grid to address each pixel individually.

Because each pixel is powered individually, generating its own light and the appropriate color, a much brighter and more vivid picture results. Creating light instead of altering reflection provides a wider viewing angle, which allows more than one viewer to see the screen at a time. The refreshes are faster and lack the fuzziness associated with the dual-scan systems.

Naturally, the cost of having 480,000 transistors instead of merely 1,400 (on an 800 by 600 screen) makes the active-matrix screen more expensive. Another drawback is that it also requires a lot more power and drains batteries faster. Failure of a transistor causes individual "dead pixels," but this is far less noticeable than the black line caused by a transistor failure of the dual-scan screen.

The 12.1-inch screen has become the standard on high-end laptops with resolutions running at 800 by 600, or even 1,024 by 768. Many portable systems today also include PCI bus video adapters. These screens come very close to the quality of a desktop display.

Screen Resolution

An LCD display's resolution is determined as much by the screen hardware as by the drivers and amount of installed video memory. Some portables can use a "virtual screen" to achieve resolutions of 800 by 600 (and even more) on a 640 by 480 pixel screen. The larger display is held in video memory while the actual screen displays the portion that fits into a 640 by 480 window. The cursor can be used to "pan" the image so that the 640 by 480 window is moved around within the 800 by 600 display. Some manufacturers advertise an 800 by 600 display while using this method, which is a little misleading.

Like a desktop system, color depth is affected by video memory. To operate any LCD display in 16-bit or 24-bit color mode, you must have sufficient video memory available. Portables usually have the video adapter hardware permanently installed on the motherboard, which makes an upgrade virtually impossible. A few PC Card video adapters, however, allow you to connect to an external monitor and increase your video capabilities.

Note LCD technology has progressed to the point that large, flat-panel LCD-type displays are now available for desktop computers, although they're quite expensive.

Processors

Computer CPU manufacturers spend a great deal of time and effort on the design and creation of chips specifically for the portable market. In desktop systems, CPU heat is dissipated by cooling fans housed inside the case. There is no room for this solution in a portable system, so manufacturers have addressed this problem in the packaging of the chip itself.

Chip manufacturer, Intel's, solution to the size and heat problems is the *Tape Carrier Package*. This method of packaging reduces the size, power consumption, and heat generated by the chip. A Pentium mounted on a motherboard using Tape Carrier Packaging is much smaller and lighter than the pin grid array (PGA) used in desktop systems. The 49-millimeter (mm) square of the PGA is reduced to 29 mm, the thickness to approximately 1 mm, and the weight from 55 grams to under 1 gram.

The Tape Carrier Packaging processor is bonded to a piece of polyamide film (which is like photographic film) using *tape automated bonding (TAB)*. This is the same process that is used to attach electrical connections to LCD panels. The film (called tape) is laminated with copper foil etched to form the leads that connect the processor to the motherboard. When the leads are formed, they are gold-plated to protect them against corrosion, bonded to the processor chip itself, and then the entire assembly is coated with a protective resin.

After being tested, the tape is cut to the proper size and the ends folded into a "gull wing" shape that allows the leads to be soldered to the motherboard while the processor is suspended slightly above it. A thermally conductive paste is inserted between the processor chip and the motherboard, allowing heat to be dissipated through a sink on the underside of the motherboard, while keeping it away from the soldered connections. Of course, because Tape Carrier Packaging processors are soldered to the motherboard, they usually cannot be upgraded.

Some manufacturers use standard PGA processors, sometimes accompanied by fans. As well as a greatly reduced battery life, these systems can be too hot to touch comfortably. Always check the exact model of processor that is used in a system you intend to purchase, not just the processing speed. You might not want to purchase a non–Tape Carrier Packaging processor for the aforementioned reasons.

Voltage Reduction

Mobile Pentiums have operated at 3.3 volts from the days of the original 75-MHz chip, but the newer and faster models have reduced the voltage to only 2.9 volts for internal operations, while retaining the 3.3 volt interface with the motherboard. This translates into a processor that uses as little as 60 percent of the power of a desktop system.

Memory

As with desktop systems, adding memory is one of the most common upgrades performed on portable computers. Unlike desktop computers, which offer only three basic types of slots for additional RAM, there are dozens of different memory-chip configurations designed to squeeze memory upgrades into the small cases of the portable systems.

Some portables use memory cartridges that look a lot like PC Cards, but they plug into a dedicated IC memory socket. Others use extender boards like the SIMMs and DIMMs. In any case, it is strongly recommended that you only install memory modules that have been designed for your system, and only in the configurations recommended by the manufacturer. This does not necessarily limit you to products made by your system's manufacturer, however, because a number of companies manufacture upgrade modules for dozens of systems.

Portable computers use the same types of DRAM and SRAM as desktops and, thanks to advances in thermal management, today's high-end portable systems usually include SRAM cache memory.

Hard Disk Drives

Except for their size and packaging, portable hard disk drive technology is mostly similar to desktops. EIDE drives are standard in portable computers with the exception of the Macintosh computer, which uses SCSI. Internal hard drives, depending on the size of the system, are typically 12.5 mm or 19 mm tall, and use 2.5-inch platters. As with memory modules, hard drives are also mounted in the system a little differently by manufacturers. And, as with memory modules, this can cause upgrade compatibility problems.

Some manufacturers use a caddy to hold the drive and make connections to the system. This makes upgradability as simple as inserting a new hard disk drive into the caddy and then mounting it in the system. Other systems require you to purchase a specifically designed drive complete with the proper connections built into it. Replacing the hard drive can be much easier in many portable systems than in their desktop counterparts. This makes it possible for multiple users to share a single machine by simply snapping in their own hard drives. However, because laptops are specialized equipment, any servicing beyond batteries, hard drives, and memory is usually left to specialists or the manufacturer.

The support provided by the system's BIOS determines the upgradability of a system. Older systems, particularly those manufactured before 1995, might offer only limited drive-size options. BIOS chips made before EIDE hard disk drives became the standard can support a maximum hard drive size of 528 MB. A flash BIOS upgrade might be available for your system to provide additional drives. Another option for expanding hard drive space is the PC Card hard drive. This device fits into a Type III PC Card slot and can provide as much as 450 MB of additional space. External drives are also available and can be connected using a PC Card SCSI host or specialized parallel port drive interfaces—you can use any size SCSI drive you choose without being limited by your system's BIOS.

Removable Media

Portable systems are now equipped with other types of storage media that can provide access to large amounts of data. CD-ROM and Zip drives are now available, as well as standard floppy disk drives. Just as in their desktop counterparts, CD-ROM is becoming standard on portables.

The swappable drive bay is increasing in popularity. This product allows the user to switch one of several types of components in the unit. For example, you might not need a floppy disk drive when traveling, so you can insert an extra battery.

Keyboards

Portable keyboards are integrated into the one-piece unit and are therefore very difficult to repair or replace. Unfortunately, the keypad is almost always the first component to fail in a portable. The functionality and durability of the keyboard should be an important concern when purchasing a portable system.

Today's portable keyboards are approaching the size and usability of desktop systems, thanks to the larger screens found in most systems. This has created more space for manufacturers to utilize in the overall design.

Pointing Devices

Today's portable computers come with built-in pointing devices. Most of these pointing devices conform to one of three types: trackball, trackpoint, or trackpad.

Trackball

This small ball (approximately .5 inch in diameter) is partially embedded in the keyboard below the spacebar. The ball is manipulated by the user's finger. These are accurate and serviceable, but they are unpopular because of their tendency to gather dirt and dust, which dramatically reduces performance.

Trackpoint

The trackpoint was developed by IBM and many manufacturers install it in their systems. It is a small, rubberized button (approximately .25 inch in diameter) located above B and below G and H on the keyboard. The user nudges it in any direction (rather like a tiny version of a joystick) to move the cursor around the screen. It is convenient because the user's hands don't need to leave the keyboard to manipulate the trackpoint.

Trackpad

The trackpad is the most recent development of the three—it is an electromagnetically sensitive pad measuring about 1 by 2 inches located in the keyboard below the spacebar. It responds to the movement of a finger across its surface to move the cursor. Mouse clicks are simulated by tapping the pad (buttons are also provided). It's a truly innovative device, but does tend to be overly sensitive to accidental touches and taps. It is also sensitive to humidity, so moist fingers can cause unpredictable performance.

Batteries

A great deal of technology has been developed to extend battery life and improve power management in portable systems. However, battery life is still one of the biggest complaints about portable systems. Even though power management and batteries themselves have improved dramatically over the last few years, the power needed to run faster processors and external devices has increased, leaving battery life about the same. Actual battery life depends as much on how the computer is used, as it does on power-management technology. Simply put, the more you ask the computer to do, the shorter the battery life. Today, battery life is still an issue with portable-system users. Most systems use one of three types of batteries.

Nickel Cadmium (NiCad) Batteries

The oldest of the three technologies, nickel cadmium is rarely used today. It has a shorter life and is sensitive to improper charging and discharging. After being charged, NiCad batteries hold the charge very well. However, their life can be severely shortened if they are not fully discharged before recharging, or if they are overcharged.

Nickel Metal Hydride (NiMH) Batteries

NiMH batteries have a longer life than NiCad (about 50 percent longer), and are less sensitive to improper charging and discharging. They are more expensive than NiCad and don't hold a charge as well when not used. They usually cannot be recharged as many times. They are, however, used in most portable systems, especially those at the lower end of the market.

Lithium Ion (Li-Ion) Batteries

Li-Ion batteries cannot be overcharged, hold a charge well when not in use, and are longer lived than the other two types of batteries. They are also proficient at handling the heavy-duty power requirements of today's higher-end portables. Unfortunately, Li-Ion batteries can be used only in systems specifically designed for them.

Caution   Never install a Li-Ion battery in a system designed for a NiCad or NiMH battery. Doing so could result in a fire.

Because they are the most expensive of the three battery technologies, Li-Ion batteries are usually found only in high-end systems.

Sometimes, buying a system with a Li-Ion battery does not mean you will realize a longer battery life. Some manufacturers take the opportunity to make the battery smaller because it is more powerful, thereby saving some space inside the computer while delivering the same performance as a NiCad or NiMH.

New Technology

Battery technology has trailed behind nearly all the other advancements of the portable system. A battery life of two hours is considered very good even when a system's power-saving features are utilized. Some manufacturers are designing systems that hold two batteries to try to overcome this limitation.

A fourth type of battery technology—the Lithium Polymer—has been in development for several years, but it has not yet appeared on the market. Lithium Polymer batteries can be formed into thin, flat sheets and installed behind the LCD panel. They provide approximately 40 percent more battery life while adding far less weight to the system.

Tip   All battery types function best if they are completely discharged before recharging. Even Li-Ion batteries perform better and last longer if they are discharged before being recharged. Another tip is to store charged batteries in the refrigerator. This helps them maintain their charges longer.

Power Management

Some components in a computer system do not need to run continuously. The purpose of power management is to conserve battery life by shutting down these components when they're not needed.

Most portable computers include power-saver modes that suspend system operations when the computers are not in use. Different manufacturers have different names for their power-saver modes such as: *suspend*, *hibernate*, or *conserve*, but they all usually refer to two different states of power conservation: one state continues to power the system's RAM, while the other does not.

Generally, the suspend mode virtually shuts down the entire system after a certain period of inactivity. However, power continues to be supplied to RAM, and the system can be reawakened almost immediately.

The hibernate mode writes the entire contents of memory into a special swap file and then shuts down the system. When reactivated, the file is read back to memory. The hibernate mode takes a little longer to reactivate than the suspend mode, but conserves more battery life. In some systems, the swap file used for the hibernate mode is located in a special partition of the hard drive. If it is inadvertently destroyed, it might require a special utility from the manufacturer to re-create it.

A document jointly developed by Intel and Microsoft—known as the Advanced Power Management (APM) standard—has been, for the most part, responsible for defining the interface (interaction) between the power-management policy driver and the operating system. This interface is usually implemented in the system BIOS.

Another standard currently under development by Intel, Microsoft, and Toshiba is called the Advanced Configuration and Power Interface (ACPI). This standard is designed to place the power-management functions under the control of the operating system. As power-management techniques develop, it becomes difficult for the BIOS to maintain the complex information states needed to run the more advanced functions. Placing power management under the control of the operating system allows applications to interact with the operating system to let it know which of its activities are crucial and which can wait until the next time the hard disk drive is activated.

Lesson Summary

The following points summarize the main elements of this lesson:

- Portable computers are classified as laptops, notebooks, or palmtops.
- PCMCIA cards provide expandability to portable computers.
- Type I PCMCIA cards are used for memory; they are 3.3 mm thick.
- Type II PCMCIA cards are used for expansion devices; they are 5.0 mm thick.
- Type III PCMCIA cards are used for hard drives; they are 10.5 mm thick.
- Display screens for portable computers are either dual-scan or active-matrix.
- Tape Carrier Packaging is used to make processors consume less energy and put out less heat.
- Good power management is the key to long battery life in a portable computer.

Chapter Summary

The following points summarize the key concepts in this chapter:

Networks

- The benefits provided by a network are connections, communications, and services.
- There are two types of networks: server networks and peer-to-peer networks.
- A network topology describes the physical layout of the network. There are three basic topologies: bus, star, and ring.
- In order to function on a network, each computer must have a network interface card (NIC) and a network operating system (NOS).
- The three types of network cabling are twisted-pair, coaxial, and fiber-optic.

Portable Computers

- Early "portable" computers were heavy, and usually more worthy of the term "luggable."
- Today's laptops and notebooks have most of the features of a desktop machine in a very compact package—but at a much higher cost.
- A computer technician should know the four types of PCMCIA cards and their uses.
- Batteries and power management are key factors to consider when maintaining portable computers.

Review

1. Name the three basic elements required to create a network.

2. The primary benefit of a LAN is its ability to share resources. Name some of the other benefits of networking.

3. What is the difference between a peer-to-peer and a server-based network?

4. Name the three network topologies.

5. What type of cabling do thin Ethernet and UTP cabling require?

6. What is the function of a network interface card?

7. Name the three main types of network cabling. What are their advantages?

8. What is the purpose of network protocols?

9. Describe the functions of a router, a bridge, and a gateway.

10. What is the most widely used network protocol?

11. What is the difference between a LAN and a WAN?

12. Your network is showing signs of reduced bandwidth. What is causing this problem?

13. What is an ISP?

14. Name some of the most common Internet domain extensions.

15. What does URL stand for?

16. Besides A+ Certification, what other computer-related certifications are available?

17. Name the three main types of portable computers.

18. What is a docking station?

19. What is the purpose of PCMCIA cards?

20. Describe the different PCMCIA card types.

21. How do you configure a computer card?

22. What are the two kinds of displays found on laptop computers?

23. Why is heat dissipation a concern in computer-chip technologies for portable computers?

24. With the exception of Macintosh, what drives are standard in a portable computer?

CHAPTER 19

Maintaining Computer Hardware

About This Chapter

The best way to repair a failure is to prevent it from happening in the first place. It is a well-known fact of life that failures occur at the most inopportune times. A little preventive maintenance can minimize the impact by either catching and repairing the failure before it happens, or preventing it altogether. The concepts of preventive maintenance and safety have been emphasized throughout this book. Likewise, safety issues are prevalently featured throughout the A+ certification exam. In fact, one objective (10 percent) of the core exam is devoted to this subject. Because of their importance, this chapter focuses on reviewing and expanding upon these issues.

Before You Begin

This chapter is, in itself, a review of many concepts discussed in previous chapters. Therefore, you should review all chapters on hardware before completing this chapter.

Lesson 1: Preventive Maintenance

Computers are, by design, very rugged and dependable pieces of equipment. However, like other machines, they age. Several basic procedures, when performed on a regular basis, can prevent premature failures. This lesson discusses how to keep computer hardware running smoothly and reliably.

After this lesson, you will be able to:

- Extend the useful life of computer hardware.
- Avoid major problems caused by unexpected downtime.

Estimated lesson time: 15 minutes

Cleaning

For the most part, computer equipment is very reliable and lasts a long time. However, as with any piece of equipment, dirt and other airborne contaminants will greatly accelerate the deterioration caused by normal use. Therefore, the best preventive maintenance is to keep the equipment clean.

The first step is to be sure that the computer is installed in a computer-friendly environment. This means that it should be in a dust-free (relatively speaking), smoke-free, and humidity-controlled (within a range of 50 to 70 percent relative humidity) location. For the most part, a normal office environment will qualify as computer-friendly. However, a normal office environment is not the only place that we find computers. Many computers are located on a warehouse floor, in a shop, or grouped together with a large industrial piece of equipment. In the event that the location of a computer is not as desirable as it should be, the frequency of preventive maintenance (cleaning) should be accelerated. In these instances, consideration should be given to establishing a computer-friendly zone around the computer, for instance, installing it into a cabinet and providing a source of clean fresh air. The following table describes what a computer technician should include in a basic cleaning kit.

Item	Usage
Lint-free chamois cloth	A cloth is useful for cleaning the outside surfaces.
Cleaning solution	Simple soap and water should be followed by a clear water rinse. Standard household cleaning solution (not extra strength) can also be used. The solution should be applied to the lint-free cloth and then applied to the computer surface. Do not use aerosol sprays. These generally use solvents as a propellant. Solvents can damage the plastic as well as the electrical components of a computer.

continued

Item	Usage
Foam swabs	Use these with cleaning solutions to clean small parts such as the wheels inside a mouse. (Cotton swabs are not recommended, because the cotton fibers can come off and be a contaminant themselves.)
Antistatic spray	An antistatic spray or solution should follow any cleaning. A solution composed of 10 parts water to 1 part common household fabric softener will do.
Small paintbrush and/or small hand-held vacuum cleaner	Used to remove dust from around the computer and inside its cabinet. The vacuum can be used to remove dust from the keyboard and other input devices.
Can of air	For removing dust from the power supply fan or from inside a computer. These can be purchased from any computer supplier; they are made especially for removing dust from electronic equipment.

Caution   Never use liquids to clean inside a computer. Never apply liquids directly to the surface of a computer. Never use solvent-based cleanser or aerosols.

The proper placement or location of a computer relative to its environment is important for ease of maintenance and long life. Let's sum up good practices for placement of computer equipment. A computer should be:

- Located in a dust-free and smoke-free environment.
- Subjected to controlled humidity (50 to 70 percent relative humidity).
- Subjected to controlled temperature (do not place too close to a heater or in direct sunlight—avoid temperature extremes).
- Have good ventilation (make sure fan/ventilation vents aren't blocked).

Preventive Maintenance

For the most part, the MTBF (mean time between failures) of a computer and its peripheral devices is quite long. By following the general cleaning and safety measures just described, you can extend this time. This section describes several components and their special maintenance requirements.

Monitors

Monitors require very little maintenance. To keep a monitor in peak condition:

- Keep it clean—use periodic cleaning, dusting, and good common sense with a monitor.
- Use simple cleaning solutions, not aerosol sprays, solvents, or commercial cleansers. DON'T use windows sprays on a monitor screen.

- Do not leave monitors on unattended for extended periods of time. Use a screen saver or the computer's power-conservation features to prevent burn-in of the monitor screen.

- Don't attempt to work inside the cabinet unless you are properly tranied to do so.

- Don't tamper with the monitor. Monitors emit x-ray radiation. Changing the settings or operating the monitor with the cover removed can disable manufacturer's safety devices, thus increasing the hazard.

Hard Disk Drives

Hard disk drives are another type of device that requires very little intervention to keep running. Mechanical failure of hard drives is rare, and when it does occur the solution is generally replacement. The most common problem with hard drives is corrupted sectors. Often they can be repaired with tools such as ScanDisk (part of the Windows 95 and 98 system tools) or one of the many after-market utility software packages available. Here are a few suggestions for preventing problems with hard drives:

- Avoid rough handling.
- Never move a hard disk when it is still spinning.
- Never expose the internal housing to open air.
- Perform regular data backups.
- Use software utilities to maintain the condition of the device (CHKDSK and ScanDisk; hard drive defragmentation programs and antivirus programs).

Floppy Disk Drives

Floppy disk drives are highly susceptible to failure. This is due mostly to the fact that they are exposed to the environment (through the disk slot) and are prone to mechanical damage from inserting and removing the disk. When they fail, the best solution is usually to replace them because they are inexpensive and simple to install. Here are a few tips to increase the life of floppy drives and disks:

- Do not expose the disks to magnets.
- Never touch the exposed surface of a floppy disk.
- Do not allow smoking near a computer.

Clean the read/write heads. Special head-cleaning diskettes and solutions such as isopropyl alcohol and methanol that do not leave a residue when they dry are available. Cotton swabs are not recommended because of the fibers they shed. Use cellular foam swabs or a lint-free cloth.

Keyboards and Pointing Devices

Keeping a keyboard and mouse clean is key to prolonging their lives. Never place drinks (coffee, soda, tea, and so on.) around a keyboard; spilling liquids is a common cause of keyboard failures. Here are a few tips to increase the life of a keyboard and mouse:

- Use a hand-held vacuum cleaner to remove dust from the small crevasses.
- Never use spray cleaners.
- Clean a mouse or trackball by removing the ball and cleaning the x and y rollers.
- When using a light pen, never touch the ends with your finger.

Printers

Printers are more mechanical than other peripherals and therefore require more attention. Because they use paper, ink, or carbon, printers generate pollutants that can build up and cause problems. Always check the manufacturer's recommendations for cleaning. Here are a few steps for cleaning the most popular types of printers:

Dot-Matrix Printers
- Adjust the print-head spacing.
- Check the tension on the print-head positioning belt. Use a non-fibrous swab dipped in alcohol to clean the print head.
- Clean the printer's roller surfaces.
- Clean the surface of the platen.
- Clean the gear train of the paper-handling motor.
- Apply light oil to the gears using a foam swab.
- Turn the platen to distribute the oil.
- Apply a light coating of oil to the rails.
- Move the carriage assembly to distribute the oil.

Ink-Jet Printers
- Adjust the print-head spacing.
- Check the tension on the print-head-positioning belt.
- Clean the printer and its mechanism.
- Clean the printer's roller surfaces.
- Clean the surface of the platen.
- Clean the surface of the ink-jet print head.
- Clean the gear train of the paper-handling motor.

- Apply light oil to the gears using a foam swab.
- Turn the platen to distribute the oil.
- Apply a light coating of oil to the rails.
- Move the carriage assembly to distribute the oil.

Laser Printers

- Vacuum to remove dust buildup and excess toner from the interior. Remove the toner cartridge before vacuuming.
- Clean the laser printer's rollers using a damp cloth or denatured alcohol.
- Clean the gear train of the paper-handling motor using a foam swab.
- Apply light oil to the gears using a foam swab.
- Distribute the oil throughout the gear train.
- Clean the writing mechanism thoroughly using compressed air. If possible, wipe the laser lens with lint-free wipes to remove fingerprints and stains.
- Clean the corona wires using a swab dipped in alcohol. Be careful not to break any of the strands because if you do, your printer will be rendered useless until they are repaired!

Preventive Maintenance Schedule

There are no universal preventive maintenance schedules that work on every computer. Each schedule must be individualized to meet the needs of the work environment. Use the following suggestions as maintenance guidelines:

Do This Daily

- Back up data.
- Check computer ventilation to ensure that it is clear. Remove any paper, books, or boxes that might impede the flow of air into or out of the computer.

Do This Weekly

- Clean the outside of the case.
- Clean the screen.
- Run CHKDSK or ScanDisk on all hard disk drives. Windows 95 and 98 come with scheduling programs to help you accomplish this on a regular basis.
- Run a current antivirus program and check all drives. These programs also come with scheduling features so this can be accomplished on a regular basis. They will also remind you when to update the virus list (usually done through the manufacturer's Web site).
- Inspect all peripheral devices.

Do This Monthly

- Clean the inside of the system.
- Clean the inside of any printers.
- Vacuum the keyboard.
- Clean the mouse ball and x and y wheels.
- Defragment all hard disk drives.
- Delete any unnecessary temporary files.

Do This Every Six Months

- Perform an extensive preventive maintenance check.
- Apply an antistatic solution to the entire computer.
- Check and reseat all cables.
- Run the printer's self-test programs.

Do This Annually

- Reformat the hard disk drive and reinstall all software. Don't forget to back up data first.
- Check all floppy disk drives.
- Consider an upgrade to your computer. Check to see that your components can handle your workload.

Lesson Summary

The following points summarize the main elements of this lesson:

- The best preventive maintenance is to keep a computer clean.
- Never use solvent-based cleaners on a computer.
- Never use liquids on the electrical components inside a computer.
- Create and implement a regular maintenance program for each computer under your care.

Lesson 2: Safety and the Environment

Lesson 1 discussed several ways in which to keep a computer's hardware running at peak performance. When maintaining or servicing a computer, several guidelines should be followed to protect you and the environment. This lesson summarizes how to maintain a safe workplace and minimize negative impacts on the environment.

After this lesson, you will be able to:

- Prepare a safe work environment and prevent damage to the computer, yourself, and the environment.

- Manage the components of a computer that have negative effects on our environment.

Estimated lesson time: 15 minutes

General Safety

Computers and their peripheral devices are electronic equipment, consequently, most safety issues relate to electrical power. However, when you work on this equipment, there are several other concerns to take into consideration, as listed in the following table.

Problem	Prevention
Back injuries	Some equipment, such as printers, monitors, and even the computer itself, can weigh several pounds (10 to 20 pounds or more for newer, larger monitors). This might not seem like much; however, when the equipment is improperly picked up (or dropped), back or other injuries can result. Be especially careful when removing a component from its original packaging. These components are generally packaged very tightly to provide protection during transport and can be difficult to remove.
Cuts	Be very careful when removing covers from computer components. The frames of the cases are often made of thin metal with sharp edges. Also, poorly cut or stamped parts might still have metal burrs, which are very sharp. Devices such as scanners and monitors have glass components that can break.
Tripping hazards	Computers tend to have many cables and wires. If not properly installed, these wires and cables can constitute a serious tripping hazard. Use cable ties to bundle up cables and reduce the "spaghetti" effect. Also avoid running cables under carpets and where people walk.

When installing or working on any equipment, make sure that the work done conforms to all applicable local and national safety codes, such as OSHA (Occupational Safety and Health Administration) and NEC (National Electric Code) standards. Most companies have their own internal safety departments and safety manuals. Be sure that you are familiar with them as well.

Power and Safety

Power is the primary safety hazard encountered when servicing a computer. Be familiar with the following guidelines when working with electrical devices and components.

ESD

The primary electrical-power concern when working with computers is ESD (electrostatic discharge). This subject was covered fully in Chapter 13, "The Basics of Electrical Energy." Remember that while ESD can destroy sensitive computer parts even when the discharge is imperceptible and harmless to humans. If proper ESD tools are not available, touching the case (specifically, the power supply) while working on the computer or its components will provide some protection. However, this will only work if the power supply is plugged into a properly grounded electrical outlet. For a review of power supplies and how to work with them, see Chapter 5 "Supplying Power to a Computer."

Grounds

When used to refer to electronic equipment, the term "ground" can be confusing. Generally speaking, a ground is any point from which electrical measurements can be made. In most cases, a ground means *earth ground*. With early electrical systems, the earth was used as a path for electrical current to return to its source. This is why telegraphs required only one wire (the earth ground serves as the other conductor). In most instances, the frame of the computer is at ground potential or earth ground, as long as the power cord is installed and connected to a properly grounded system. Some electronic equipment uses a special path or conductor for its ground. This is known as signal ground and is not the same as earth ground.

Electronic equipment is both susceptible to and a source of electromagnetic interference (EMI). A properly grounded computer will both prevent the transmission of EMI and protect itself from other sources of EMI. Unchecked, EMI will distort images on a video display, as well as corrupt communications equipment and data on floppy disks.

High Voltages

For the most part, a computer uses ±5 and ±12 volts DC. However, two devices use much higher voltages: power supplies and monitors. With these two exceptions, there are generally no electrical hazards inside a computer.

Power Supplies

The power supply uses 120 volts AC. This voltage is found inside the power-supply case. In most cases, there is no need to open the power-supply case and work on the power supply. The cost of a new power supply is low enough that it is generally easier to replace than repair. However, should you decide to open the case, be careful. Remember, the power switch on most computers (usually located on the front of the computer) also uses 110 volts AC to turn the power supply on or off. If you are working on a computer and leave it plugged in to provide proper grounding, this could present a hazard.

Monitors

Monitors use very high voltages (30,000 volts) to drive the CRT. Remember that monitors are dangerous even when unplugged. They can store this high voltage and discharge it if you touch the wrong parts. Working inside the monitor case should be left to a properly trained technician with the necessary tools.

Power Safety Guidelines

The following are some general guidelines to follow when working around computers:

- Never wear jewelry or other metal objects when working on a computer. These items pose an electrical threat that can cause shorts, which will destroy components.

- To avoid spills, never use liquids around electrical equipment.

- Do not defeat the safety feature of the three-prong power plugs by using two-prong adapters.

- Replace any worn or damaged power cords immediately.

- Never allow anything to rest on a power cord.

- Avoid using extension cords. These can become tripping hazards. Also, they may not be rated to carry the current requirements of the system.

- Keep all electrical covers intact.

- Make sure all vents are clear and have ample free-air space to allow heat to escape.

- Some peripheral devices such as laser printers and scanners use high voltages. Before removing any covers or working on any of these devices, be sure to read the manufacturers' manuals carefully.

Fire

Fire is not pleasant to think about, but it is a fact of life. A workplace fire can be disastrous both in terms of lost equipment and injury to people. Knowing what to do in the event of a fire can save valuable equipment and, most importantly, lives. Here are a few tips to help prevent fire and protect yourself:

- Always know the emergency procedures to be carried out in case of fire at your workplace.
- Know the location of the nearest fire exits.
- Know the location of the nearest fire extinguishers and how to use them.
- Don't overload electrical outlets.

Simply knowing the location of a fire extinguisher is of no value unless you know how to use it. If you don't, contact your safety department or local fire department. They will be glad to help you get the training you need. Also, remember that using the wrong type of fire extinguisher can be worse than not using one at all.

There are three basic types of fire extinguishers as shown in Figure 19.1.

Fire Extinguishers

Type A is used to extinguish ordinary combustibles
Type B is used to extinguish flammable liquids
Type C is used to extinguish electrical fires

Figure 19.1 Fire extinguisher types

Environmental Issues

Many computers and peripheral devices (especially printers) use consumable or recyclable components. In order to help keep our environment safe, you should be aware of these items and use them properly.

Examples of recyclable items or items that require special disposal are:

- Batteries.
- Toner and cartridge kits.
- Circuit boards.
- Chemical solvents.
- Monitors (CRTs).

Be sure to follow the manufacturers' recommendations for recycling or disposal of any of these items. Some items, such as toner cartridges even have prepaid shipping labels so that they can be returned for proper disposal.

When purchasing or using any kind of chemicals (cleaners, for example) that you are not familiar with the proper use and disposal of, be sure to check the MSDS (material safety data sheet). This is a form that describes the nature of any chemicals manufactured. It includes generic information about the product's chemical makeup and any recognized hazards (including what to do and who to call if there is a problem). These forms are required by law, so ask to see them. Chemical suppliers must provide the purchaser with the MSDS for products, if requested. Also consider purchasing sprays with a manual pump dispenser or compressed air rather than CFCs or other propellants that can be harmful to the environment.

Lesson Summary

The following points summarize the main elements of this lesson:

- Electrical safety is your responsibility—know what is dangerous and how to be safe.
- Beware of potential ESD problems, and maintain good electrical grounds.
- Know where your fire extinguishers are and how to use them.
- If in doubt about particular chemicals, ask the vendor for the MSDS and be sure to read it.
- Choose chemicals that are safe for the environment.

Chapter Summary

The following points summarize the key concepts in this chapter:

Preventive Maintenance

- The life of computer hardware can be extended through preventive maintenance. Implementation of a scheduled preventive maintenance program is recommended.

- The most important preventive maintenance procedure is periodic cleaning.

- A computer technician should include a simple cleaning kit along with other tools.

Safety and the Environment

- Know your fire extinguishers and how to use them.

- Be sure you know how to properly use and dispose of any chemicals required in your workplace.

- Be aware of possible electrical hazards and take appropriate steps to reduce risk of shock.

Review

1. What items should be included in a cleaning kit?

2. Why is ESD dangerous to computers?

3. Will a properly grounded computer help prevent EMI?

4. Describe some safety precautions you can take to protect yourself from high voltage when working on a computer.

5. What type of fire extinguisher is used for an electrical fire?

6. How do you clean a keyboard?

7. How do you clean a laser printer?

8. Give one example of a recyclable item that requires special disposal.

9. Why is a toner cartridge easy to recycle?

10. What is a material safety data sheet?

CHAPTER 20

Staying on Top of Your Profession

About This Chapter

In the first chapter of this course, you learned that a computer professional must combine the skills of technician, scholar, and diplomat. So far, we have focused on technical skills. In this chapter, we focus on scholarly and diplomatic skills. This chapter is about how to stay at the top of your profession and how to work with the most important component of your business: the customer.

Before You Begin

There are no official prerequisites for this chapter, however you can make best use of the information contained in it if you have first completed the rest of the book.

Lesson 1: Becoming an A+ Technician

By virtue of choosing and completing this course, you are demonstrating a commitment to the computer industry. You have chosen to be a part of one of the most dynamic industries ever. This lesson is about how you, as a computer technician, can stay current with a profession in flux.

After this lesson, you will be able to:

- Keep up-to-date in your chosen profession.
- Provide effective customer service.

Estimated lesson time: 20 minutes

Staying on Top

There is more to being a computer professional than simply servicing computers. The simple act of studying to become A+ Certified indicates that you are committed to becoming a qualified computer technician. The truth is that the very minute you pass your A+ Certification, new technology will arrive on the scene, or someone will discover a new bug in existing technology. You have entered a dynamic, fast-growing, and rapidly changing industry. To stay at the top, a computer professional must *never* stop learning.

Repairing computers is as much an art as a science. Acquiring technical knowledge is just the beginning. The ability to apply that knowledge in a useful manner is every bit as important as possessing the knowledge. A successful computer professional must be both invisible and indispensable.

Don't Stop Learning

Continuing education is vital in the computer-repair business. Attending seminars, reading books and magazines, and listening are essential parts of the job. The formal training that you are undertaking should be the beginning of your technical education, not the end. Remember, you will never know everything, and it will often seem that as soon as you've mastered a new technology, it is revised. Knowing how to "get the answer" is often more important than guessing or thinking you know it all.

Networking

When we want to increase our computers' data capabilities, we network them. Remember that you are not the only one interested in fixing computers. Take advantage of every opportunity to make connections with your colleagues in the computer business and in the classroom.

Join a local computer users' group—one can easily be found by asking around local computer stores. These groups are great places to meet and share common interests with others.

Make yourself available to other technicians. The person you help to solve a problem (from your base of knowledge and experience) today, will be there to help you tomorrow. The best time to learn about problems, and their solutions, is before they happen to *you*.

The range of hardware, operating systems, and software available today makes it impossible for any single person to master every aspect of the personal computer environment. Your experience base, as you encounter problems, will be different from that of your colleagues. Build a network of technicians with different areas of specialization. Share your specialized expertise with your colleagues, and learn from them when the opportunity and need arises.

Get Connected!

Today's computer professional needs to be linked electronically to the Internet. You need Internet access for e-mail, Usenet newsgroups, and the World Wide Web (WWW). After all, your goal is to make computers work for others, so put yours to work for you.

E-mail

E-mail is a useful way to communicate with technical support people and colleagues. E-mail is asynchronous communication that transcends time zones; a question can be posed at any time of the day, and answered anytime, without fear of inconveniencing the other party. It is also a good method for providing customer service.

Usenet

Usenet newsgroups are good places to acquire detailed information about computers. In a newsgroup, you can get information from other users. You are more likely to get a frank opinion than to hear "the company line." There are thousands of Usenet groups, and hundreds are dedicated to computers. Be sure to look for FAQs lists (Frequently Asked Questions). They are great for answering basic questions and giving guidance on how to use a particular newsgroup.

Newsgroups are also invaluable when you come across a situation that stumps you. Write up the problem and post it to an appropriate newsgroup (or more than one, but don't cross-post!). You will often be amazed at the responses you'll get from helpful colleagues—everything from "try this" suggestions, to the actual solution to your problem from someone who has encountered it before.

The World Wide Web

The Web is quickly becoming the best place to get computer information. Most suppliers have a presence on the Web. Suppliers often provide upgrades, patches, and work-arounds for most problems users encounter with their products. Many maintain technical databases full of information about both their legacy products and the most current ones. This information is usually free, but the fact that it exists is not always advertised. It is not uncommon today for a supplier to post a fix or upgrade on its Web site without notifying registered users.

Finding the correct Web site can often be challenging. A good starting place is a portal site that caters to technicians who frequently upgrade computers. These sites help you search for a source for buying parts and have links to the major computer industry manufacturers.

If you don't have luck with portals, use search engines. You might feel over-whelmed at first with your search results, because responses can literally number in the thousands. Learn how to use "advanced" search techniques and try *suppliername*.com to find the correct domain (it works more often than not).

A good example, and an excellent resource, is www.microsoft.com. Go to the support page and access the Knowledge Base. You will find a wealth of information regarding Microsoft products. After you find a good source, don't forget to use the Web browser's Favorites, Bookmarks, or similar feature to organize folders with links to the most useful resources you've found online. For example, you could create folders for tech support by company or product.

Commercial Networks

There are a number of major commercial networks such as The Microsoft Network (MSN) available. Many of the smaller Internet service providers host forums for computer users, similar to the newsgroups previously discussed. The difference is that they are private, available only to the users of the service. They work similarly to a bulletin board service (BBS) where you can post questions and answer other questions.

Practice

Knowledge that does not get used gets lost. Practicing is the only way to keep your skills sharp. However, use caution when trying things out for the first time or when experimenting (especially on someone else's computer). Having to explain that you crashed because you were "playing" with a new technique or piece of hardware can be a painful experience for all involved.

However, it doesn't hurt to keep some equipment on hand for the sole purpose of playing. For many technicians, extra equipment at work is rare and their personal machines become their test machines, constantly being ripped apart and experimented upon. If a system or two can be kept around for experimentation and education, you can greatly magnify the value of any other training you receive and reduce costs overall.

Read, Read, and Read Some More!

Keep up with the computer-industry press. There are many good computer books available, but remember that the lead time required to publish a book almost guarantees that computer books are out-of-date the moment they come off the press. At the very least, computer books have a relatively short "shelf life" in an industry that is the most rapidly changing industry in the world. Computer magazines are a great source for keeping up with new developments. There are many good computer magazines, each with its own strengths and weaknesses. Much magazine coverage overlaps; pick two or three magazines to read every month and *make* the time to read them.

Don't forget that most print magazines have online editions, and some excellent ones exist only online. These E-zines offer in-depth reviews and industry advice long before it appears in hardcopy publications.

Subscribing to a computer magazine usually means that your name will appear on a number of mailing lists that are sold to computer companies. If you can overcome sensitivity to privacy issues and tolerate junk mail, the ads that will begin to fill your mailbox offer another way to keep track of new products as they become available.

Technical Support

You might ask yourself why you need to get technical support if you are yourself an A+ Technician. The answer is simple: you can never know everything. The ability to use technical support wisely is part of your technical growth and part of staying on top. The unlimited technical support by phone that we once took for granted is rapidly disappearing. It is being replaced by limited technical support transmitted through e-mail and the Web. This means that increasingly we are expected to get the job done without direct support from the original equipment manufacturer (OEM). Technical support is out there, but it must be used wisely to be cost-effective.

Telephone Support

Many telephone-line support systems are geared toward novice and home users, not to knowledgeable, well-trained technicians, and many try to walk all callers through basic installation procedures. Patience is the rule when talking to someone at this level (who most probably had to complete a basic troubleshooting procedure required by their employers); that person must follow the rules and procedures of their company. Also, don't be blinded by how much you *think* you know. The individual providing phone support just might cover something that you missed or lead you in another, more fruitful, direction. If the problem remains unresolved, you'll usually have to convince support personnel to send you to the next level of support.

After you get to that next level, always ask the "level 2 technician" to give you the phone number for the direct technical-support line. Some technicians are reluctant to give out that number unless the caller promises not to distribute it and not to call about trivial matters. Every computer technician should build up a collection of technical-support phone numbers, including as many direct numbers that bypass the usual voicemail routing system as possible. The major drawback to technical-support lines is the amount of time callers spend on hold. Hold times of up to several hours are not uncommon. If you are going to rely on telephone support, invest in a speakerphone. You will need it.

Tip   It is a good idea to have the problem computer in front of you when you call. Often, you will be asked to follow some basic instructions while you are on the line with the technician. It is more believable to the technician to hear you describe the failure in real time, rather than simply telling the technician that you have already tried the recommended solution to no avail.

Online Support

Online technical support is becoming a better option. Most phone support today is free only to registered owners, and only for a limited time. If you want serious support, you will have to subscribe to a service or use a pay-as-you-go phone line. Checking the vendors' websites or online forums on commercial networks such as MSN often provides a solution without the need to contact the company. Many forums have libraries of technical support questions that have been posed about particular products. By searching these libraries, you can often get immediate answers to your questions. Some sites also have troubleshooting "wizards" that walk you through a diagnosis and solution to your problem. If not, post questions and hope for an answer, either from the OEM or from another user.

Remember, if support is essential to you and your OEM does not provide the level of service you need, you can always change OEMs (if you work in a large company, inform your supervisor of the problem). Before taking that step, tell the OEM you are considering another OEM and why. You could also point out that if the way you've been treated is typical of their service and support, you'll post it as a cautionary tale in a newsgroup or two.

Your Own Technical Support

As an A+ Technician, you will find technical support to be a two-way street. You will often find yourself giving technical support as well as receiving it. In these cases, the best advice is to remember what it is like to be on the other side and—most importantly—listen to your customer.

The Bottom Line

Often computer owners get so caught up in the excitement over new technology that they forget the reason they bought their computer in the first place. Whether it was to increase productivity in the office, provide an educational resource for the kids, play games, or access the Internet—if it is meeting their expectations, the rule should be "if it isn't broken, don't fix it!" Finding ways to get better performance from a computer is fine. But any time changes are made to a system that is already working properly, there is the chance it will not work at all (at least for some period of time).

While there is no reason to discourage customers from upgrading and enhancing the capabilities of their computers, keep in mind what *they* want their computers to do for them. If they use the family computer only for word processing, then perhaps the 386 will suffice until they have greater need for more complex applications. If the computer or software is too complex for the user, then it might as well be broken; it is not working properly—for that user.

Learning to interact with the people using computers is often underemphasized. Listen carefully to the end user—it's the most important part of the troubleshooting process. Remember, it is end users who determine your success or failure. They must feel that the computer is working for them, not that they are working for the computer.

These rules apply to both workplace and individual computer users. A good computer professional matches the computer with the job and the operator. It might be nice to drive a Ferrari, but does someone whose transportation needs are limited to a 35-mph speed zone, carpooling three kids, or hauling camping gear really need a Ferrari?

Tools of the Trade

Nothing is more important than having the right tools for the job. To be an effective computer professional requires owning four sets of tools:

- **Hardware Toolkit:** Use this to take things apart and put them back together; also to build up a collection of screws, jumpers, cables, splitters, and other goodies that can save a trip to a supply store.

- **Software Toolkit:** Use this to troubleshoot and correct operating systems, hardware, drivers, and application problems. These days, your software toolkit should also include good, routinely updated virus checkers. And include a bootable disk with key diagnostic and system files for each operating system you work with.

- **Technical Library:** Use this to help you keep track of the ever-growing base of information and provide answers to "I never saw that before" problems.

- **Spare Parts:** Keep these computer-system components—such as power supply and expansion card that can be easily replaced when you're on location—at hand.

Tip Keeping track of technical information is always a problem. There is always too much to remember. It can be helpful to keep track of technical information and problem resolution by using a free-form note-taking and database system with searching and indexing capabilities. There are many software packages commercially available for this purpose; however, with a little creativity, you can create your own custom database.

Hardware and Software Toolkits

A good hardware and software toolkit is an important part of a technician's life. Lesson 1: Computer Disassembly and Reassembly of Chapter 14 covers the details of creating a basic toolkit. Only over time will you be able to perfect the contents of your toolkit. Your customer base (and the type of computers and software they use) will eventually determine the contents you need to carry. When creating your toolkit, remember two things:

- The more tools you have, the more you will have to carry.

- There is nothing more embarrassing than arriving on a job site without the tools to do the job.

Somehow—but only with experience—you will be able to overcome the contradiction inherent in these statements.

Technical Library

Keeping up with new developments in the ever-growing computer industry is a necessity. However, a good, old-fashioned technical library is also necessary—to keep up with the past. It is not uncommon to encounter an older machine that is still performing its assigned task but that has developed an ailment. It might not be cost-effective to replace the machine at this time, and you'll have to dust off the old books just to remind yourself what you used to do.

A technical library also helps keep up with the present. There are so many software and hardware packages in use that it is impossible to keep track of all the details. Further, many manufacturers no longer provide documentation. A good after-market reference manual can help. Check with your local computer/software stores and bookstores.

Not all the information in your library needs to be purchased. Keep a record of problems and their resolutions. Any time you need to download technical information from the Internet or assemble product documentation, file it for future reference. You never know when you might need it again.

Tip   If you do a lot of on-site troubleshooting, you should consider a notebook computer with a CD-ROM or DVD drive. You can take it with you to gain access to your searching/indexing software. There is even a version of a Web search engine that you can use to search for files on your own hard disk.

Spare Parts

As mentioned, it doesn't hurt to keep a few spare parts for testing purposes. When in doubt, exchanging a problematic part with a known-to-be working part will help you troubleshoot. Be careful to collect only parts that you're sure work. Exchanging a bad part with another bad part won't help the troubleshooting process and can even make matters worse.

Some suggested parts to keep on hand include the following:

- Keyboard
- Power supply
- I/O card
- Floppy drive
- RAM
- Network card
- Variety of cables and connectors
- Mouse
- Video card

Troubleshooting

Troubleshooting is perhaps the most difficult task of a computer professional. After a problem has been diagnosed, there are usually several resources, or given procedures, available to correct the problem. Frequently, the problems as reported are really just symptoms, not the cause. To make matters worse, computers never fail at a convenient time. They fail in the middle of a job or when there is a deadline and the user must have the problem fixed *now*.

Troubleshooting is more of an art form than an exact science. However, to be an efficient and effective troubleshooter, you must approach the problem in an organized and methodical manner. Remember, you are looking for the cause, not the symptom. As a troubleshooter, you must be able to quickly and confidently eliminate as many alternatives as possible so that you can focus on the things that might be the cause of the problem. In order to do this, you must be organized.

Understanding the following five phases of troubleshooting will help you focus on the cause of the problem and lead you to a permanent fix.

Phase I: Define the Problem

The first phase is the most critical and, often, the most ignored. Without a complete understanding of the entire problem, you can spend a great deal of time working on the symptoms instead of the cause. The only tools required for this phase are a pad of paper, a pen (or pencil), and good listening skills.

Listening to the client or coworker (the computer user) is your best source of information. Don't assume that just because you are the expert, the operator doesn't know what caused the problem. Remember, you might know how the computer works and be able to find the technical cause of the failure, but the users were there before and after the problem started and are likely to recall the events that led up to the failure.

Ask a few specific questions to help identify the problem and list the events that led up to the failure. You might want to create a form that contains the standard questions that follow (and other questions specific to the situation) for taking notes.

- When did you first notice the problem or error?
- Has the computer been moved recently?
- Have you made any changes to software or hardware?
- Has anything happened to the computer? Was it dropped or was something dropped on it? Was coffee or soda spilled on the keyboard?
- When exactly does the problem or error occur? During the startup process? After lunch? Only on Monday mornings? After using e-mail?
- Can you reproduce the problem or error?
- If so, how do you reproduce the problem?
- What does the problem or error look like?
- Describe any changes in the computer coinciding with the problem (such as noise, screen changes, lights, and so forth).

Phase II: Zero In on the Cause

The next step involves the process of isolating the problem. There is no particular correct approach to follow, and there is no substitute for experience. The best you can do is to eliminate any obvious problems and work from the simplest problems to the more complex. The purpose is to narrow your search down to one or two general categories. The following table provides 14 possible categories you can use to narrow your search.

Category	Subcategory	Symptom
Electrical Power	Electric utility Fuse box Wiring Plugs/cords Power supply Power connectors	Dead computer. Intermittent errors on POST. Intermittent lockups. Device not working/not found.
Connectivity	External cables Internal cables Properly seated cards (chip/boards) SCSI chain Front panel wires (lights and buttons)	Device not working. Device not found. Intermittent errors on a device.
Boot	Boot ROM CMOS (chip and settings) CMOS battery Flash ROM	Dead computer. Consistent errors on POST. Beep errors. CMOS text errors. RAM, hard disk drive, floppy disk drive, video errors.
Memory	DRAM—proper type and setup DRAM CMOS settings SRAM—proper type and setup SRAM CMOS settings Motherboard jumpers	Dead computer. Parity errors. GPF with consistent addresses. HIMEM.SYS errors.
Mass storage	Hard disk drives, floppy disk drives, CD-ROM drives, Zip drives, tape drives Partitions File structure FATs Directory structure Filenames and attributes	Error messages: "Missing operating system" "File not found" "No boot device" "Abort, Retry, Fail"
Input/output	IRQ settings I/O addresss DMA settings Serial port settings Parallel port settings SCSI settings Card jumper settings	System locks up. Device not responding. Bizarre behavior from a device.

(continued)

continued

Category	Subcategory	Symptom
Operating system	BUFFERS FILES FCBs (File Control Blocks) Stacks IO.SYS/MSDOS.SYS Set statements Paths and prompts External MS-DOS commands Multiboot CONFIG.SYS	Error messages: "Missing operating system" "Bad or missing command interpreter" "Insert disk with COMMAND.COM" "Stack overflow" "Insufficient File Handles"
Applications	Proper installation Proper configuration Knowledge of capabilities Knowledge of bugs, incompatibilities, work-arounds	Application doesn't work properly. Application-specific errors. Application-specific GPFs. Lock-up only in specific application.
Device drivers	All devices in CONFIG.SYS, SYSTEM.INI, or Registry Proper versions Proper configuration	Device lockups on access. Intermittent lockups. Computer runs in safe mode only.
Memory management	HIMEM.SYS settings EMM386.EXE settings MSDOS.SYS options (Win95) SYSTEM.INI/WIN.INI Virtual memory Windows resource usage UMB management	"Not enough memory" error. Missing XMS, EMS memory. Device lockups. GPFs at KRNL386.EXE. GPFs at USER.EXE or GDI.EXE.
Configuration/ setup	Files used for initialization Basic layout of initialized files	Programs refuse to do something they should. Missing options in program. Missing program or device.
Viruses	Virus-management procedures Knowledge of virus symptoms Virus-removal procedures	Computer runs slow. Intermittent lockups. Storage problems. Operating-system problems. Mysterious symptoms.
Operator Interface	Lack of training/ understanding Fear of the computer Poor attitude	"I didn't touch it!" "It always does that!" Multiple users.
Network	Logon errors Communication errors	User forgets password. Expired password. Cable or NIC card problems.

Be sure to observe the failure yourself. If possible, have someone demonstrate the failure to you. If it is an operator-induced problem, it is important to observe *how* it is created, as well as the results.

Intermittent problems are the most difficult ones to isolate. They never seem to occur when you are present. The only way to resolve them is to be able to re-create the set of circumstances that causes the failure. Sometimes, moving step-by-step to eliminate the possible causes is all you can do. This takes time and patience. The user will have to keep a detailed record of what is being done before and when the failure occurs. In such cases, tell the user to not do *anything* with the computer when the problem recurs, except to call you. That way, the "evidence" will not be disturbed.

Tip   For a totally random, intermittent problem, always suspect the power supply.

Phase III: Conduct the Repair

After you have zeroed in on a few categories, the process of elimination begins.

Make a Plan

Create a planned approach to isolating the problem based on your knowledge at this point. Your plan should start with the most obvious or easiest solution to eliminate and move forward. Put the plan in writing!

The first step of any plan should be to *document* and *back up*.

If possible, make no assumptions. If you must make any assumptions, write them down. You might need to refer back to them later.

Follow the Plan from Beginning to End

Once a plan is created, it is important to follow it through. Jumping around and randomly trying things can often lead to more serious problems.

Document every action you take and its results.

If the first plan is not successful (they won't always be), create a new plan based on what you discovered with the previous plan. Be sure to refer to any assumptions you might have made.

Repair or Replace

After locating the problem, either repair or replace the defect. If the problem is software-oriented, be sure to record the "before" and "after" changes.

Phase IV: Confirm the Results

No repair is complete without confirmation that the job is done. Confirmation involves two steps:

- Make sure that the problem no longer exists. Ask the user to test the solution and confirm client satisfaction.

- Make sure that the fix did not create other problems. You have not done a professional job if the repair has been completed at the expense of something else.

Phase V: Document the Results

Finally, document the problem and the repair. There is no substitute for experience in troubleshooting. Every new problem presents you with an opportunity to expand that experience. Keeping a copy of the repair procedure in your technical library will come in handy in a year or two when the problem (or one like it) occurs again. This is one way to build, maintain, and share experience.

Lesson Summary

The following points summarize the main elements of this lesson:

- Learning doesn't stop with certification. To stay at the top of your profession, you must keep learning.
- Staying connected with your peers is an important part of learning.
- Maintain a proper set of the tools of the trade.
- Know where and how to get technical support.
- Good troubleshooting requires a plan. To be successful, you must stick to your plan.

Lesson 2: Customer Service

Whether you're in business for yourself or part of a large organization, there is more to becoming a computer professional than just fixing computers. Lesson 1 focused on how to stay on top of your profession. This lesson focuses on perhaps the most important element of the professional configuration—the customer. Remember that whether you are a consultant, a contractor, or on the staff of a large organization, you are working on an individual's computer and that individual is your customer. Your customers are your business.

After this lesson, you will be able to:

- Identify the level of support needed to resolve a problem.

- Put techniques for offering good customer service to use.

Estimated lesson time: 15 minutes

Getting Organized—Keeping Records

Repairing computers can be a time-consuming job. When a computer goes down or has some kind of glitch, the owner or operator is inevitably in the middle of a major project and rarely has time or patience to address the problem. Therefore, being an efficient and effective service provider is as important as being able to resolve hardware or software problems. It is as important to work smart as it is to work hard. Being organized and keeping good records is the key to becoming efficient, effective, and successful.

How much time does it take you to check IRQs every time you install a new card on the same computer? Do you spend too much time rebuilding CONFIG.SYS and AUTOEXEC.BAT files when an end user accidentally erases them? Spending a few minutes reviewing and updating your records each time you install a new system or perform maintenance and can save you hours in the long run.

Keep a simple set of documents that contains essential information for each computer you work on. Create a database, spreadsheet, or word processor file to make updating easy. Be sure to back up the data and keep a hard copy on file for quick reference. The following table provides some suggestions about the information you might want to keep.

Suggestion	Usage
Name each computer.	Which name you choose does not matter, but make it unique and descriptive. Establish naming conventions to make remembering them easier. Use names in addition to serial numbers.
Document all technical information.	Include the operating system name and version, CONFIG.SYS, AUTOEXEC.BAT, IRQs, I/O base address, DMA channels, device driver names, processor type and speed, size of cache, RAM, BIOS, monitor, video card, modems, and sound cards.
Save startup data to floppy disks (unique data).	Include the startup disk (based on the current version of the operating system, AUTOEXEC.BAT, and CONFIG.SYS), device driver disks, and recovery disks—as required by antivirus program or system.
Keep an incident log.	In your log of events for each computer include such things as the user, application installations (date and version), upgrades (hardware), and problems (cause of failure and actions taken for resolution).

Levels of Support

In an organization or corporate environment with a large number of computers and peripheral devices, it is often wise to separate support functions into several levels or categories. Depending on the size of the organization and the degree of knowledge of the end users, some technical support can be delegated or handled over the phone. By properly delegating responsibility for technical support, you can avoid being tied up with trivial problems, saving time for you and your end users.

Level 1: Designated, On-Site User

It is usually possible to designate someone within each department, or section, to handle simple technical-support questions. Find someone with a basic familiarity with computers and designate that individual as the key contact. They can handle many of the trivial problems that often plague inexperienced users (for instance, the computer/mouse/keyboard/printer is not plugged in) and can also handle basic maintenance (such as performing backups). By delegating these tasks locally, you can ensure that technical support will be available when more serious problems arise. You will also have a knowledgeable source onsite to be your eyes and ears.

How you apply this level of support will depend on your situation. If, for example, you are an independent consultant or working at a service desk for a computer supplier, you most likely will be dealing with the owner/user and this won't apply.

Level 2: Telephone Support

Handle as many problems as possible over the phone. Phone support offers the quickest solution to many common problems. In addition, by getting as much information about the problem as possible over the phone, you can be sure to have the right tools at hand and an appropriate plan if and when you arrive on the scene.

Level 3: On-Site Service

For those jobs that cannot be handled over the phone, you will need to decide whether to service the machine on-site or to bring it back to your own workspace. Consider these questions when making this decision:

- Will your repairs interfere with your end user's work?
- Will the end user's location interfere with your work?
- Is the computer in a high-traffic area?
- Is there a lot of activity in the area?
- Will the end user want to help? (Also consider whether or not this would be a benefit.)
- Do you have enough space to do the work?

Tip   If the work will take more than a few minutes, you might do better to take the machine back to your own workspace.

Spare Parts

Possessing a large supply of spare parts can definitely shorten the time to complete a repair; however, having too many spare parts can be a problem as well. Maintaining a large inventory is expensive, especially if you have 100 items that just became obsolete. You will need to keep spare parts in stock and you will need to manage them. Consider the following tips when determining how to manage your spare parts inventory:

- Know the frequency of failures and, therefore, the number of the replacements you are likely to need for your organizational situation.
- Know how long it takes to get replacements and order appropriately.
- Know your suppliers and how quickly they can provide parts when you need them. This way you need keep only what you need on your shelf.
- Buy spare components in bulk whenever possible, especially inexpensive components such as floppy disk drives, cables, mouse devices, ink-jet cartridges, and so forth.
- Standardize your parts to keep your inventory small (see the next section).

Standardization

Standardizing equipment is very desirable in large organizations. It reduces the number of spare parts required and simplifies installations. But although desirable, it is not always possible. Many organizations purchase equipment, such as computers, solely on the basis of the best price available at the time of purchase. Therefore, whichever manufacturer happens to be offering a special deal at that time is likely to be the one to get the contract. The result is that the organization eventually assembles a wide assortment of computer equipment, making standardization difficult.

In cases such as this, you can standardize what you have control over, and group the rest as well as you can. If you have several identical systems, by using an identical configuration, with standard CONFIG.SYS, AUTOEXEC.BAT, and IRQ assignments, you can simplify the troubleshooting process. Even if you have many computers with little in common, adopting certain standards can be worthwhile. For example, establish common IRQs for standard equipment such as modems, sound cards, network cards, and mouse and SCSI devices.

Customer Service

The bottom line in computer repair is customer service. Whether you work for a large organization or as an independent consultant, the end user is your customer. This section discusses general guidelines for setting up and managing customer service.

Support Calls

There are generally two methods for handling initial support calls to a technical service department. The first method, and perhaps the most common, is the help desk. Each call is routed through a central location or phone. At this point, the call is evaluated, classified according to the nature and urgency of the problem, and then routed to the appropriate member of the support team for action.

In the second method, any member of the support team can respond to a call and attempt to solve the problem. If that fails to resolve the issue, the problem is handed on to a more knowledgeable team member for action.

It is at this stage that you have the opportunity to put your customer service skills in action. The person who calls you will be sensitive not only to how you resolve the technical problem, but to how you treat that individual personally. Chances are, if someone needs to call you, the day is already going badly. Your demeanor and expertise can improve it or make it worse. This is especially important if you are in business for yourself; it can mean the difference between building your business with repeat calls and referrals—or bankruptcy.

When you receive a call requesting you to provide technical support, going through the following four simple steps should lead to a successful conclusion of the encounter:

- **The Greeting:** During this stage, which should be as brief as possible, your purpose is to establish the identity of the caller and the nature of the problem. In some cases, it can also lead to initiating a work order or tracking code to follow and record the event. Following good telephone etiquette is critical, especially if it is your business and your caller is a potential customer who is shopping around for a computer-repair professional. This is likely to be your potential customer's first impression of your company.

- **The Description:** During the second stage, your task is to obtain a description of the problem. It is important to avoid any miscommunication. Try to pick up audible clues (note significant points, caller's level of expertise, and sense of urgency) and guide the conversation (keep it focused). However, appreciate that you, not the caller, are the expert. Don't become frustrated (or sound frustrated) by the caller's lack of understanding of the problem. After all, if the exact problem were known already, chances are you would not be needed to fix it.

- **The Interview:** Use this stage to ask questions. (See "Troubleshooting" in the previous lesson.) Keep your questions short, logical, and as simple as possible. This is not the time to try to impress a customer with your expertise. Keep your questions at a level that will not confuse or intimidate the caller.

- **The Closure:** By the fourth stage, the end of the conversation, you should be able to assess and evaluate the information. You will be able to provide the client with a plan of action, including what the next step will be, who will be handling the problem, and when they should expect action.

Take the time to create a form and/or a database for tracking calls. This will provide a source of information for future use. Basing the form on keywords chosen to describe the problem briefly, will allow easy creation of reports.

Reports and Logs

If you work independently, you should also keep a client profile log that includes a few paragraphs describing each of your clients and their business. Include notations of any relevant facts about clients that you can use in future conversations with them. Also, take note of any client plans for future expansion or equipment upgrades that might need your help. It is best to get in a habit of writing this down as soon as possible after your service call, when the important details and observations are still fresh in your mind.

Referrals are the lifeline of any small business. If you feel that your client is satisfied with your work, do not hesitate to ask for referrals and ask if you can use the client's name as a reference. Keep a written record of referrals you receive and contact the referred individual with a phone call or letter as quickly as possible. Also, leave a few business cards with your clients and encourage them to give the cards to anyone who might need your services. Call your clients within a few days after you have serviced their equipment, and confirm that their problems have been resolved. They will appreciate it. Even technicians who work in a corporate setting can find this procedure helpful as well.

Difficult Clients and Coworkers

You will inevitably encounter difficult clients or coworkers. Keep in mind that it is your job to identify, and to try to resolve these problems too, not just those that are mechanically based. Here are a few suggestions for handling difficult clients and coworkers:

- If the user needs training, ensure that information about appropriate courses is available. If the individual is one of your coworkers, speak to the user's manager and identify training needs. If it is a client, gently point out the benefits of obtaining specific training or offer some of your time and expertise for tutoring.

- If the client has difficulty remembering instructions, put them in writing. Give the client a memo or sheet with written instructions—and save the instructions for future use.

- Dealing with technophiles (those who think they are experts) can be a challenge. The best approach is to listen carefully and make them part of the solution, not part of the problem. Remember, they came to you for help. In a corporate or large organizational setting, start an advanced users group and make them responsible for developing solutions, or at least for being part of the solution.

- Require users who are coworkers and constantly complain about trivial problems to put them in writing. Include their notes as part of your records. If the complainants are your clients, charge them for your time.

Escalating Problems

Because new devices and software are introduced every day, it is not uncommon to encounter problems that are outside the scope of the support group or your current level of experience. In such cases, addressing the problem requires gaining the assistance of the hardware or software supplier. Whether you turn to a more-experienced team member or an original equipment manufacturer (OEM), be sure to track the progress of the problem and who retains responsibility.

Of course, if you are an independent service person, you will be responsible for doing the research to find a solution to the problem. Keep a record of your resources (phone numbers, individuals' and company names, Internet URLs, documentation sources) for future reference.

If the problem is resolved by making previously undocumented changes (such as a patch or upgrade by the OEM), be sure to pass along the information to other team members. Also, be sure to keep good documentation of the solution because you may need it for future reference.

Conclusion

After a service call is concluded (successful or not), there is one more action to take: document the closure. Make this report as detailed as possible. Include what was done to resolve the problem—or what steps were taken to *try* to resolve the problem—and the results of your efforts. If the problem was not resolved, explain to the user why it could not be fixed and provide some alternatives. This might include advising the user to return the computer to the dealer from which it was purchased, if it is a relatively new unit. If you are unable to resolve the problem, do not be afraid to pass it on to someone with more experience or who specializes in that type of problem.

Lesson Summary

The following points summarize the main elements of this lesson:

- The customer is most important.
- Keep good records.
- Technical support can be provided at three levels: through a designated on-site user, telephone support, or on-site service. Categorizing jobs by these levels will make your work more efficient.

Chapter Summary

The following points summarize the key concepts in this chapter:

Becoming an A+ Technician

- A computer technician must never stop learning.

- Network with others in your field and learn how to get technical support when you need it.

- To be effective, a computer professional requires a hardware toolkit, software toolkit, a technical library, and spare parts.

- Effective troubleshooting requires approaching the problem in an organized and methodical manner. Make a plan and stick to it, and don't forget to document!

Customer Service

- Good recordkeeping is the key to becoming an efficient and effective service provider.

- Recognize the three levels of support—designated on-site user, telephone support, and on-site service—and know how to delegate to the appropriate level.

- Providing outstanding customer service will be the key to your success.

Review

1. Name five ways to stay on top of your profession.

2. How and where can you obtain technical support?

3. What are the four categories of tools used by computer technicians?

4. Which files are essential to include in a software toolkit?

5. What are the five phases of troubleshooting?

6. How important is recordkeeping?

7. What are the three levels of technical support?

8. Why is it important to standardize equipment in large organizations?

9. What four stages should you go through when you receive a service call?

10. Describe some ways of coping with a difficult client or coworker.

APPENDIX A

Questions and Answers

Chapter 1

Page 10

1. Give several examples of early electronic computers.

   Among the early electronic computers were the Atanasoff-Berry Computer (ABC), ENIAC (Electronic Numerical Integrator and Computer), and Colossus.

2. What are the three roles that today's computer service professional needs to assume?

   Today's computer professional needs to be a technician, a scholar, and a diplomat.

Chapter 2

Page 23

1. What is the definition of a bus in a computer?

   A computer bus is a group of electrical conductors (usually wires) running parallel to each other. These conductors can be copper traces on a circuit board or wires in a cable. Usually, they are found in multiples of eight (8, 16, 32, 64, and so on).

2. What is the purpose of the computer bus?

   The purpose of the computer bus is to provide a common path to transmit information, in the form of code, to all parts of the computer.

3. Define the term "digital."

   Digital, as it is used in this book, refers to the binary digits 0 (off) and 1 (on).

4. Describe the difference between serial and parallel communication.

   Serial communication sends each piece of information one bit at a time on one wire, and parallel communication sends as many bits of information at a time as there are parallel wires.

5. What is binary code language?

Binary code language is computer language. The language is called binary because it is based on two states or numbers (0 and 1) represented by a switch condition being set either on or off.

6. How does ASCII use binary code to represent numbers or characters?

Computers use the binary system for communication, based on eight bits (or one byte) of information being transmitted at one time. To support this, a standard code called ASCII (American Standard Code for Information Interchange) was developed as the basis for computer communication. Basic ASCII consisted of 128 binary codes that represented the English alphabet, punctuation, and certain control characters.

7. Define a bit.

A bit is the smallest unit of information that is recognized by a microcomputer. It is similar to a light bulb in that it can exist only in two states—it is either on or it is off.

8. Define a byte.

A byte is a group of eight bits. To represent one character of information requires one byte.

9. Which decimal number does the following binary number represent: 00001001?

This binary number represents the number 9.

10. What do 1s and 0s represent in computer operation?

1s and 0s represent voltage to a computer: the absence of voltage represents a 0 bit, and the presence of voltage represents a 1 bit.

11. Computer buses are usually found in multiples of _____ wires or traces.

Computer buses are usually found in multiples of 8 wires or traces.

Chapter 3

Page 38

1. What are the three stages of computing?

The three stages of computing are input, processing, and output.

2. What is the purpose of the central processing unit (CPU)?

The central processing unit (CPU) is the heart and brain of the computer. This one component or "chip" does all the number crunching and data management.

3. Describe two devices that process information inside a computer.

   The CPU and the chip set process information inside a computer.

4. What is a chip set?

   A chip set is a group of computer chips or ICs (integrated circuits) that, when working in harmony, manage and control the computer system.

5. Give three examples of input devices.

   The mouse, keyboard, microphone, and scanner are examples of input devices.

6. What type of device is a scanner?

   A scanner is an input device.

7. Give three examples of output devices.

   The printer, monitor, and speakers are examples of output devices.

8. What is I/O?

   Many devices can handle both input and output functions. These devices are called I/O devices.

9. Give four examples of I/O devices.

   The floppy disk drive, hard disk drive, modem, and network interface card are examples of I/O devices.

Chapter 4

Page 76

1. What is the language of the computer?

   Binary code is the language of the computer.

2. What is an external data bus?

   The external data bus is the primary bus for handling the flow of data. All devices that process data are connected to the external data bus.

3. Describe an integrated circuit (IC).

   An integrated circuit is an electronic device consisting of many miniature transistors and other circuit elements (resistors and capacitors, for instance).

4. Define a clock cycle.

   The timing for all activities within a computer is set by the computer's clock (but not the one that keeps time). Each pulse of voltage produced by the clock is called a "clock cycle."

5. What are the advantages of a Pentium processor over a 486?

   Many improvements were made to the Pentium chip that made it superior to the 486, including:

   - **Faster speeds.**
   - **A 32-bit address bus and 32-bit registers.**
   - **A 64-bit data path to improve the speed of data transfers.**
   - **A dual pipeline, 32-bit data bus that allows the chip to process two separate lines of code simultaneously.**
   - **A write-back cache of at least 8-KB for data and an 8-B write-through cache.**
   - **Branch prediction—the program cache attempts to anticipate branching within the code.**

6. What is the difference between "SX" and "DX" in a 386 chip?

   The 80386DX was a true 32-bit processor with a 32-bit external data bus, 32-bit registers, and a 32-bit address bus (enabling 4 GB of memory to be accessed). The 80386SX was similar to the DX except that it had a 16-bit external data bus and a 24-bit address bus (it could address only 16 MB of memory).

7. Which computers use the Motorola 68040 chip?

   Some Apple Macintoshes use the Motorola 68040 chip.

8. Define microprocessor.

   A microprocessor is an integrated circuit that contains a complete CPU on a single chip.

9. In computer code language _____ means on and _____ means off.

   In computer code language the number 1 means on and the number 0 means off.

10. Define clock speed.

    Clock speed, a main selling point for today's PC computer, is the system clock rate, measured in megahertz (MHz). One MHz equals one million cycles per second. Clock speed is the number of times per second that a computer can process an instruction.

11. What is the function of the address bus?

    The CPU accesses memory through an additional bus called the address bus. The number of conductors in the address bus determines the maximum amount of memory that can be used by the CPU.

12. Microprocessor chips (CPUs) are manufactured in a variety of sizes and shapes. Name as many different kinds as possible.

    Examples of chip packages are DIPP, PGA, PLCC, and PQFP.

13. Name the basic types of CPU sockets.

The LIF (low-insertion-force) and ZIF (zero-insertion-force) sockets are the two basic CPU sockets. The Pentium II and later Intel processors use Slot 1 sockets.

14. If a customer brought you an old Pentium 60-based computer and asked you to install a new processor, what would your advice be?

Consider upgrading the CPU and motherboard to a newer CPU and matching motherboard.

Chapter 5

Page 91

1. Explain the difference between spikes, surges, and sags.

Spikes and surges are brief, but often catastrophic, increases in the voltage source (very high voltage for a very short time). These can be caused by the power source (the local power company), but most often are caused by lightning strikes. A spike (or transient) is a very short over-voltage condition measured in nanoseconds, while a surge is measured in milliseconds. A sag is a brief decrease of voltage at the source.

2. What are the two types of power-supply connectors to the motherboard?

AT style with two plugs—P8 and P9, and the ATX style with a single connector.

3. What are the two types of power-supply connectors to devices such as drives?

The Molex, a 5-volt connector, is used for hard disk drives, and the mini 3.3-volt is used for floppy disk drives and similar devices.

4. Name two benefits to having a UPS on a system.

The UPS (uninterruptible power supply) buys the user some time in which to save data and properly shut down a system, in the event that a power outage has occurred. And the UPS conditions the line in the event of a spike or surge.

5. Describe the difference between a brownout and a blackout.

A brownout is a decrease in the voltage in the power supply. A blackout is a total power failure.

6. When you purchase a UPS, what is the most important thing to consider?

That the UPS offers enough time to power the computer until all data can be saved and the computer can be properly shut down.

7. Will all surge suppressors provide protection against lightning strikes?

No, surge suppressors offer limited protection, and it decreases with age. Also, nothing can totally protect against a nearby full-force lightning strike.

8. What is the best defense against spikes caused by lightning?

   To protect against spikes from lightning, unplug your computer from the wall outlet.

9. What is the most important thing to remember when connecting a P8 and P9 connector to a motherboard?

   The black (ground) wires must be installed next to each other.

10. Explain the difference between the mini connector and the Molex connector.

    The Molex connector is the most common connector, and is used primarily for devices that need both 12-volt and 5-volt power, such as older floppy disk drives, hard disk drives, and CD-ROM drives.

    The mini connector is used primarily on 3.5-inch floppy drives. Most systems provide a mini connector.

11. Describe the best way to make sure a new power supply matches the one you are replacing.

    Take the old one with you and match its physical size, as well as the power ratings and number of connectors, to the new one.

12. What is the primary use of mini connectors?

    Mini connectors are primarily used for 3.5-inch floppy disk drives.

13. A computer power supply has both 5-volt and 12-volt outputs. The 5-volt output is used to power _____, and the 12-volt output is used to power _____.

    The 5-volt output is used to power devices that manage data only, and the 12-volt output is used to power devices that have moving parts, such as drives and fans.

Chapter 6

Page 117

1. What is the main function of the motherboard?

   The motherboard is the primary card in the computer. It defines the limits for CPU type, speed, memory, and expandability.

2. Name the typical chips found in a chip set.

   A motherboard comes with several chips soldered in place. They constitute the chip set and are designed to work with the CPU. These chips are highly complex and coordinated ICs that help the CPU manage and control the computer's system. Included in the chip set are the clock generator, bus controller, system timer, interrupt controller, DMA controller, CMOS, and keyboard controller.

3. What is EMI?

EMI stands for electromagnetic interference. EMI is the same thing as radio frequency interference (RFI), but EMI is a newer term. EMI is considered to be any radio frequency that is emitted from an electrical or electronic device that is harmful to the surrounding equipment or that interferes with the operation of another electrical or electronic device.

4. What are ROM chips used for?

ROM chips are used extensively to program the operation of computers, but ROM plays a limited role in the PC; it holds the BIOS information used to describe the system configuration and the instructions for performing the POST routine.

5. Name the three types of ROM chip.

The first type of ROM chip is called the core chip and includes hardware that is common, necessary, and unchanging. The second type of ROM chip is hardware that is common, necessary, and changeable; these chips are called updatable chips. The third type of chip includes any chip other than the first two types of chips.

6. Describe what makes the CMOS special.

The CMOS chips are updatable, and that makes them special. They do not store programs like other ROM chips do; they store only data that is used by BIOS for the programs needed to communicate with changeable hardware. The CMOS chip also maintains date-and-time information when the computer is powered off.

7. How can a technician use the POST beep codes?

The purpose of the first POST (power-on self test) is to check the most basic components. Because the video integrity has not been confirmed, any errors that occur in this phase are indicated by a series of beeps. A technician can use the beep codes to interpret any problems that occur before the video is confirmed.

8. What is a device driver?

A device driver is a program that acts as an interface between the operating system and the control circuits that operate the device.

9. What information is contained in the CMOS?

Typically, the CMOS contains at least the following information: floppy and hard disk drive types, CPU and memory size, date and time, and serial- and parallel-port information.

10. Define the POST and describe its function.

Every time a computer is turned on or reset, the entire system is reset. From this on or reset state, it begins to carry out software instructions from its BIOS program. The first set of instructions it initiates is a special program (stored on a ROM chip) called the power-on self test (POST). The POST sends out standardized commands that check every device (in more technical terms, it runs an internal self-diagnostic routine).

Chapter 7

Page 144

1. What is hexadecimal shorthand used for?

Hexadecimal shorthand (hex, for short) is a numbering system used by designers and programmers to simplify the representation of numbers and notations. Known as "base-16 mathematics," it is a complete numbering system based on 16 instead of 10. Just as in the base-10 system, you can add, subtract, or do trigonometry with hex.

2. Define the following terms: conventional memory, expanded memory, extended memory, HMA, shadow RAM.

Conventional memory is the first 640 KB of memory in a computer. The first 1 MB of memory was divided into two sections: 384 KB of RAM (designated upper memory) for running the computer (BIOS, video RAM, and ROM), and 640 KB for applications (designated).

Expanded memory is memory that conforms to the EMS specification, developed by Lotus, Intel, and Microsoft. It requires a special device driver. EMS is accessed through 64-KB blocks of the upper memory.

Extended memory is any memory beyond the first 1 MB.

HMA is the first 64 KB of extended memory on machines with 80286 or higher processors.

Shadow RAM rewrites (or shadows) the contents of the ROM BIOS and/or video BIOS into extended RAM memory (between the 640-KB boundary and 1 MB). This allows systems to operate faster when application software calls for any BIOS routines.

3. Describe the difference between ROM and RAM.

ROM is read-only memory and cannot be changed. It is usually used for BIOS or other data that cannot be lost if the power is off.

RAM is random access memory and is constantly changing. It is used as the main working memory for a computer. RAM memory is lost if the power is turned off.

4. How many 30-pin SIMM boards are required for one bank of memory on a computer with a 486 processor?

Because a 486 computer has a 32-bit external data bus, it requires four 30-pin SIMMs per bank. Remember, a 30-pin SIMM is only one byte (8-bits) wide; therefore, you need to divide the width of the bus by the width of the SIMM—that is, 32 (the width of data bus) divided by 8 (the number of bits per SIMM module).

5. What is the difference between "write-through" and "write-back" cache?

Some caches immediately send all data directly to RAM, even if it means hitting a wait state. This is called write-through cache. Some caches store the data for a time and send it to RAM later. This is called a write-back cache.

6. What is DRAM?

DRAM (dynamic random access memory) is volatile memory that works only when the computer has power. This is the "scratch pad" that the CPU uses to manipulate data.

7. Define access speed.

The time required to complete a memory read or to write actions is known as the access speed of the memory chip. This time is usually very small and is measured in nanoseconds (one-billionth of a second—abbreviated as ns). The faster the chip, the smaller the access-speed number.

8. Describe the major difference between SIPPs and SIMMs.

A SIPP (single inline pin package) is a printed circuit board with individual DRAM chips mounted on it. SIMMs (single inline memory modules) are the new generation of memory chips. They are similar to SIPPs, with one exception—SIMMs have no pins, as such. 30-pin SIMMs have 30 contacts along the edge.

9. Define cache memory.

To cache means to set something aside, or to store nearby, for anticipated use. Mass storage (disk drives) is much slower than RAM, and RAM is much slower than the CPU. Caching increases the speed of the system by creating special storage areas in high-speed memory.

10. One of the differences between DRAM and SRAM is that SRAM does not have to be refreshed. What does this mean, and how does it affect the cost of each type of chip?

Refreshing means that the information must be updated constantly or it will be lost. SRAM does not require that extra step that can slow things down (nothing can access the memory during a refresh). Because SRAM is faster, the circuitry required is more expensive.

Chapter 8

Page 181

1. What is the purpose of an IDE drive?

   The IDE (Integrated Drive Electronics) drive was introduced in the early 1990s. The IDE quickly became the standard for general-purpose computers. The purpose of the IDE specification was to increase data throughput, support non-hard disk drive storage devices, increase the capacity of hard drives beyond the 528-MB barrier, and to allow connection of up to four devices instead of only two.

2. How many drives can be connected to a single IDE connector?

   Two drives can be connected to one IDE connector.

3. What is the best method of determining the number of drives available on a computer?

   The best method of determining the number of drives available on a computer is to run the CMOS setup program. Originally, the CMOS would only allow for two drives. Later versions allow up to four drives.

4. What three things should be checked when a floppy disk drive fails?

   Three things to check when a floppy disk drive fails are the floppy disk itself (not the drive), the CMOS setup, and the drive controller/power supply cables.

5. What is the best way to ensure long life from a floppy disk drive?

   To ensure long life from a floppy disk drive, keep it clean.

6. When you purchase a new floppy disk drive controller, what can you expect to receive with it?

   Floppy disk drive controller cards also include some or all of the following: hard disk drive controllers, serial ports, parallel ports, and game ports. If the new card contains any ports that duplicate ports already present elsewhere on the computer (on the motherboard, for instance), a potential conflict exists.

7. Other than physical size, what are the only differences between a 5.25-inch floppy disk drive and a 3.5-inch floppy disk drive?

   The only difference between a 5.25-inch and a 3.5-inch drive (other than physical size) is that a 5.25-inch drive has a slot connector and a 3.5-inch drive has a pin connector for engaging and spinning the disk.

8. What type of cable is used to connect a floppy disk drive to the external data bus?

   All floppy disk drives are connected to the motherboard (external data bus) by a 34-conductor ribbon cable. This cable has a seven-wire twist in lines 10 through 16. This ensures that when two floppy disk drives are attached, the drive-select and motor-enable signals on those wires can be inverted to "select" which drive becomes the active target. The other wires carry data and ground signals.

9. What is the proper way to install a floppy disk drive cable?

   The connector end of the cable, with the twist, always goes toward the drives.

10. To which pin must the Number 1 wire of the floppy disk drive control cable be connected?

    This red (or sometimes blue) wire is connected to the number 1 pin on the drive's controller connector. (The number 1 pin is usually located next to the power connection.)

11. You've received the following error message: "General failure reading Drive A:". What is the most likely problem?

    The CMOS settings for the A drive are the most likely cause. Always double-check the CMOS if you are experiencing a recurrent drive failure. Checking is quick, easy, and can save you time.

12. Are floppy disk controllers sensitive to ESD?

    Yes, floppy disk controllers are sensitive to ESD (electrostatic discharge).

13. You receive an error message that ends with "Abort, Retry, Fail?" What is the most likely cause of the error?

    This error message indicates a failure to read the drive. These errors are the easiest to fix and can usually be attributed to a bad sector on the drive.

14. Why is a voice coil actuator arm better than a stepper motor actuator arm?

    A voice coil actuator arm has several advantages over the stepper motor actuator arm. The lack of mechanical interface between the actuator arm and the motor provides consistent positioning accuracy. When the drive is shut down (the power is removed from the coil), the actuator arm (which is spring-loaded) moves back to its initial position, thus eliminating the need to park the head. In a sense, these drives are self-parking.

15. Define hard disk drive geometry.

    Hard disk drives are composed of one or more disks, or platters, on which data is stored. The geometry of a hard drive is the organization of data on these platters. Geometry determines the maximum storage capacity of the drive.

16. What is the best way to determine the geometry of an unknown drive?

The geometry or type of many hard disk drives is labeled directly on the hard drive itself.

17. Describe HDI.

Head to Disk Interference (HDI) is another term for head crash.

18. The BIOS limits the number of heads to a maximum of _____.

The maximum number of heads is 16.

19. The BIOS limits the number of cylinders to a maximum of _____.

The maximum number of cylinders is 1024.

20. How many bytes of data does a sector hold?

One sector holds 512 bytes of data.

21. What is the maximum number of sectors per track?

The maximum number of sectors per track is 63.

22. What does CHS stand for?

CHS stands for cylinders, heads and tracks per sector.

23. What type of drive is standard on today's personal computer?

The IDE is the standard drive on today's personal computers.

24. Describe the characteristics of the different hard disk drive types.

The first hard disk drives for personal computers used the ST-506/412 interface. The ST-506/412 was the only hard drive available for the IBM computer and the first to be supported by the ROM BIOS chip on the motherboard.

The Enhanced Small Device Interface (ESDI) was introduced in 1983 by the Maxtor Corporation. Beginning with this drive, most controller functions were incorporated directly onto the hard disk drive itself.

The Small Computer System Interface (SCSI) has been around since the mid 1970s in one or another form. Apple adopted the SCSI as its expansion bus standard. The SCSI bus functions as a communications pathway between the computer system bus and the SCSI device controller.

25. What is a partition? What are the two types of partition?

Partitions are logical divisions of a hard disk drive. A computer might have only one physical hard drive (called hard drive 0), but it can have anywhere from one to 24 logical drives, called C to Z.

There are two types of partitions: primary and extended.

26. Define a cluster.

A cluster is a combined set of contiguous sectors which the FAT treats as a single unit. The number of sectors in each cluster is determined by the size of the partition. There can never be more than 64,000 clusters.

27. What is the FAT and how does it work?

The FAT (file allocation table) is simply an index that keeps track of which part of the file is stored in which sector. Each partition (or floppy disk) has two FATs stored near the beginning of the partition. These FATs are called FAT 1 and FAT 2. They are identical. Each FAT can be looked at as a two-column spreadsheet.

28. What is fragmentation?

Fragmentation is the scattering of parts of the same disk file over different areas of the disk. When files are scattered all over a drive in noncontiguous clusters they are said to be fragmented.

29. How can you minimize the impact of a hard disk drive failure?

To minimize the impact of a hard disk drive failure, perform comprehensive, frequent backups, and save a copy of the boot sector and partition table.

30. What is the function of ScanDisk?

ScanDisk performs a battery of tests on a hard disk. These include looking for invalid filenames, invalid file dates and times, bad sectors, and invalid compression structures. In the file system, ScanDisk looks for lost clusters, invalid clusters, and cross-linked clusters.

Chapter 9

Page 218

1. Name four methods of overcoming the 528-MB hard disk limitation.

The first method utilizes Logical Block Addressing (LBA mode)—a means of addressing the physical sectors on a hard disk drive in a linear fashion.

The second method utilizes Enhanced CHS—a standard that competes with LBA. This standard allows drives to be manufactured a little faster and more easily than LBA.

The third method utilizes Fast ATA, which uses PIO mode 3, and Fast ATA-2, which uses PIO mode 4.

The fourth method utilizes logical cylinders, heads, and sectors (L-CHS)— a value used by the operating system (for instance, MS-DOS, Windows 95 and Windows 98, OS/2) to determine the size of the hard drive.

2. How do multiple block reads speed up a computer?

The ATA standard requires each drive to activate its IRQ every time it sends one sector of data. This process helps to verify good data transmission, but it slows down the computer. Multiple block reads speed up the process by reading several sectors of data at a time.

3. How many devices can be installed on a SCSI chain?

Eight devices can be installed on a single SCSI-1 chain. However, one of those devices must be reserved for the SCSI controller. SCSI-2 and later host adapters allow up to 16, with one reserved for the host adapter. Some SCSI cards offer multichannel support and can handle even more.

4. What is the effect of improper termination on a SCSI chain or device?

Improper termination can cause a failure to boot, the "disappearance" of a device from the SCSI chain, erratic behavior, and—in extreme cases—can even destroy a SCSI device.

5. What is the BIOS protocol for SCSI devices?

The BIOS protocol for SCSI devices is the Advanced SCSI Programmers Interface (ASPI).

6. Sometimes the SCSI device driver conflicts with other drivers. What steps need to be taken to resolve the problem?

Often, the only way to tell if there will be a conflict is to try the driver and see what happens. Remember to document every step you take so that you can undo any changes. Load only the device drivers for the SCSI devices.

If the problem occurs, use the F8 key to determine which driver conflicts. (Press F8 when starting MS-DOS or Windows 95 or Windows 98—this will allow step-by-step confirmation of the startup process.)

If the device driver is an executable file, try running it with the "/?" option. This will usually show a variety of command-line switches for the device driver (for example, "mouse.exe /?").

7. Describe at least three advantages of using a CD-ROM drive.

Advantages of using CD-ROM drives include: large storage capacity, sturdiness, portability, and the fact that data on the disk cannot be changed.

8. What are the four steps required to install a CD-ROM drive?

1. Install the drive controller card, if needed.

2. Install the CD-ROM drive in the computer case.

3. Attach the data and power cables.

4. Install the necessary drivers and set up the CD-ROM drive.

9. Is a 16X CD-ROM drive 16 times faster than a 1X?

No, it is not. The 16X CD-ROM data transfer rate will be 16 times faster, but the mean access time is not 16 times faster.

10. How would you determine which type of CD-ROM drive to install in a computer?

You first have to determine whether or not there is room inside the case and if there are any available IDE controller connections. If not, then consider an external drive. If you want a SCSI controller, you will have to make sure there is an available slot in the expansion bus.

11. Why would you use the MSCDEX.EXE real-mode driver with Windows 95?

Windows 95 and Windows 98 use virtual drivers and do not need the MSCDEX.EXE real-mode driver. However, if you intend to use a CD-ROM drive in the MS-DOS mode (from a bootable disk), the real-mode drivers will have to be installed and added to the CONFIG.SYS and AUTOEXEC.BAT files of the boot disk.

12. Instead of using magnetic energy for storing data, a CD-ROM uses _____ technology.

A CD-ROM uses laser technology.

13. Name some possible controller card combinations.

There are several ways to combine controller cards: use the secondary IDE controller on the motherboard; use a new controller card (supplied with the CD-ROM); use an existing SCSI chain; use a SCSI host adapter, create a new SCSI chain; or use an existing sound card with a CD connection.

14. What software is required for a CD-ROM drive installation?

The driver that came with the CD-ROM and the Microsoft MSCDEX.EXE program, are required for a CD-ROM drive installation.

Chapter 10

Page 244

1. Why does a computer need an expansion bus?

Expansion slots on the motherboard are standardized connections that allow the installation of any device not soldered to the motherboard. By providing this connection to the expansion bus, computers can be customized to meet the requirements of the user.

2. Name the available expansion buses.

The available expansion buses are: ISA, MCA, EISA, VESA, AGP, and PCI.

3. What happens if two non-PCI devices use the same I/O address?

The computer will lock up.

4. How many IRQs are available on most PCs?

There are 15 IRQs available, although some of them are permanently assigned.

5. Under what conditions would a second modem—installed and assigned to COM3—not work?

If the first modem had been using COM1, the failure would be the result of an IRQ conflict. Devices assigned to COM1 and COM3 both make use of IRQ4. If the first modem has already been assigned to COM1, a conflict will occur when both modems make use of IRQ4.

One solution is to assign COM3 an available interrupt such as IRQ10.

6. Identify the two divisions of the external data bus and describe the purpose of each.

The two divisions of the external data bus are the system bus and the expansion bus. The system bus supports the CPU, RAM, and other motherboard components. The system bus runs at speeds that support the CPU.

The expansion bus supports any add-on devices via the expansion slots and runs at a steady 7.16 MHz.

7. What is the standard that governs computer buses?

IBM established the ISA industry standard, thus generating the market for clones. The term ISA (Industry Standard Architecture) did not become official until 1990.

8. What is the difference between ISA and EISA cards?

EISA uses a double slot connector that is compatible with ISA devices. Physically, the EISA bus is the same size and looks similar to the ISA. However, they differ in the number of contacts and the depth of the slot. On close inspection, you can see a double set of contacts (one above the other).

9. Why was VESA created?

The Video Electronics Standards Association (VESA) is a trade association of display-adapter vendors. It was created to address the need for faster video to support the increased demands of new graphical operating systems like Windows and OS/2. These environments called for far better graphics and color management than the older character-based operating systems like CP/M.

10. What is bus mastering?

Bus mastering allows a device to gain control of the bus to perform special tasks without processor intervention.

11. Describe ways in which the PCI bus is better than previous technologies.

The PCI (Peripheral Component Interconnect) bus was designed by Intel to be a stronger, more flexible alternative to the current expansion buses while maintaining backward compatibility. It is independent of the CPU, so it is better than the VL bus and is not limited to use in 486-based computers.

12. How does the CPU use I/O addresses?

The CPU uses the unique address (actually a block of addresses) to communicate with a device in the system using the bus.

13. What is the I/O port address of COM2?

The I/O port address of COM2 is 2F8.

14. What are the functions of IRQs?

An IRQ is used by a device to send a request to the CPU for permission to transmit data so that all devices do not attempt to communicate at the same time.

15. List as many of the standard IRQ assignments as you can.

Here is a list of IRQ assignments. How many did you get?

IRQ	Function
IRQ 0	System timer
IRQ 1	Keyboard controller
IRQ 2/9	Available
IRQ 3	COM2, COM4
IRQ 4	COM1, COM3
IRQ 5	LPT2
IRQ 6	Floppy disk controller
IRQ 7	LPT1
IRQ 8	Real-time clock
IRQ 10	Available
IRQ 11	SCSI/available
IRQ 12	Available
IRQ 13	Math coprocessor
IRQ 14	Primary IDE controller
IRQ 15	Secondary IDE controller

16. What is the function of the DMA chip?

The only function of the DMA chip (8237) is to move data. It handles all data passing from peripherals to RAM and vice versa.

17. Why is it important not to assign an IRQ to more than one device?

If two devices have the same IRQ and try to communicate with the CPU at the same time, the resulting conflict will lock up the computer.

18. What is the difference between COM ports and LPT ports?

COM ports are for serial communications, and LPT ports are parallel ports normally used with printers.

19. Why is it important to document IRQs, DMAs, and I/O addresses?

Because these three things cause more conflicts than perhaps anything else in a computer, you will be able to reduce installation times and correct conflicts.

Chapter 11

Page 267

1. Describe the three elements that make up one dot of color.

One dot of color is made up of three smaller dots: one red, one green, and one blue.

2. What is the advantage of interlacing? Is it worth doing?

Interlacing is a way of arranging a video display so that the CRT sweeps all the odd-numbered rows and then all the even-numbered rows (or vice versa). The intention of interlacing is to reduce the flicker on the screen by increasing the refresh rate (in other words, scanning the screen twice as often). An interlaced monitor can be well-suited for stand-alone servers or computers that run for long hours unattended. It might be a good choice when there will be little interaction by an operator or when cost is a primary factor. Interlacing should be avoided for normal use, because it can lead to eyestrain and headaches.

3. Should a monitor be turned on and off, or left on all day?

The most basic form of power management is to turn off the monitor, using the power switch. At the same time, the CRT is the most expensive component of a monitor and can be damaged when it is turned on and off too frequently. Because these two concepts contradict each other, there is no single correct answer. You will have to make a decision based on the customer's individual circumstances.

4. What is the "standard" type of video card used with today's computers?

Some variation of the SVGA video card is used on most computers sold today.

5. What is the formula for calculating the required memory for a monitor/video card combination?

The formula is: video memory requirement = horizontal pixels x vertical pixels x color depth.

6. What does CRT stand for?

   It stands for cathode-ray tube.

7. What are HRR and VRR?

   The number of times per second an electron beam sweeps is called the refresh rate. The speed at which the electron beam completes one horizontal trace is known as the horizontal refresh rate (HRR). The time taken by the monitor to complete all horizontal traces and return to the top of the screen is the vertical refresh rate (VRR).

8. Define resolution.

   Resolution is the measurement of image detail produced by a monitor or printer. Monitor resolution is expressed as the number of horizontal pixels by the number of vertical pixels.

9. What is bandwidth?

   With computer monitors, bandwidth is the maximum number of times per second an electron gun can be turned on and off. Bandwidth is measured in megahertz (MHz—millions of cycles per second). A typical value for a high-resolution, 17-inch color monitor would be around 100 MHz.

10. Why is it dangerous to open the monitor's cover?

    The CRT part of a monitor acts like a large capacitor and is capable of holding a very large charge (30,000 volts).

11. Name four common sources of video problems.

    The video-signal cable, video controller card, video-driver software, and the monitor are the four primary sources of video problems.

12. Explain one similarity and one difference between VRAM and WRAM.

    Both offer dual port reads and writes, but WRAM is faster and less expensive.

13. What is a raster?

    Video data is displayed on the monitor by sweeping the electron gun(s) in a series of horizontal lines or traces across the display. The line created by each sweep is called a raster. The number of rasters is used to describe the vertical resolution of a monitor.

14. What type of connector is used for an SVGA monitor?

    The PGA, VGA, and SVGA monitor each use a 15-pin, three-row, female DB connector.

Chapter 12

Page 311

1. Name three types of printers and describe their advantages and disadvantages.

   Impact printers produce an image on paper by physically striking an inked ribbon against the surface of the paper. The advantages of impact printers are that they tend to be inexpensive and print at a relatively high speed. Impact printers were very popular in the late 1980s. Some disadvantages of impact printers are lower print quality and noise.

   Ink-jet printers have replaced dot-matrix printers at the low end of the market. Many computer manufacturers and large computer stores offer ink-jet printers along with computers as part of package deals. They produce good-quality printing and are relatively fast, while requiring little maintenance beyond replacing the cartridge. What makes them attractive is their ability to easily produce color, as well as standard black-and-white images. High-quality color ink-jet printers are available; however, high-quality color printing comes at a cost. It requires a good printer and special paper that will prevent "wicking" of the ink, which causes a fuzzy appearance.

   Laser printers have become one of the most popular types of printer for home use and are a must for most office environments. They produce high-quality, high-speed printing. Early laser printers were notorious for generating lots of heat and consuming lots of power.

2. The dot-matrix printer is an _____ printer. Name at least one advantage of this type of printer. Name at least one disadvantage.

   A dot-matrix printer is an impact printer. Its main advantages are its ability to print forms (multiple pages) and its high reliability and low operating cost. Its disadvantages are its noise, slow speed, and generally low-quality (by today's standards) images.

3. What are the six steps of laser printing?

   1. Clean the drum.
   2. Charge the drum.
   3. Write the image.
   4. Transfer the toner.
   5. Transfer the image.
   6. Fuse the image.

4. Which components are usually included in a laser printer's replaceable toner cartridge? Why?

   Many of a laser printer's critical components, including those that experience the most wear and tear, are incorporated into the toner cartridge. The most important is the photosensitive drum. By incorporating these components into the toner cartridge, chances of failure are reduced because the primary-wear components are constantly replaced.

5. What causes black spots to appear on a document that has been printed on a laser printer? How can this problem be resolved?

   If residual particles remain on the drum, they will appear as random black spots and streaks on the next printed page. The drum will need to be cleaned to clear this problem.

6. What is the IEEE 1284 standard?

   There is a vast array of printers available and in order to ensure that you are obtaining optimum performance, the printer, the printer driver, and the software using the printer must be configured for the same mode. The IEEE 1284 standard establishes the standards to ensure printer compatibility.

7. What kinds of signals do telephones use? What kinds of signals do computers use?

   Computers transfer data by means of parallel wires or buses. Computer modems use serial communication. Telephone systems use only two wires.

8. What is the purpose of a modem?

   A modem is a peripheral device that enables computers to communicate with each other over conventional telephone lines and through wireless communication.

9. Which AT command is used to take the phone off the hook?

   The ATH command takes the phone off the hook.

10. What is the difference between baud and bps?

    Baud is limited to 2400 cycles per second. Baud rate is limited by the capability of copper wires to transmit signals. Bps represents the actual number of data bits that can be transmitted per second.

11. What is the name of the chip that converts data from parallel to serial?

    This chip is called a UART (universal asynchronous receiver-transmitter).

12. Name three transfer protocols.

    Three protocols for synchronous communication are Xmodem, Ymodem, and Zmodem.

13. What is Zmodem? What are its advantages over other protocols?

    Zmodem shares all the features found in Xmodem and Ymodem protocols. It also adds a few new features, including crash recovery, automatic downloading, and a streaming file-transfer method. It is the protocol of choice for most telecommunication operations.

14. Define handshaking.

    Handshaking is the negotiation of the rules (protocols) of communication between two modems.

15. What are AT commands and how can a computer technician use them?

   AT commands are text commands that can be used to provide instructions to a modem. They are all preceded by the letters "AT." These commands are very useful as diagnostic tools for today's computer professional. To use these commands, make sure the communication software is loaded and the computer is in terminal mode. Unless the modem is set up to autoconnect (online mode), it will be in command mode and ready to accept AT commands.

16. Explain the difference between half-duplex and full-duplex. What makes them different? Where or when is each used?

   In half-duplex, the RJ-11 plug has only two wires; therefore, only one signal can be sent or received at a time. Half-duplex is used to send messages in only one direction, like a fire alarm signal.

   In full-duplex, the RJ-12 plug uses four wires (for two phones). It is the same size as the RJ-11 but with two additional wires. This enables users to send and receive data simultaneously.

17. What is the difference between synchronous and asynchronous communication?

   Asynchronous communication is data transmission in which the length of time between characters may vary. Timing is dependent on the actual time it takes for the transfer to occur. This differs from synchronous communication, which is timed rigidly by an external clock.

   Synchronous communication is a form of communication in which blocks of data are sent at strictly timed intervals. Because of this timing, no start or stop bits are required. Synchronous communication is more reliable than asynchronous and, therefore, more widely used.

18. Why are fax standards different from modem standards?

   Faxes involve a different technology from that used by modems and are developed by different standards committees and operate on technology defined in a different standard than modems. A fax can be a stand-alone machine or incorporated into a computer. Computer faxes allow you to use the same format as picture reproduction (they paint a page of black-and-white pixels).

19. Describe a null-modem cable.

   Null-modem cables are used to directly connect two computers together without the need for a modem. The transmit and receive wires in the cable (wires 2 and 3) are switched to make the computers "think" they are using modems.

20. In addition to the cost of the printer, what other costs should be considered when purchasing a printer?

You should always consider the total operating cost, including the cost of paper and ink or toner.

21. What does bps stand for?

Bps stands for bits per second.

22. Identify as many cables and connectors as you can.

Here is a table of connectors. How many did you get right?

Name	Uses
DB-9	Serial ports—external modem, mouse, printer.
DB-25	Parallel Port—printer, scanner, removable drive.
RJ-11	Standard telephone connector—2 wires.
RJ-12	Standard telephone connector—4 wires—used with dual phone connections.
RJ-45	Network connector.
PS/2 (mini-DIN)	Mouse, scanners.
Centronics	Printers.
USB	Universal serial bus—Technology that allows multiple peripherals to be attached to one cable.

23. What type of connector is used for a parallel port on the computer?

A 25-pin female connector is used for a parallel port on the computer.

24. What type of connector is used for a parallel port on the printer?

The most common parallel connector on the printer is the Centronics connector.

Chapter 13

Page 339

1. What is Ohm's Law?

Ohm's Law states that the current (electrons) flowing through a conductor, or resistance, is in linear proportion to the applied potential difference (volts).

2. What is the formula for Ohm's Law?

The formula for Ohm's Law is voltage is equal to the current multiplied by the resistance ($V = I\ R$).

3. What is the difference between AC and DC?

AC is alternating current in which the voltage varies from positive to negative. DC is direct current in which the voltage stays the same all the time.

4. What instrument is used to measure the various components of electricity?

The instrument used to measure the various components of electricity is VOM—Volt-Ohm Meter (sometimes referred to as DVOM or Digital Volt-Ohm Meter).

5. How do you test for continuity?

Continuity is a term used to indicate whether or not there is a connection from one point to another. It is used to determine the presence of breaks in wires and electrical circuits. If no continuity setting is available, use the resistance setting. If the multimeter measures infinite resistance, then there is no continuity, indicating a break in the circuit. If the multimeter shows little or no resistance, then there is continuity and the circuit is complete.

6. What is "AC Ripple?" How do you test for it?

A power supply converts AC to DC voltage. When working properly, a pure DC signal will be produced. Sometimes, however, as the power supply ages, its ability to produce pure DC falters. A power supply uses capacitors to filter or smooth the voltage after being converted from AC to DC. These capacitors are second only to fuses as the part of a power supply most likely to fail. When a capacitor begins to fail, it allows more and more AC voltage to pass through. This AC voltage is superimposed on top of the DC voltage and is called noise or ripple.

To test for ripple, set a meter to read AC. Then connect a .1μfd capacitor to the red lead. With the power turned on, measure the DC voltage to ground. Any ripple present will be displayed as an AC voltage.

7. Describe ESD and how to prevent it.

Just as high voltages generated by electrical and electronic equipment can do severe damage to humans, high voltages generated by humans can do damage to computers. We have all seen what a short circuit can do to electrical equipment (smoke, fire, and destruction). Electrostatic discharge (ESD) is an unseen (and sometimes unheard) force, created by humans, that is just as deadly to a computer.

The key to ESD prevention is to keep all electronic components and yourself at the same electrical potential. This usually means ground potential or zero volts. Maintain a habit of "grounding" yourself to the computer chassis whenever you attempt a repair. An ESD wrist strap is the tool most commonly used by technicians to prevent ESD.

8. What is a latent failure? What makes it especially troublesome?

This type of ESD problem occurs when a transistor junction becomes weakened. A transistor in this condition may pass all quality tests but, over time, will generate poorer system performance and eventually fail completely.

9. What is a catastrophic failure?

Catastrophic failure is the destruction of a part because of the heat generated during the mishandling and misapplication of a power source, cable, or test instrument.

10. When working with a computer, when is it acceptable to use an AC power supply that is not grounded?

It is never acceptable to use an AC power supply that is not grounded.

Chapter 14

Page 366

1. Describe a basic sample toolkit for the computer professional.

The basic toolkit should include screwdrivers, a Torx driver, tweezers, needlenose pliers, chip removers, a tube for small parts, a can of compressed air, ESD tools, a multimeter, a flashlight, a nut driver set, and curved hemostats.

2. What is a Torx driver used for?

A Torx driver is used to remove the star-shaped screws found on some proprietary computers. (Sizes T-10 and T-15 should meet the needs of most computers.)

3. How many bootable floppy disks are needed for a computer professional's tool kit?

One bootable floppy disk is needed for every operating system that you will be working on.

4. You are only going to check the memory chips. Do you need to follow ESD (electrostatic discharge) safety practices?

Always use ESD safety practices.

5. SIMMs are available in two physical configurations. What are they?

SIMMs (single inline memory modules) are provided in two basic (physical) formats: a 30-pin and a 72-pin chip.

6. You have an extra 16 MB of RAM on a single 30-pin SIMM, and a friend has a computer and needs more memory. What do you need to check in order to determine if this memory module can be used on your friend's computer?

You first have to determine whether there are any 30-pin slots available, then check the bus width to determine how many you will need to complete the job. For example, if the machine is a 486, you will need four modules to complete the job.

7. What is parity? Can parity chips be mixed with nonparity chips?

   Parity is used to check the reliability of data. Parity requires one additional bit (chip). Memory can be purchased with or without parity. Parity adds about 10 percent more to the cost of memory. You cannot mix parity and nonparity chips.

8. Can L1 cache memory be upgraded?

   L1 cache is part of the CPU and cannot be upgraded.

9. Your client wants to install an internal modem. How would you determine whether this internal modem could be installed on your client's machine?

   First, the machine must have an available expansion slot. Second, there must be available resources such as IRQ and an address.

10. A friend just got a bargain on a new Plug and Play sound card and wants to install it on her 486SX computer. Will it work?

    It will probably work, but will have to be manually configured either through software or jumpers.

11. How do you determine whether to upgrade the CPU or install another motherboard?

    First, you must evaluate the existing motherboard to see if it can be upgraded and then determine the highest CPU that you can use. Second, you must determine the needs of the customer, particularly whether the CPU upgrade will meet the customer's operational requirements.

12. What is the advantage of Plug and Play?

    Plug and Play, the latest technology available for installing expansion cards, is an independent set of specifications developed by a group of hardware and software companies. This specification allows the user to make configuration changes with minimal adjustments. The user simply installs the card, turns on the computer, and uses the device.

13. What are the four requirements that must be addressed before installing a new drive in a computer?

    1. **Will the drive physically fit inside the computer?**

    2. **Will the computer's BIOS and operating system support the size (storage capacity) of the drive?**

    3. **Will the drive controller support the new drive?**

    4. **Are there sufficient cables (data and power) to install the drive?**

Chapter 15

Page 410

1. What does DOS stand for?

   DOS stands for disk operating system.

2. What was DOS created to do?

   The original version of DOS was designed to support the operation of floppy disk drives.

3. Which version of MS-DOS is bundled with Windows 95?

   The version bundled with Windows 95 is referred to as MS-DOS 7.0.

4. Describe the core operating systems within MS-DOS.

   - **IO.SYS: This system is the interface between the hardware and the operating system code.**

   - **MSDOS.SYS: This system is the main operating-system code.**

   - **COMMAND.COM: This system is the interface between the user and the operating-system code.**

5. What are the two MS-DOS startup files?

   - **CONFIG.SYS: This startup file loads extra hardware and device drivers not built into the IO.SYS.**

   - **AUTOEXEC.BAT: This startup file loads terminate-and-stay-resident (TSR) programs selected by the user and sets up the environment variables such as TEMP and PATH.**

6. Which MS-DOS command is used to determine the amount of free space left on a disk?

   From the command prompt in the root directory, the MS-DOS command DIR or directory will return the list of all the files on the drive and indicate the amount of free space available.

7. Describe the difference between real mode and protected mode.

   MS-DOS operates with a 1-MB memory limit. This is called real mode. Windows broke out of the MS-DOS 1-MB barrier by engaging 286-level protected mode (Windows 2.0). Protected mode Windows could address up to 16 MB of RAM. Although MS-DOS programs could run only in the first megabyte of memory, specialized programs were written that would run in (and only in) the extended memory controlled by Windows. Protected mode refers to using protected memory.

8. Windows provides a GUI for the user. What does "GUI" stand for? What is its advantage over the older MS-DOS system?

   GUI stands for graphical user interface. MS-DOS used a text or command-line interface. With MS-DOS, you had to memorize and type commands. With a GUI interface, you work in a graphical environment and use a mouse with icons or menus to simplify tasks.

9. Describe the three kinds of fonts used in a Windows environment.

Windows provides three types of font files. Each font contains a complete character set for a particular typeface.

- **Vector fonts are designed as a set of lines drawn between two points. Each character represents a mathematical model that can be scaled to virtually any size.**

- **Raster fonts are bitmap fonts made up of a set of dots. Each character or set of dots is "painted" on the screen or printer. Because each character requires separate data for each size, only limited scaling is possible.**

- **TrueType fonts are made from an "outline" of each character. When printing (on the screen or on a printer), these outlines are filled in.**

10. Name five settings that can be changed from the Windows Control Panel.

Many settings can be changed from the Windows Control Panel.

Some of these are Screen colors, Other desktop options (screen savers, wallpaper, and so on), Fonts, Printer, Keyboard, Mouse, International settings, COM port settings, Network settings, Date and Time, Sounds (used by the system), Drivers for hardware, and Multitasking and virtual-memory settings.

11. Which wildcard character can be used to replace a single character in a search string?

The single character wildcard is the question mark (?).

Chapter 16

Page 467

1. Name three ways that Windows 95 differs from Windows 3.x.

Installing devices, managing memory, optimizing the system, and trouble-shooting are handled differently in Windows 95 than in Windows 3.x.

2. What is Plug and Play? What is required for a component to be Plug and Play-compliant?

The ultimate goal of any computer user is to be able to simply plug any device into a computer, turn it on, and have it work. This is the concept upon which Plug and Play is founded. A well-designed Plug and Play system eliminates the need for jumpers, switches, and installation software.

The three requirements of Plug and Play are: a Plug and Play BIOS, a Plug and Play device, and a Plug and Play operating system (such as Windows 95).

3. Does Windows 95 still require MS-DOS?

Windows 95 does not require MS-DOS. MS-DOS is provided mostly for backward compatibility.

4. Which version of MS-DOS comes with Windows 95?

   DOS 7.0 comes with Windows 95.

5. Is CONFIG.SYS required to install GUI drivers?

   CONFIG.SYS is not required to install GUI drivers; however, it is required if you want to use any real-mode drives.

6. Why would you want to set the swap-file size in Windows 95?

   The VCACHE that comes with Windows 95 is quite different from Windows 3.x in that the cache is "sized dynamically." As Windows needs more RAM, it takes away from the cache and vice versa. Unfortunately, the cache-sizing algorithms are very slow, especially when used with the swap file; therefore, the swap file needs to be limited in size.

7. What is the main difference between Windows 3.x and Windows 95?

   Windows 3.x is basically an operating environment created to run on top of MS-DOS; its purpose is to provide a GUI and other features in order to run programs and manage files easily. Windows 95 is a complete operating system that includes an improved GUI as well as other useful features.

8. Why can't older versions of disk utilities be used with Windows 95?

   Older disk utilities do not understand many of the improvements of Windows 95, such as long filenames.

9. After turning on the power to the computer, what is the first step in the boot-up process?

   The first step in the boot-up process is to run the POST.

10. In which directory do you find the external MS-DOS commands?

    MS-DOS external commands reside in the windows\command directory of the bootable drive.

11. What is FDISK used for?

    FDISK for Windows 95 is no different than for Windows 3.x; it is used to partition hard drives. Windows 95 OSR2 and Windows 98 do give the option of using FAT32 file system instead of FAT16.

12. Define virtual memory.

    Virtual memory uses disk space to simulate RAM. This hard disk drive space is called the swap file.

13. The Registry is composed of two binary files. Name them.

    The two binary files that hold the Registry database are called SYSTEM.DAT and USER.DAT.

14. What is the difference between an MS-DOS session and MS-DOS mode?

An MS-DOS session runs inside a window in the GUI. Windows 95 has the new MS-DOS mode that allows creation of custom CONFIG.SYS and AUTOEXEC.BAT files for tough MS-DOS applications. MS-DOS mode exits the GUI—therefore, you might have to configure real-mode drivers to access hardware.

15. If you are running in MS-DOS mode and the CD-ROM does not run, what must you do to get it running?

You must create (or edit) the CONFIG.SYS and AUTOEXEC.BAT files to load the appropriate real-mode drivers for the CD-ROM. You will also need to run the MSCDEX.EXE application.

16. Do you need a .PIF file to run an MS-DOS program in Windows 95?

Windows 95 no longer creates .PIF files by using the PIF editor. PIF settings are created by accessing the Properties value that appears when an MS-DOS application is right-clicked.

17. What are the five steps of a Windows 95 installation?

The five steps are startup and system check; information collection; hardware detection; startup disk creation and file installation; and windows configuration.

18. Which version of Windows 95 uses FAT32?

Only the OSR2 version uses FAT32.

19. What is safe mode and what is it used for?

Safe mode starts Windows 95 with a minimum of drivers. This mode is considered to be the Windows 95 troubleshooting mode.

20. What are the three Registry backup tools provided with Windows 95?

The three primary Registry backup tools available in Windows 95 are: Microsoft Configuration Backup (CFGBACK.EXE), Emergency Recovery Utility (ERU.EXE), and REG files.

Chapter 17

Page 492

1. In Windows 95, which Windows 3.x program was replaced by Windows Explorer?

Windows Explorer replaced the Windows 3.x File Manager—the more advanced Explorer is the better choice for computer professionals.

2. What utilities are provided for managing files in Windows 95?

Windows 95 uses two programs for managing files: My Computer and Windows Explorer.

3. How do you partition a drive in Windows 95?

Use the FDISK program that came with Windows 95 to partition hard disk drives.

4. What is the function of the Recycle Bin?

The Recycle Bin provides temporary storage for discarded or deleted files.

5. What is the System Monitor used for?

The System Monitor provides real-time reports on how different system processes are performing. It displays various functions using either a line graph, a bar graph, or a numeric graph.

6. What is the Resource Meter used for?

The Resource Meter is used to monitor the use of system resources in real time. When activated, it adds a small bar graph to the taskbar (in the notification area) that indicates the percent of free resources (based on the computer's total resources).

7. Loading which file will cause Windows 95 to report an appropriate version of MS-DOS to older MS-DOS applications?

With SETVER.EXE loaded, Windows 95 will report a compatible version number to your MS-DOS application.

8. Identify the four basic kinds of viruses and describe how they are transmitted.

1. **File infector viruses attach themselves to executable files and spread to other files when the program is run.**

2. **Boot sector viruses replace the master boot record (or boot sector on a floppy disk). They write themselves into memory any time the computer is booted.**

3. **Trojan horse viruses appear to be legitimate programs, but when loaded, begin to harm or destroy the system.**

4. **Macro viruses are major nuisances. These viruses commonly infect Word documents. Attaching themselves as executable code to documents, macro viruses run when the documents are opened. (They can also attach to some kinds of e-mail.)**

Your best protection is to acquire and use an antivirus program. Remember to keep it up-to-date as new viruses are created every day.

Chapter 18

Page 526

1. Name the three basic elements required to create a network.

   The three basic elements required to create a network are connection, communication, and services.

2. The primary benefit of a LAN is its ability to share resources. Name some of the other benefits of networking.

   In addition to the ability to share resources, LANs are resilient, act as communication gateways, and facilitate electronic mail.

3. What is the difference between a peer-to-peer and a server-based network?

   In a peer-to-peer network, each computer acts as a server or a client depending on the user's needs. Each user, or workstation, establishes its own security and determines which resources are available to other users.

   In a server network, a central server (dedicated computer) manages access to all shared files and peripherals. This is a secure environment suitable for most organizations.

4. Name the three network topologies.

   The three network topologies are star, bus, and ring.

5. What type of cabling do thin Ethernet and UTP cabling require?

   Thin Ethernet uses a round BNC connector and UTP uses an RJ-45 connector (similar to a telephone jack).

6. What is the function of a network interface card?

   Network interface cards (NICs) link the computer to the network cable system. They provide the physical connection between the computer's expansion bus and the network cabling.

7. Name the three main types of network cabling. What are their advantages?

   - **Twisted-pair cable is very common, easy to install, and inexpensive.**

   - **Coaxial cable is found in two types: thin (ThinNet) and thick (ThickNet). When compared to twisted-pair, coaxial cable is the better choice even though it costs more. It is a standard technology and resists rough treatment and electromagnetic interference (EMI). Although more resistant, it is still susceptible to EMI and eavesdropping.**

   - **Fiber-optic cable is made of light-conducting glass or plastic fibers. It carries data signals in the form of modulated pulses of light. Although it is no less expensive (in both installation and cable cost) than twisted-pair or coaxial cable, it has advantages. It is immune to EMI or detection outside the cable. It supports very high bandwidths (the amount of information the cable can carry) and can handle thousands of times more data than twisted-pair or coaxial cable.**

8. What is the purpose of network protocols?

A network protocol is a set of rules governing the way computers communicate over a network. In order for computers using different software to communicate, they must follow the same set of networking rules and agreements, or protocols. A protocol is like a language. Unless both computers trying to communicate are "speaking" and "listening" in the same language, no communication will take place.

9. Describe the functions of a router, a bridge, and a gateway.

Bridges work like repeaters but offer additional advantages. They can isolate network traffic or problems. The traffic within a segment will not be sent to the entire network unless its destination is in another segment. Bridges can also link unlike segments (Ethernet and token ring).

Routers provide interconnectivity between like and unlike devices on the LAN and WAN. Routers work like bridges, but can connect networks using different protocols and can select the best route from network to network based on traffic load. Routers route data based on factors such as least-cost, minimum delay, minimum distance, and least congestion. Routers are generally used to create a wide area network and to connect dissimilar networks.

Gateways provide as much interconnectivity and even greater functionality than routers and bridges do. A gateway usually resides on a dedicated computer that acts as a translator between two completely dissimilar systems or applications. Since a gateway is both a translator and a router, it tends to be slower than bridges or routers. Gateways also provide access to special services such as e-mail or fax functions.

10. What is the most widely used network protocol?

TCP/IP is the most widely used network protocol. It is the protocol of the Internet.

11. What is the difference between a LAN and a WAN?

A LAN is a local area network; it is usually confined to a limited space such as a building or a room. A WAN is a wide area network and can span long distances (even worldwide).

12. Your network is showing signs of reduced bandwidth. What is causing this problem?

This type of problem is called a bottleneck. A bottleneck on a system is the resource that limits the rate at which a task can be completed. If your task uses the processor, network and disk resources, and spends more of its time transferring data to and from the disk, you might have a memory bottleneck. A memory bottleneck might require adding more RAM.

13. What is an ISP?

An ISP (Internet Service Provider) provides the connection between dial-up (modem) users and the Internet.

14. Name some of the most common Internet domain extensions.

Here is a table of common Internet domain extensions. How many did you get?

.com	Commercial organizations
.net	Networks
.edu	Educational institutions
.org	Nonprofit organizations
.gov	US Government nonmilitary institutions
.mil	US Government armed services
.xx	Two-letter country code

15. What does URL stand for?

URL stands for Uniform Resource Locator, the address system used on the World Wide Web.

16. Besides A+ Certification, what other computer-related certifications are available?

Other certifications available are Novell CNN and CNE, or Microsoft MCP and MCSE.

17. Name the three main types of portable computers.

The three types of portable computers are laptop, notebook, and subnotebook or palmtop computers.

18. What is a docking station?

Docking stations (also known as docking ports) are specialized cases that allow entire notebook computers to be inserted within them. This allows the notebook to be connected to desktop I/O devices such as full-sized keyboards, CRT monitors, and network connections.

19. What is the purpose of PCMCIA cards?

In order for laptop and notebook computers to have the same degree of expandability that is associated with desktop computers, the Personal Computer Memory Card International Association (PCMCIA) established several standards for credit-card-sized expansion boards that fit into small slots on laptop and notebook computers.

20. Describe the different PCMCIA card types.

There are four types of PCMCIA cards:

- **Type I is the original computer-card standard and is now referred to as the Type I standard. These cards are used only for memory. Type I cards are 3.3 mm thick.**

- **Type II cards support most types of expansion devices (like communication hardware) or network adapters. Type II cards are 5 mm thick.**

- **Type III cards are primarily for computers that have removable hard disk drives. This standard was introduced in 1992. Type III cards are 10.5 mm thick, but they are compatible with Type I and Type II cards.**

- **Type IV cards are intended to be used with hard disk drives that are thicker than the 10.5-mm Type III card.**

21. How do you configure a computer card?

PCMCIA (PC-Card) is part of the Plug and Play standard. Plug and Play-compatibility means being able to add components without turning off or rebooting the computer. PCMCIA buses are not configured with jumper settings (because they don't have any) but with software.

22. What are the two kinds of displays found on laptop computers?

The two types of displays found on laptop computers are active-matrix and dual-scan.

23. Why is heat dissipation a concern in computer-chip technologies for portable computers?

In desktop systems, CPU heat is dissipated with the use of cooling fans housed inside the case. There is no room for this solution in a portable system, so manufacturers have addressed this problem in the packaging of the chip itself.

24. With the exception of Macintosh, what drives are standard in a portable computer?

Except for the size and packaging, hard disk drive technology is similar to desktop technology. EIDE drives are standard in portables, with the exception of Macintosh, which uses SCSI.

Chapter 19

Page 542

1. What items should be included in a cleaning kit?

A cleaning kit should contain at least the following: lint-free cloth, cleaning solution, foam swabs, and antistatic spray.

2. Why is ESD dangerous to computers?

ESD (electrostatic discharge) will destroy electronic components.

3. Will a properly grounded computer help prevent EMI?

   Yes, a properly grounded computer will help prevent EMI (electro-magnetic interference).

4. Describe some safety precautions you can take to protect yourself from high voltage when working on a computer.

   Never work above your skill level when it comes to safety! Working inside the monitor case should be left to a properly trained technician with the necessary tools to protect against high voltages.

   The power switch on some computers, usually located on the front of the computer, uses 110 volts AC to turn the power supply on or off. If you are working on a computer and it is plugged in to provide proper grounding, this could present a hazard.

5. What type of fire extinguisher is used for an electrical fire?

   Type C fire extinguishers are used for electrical fires.

6. How do you clean a keyboard?

   To clean a keyboard, use a hand-held vacuum to remove dust from the small crevasses.

7. How do you clean a laser printer?

   To clean a laser printer, complete the following steps:

   1. **Remove the toner cartridge.**
   2. **Vacuum dust build-up and excess toner from the interior.**
   3. **Clean the laser printer's rollers using a damp cloth or denatured alcohol.**
   4. **Clean the paper-handling motor's gear train, using a swab.**
   5. **Apply light oil to the gears, using a swab.**
   6. **Distribute the oil throughout the gear train.**
   7. **Clean the writing mechanism thoroughly, using compressed air.**
   8. **If possible, wipe the laser lens with lint-free wipes to remove fingerprints and stains.**
   9. **Clean the corona wires using a swab dipped in alcohol. Be careful not to break any of the strands; if they are broken, your printer will be rendered useless until they are repaired.**

8. Give one example of a recyclable item that requires special disposal.

   Examples of recyclable items that require special disposal are batteries, toner and cartridge kits, circuit boards, chemical solvents, and monitors (CRTs).

9. Why is a toner cartridge easy to recycle?

Often the manufacturer provides a prepaid shipping box to return the cartridge.

10. What is a material safety data sheet?

When purchasing or using any kinds of chemicals (for instance, cleaners) be sure to look at the MSDS (material safety data sheet). This form describes the nature of any chemicals manufactured. It includes generic information about the chemical makeup and any recognized hazards of the product (along with what to do and who to call if there is a problem).

Chapter 20

Page 565

1. Name five ways to stay on top of your profession.

Five ways to stay on top of your profession are to: keep learning; network with others; take advantage of opportunities to connect with your peers through professional groups and trade shows; practice your skills; and read widely.

2. How and where can you obtain technical support?

The unlimited free technical telephone support that we once took for granted is being replaced by support offered through e-mail and the Web. This means that increasingly we are expected to get the job done without free direct phone support from the original equipment manufacturer (OEM). Technical support is out there, but it must be used wisely to be cost-effective.

3. What are the four categories of tools used by computer technicians?

Four categories of tools used by computer technicians include hardware toolkit, software toolkit, spare parts, and access to a technical library.

4. Which files are essential for a software toolkit?

The bare minimum software toolkit should include: ATTRIB.EXE; DEFRAG.EXE; EDIT.COM; EMM386.EXE; EXPAND.COM; FDISK.EXE (.COM); FORMAT.EXE (.COM); HIMEM.SYS; LABEL.COM; MEM.EXE; Memmaker; MSCDEX.EXE; MSD.EXE (.COM); QBASIC.EXE; SCANDISK.EXE; SHARE.EXE; SIZER.EXE; SMARTDRV.EXE; and SYS.COM.

5. What are the five phases of troubleshooting?

Phase 1 is to define the problem.

Phase 2 is to identify the cause.

Phase 3 is to make the repair.

Phase 4 is to confirm the repair.

Phase 5 is to document the incident.

6. How important is record keeping?

Good recordkeeping is essential if you are to become a success at your profession. Recordkeeping is the process by which you keep track of which techniques worked and which did not work. In short, it becomes your experience database. Good records will save you valuable time in the long run.

7. What are the three levels of technical support?

Level 1 is to provide local support by assigning a knowledgeable person onsite to address minor problems.

Level 2 is to provide telephone support.

Level 3 is to provide on-site support.

8. Why is it important to standardize equipment in large organizations?

Standardization of equipment in large companies reduces the number of spare parts required and simplifies installations.

9. What are the four stages to follow when you receive a service call?

The four stages of a service call are the greeting, the description, the interview, and the closing.

10. How would you deal with a difficult client or coworker?

If the individual needs training, ensure that they have information about available courses.

If the individual is a coworker, speak to the person who supervises them and identify their training needs.

If the individual is a client, gently suggest that it would be beneficial to obtain specific training.

Send the client a memo or instruction sheet to follow. Save the instructions for future use.

Dealing with technophiles (or those who think they are experts) can be a challenge. The best option is to listen carefully and make the individual part of the solution, not part of the problem. Remember, they came to you for help.

In a corporate setting, form an advanced users group and give participants responsibility for finding solutions to issues. Ask coworkers (or users) who constantly complain about trivial problems to put all complaints in writing. Keep their notes as part of your records.

APPENDIX   B

Table of Acronyms

This appendix presents many of the acronyms used in this book. Be aware that—as with all acronyms—some have more than one meaning, depending on the context.

AC	Alternating current
AGP	Accelerated Graphics Port
ALU	Arithmetic logic unit
ANSI	American National Standards Institute
ASCII	American Standard Code for Information Interchange
ASPI	Advanced SCSI Programming Interface
BBS	Bulletin board system
BIOS	Basic input/output system
BPS (bps)	Bits per second
CAM	Common Access Method
CCITT	Comité Consultatif Télégraphique et Téléphonique
CD-ROM	Compact disc read-only memory
CGA	Color/Graphics Adapter
CHS	Cylinder head sector
CISC	Complex instruction set computing
CMOS	Complementary metal-oxide semiconductor
COM port	Serial communications port
CPU	Central processing unit
CRT	Cathode-ray tube
DC	Direct current
DDE	Dynamic Data Exchange
DIMM	Dual inline memory module
DIPP	Dual inline pin package

DLL	Dynamic link library
DMA	Direct memory access
DOS	Disk operating system
dpi	Dots per inch
DPMI	MS-DOS Protected Mode Interface
DPMS	Display Power Management Signaling
DRAM	Dynamic random access memory
DTE	Data Terminal Equipment
DVD	Digital video disc
EDB	External data bus
EDO	Extended data out
EGA	Enhanced Graphics Adapter
EIDE	Enhanced Integrated Drive Electronics
EISA	Extended Industry Standard Architecture
EMI	Electromagnetic interference
EMS	Expanded Memory Specification
ESD	Electrostatic discharge
ESDI	Enhanced Small Device Interface
ETX	End-of-text
FAT	File allocation table
FPM	Fast-page mode
FTP	File Transfer Protocol
GB	Gigabyte
GDI	Graphical Device Interface
GPF	General Protection Fault
GUI	Graphical user interface
HMA	High memory area
HRR	Horizontal refresh rate
HTTP	HyperText Transfer Protocol
I/O	Input/output
IDE	Integrated Drive Electronics or Integrated Device Electronics
IEEE	Institute of Electrical and Electronics Engineers
IOR	Input/output read wire
IOW	Input/output write wire
IP	Internet Protocol
IPX/SPX	Internetwork Packet Exchange/Sequenced Packet Exchange

IRQ	Interrupt request
ISA	Industry Standard Architecture
ISDN	Integrated Services Digital Network
ISO	International Organization for Standardization (often incorrectly identified as International Standardization Organization)
ISP	Internet service provider
ITU-T	International Telecommunications Union—Telecommunication Standardization Sector
KB	Kilobyte
LAN	Local area network
LBA	Logical Block Addressing
LIM	Lotus/Intel/Microsoft
LPT	Line printer
MB	Megabyte
MCA	Micro Channel Architecture
MCC	Memory controller chip
MDA	Monochrome Display Adapter
MDRAM	Multibank DRAM
MFM	Modified frequency modulation
MHz	Megahertz
MOS	Metal-oxide semiconductor
MSD	Microsoft Diagnostics
MTBF	Mean time between failures
NDIS	Network Driver Interface Specification
NetBIOS/ NetBEUI	Networked Basic Input/Output System/NetBIOS Enhanced User Interface
NIC	Network interface card
NTSC	National Television Standards Committee
OLE	Object linking and embedding
PC	Personal Computer
PCI	Peripheral Component Interconnect
PDI	Post DMA-IRQ card
PDL	Page-description language
PGA	Pin grid array or Professional Graphics Adapter
PIO	Programmed Input/Output
PLCC	Plastic leadless chip carrier
PM	Preventive maintenance

POST	Power-on self test
POTS	Plain Old Telephone Service
PPP	Point-to-Point Protocol
PPTP	Point-to-Point Tunneling Protocol
PQFP	Plastic Quad Flat Pack
RAID	Redundant array of independent disks
RAM	Random access memory
RISC	Reduced Instruction Set Computing
RLL	Run-length limited
ROM	Read-only memory
SCSI	Small Computer System Interface
SDRAM	Synchronous dynamic random access memory
SGRAM	Synchronous Graphics RAM
SIMM	Single inline memory module
SIPP	Single inline pin package
SMM	System Management Mode
SPA	Software Publishers Association
SRAM	Static random access memory
TB	Terabyte
TCP/IP	Transmission Control Protocol/Internet Protocol
TSR	Terminate-and-stay-resident program
UART	Universal asynchronous receiver-transmitter
UMB	Upper memory block
UPS	Uninterruptible power supply
USB	Universal serial bus
VESA	Video Electronics Standards Association
VGA	Video Graphics Adapter
VLB	VESA local bus
VOM	Volt ohm meter
VPN	Virtual private network
VRR	Vertical refresh rate
WAN	Wide area network
WRAM	Window random access memory
XMS	Extended memory specification
ZIF	Zero insertion force

Glossary

A

Accelerated Graphics Port (AGP) An Intel-design expansion port found on Pentium II and later computers that allows a separate data path for display adapters.

access speed The time required to complete read or write instructions as required by the memory controller chip. Usually measured in nanoseconds (ns) for memory chips and milliseconds (ms) for disk drives. Most manufacturers rate average access time on a hard disk as the time required for a seek across one-third of the total number of cylinders plus one half of the time for a single revolution of the disk platters.

address bus A group of parallel conductors (circuit traces) found on the motherboard that are used by the CPU to "address" memory locations. Determines what information or code is sent to or received from the data bus.

ampere A measurement of electrical current strength.

ASCII file Commonly used term to refer to a text file that contains only data as set forth by the **American Standard Code for Information Interchange** to conform to their standard.

asynchronous Not synchronized—the computer is free to transmit any number of characters at any time. The bits constituting a single character are transmitted at a fixed rate, but the pauses between transmission can be of any duration.

attachment A file attached to e-mail; most e-mail clients allow the user to append files (for instance, graphics files like GIFs or JPEGs) to e-mail as a handy way of sending information to other people.

B

backslash (\\) Symbol used to separate each directory level, for instance C:\Windows\Utilities. For this reason, it is a reserved character and cannot be used as part of a filename.

bandwidth Used in several ways to denote the amount of data or load capacity of a medium. 1) The range of frequencies that an electronic system can transmit. High bandwidth allows fast transmission or the ability to transmit many signals at once. 2) On a monitor screen, a higher bandwidth that provides a sharper image. 3) The rate at which data can be send over a modem or other telecommunication device.

battery A power source for use outside or as an alternate to the electrical mains. Prevents unique information about the setup of the computer from being lost when the power is turned off. Also maintains the external clock time (not to be confused with the CPU's clock).

baud Roughly speaking, a measurement of how fast data can be sent over telephone lines.

BBS (bulletin board system) A local computer system that is not part of the Internet. It allows users to dial in and chat with others and download or upload files.

Bi-Tronics A modified Centronics connection created by Hewlett-Packard. It utilizes bidirectional communication, allowing the printer to send messages to the computer (out of paper, paper jam, and so forth).

binary file A file type in the form of pure data (1s and 0s) that needs to be converted to image, sound, or application to be used. Contrast this to an ASCII file.

binary system The language used by computers—it is based on something being either on or off. There are only two digits used in binary language; 1 equals on and 0 equals off.

BIOS (basic input/output system) Software that includes hundreds of little programs stored on ROM chips, used during the startup routine to check out the system and prepare to run the hardware.

bit The smallest unit of information that is recognized by a microcomputer. Shorthand term for binary digit. There are only two possible binary digits: 0 and 1.

boot partition A hard-disk partition containing the portion of the operating system needed to launch the operating environment.

boot up To start a computer; drawn from the phrase "pulling oneself up by one's own boot-straps."

bps (bits per second) The speed at which a modem transmits data. Typical rates are 14,400, 28,800, 33,600 and 56,600 bps. This represents the actual number of data bits that can be transmitted per second.

bridge A device that provides communication between two or more network segments, thereby forming one logical network.

broadband A network with high bandwidth (greater than 256 bps).

browser Software used to navigate the World Wide Web, such as Microsoft's Internet Explorer and Netscape Navigator.

bulletin board system *See* BBS

bus The main communication avenue in a computer. It consists of a set of parallel wires that are connected to the CPU, memory, and all input/output devices. The bus can transmit data in either direction between any two components. If a computer did not have a bus, it would need separate wires to connect all the components.

bus mastering The ability of a device to control its own data bus, only making use of the main system bus when data must be sent to the CPU or another device. This reduces CPU and system bus traffic, improving overall performance.

bus network A network in which all computers are connected to a single linear cable. Both ends of the cable must be terminated. Because there is no central point, it is harder to isolate problems in a bus network than in a star network topology.

byte A group of 8 bits that represents 1 character of information (for instance, pressing one key on the keyboard). A byte is the standard unit of measuring memory in a microprocessor. Memory size is measured in terms of kilobytes (KB) or megabytes (MB). 1 KB of RAM is 1024 bytes; 1 MB is approximately one million bytes.

C

cache A place where data is stored so that it does not need to be read from a slower device. Copies of frequently used disk sectors are stored in RAM so they can be accessed without accessing the hard disk.

case sensitivity The ability of the operating system to distinguish between uppercase and lowercase letters. MS-DOS commands are not case-sensitive; UNIX commands are.

cathode-ray tube *See* CRT

CD-ROM (compact disc read-only memory) A disc similar to an audio compact disc, but it contains computer data.

central processing unit *See* CPU

CGA (Color Graphics Adapter) An early color graphics adapter standard with resolutions of 320 pixels by 200 pixels or 640 x 200. CGA supported no more than four colors.

chip The ultimate integrated circuit; contains the complete arithmetic and logic unit of a computer. *See* microprocessor

chip set A group of computer chips or ICs (integrated circuits) that, when working in harmony, manage and control the computer system. This set includes the CPU and other chips that control the flow of data throughout the system. Typical chip sets consist of a bus controller, a memory controller, data and address buffer, and a peripheral controller.

CISC (complex instruction set computing) A computer with many different machine-language instructions.

client A computer that connects to a network and uses the available resources provided by the server.

clock Establishes the maximum speed at which the processor can execute commands. Not to be confused with the clock that keeps time.

clock speed Measured in megahertz (MHz)— millions of cycles per second—it is the speed at which a clock can cycle, or how fast a CPU can execute a command.

clone A term that derives from the early days of personal computing used to denote a computer compatible with, but not manufactured by, IBM.

clusters A unit of storage on a mass-storage device such as a hard disk drive or CD-ROM disc. On a hard drive a cluster usually consists of two to eight sectors. The actual amount of data a cluster can hold is dependent on the operating system and controller type.

CMOS (complementary metal-oxide semiconductor) A chip that gets its name from the way it is manufactured and not the information it holds. Unlike other ROM chips, CMOS chips store data that is read by the BIOS to complete the programs needed to talk to changeable hardware.

CMOS battery Prevents unique information about the setup of the computer from being lost when the power is turned off. Also maintains the external clock time (not to be confused with the CPU's clock).

coaxial cable Made of two conductors that share the same axis. The center is a relatively stiff copper wire encased in insulating plastic. A wire-mesh tube around the insulation serves as shielding. The outside is a tough insulating plastic tube.

code A way of representing information on a machine or in some physical form so that the information can be placed on the external data bus to be read by all devices. Also, statements (source code) written in a programming language, which are compiled into executable instructions (object code).

cold boot The process of restarting a computer after it has been powered down.

COM1, COM2 The names assigned to the first two serial ports on a PC.

command mode The character mode used in an operating system such as Microsoft Windows, MS-DOS, or UNIX that has a prompt and in which actions take place while the user enters text strings to execute commands.

compression "Squeezing" a file down in size by getting rid of all the bits it doesn't really need. Many files (especially those with graphics) are very large and require a long time to travel over the Internet, so they are best compressed before sent.

conferences Different areas of conversation in an e-mail system that are topic-specific rather than individualized.

conventional memory The memory area between 0 and 640 KB that is designated for running MS-DOS and MS-DOS applications.

coprocessor A separate circuit inside a computer that adds additional functions to the CPU or handles extra work while the CPU is busy.

CPU (central processing unit) The part of a computer in which arithmetic and logical operations are performed and instructions are decoded and executed. It controls the operation of the computer.

CRT (cathode-ray tube) The main component of a monitor. One end of the tube is a very slender cylinder containing an electron gun(s). The fatter end is the display screen.

cursor When entering data, whether in an application or in an MS-DOS command, the cursor (often a small flashing line) indicates the place at which the characters will be inserted.

D

data bus A group of parallel conductors (circuit traces) found on the motherboard that is used by the CPU to send and receive data from all the devices in the computer. Also called the external data bus.

Data Communications Equipment (DCE) The receiver in a telecommunications connection.

default drive The active drive on the computer. Each drive has its own letter designation. Unless otherwise specified, any commands are performed upon the default drive.

defragmentation Running a program to organize the files on a hard disk so that the various clusters of data for each file are once again contiguous. This helps to speed up the hard disk.

device driver A program that extends the operating system to support specific devices.

direct memory access (DMA) Allows a peripheral device to access the memory of a computer directly, without going through the CPU. This speeds up the transfer of data to or from external devices.

directory A location where files are grouped together on the disk. In the Microsoft Windows environment and Apple Macintosh operating systems, these are known as folders.

DLC (Data Link Control) A protocol developed by IBM to connect token-ring-based workstations to IBM mainframe computers. Printer manufacturers have adopted the protocol to connect remote printers to network print servers.

DMA *See* direct memory access

DOS (disk operating system) The system used by most early PCs as the operating system software to manage hardware, data, and applications.

DOS prompt Displays the active drive letter (for instance, C:) and directory. This indicates that the operating system is ready to accept the next command.

DOS Protected Mode Interface (DPMI) Specification that allows multiple applications to access extended memory at the same time. It has been endorsed by most memory manager producers and application developers. Microsoft Windows uses the DPMI specification.

download The ability to transfer a file from a remote computer.

dpi (dots per inch) Units used to measure the resolution of images on many printers and scanners. Keep in mind that dpi is an exact measurement in laser printers, but often used as an approximation in ink jet printers.

DRAM (dynamic random access memory) Memory that requires a refresh signal to be sent to it periodically.

Dynamic Data Exchange (DDE) A data exchange protocol that allows for the automatic updating of a file or open application when the source is modified.

E

ECC (error-correction coding) The use of a code to verify or disprove that a data string received is the same as the data sent.

ECP (Extended Capabilities Port) Developed by Hewlett-Packard and Microsoft. It features 2 MB per second data transfer and bidirectional 8-bit operation. ECP specifies whether transmitted information consists of data or commands for the peripheral.

EGA (Enhanced Graphics Adapter) An improvement on the older CGA standard. Supports a resolution of up to 640 pixels by 350 pixels at 16 colors in text-only mode or 640 x 200 at 2 colors in graphics mode. The EGA standard was not fully backward-compatible with CGA and MDA.

e-mail (electronic mail) The transmission of messages by computer from one person to another, often via the Internet.

Enhanced IDE (EIDE) A standard developed in order to increase the size of available disk drives and the speed of data transfer between the host and the disk drive. *See also* Integrated Drive Electronics (IDE)

EPP (Enhanced Parallel Port) Features 2 MB per second data transfer rates, bidirectional 8-bit operation, and addressing to support multiple (daisy-chained) peripherals on a single computer.

error messages Brief technical messages that are displayed when an error occurs.

Ethernet A type of local area network in which communication takes place by means of radio frequency signals carried by a coaxial cable.

Expanded Memory (EMS) A technique, developed by Lotus/Intel/Microsoft (LIM), that adds addressable memory to a computer system, overcoming the original MS-DOS upper memory limit. The LIM expanded memory specification uses a 64-KB section of memory (usually in upper memory) to provide a "window" into which data can be written. Once in this area, the data can be transferred to the expanded memory. The memory chips are located on an expansion card installed inside the computer.

expansion buses Provide the connection between expansion cards (drive controllers, video cards, modems and so forth) and the system bus.

expansion slots Specialized sockets that allow additional devices (circuit boards/adapter cards) to be attached to the motherboard (by means of the expansion bus). These are used to expand or customize a computer. They are an extension of the computer's bus system.

extended memory (XMS) RAM above the 1-MB address. Extended memory is accessed through an extended memory manager (HIMEM.SYS for DOS).

F

fiber-optic cable A cable that is made out of light-conducting glass or plastic fibers. Multiple fiber cores can be bundled in the center of its protective tubing.

filenames (also filespec) Ways to designate files. A filename is made up of three parts—a name of up to eight characters, a period, and extension of up to three characters. The name can include any number, character, or the following symbols: _()~'!%$&#. For example: "myfile.doc." Spaces cannot be used in MS-DOS filenames.

File Transfer Protocol (FTP) 1) An application used for transferring files to and from another computer, usually over the Internet. 2) The protocol by means of which these transfers take place.

floppy disk drive Low-capacity magnetic removable storage drive.

form factor The standard physical configuration of a typical device such as a motherboard or a 3.5-inch hard disk drive.

fragmentation Scattering of data in files throughout a disk drive caused by the continual addition and deletion of files. Although not harmful to the computer, fragmentation will slow down a hard drive because it causes the computer to access two or more places to retrieve a file.

G

gateway A link between different computer networks. It is usually a computer that acts as a translator between two completely dissimilar systems. Because it is both a translator and a router, it is usually slower than a bridge or router alone.

Gopher A system of information retrieval that "digs" down through layers of menus to reach what you want. A Gopher system is generally text-based and is best for finding documents buried in archives such as university libraries. Some Web sites offer access to Gopher, but Gopher has been largely replaced by information archives on Web sites.

GPF (General Protection Fault) An error that occurs in Microsoft Windows when a program tries to access a memory location that is not allocated to it.

greater than (>) This symbol is used to indicate that a command can be redirected to an output device. For example, to redirect the directory command to a printer, type **dir > lpt1**.

GUI (graphical user interface) Microsoft Windows is a GUI-based operating system. A GUI allows users to choose commands and functions by pointing to a graphical icon using either a keyboard or pointing device such as a mouse.

H

handshaking A term used to describe the sequence of data and related tones used to align and synchronize two modems before working data is sent between the devices.

hard disk drive High-capacity magnetic disk for data storage and program files. Also called a fixed disk.

hardware The physical elements of the computer system.

high memory area (HMA) An irregularity found in the Intel chip architecture that allowed MS-DOS to address the first 64 KB of extended memory on machines with a 80286 or higher processors. This special area is called the high memory area.

High Sierra format An industry-wide format specification for the logical structure, file structure, and record structures on a CD. The specification is named after a meeting on CD-ROM held near Lake Tahoe in November 1985. It served as the basis for the international standard ISO 9660.

host A computer that you connect to in order to access information. For instance, a computer at an ISP that lets you access the Internet is a host.

HRR (horizontal refresh rate) The speed at which the electron beam in a CRT completes one horizontal trace.

HTML (Hypertext Markup Language) An application of SGML (Standardized General Markup Language) used to create Web pages.

HTTP (Hypertext Transfer Protocol) The protocol used to transmit data in the HTML format.

I

I/O address A unique name assigned to each device that allows the CPU to recognize the device with which it is communicating.

icon A small picture on a computer screen that represents a group of files, an object, or operations. A user accesses the item he or she wants by clicking on the picture with the mouse.

Industry Standard Architecture (ISA) One of several common expansion slot and card designs.

integrated circuit (IC) An electronic device consisting of many miniature transistors and other circuit elements (resistors and capacitors and so forth).

Integrated Drive Electronics (IDE) The most common standard for interfacing hard disk and CD-ROM drives in the PC environment. Much of the actual work of controlling the hard disk drive is handled by the system BIOS. This reduces hardware cost, but introduces an overall system performance penalty during I/O operations. *See also* Enhanced IDE (EIDE)

internal cache High-speed memory built into the processor to store frequently used data. This avoids accessing slower devices such as RAM or hard drives.

International Organization for Standardization (ISO) Groups of experts drawn from the industry that set standards for various technologies. The work of these teams has led to development of SCSI, SMAL and the Internet, and the ASCII character set.

Internet A system that links computer networks all over the world.

IP (Internet Protocol) The protocols used to define how data is transmitted over the Internet.

IP address (Internet Protocol address) A unique address that identifies every network and host on the Internet. (A host is defined as the TCP/IP network interface within the computer, not the computer itself—a computer with two network cards will have two IP addresses.)

IPX/SPX (Internetwork Packet Exchange/Sequenced Packet Exchange) NetWare core protocol developed by Novell in the early 1980s.

IRQ (interrupt request) A wire used by the CPU to control the flow of data. It prevents devices from trying to communicate with the CPU at the same time by "interrupting" and temporarily stopping the CPU to deal with a particular request.

ISDN A telecommunication standard that allows a channel to carry voice and data in digital form over a single line.

ISP (Internet service provider) A host computer that users can dial into over a modem to connect to the Internet.

K

keyboard A primary input device for a computer, used for entering text and shortcuts for command functions.

kilobyte (KB) A unit of memory equal to 1,024 characters or bytes (1 KB = one kilobyte).

L

LAN (local area network) A network that covers a limited distance (such as a single building or facility) to allow computers to share information and resources.

link Means, also known as a hyperlink, by which reader is moved to a different location on the Internet when the link is activated. When text is used for a hyperlink, it is often colored differently from the body text of the page so it stands out.

local bus A separate bus in the computer designed to provide extra-fast access to the CPU for certain devices, such as video cards.

logging on Means by which—when connecting to a remote computer—the host computer (the one that is called) gives permission to connect. The process of sending the appropriate information to sign on is called logging on. Often a user name and password are required.

LPT1, LPT2, LPT3 The names assigned to the parallel printer ports on a PC.

M

mailing list A list of subscribers to a particular discussion group. This database can be used to distribute eZines (electronic magazines).

Mainboard *See* motherboard

MDA (Monochrome Display Adapter) Displays text only at a resolution of 720 pixels by 350 pixels. An MDA is perfect for use with MS-DOS-based word-processing and spreadsheet programs. The MDA uses a 9-pin male connector.

megabyte (MB) An amount of computer memory equal to 2^{20}. 1,048,576 bytes = 1024 kilobytes. One megabyte can store more than one million characters.

megahertz (MHz) One million hertz (one million cycles per second). A measurement of clock speed.

memory The area within a computer where information is stored while being worked on. It stores information (in the form of data bits) that the CPU and software need to keep running.

Micro Channel Architecture (MCA) A short-lived 32-bit expansion bus that was a proprietary design of IBM used on the IBM PS/2 computer. By abandoning the open design of the existing PC market, IBM limited the willingness of developers and buyers alike to use MCA.

microphone Just like the microphone on a tape recorder. Allows input of voice or music to be recorded and saved to a computer file.

microprocessor An integrated circuit containing the entire CPU of a computer, all on one chip, so that only the memory and input/output devices need to be added.

mini connector A type of power supply connector primarily used on 3.5-inch floppy disk drives.

modem (MOdulator/DEModulator) Converts computer data to information that can be transmitted via wires (telephone, ISDN, fiber optics, as well as wireless communication). Allows communication between computers over long and short distances.

Molex connector Type of power supply connector primarily used for devices that need both 12-volt and 5-volt power (floppy disk drives). The most common type of connector.

monitor The primary output device that resembles a television set—it visually displays text and graphics.

motherboard Also known as a PWB or printed wiring board. The large circuit board found inside the computer. For all practical purposes, it is the computer. It contains the following items: chip set, data bus, address bus, expansion slots, clock, battery, and memory.

mouse Device used with graphical environments to point and select objects on the system's monitor. They come in a variety of shapes and sizes.

MTBF (mean time between failures) A standard means by which vendors estimate the expected lifespan of a given product line.

multitasking The operation of more than one application at what appears to be the same time on the same PC. The CPU quickly switches between the various programs, making it possible to work in more than one program at once.

N

nanosecond (ns) One-billionth of one second. The time increment used to measure access speed of the memory chip.

NetBIOS/NetBEUI (networked basic input/output system/NetBios Enhanced User Interface) A local area protocol developed by IBM and refined by Microsoft; originally, the native protocol for LAN Manager and Windows NT. IBM developed NetBIOS as a way to permit small groups of computers to share files and printers efficiently. NetBIOS is the original edition; NetBEUI is an enhanced version for more powerful networks in the 32-bit operating system.

network A group of computers connected together in order to share data and resources.

network card An expansion card that connects a computer to a group of computers so they can access information and programs. Also known as a network interface card, NIC, and network adapter card.

O

offline Networked computers that are not actively connected so that transmission of data is not possible.

offline reader A program to display e-mail messages that have been downloaded to a computer.

ohm A unit of electrical resistance.

online The state in which two or more computers are connected to each other, making possible data transmission.

operating system The program that controls a PC and makes it possible for users to run their own applications. The operating system provides the built-in routines that allow the computer to recognize commands, manage files, connect devices, and perform input/output operations.

P

packet A group of consecutive characters transmitted from one computer to another over a network.

parallel The transmission of several bits at the same time over separate wires.

parity bit A very basic method of error-correcting code that uses the value of an extra bit sent at the end of a data string. The bit must have a set value based on an algorithm to verify that the data at the receiving end is correct.

path The address to a file. The path consists of the drive name, the location of the file in the directory structure, and the filename. Example: C:\Mystuff\Myfile.doc.

peer-to-peer network A network in which each connected computer acts as either a server or a client depending on the users' needs. Each user or workstation establishes its own security and determines which resources are available to other users. These networks are limited in size, usually 15 to 20 workstations.

peripheral An external device connected to a computer such as a printer, scanner, modem, or joystick.

persistence The amount of time a pixel stays visible on a monitor screen, which is a factor of the decay of activity in the phosphor coating.

PGA (Professional Graphics Adapter) An adapter that was originally marketed to the engineering and scientific communities. It was expensive and required three ISA slots when fully configured. This system offered 3-D rotation and 60 frames per second animation. It used a 15-pin, three-row, female DB-type connector. It gained limited use in CAD environments, but was quickly replaced by better mass-market solutions.

pixel Short for "picture element." One of the dots that make up a graphical image.

plotter Similar to a printer, but uses pen(s) to draw an image. Used most often with graphics and drawing programs.

port Specific channel used by a network service. For example, Gopher often uses port 70, while some Web sites use port 80.

power The strength or force actually put forth by electricity. Electrical power is measured in watts, which is measured by multiplying voltage by current.

power supply Takes alternating current (AC) power from a local source (a wall outlet) and converts it to direct current (DC) for on-board electronics use.

printer A peripheral device that transfers computer output to paper or other form of hard copy.

prompt The command prompt—a user interface provided by COMMAND.COM to signal to the user that the computer is ready to receive input (for example, C:\> or A:\>).

protected mode A mode introduced with 80286 processors that used an operating system like OS/2 or Windows to allow creation of "virtual machines." These provided the functionality of a standard computer in real mode but allowed multiple tasks to take place at the same time. The term refers to the fact that processor, memory, and other hardware are "protected" from the software applications by the operating system, which allocates the memory and processor time.

protocol A set of rules that govern the transfer of information. The format used to upload or download files to allow two different computers to communicate in a standard format.

R

RAID (redundant array of independent disks) The combining of several drives using either hardware or software controls to make them seem to be one drive.

RAM (random access memory) The main memory where a computer temporarily stores data.

read-only memory *See* ROM

real mode An MS-DOS mode in which a computer can perform only one operation at a time and an application expects full control of the system. Real mode operates within the MS-DOS 1 MB limitation.

register Temporary memory storage areas located inside the CPU. Used to hold the intermediate results of calculations or other operations.

Registry A file or set of files in Windows 95 and later that stores information about a computer's hardware and software configuration.

repeater A device that works like an amplifier; it increases or boosts a signal to allow transmissions over longer distances.

resolution A measurement of the detail of images produced by a monitor or printer. Normally measured by a horizontal and vertical number of pixels for monitors or dots per inch for laser printers. The higher the number, the better the quality and more memory required by the system.

ring network A type of network in which all the servers and clients are connected in a closed loop.

RISC (Reduced Instruction Set Computing) Uses a smaller and simpler set of instructions to control the processor thereby greatly enhancing the processing speed.

ROM (read-only memory) Computer memory that contains instructions that do not need to be changed, such as operating system startup instructions. The computer can access data from ROM but cannot put new data into it.

router A device that works like a bridge but is able to select the best route from network to network based on traffic load. A router can also connect dissimilar networks.

S

scanner A peripheral that converts information from the written page (or a printed graphic) to digital information that can be used by the computer. Works similarly to the scanning process in a photocopy machine.

scanning A process that converts a photograph, graphic, or even text image found on paper into an electronic computer file.

SCSI (Small Computer System Interface) A standard way of interfacing a computer to disk drives and other devices that require high-speed data transfer. Up to 16 SCSI devices, including the host adapter, can be connected in a daisy chain fashion. These devices can be hard disk drives, CD-ROMs, scanners, or printers. SCSI is the only common computer interface that allows adding both internal and external devices on the same chain. (Pronounced "scuzzy.")

search engine A program that searches indexes of Internet addresses using keywords. There are hundreds of search engines located on servers throughout the Internet. Some popular search engines are AltaVista, Yahoo, HotBot, and Excite.

serial Transmission of 1 bit at a time over a single wire.

server The computer that runs the network operating system, manages security, and administers access to resources. Strictly speaking, any computer that stores information and allows outside users to get copies of that information.

server network This type of network requires a central server (dedicated computer) to manage access to all shared files and peripherals.

shadow RAM Many high-speed motherboards use shadow RAM to improve the performance of a computer. Shadow RAM rewrites (or shadows) the contents of the ROM BIOS and/or video BIOS into extended RAM (between the 640-KB boundary and 1 MB). This allows systems to operate faster when application software calls BIOS routines. In some cases, system speed can be increased up to 400 percent.

software Any program (set of instructions) that causes a computer to carry out a task or function.

spooling Holds computer output before sending it to a printer. This enables the main program to run more quickly because output is handled by the print spooler, which then distributes it to the printer at the proper speed.

star network A type of network configuration in which all computers are connected to a central point called a hub. The hub collects and distributes the flow data within the network. In large networks, several hubs may be connected. This is the easiest form of network topology to troubleshoot because all information goes through a hub, making it easier to isolate problems.

superscalar Technology found in Pentium processors allowing the Pentium to have two instruction pipelines, thereby increasing the speed of processing.

surge suppresser Used to prevent large power spikes (such as from lightning) from damaging a computer.

SVGA (Super Video Graphics Array) A video standard. The minimum requirement for SVGA compatibility is 640 pixels by 480 pixels at 256 colors. At the low end, typical SVGA systems are operated at 800 x 600 at any color depth. Today, most SVGAs run at 1024 x 768 at 256 with 64K colors or better.

switch box Allows the user to manually (or automatically) switch cable connections so that one computer can use several different printers or devices with one parallel port.

synchronous Form of computer communication in which data is transmitted in packets containing more than one character. This is faster than asynchronous transmission because there is no start/stop bit between each individual character.

syntax Specific rules that prescribe how the symbols of a programming language can be written in order to form meaningful statements that will be understood by the PC.

sysop (system operator) The system operator of a small BBS. (Pronounced "SIS-op.")

system bus Supports the CPU, RAM, and other motherboard components that provide the controlling element to the computer. It is responsible for coordinating the operation of the individual system components and central to the communications system of a computer. Also called the control bus.

system crystal Determines the speed at which a CPU is operated (sets the clock speed); it is usually a quartz oscillator.

T

tape drive A high-capacity removable magnetic data storage device. Ideal for backups and retrieval of large amounts of data. Works like a tape recorder and saves information is a linear format.

TCP/IP (Transfer Control Protocol/Internet Protocol) The name given to a collection of protocols that were designed in the 1970s for use on the large-scale mixed-platform that became the Internet.

telecom software An application that allows two computers to communicate. Both computers must use compatible software for communication to take place.

telecommunications The ability to transmit data over telephone lines to a remote computer.

telnet A terminal emulation program that allows you to log into another computer system over the Internet. You can then run programs on that machine as though you dialed in directly.

Topology The layout scheme that describes the way in which network nodes are wired in relation to each other.

transistor An electronic device that allows a small current in one place to control a larger current in another place; commonly used as amplifiers in radio and audio circuits.

TSR (terminate-and-stay-resident program) A computer program, also known as a memory-resident program, that remains in memory after being run so that it can be called up later. These extend the capabilities of the operating system or provide "pop-up" functions (such as a calendar or calculator) that can be brought up in the middle of another program without disturbing that program. These programs were popular in the days of MS-DOS, but lead to lots of problems due to memory usage conflicts.

twisted-pair cable Consists of two insulated wires twisted around each other to form a pair. One or more twisted pairs are used in a twisted-pair cable.

U

universal serial bus (USB) A new external expansion bus that is popular for use with low-speed mass storage devices such as ZIP drives, modems, and printers.

upload The ability to transfer (send) a file from one computer to a remote computer.

upper memory area (UMA) The area from 640 KB to 1024 KB that is designated for hardware needs such as video RAM, BIOS, and memory-mapped hardware.

upper memory blocks (UMB) The unused spaces in upper memory that can be divided into blocks. These empty blocks have no RAM associated with them and are simply reserved space. This unused space is valuable because, unlike expanded and extended memory, MS-DOS can run programs in UMB.

UPS (uninterruptible power supply) Acts as both a surge suppresser and a power leveler to provide the computer with a constant source of power. It also provides power during a power failure or interruption so the user can safely save data before shutting down.

Usenet The vast collection of discussion groups and newsgroups on the Internet.

V

VGA (Video Graphics Array) A graphics adapter that offers 16 colors at a resolution of 640 pixels by 480 pixels. To gain more colors, VGA uses an analog video signal instead of a digital signal. With the analog signal, the VGA standard is able to provide 64 distinct levels for each color, giving users 64^3 or 262,144 possible colors. It uses a 15-pin, three-row, female DB-type connector.

Virtual Control Program Interface (VCPI) A memory management specification that accesses extended memory for MS-DOS-based applications. It allows only one application to control extended memory and does not support multi-tasking. Windows is not compatible with the VCPI specification.

virtual memory Hard disk space that can be used as additional memory for holding data not immediately required by the processor.

volts The unit of electromotive force, or the potential energy, that will produce a current of 1 ampere when steadily applied against a resistance of 1 ohm. Voltage is also considered the potential energy of a circuit.

VRR (vertical refresh rate) The speed at which a monitor completes all vertical traces.

W

WAN (wide area network) A network that spans a large geographical area. The network is connected by means of telephone lines, ISDN (Integrated Services Digital Network) lines, radio waves, or satellite links.

warm boot The process of restarting a computer that is already running by holding down the CTRL, ALT, and DELETE keys simultaneously. It can also refer to choosing a "Shut-down and Restart" option under Windows 9x or Windows NT.

wildcards A keyboard character that represents one or more characters in a string, usually for specifying more than one file by name. The question mark (?) matches any character in a specified position, and the asterisk (*) matches any number of characters up to the end of the filename or extension.

Word The largest amount of data that can be handled by the microprocessor in one operation and also, as a rule, the width of the main data bus.

Index

C

M

neutral wire, 318, 319, 321, 322

Newman, Max, 4

newsgroups, 545

NextGen, 63

nibbles, 13

nickel cadmium (NiCad) batteries, 522

nickel metal hydride (NiMH) batteries, 522

noise, electrical, 211

nonvolatile memory, 120
    See also read-only memory (ROM)

NOS (network operating system), 499

notation. *See* binary system; decimal notation;
    hexadecimal notation

notebook computers, 515
    See also portable computers

Novell
    DR-DOS, 370
    NetWare, 499
    network certification programs, 509

null-modem cables, 307

numbering systems. *See* binary system;
    decimal notation; hexadecimal notation

nut drivers, 344

O

Occupational Safety and Health Administration
    (OSHA), 537

odd parity, 290

offline, 285, 617

offline readers, 285, 617

ohms
    defined, 317
    glossary definition, 617
    measuring resistance, 323
    and Ohm's Law, 317

Ohm's Law, 317–18

online, 285, 617

online technical support, 548

operating systems
    carrying on disk, 345
    defined, 370
    glossary definition, 617

operating systems *(continued)*
    MS-DOS. *See* MS-DOS
    and Windows 3.1, 373–76, 388–408
    Windows 95. *See* Windows 95
    Windows 98, 376, 411, 417, 418, 427
    Windows 2000, 377
    Windows NT, 377

.org domains, 512

OSHA (Occupational Safety and Health
    Administration), 537

Out of memory messages, 400

output
    in databases, 28
    defined, 27
    examples of devices, 27, 32
    in games, 28
    relationship to input and processing, 26
    in spreadsheets, 28
    in word processors, 28

output devices, 32. *See also* monitors; printers

P

packets, 289, 291, 299, 617

paging memory, 470

palmtop computers, 516. *See also* portable computers

paper, printer, 270, 271

paper trays, 270

parallel communication, 16, 287, 288–89, 617
    See also LPT ports

parity, 122, 290–91, 352

parity bit, 122, 290–91, 617

partitioning hard disk drives
    background, 169
    and FATs, 172, 415, 480
    how to do it, 171–72
    loss of key information, 179
    primary vs. active partition, 171
    primary vs. extended partitions, 169–70
    steps in procedure, 171–72
    using FDISK utility, 169–72, 415, 480
    when to use, 169
    from Windows 95, 415, 480

S

T

MICROSOFT LICENSE AGREEMENT

Book Companion CD

IMPORTANT—READ CAREFULLY: This Microsoft End-User License Agreement ("EULA") is a legal agreement between you (either an individual or an entity) and Microsoft Corporation for the Microsoft product identified above, which includes computer software and may include associated media, printed materials, and "online" or electronic documentation ("SOFTWARE PRODUCT"). Any component included within the SOFTWARE PRODUCT that is accompanied by a separate End-User License Agreement shall be governed by such agreement and not the terms set forth below. By installing, copying, or otherwise using the SOFTWARE PRODUCT, you agree to be bound by the terms of this EULA. If you do not agree to the terms of this EULA, you are not authorized to install, copy, or otherwise use the SOFTWARE PRODUCT; you may, however, return the SOFTWARE PRODUCT, along with all printed materials and other items that form a part of the Microsoft product that includes the SOFTWARE PRODUCT, to the place you obtained them for a full refund.

SOFTWARE PRODUCT LICENSE

The SOFTWARE PRODUCT is protected by United States copyright laws and international copyright treaties, as well as other intellectual property laws and treaties. The SOFTWARE PRODUCT is licensed, not sold.

1. **GRANT OF LICENSE.** This EULA grants you the following rights:

    a. **Software Product.** You may install and use one copy of the SOFTWARE PRODUCT on a single computer. The primary user of the computer on which the SOFTWARE PRODUCT is installed may make a second copy for his or her exclusive use on a portable computer.

    b. **Storage/Network Use.** You may also store or install a copy of the SOFTWARE PRODUCT on a storage device, such as a network server, used only to install or run the SOFTWARE PRODUCT on your other computers over an internal network; however, you must acquire and dedicate a license for each separate computer on which the SOFTWARE PRODUCT is installed or run from the storage device. A license for the SOFTWARE PRODUCT may not be shared or used concurrently on different computers.

    c. **License Pak.** If you have acquired this EULA in a Microsoft License Pak, you may make the number of additional copies of the computer software portion of the SOFTWARE PRODUCT authorized on the printed copy of this EULA, and you may use each copy in the manner specified above. You are also entitled to make a corresponding number of secondary copies for portable computer use as specified above.

    d. **Sample Code.** Solely with respect to portions, if any, of the SOFTWARE PRODUCT that are identified within the SOFTWARE PRODUCT as sample code (the "SAMPLE CODE"):

    i. **Use and Modification.** Microsoft grants you the right to use and modify the source code version of the SAMPLE CODE, *provided* you comply with subsection (d)(iii) below. You may not distribute the SAMPLE CODE, or any modified version of the SAMPLE CODE, in source code form.

    ii. **Redistributable Files.** Provided you comply with subsection (d)(iii) below, Microsoft grants you a nonexclusive, royalty-free right to reproduce and distribute the object code version of the SAMPLE CODE and of any modified SAMPLE CODE, other than SAMPLE CODE, or any modified version thereof, designated as not redistributable in the Readme file that forms a part of the SOFTWARE PRODUCT (the "Non-Redistributable Sample Code"). All SAMPLE CODE other than the Non-Redistributable Sample Code is collectively referred to as the "REDISTRIBUTABLES."

    iii. **Redistribution Requirements.** If you redistribute the REDISTRIBUTABLES, you agree to: (i) distribute the REDISTRIBUTABLES in object code form only in conjunction with and as a part of your software application product; (ii) not use Microsoft's name, logo, or trademarks to market your software application product; (iii) include a valid copyright notice on your software application product; (iv) indemnify, hold harmless, and defend Microsoft from and against any claims or lawsuits, including attorney's fees, that arise or result from the use or distribution of your software application product; and (v) not permit further distribution of the REDISTRIBUTABLES by your end user. Contact Microsoft for the applicable royalties due and other licensing terms for all other uses and/or distribution of the REDISTRIBUTABLES.

2. **DESCRIPTION OF OTHER RIGHTS AND LIMITATIONS.**

    - **Limitations on Reverse Engineering, Decompilation, and Disassembly.** You may not reverse engineer, decompile, or disassemble the SOFTWARE PRODUCT, except and only to the extent that such activity is expressly permitted by applicable law notwithstanding this limitation.

    - **Separation of Components.** The SOFTWARE PRODUCT is licensed as a single product. Its component parts may not be separated for use on more than one computer.

    - **Rental.** You may not rent, lease, or lend the SOFTWARE PRODUCT.

- **Support Services.** Microsoft may, but is not obligated to, provide you with support services related to the SOFTWARE PRODUCT ("Support Services"). Use of Support Services is governed by the Microsoft policies and programs described in the user manual, in "online" documentation, and/or in other Microsoft-provided materials. Any supplemental software code provided to you as part of the Support Services shall be considered part of the SOFTWARE PRODUCT and subject to the terms and conditions of this EULA. With respect to technical information you provide to Microsoft as part of the Support Services, Microsoft may use such information for its business purposes, including for product support and development. Microsoft will not utilize such technical information in a form that personally identifies you.

- **Software Transfer.** You may permanently transfer all of your rights under this EULA, provided you retain no copies, you transfer all of the SOFTWARE PRODUCT (including all component parts, the media and printed materials, any upgrades, this EULA, and, if applicable, the Certificate of Authenticity), **and** the recipient agrees to the terms of this EULA.

- **Termination.** Without prejudice to any other rights, Microsoft may terminate this EULA if you fail to comply with the terms and conditions of this EULA. In such event, you must destroy all copies of the SOFTWARE PRODUCT and all of its component parts.

3. **COPYRIGHT.** All title and copyrights in and to the SOFTWARE PRODUCT (including but not limited to any images, photographs, animations, video, audio, music, text, SAMPLE CODE, REDISTRIBUTABLES, and "applets" incorporated into the SOFTWARE PRODUCT) and any copies of the SOFTWARE PRODUCT are owned by Microsoft or its suppliers. The SOFT-WARE PRODUCT is protected by copyright laws and international treaty provisions. Therefore, you must treat the SOFTWARE PRODUCT like any other copyrighted material **except** that you may install the SOFTWARE PRODUCT on a single computer provided you keep the original solely for backup or archival purposes. You may not copy the printed materials accompanying the SOFTWARE PRODUCT.

4. **U.S. GOVERNMENT RESTRICTED RIGHTS.** The SOFTWARE PRODUCT and documentation are provided with RESTRICTED RIGHTS. Use, duplication, or disclosure by the Government is subject to restrictions as set forth in subparagraph (c)(1)(ii) of the Rights in Technical Data and Computer Software clause at DFARS 252.227-7013 or subparagraphs (c)(1) and (2) of the Commercial Computer Software—Restricted Rights at 48 CFR 52.227-19, as applicable. Manufacturer is Microsoft Corporation/One Microsoft Way/Redmond, WA 98052-6399.

5. **EXPORT RESTRICTIONS.** You agree that you will not export or re-export the SOFTWARE PRODUCT, any part thereof, or any process or service that is the direct product of the SOFTWARE PRODUCT (the foregoing collectively referred to as the "Restricted Components"), to any country, person, entity, or end user subject to U.S. export restrictions. You specifically agree not to export or re-export any of the Restricted Components (i) to any country to which the U.S. has embargoed or restricted the export of goods or services, which currently include, but are not necessarily limited to, Cuba, Iran, Iraq, Libya, North Korea, Sudan, and Syria, or to any national of any such country, wherever located, who intends to transmit or transport the Restricted Components back to such country; (ii) to any end user who you know or have reason to know will utilize the Restricted Components in the design, development, or production of nuclear, chemical, or biological weapons; or (iii) to any end user who has been prohibited from participating in U.S. export transactions by any federal agency of the U.S. government. You warrant and represent that neither the BXA nor any other U.S. federal agency has suspended, revoked, or denied your export privileges.

DISCLAIMER OF WARRANTY

NO WARRANTIES OR CONDITIONS. MICROSOFT EXPRESSLY DISCLAIMS ANY WARRANTY OR CONDITION FOR THE SOFTWARE PRODUCT. THE SOFTWARE PRODUCT AND ANY RELATED DOCUMENTATION ARE PROVIDED "AS IS" WITHOUT WARRANTY OR CONDITION OF ANY KIND, EITHER EXPRESS OR IMPLIED, INCLUDING, WITHOUT LIMITA-TION, THE IMPLIED WARRANTIES OF MERCHANTABILITY, FITNESS FOR A PARTICULAR PURPOSE, OR NONINFRINGEMENT. THE ENTIRE RISK ARISING OUT OF USE OR PERFORMANCE OF THE SOFTWARE PRODUCT REMAINS WITH YOU.

LIMITATION OF LIABILITY. TO THE MAXIMUM EXTENT PERMITTED BY APPLICABLE LAW, IN NO EVENT SHALL MICROSOFT OR ITS SUPPLIERS BE LIABLE FOR ANY SPECIAL, INCIDENTAL, INDIRECT, OR CONSEQUENTIAL DAM-AGES WHATSOEVER (INCLUDING, WITHOUT LIMITATION, DAMAGES FOR LOSS OF BUSINESS PROFITS, BUSINESS INTERRUPTION, LOSS OF BUSINESS INFORMATION, OR ANY OTHER PECUNIARY LOSS) ARISING OUT OF THE USE OF OR INABILITY TO USE THE SOFTWARE PRODUCT OR THE PROVISION OF OR FAILURE TO PROVIDE SUPPORT SERVICES, EVEN IF MICROSOFT HAS BEEN ADVISED OF THE POSSIBILITY OF SUCH DAMAGES. IN ANY CASE, MICROSOFT'S ENTIRE LIABILITY UNDER ANY PROVISION OF THIS EULA SHALL BE LIMITED TO THE GREATER OF THE AMOUNT ACTUALLY PAID BY YOU FOR THE SOFTWARE PRODUCT OR US$5.00; PROVIDED, HOWEVER, IF YOU HAVE ENTERED INTO A MICROSOFT SUPPORT SERVICES AGREEMENT, MICROSOFT'S ENTIRE LIABILITY REGARDING SUPPORT SERVICES SHALL BE GOVERNED BY THE TERMS OF THAT AGREEMENT. BECAUSE SOME STATES AND JURISDICTIONS DO NOT ALLOW THE EXCLUSION OR LIMITATION OF LIABILITY, THE ABOVE LIMITATION MAY NOT APPLY TO YOU.

MISCELLANEOUS

This EULA is governed by the laws of the State of Washington USA, except and only to the extent that applicable law mandates govern-ing law of a different jurisdiction.

Should you have any questions concerning this EULA, or if you desire to contact Microsoft for any reason, please contact the Microsoft subsidiary serving your country, or write: Microsoft Sales Information Center/One Microsoft Way/Redmond, WA 98052-6399.

System Requirements

To get the most out of the *A+ Certification Training Kit*, including the companion CD, you should have a computer equipped with the following minimum configuration:

- 486 DX or higher processor and motherboard
- MS-DOS version 5.0 or later (version 6.2 recommended)
- Microsoft Windows 3.1 *and* Windows 95, Windows 98, or later
- 16 MB of RAM
- 500-MB hard disk drive and 15 MB of available disk space
- 3.5-inch floppy disk drive
- CD-ROM drive (8× minimum recommended)
- Mouse or other pointing device (recommended)
- A simple printer

To view the electronic version of the book on the companion CD, you will need Microsoft Internet Explorer 4.01 or later. A version of Microsoft Internet Explorer 5 that allows you to view the electronic version of the book is supplied on the companion CD. See the README.TXT file on the companion CD for instructions on how to use this supplied version of the Internet Explorer browser to view the electronic version of the book.

**For information about Microsoft Press®
products, visit our Web site at
mspress.microsoft.com**